BRUCÉ
LOUPIA

Human Information Processing

AN INTRODUCTION TO PSYCHOLOGY

HUMAN INFORMATION PROCESSING

An Introduction to Psychology

PETER H. LINDSAY and DONALD A. NORMAN

University of California, San Diego

ACADEMIC PRESS

New York and London

A Subsidiary of Harcourt Brace Jovanovich, Publishers

ACADEMIC PRESS, INC.
111 Fifth Avenue, New York, New York 10003

United Kingdom Edition published by
ACADEMIC PRESS, INC. (LONDON) LTD.
24/28 Oval Road, London NW1

Library of Congress Catalog Card Number: 70–182657

PRINTED IN THE UNITED STATES OF AMERICA

Cover design by Leanne Hinton
Text design by Wladislaw Finne

Contents

It all started in the summer of 1966 when the two of us first met at a conference in Driebergen, The Netherlands. We were both on circuitous paths to La Jolla—PHL from Toronto, DAN from Harvard. The University of California had just started its new campus at San Diego and the undergraduate program in psychology did not yet exist. We decided to teach an introductory course jointly. So began Psychology 11.

Our goal was to try to convey the excitement of modern experimental psychology to the beginning student. We wanted to explain what we, as researchers, were doing in our laboratories. We wished to get the students actively involved in working with the concepts of psychology, rather than simply committing to memory long lists of facts and experiments. We wanted to communicate how we think and how we approach the study of the human mind.

We did not meet with immediate success. It was painful to discover that things that seemed so interesting to us were not always so interesting to the student: but gradually we learned how to teach introductory psychology. As our experience developed, so did our backlog of notes and ideas. The course took hold, the enrollment climbed. But we were hampered by lack of a suitable text. The only way to get one seemed to be by writing it ourselves.

So here it is. We have learned in the teaching and writing of this material. It has forced us to crystallize our ideas and today we are even more excited about psychology than when we began. We wait with impatience the advances that will occur during the next few years. The framework presented within this book has become our guide to the study of psychology.

Acknowledgments

Many people have unselfishly given us their time, their efforts, and their thoughts. We owe a great deal to David Rumelhart for his intellectual stimulation as he collaborated with us in our research and in our teaching. He has played an extremely influential role in the development of the memory model: the material from which Chapters 10 and 11 were developed, the guide for Chapters 12 and 13. [See the paper by Rumelhart, Lindsay, and Norman (1972).]

In a similar manner, over the years the participants of the "LNR research group" have been instrumental in the development of much of our thinking, from perception through cognition. Numerous graduate-student teaching assistants have helped us develop the course from which this book has come (perhaps fifty of them). They individually and collectively deserve much credit. In particular, however, we wish to acknowledge the assistance of Richard Meltzer, Jim Levin, and Marc Eisenstadt for their guidance as "chief TA's."

Leanne Hinton has aided us throughout the writing of the book. First, she tape-recorded, transcribed, and reorganized our original lectures, checked our references, and helped out in all phases of the work. Then, that job done, she researched and prepared the original sketches from which the final art was prepared. Her anatomical drawings, delightful demons, and misshapen bodies helped set the tone for the book and clarify the text.

Cathy Cox helped us transcribe the lectures on audition that became Chapters 6 and 7. Margaret Jackson helped us in the editorial work necessary to complete the book. Julie Lustig has watched over the final year, checking, supervising, and needling when necessary. Marlene Farnum, Julie Lustig, and Martha Norman did the Subject Index in a long, protracted marathon weekend.

A number of people have read and commented on the chapters for us. Peter Dean helped with problem solving and with contemporary art. Larry Squires has read and commented on Chapter 8, Allen Newell, Chapter 14, George Mandler, Chapter 17, and Ed Fantino, the material on operant learning. Jack Nachmias and Charles Harris commented on an early version of Chapters 1–7, and Ulric Neisser, along with several anonymous reviewers, helped with the entire book. We wish especially to thank the man we have come to know as "Reviewer 3." His comments, although painful, have been insightful and important.

Finally, our long-suffering publishers deserve credit for helping us get the thing done. The view from New York and San Francisco must have seemed foggy and chaotic at times, but their support made it possible for us to get the editorial assistance that made completion possible.

FIGURE AND TABLE CREDITS		
Figure 1-38	From M. Luckiesh, *Visual illusions.* New York: Dover Publications, Inc., 1965. Reprinted through permission of the publisher.
Figure 1-45	From R. M. Pritchard, Stabilized images on the retina. Copyright © 1961 by Scientific American, Inc. All rights reserved.
Figure 2-1	From Pomeranz and Chung (1970). Copyright 1970 by the American Association for the Advancement of Science.
Figures 2-6 and 4-7	From S. Polyak, *The vertebrate visual system.* Copyright © 1957 by the University of Chicago Press and used by permission.
Table 3-2 and Figures 6-4 and 6-5	From Denes and Pinson (1963). Courtesy of Bell Telephone Laboratories, Incorporated.
Figure 5-8	From S. S. Stevens (1961b). Copyright 1961 by the American Association for the Advancement of Science.
Figure 5-18	From D. B. Judd, Basic correlates of the visual stimulus. In S. S. Stevens (Ed.), *Handbook of experimental psychology.* New York: Wiley, 1951. By permission of John Wiley & Sons, Inc.
Figure 5-28	From Wald (1964). Copyright 1964 by the American Association for the Advancement of Science.
Figure 5-29	Based on DeValois and Jacobs (1968). Copyright 1968 by the American Association for the Advancement of Science.
Figure 6-11	After G. L. Rasmussen and W. F. Windle (Eds.), *Neural mechanisms of the auditory and vestibular systems,* 1960. Courtesy of Charles C Thomas, Publisher, Springfield, Illinois.
Figure 6-13	Photo is from Bredberg *et al.* (1970). Copyright 1970 by the American Association for the Advancement of Science.
Figure 7-1	From Robinson and Dadson (1956). By permis-

sion of the Institute of Physics and the Physical Society.

Figure 7-2 — Illustration courtesy of C. G. Conn, Ltd., Oak Brook, Illinois.

Figures 7-6 and 7-8 — From E. Zwicker and B. Scharf, Model of loudness summation. *Psychology Review*, 1965, **72**, 3–26. Copyright 1965 by the American Psychological Association, and reproduced by permission.

Figures 7-11, 7-12, and 7-21 — From J. Zwislocki, Analysis of some auditory characteristics. In D. R. Luce, R. R. Bush, and E. Galanter (Eds.), *Handbook of mathematical psychology*, Vol. III. New York: Wiley, 1965. By permission of John Wiley & Sons, Inc.

Figure 7-18 — From R. R. Fay, Auditory frequency stimulation in the goldfish (*Carassius Auratus*). *Journal of Comparative & Physiological Psychology*, 1970, **73**(2), 175–180. Copyright 1970 by the American Psychological Association, and reproduced by permission.

Figure 8-15 — Graph from E. H. Lenneberg, *Biological foundations of language*. New York: Wiley, 1967. By permission of John Wiley & Sons, Inc.

Figure 9-8 — From B. B. Murdock, Jr., The retention of individual items. *Journal of Experimental Psychology*, 1961, **62**, 618–625. Copyright 1961 by the American Psychological Association, and reproduced by permission.

Figures 9-11 through 9-14 — From B. B. Murdock, Jr., The serial effect of free recall. *Journal of Experimental Psychology*, 1962, **64**, 482–488. Copyright 1962 by the American Psychological Association, and reproduced by permission.

Table 12-2 — From R. Brown and C. Hanlon, Derivational complexity and order of acquisition in child speech. In J. R. Hayes (Ed.), *Cognition and the development of language*. New York: Wiley, 1970. By permission of John Wiley & Sons, Inc.

Figure 14-7 — From Herbert A. Simon and Allen Newell, *Human problem solving* © 1971. By permission of Prentice-Hall, Inc., Englewood Cliffs, New Jersey.

Figures 16-4 and 16-5	From S. Siegal and L. E. Fouraker, *Bargaining and group decision making: Experiments in bilateral monopoly.* Copyright 1960 by McGraw Hill, Inc. Used with permission of McGraw-Hill Book Company.
Figure 17-14	From N. Kleitman, *Sleep and wakefulness* (2nd ed.). Copyright © 1963 by the University of Chicago Press, and used by permission.
Figure 17-15	Reprinted from D. B. Lindsley, Psychophysiology and motivation. In M. R. Jones (Ed.), *Nebraska symposium on motivation,* by permission of University of Nebraska Press. Copyright © 1957 by The University of Nebraska Press.
Figures A-3 and A-6 and Table A-3	Reprinted from S. S. Stevens, The psychophysics of sensory function in W. A. Rosenblith (Ed.), *Sensory communication* by permission of The M.I.T. Press, Cambridge, Massachusetts. Copyright © 1961 by the M.I.T. Press.
Figures A-4 and A-5	From Stevens (1966a). Copyright 1966 by the American Association for the Advancement of Science.

QUOTATION CREDITS

P. 311	From B. Milner, S. Corkin, and H. L. Teuber, Further analysis of the hipocampal amnesic syndrome: 14 year follow-up study of H. M. *Neuropsychologica,* 1968, **6,** 215–234. Reprinted with permission from Pergamon Press.
P. 322	From Michael S. Gazzaniga, *The bisected brain.* Copyright © 1970 by Meredith Corporation. Reprinted by permission of Appleton-Century-Crofts, Educational Division, Meredith Corporation.
Pp. 474, 480	From B. Spock, *Baby and child care.* New York: Pocket Books, Inc. Copyright © 1945, 1946, 1957, 1968 By Benjamin Spock, M.D. Reprinted by permission of Pocket Books, a division of Simon and Schuster, Inc.
P. 527	From the book *Now we are six* by A. A. Milne. Copyright 1927 by E. P. Dutton, Inc. Renewal © 1955 by A. A. Milne. Published by E. P.

Dutton & Co., Inc. and Methuen & Co., Ltd., and used with their permission.

Pp. 553ff.

From *Khrushchev remembers, with an introduction, commentary, and notes by Edward Crankshaw.* Translated and edited by Strobe Talbott. Copyright © 1970 by Little, Brown and Company, Inc. and used with their permission and that of André Deutsch, Ltd.

Pp. 568ff.

From S. Milgram, Behavioral study of obedience, *Journal of Abnormal and Social Psychology,* 1963, **67,** 371–378. Copyright 1963 by the American Psychological Association, and reproduced by permission.

P. 570

From S. Milgram, Some conditions of obedience and disobedience to authority. *Human Relations,* 1965, **18,** 57–75. Reprinted by permission of Plenum Publishing Corp.

We do not know all about the human mind. But we have learned how to go about looking for what we do not know. This book introduces some of the techniques that have been used in that search. More than merely telling what is and is not known, we emphasize the way things are learned. Throughout the book, we attempt to develop specific models of particular phenomena. By using these models, we can uncover the reasoning underlying particular theoretical explanations as well as point up the strengths and weaknesses of the theories.

Although the models in this book cannot accurately reflect the complexity and sophistication of human thought processes, they do help to clarify the issues and pinpoint the important and unimportant aspects of a problem. But the simplicity of our models is to be expected. Man is just beginning to understand his own mind.

In the first seven chapters of the book we introduce some problems in perception and ask what kind of a system is needed to produce the properties of human perception. After grappling with some of the theoretical problems, the actual physiological mechanisms are presented in some detail. The ways in which neurological circuits can be constructed to perform many of the necessary first steps in pattern recognition is considered. After examining the basic properties of neural circuits and of seeing and hearing, we return to the general problem of perception to show that what is known about the physiological mechanisms cannot provide the whole explanatory picture: Some major psychological problems remain unsolved.

We move from perception and pattern recognition to memory, which occupies the next section of the book, Chapters 8–11. Memory plays an essential role in all human intellectual activity, and its nature and function must be thoroughly explored. We begin with an examination of intellectual processes in humans, centering around the properties of the memory system. In Chapter 8 the neural basis of memory is studied, including what is known about physiological substrates of memory and the impairments to human memory caused by various types of physiological disorders. Chapter 9 introduces the literature on short-term memory and on attention. The reconstructive nature of short-term memory and its role in a number of aspects of human performance is explored.

In Chapters 10 and 11 we consider a possible model for representing the storage of information within long-term memory. This is an area of investigation that is relatively untouched in modern psychological investigations, yet is fundamental for understanding many of the higher mental processes in humans. This memory model plays a central role in the chapters that follow.

In the final tacit division of the text, Chapters 12–17, we examine cognitive process. Building on the material of Chapters 10 and 11, Chapter 12 presents the study of language as a means of communication. Communication is emphasized because it is the central reason for the existence of language. The development of language in children is analyzed from this framework. Chapter 13 examines the mechanisms for learning, and the stages of intellectual development that a child goes through from birth through adolescence.

In Chapters 14–16 we consider adult intellectual behavior, with an analysis of problem-solving behavior, an examination of decision making, and an analysis of social influences upon human decisions. In the last chapter, motivation and emotion are discussed. In doing so, we return to some of the problems raised in Chapters 1 and 3. Starting with a prototypical model of a motivational system, we explore the way in which the chemical and biological states of the body interact with cognition to control emotions and human behavior.

Chapters 1–17 complete the text, but the appendices, which present some of the more technical material, remain. Appendix A briefly discusses the problem of measurement in psychology and then, at greater length, discusses magnitude estimation procedures, including some sample tasks. Appendix B presents a problem in decision making and introduces the important technique of operating characteristics (commonly known as d' and ROC curves).

The literature of a science constitutes its foundation. We introduce this literature in two ways. References to the points discussed in the book are cited in the chapter text and in the "Suggested Readings" at the end of each chapter. This special section serves several purposes. First, there is an expansion, with brief comment, of the references used for the chapter material. This is where major credit is given to the sources of the materials in the text. By following both the references given in the chapter itself as well as those in the "Suggested Readings," it is possible to trace the history and the details of the material presented within the chapter.

Second, there is a list of reading matter that can be used to guide those who wish to pursue any of the topics in more detail. General review articles and books that cover the material are cited. These sources will in turn lead to even more specific (and usually more advanced) readings. We often cite works that we found interesting in the course of our studies, even though they may not have been used directly in the material within the chapter itself. Information on how to search for additional reference material is given in the section "Using Basic Reference Material" at the end of the book. The complete reference for any citation given in the text or "Suggested Readings" can be found in the "References" at the end of the book.

1

Human perception

The goal is to understand the mechanisms of perception. The task before us is to discover the psychological processes that are operating and as much as possible of the wiring diagram of the neural networks that are involved. The problems are numerous. When we read the printed letters on a page of text, the conversion from the visual symbols on the page to meaningful phrases in the mind is performed rapidly and without effort. Similarly, speech is heard as meaningful words, not as a jumble of sounds that must somehow then be translated to make sense. When we walk about in the environment, we recognize the objects before us immediately and without effort. If there is a sound on the left, we hear it on the left. When we come to a curb, we step up or down at the right time, and when we pick up a pencil, no conscious thought processes are involved, either in the recognition of that object as a pencil, in the control of the arms and hands to grasp the object, or in the way by which the pencil gets put to use.

We start the story of perception with the study of pattern recognition: how the external signals arriving at the sense organs are converted into meaningful perceptual experiences. Ordinarily, the objects and events around us are recognized with such apparent ease and immediacy that it is easy to assume that the operations involved are simple and direct. But the experience of engineers has proven the illusiveness of the task. There exists no machine that is capable of recognizing sounds and symbols normally encountered in the environment. The numerous attempts to build pattern recognition systems have failed to achieve the flexibility and power of the perceptual systems of even primitive animals. Let us start by seeing why the task is so difficult.

INTERPRETING
SENSORY MESSAGES

Matching templates

Template matching is the simplest of all the possible schemes for classifying and recognizing patterns. For template matching, there must be some representation—a template—for each of the patterns to be recognized. Recognition is accomplished by matching the external signal against the internal template. The one that matches best identifies the pattern present.

Consider how a template scheme might work in detecting signals that are presented visually. Suppose the task is to recognize letters of the alphabet. For the present discussion, assume that when a letter is presented, its image falls upon the rear surface of the eye, the area called the *retina*. The retina is composed of many hundreds of thousands of light-sensitive nerve cells, called *receptors*. Details of how these receptors operate will be discussed in later chapters; for the moment, let us see how they might be interconnected to recognize the letters of the alphabet.

FIGURE 1-1

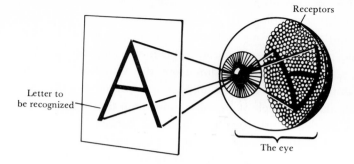

If the letter **A** is presented to the eye, it excites a pattern of receptors on the retina. If we were to interconnect these receptors together to a single detector cell, we would have a template of receptor cells specifically designed to detect the occurrence of the letter **A**. Thus, a possible template for **A** is shown in Figure 1-2.[1] When the light pattern

FIGURE 1-2

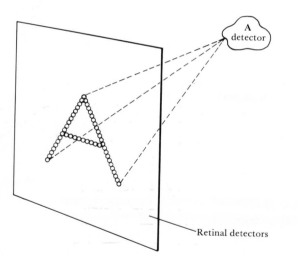

stimulates just the right set of receptors, the "**A** detector" begins responding vigorously.

---

[1] In the diagrams that follow, the fact that the lens of the eye inverts the image is conveniently ignored. This makes it easier to draw the diagrams and talk about the various pattern recognition schemes. Obviously, the principles of connecting together the receptors are unchanged whether the retinal image be upside down or rightside up.

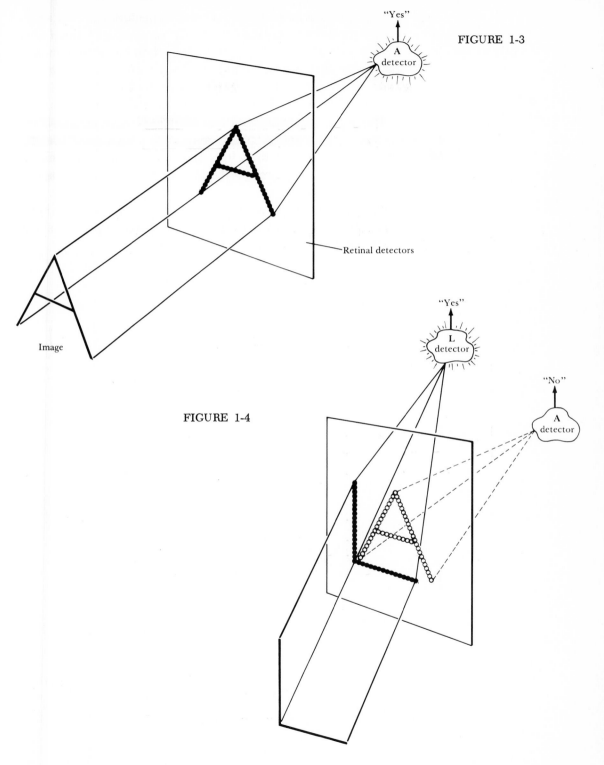

"Yes"

A
detector

FIGURE 1-3

Retinal detectors

Image

"Yes"

L
detector

"No"

A
detector

FIGURE 1-4

A different selection of receptors makes a template for **L**. Still another arrangement produces a template for **N**. By continuing in this fashion, it is possible to make templates for each pattern to be recognized.

Figure 1-4

Template matching is a straightforward scheme for recognizing patterns. Note that it does have one interesting feature: It matches the incoming pattern against all of the possible templates simultaneously. That is, it doesn't have to go through the cumbersome procedure of trying out a succession of templates one at a time to find the one that fits best. It looks for all of the letters at the same time: The template that provides the closest match to the incoming pattern is the one that is most strongly activated.

This simple version, however, is easy to dismiss as a model of human pattern recognition. Look what happens if the letter is printed slightly crooked, too big, or too small, respectively:

FIGURE 1-5*a*

TEMPLATE MATCHING ORIENTATION

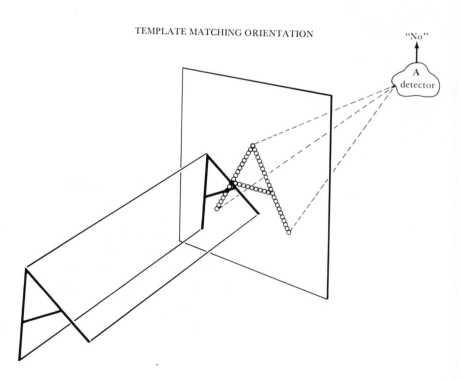

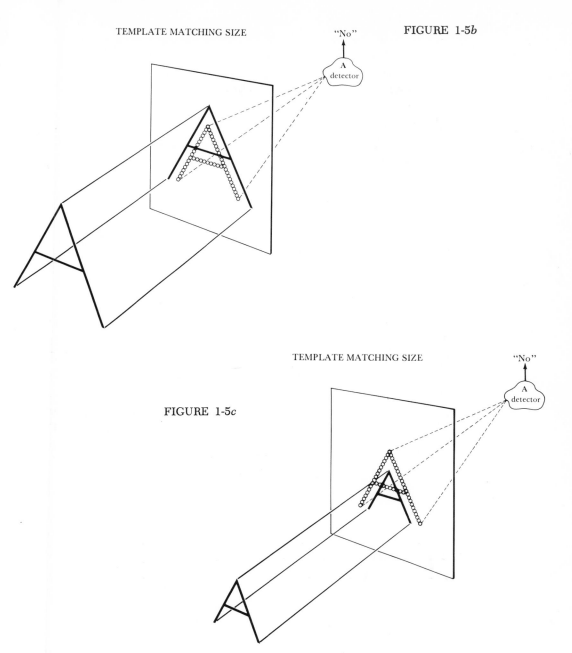

TEMPLATE MATCHING SIZE   "No"   FIGURE 1-5*b*

TEMPLATE MATCHING SIZE   "No"

FIGURE 1-5*c*

Thus, the system fails unless it has an exact template for the incoming ✳ pattern.

There is a choice of strategies for modifying the template scheme to handle these problems. More templates can be added—one for each possible size and orientation of the letter to be recognized:

TEMPLATE MATCHING DIFFERENT SIZES   "Yes"   **FIGURE** 1-6

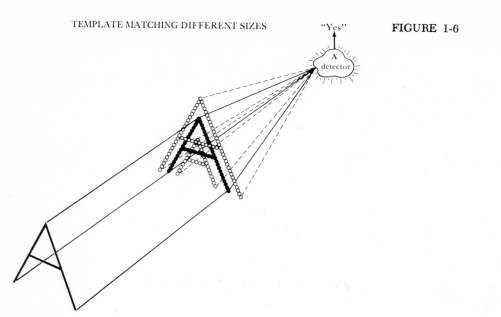

Alternatively, the symbols can be preprocessed to put them into a standard format before attempting a template match.

Many computer programs and machines that use a template system for recognizing patterns perform preprocessing. Before attempting to recognize the pattern, the letter is rotated so that its long axis is vertically oriented. It is then scaled in size to a preset height and width. Finally, the preprocessed signal is matched against a standard set of templates.

FIGURE 1-7

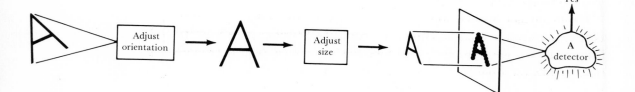

The best known working example of a template-matching scheme illustrates some of its limitations as a method for pattern recognition. On the bottom of bank checks, the serial number and checking account number are printed in special characters that can be read both by humans and by the check-sorting machines connected to the computers of the bank's clearing house. The characters are read off the check by a scanning device and are identified by an electronic template-matching system. Note the characters.

SOUTHERN CALIFORNIA FIRST NATIONAL BANK
LA JOLLA SHORES OFFICE
2256 Avenida De La Playa, La Jolla, California 92037

⑈2345⑈67891⑈ 12345678⑈

FIGURE 1-8

A great deal of effort went into designing them to be as distinct as possible from one another. They must be printed on the checks with a special machine to ensure the exact size and positioning of the letters. When the checks are read by the scanning device, misalignment can lead to errors. Template matching is the simplest scheme to build; it is also the easiest to go wrong.

It seems unlikely that templates could account for human pattern recognition. The variety in the patterns that must be dealt with poses considerable problems for a template scheme. They can be handled, but each must be treated as a special case, and the system soon becomes very complex and unwieldy. Moreover, a template scheme cannot recognize novel versions of patterns for which it has no template. Humans can succeed. Clearly then, a more powerful and flexible system is needed to account for the capabilities of human pattern recognition.

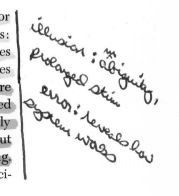

Analysis by template matching fails. We need no experiments to discover this; simple logic is enough. But what are the alternatives? It is time to examine the phenomena of perception.

PATTERN
RECOGNITION

Things do not always appear as they actually are. What we see or hear is not always what is. Often, the perceptual system makes errors: Sometimes we see illusions, sometimes the perceptual system requires time to recover from prolonged stimulation, and sometimes it requires time to interpret the image presented to it. All these phenomena are valuable to us because the mechanics of a system are frequently revealed primarily through its errors and distortions. When all works smoothly and properly, it is difficult to know where to begin the search. But when failures occur, the analysis of those failures can be very revealing. So now let us examine some perceptual phenomena for the basic principles that can be extracted from them.

Let us start by examining how sensory information gets interpreted.

FIGURE 1-9   *R. C. James (photographer). Courtesy of the photographer.*

We bring the interpretation process into awareness through tricks. First, we *degrade the image,* making interpretation difficult (if not impossible). Second, we provide *competing organizations,* making possible several conflicting interpretations of the same image. Third, we provide *organization without meaning* to see how past experience affects the process.

Organizing degraded images   Ordinarily, the interpretation of sensory messages proceeds so rapidly and automatically that we are seldom aware of the complexity of the task. The processes must be slowed up a bit so that the mechanisms involved become apparent. One way of doing this is by reducing the amount of visual information available. For example, look at Figure 1–9.

Here we see some of the organizational processes that are operating during the interpretation of a visual image. To see that it is a picture of a dalmation dog (facing to the left), information not present in the picture must be added. Once the dog can be seen, it is difficult not to see it. The knowledge that the picture is of a dog seems to speed up the whole interpretive process: When you know what to look for, it is easier to see it.

An image may be ambiguous because of a lack of relevant information or a surplus of irrelevant data. It can also be ambiguous because of the existence of several different ways of constructing a meaningful interpretation. Under these conditions, we have difficulty in interpreting the image in two distinct ways at the same time. A work by the artist Salvador Dali illustrates the point.

Competing organizations

Salvador Dali, "The Slave Market with Disappearing Bust of Voltaire." FIGURE 1-10
Collection: Mr. and Mrs. A. Reynolds Morse. Photograph courtesy of Salvador Dali Museum, Cleveland, Ohio.

The title gives the clue to the alternative interpretations of Dali's work: *Slave Market with Disappearing Bust of Voltaire*. In the very center of the picture are two undersized nuns standing shoulder to shoulder. But with a different perceptual organization, the faces of the nuns become the eyes of Voltaire, the joining of their shoulders becomes a nose, the slash of white across their waists becomes a chin. One way of putting the information together produces a perception of miniature figures, the alternative way produces an oversized sculpture of a head. The two perceptions are, to some extent, incompatible ways of organizing the visual information: It is difficult to perceive both views simultaneously.

ORGANIZING AUDITORY PERCEPTIONS

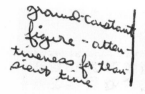

The tendency to attend to and organize selectively the data provided by sensory systems is a very general characteristic of all perceptual experiences. When one conversation is extracted from out of the many around us, that conversation becomes _figure_. All other sounds in the environment become ground. The effect is most noticeable in a crowded party, where it is possible to switch attention from one conversation to another. Each time, the new conversation stands out clearly and sharply in consciousness while the others recede fuzzily into the background.

In music, the organization of our perceptions into figure and ground is well known. Composers often present different melodic lines simultaneously, knowing that the listener will attend primarily to one. In fact, it is possible to make one solo instrument sound as if it were playing two melodic lines at the same time. The player alternates between a high series and a low series of notes. The listener finds that he can listen to the high notes and find one line of the music or to the low notes and find the other line. He perceives the alternating notes as two distinct themes.

Look at this example of the technique in a segment of music from a piece for a solo flute. We have separated the two themes for you by screening the lower line. Note that the composer (Telemann) maintains a clear separa-

FIGURE 1-11

tion between the themes by separating the notes and forcing the flute player to alternate between one theme and the other. The listener can choose to follow either the high or the low theme. Whichever line is attended to becomes the figure. The intervening notes are heard as background accompaniment.

Figure 1-11

In many ways the richness of music depends upon perceptual organizations. We pick out a theme and follow it. We hear the bass, pick it up for a while, then pass on to another instrument. We learn to follow the pattern from instrument to instrument. As the same piece of music is listened to over and over again, new themes can be discovered. The theme attended to at the moment is the figure. Everything else is the ground. Go back and listen to some music, something complex like Bach or Stravinsky or some good jazz or rock. Try out different ways of listening to the music. The variety of possible organizations is not obvious until you begin to notice them. It may take dozens of listenings to a piece before a particular pattern stands out clearly and distinctly. Like visual perceptions, knowing what to listen for seems to help, but once a particular way of organizing the music has been found, it is difficult to avoid from then on.

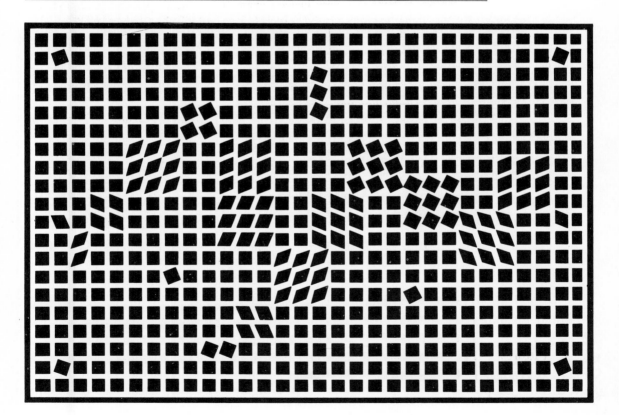

Victor Vasarely, "Tlinko." 1956. From Vasarely 1, p. 120, Editions du Griffon, Neuchâtel-Suisse.

FIGURE 1-12

FIGURE 1-13   *François Morellet, "Screen Painting: 0°, 22°5, 45°, 67°5." Collection: Museum of Modern Art, Paris. Courtesy of the artist.*

Organization without meaning

*Pics art dis-
tinguishable
Characteristic
from unfamiliar
phenomenon*

Does the ability to organize and separate out particular components of the visual image rely entirely on being able to construct familiar perceptions? Not at all. During the interpretation of a visual message, we seem to segregate and treat as a unit any grouping which has some distinguishing characteristic. Clusters of similar shapes or breaks in a repetitive pattern stand out as figures. A classic maxim for composing an interesting graphic pattern is to make sure to provide a focal point of interest by including some type of break in any repetitive pattern. Many contemporary artists are masters at discovering the variety of compositions that can be used to provide interesting groupings of figure and ground. We have just seen some samples of their works.

Figures 1-12 & 1-13

How do you break up these images? What do you look at? Why do the organizations keep changing in some of the pictures? These paintings have illustrated several different points. First, the objects need be neither meaningful nor familiar for the organizational principles to work. Second, it is difficult, if not impossible, to prevent the organization of information. Look at these figures carefully. The organization fluctuates, sometimes taking one form, sometimes another. But there is usually some structure to the pictures, even if the artist has deliberately tried

information organization unavoidable, always try to make sense of Chaotic world, Human

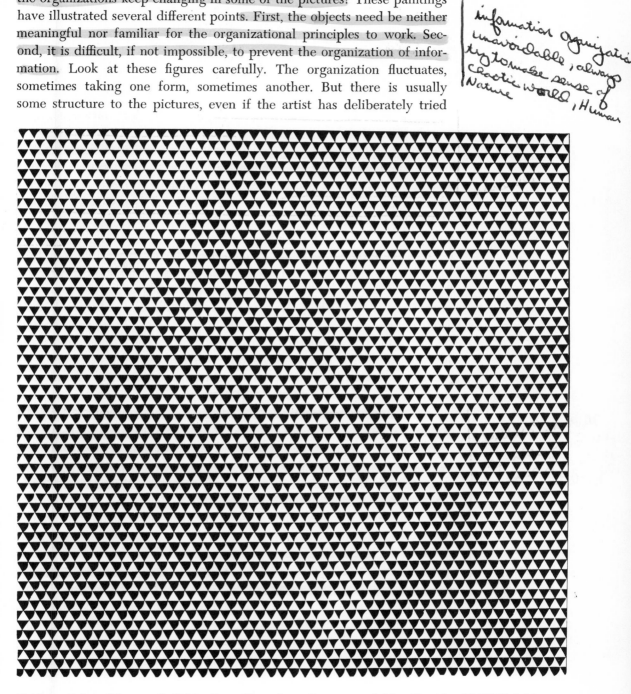

Bridget Riley, "Tremor." 1962. 48 × 48 inches. Courtesy of Mr. David M. Winton.   FIGURE 1-14

to avoid standard forms of organization. The viewer puts it in. Figure 1-14 is especially interesting, since it can be perceived as a set of long, horizontal, rectangular tubes, or vertical ones, or simply as patterns of large, shifting triangles. But whatever the pattern, one is almost always present. Whether the figure be meaningful or not, familiar or novel, the visual and perceptual processes impose organization upon it.

Making the
sensory data fit
the interpretation

illusion

Other important aspects of the organization of visual information can be demonstrated by illusions. The point of an illusion is to design an ambiguous set of sensory inputs in order to tease out some characteristics of the perceptual system through an analysis of the kinds of errors made. In this way, it is often possible to examine in more detail operations of the system that normally are not observable. Consider Figure 1-15. It could represent either an object lying down (Figure 1-16) or standing up (Figure 1-17).

To make the object,[2] take a piece of fairly heavy paper, fold it and set it up as shown in Figure 1-18. When you have set it up, view it with one eye closed from a point directly in line and slightly above the fold: The point labeled O. At first, the paper looks like the one in Figure 1-16. If you continue to stare at it intently, the paper will suddenly stand up and look like the one in Figure 1-17. It takes a little concentration and practice, but do it. The illusion is worth it. When you see it as in Figure 1-17, gently move your head slowly back and forth (remember to use only one eye). Note what happens to the object.

Motion Parallax:
pattern of stim. for
parts of a scene at
dif depths

There are two distinct ways of organizing the image of the figure. When the object is perceived as lying down, all of the depth information fits together. When it is standing up, the shadows and contours are not quite what they should be (which makes the object appear somewhat luminous). When you move your head, the object seems to be made of a rubbery substance that twists and turns. This comes about because when the head is moved, the image of the near point of the fold moves across the retina faster than the image of the far point. This is the normal pattern of stimulation for parts of the scene at different depths—a phenomenon known as *motion parallax.* When the object is seen in its true orientation, this motion parallax cue coincides with the motion. When the object is seen as standing up, however, all the points along the fold appear to be equally distant. The only way the motion cues can be consistent with the vertical organization is if the object itself twists

---

[2] It is instructive to try out all of these illusions yourself: Little can be learned simply by reading about them.

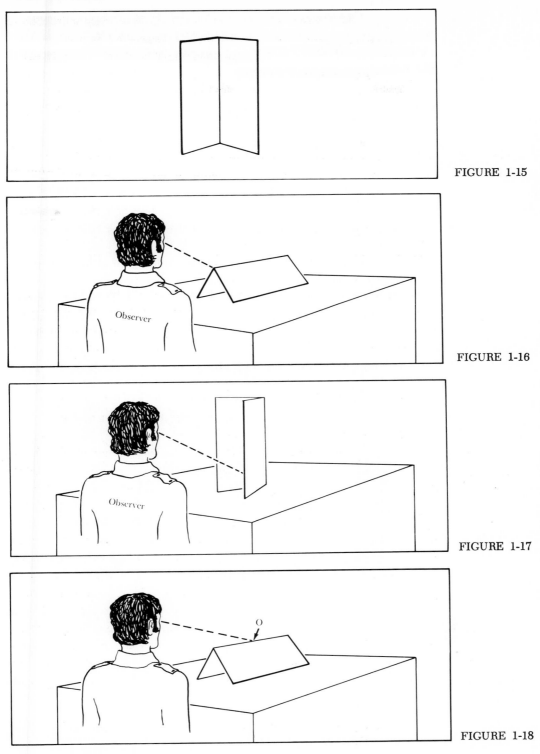

FIGURE 1-15

FIGURE 1-16

FIGURE 1-17

FIGURE 1-18

and turns. Even though you know very well that the object cannot be behaving in that way, the sensory data force you to perceive it as though it were. All of the sensory data are used to construct a consistent interpretation of the visual world.

Before you put away the paper, try it once more. This time, place the paper so that it is strongly lit from the side. When it switches from a horizontal to a vertical orientation, pay particular attention to the changes in the apparent brightness of the side of the object that is in the shadow. Can you explain these brightness differences?

THE IMPORTANCE OF RULES   The last few examples have all illustrated a common theory: Sensory evidence must be interpreted. But what are the rules that govern the interpretation?

Look at Figure 1-19. The immediate perception is of a group of three-dimensional blocks, some overlapping others. The question is, what information is used to determine how the different areas in the block combine to form figures? How is it known that areas 20 and 18 come from the same figure, or, to pick a more difficult example, areas 3 and 29? To do this task requires considerations of the lines and angles extracted from the image. It turns out that there are several methods by which

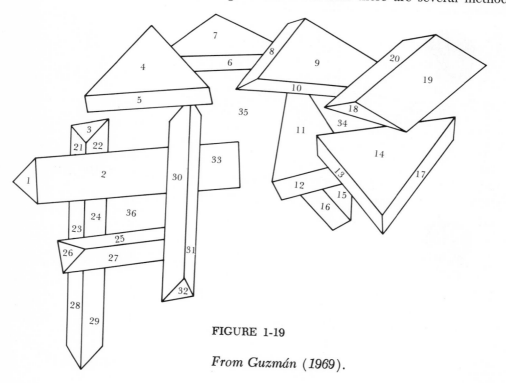

FIGURE 1-19

From Guzmán (1969).

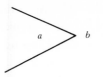

L – Vertex where two
lines meet

Fork – Three lines forming angles
smaller than 180°

Arrow – Three lines meeting at a
point, with one of the angles
bigger than 180°

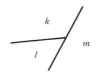

T – Three concurrent lines, two
of them collinear

K – Two of the vertices are collinear
with the center, and the other
two fall in the same side of such
a line

X – Two of the vertices are collinear
with the center, and the other
two fall in opposite sides of
such a line

Peak – Formed by four or more lines,
when the central vertex is the
tallest part of the intersection.

Multi – Vertices formed by four or more
lines, and not falling in any
of the preceding types

FIGURE 1-20

*From Guzmán
(1969).*

this figure can be disentangled. This particular diagram comes from the work of Guzmán (1969), a computer scientist interested in determining rules by which computers might do the task.

Guzmán analyzed a number of scenes of this type and concluded that the most important information about overlap came from a consideration of intersections, the spot where several contours intersect each other (see Figure 1-20). If the intersection forms an **L**, for example, it is likely that the surface to the left (*a*) belongs to a different body than the surface to the right (*b*). With a **fork,** however, all three surfaces can belong to the same body: *d*, *e*, and *f*. An **arrow** usually signifies two bodies, one that contains surfaces *h* and *i*, the other containing *j*.

It is the intersection labeled **T** that often contains the most important clues for the construction of the final picture. A **T** often signifies that one object is in front of another, so that surfaces *k* and *l* belong to one body that passes behind body *m*. Hence, when one **T** is found, it is important to see if others are around, other **T**'s that will line up properly with the first.

In Figure 1-21 the two **T**'s that are marked are sufficient to identify that surfaces *o* and *p* belong together, surfaces *r* and *s* belong together, and that *o* and *r* are the same surface, as are *p* and *s*. With the additional information provided by the **fork** that *r*, *s*, and *z* are part of the same body, the entire figure is unambiguously interpreted: *q* is one body: *o*, *p*, *r*, *s*, and *z* is another; *u* is the background.

Here we see a situation that clearly makes use of two different sources of information: first, the specific information about the picture gathered by analysis of the intersecting lines; second, an interpretation of the meaning conveyed by those intersections. In this case, there is a combination of the information conveyed by the local features of the picture with a consideration of the global interpretation. This dual process—of feature extraction and interpretation—will come up repeatedly as we examine the perceptual experience. Moreover, the implications of this dual process of perception make themselves felt not only in the analysis of things like blocks, but also in situations where there is conflict between the implications of the local features and the global interpretation. When these contradictions arise, the resulting perception shows the conflict in rather obvious ways.

FIGURE 1-21

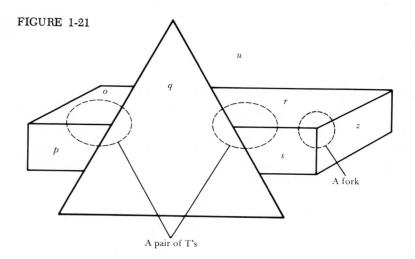

L – Vertex where two
lines meet

Fork – Three lines forming angles
smaller than 180°

Arrow – Three lines meeting at a
point, with one of the angles
bigger than 180°

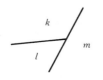

T – Three concurrent lines, two
of them collinear

K – Two of the vertices are collinear
with the center, and the other
two fall in the same side of such
a line

X – Two of the vertices are collinear
with the center, and the other
two fall in opposite sides of
such a line

Peak – Formed by four or more lines,
when the central vertex is the
tallest part of the intersection.

Multi – Vertices formed by four or more
lines, and not falling in any
of the preceding types

FIGURE 1-20

*From Guzmán
(1969).*

this figure can be disentangled. This particular diagram comes from
the work of Guzmán (1969), a computer scientist interested in determining rules by which computers might do the task.

Guzmán analyzed a number of scenes of this type and concluded that
the most important information about overlap came from a consideration
of intersections, the spot where several contours intersect each other (see
Figure 1-20). If the intersection forms an **L**, for example, it is likely that
the surface to the left (*a*) belongs to a different body than the surface
to the right (*b*). With a **fork**, however, all three surfaces can belong to
the same body: *d, e,* and *f*. An **arrow** usually signifies two bodies, one
that contains surfaces *h* and *i*, the other containing *j*.

It is the intersection labeled **T** that often contains the most important clues for the construction of the final picture. A **T** often signifies that one object is in front of another, so that surfaces k and l belong to one body that passes behind body m. Hence, when one **T** is found, it is important to see if others are around, other **T**'s that will line up properly with the first.

In Figure 1-21 the two **T**'s that are marked are sufficient to identify that surfaces o and p belong together, surfaces r and s belong together, and that o and r are the same surface, as are p and s. With the additional information provided by the **fork** that r, s, and z are part of the same body, the entire figure is unambiguously interpreted: q is one body: o, p, r, s, and z is another; u is the background.

Here we see a situation that clearly makes use of two different sources of information: first, the specific information about the picture gathered by analysis of the intersecting lines; second, an interpretation of the meaning conveyed by those intersections. In this case, there is a combination of the information conveyed by the local features of the picture with a consideration of the global interpretation. This dual process—of feature extraction and interpretation—will come up repeatedly as we examine the perceptual experience. Moreover, the implications of this dual process of perception make themselves felt not only in the analysis of things like blocks, but also in situations where there is conflict between the implications of the local features and the global interpretation. When these contradictions arise, the resulting perception shows the conflict in rather obvious ways.

FIGURE 1-21

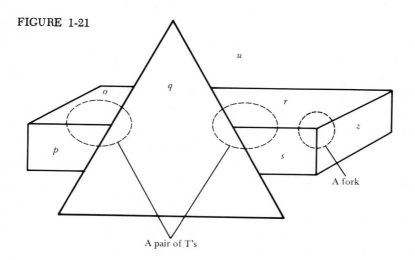

We normally perceive space to be three-dimensional. Distant objects take up a smaller angle than they do when close up. Textures change with distance and with viewing angle. Lines converge in the distance. Assuming that humans normally live and move about in a three-dimensional world, it makes sense that the visual apparatus has evolved to piece together a three-dimensional representation of the images that it sees. Let us try out some rules that it might have adopted to see how they work in explaining some phenomena.

Whenever a visual pattern is encountered in which lines or edges are converging, there are two options in interpreting it. It could be a two-dimensional object viewed straight on, in which case the lines are truly converging, or, it could be a three-dimensional object viewed at an angle, in which case the lines may really be parallel and the apparent convergence is a result of distance. The choice of interpretation seems to be based on an analysis of all of the available evidence. Consider the two cone shapes in this picture by Magritte (Figure 1-22).

They are drawn almost identically, yet they represent quite different objects. The cone on the left is obviously oriented vertically. The sides do not appear to be parallel. The same size cone on the right is a street receding away to the distance. The sides appear parallel. The same visual information can be interpreted quite differently.

The ability to see things in depth does not depend on familiarity with the objects. In Figure 1-23, a painting by Jeffrey Steele, a compelling illusion of depth is created by a very precise use of perspective in an endlessly repeated pattern.

Horizontal contours that are equally spaced in the environment are projected onto the retina with smaller and smaller separations. Look at this design (Figure 1-24).

If we start at the middle of the pattern and follow up to the right, it appears to recede in the distance because the line spacing is systematically reduced. In fact, if you examine the geometry of the figure with care, you see that the gradient of line spacings gives rather precise angle and distance information. This is illustrated in Figure 1-25, where the different line gradients seen by an observer are shown as a plane surface that has a series of equally spaced horizontal lines tilted away from him. The spacing of the lines tells unambiguously the angle of the surface. Distance is not known, however, since in this diagram, the same gradient of line spacings can be the result of any distance from the eye (assuming that there is no way of knowing the actual spacing of the horizontal lines). Note, however, that if the information about the sides of the surface is available, as it is in the figure, then further constraints are put upon the situation.

Perception of space

Normally 3-Dim.

2 Dim viewed from straight on OR 3 dim. viewed from angle

FIGURE 1-22   Rene Magritte, "Les Promenades d'Euclide." Courtesy of The Minneapolis Institute of Arts.

Jeffrey Steele, "Baroque Experiment: Fred Maddox." Collection: Hon. FIGURE 1-23
Anthony Samuel. Courtesy of the artist.

FIGURE 1-24   *From Carraher and Thurston (1968).*

optical illusion —
distance gradient

In Figure 1-25 the plane surface was tilted, so that not only did the equally spaced horizontal lines become more tightly packed in the furthest parts of the retinal image, but the projected length of the lines also decreased. This phenomenon, the well-known distance gradient, is responsible for many optical illusions.

The first illusion can be seen in Figure 1-24, where the end of the object that is perceived to be more distant is also perceived to be larger, even though (actually, because) the vertical lines of the drawing are all the same length. This diagram presents conflicting information to the observer, so it is no surprise that the resolution of the interpretation is also a conflict (see also Figure 1-37, page 29).

It does not take much to present depth information. Many different types of surface gradients will do the trick, as shown in Figure 1-26. When a rectilinear object is viewed straight on, the intersecting lines formed by its contours form right angles. As the object is tilted and rotated in space, the angles in the retinal image diverge from right angles. The degree of divergence depends on the orientation of the object in space. By interpreting that divergence from right angles as a result of depth, distance information can be extracted.

For example, in Figure 1-27 it is easy to see which of the cross bars intersects the vertical line at right angles. Yet, the same set of crosses is normally interpreted differently when accompanied by information about depth, as in Figure 1-28.

FIGURE 1-25

Observer  Plane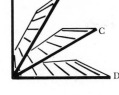

WHAT IS SEEN   WHAT THE SITUATION IS

From the side   From the top

A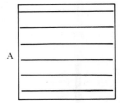

B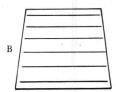

C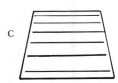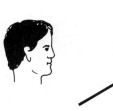

D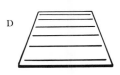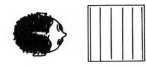

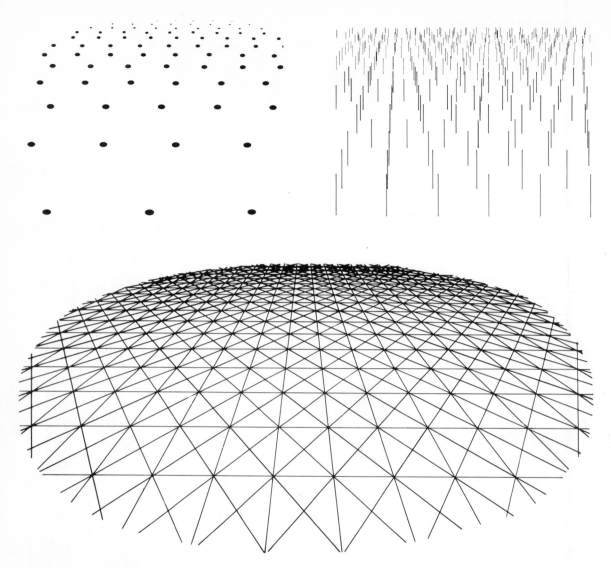

FIGURE 1-26   *From Gibson (1950).*

FIGURE 1-27   FIGURE 1-28

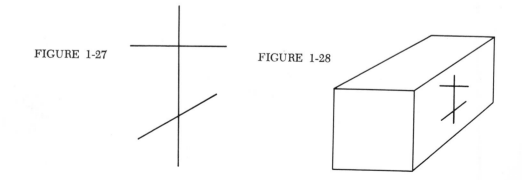

Impossible organizations. Another way of demonstrating the operation of the attempt to put objects into three dimensions during their interpretation is to construct pictures whose parts cannot be fit together to make a logical story. Here are some bits and pieces of a picture.

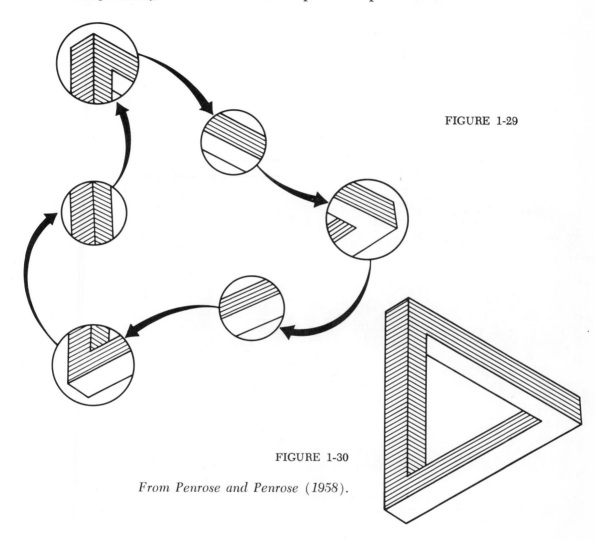

FIGURE 1-29

FIGURE 1-30

From Penrose and Penrose (1958).

They look like corners and sides of some three-dimensional object. Now we put them all together.

What happened? The pieces do not quite fit; the figure is impossible. But there is nothing inherently impossible about the collection of lines and angles that make up the drawing. The individual features conflict with the global interpretation. Here are some more examples to mull over.

Figure 1-30

ind. features conflict
with global interp ∴
Producing an
im →
Figures 1-31, 1-32, & 1-33
possible image

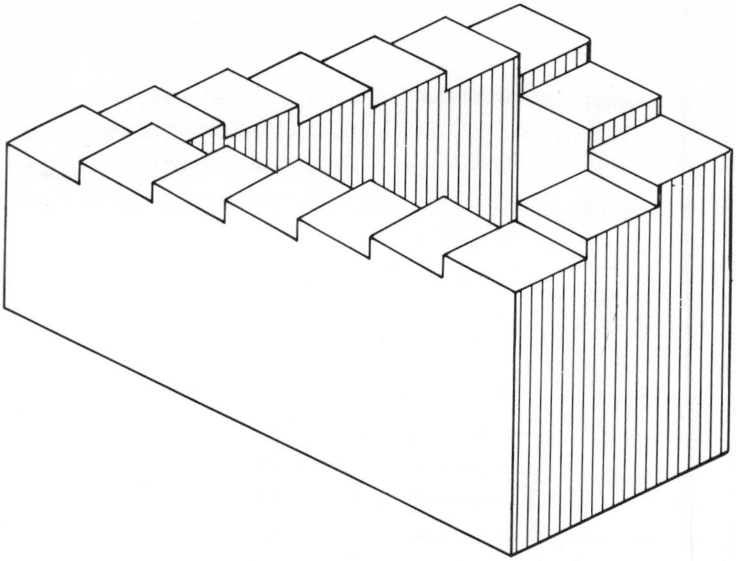

FIGURE 1-31

From Penrose and Penrose (1958).

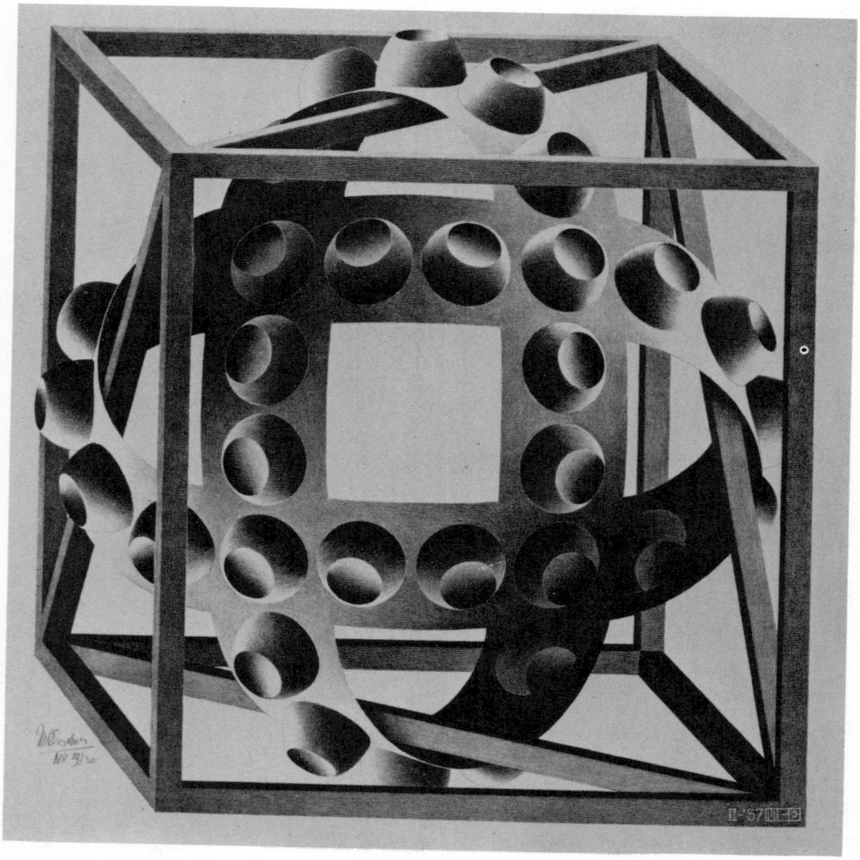

FIGURE 1-32 *M. C. Escher, "Cube with Magic Ribbons." Collection: Haags Gemeentemuseum—The Hague.*

Josef Albers, "Structural Constellations." 1953–1958. From Despite Straight Lines, pp. 63, 79. Courtesy of the artist. FIGURE 1-33

*The importance of
context*

Nothing is dealt with in isolation. All the information must be integrated into a consistent overall interpretation of the visual scene. The three barrels in Figure 1-34 obviously have different sizes. Yet, it is easy to change their apparent relative sizes; just add information that provides the appropriate context.

FIGURE 1-34

FIGURE 1-35

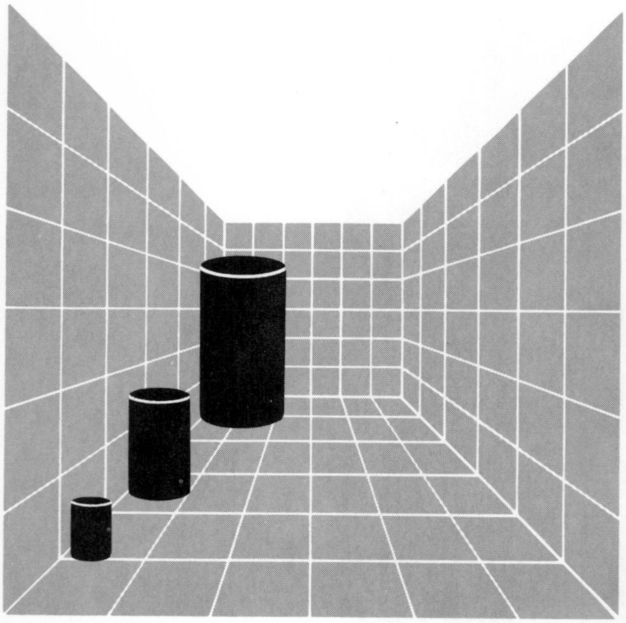

FIGURE 1-36

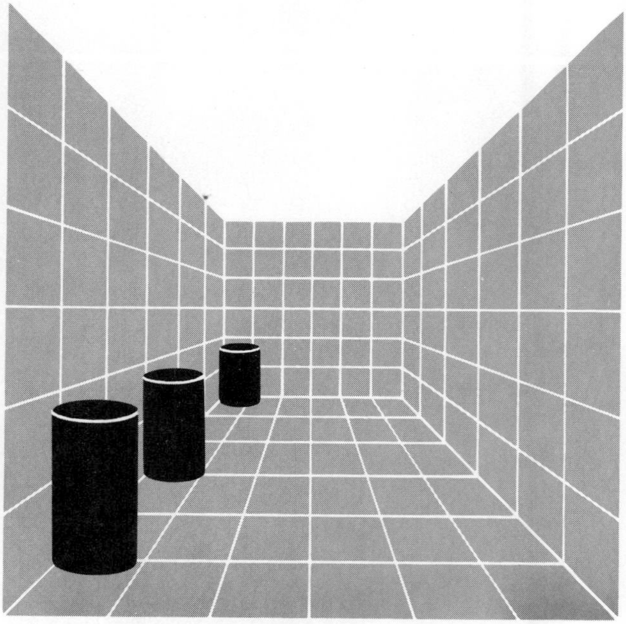

Again, the effects of context do not depend on working with familiar objects. Subtle effects seem to be present even in the meagerest of line drawings.

Figures 1-37 & 1-38

Normally, all contextual information fits together. As objects move away, their image size changes by just the right amount. The relative sizes and distances and what they should be. Neither the artist nor

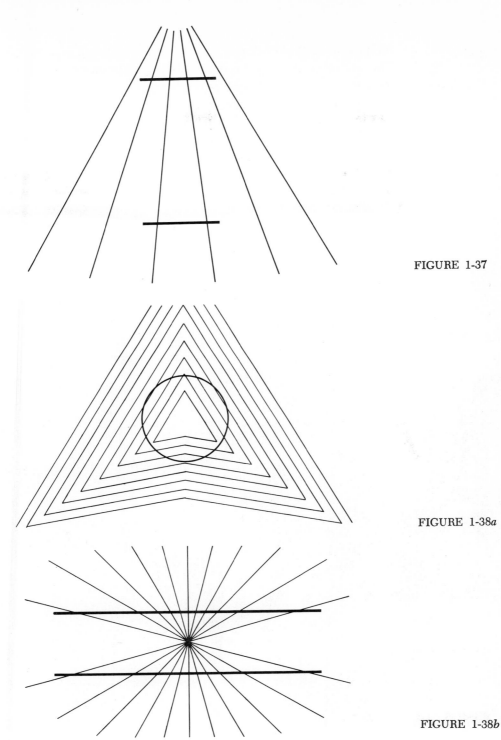

FIGURE 1-37

FIGURE 1-38*a*

FIGURE 1-38*b*

The two horizontal lines of Figure 1-37 are the same length. Figure 1-38a contains a perfect circle. The two horizontal lines of Figure 1-38b are parallel. From Luckiesh (1965).

Figure 1-39

the psychologist, however, is constrained to studying real-life situations. The surrealist delights in discovering and intentionally violating the rules for constructing logical perceptions.

We could accommodate the apple if we could assume the room was very tiny. Magritte has been meticulously careful to portray a lifelike room and apple so that neither can be easily scaled down in size. He violates the rules to provide an interesting image.

All these phenomena suggest that when piecing together sensory information, a consistent image of the world must be produced. In the laboratory, we can construct situations in which the information seen is

FIGURE 1-39 *Rene Magritte, "The Listening Room." Collection: Mr. William N. Copley.*

ambiguous or incomplete. Thus, in the folded paper trick, the information about the true orientation of the figure was eliminated by viewing the object with one eye closed from a relatively stable head position. Only once the perceptual illusion had been achieved was it possible to move the head again, adding new depth cues. This time, however, the motion cues were interpreted in terms of the novel perception. As long as the interpretation was still possible (no matter whether it was unique or unfamiliar), the illusion was maintained.

Feature Analysis based on producing a consistent image of an

The last section concentrated on the interpretation of sensory features, on the rules of perception. But what can we say about the features themselves? What information does the nervous system extract from the signals arriving at the sense organs? Again, we make progress by looking for anomalies of perception. Actually, in studying the operations of sensory systems, it is possible to use physiological recording techniques and measure the operations of the nerves themselves. The evidence from investigations of this type will be presented in Chapter 2 and again in Chapters 4 through 7. But before going into the nervous system, it helps if we examine some of the more general properties of the feature extraction scheme by looking at their effects on perception.

FEATURE ANALYSIS

Examine Figures 1-40 and 1-41. In Figure 1-40, there is a tiny gray spot at the intersection of all the white lines, with the exception of the intersection at which you are looking. In Figure 1-41, the inner gray squares look to be different shades of gray: In fact, they are all the same. These two figures illustrate one principle of sensory analysis: Neural cells interact with each other. Thus, the receptors at one part of the visual image are affected by the operation of neighboring receptors. Neither of these effects would occur if the receptors were independent of one another so that they simply sent a pure, uninterrupted signal to the brain. Indeed, in the one spot in the eye where the receptors do not interact much with one another, the darkening of the intersections does not take place: the small area right at the point on which the eye is focused. (This area is called the *fovea*—more about it in Chapters 4 and 5.) Figure 1-42 shows a similar result. See the faint diagonal lines running between the squares? Well, they are actually not there. The neural interaction adds them to the image.

Sensory analysis: neurons interact with one another

Here in simple demonstrations are strong influences of the feature extraction system, but these demonstrations do not tell us how they operate. It is possible to obtain more information about the operation of the feature extraction mechanism through two psychological procedures:

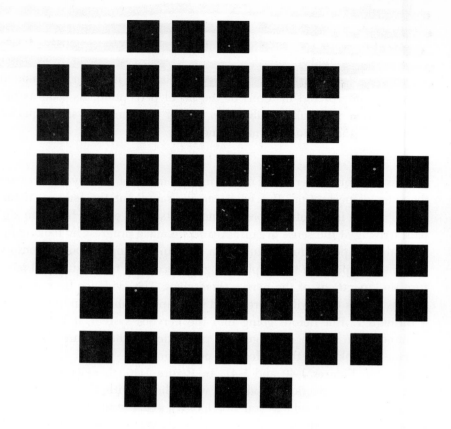

FIGURE 1-40   *The Hering grid: Gray spots appear at each intersection, except the one you are looking at.*

FIGURE 1-41   *Simultaneous contrast: The small squares all have the same intensities. From Cornsweet (1970).*

This illusion, the appearance of faint, diagonal lines (which are not actually there) was discovered by Robert Springer.   FIGURE 1-42

- First, the eyes are in constant motion. If that motion is stopped, the images seen by the eyes disappear. The way in which the visual image fades away when the eye is stopped suggests some of the properties of the feature extraction mechanism.
- Second, prolonged viewing of an image leaves its mark on future perceptions. The effects of these afterimages provide another clue to the operations of the visual system.

The image on the eye is in constant motion, not simply because of movements in the environment, but because of a continuous tremor in the eye—small jiggling movements called *physiological nystagmus*. In fact, there are a number of different types of eye movements which go on without our noticing them. One is very small and fast: The eye moves in an angle of about 20 seconds of arc, 30 to 70 times each second. (There are 60 seconds of arc to each minute and 60 minutes of arc to a degree—thus, 20 seconds is $\frac{1}{180}$ of a degree.) Another is a large, oscillatory motion. Still another is a slow drift of a few visual minutes one way or the other. And finally, there are some rapid jerks, with an amplitude of about 5 minutes of arc, often correcting for the slow drifts. You can see the effect of these eye movements with this demonstration.

Stopping the image

Figure 1-43

FIGURE 1-43

*From Verheijen
(1961).*

Look at the black fixation point of Figure 1-43 steadily (the dot in the center of the figure), trying to keep your eyes as still as possible. Keep looking until the black and white parts of the picture appear to shimmer (about 30 sec). Then move your gaze to the white dot. You should see a set of white blocks on a dark background, superimposed on the picture itself. The afterimage of the grid will continually shift about on the pattern, no matter how carefully you try to hold the image steady. This is physiological nystagmus.

What is interesting, however, is not so much that the eye is in continuous motion, but that if all movements are stopped, the visual image disappears. This phenomenon gives us some basic information about the way the receptor and sensory analyzing systems are working.

Movements of the visual image across the surface of the retina can be stopped using several techniques (Riggs, Ratliff, Cornsweet, & Cornsweet, 1952). One of them is shown in Figure 1-44. Here a small mirror is attached to a contact lens on the eye. The image to be seen by the subject is projected at this mirror, which bounces it off onto the viewing surface. With this system, when the eye moves to the right, the mirror does too, and thus the image is displaced to the right. With careful calibrations, it is possible to make the image move through exactly the same visual angle as the eye, so that the image seen at the retina does not change its position, regardless of eye movements.

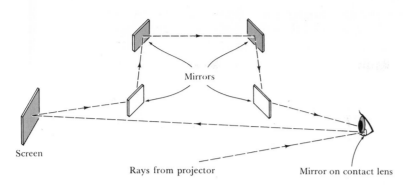

Mirrors

Screen

Rays from projector

Mirror on contact lens

FIGURE 1-44

From Riggs, Ratliff, Cornsweet, and Cornsweet (1953).

When a visual scene is viewed through such an apparatus, after a few seconds the patterns begin to disappear. Gradually, nothing is left but a blank, homogeneous field. The image disappears in a peculiar way. It does not simply fade away. It disappears in meaningful chunks. Whole segments go at once, leaving other parts still visible. The more meaningful the image, the longer it lasts. The part of the image that is consciously attended to lasts longest of all.

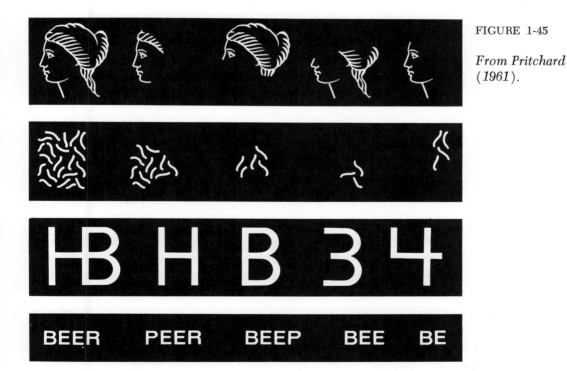

FIGURE 1-45

From Pritchard (1961).

BEER   PEER   BEEP   BEE   BE

You can observe the disappearance for yourself by examining Figure 1-46, *Looking Glass Suite No. 9* by the English artist Peter Sedgley, reproduced in color on page 216a. First notice some of the characteristics of the picture. The edges of the concentric circles are blurred. That is deliberate. In fact, it is one of the secrets to its operation. Now, stare at the center of the picture from close up without moving your eyes. Stare for awhile; it takes time. What should happen first is that the middle circle will go away. Then parts of the circles will be eliminated, not gradually, but in large segments. Finally, both circles will disappear, leaving only a constant, homogeneous yellow field. If you move your eyes even slightly, it will return. (Do not be disappointed if it takes you a long time to make the picture go away. There is a practice effect: The more you do it, the easier it becomes. The first time is sometimes extremely difficult. But the experience is worth the trouble.)

Notice that when the circles disappear, the yellow field fills in to take their place. Whenever the neural circuits cease to operate normally, their absence is not noted. In this case, the evidence for the circles is not present, but the color information is: Hence, we see only the latter.

What accounts for these effects? The most popular explanation is that perception of the pattern depends on the activity of very complex feature detectors, neural circuits that detect lines, edges, angles, and perhaps circles. So long as enough information is being provided by the neural receptors in the eyes, the complex feature detector continues to respond, and the pattern can be seen intact. When the eye stops its movements the receptors in the eye cease their responses. When there are no longer enough responses coming from the eyes to drive the complex detector, it ceases to respond and the pattern disappears as a whole. Hence, the relatively long life of complex images compared with simpler ones; hence the abrupt way in which whole segments of the image fade in and out of view; hence the distortions of complex images that occur when the fading sensory signal causes the perceptual mechanisms to err in their interpretations of those data that are still available.

Two questions remain. One, do other senses behave in this way: Does a constant auditory tone become inaudible after awhile? Two, why did Sedgley's circles disappear even though no special equipment was used to stop the eye movements? The answer to the first is easy. A constant auditory signal does not exist. Even tones which appear to have a constant pitch and loudness are, in reality, a continuously changing pattern of air pressure. Auditory signals have their motion built in: The visual system must add it artificially. Other systems, such as taste and touch, do adapt. The band of a wrist watch is no longer felt after a few minutes. You notice it only when it moves. A constant taste sensation or odor disappears after awhile. All sensory systems seem to require changes in stimulation in order to maintain perception. Stop the image, and you stop the perception.

What about the second question? The picture disappeared because it was cleverly constructed with blurred edges. Even though the eye did move slightly as the picture was viewed, the resulting vibratory pattern on the retina of the eye was of a blur moving across the receptors (see Figure 1-47). The transition from one color to the next was done so smoothly that the movement of the blur was not sufficient to cause the receptor cells to note the change in stimulation.

One must be very cautious in making deductions about neural mechanisms from behavioral data such as these. Alternative explanations should be carefully considered. The disappearance and reappearance of the patterns may be due to technical difficulties in the apparatus, such as slippage of the lens. Maybe the image is not perfectly stopped. Perhaps you only think that the disappearance occurs in meaningful components, because these are the only changes in perceptions that can readily be described.

These questions should not, of course, be taken as grounds for dismissing the phenomenon, but rather as spurs toward further research. The work on stopped images provides a potentially useful bridge between our perceptual experiences and the neural mechanisms underlying human vision.

A second important source of information about human perception comes from a consideration of the aftereffects of strong stimulation. If one stares at a brightly colored light for a while and then looks at a smooth, white surface, the image is seen, but in the complementary color. If the original light was red, the afterimage is green. If the original was blue, the afterimage is yellow: If it was black, the afterimage is white.

Aftereffects

Similarly, if you stand in a doorway and push hard against the doorjambs with your arms as if you were trying to raise them up over your head, you discover when you move away and let both hands relax normally, your arms slowly rise up in the air, as if of their own accord. Again, the aftereffects of intense stimulation make themselves felt in ways that tell us something about the internal functioning of the system.

Motion aftereffects.   A particularly compelling aftereffect involves motion. Watch a moving object for a while. The classical object is a waterfall, but many other movements will do. The important thing is that you be able to stare fixedly at one spot, being careful not to move your eyes for several minutes while the motion takes place.

Now if you shift your gaze to a textured object (a wall, or better,

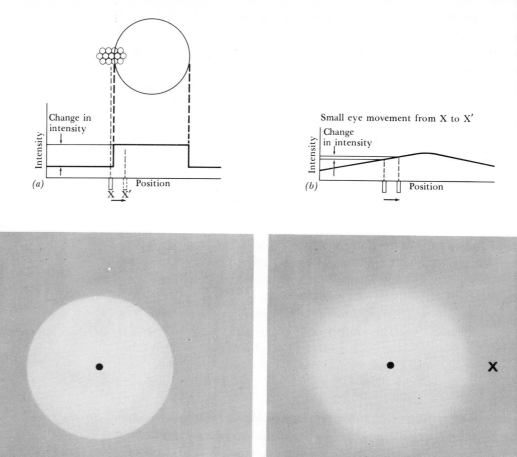

FIGURE 1-47   *Top: An explanation of why the blurred disk disappears, but the sharp one does not. Involuntary eye movements (nystagmus) produce strong intensity changes on the retina when the sharp disk (a) is fixated, but the same eye movement produces only a slight change in intensity with the blurred target (b).*

Is this the explanation for the disappearance of the rings in the picture by Peter Sedgley (Figure 1-46 in the color plates)?

Bottom: A demonstration of the role of abrupt changes in intensity. If you fixate the dot of picture (b) steadily (closing one eye helps), the blurred disk will disappear. It will reappear if you blink or if you shift your fixation to the X. The sharp disk (a) will probably not disappear for you.

These figures come from Cornsweet (1969).

some finely textured material such as curtains or bedspreads), you will see the appearance of motion in the direction **opposite** to that of the original object. If the object was moving down, after motion moves up; if you watched a contracting spiral, the aftermotion is that of expansion. If you examine the textured surface with care, you will note that the motion is really not there: The visual image is not moving. There is the appearance of motion in the absence of a moving image.

WHAT TO LOOK AT FOR MOTION AFTEREFFECTS

An extremely effective source of motion is a moving wheel that rotates some three or four times each second. The wheel should be marked with lines of high contrast so that the movement is easily observed. The best movement effects come from watching a spiral mounted on a rotating wheel: As the spiral rotates it will appear to be contracting or expanding, depending upon the direction of rotation.

To help you view the phenomenon of motion aftereffects, we have provided you with a spiral (Figure 1-48) that can be traced from the drawing in the book and then mounted on a rotating phonograph turntable. This spiral is designed to be rotated at 33⅓ rpm. If you lack a phonographic turntable, you can try inserting a pencil in the center hole and spinning the spiral around that. But rotate the spiral slowly: about the same speed as that of a 33⅓ rpm record.

Now, stare intently at the center of the rotating spiral for at least 30 sec. Do not let your eyes wander from the center. Now look at other objects around your room, or at someone's face.

As we have mentioned, the original form of the motion aftereffect came from prolonged observation of a waterfall. If you are unable to find a waterfall and do not wish to or cannot construct the wheel, then there are still some alternative methods of finding motion. One method is to use the television set, first adjusting the image to have maximum brightness and maximum contrast, second, by carefully fiddling with the vertical hold controls, to adjust the picture so that it continually drifts up or down across the screen. Unfortunately, the television image, especially on a good set, will move jerkily, hindering the effect, so that you might have to look at the image longer (please turn off the sound).

Finally, you could simulate a waterfall by turning on the water in the bathtub or shower so as to make as big a stream as possible. Stare intently at this for at least 1 min. This method is not particularly recommended, but it does seem to work.

Color aftereffects. Examine Figure 1-49 (in color on page 216a). Stare intently at the black dot in the left panel, the one with all

FIGURE 1-48   *If this spiral (or a facsimile) is placed on a rotating turntable and the center stared at for 30 sec, a motion aftereffect will occur. From Gregory (1970).*

the green hearts. Keep your head and eyes steady and keep staring until the whole figure starts to shimmer. Then look at the right black dot in the figure, the one in the white area. You should see a series of red hearts (it helps to blink a few times to get the afterimage started). The afterimage that results from intensive examination of a color is the appearance of the complementary color—the opposite color, if you will. You can notice this color aftereffect with any brightly colored surface, including most of the other figures included in the color plates.

Notice two aspects about aftereffects. First, the aftereffect is always the opposite or complement of the original movement or muscle pressure or color (when we discuss the mechanisms of color vision we will see why red is the complementary color to green). This suggests the operation of two antagonistic systems pitted against each other. The second point is that the aftereffect requires prolonged stimulation of one of the antagonistic systems: Prolonged exposure to one of complementary colors or continued movement in one direction. This suggests that the responsiveness of the underlying neural mechanisms can be adapted or fatigued to have a reduced sensitivity to the input.

The explanation of aftereffects

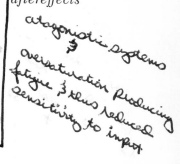

Consider the motion aftereffect. Suppose that there were specific neural detectors for movement, with the detectors for movement in one direction paired up with those for movement in the exactly opposite direction. Suppose further that these two detectors act against each other, with the action of one causing a decrease in the action of the other. Now we need further to assume that the motion detectors are connected together to form a new detector unit, one that responds with increased neural responses when movement in one direction occurs and with decreased neural responses when movement in the other direction occurs. When there is no movement, the two detectors balance each other out and the output of the new detector unit is simply a low level, background response—one that indicates no movement.

All that is needed now is to assume that either class of detectors feeding into the circuit can be fatigued by prolonged stimulation. Then, after overstimulation (and fatigue) to movement, when a stationary object is viewed, the fatigued detectors do not make their normal contribution to balance the activity in the pair of opposed motion detectors. The circuit will signal movement in the opposite direction.

The explanation of color aftereffects follows a similar line of reasoning. Again, neural cells are paired, so that cells that respond in one way are connected with cells which respond in the other, the output of the pairing being simply the difference between the two. If a **red** receptor is paired with a **green** one, both respond equally in the presence of white light, leading to no output from the combined cells. The **red** cell fires with **red** light leading to a positive output, the **green** cell with **green** light, leading to a negative output. Normally, with white light present, both **red** and **green** respond equally, leading to no output from the combined cells. Now suppose the eye focuses upon a **red** color for some period of time. By fatigue, the **red** cell loses its ability to respond. Now if the eye looks upon a white light, the **green** responds normally, but the normal response of the **red** is inhibited. The result, of course, is that the **green** responses outweigh the **red,** and the white light is seen as **green.**

Although aftereffects indicate that fatiguing is occurring somewhere in the chain of events leading to perception, the simple existence of the effect does not give any information about what parts of the system are being fatigued. To determine where the fatigue occurs, additional data are needed. The main technique is to test whether the aftereffect transfers between eyes: Stimulate one eye until fatigue takes place, then test the other eye for the aftereffect. If the aftereffect is not observed, peripheral mechanisms are assumed to be responsible. The color after-effects just described do not transfer between eyes. Thus, they are a result of fatigue or adaptation in peripheral mechanisms, probably due to the depletion of the chemical reserves in the color receptors of the eye itself.

The exact locus of fatigue underlying the motion aftereffects is less clear. Some studies have reported transfer of the aftereffect between eyes suggesting central processes are being fatigued. Others have failed to find such transfer.

The conclusion, of course, is that these aftereffects imply the operation of specific types of neural circuits in the sensory analyzing system. They suggest the presence of specific detectors for movement and for color.

Orientation-specific color adaptation One intriguing set of aftereffects has been found relatively recently. The phenomenon was first reported by McCollough in 1965, and it bears her name: the McCollough Effect (McCollough, 1965). Again the rationale behind the effect comes from a consideration of the possible feature detectors in humans.

We have suggested that there might be special detectors for lines: Suppose there were not only line detectors, but colored line detectors in the human visual system. How could one demonstrate their existence? Following the reasoning in the preceding section, one strategy is to fatigue one set of line detectors, then present a neutral object. If the complementary set of features exists, they should show themselves.

Suppose there are both red and green horizontal line detectors. After

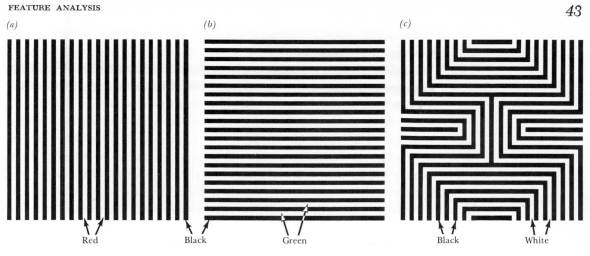

(a) (b) (c)

Red   Black   Green   Black   White

FIGURE 1-50

prolonged exposure to green horizontal lines, white horizontal lines should then appear reddish (white has equal amounts of red and green). Is this effect specific to horizontal lines, or just an overall color adaptation to green? To find out, simultaneously fatigue the red vertical-line detectors so that white vertical lines will subsequently appear green.

This is the McCollough Effect. For 5 min subjects are alternately shown red vertical lines (Figure 1-50*a*) and then green horizontal lines (Figure 1-50*b*), each pattern being left on for about 5 sec. Then a test pattern consisting of black and white lines at various orientations is presented to the subject (Figure 1-50*c*): the horizontal white lines look reddish; the vertical white lines look greenish; oblique lines look white. If the head is tilted to the side so that oblique lines now become vertical or horizontal, they too take on the appropriate coloration.

The effect has several surprises. For one thing, it is very persistent. Some people still see white lines as colored for 8 to 10 hours after the stimulation. In fact, some claim to see the aftereffects for as long as a week: an unusually long time for such a simple perceptual phenomenon to last. The effect is not a simple afterimage of the type that makes a black square leave a white afterimage. Afterimages require prolonged stimulation without any eye movements. But most surprising of all, the effect does not agree with two intuitions about line detectors.

If the specific color adaptations were due to specific circuits for detecting lines, then one would suspect that blurring the contours between the black and white stripes of the test pattern would destroy the effect (the lines are not seen sharply). On the other hand, changing the contrast between the white and black lines on the test pattern should have no effect, since the lines would still be seen clearly. The reverse is

From Gibson and Harris (1968).

true: Changing focus has no effect; increasing the intensity differences increase the aftereffect.

The McCollough Effect does demonstrate the operation of two complementary systems sensitive to certain patterns in the visual stimulus. And, in fact, as we shall see, a small number of colored line detectors—units which are maximally sensitive to a line of a specific color—have been found recently in the brains of monkeys. Be careful, however, in jumping to conclusions. Line detectors are far more complex than what is needed to explain the perceptual phenomenon. When we come to discuss the neural circuits for recognizing features, we will find that a much simpler type of detector perhaps gives an even better account of the data (see page 100).

Before leaving the McCollough Effect, it is interesting to note that it also works for moving images. We set up a band of horizontal stripes that can move up or down. When the stripes move up they are colored green; when they move down they are red. Each direction of movement is maintained for about 5 sec: The directions alternate while someone watches them for a total time of approximately 5 min. Now, we present a test image of black and white horizontal lines moving either up or down. When the test image moves up, the lines appear reddish; when it moves down, the lines appear to be greenish (Stromeyer, 1969; Stromeyer & Mansfield, 1970).

This is the exact analog of the McCollough Effect. All that has been changed is to substitute up and down movement for stationary lines at different orientations. Does this mean that there are color-sensitive movement detectors?

PERCEPTION WITHOUT FEATURES

The work on stopped images and aftereffects illustrates some of the techniques for studying the kinds of feature detectors that may be operating in human vision. There can be no question that specific feature detectors do exist in humans. But there is doubt about the exact types of detectors operating and their overall role in human perception. At least one noted neurophysiologist (Spinelli, 1967) maintains that specific detectors are important for lower animals, but their presence in man is simply an evolutionary oversight (that is, they are excess evolutionary baggage). There are characteristics of human perception that cannot be handled easily by an appeal to feature-detection systems.

Go back through the illustrations of this chapter. Look at the dog, or at some of the other pictures. What features are present? How do you construct a dog out of the miscellaneous blobs, where no straight lines or edges exist? How are competing organizations of the picture by Dali, or the different interpretations of the same cone shape in the picture by Magritte, explained through feature analysis? Consider the problem of "seeing" a sensation on the skin.

If someone traces a large capital letter on your arm or back, you have no difficulty in determining what that letter is. It is unlikely that you have feature detectors in the skin appropriate to this task. To interpret these tactile sensations requires a constructive effort on your part to recreate the path of the finger and decide on the appropriate pattern. If pattern recognition can be carried out in this novel way without feature detectors, are they truly needed in normal vision?

Seeing with the skin

Consider a more controlled situation where a complex visual image is painted onto the touch receptors of the skin rather than the light receptors of the eye. The data come from some recent work on vision substitution systems for the blind.

The apparatus for translating a visual image into a tactile one consists of a television camera that is connected to a set of tactile vibrators for stimulating the touch receptors. In one such apparatus, the visual image is transformed to a tactile impression by sending the image to a bank of 400 tactile vibrators arranged in a 10-inch square mounted on the back of a barber chair. (This apparatus was built and tested by White, Saunders, Scadden, Bach-y-Rita, and Collins, 1970.) The observer sits on the chair with his back against the vibrators. Regions of high light-intensity in the visual scene activate the vibrators in the corresponding region in the vibrator array. For low-intensity regions in the visual image, the vibrators are inactive. Thus, as the observer moves the television camera across the scene, the patterns of light intensity in the

FIGURE 1-51

From White, Saunders, Scadden, Bach-y-Rita, and Collins (1970).

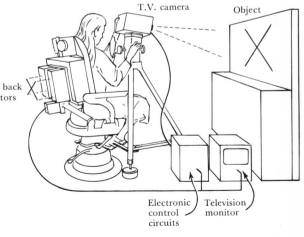

T.V. camera   Object

Image is transmitted to back via a bank of 400 vibrators

Electronic control circuits   Television monitor

Figure 1-51 visual scenes are reproduced in successions of tactile images impressed on the touch receptors of his back.

Given the crudeness of the tactile image, both sighted (but blindfolded) and blind observers show a rather remarkable recognition capacity using this device. They can easily distinguish horizontal from vertical bars on their first attempt. They quickly learn to identify simple geometric shapes—circles, triangles, and squares. More experience is required for recognizing more complicated objects such as coffee cups and telephones. With practice, however, both blind and sighted subjects can learn to identify up to 25 common objects on the basis of their tactile images. Moreover, when the objects are arranged on a table and viewed from slightly above, the observers can also report the relative positions and depths of the objects in the scene.

This last finding, the ability to perceive depth in a two-dimensional tactile image, is particularly interesting. A major clue to depth seems to be the relative height of objects at different distances. Some of the observers also noted the relationship between the image size and the distance of the object in the environment. In one example, a blind psychologist, who had frequently taught students about changes in image size with distance, reported a genuinely insightful discovery (an "aha" experience) when he first perceived the changes in the tactile image as an object was moved from a distance in close to the camera lens.

Generally, congenitally blind observers perform as well with the vision substitution system as normally sighted observers. If a blind observer has not experienced the object by touch before, he has to feel its shape before he can recognize its tactile image. Finally, allowing the observer to control the camera seemed to be crucial for accurate recognition. Many objects which observers simply could not learn to recognize with the camera held in a fixed position could readily be identified when they were allowed to sweep the image back and forth across the tactile receptors of their back.

The study of visual substitution systems raises some fundamental questions about the structure of perceptual analyses. Here, a discrete pattern of points is impressed into our skin—a crude analogy to the light pattern striking retinal receptors. Yet complex patterns can still be recognized. Some of the visual illusions that are often attributed to higher levels of analysis are also experienced when the equivalent tactile stimuli are used, so that the lines making up the drawings are felt rather than seen. Thus, the blind also experience "optical" illusions.

Does all this mean that the neural channels carrying tactile information are wired up the same way as those transmitting visual data? Are there line detectors and angle detectors for analyzing tactile information? If not, then how can these complex tactile patterns be analyzed? Maybe complex detectors are not needed. Perhaps they are simply a built-in luxury in the visual system. These are provocative questions, but we do not know enough yet to answer them.

Note especially the critical role of active movement in recognizing tactile images. Movement is very important in the processing of visual information. Apparently, perceptual systems in general are designed to extract more information from the succession of events produced by a moving pattern than from the responses to a static signal in the environment. Note, however, that movement only helps if the observer himself does the moving. When someone else moves the object (or the television camera), movement does not help. An analogous finding occurs with the active and passive movement of the eyes. If the eyes are moved naturally, by active control of the eye muscles, the world looks normal. If the eyes are moved passively, by pushing at them gently with the fingers, the visual scene appears to move about. Compensation for eye movement does not occur unless it is produced actively. The same might be true of tactile movements.

We have just started on the trail of the exploration of pattern recognition. In the next two chapters, we examine some of the problems in more detail: Both the exact neurological operations of the cells responsible for the initial processing of the signals and the status of some theories of pattern recognition will be discussed. We shall see that the extraction of features plays an important role both in the study of the physiological mechanisms and in the theoretical structures. But, as the discussions of this chapter have suggested, feature analysis will not be sufficient to explain all of the properties of human perception.

SUGGESTED READINGS

Perception

A good start is with the lovely little books by Gregory: *Eye and Brain: The Psychology of Seeing* (1966) and *The Intelligent Eye* (1970). You will find his books to be interesting and easy reading. The books on *Light and Vision* (Mueller, Rudolph, & Editors of Time-Life Books, 1969) and *The Mind* in the Life Science Series are also excellent.

Gibson has done more than anyone else to emphasize the importance of the physical cues in perceptual phenomena, and his two books (Gibson, 1950, 1966) are filled with illustrations of his ideas. We have used some of his ideas and illustrations, although we disagree with some of his views about the role of cognition in perception. All in all, we have profited immensely from our written and verbal disagreements with him, and we recommend his books to you.

A good book on perception is the little monograph by Hochberg (1964: paperback). This is one of the clearer presentations of the issues and phenomena of perception. In addition, you might want to see Hochberg's article, *In the Mind's Eye* (1968), which is reprinted in the book of readings collected by Haber (1968). The readings themselves are valuable, since you will probably be interested in many of the other articles reprinted there as well. [In addition, a second set of readings (Haber, 1969b) is also available, but not quite so relevant to this chapter of our book.] Still another good collection of papers can be found in Vernon's *Experiments in Visual Perception* (1966: paperback).

The work on stopped images and aftereffects will be discussed in later chapters. For more information on pattern recognition, see the *Suggested Readings* for Chapter 3. For more on the McCollough Effect, see the *Suggested Readings* for Chapter 2.

Art Good classical discussions of art come from the works of Arnheim, and his several books (Arnheim, 1969a,b), as well as Gombrich's book, *Art and Illusion* (1960). Our emphasis on illusions, optical art, and other contemporary art comes from our own wanderings through the museums and galleries. Excellent catalogs of optical art are available both from the museums, such as the Museum of Modern Art in New York [see, e.g., *The Responsive Eye* by Seitz (1965)] and the Arts Council of Great Britain. (*The Responsive Eye* is also available as a slide set from Sandak Color Slides, Set No. 617.) Our selection of Magritte's pictures comes from one of two catalogs, one from the Museum of Modern Art (Soby, 1965), and the other from the Arts Council of Great Britain (Sylvester, 1969). A fascinating (but expensive) book is available on Vasarely (1965), and Escher's works are also available in a book, *The Graphic Work of M. C. Escher* (Escher, 1967). In addition, the work of Bridget Riley (de Sausmarez, 1970), and the books of Albers (1963) and Kepes (1965) should be examined by anyone who is seriously interested in the perception of art. [The figures by Albers reproduced in this chapter come from the lovely discussion of geometric illusions in Bucher's (1961) book entitled *Joseph Albers. Despite Straight Lines.*]

An interesting discussion of the history and development of perspective in art is provided by Pirenne's *Optics, Painting, and Photography* (1970). This book treats the optical properties of the eye in some detail.

Many excellent examples of optical art and other illusions are reprinted in *Optical Illusions and the Visual Arts* (Carraher & Thurston, 1968). Luckiesh's (1922) book, *Visual Illusions,* provides a rich source to play with.

But above all, to enjoy the perceptual bases of art, tour the art galleries, both private and public. Many artists are experimenting with very sophisticated phenomena, and the only way to discover the artists is to go and seek them out. This is especially true with nonobject art: The artist's works may last only as long as he wishes them to, if they ever had a physical presence at all. We have found the material discussed in this chapter to be an excellent foundation for holding intelligent conversation with the artists, something that formal training in art may not let you do.

2

Neural information processing

How does one begin the study of neural information processing? What does one look for? One approach is that of Lettvin, Maturana, McCulloch, and Pitts (1959), the authors of a now classic paper on the visual system of a frog:

> We decided then how we ought to work. First, we should find a way of recording from single . . . fibers in the intact optic nerve. Second, we should present the frog with as wide a range of visible stimuli as we could, not only spots of light but things he would be disposed to eat, other things from which he would flee, sundry geometrical figures, stationary and moving about, etc. From the variety of stimuli we should then try to discover what common features were abstracted by whatever groups of fibers we could find in the optic nerve. Third, we should seek the anatomical basis for the grouping.

What should these investigators find inside the eye of a frog? From external appearances, frogs do not live in a very rich visual world. Generally, they appear to ignore most of their visual environment and show relatively little exploratory behavior. Because of their lack of active scanning and exploration they can be easily caught, provided they are approached from the rear. They seem to rely mainly on the presence of moving shadows to warn them of predators and possible danger. In fact, the only feature that stands out about a frog's use of vision is its ability to catch fast-moving flying insects. It manages this by waiting until they come within range, then lashing out quickly and accurately with its tongue.

Lettvin and his collaborators found a visual nervous system that corresponded to the frog's visual behavior. The frog's eye appears to extract only four patterns of information from the visual signal. Three of the four kinds of detectors are associated with relatively general characteristics in the visual scene: *edge detectors* that respond strongly to the border between light and dark regions, *moving contrast detectors* that respond when an edge moves, and *dimming detectors* that react when the overall illumination is lowered.

But it is the responses of the fourth class of detectors that are the most fascinating: *convex edge detectors* that respond only when a small, dark object moves into the field of vision. For there to be a response the object must be dark, must be moving, and must have a roughly circular shape. When this type of object first enters the field of view, a convex edge detector begins responding at a slow rate. As the object moves closer to the frog, the detector responds more and more vigorously. The response will continue even if the object suddenly disappears from view (but it can be stopped by a sudden change in illumination, such as that caused by an eyeblink). This, of course, is a bug detector: It provides exactly the visual information needed for efficient fly-catching behavior.

This investigation, then, suggests that the eye of the frog has in it a neural template for bugs. The frog has an exceedingly primitive brain. By putting the bug detector in the eye, the processes needed for the precise visual-motor coordinations involved in fly-catching are simplified. But place a frog in a new environment, perhaps one in which he is surrounded by hundreds of freshly killed flies, all suitable for eating, but with no movement: The template fails, and the frog will starve to death. The specialization of the frog's eye marks a high point for neural efficiency and sophistication, but a low point for adaptability. This visual pattern recognition system is simply not flexible enough to adapt to new conditions.

THE ANATOMY OF DETECTORS

The differences in function of the four classes of detectors found in the eye of the frog appear to be reflected in the neural organization of the cells, as well as in their visual appearance. The four classes of receptors go to different areas of the brain; moreover, the four types of detectors also look different.

Figure 2-1 shows three things: (a) the predicted classification of cells by Lettvin, Maturana, Pitts, and McCulloch (1961); (b) the actual classification in tadpoles found by Pomeranz and Chung (1970); and (c) photographs of the cells found by Pomeranz and Chung.

It is not easy to determine what each type of receptor looks like. It is possible to dissect the frog's eye and examine it under a microscope. And then, indeed, four different types of cells can be seen. The problem remains: Which is which?

Some tricks were necessary to determine what type of cell corresponded to which type of detector. The main problem is that the dissection kills the cells: It is not possible to record from a cell and also to examine it under a microscope, since the normal operation of a cell will not take place unless the neural structures are undisturbed. The surgical dissections required to expose the cells for study under the microscope would interfere with their normal functioning as pattern detectors. Hence, Pomeranz and Chung resorted to some deductive logic. They studied the tadpole, not the frog.

There seem to be only three different kinds of cells present in the eyes of tadpoles, not four. That identifies the missing cell, for if careful physiological recordings are made from living tadpoles, the edge response is found to be missing. Evidently, the *edge detector* develops only in the more mature animal.

FIGURE 2-1

PREDICTED CLASSIFICATION		ACTUAL CLASSIFICATION	
Physiology	Anatomy	Physiology	Anatomy
Class 1 edge detector	Constricted tree	Class 1 edge detector	Constricted tree
Class 2 convex edge detector	E tree	Class 2 convex edge detector	E tree
Class 3 moving contrast detector	H tree	Class 3 moving contrast detector	H tree
Class 4 dimness detector	Broad tree	Class 4 dimness detector	Broad tree

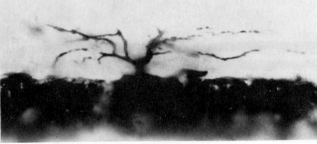

Photomicrographs (at the same magnification) of the three types of ganglion cells found in the tadpole retina. From Pomeranz and Chung (1970).

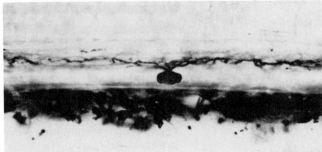

There is only one kind of cell in the periphery of the tadpole eye. By recording the responses of live tadpoles to signals presented peripherally, this detector is identified as the *convex edge detector*. Now there are two cells left to be identified: the *moving contrast detector* and the *dimness detector*. These two are determined by logical deduction. Of the two remaining cells, one has two layers, the other only one layer. Moreover, the two-layer cell is less spread out than the one-layer cell. These cues unlock the puzzle. The dimness detector has a larger receptive field than the moving contrast detector. Moreover, it clearly is a simpler circuit, so it should be the simpler cell, one layer, not two.

The study of the frog's eye illustrates the procedures and philosophy of physiological investigators. The results demonstrate that the frog has developed a highly sophisticated sensory analysis designed to extract specific information from a visual image. Of course, we do not expect to find that all animals have bug detectors. In fact, the sensory information processing performed in higher species than frogs is, in some sense, much simpler but also more elegant and flexible. It proceeds by small steps, employing simple but powerful principles for combining, rearranging and analyzing the data flowing in through the receptors from the environment. To understand it, we must understand the operation of the basic unit in the nervous system—the neuron—and the techniques for studying its behavior. We must explore how these units are put together to construct the neural circuits that analyze the information provided by the sensory systems.

PHYSIOLOGICAL
PROCEDURES
The neuron

The basic building block of the nervous system is the *neuron*, the cell that handles intercommunication of information among the various parts of the body. For our purposes, a simplified schematic knowledge of a neuron is sufficient. A *neural unit* consists of several parts (see Figure 2-2): a *cell body* (also called the *soma*), a *nerve fiber* (also called the *axon*) that carries information from one neuron to another, and a terminal *junction* (a *synapse*) at which the activity of one neuron influences the electrical characteristics of the cell body of another.

Junctions between neurons occur either on the cell body itself or on tiny extensions of the cell body called *dendrites*. Moreover, a single axon may send out only a few branches at its ending, or it may send out a large number of branches to make synaptic connections with adjoining cells. Similarly, the cell body may only have a few incoming connections which influence it, or may receive inputs from thousands of different neurons.

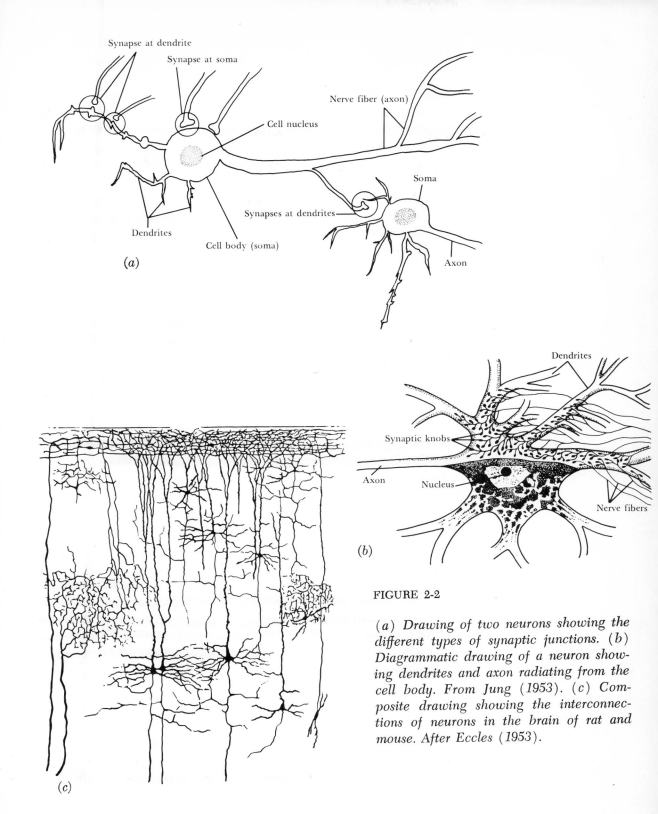

FIGURE 2-2

(*a*) *Drawing of two neurons showing the different types of synaptic junctions.* (*b*) *Diagrammatic drawing of a neuron showing dendrites and axon radiating from the cell body. From Jung (1953).* (*c*) *Composite drawing showing the interconnections of neurons in the brain of rat and mouse. After Eccles (1953).*

Nerve fibers and dendrites can be treated as insulated conductors for transmitting the basic signals of the nervous system—electrical impulses. These electrical (more accurately, ionic) inputs are generated in the cell body in response to activity at the incoming synapses. At the synapse itself, an incoming impulse triggers the release of a chemical *transmitter substance*, which travels across the small gap between the axon of the arriving neuron and the receptor location of the new neuron. The arrival of transmitter substance at the new cell body causes a change in its normal electrical potential. If enough transmitter is received, the change in electrical potential in the cell body will be sufficient to initiate an impulse, which then travels down the axon to the next synaptic junction, where the whole process is repeated.

It is seldom the case that activity at a single synaptic connection is sufficient to generate an impulse in the receiving cell. Usually a large number of impulses must arrive at a cell before it responds with its own impulse. Synaptic junctions are of two forms: *excitatory*, in which the effect of the arriving impulse is to increase the chance that the cell will respond, or *inhibitory*, in which the arriving impulse reduces the chance that the receiving cell will respond.

A cell's response to the pattern of activity on the incoming synapses is the result of a kind of chemical vote in which the balance of excitatory and inhibitory influences determines the final activity level of the cell. The response rate of a receiving cell generally depends on the rate and pattern of the impulses arriving at the incoming synapse, but there are limitations. After emitting an impulse, a cell requires about $\frac{1}{1000}$ sec in order to recover. Thus, in theory, the most frequently any cell could respond with an impulse is around 1000 impulses per second, and in practice the maximum observed response rates are much lower—on the order of 300 to 800 impulses per second.

There are actually many different types of neural cells, each of which performs specialized functions. For our purposes, the most important specialized cell is the *receptor* or *transducer* cell. These units are responsible for converting the energy in an external physical signal into electrical impulses. The *rods* and *cones* in the eye are examples of transducers that convert the electromagnetic energy in the incoming light pattern into neural responses. Similarly, the *hair cells* of the inner ear are transducers that convert the mechanical energy in acoustic signals into a neural code.

Recording neural responses   Since a neural response is a brief electrical discharge, for us to monitor neural activity patterns requires us to be able to connect electrical conductors to the neurons. The device used is an *electrode*. Usually the electrode is connected to an electronic amplifier to amplify the small electrical impulses. The output of the amplifier is then fed into electronic monitors that allow the experimenter both to hear and see the neural responses produced by an external signal.

An oscilloscope is usually used to plot a picture of the voltage changes in the neuron as a function of time. Neural impulses produce brief blips or spikes on the screen when the impulse travels past the recording electrode. If the signal is sent to a loudspeaker, it is possible to hear a click every time an impulse is generated in the neuron. In addition, the neural response patterns are often recorded for subsequent analysis on a tape recorder, or the screen of the oscilloscope may be photographed, or the analysis may be done by a digital computer as the impulses occur.

FIGURE 2-3

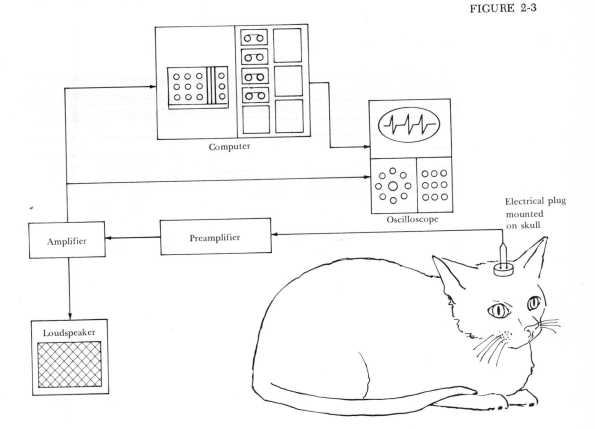

Computer

Oscilloscope

Electrical plug mounted on skull

Amplifier

Preamplifier

Loudspeaker

Nerve fibers in most sensory systems are small—typically about 3 to 5 microns (μ) in diameter (a micron is one micrometer: one thousandth of a millimeter). To isolate the activity in a single neuron, then, a very small electrode, a *microelectrode*, is needed. The recording tip of a microelectrode may vary from .1 to 1 μ in diameter depending on the type of electrode. Alternatively, a slightly larger electrode, a *macroelectrode*, can be used to monitor the combined activity in a group of neighboring fibers. The tip of a microelectrode is often so small that it cannot be seen with a light microscope, an electron microscope must be used.

Both types of electrodes are useful. Often, large numbers of neighboring neurons appear to be extracting similar types of information from an incoming signal, with no single fiber being solely responsible for providing the pertinent data to the brain. In this case, it is useful to study the characteristics of the average response activity of neighboring fibers with macroelectrodes. In other situations, microelectrodes are needed. Individual neurons frequently interact with one another in complex ways during the analysis and coding of sensory signals. To discover the nature of the interactions, the detailed response patterns of each individual unit must be examined.

Where should the electrode be placed? In sensory systems, the synapses of fibers carrying sensory messages tend to be clustered together in a local region called a *synaptic station* or a *relay station*. Since most of the computations carried out by the nervous system are performed at the junctions between neurons, these relay stations are profitable places to begin investigations. By studying both the input and output we try to determine how the sensory information is rearranged as it passes through a synaptic station.

The choice of experimental animal depends upon many factors. A number of the basic studies have been performed on the eye of the *Limulus*, or *horseshoe crab*, mainly because its retinal cells are relatively large and easy to monitor. More advanced animals are required if we wish to learn about systems more directly applicable to the human. Cats and monkeys are usually used for this purpose. Other animals, such as fish and, infrequently, birds, are studied when their sensory systems offer some particular advantages for investigating certain types of neural coding. Humans are only occasionally used, almost always when some brain surgery needs to be done, and the recording of neural responses is either only a very minor digression in the operative steps to be performed or is one of the procedures necessary for the operation itself.

DESIGNING NEURAL
CIRCUITS

At this point we have the tools to put together neural circuits. Consider the problem of detecting a moving object. How do we go from the simple responses of the light-sensitive receptors of the eye to a neuron that responds only if an object moves across the visual field from right to left? What is the circuit theory of the nervous system?

In the pages that follow, we construct neural circuits that detect the edges of a figure, movement, color, and other patterns. We start with the simpler interactions of the system and work our way to the point where, at the rate we would be proceeding, we could, in theory, produce a set of neurons that respond only when a very complex object like your grandmother comes into sight. We stop just before that point, however, since we would have returned to the problems encountered in the opening chapter of the book. Is it really possible to construct a grandmother detector? Is there really a specific cell in the brain that responds only when she comes into view? The analysis and recognition of complex patterns will be the topic of the next chapter. Meanwhile, before discussing that problem completely, we need to gain some experience in putting together neurons to do things.

We start with the simpler circuits and work our way to the more complex ones. This means that we start with the sensory systems and then follow the neural pathway to the brain. The analysis is based on the visual system, both because it serves as a convenient source of material and because more is known about the hookup of neurons in the eye and visual centers than for other systems. But the basic neural building blocks are similar for all sensory modalities. Once the principles for constructing the circuits that analyze visual signals are known, it is not difficult to put together circuits for other systems.

Before we start, a word of caution. When considering the types of analyses performed in sensory systems, it is wise to keep in mind the complexity facing anyone who would trace the wiring diagram of the brain. In the visual system of man there are about 125 million basic receptor elements in each eye. In the brain, there are approximately 40 million synapses per cubic centimeter (or, equivalently, some 600 million synapses per cubic inch). Each individual cortical neuron (and there are hundreds of millions) has from 6,000 to 60,000 synapses on it, depending upon which section of the brain it is in. In the face of these numbers, and considering the delicacy of the electrode required to record from a single cell and the many biological, electronic, and mechanical details that go into making a successful experiment, it is remarkable that so much has been learned.

Some of what we present in this chapter is well-established fact. Other is speculative theory. Some is generally accepted; some is still under dispute. In reading these sections, it is wise to remember that the exploration of specific functions of single cells in the brain is in its infancy. The results to this date are exciting and provoking. But they are far from complete.

BASIC CIRCUITS

The building blocks

transform - rec.
combine - gang.

When we study the construction of sensory circuits, two levels of the system have to be considered: the set of cells that **transform** the external physical signals into a neural output—the *receptors* or *transducers,* and the cells that **combine** neural signals in various ways—simply called *neural cells,* or sometimes *bipolars* or *ganglion cells*. We will not always be scrupulously accurate with the neurological labels. Often abstract concepts like receptors and ganglions are used when really a whole complex of elements are involved—amacrine cells, horizontal cells, receptors of various sorts, and a variety of synaptic mechanisms. But the important points of neural circuits can be made most easily by restricting ourselves to two basic types of devices: **transformers** and **combiners,** or in neural terms, **receptors** and **neural** cells.

The receptor. The receptor reacts to external signals—sound, light, touch, taste—and puts out a neural response. The symbol for a receptor is shown in Figure 2-4. We represent the output of a receptor by a number—the rate at which neural responses are produced. In general, we simplify things by ignoring the mechanisms for translating a physical intensity into a particular response rate. Thus, we specify intensity of a signal simply by the number of neural responses it produces in the receptor. A signal of intensity 5 means a signal with an intensity that produces 5 units worth of neural response. The figure illustrates the symbols and how they are used.

The neural cell. This is a general purpose device for mixing together neural inputs. The symbol for the neural cell is a circle. There are two kinds of connections or *inputs* to a neural cell; one is *excitatory,* the other *inhibitory*. As many inputs as necessary go to a neuron, but there is only one output (although it may go to several different locations).

A neuron often has a background rate of responding. That is, even when there are no signals coming in, there still may be an output from the cell. In the circuits that follow, the background rate corresponding to spontaneous activity is often set at 100. For particular applications this number may vary, sometimes being higher, sometimes lower, and sometimes being 0.

Each input to a neural cell is assigned a positive or negative number. The number is the *gain* of that input. An input with a positive (+) gain is excitatory; an input with a negative gain (—) is inhibitory. For example, suppose an input has a gain of .5. This means for every 100 units of neural activity in the input, the output of the neuron is increased by $.5 \times 100$ or 50 units. If the gain were —.5, the output of the neuron would be *decreased* by 50 units for every 100 units input. To simplify the use of the drawings, excitatory connections are signified

FIGURE 2-4

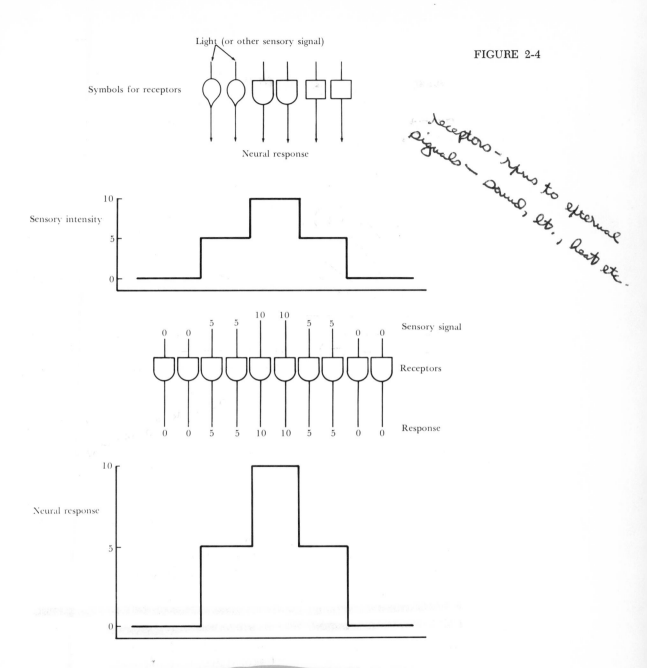

Light (or other sensory signal)

Symbols for receptors

Neural response

Sensory intensity

Sensory signal

Receptors

Response

Neural response

[handwritten margin note:] Receptors - rspns to external signals - sound, lt., heat etc.

by arrows; inhibitory connections are signified by dots. The output of a neuron is the algebraic sum of the background rate plus the contribution of all excitatory inputs, minus the contribution of all the inhibitory units.

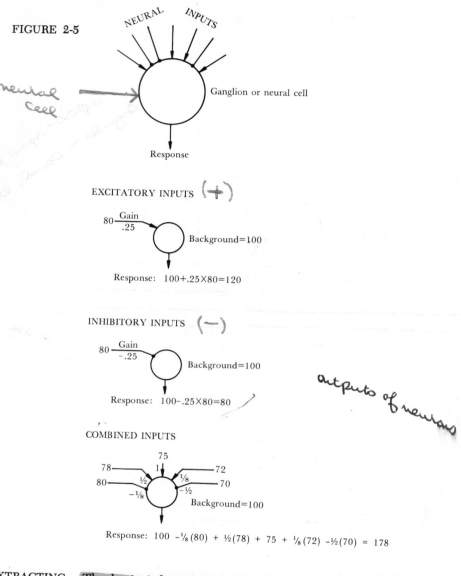

FIGURE 2-5

neural cell

NEURAL INPUTS

Ganglion or neural cell

Response

EXCITATORY INPUTS $\left(+\right)$

80 — Gain .25

Background=100

Response: 100+.25×80=120

INHIBITORY INPUTS $\left(-\right)$

80 — Gain −.25

Background=100

Response: 100−.25×80=80

outputs of neurons

COMBINED INPUTS

75

78 — 1

80 — ½

−⅛ ⅛ ½ −½

72

70

Background=100

Response: $100 -\tfrac{1}{8}(80) + \tfrac{1}{2}(78) + 75 + \tfrac{1}{8}(72) -\tfrac{1}{2}(70) = 178$

EXTRACTING CONTOURS The basic information in a visual image is carried by variations in the light intensities striking different parts of the retinal surface. These variations may be spread out over a large part of the visual scene, corresponding to variations in the brightness of different components of the scene. At places corresponding to the contours of objects, the change in intensity may be abrupt and large. The arrangement of neural interconnections in the receptor apparatus determines how these light patterns are encoded into neural impulses by the visual nervous system.

On the one hand, it is desirable to have sensory systems as sensitive as possible to the signals occurring in the environment. On the other hand, a sensory system should preserve as much as possible the details of the energy pattern in the external signal. These two requirements conflict. Consider the basic arrangement of receptors in a sensory system, the light detectors of the eye (the rods and cones).

Sensitivity versus specificity

Photomicrograph of human foveal cells, seen head on. From Polyak (1957).   FIGURE 2-6

Here there are numerous individual receptor elements packed tightly together. Light energy falling on the eye is scattered across these receptors. To make a sensitive system, the simplest way to connect receptors to the next level of cells in the system (called the *ganglion cells*), is to add up the responses of a number of receptors and feed them into a single ganglion cell.

Figure 2-7

The more receptors connected to a single ganglion cell, the more sensitive the system is to weak light signals. To obtain the maximum response, a ganglion cell should be adding up the responses of as many receptors as possible.

But increased sensitivity comes at a price. If one ganglion cell is adding up the receptor responses over a large region of the retina, the ability to discriminate different light patterns within that region is lost. The receptive fields of a ganglion cell should be small if the details of the light patterns are to be preserved. Thus, when considering possible ways in which receptor information can be rearranged at the first level of sensory processing, we find a tradeoff between maintaining sensitivity and recording the details of the signal pattern.

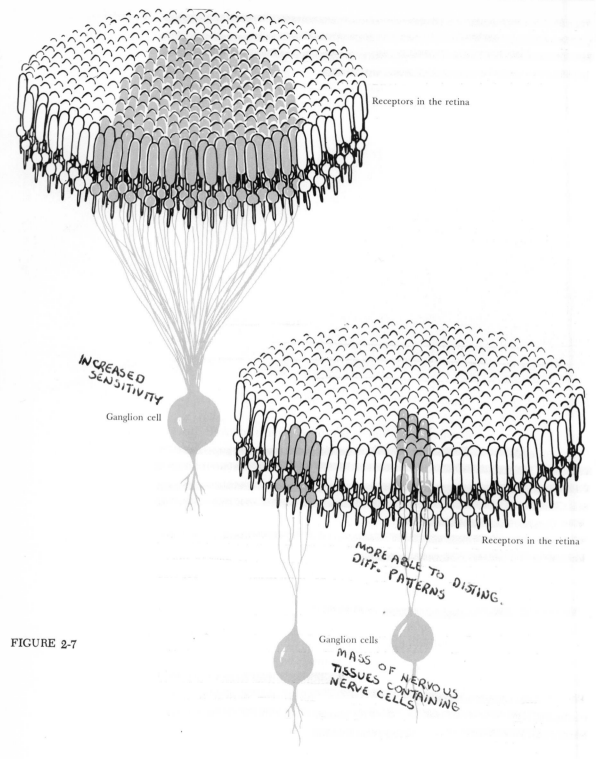

Receptors in the retina

INCREASED
SENSITIVITY

Ganglion cell

Receptors in the retina

MORE ABLE TO DISTING.
DIFF. PATTERNS

FIGURE 2-7

Ganglion cells

MASS OF NERVOUS
TISSUES CONTAINING
NERVE CELLS

The techniques required to discover the wiring diagram of the eye are *Lateral inhibition*
tricky. Only a few different individual cells can be monitored at any
one time. Much of the structure of the neural interconnections must
be deduced by some clever experimentation.

A good deal of the basic knowledge of the eye comes from the study
of the *Limulus* or horseshoe crab.

Lateral Eye

Limulus, the horseshoe crab. From Cornsweet (1970).   FIGURE 2-8

This animal has an easily accessible eye with large, easy-to-dissect nerve
fibers. The first step is to dissect the eye so that individual receptors
can be stimulated directly without going through the lens and biological
matter.   Figure 2-9

This allows the experimenter to stimulate an individual receptor cell
in the eye. Next, the electrode is placed at a ganglion cell and a light
is turned on.

Suppose we watch the responses at the ganglion cell as light is directed
toward the receptor labeled A in Figure 2-10. If the neural response
of the ganglion cell increases, then apparently this cell is monitoring
activity in receptor A.

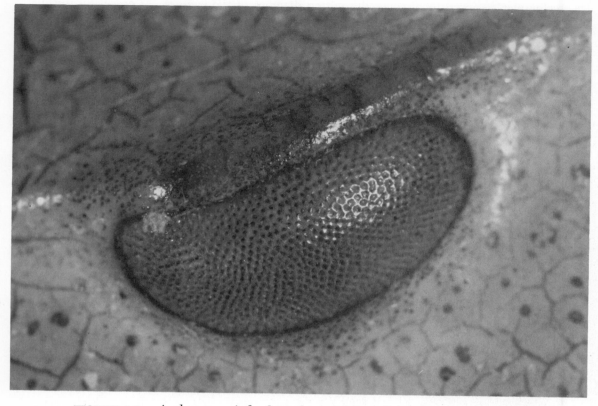

FIGURE 2-9   *A close-up of the lateral eye of Limulus. From Cornsweet (1970).*

FIGURE 2-10   FIGURE 2-11

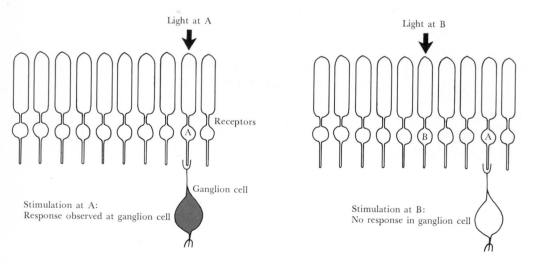

Suppose the light is moved to receptor B and turned on. This time, the electrode records no change in the activity of the ganglion cell. Apparently, receptor B is not influencing the ganglion cell at A. But before concluding that **only** receptor A affects this ganglion cell, consider what happens with a combination of lights. Begin again with a light at A. Then turn on a second light at B: The neural response of the ganglion cell **decreases.**

Figure 2-11

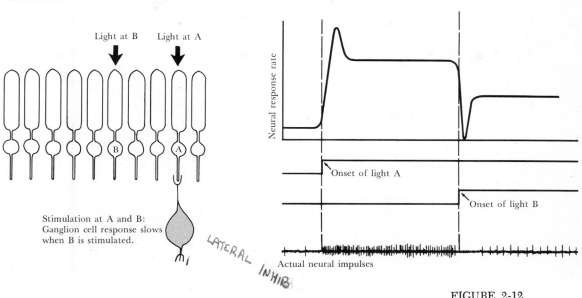

Light at B   Light at A

Stimulation at A and B:
Ganglion cell response slows
when B is stimulated.

LATERAL INHIB

Neural response rate

Onset of light A

Onset of light B

Actual neural impulses

FIGURE 2-12

Although lights on receptors other than A cannot initiate a response in the ganglion cell, they can decrease any ganglion cell activity that is already in progress.

This simple experiment demonstrates one of the most important mechanisms of sensory information processing: *lateral inhibition.* The activity in one cell is modified by the activity of its neighbors. Conceptually, the notion is simple. It reflects the operation of an inhibitory process, which causes the responses of one cell to be subtracted from the responses of another: computing the difference between two inputs. The simplicity is deceptive. It provides all the computing power needed to convert a complex light pattern falling on the receptors into the abstract rearranged sensory message that is eventually sent to the higher centers in the brain.

With the mechanism of lateral inhibition to work with, consider the basic properties of a network that extracts the contours in a figure. Begin with a one-dimensional network with the receptors all lined up

*Circuits for
extracting contours*

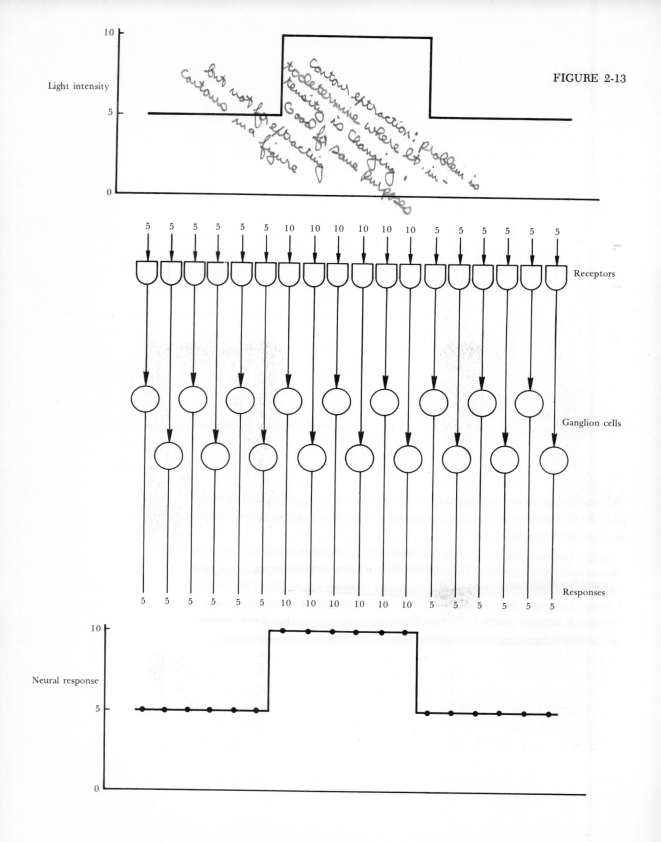

FIGURE 2-13

Contour extraction: problem is to determine where lt. in-tensity is changing.
Good for extracting some purposes
but not for extracting contours in a figure

in a row. A light shines on the receptors. The problem of detecting contours is to determine where the light intensity is changing. If there were a simple, straightforward connection between receptors and ganglion cells, nothing much would be accomplished.

Figure 2-13

The neural response pattern would be simply a relatively faithful reproduction of the pattern of lights falling on the receptors. This is fine for some purposes, but it does not yield any mechanism for extracting contours in a figure. Something must be added to the system.

Basically, for contour extraction we would like to have relatively little response activity wherever the lights have a constant intensity and a large amount of activity wherever there are changes in illumination. One way of achieving this is to use inhibition so that responses of one receptor are modified by the receptors on either side of it. For example, suppose there is a constant light source of 10 units: The excited receptor produces a response rate of 10. We want no output at all from the ganglion cell to this light source. Thus, we need to subtract 10 units of activity, possibly by subtractions of 5 units from each side. This is easily done by setting the connection between the ganglion cell and its neighboring receptor at −.5.

Figures 2-14 & 2-15

Here the figures show a system that responds only to the contours in the light pattern. In fact, if you study it carefully, you will see that it only responds when the **differences** in the light intensities striking successive pairs of neighboring cells change.

This circuit illustrates several points. First, we see the need for background activity. If there were no background rate, the negative part of the response to the input would not be observed, since a negative firing rate is meaningless. With a background rate, however, then both the positive and negative responses would be observed as increases and decreases in the normal rate at which the ganglion responds. This is illustrated in the right-hand vertical coordinates of the last part of Figure 2-15 where the background rate is assumed to be 20 responses per second.

This circuit responds only to the edges: It turns the world into a cartoon drawing. Differences in the overall intensity of various regions in the visual scene are not encoded: Perhaps the circuit has accomplished too much.

It makes sense to find a compromise between the first system which did nothing to the signal and the second which left only the edges. One way to do this is to reduce the effect of the inhibitory connections. Suppose we try a gain of −.2.

Figure 2-16

Here is a useful result. The most vigorous response occurs at the contours, but information about the relative intensities of different regions is still preserved.

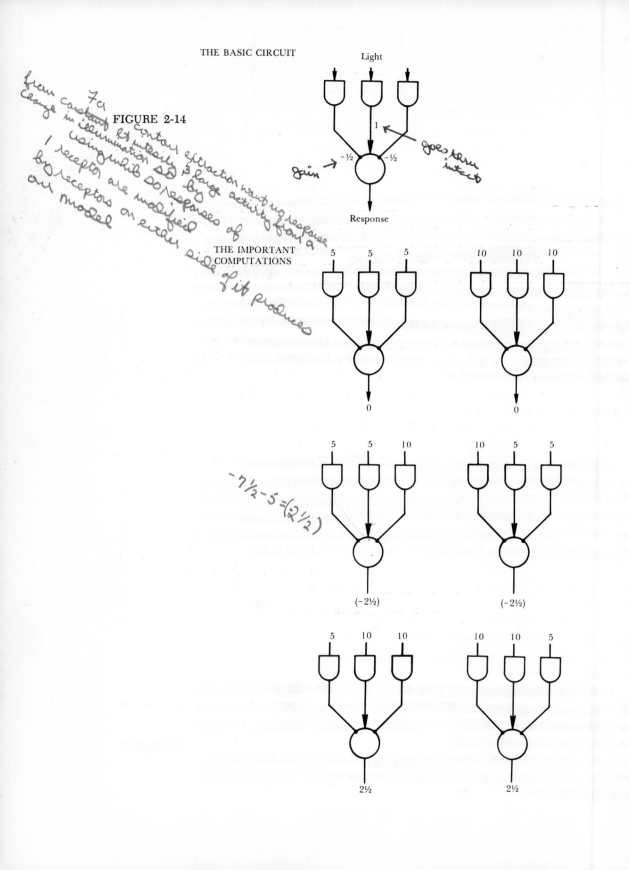

THE BASIC CIRCUIT

FIGURE 2-14

THE IMPORTANT
COMPUTATIONS

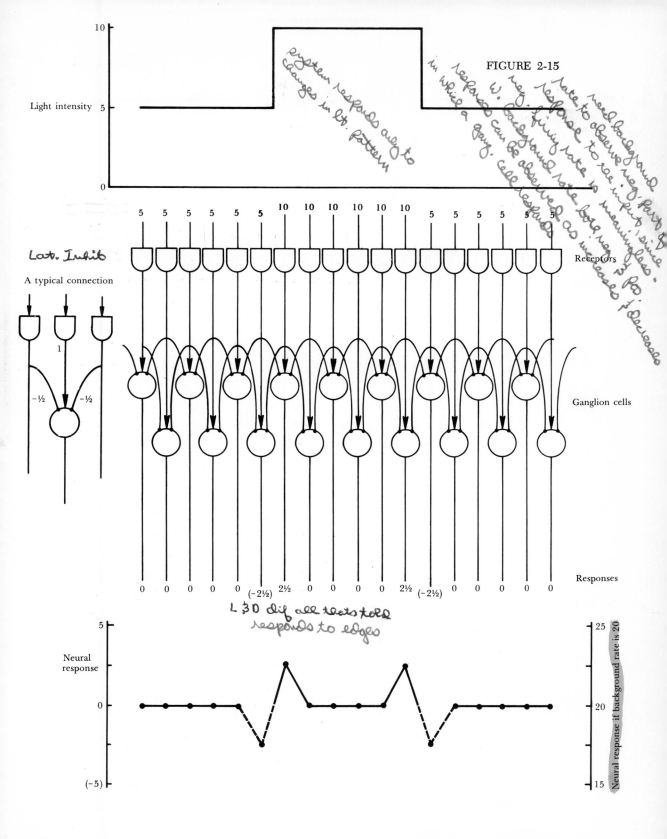

FIGURE 2-15

Light intensity

Lat. Inhib

A typical connection

1

−½   −½

Receptors

Ganglion cells

Responses

5 5 5 5 5 5 10 10 10 10 10 10 5 5 5 5 5 5

0 0 0 0 0 (−2½) 2½ 0 0 0 0 2½ (−2½) 0 0 0 0 0

Neural response

(−5)

Neural response if background rate is 20

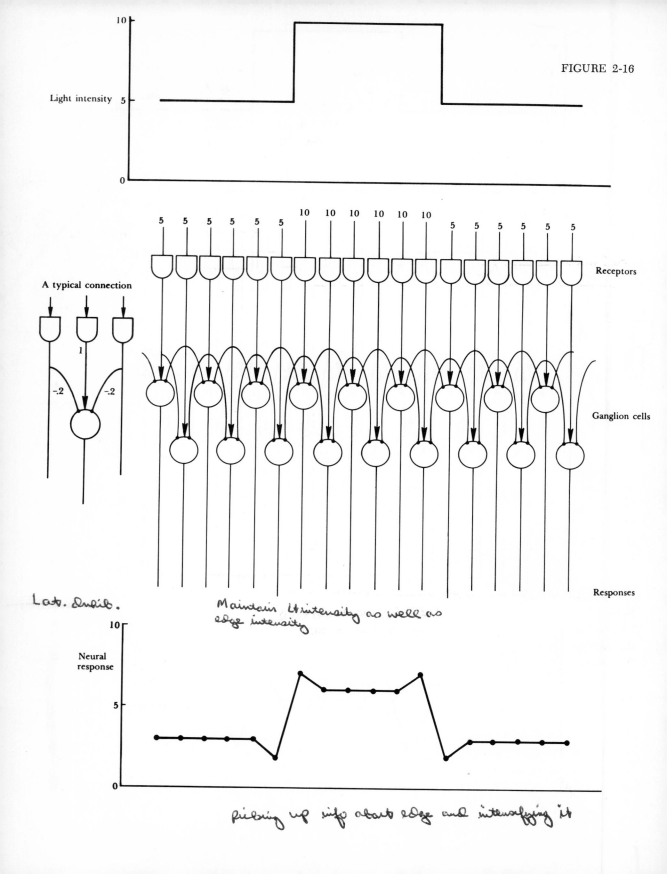

FIGURE 2-16

Light intensity

A typical connection

Receptors

Ganglion cells

Responses

Lat. Inhib.

Maintain Lt intensity as well as edge intensity

Neural response

picking up info about edge and intensifying it

With the same basic network then, adjustments in the relative strength of inhibitory processes alter the kinds of information that is extracted from the visual image. To find the typical values of inhibition in a real nervous system, careful measurements must be made. Here are graphs of some neural recordings made in a situation almost identical to the one described previously.

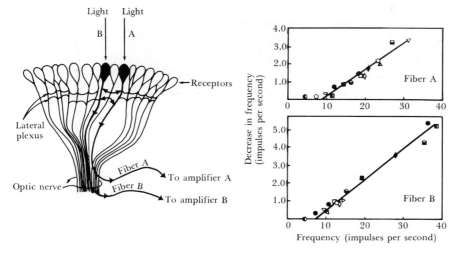

FIGURE 2-17

From Hartline and Ratliff (1957).

As before, the rate of neural impulses is decreased when light A comes on. The effect of one neuron on another is mutual: A affects B in the same way that B affects A. Also notice that there appears to be a threshold for the operation of inhibitory processes. There are no changes in the firing rate of A until B responds above 8 or 9 impulses per second. Once the inhibition begins to take effect, however, the diminution of neural rate is linear. The straight sloping line in the diagram indicates that the amount one unit affects another is directly proportional to the rate at which it is responding. Specifically, the coefficient of proportionality is .16. For every increase in firing rate by 10 impulses per second, the neuron receiving inhibition decreases by 1.6 impulses per second. Thus, the inhibitory gain in this circuit is —.16, very close to the —.20 value for the circuit just designed. The response pattern in the crab's eye, then, should look very much like those shown in Figure 2-16.

Figure 2-18 illustrates actual neural response rates measured at the eye of the crab. The photograph shows the test pattern: exactly the same light pattern we have been examining. The recording electrode was located at one ganglion cell. Thus, to see the response caused by this light pattern, it was necessary to move the light, holding the elec-

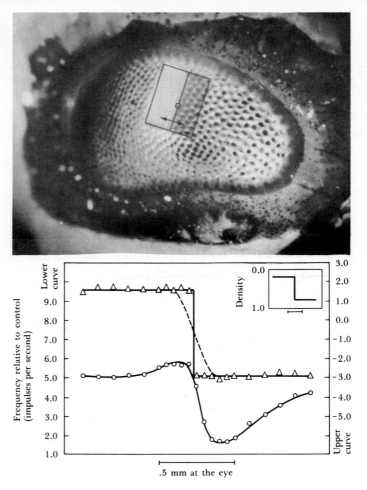

FIGURE 2-18

Top: From Ratliff (1965). Bottom: From Ratliff and Hartline (1959).

trode constant, as shown by the arrows on the light pattern. This is obviously both easier than, and completely equivalent to, keeping the light steady and moving the electrode. First, the light was covered over by placing a mask with a tiny opening right over the part of the eye where the recording electrode was placed—the spot marked with the symbol ⊗. Only the excitatory part of the receptive field receives light, so the neural responses (△) reflect the result of the neural activity with no inhibition. We see from the diagram that this neural response gives a rather accurate portrayal of the light pattern.

The mask was then removed and the total pattern of light exposed to the eye. This allowed all the inhibitory factors to enter into action; the resulting neural activity is shown on the bottom curve (○). No longer is the network response a simple reproduction; the boundaries of rapidly changing intensities have been enhanced.

Before leaving this experiment, examine the pattern shown in Figure 2-19. Look at it carefully. Do the lines look like a set of evenly darkened bands? Do the bands appear to have a constant intensity throughout?

Try analyzing the neural response that the circuit of Figure 2-16 would produce to such a pattern—it should match your perception.

Each step in the photograph has a uniform intensity, but the perceived   FIGURE 2-19
intensity of each step is not uniform. The output pattern (solid line)
predicted for the dashed input intensity distribution. From Cornsweet
(1970).

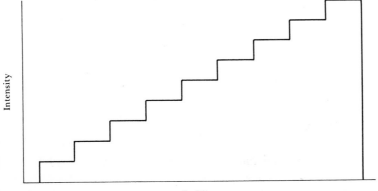

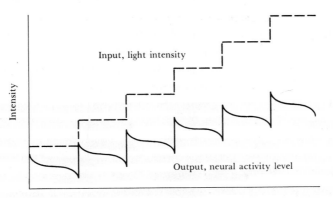

All sensory systems so far studied appear to have contour extracting mechanisms based on the principles of lateral inhibition. Moreover, this basic mechanism has a great deal of flexibility, and can be used to perform other types of analyses of the visual image. It is instructive to try to design these circuits.

Center–surround fields

In more complex organisms, such as mammals, the retinal operations differ somewhat from those of a crab, but the basic features of the analysis are similar. However, several problems arise in studying these more complex visual systems. First, an individual receptor may be connected to many different ganglion cells, making it impossible to restrict the light source so that only one ganglion cell is excited by the signal. Second, interconnectors between receptors and ganglion cells in higher organisms are both excitatory and inhibitory. In the eye of a crab, one cell can have only a negative effect on its neighbor. This is not so with other animals. Neighboring receptor cells can both increase and decrease the response of a ganglion cell.

Consider this typical recording from the retina of the cat. First, the electrode is placed in a ganglion cell and the responses to light are recorded. Then the region of the retina where light stimulation increases the rate of responses—the excitatory area—is found by moving the spot about. This is shown in Figure 2-20. Notice the new feature that has been added to the neural-response patterns. The unit responds to the light shown with an initial burst of activity greater than its sustained response rate. In fact, the sustained rate after the initial burst may be barely above spontaneous activity levels.

Now the light is carefully moved around to determine the exact region of the retina that can activate the ganglion cell. Typically, the excitatory area is an elongated circle, with an average diameter of somewhere between .1 and 1.0 mm (between 4 and 40 thousandths of an inch). When the light source moves outside the circular, excitatory region, a different type of response occurs. Rather than simply returning to its normal background rate, turning off the light causes the ganglion cell to increase its response rate substantially for a brief time. The region producing responses to light extinction is also circular in shape and surrounds the central excitatory area.

Figure 2-21

This ganglion unit and its corresponding receptive fields are referred to as an *on-center, off-surround unit*. Light to the center region causes an increase in the response of the ganglion; light to the surround causes a decrease in response rate with a brief burst of activity when the light it turned off. A diffuse light over the whole receptive region—both center and surround—may produce no perceptible response at all.

Figure 2-22

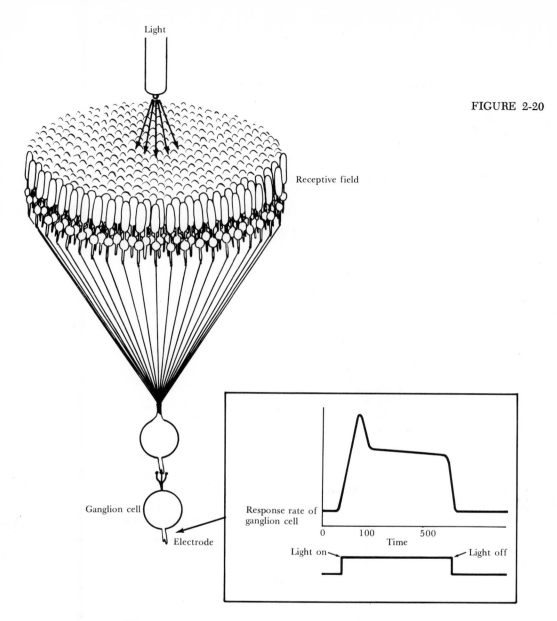

Light

FIGURE 2-20

Receptive field

Ganglion cell

Electrode

Response rate of
ganglion cell

0   100   500
Time

Light on

Light off

In general, the nervous system is quite symmetrical. Whenever one kind of neural response is found, we can also expect to find the complementary type of response. In addition to the on-center, off-surround unit, there are equal numbers of units where the response pattern is reversed: the unit is inhibited by stimulation in the central region and excited by stimulation in the surround—referred to as an *off-center, on-surround unit*.

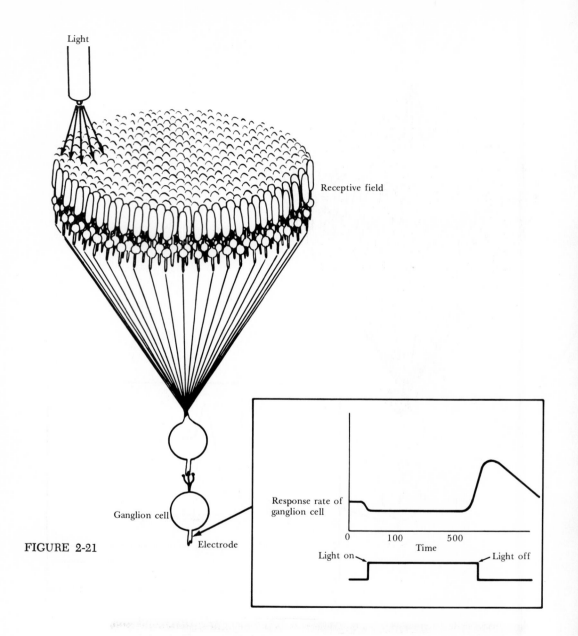

Light

Receptive field

Response rate of
ganglion cell

Ganglion cell

Electrode

0   100   500
Time

Light on

Light off

FIGURE 2-21

On–off circuits   What are the neural mechanisms that lead to this complementary on–off pattern? Using the basic receptor–ganglion mechanisms of the previous section, it is not too hard to devise circuits to do the job. But what system does the nervous system **actually** use? There are several possibilities still being debated.

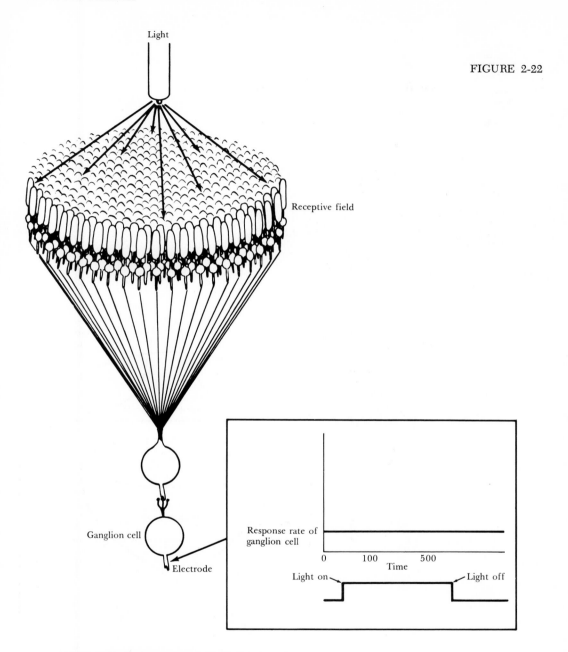

Light

FIGURE 2-22

Receptive field

Ganglion cell

Electrode

Response rate of
ganglion cell

0   100   500
Time

Light on   Light off

Consider the on-center, off-surround system. One possibility is that the central region is entirely connected to an excitatory on-system, and the surround is entirely connected to an inhibitory off-system. This possibility is shown in the diagram by the introduction of a new cell called a *bipolar cell*. One bipolar collects receptor activity in the

Figure 2-23

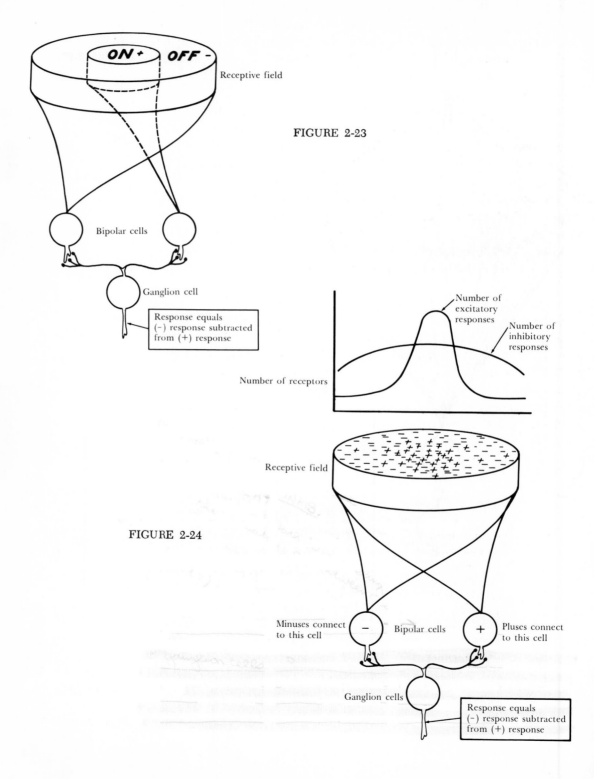

FIGURE 2-23

FIGURE 2-24

on region; the other monitors activity in the off region. The two bipolars then converge on the same ganglion cell. This is a rather straightforward, simple implementation of the on–off system. It assumes, of course, that there is a very clean distinction between the central region and the surround. What if things are not so neat, and the distinction is more ambiguous?

Suppose that the responses of receptors could be both excitatory and inhibitory throughout the entire receptor field, but with more excitatory connections in the on region and more inhibitory connections in the off region. There will still be the same pattern of responses. In the central region, excitatory connections pervail, leading to **on** responses. In the surround, there are more inhibitory connections, leading to **off** responses. The response to signals at any point in any given region depends on the difference between the excitatory and inhibitory activity produced. For off-center, on-surround, the arrangement is simply reversed. Either method of connecting the receptor cells leads to substantially the same result.

Figure 2-24

In the retina of the cat, about 30–50% of the ganglion cells respond in the center–surround manner. The remainder of the cells show various idiosyncracies. Some may respond only to light onset or only to light extinction, but without the concentric receptive field. Many ganglion cells are of the center–surround type, but with peculiarly shaped receptive fields. Some seem entirely unresponsive to any of the standard test patterns used during typical experiments. Even the simple type of concentric receptive field can give complicated response patterns under different conditions. In Figure 2-25, the neural responses from an on-center, off-surround ganglion unit are shown. In *a*, light falls in the **on** area at two different levels

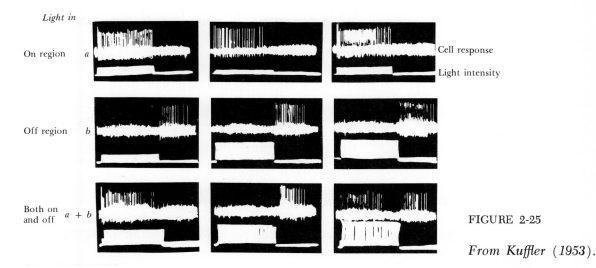

FIGURE 2-25

From Kuffler (1953).

of intensity: medium intensity in the first picture, low intensity in the second, and medium intensity again in the third. In *b*, the light is stimulating the off region and the responses to medium intensity and high intensity signals are shown. Note the **off** response burst when the light is turned off. The third row shows the response when patterns *a* and *b* are combined. The result depends upon the relative mixture of the light at the **on** and **off** regions.

The basic center–surround mechanism can also operate with lights

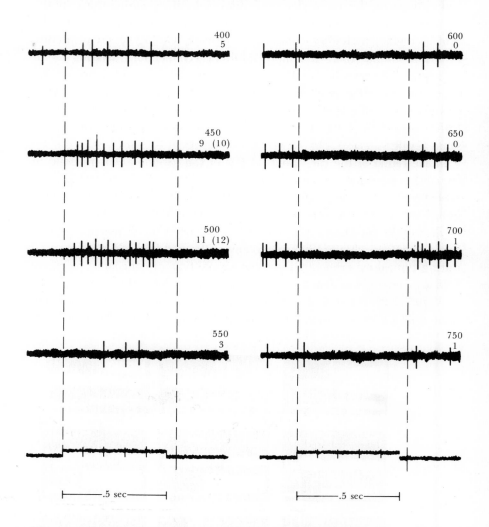

FIGURE 2-26   *The impulses discharged from goldfish retinal ganglion cell in response to .5-sec flashes of light. Wavelength in nanometers indicated at the right-hand end of each record. From Wagner, MacNichol, and Wolbarsht (1960).*

of different colors rather than for white lights in different regions. Figure 2-26 shows the responses of a ganglion cell in the retina of a goldfish to different colors of lights. The same part of the receptive field is stimulated, but the wavelength of the light is varied. The cell changes from an on-center to an off-center response just by changing the wavelength of the illuminating light. This is an important property of color-sensitive cells and will be discussed in more detail in the section on color in Chapter 5.

Figure 2-26

We have noted the transient burst of activity that typically accompanies the onset of a light. It is not clear whether this response pattern represents an adaptive mechanism to slow down the responses and make the system less sensitive to prolonged stimulation, or whether it represents a special sensitivity to transient illumination. Whatever the mechanisms, the transient response can have great effect. Here is a recording of the transient process in operation. A light is turned on over a group of receptors for 2 sec. The open circles show the response of a ganglion connected in an on fashion. First its response rate increases rapidly to around 80 impulses per second, then abruptly decreases to a sustained rate of about 40 impulses per second. This rate is maintained until the light is turned off. In this case, the sustained rate is slightly higher than its normal background activity level of 30 impulses per second.

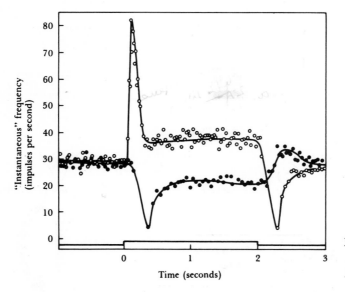

FIGURE 2-27

From Ratliff (1961).

The filled circles on the graph show the response to a unit inhibited by the light. Here there is a transient decrease in response rate all the way down to about 5 impulses per second, a rate much lower than the response level sustained during the remainder of the signal.

Circuits for producing transient responses It is simpler to design neural mechanisms that produce a transitory response than it is to decide how the nervous system actually does it. The former requires only some careful work with the basic circuits; the latter requires elaborate and painstaking investigation of the micro-anatomy of single cells. At the moment, we do not have the latter evidence; meanwhile, let us see what we can invent.

A simple way to produce a transient response is to insert an inhibitory path paralleling the excitatory one between two neural cells. In the case illustrated in Figure 2-28, there is a connection between the levels of the bipolar cells and the ganglion cells. When the light comes on, its excitatory tendency is counteracted by the parallel inhibitory path. In order not to block the response altogether, assume the inhibitory processes get underway more slowly than the excitatory ones. Thus, at the onset of the light, neural activity starts building up through the faster acting excitatory system. As the inhibition circuits begin to function, the rate of buildup slows up, then starts declining and eventually dies out altogether. The ultimate sustained rate will depend on relative gains in the excitatory and inhibitory channels.

An alternative circuit for producing transient behavior is to let the

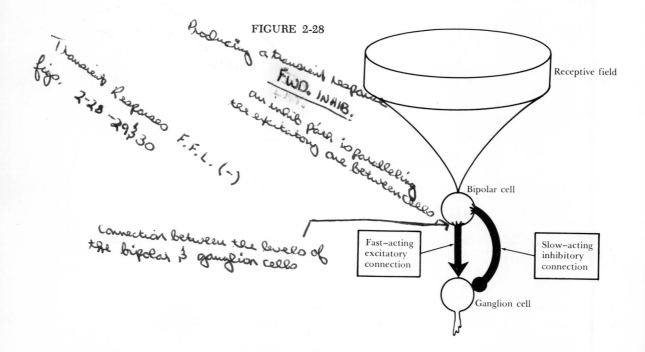

FIGURE 2-28

Receptive field

Bipolar cell

Fast–acting excitatory connection

Slow–acting inhibitory connection

Ganglion cell

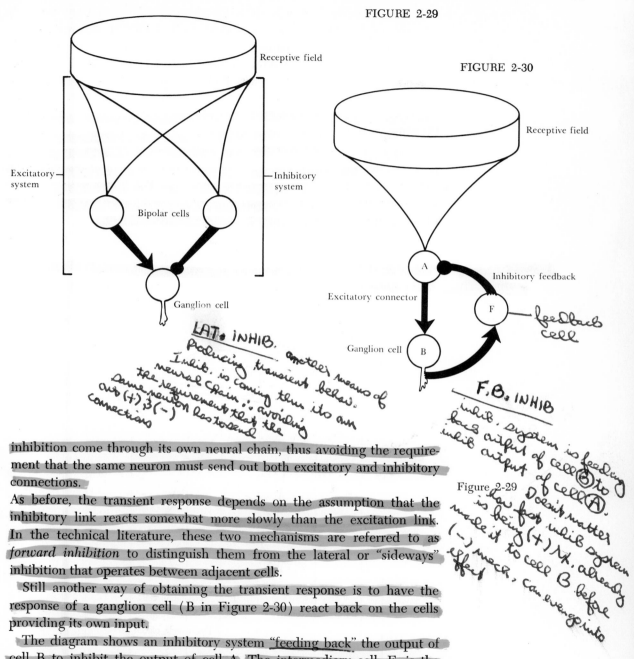

FIGURE 2-29

FIGURE 2-30

Handwritten annotations (Figure 2-29 area):

LAT. INHIB. another means of producing transient behav.

Inhib. is coming thru its own neural chain; avoiding the requirement that the same neuron has to send out (+), 3 (−) connections

Handwritten annotations (Figure 2-30 area):

feedback cell

F.B. INHIB

inhib. system is feeding back output of cell B to inhib output of cell A. Doesn't matter how fast inhib system is being (+) M. already made it to cell B before (−) mech. can even go into effect

Figure 2-29

inhibition come through its own neural chain, thus avoiding the requirement that the same neuron must send out both excitatory and inhibitory connections.

As before, the transient response depends on the assumption that the inhibitory link reacts somewhat more slowly than the excitation link. In the technical literature, these two mechanisms are referred to as *forward inhibition* to distinguish them from the lateral or "sideways" inhibition that operates between adjacent cells.

Still another way of obtaining the transient response is to have the response of a ganglion cell (B in Figure 2-30) react back on the cells providing its own input.

The diagram shows an inhibitory system "feeding back" the output of cell B to inhibit the output of cell A. The intermediary cell, F, is the feedback cell. Unlike the other circuits, the delay of inhibition is built into this mechanism; all the loops shown can operate at the same speed. Of course, it is quite possible to simplify this feedback loop. To start with, cell F can be eliminated, so that B directly inhibits A. In fact, cell A can be eliminated so that the output of B goes right back to the input of B—the cell directly inhibits itself. Such systems are common in electronic circuits. Whether or not they are possible to neurological circuits is not known. Observe that only this feedback method of inhibition accounts automatically for the burst of rapid responding that occurs when the signal is turned off.

We have explored three different kinds of excitatory–inhibitory mechanisms: lateral, forward, and feedback. Lateral inhibition acts to sharpen contours: It is selectively responsive to variations in the spatial patterns of illumination. Forward and feedback inhibition act to sharpen neural responses to temporal changes in illumination. The basic strategy seems to be to give preferential treatment to the changing aspects of external signals; extract changes; suppress aspects that are constant.

RESPONDING TO MOVEMENT   A final basic problem that the visual nervous system must solve is that of movement. Most of the receptors discussed so far are not primarily

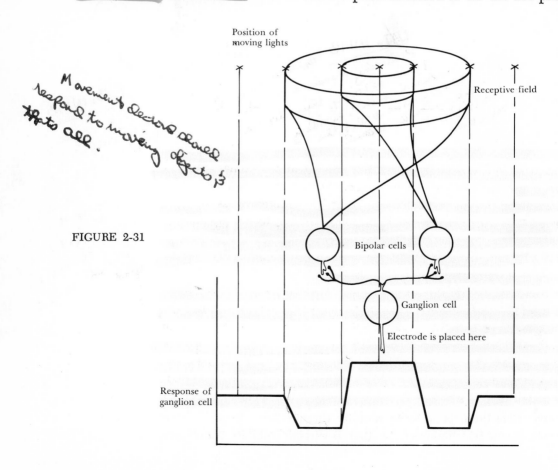

FIGURE 2-31

Movement detectors respond to moving objects that's all. [handwritten note]

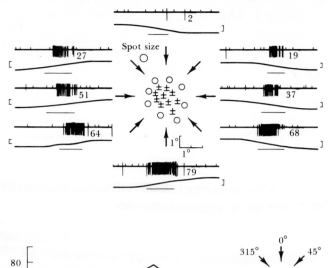

FIGURE 2-32

After Barlow, Hill, and Levick (1964).

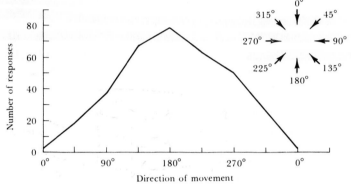

concerned with distinguishing between moving and stationary objects. Certainly, they respond to moving objects as well as to stationary ones. For example, if we move a light beam from left to right across a center-surround unit, the response changes corresponding to the location of the light on the receptive field: First, when the light is just left of the surround, we have the background rate, then inhibition, then excitation, and then the background rate again.

Figure 2-31

These responses do not qualify the unit as a movement detector. Movement detectors should respond only when an object is moving, and at no other time. Ideally, they should also be selective about the direction and perhaps the speed of the moving pattern.

If we search for movement detectors in the visual nervous system, we do find them. The retinas of rabbits, squirrels, and frogs have units that are selectively sensitive to particular types of movement. Examine these data from the rabbit's visual system.

Figure 2-32

In the center of the diagram, the layout of the receptive fields is shown.

The central region produces on–off responses (denoted by the symbol ±), and light stimulating the region surrounding this central part apparently produces no response (denoted by the symbol 0). The arrows show the direction of movement of a test spot swept across the receptive field: The response rates are shown for each direction. The maximum response (79 impulses) occurs to a spot moving straight up. The minimum response (2 impulses) occurs to movement in exactly the opposite direction—straight down. The number of responses produced by movement in intermediate directions is shown in the lower graph.

Circuits for detecting movement   How does the movement detector work? A normal receptive field contains lateral inhibitory mechanisms. We have seen that these circuits are especially sensitive to contours, but do not respond differentially depending on the direction of movement. Two characteristics are needed to make them directionally sensitive. The first is that the inhibitory connections be asymmetrical; the second is that the lateral inhibition contain some delay. Here is the basic circuit with the gain indicated on each connection; let us work through the calculations.

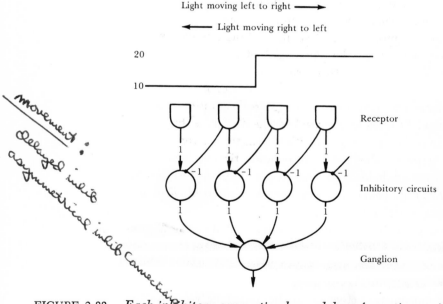

FIGURE 2-33   *Each inhibitory connection has a delay of one time unit.*

The light moves from left to right. Examine Figure 2-34. Here the numbers indicate actual response rate, not gain. At first, there is no response from the ganglion cell. The light intensity is initially at 10 units. Thus, the output of each receptor is 10. This is exactly cancelled by the inhibitory effect of the cell to the right. But when the bright part of the light (which has an intensity of 20) reaches the first receptor, it excites it to a response of 20, yet this receptor is still only inhibited by a value of −10 from the receptor on its right. Thus, the ganglion cell begins responding at 10 units (see Figure 2-34*b*).

In Figure 2-34*c*, the light has moved across two receptors. Since the inhibitory influences are delayed, however, the first cell has not yet received the increased level of inhibition. Two cells are excited by 20 units and inhibited by −10: The combined output of the ganglion cell is 20. At D, the light has moved across one more receptor and the inhibition starts to take effect. Here three receptors are being activated by the higher intensity. Enough time has elapsed since the light reached the second receptor so that its inhibitory influences have built up to shut down the first cell; hence, although three receptors are activated by the higher intensity, the response of the ganglion cell remains constant at 20 units.

As the light continues moving, exactly analogous computations are performed. The ganglion response will remain at 20 units until the light has passed out of the receptor field and sufficient time has elapsed for the delayed inhibitory actions to take place. At that point, the ganglion cell returns to its baseline level (0, in this case).

The light moves from right to left. An entirely different response pattern occurs when the light moves from right to left (Figure 2-35). At position B, although the light has reached the first receptor, there is still no response from the ganglion. Inhibition from the far right comes into effect just as the first receptor is stimulated, thus preventing a response. The increased inhibition from the first receptor to the second has yet to occur. Without a delay in inhibition, the first receptor would immediately increase its inhibitory influence, thus reducing response activity in the second unit and ultimately the ganglion cell to −10 units. The movement could be detected by the decrease in rate below the normal background level. Because of the delay, no change occurs at the ganglion cell, neither an increase nor a decrease.

We have constructed a directionally sensitive movement detector. The unit responds neither to constant light sources, nor to movement from right to left. The delay of inhibition is extremely important. In fact, this turns out be to a general requirement for the circuit: Movement detectors must have a delay.

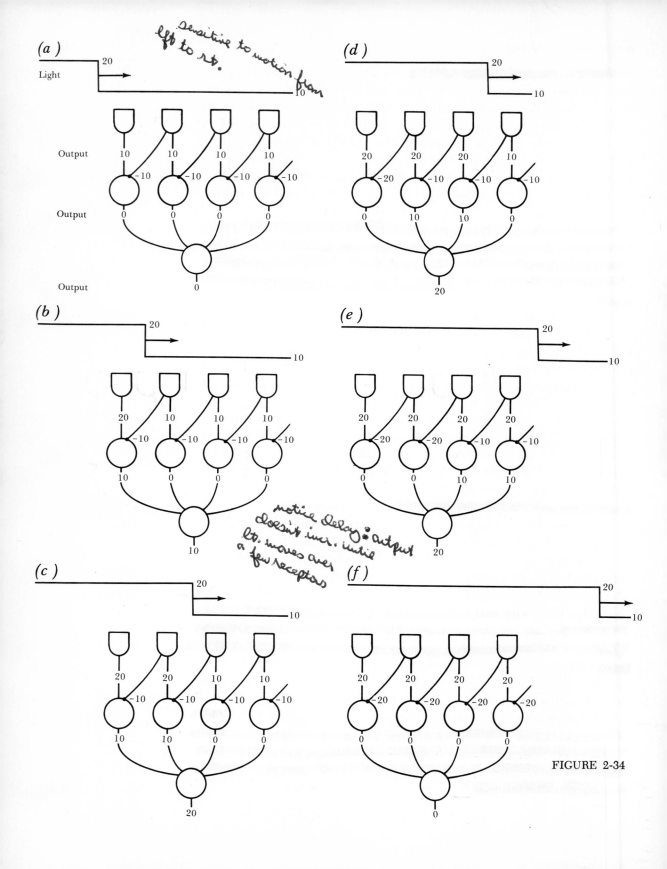

FIGURE 2-34

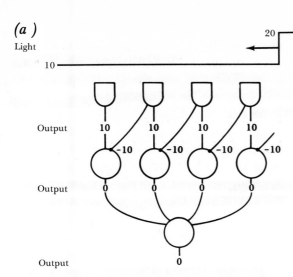

(a)

Light

10   20

Output   10   10   10   10

−10   −10   −10   −10

Output   0   0   0   0

Output   0

(b)

10   20

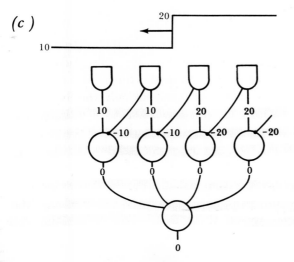

10   10   10   20

−10   −10   −10   −20

0   0   0   0

0

(c)

10   20

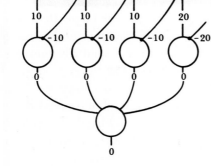

10   10   20   20

−10   −10   −20   −20

0   0   0   0

0

(d)

10   20

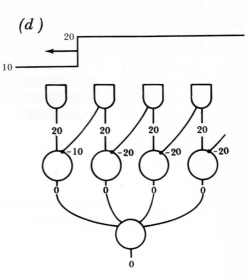

20   20   20   20

−10   −20   −20   −20

0   0   0   0

0

(e)

10   20

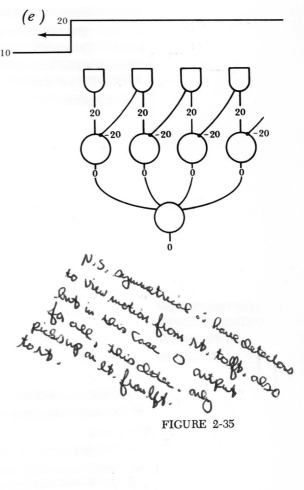

20   20   20   20

−20   −20   −20   −20

0   0   0   0

0

N.S. symmetrical ∴ have detectors
to view motion from rt. to lft. also
but in this case 0 output
to all, this detec. only
picks up a lt. from lft.
to rt.

FIGURE 2-35

Quite sophisticated movement detectors can be constructed using this same basic design. Notice, for example, that the movement detector should respond maximally to a target traveling at a specific speed—the speed corresponding to the rate at which the inhibitory influences move out across the receptive fields. And the delay of inhibition received by a given receptor region could depend on how far away the region is from the moving target. Moreover, the reaction times of both excitatory and inhibitory processes in the nervous system depend on the intensity of the signal. Thus we might expect the responses of movement detectors to depend on the intensity of a signal as well as its speed of movement.

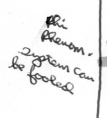

Phi Phenom. system can be fooled

Although these circuits illustrate possible mechanisms for detecting movements, they do not solve all the problems involved in dealing with a dynamic visual environment. It should be possible, for example, to trick a movement detector. Simply flash a light for a brief duration on one receptor, then wait for the proper time and flash a light on the neighboring receptor. This should produce a response pattern similar to moving the light continuously through the field. In fact, we do see continuous motion if two lights alternately flash on and off at some distance apart—a phenomenon called the *phi phenomenon*. The distances over which phi movement is perceived are far larger than the receptive field of the average movement detector found in typical visual systems.

Nothing in the circuits so far discussed would discriminate between movements caused by the head and eyes and those produced by actual movements of external objects. Somehow, higher brain mechanisms must coordinate the information provided by retinal movement detectors with the motor commands controlling the eyes and head, if it is to distinguish changes in the retinal patterns produced by head and eye movements from those produced by movements in the external world.

SIGNAL PROCESSING IN THE LATERAL GENICULATE NUCLEUS

The analysis just completed describes mechanisms that extract basic features from the visual image. In most animals, the cells studied thus far are located right in the eye itself, within the three layers of cells that make up the retina. These processes represent only the first levels of signal analysis. The neural signals are then conducted by the optic nerve to the more advanced stages of processing (see Figure 2-36). Now it is time to follow the trail of the visual information up into the brain.

Neural signals that leave the retina travel upward along the axons of the retinal ganglion cells until they arrive at the next relay station—the *Lateral Geniculate Nucleus (LGN)*. Here the fibers from retinal cells

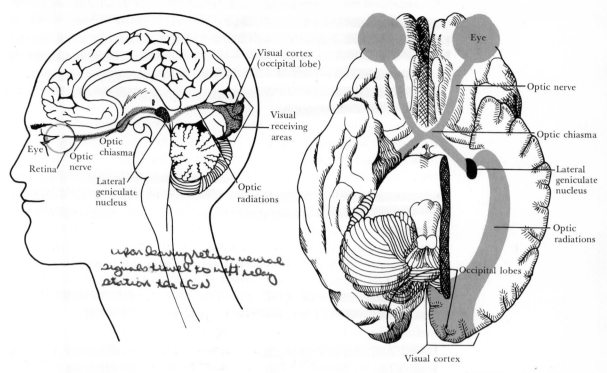

[handwritten annotation: upper half retina neural signals travel to left relay station the LGN]

FIGURE 2-36

make synaptic connections with new cells that will carry the sensory message to the cortical receiving areas of the brain (see Figure 2-36). Fibers that come from adjacent regions in the retina terminate in adjacent parts of the LGN. Thus, neighboring regions in the LGN receive neural information from neighboring parts of the visual field.

The LGN is constructed in separate layers lying on top of each other like pancakes, three layers in the cat, six in the monkey and man. Each layer receives nerve fibers from only one eye, with alternate layers receiving information from alternate eyes. The layers are in registration so that when an object is looked at, the neural activity that results in one eye goes to a particular region of one layer of the LGN, and activity at the corresponding retinal region of the other eye goes to corresponding regions in the LGN layers directly below and above.

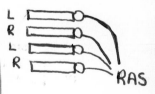

The elegant data-processing operations found in the synaptic junctions of the retina and the neat anatomical organization of the LGN suggest that further reorganization and analysis of the sensory information would occur at this higher brain center. These expectations fail to materialize. To this date, the neat anatomical layout of the LGN remains a puzzle.

The LGN does not seem to change the sensory messages arriving from the retina in any major way. Fibers leaving the LGN have receptive fields almost identical to those found in the ganglion fibers of the retina. They have a similar circular center–surround arrangement, and the fields are similar in size. Thus the LGN appears to be a true relay station: It faithfully transmits the visual information without distortion on to the next level of processing.

Nerve channels, however, unlike other communication systems, do not require any amplification to keep the signals going. So what other purpose could the LGN serve? This puzzle has not been solved, but some possibilities seem likely. For one thing, inputs to the LGN do not come exclusively from the retina. Other parts of the brain also send signals into the LGN, in particular, a midbrain area called the *reticular formation* (we consider this neural structure again on page 623 in our study of activation). There is a suspicion that activity in these non-sensory pathways may help to determine whether the signals that arrive at the LGN are sent on to the next higher level of the system. Thus, it seems possible that the LGN may normally act like an intensity control over the visual signals traveling from the eye to the brain. This is a fascinating possibility, but it is yet to be proved.

After leaving the LGN, there are no more interruptions in the path before the visual information arrives at the *cortical receiving areas* of the brain. Here, in the *visual cortex*, there again appear neural circuits for processing the signals, circuits very similar in their operation to those found in the retina.

EXTRACTING
FEATURES

Three separate areas in the cortex are involved in the analysis of visual messages arriving from the LGN. At each of the visual receiving areas, fibers from adjacent regions of the retina end up at adjacent parts in the cortical receiving centers. Two of the areas receive direct inputs from the LGN, and all three areas are richly interconnected. The fibers leaving the visual receiving areas primarily go to the *temporal lobes* at the side of the brain, an area that seems to be involved in the learning and retention of visual habits.

Like the LGN, the visual cortex is organized in layers, this time five of them. Counting inward from the external surface of the brain, the incoming fibers from the LGN terminate mainly in the fourth and fifth layers down. But in the cortex, unlike the LGN, there seem to be many interconnections among the layers. The analysis of a sensory message starts at the fourth and fifth layers and is elaborated through successive cortical layers until the information finally leaves the visual areas and travels to other parts of the brain.

The general picture of cortical processing is one of a progressive rearrangement and analysis of specific aspects of the signal. The analysis is carried out region by region, with a large number of different cortical detectors responsible for the features of any particular region. Is there a contour? Is it an edge? A dark line? Does it have a light background? Or is it a slit of light on a dark background? What is its orientation? Does it extend beyond the specific region? Does it change direction? These are the questions answered by cortical detectors.

Response characteristics. The lateral geniculate nucleus feeds information directly to the fourth layer of the cortex, so we start our analysis there. If we record the electrical activity at the fourth layer, carefully lowering the electrode through the top of the brain down the fraction of an inch required to penetrate the top three layers, we find cells that respond whenever a small test light is moved across the retina. There is a difference between these cells and those on the retina, however. The detector cells at the retina are quite specific in their response. They monitor a small region of the retina—the receptive field—and unless the light falls within that small receptive field, no response is evoked at the ganglion cell. In the cortex, however, there is a different type of organization; responses are no longer restricted to the small circular receptive field.

A typical arrangement is one in which shining the spot of light anywhere along a line increases the response of the cell. Usually, whenever such an excitatory line is found, then right beside it there is also a parallel line that causes the cell's response to decrease whenever it is excited by light. Thus, there would appear to be two parallel receptive fields, each in the shape of a straight line, one excitatory, one inhibitory.

This configuration of excitatory and inhibitory fields yields an *edge detector:* The cell responds maximally to an edge of light aligned perfectly with the axis of the fields. Any other signal pattern produces less than maximal reaction.

Other simple cells have other types of receptive fields. Another scheme, similar but a bit more advanced, is a *slit detector*. Here, there is an inhibitory zone on both sides of the excitatory region. Thus, the maximum response is produced by a bright line surrounded by two dark areas; the minimum response is produced by a dark line surrounded by two bright areas. Remembering the usual symmetry of the nervous system, whenever there is one arrangement of fields—inhibitory–excitatory–inhibitory—there should also be the complementary arrangement: Indeed, there is. If the first arrangement is represented by the symbols — + —, then the second can be represented as + — +. If the former is a *slit detector*, the latter is a *line detector*.

Simple cells

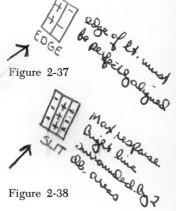

Figure 2-37

Figure 2-38

RESPONSES TO A TEST SPOT

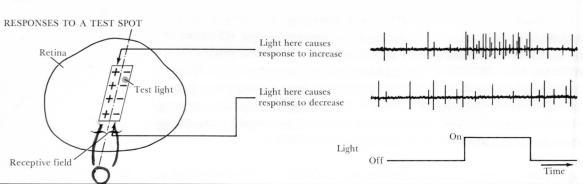

Light here causes response to increase

Light here causes response to decrease

Light

MAXIMUM RESPONSE OCCURS TO A BRIGHT – DIM EDGE

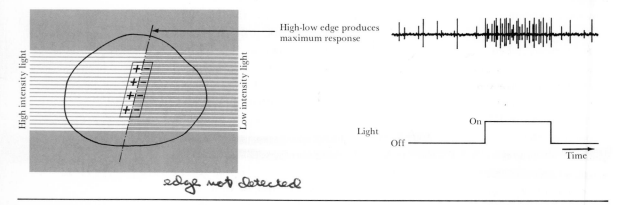

High-low edge produces maximum response

edge not detected

MINIMUM RESPONSE OCCURS TO A DIM – BRIGHT EDGE

Low-high edge produces minimum response

edge detected

FIGURE 2-37

By the way, note that information comes from the cell both when it decreases and when it increases response rate. Either reaction is informative; neither response can be considered more basic or more important than the other. The nervous system uses both increases and decreases in neural rates as signals, so it would be a mistake to assume that **on**-type responses are more basic or more important than **off** responses. The important point is that some change in the activity does occur.

Edge, slit, and line detectors monitor specific regions of the retina. Within a specific region, the edge or slit must be lined up perfectly to produce the maximum response. Thus, although these cells are reacting to more complex features in the visual image, they are still selective in the position and type of signal needed to produce a response.

FIGURE 2-38

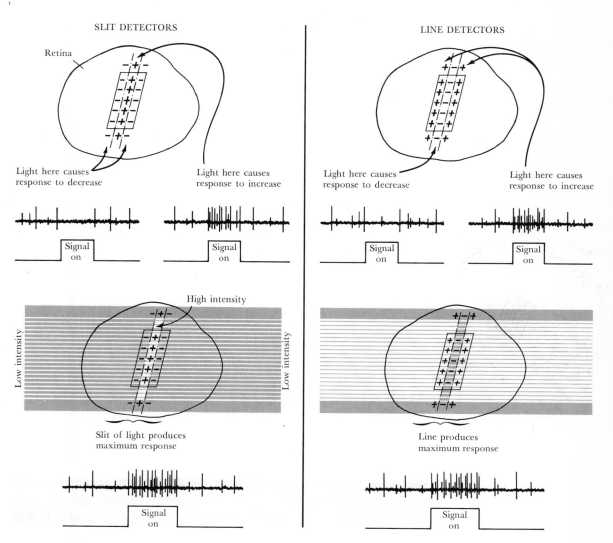

How to build slit and line detectors. Let us see what it takes to put together these simple circuits. This must be speculative, since no one has yet traced out the circuits. Start with the information coming from the retina. The basic question is how the information coming from the center–surround units of the retina is combined to produce units that respond to lines and slits. To simplify the diagrams, from now on we will use a pair of concentric circles to represent response patterns of ganglion cells.

FIGURE 2-39

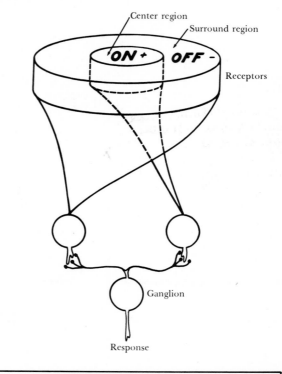

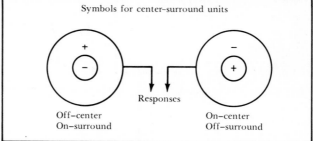

The most direct method for creating a line or slit detector is to collect the responses from ganglion cells that lie along a line in a local region of the retina and feed their outputs to a single cortical cell. Either

a line or a slit detector is produced, depending upon whether the
ganglion cells are on-center, off-surround (slit) or off-center, on-surround
(lines).

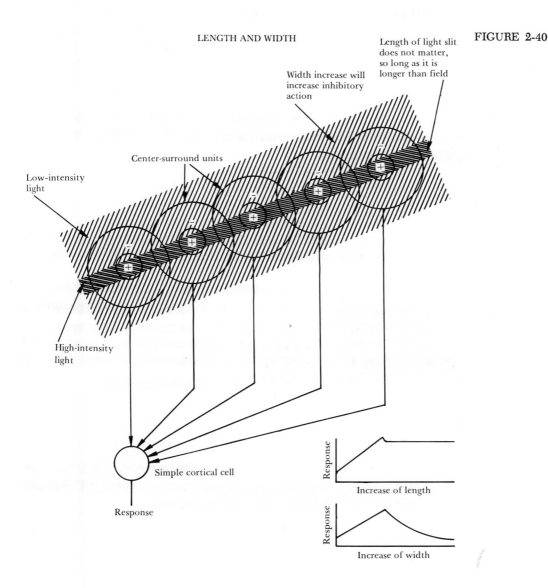

LENGTH AND WIDTH

Length of light slit
does not matter,
so long as it is
longer than field

FIGURE 2-40

Width increase will
increase inhibitory
action

Center-surround units

Low-intensity
light

High-intensity
light

Simple cortical cell

Response

Response

Increase of length

Response

Increase of width

Consider the response characteristics of this circuit. Start with a slit
positioned directly over the central excitatory region of the ganglion
cells, exactly as shown in Figure 2-40. The slit detector responds maximally. Extending the length of the line beyond the region where there

are receptors should have no effect on the detector's response, since there are no cells to detect the change in length. If the line is shortened, however, the cortical response rate should decrease until the number of center-surround cells activated becomes insufficient to drive the cortical slit detector.

Starting again with an ideal slit positioned directly over the central excitation regions, consider what happens when the width of the slit is increased. As light begins to spill over into the regions of the receptive fields occupied by the surround, the excitatory effects from the center are counteracted by the inhibitory effects of the surround, and the response rate decreases. With a wide enough slit, the two influences should cancel each other out and the cortical unit will return to its spontaneous firing rate.

What about orientation? Look at Figure 2-41. As the slit is rotated away from the optimal orientation, fewer and fewer of the excitatory centers feeding the detector are activated. The impulse flow in the visual nerve dies down, and the cortical receptor once again returns to spontaneous activity levels. The exact response for any particular angle depends upon the exact amount of excitatory and inhibitory field covered by the light.

The general picture is clear. Basic center–surround units can be put together to provide complex-pattern recognition units. There is a fair amount of freedom here, since not only can units be constructed with both on-center and off-center responses, but they can be combined in different ways. The on-center units could have inhibitory connections to the cortical cell, while off-center might be excitatory. Other types of retinal units with different shapes and types of receptive fields could be used. It is clear that a wide variety of detectors can be constructed at this first level of signal processing in the cortex.

As an example, earlier we showed how detectors could be constructed to respond only to moving spots of light. It is also possible to design moving line detectors: Units that respond only to a line of the proper orientation that moves in the proper direction. Such a unit could be built so that it responds neither to stationary lines nor to lines with the proper movement, but the wrong angular orientation or lines with the correct orientation, but the incorrect direction of movement.

DIPOLES

Remember the McCollough Effect (page 42)? After prolonged stimulation of red horizontal lines, white horizontal lines were subsequently perceived as green. One of the possible explanations was that colored-line detectors

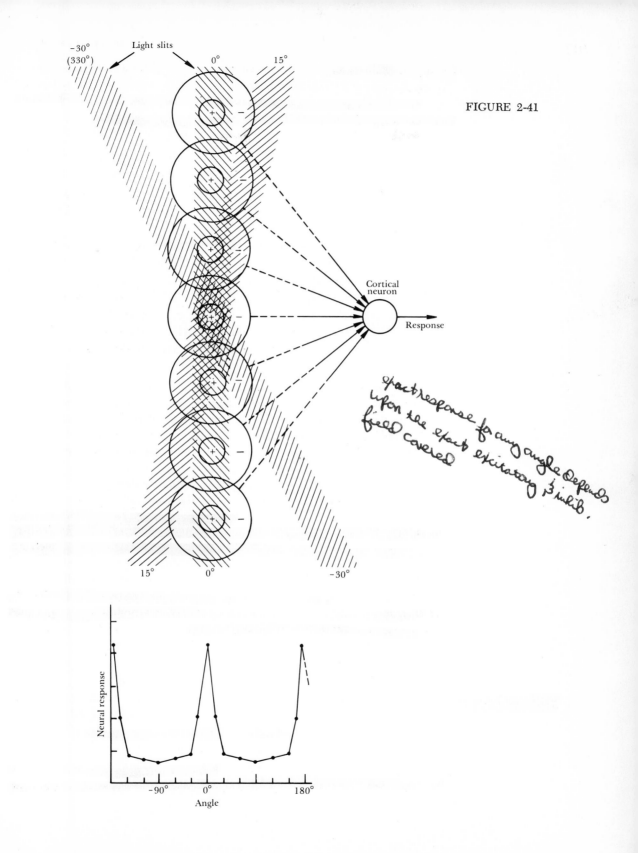

FIGURE 2-41

-30°
(330°)

Light slits

0°

15°

+ −

+ −

+ −

+ −

+ −

+ −

+ −

Cortical
neuron

Response

15°

0°

-30°

effect response for any angle depends
upon the effect excitatory & inhib.
field covered

Neural response

-90°

0°

180°

Angle

were being fatigued. However, a simpler type of orientation-sensitive device might be involved. The neural circuit is called a *dipole* (Harris & Gibson, 1968). A dipole is any asymmetric device that is more sensitive to one input on one side and to another on the other (see Figure 2-42). A dipole, for example, might be sensitive to red on one side, green on the other.

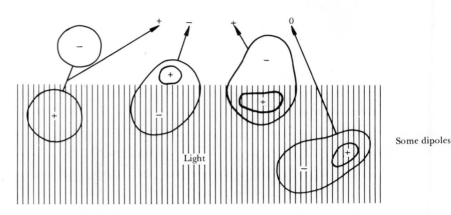

Some dipoles

FIGURE 2-42

A dipole could be any two fields of any shape that are not lined up very exactly. It could be one of many shapes. It could even be "circular," with two parts, an inner part sensitive to one of the colors, the surround to the other. This "circular" unit would not be exactly concentric circles, but rather odd-shaped and not symmetrical. Any center–surround unit could be a dipole if the two parts were not exactly concentric.

We have already noted that color-sensitive cells are indeed of the center–surround type, with green opposed to red (and also some cells have blue opposed to yellow, see page 82). Moreover, center–surround cells are usually asymmetrical. They are seldom perfectly round. The dipole provides us with a basic orientation-sensitive device much simpler than that of a line detector. If a bar of light covers the whole dipole, it does not respond. So long as the light covers only one of the two parts of the detector, it will respond, and it can adapt. By not being a precise line detector, the dipole is not sensitive to blurring of the test image. It is sensitive to the intensity. Dipoles are clearly less complex than line detectors. They explain the McCollough Effect better than do colored-line detectors.

Complex cells   At the next level of the cortical processing, things change somewhat. There are still the same basic types of features involved—edges, lines, slits, moving lines, etc.—but without some of the restrictions. In simple cells, a line detector responded only when the line was located at a very precise position on the retina. At the next higher level, the line must still have the right width and orientation but position is not so

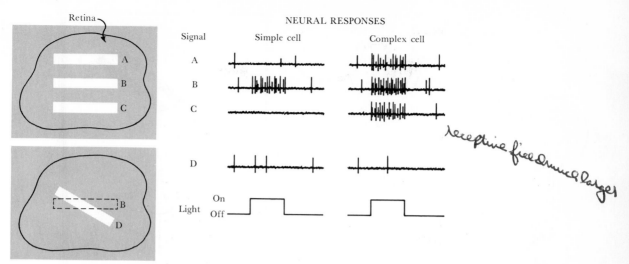

Typical response patterns of simple and complex cells.   FIGURE 2-43

critical: It can be located any place within a rather wide region of the retina (see Figure 2-43). These cells are more complex than the ones at the lower cortical level. Hence, the convention adopted for the names of the cells: If those are simple, these must be complex.

Like the simple cells below them, complex line and edge detectors are not affected by extending the stimuli beyond the receptive field. Also, in common with the simple cells, complex cells react when the appropriate signal is moved through their receptive fields, and frequently they have a preferred direction.

For complex cells, then, the type, direction, and width of the stimulating signal still critically determine the response. The information provided by these detectors, however, is somewhat more abstract than at lower levels, since the position of the contour within the visual field is less important. Thus, the retinal areas over which complex detectors react to their preferred stimuli are considerably larger than the receptive field for simple cortical detectors.

How to build complex cells. What is a complex cell? The easiest explanation is that it is the product of a combination of a number of simple cells. In Figure 2-44 we show how the combination of responses from eight simple cells might produce a complex cell. If any simple cell becomes active, the complex line detector responds. Thus, as a line is moved about in the region of the retina from which the simple cells respond, the outputs of the different individual simple cells are passed on to the complex cell. Notice that width and orientation of the line

FIGURE 2-44

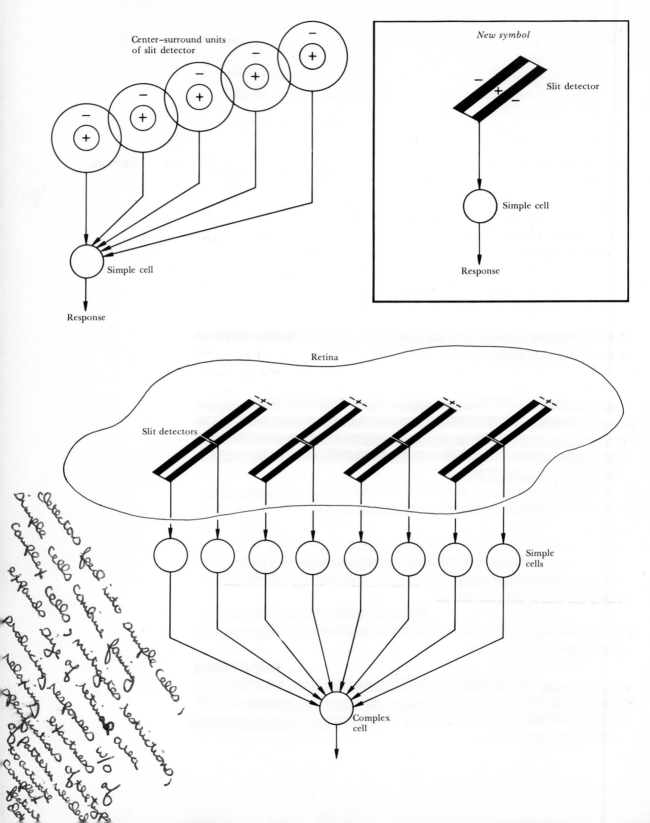

Center–surround units
of slit detector

Simple cell

Response

New symbol

Slit detector

Simple cell

Response

Retina

Slit detectors

Simple
cells

Complex
cell

detectors feed into simple ,
simple cells combine forming
complex cells) integrated reactions)
expands size of retinal area
producing responses w/o
relating spectrum of test pts
specification of pattern of test pt
to activate needed
complex
features
detect

are just as critical for activating the complex cell as for the response of the simple ones. Anything that fails to cause a simple cell to respond will also fail to drive the corresponding complex cell. This arrangement is one way of expanding the size of the retinal area which produces responses without relaxing the exactness of the specifications of the type of pattern needed to activate a complex-feature detector.

More specificity about some of the features present in the signal would be useful, for example, the length of lines. The last level of cortical cells that has been investigated appears to do just this. Here there are cells even more complex than the second level—*hypercomplex cells*.

Hypercomplex cells

The unique feature added by these cells is that the edge or line must be terminated properly in order to obtain maximum response. Figures 2-45 and 2-46 show some examples of the response patterns of hypercomplex cells. In the first diagram, the receptive field is outlined by dotted lines. It is a moving line detector: Only a horizontal line moving downward gives a response. Lines at other orientations or moving in other directions yield reduced reaction. Of course, this is a typical result of a complex cell. But note what happens when the line is extended in length beyond the receptive field: The hypercomplex cell no longer responds. This is the new dimension added at this level of processing—specificity of size.

The size specificity is not exact, as the details of the figure show. If the line is too long as in Figures 2-45 and 2-46, there will be little or no response. However, the same length line moved over so that one end of the line does terminate properly can cause the hyprcomplex cell to respond, as in Figure 2-46.

Another innovation appears in these cells. Although the very nature of a motion detector makes it specific to movements in one direction only, hypercomplex cells can sometimes show a specificity to movement in two directions. Thus, in Figure 2-47, we see that the cell responds if the line moves either up and to the right or down and to the left. Yet, if the line is too long, the response ends.

Edge detectors also show specificity of size. Figures 2-48 and 2-49 illustrate an edge detector that responds to a thin rectangle moving up into the field at any of several different locations—again, a typical complex cell response. But as soon as the rectangle is widened beyond the critical amount, the responses cease.

Still another innovation is encountered among the hypercomplex cells at this level of processing: an angle detector. Figure 2-50 shows a cell most sensitive to a right angle moving upward through the receptive

Size specificity is not exact, a line too long will elicit no response

edge a line must be terminated properly to obtain max. response

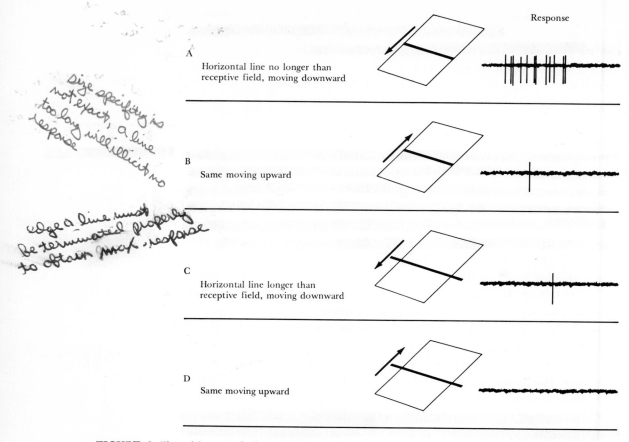

Response

A

Horizontal line no longer than
receptive field, moving downward

B

Same moving upward

C

Horizontal line longer than
receptive field, moving downward

D

Same moving upward

FIGURE 2-45   *After Hubel and Wiesel (1965).*

field. Other angles, while giving some responses, are not nearly so effective in activating the cell.

How to build hypercomplex cells. It should come as no surprise to learn that hypercomplex cells can be constructed by combining the outputs of complex ones. The major new feature is that inhibition now plays a major role: Figure 2-51 shows the connection of three complex cells to make a hypercomplex cell maximally sensitive to a line of specific orientation and length. [Note that instead of using inhibition, the same job would be accomplished by adding together the outputs of three complex cells which had a slit detector $(- + -)$ for the middle cell and the two line detectors $(+ - +)$ for the outer cells.]

The story ends at this point, for we lose track of the sensory messages as they travel into the most central regions of the brain. It is not finished—far from it—but this is the present state of the art.

FIGURE 2-46

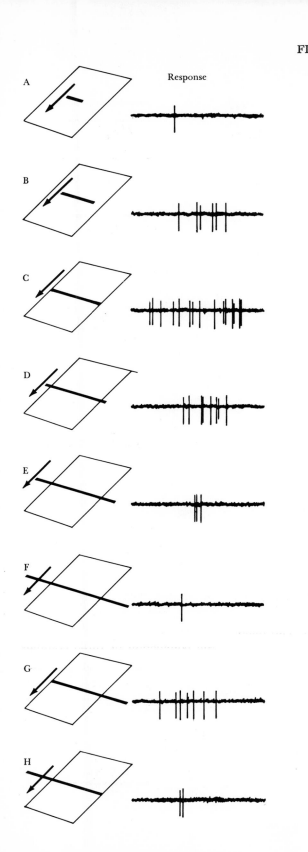

FIGURE 2-47

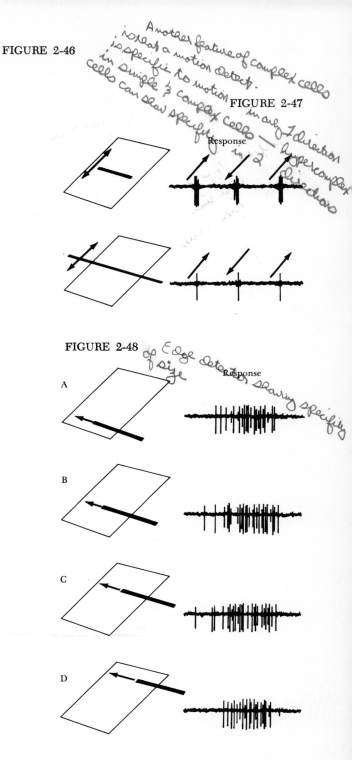

Figures 2-46 and 2-48 are after Hubel and
Wiesel (1965). Figure 2-47 is after Hubel
and Wiesel (1968).

FIGURE 2-50

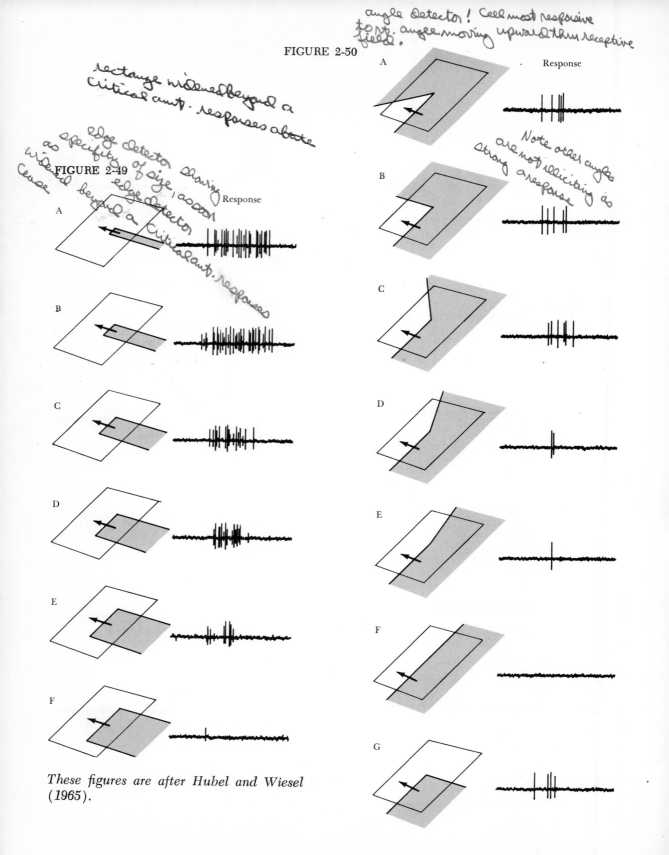

FIGURE 2-49

Response

A

B

C

D

E

F

A

B

C

D

E

F

G

Response

These figures are after Hubel and Wiesel (1965).

angle Detector! Cell most responsive to rt. angle moving upward thru receptive field.

Note other angles are not illiciting as strong a response

rectangle widened beyond a critical amt. responses abate

Edge detector sharing specificity of size, as [illegible] widened beyond a critical edge detector responses

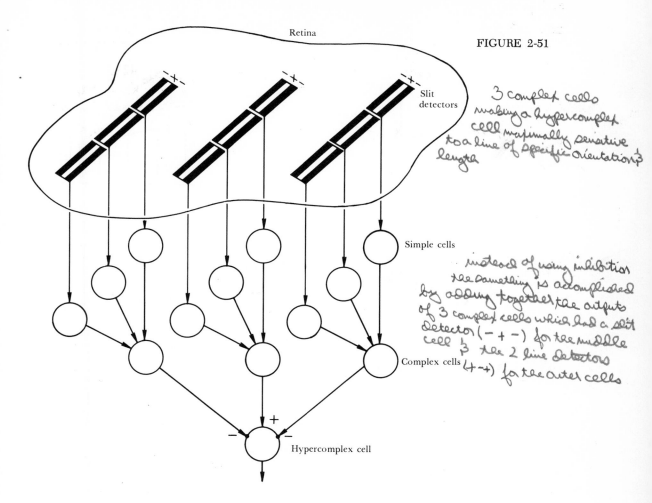

FIGURE 2-51

handwritten note (right upper): 3 complex cells making a hypercomplex cell maximally sensitive to a line of specific orientation

Labels in figure: Retina; Slit detectors; Simple cells; Complex cells; Hypercomplex cell

handwritten note (right middle): instead of using inhibition the same thing is accomplished by adding together the outputs of 3 complex cells which had a slit detector (− + −) for the middle cell & the 2 line detectors (+ −+) for the outer cells

The cells we now know about are summarized in Figure 2-52. We are still far from understanding the mechanisms of pattern recognition. The neural networks for extracting features appear to be increasingly sophisticated as we follow the sensory message into the brain, but we do not yet know where it all leads.

A number of general principles have emerged. The analysis of sensory messages seems to proceed in small steps, with each step producing a rearrangement of the information provided by preceding steps. The calculations are carried out at the interruptions in the sensory pathway—the succession of relay stations through which the messages pass

CONCLUSION

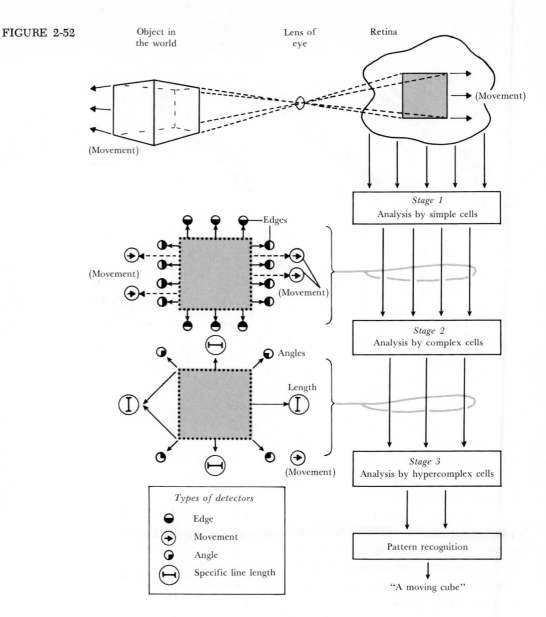

FIGURE 2-52

on the way from the eye to the central regions of the brain. With each reorganization, different features in the sensory message are extracted. Sometimes the information provided by previous states is made more specific: Line detectors at the first level in the cortex are insensitive to line length; subsequent levels are more selective and respond only to lines of specific lengths. Sometimes a more general feature is extracted by combining the responses of specific detectors at a preceding stage. The second level of cortical processing is much less sensitive to the exact position of a line than the detectors operating at the immediately preceding level.

Overall, as the sensory message proceeds upward through the system, the sheer amount of information being carried is continuously reduced. The activity in the 125 million receptors in the eye is recoded into the response patterns of the 800,000 ganglion fibers leaving the eye. As the message proceeds upward, fewer and fewer neurons respond to any given signal. A line in a specific region will cause all the simple line-detectors monitoring that region to respond. Two levels up, only the detectors sensitive to lines of that specific length will respond. At the highest levels, neural activity is primarily restricted to parts of the image where the direction of the contour changes—the angles in the stimulus pattern or the points at which a line terminates. The high spontaneous rates and the sustained response activity to continuous signals at lower levels of neural processing disappear at the higher levels in the system. The cortex is relatively quiet, interrupted only by sporadic and brief flurries of activity when the external signal changes in some way.

The reduction of information during the sensory analysis is hardly arbitrary or random. The basic rule of the nervous system seems to be to find changes in the signal pattern. Intensities in adjacent regions of the retina are compared: The responses are functions of the differences. Some circuits compare the signal present with the one just before it. If they are the same, the result is relative quiet; if different, there is vigorous response, but only briefly. The basic strategy of the analysis seems to be one of comparison: Differences are noted; constancies tend to be suppressed.

The primary mechanism for comparison is to pit excitatory and inhibitory influences against one another. The processes for adding and subtracting the inputs to a neuron provide the calculation power needed to carry out the sophisticated analysis of the visual image. These simple inhibitory and excitatory pairings form the basis of all neural circuits, in all sensory systems, in all species of animals so far investigated.

In principle, we could continue and use the same type of machinery for building even more complex detectors—detectors to recognize grandmothers, cars, and houses. Indeed, a simple extrapolation from what is known about neural information processing might suggest that this is, in fact, what is done. But we have seen in the first chapter and we will see again in the next that such extrapolations are dangerous when studying a system so complex as the human brain. A careful examination of human perception suggests that there are still a number of mysteries that cannot yet be explained by an appeal to these basic mechanisms of neural information processing.

SUGGESTED READINGS

A good introduction to the problems posed in this chapter comes from Ratliff's book *Mach Bands* (1965). A number of the illustrations used in this chapter were borrowed from that book. In addition, the reader interested in the mechanisms of neural interactions should start with the now classic papers of Barlow, Hill, and Levick (1964), the series by Hubel and Wiesel (1962, 1963, 1965, 1968), and the original, now classic paper on "What the Frog's Eye Tells the Frog's Brain," by Lettvin *et al.* (1959). Almost all the physiological information on single cells in this chapter has come from the seven references listed above. Some advanced papers on the topic can be found in the collection *Sensory Communication,* edited by Rosenblith (1961: now available in paperback).

Cornsweet (1970) and Dodwell (1970) present a review of the neural mechanisms in a fashion very similar to that presented here. Both these books are important for several chapters of this book: Cornsweet treats many problems in visual perception in excellent and elegant ways; Dodwell discusses the general problem of pattern recognition. Deutsch (1967), an electrical engineer, presents an interesting set of neurological models in his book,

Models of the nervous system

C. F. Stevens (1966) presents a primer on neurophysiology, as will almost any textbook on physiological psychology published in the 1960s or 1970s.

Eccles (1953, 1964, 1965) discusses the philosophical implications of the neurological structures, as well as providing a detailed description of the operation of synapses. Further recent and advanced literature can be found through the *Annual Review* articles, especially those by Bishop (1967) and by Creutzfeldt and Sakmann (1969) (in the *Annual Review of Physiology*).

Georg von Békésy reviews the role of lateral inhibition in many sensory modalities in his little book, *Sensory Inhibition* (1967). Basically, both Ratliff's book on *Mach bands* and Békésy's book can be considered to be required reading for anyone who has any interest at all in the material in this section. Both these books deal extensively with lateral inhibition, the primary concept involved in the construction of neural circuits. Moreover, both books are comprehensive, yet easy to read.

Some implications of movement detectors on human perception are explored in Sekuler and Ganz (1963) and Pantle and Sekuler (1968).

The studies of the McCollough Effect are proceeding so rapidly that it is best to seek out the literature through the *Psychological Abstracts* and the *Annual Reviews* (articles relevant will be in sections on perception, color vision, and physiological mechanisms of vision). Certainly, one ought to start with the articles referenced in the sections on the effect, in both Chapters 1 and 2: Harris and Gibson (1968), McCollough (1965), Stromeyer (1969), Stromeyer and Mansfield (1970). Another way to follow this phenomenon is to trace citations of McCollough's original article in the *Citation Abstracts*. (See the discussion of these bibliographic tools at the beginning of the reference section.)

3

Theories of pattern recognition

In the last chapter, we studied some of the neural mechanisms under-lying our perceptual experiences. Are these detection systems sufficient to account for human pattern recognition? A little thought about the problem immediately raises some basic questions.

If the system is to be a model of human pattern recognition it is going to have to be quite flexible. For example, it should be able to reliably recognize a given letter even though it may appear in a variety of SIZES or *orientations.* Moreover, it should not be too disturbed by various kinds of distortions in the patterns. We can easily recognize a pattern when parts of it are missing

or when there are extra irrelevant lines

or when a variety of patterns are associated with the same letter:

A a ⓐ *a* 𝒶 𝒜 *a* Ā A

˙uʍop ǝpᴉsdn pǝʇuᴉɹd ǝɹɐ ʇɐɥʇ sɹǝʇʇǝl pɐǝɹ uǝʌǝ uɐɔ ǝʍ 'pǝssǝɹd ɟᴉ 'ʇɔɐɟ uI

This is a formidable list of requirements. However, they must be dealt with if we are to understand perceptual information processing. Let us examine the kind of system that emerges when we try to combine the features extracted during visual processes with the power and flexi-bility of human perception, in an attempt to build a model of human pattern-recognition.

One possible method of using feature analysis for recognizing patterns is the system called *Pandemonium* (Selfridge, 1959). This system is composed of a succession of *demons* who work on the pattern, each performing a different job.

The first set of demons, the *image demons,* have the simplest job. They merely record the initial image of the external signal. The image is next analyzed by *feature demons.* Each feature demon looks for a par-ticular characteristic in the pattern: the presence of a certain type of line; the presence of angles of some sort; or, perhaps, certain curves

PANDEMONIUM

Figure 3-1

FIGURE 3-1

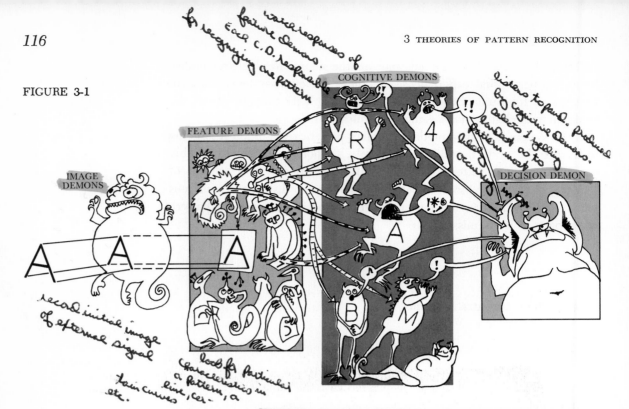

[handwritten annotations: "watch responses of feature demons.", "Each C.D. responsible for recognizing one pattern", "listens to panl. produced by cognitive demons. selects 1 yelling loudest as to pattern as to likely occurring in env."]

COGNITIVE DEMONS

FEATURE DEMONS

IMAGE DEMONS

DECISION DEMON

[handwritten: "record initial image of external signal", "look for particular characteristics in a pattern, a line, cer- tain curves, a etc."]

or contours. *Cognitive demons* watch the responses of the feature demons. Each cognitive demon is responsible for recognizing one pattern. Thus, one cognitive demon would be used for recognizing A; one for recognizing B, and so forth. The A cognitive demon tries to find evidence for the presence of the features associated with its particular pattern. When a cognitive demon finds an appropriate feature, it begins yelling. The more features it finds, the louder it yells. Finally, a decision demon listens to the pandemonium produced by the cognitive demons. It selects the cognitive demon who is yelling the loudest as the pattern that is most likely occurring in the environment.

Pandemonium, then, describes the sequence of events needed for a feature analysis of patterns. It differs from the template scheme mentioned in the first chapter only in that the image is first recoded into a set of features rather than being matched directly against an internal replica or representation. Like the template scheme, pandemonium looks for all patterns at the same time. Each cognitive demon reports the degree to which the input matches his particular set of features. It is an appealingly flexible scheme for pattern recognition. It is possible, for example, to make it learn. Each cognitive demon could gradually learn how to interpret the various features associated with its particular

[handwritten left margin: "Pandemonium & tem- plate matching dif."]

pattern. It is reasonably easy to include the effects of context by adding *contextual demons* who add their voice to the pandemonium. Moreover, the feature analysis is compatible with what we know about the way the nervous system analyzes external signals. As the previous chapters have shown, individual neurons in the perceptual system have just the type of response patterns that make them useful feature demons.

Does a feature-recognition system solve the problems associated with the changing sizes, orientations, and positions of a given pattern? Not directly. It depends on the nature of the features being analyzed. Suppose H is described as having two long vertical lines plus a short horizontal line. With this set of features, any changes in orientation would pose just as much of a problem for feature analysis as it did for template matching. Pandemonium outlines how features might be used to recognize patterns; it does not in any way tell us what features are actually being extracted from the incoming sensory information.

When we set out to design a machine to recognize patterns, we study the pattern set and try to determine the features that will uniquely classify each pattern. In principle, we are perfectly free to select any set of features we think will reliably discriminate among the patterns. The main criteria are that the feature set be as simple as possible; that it produce as few errors as possible; and that the features can be analyzed using simple circuitry. Let us go through the same process, but not in quite so arbitrary a way. Let us try to use what is known about the human nervous system to determine a set of features that might be used by the human pattern-recognition system.

Features for recognizing letters

The study of the kinds of neural responses produced by specific incoming signals suggests that the perceptual systems of most higher-level organisms extract a wealth of data about specific features in the visual image. Recall that in the brain centers which receive sensory information from our receptors, some individual neurons react only to the presence of a straight line at a particular orientation in a particular part of the retinal image. They show the same reaction regardless of the length of the line. Neighboring neurons may also respond maximally to a line of a particular orientation, but may not be so fussy about its exact location. Still others seem to be most sensitive to contours of certain shapes or to intersecting lines that form an angle of a particular size. Visual systems, then, typically extract an enormous amount of detailed information about specific features in the visual image. In fact, more

How to build pandemoniums

Problem w/ P.P.R

information is extracted than would be needed to recognize letters on the basis of a pandemonium scheme.

The information can be condensed by applying the same principle that was used to construct templates: Simply connect together a number of cells to construct a more general feature detector. For example, neurons responding to vertical lines in different parts of the retinal image could be connected together to produce a general vertical line detector. The response rate of this feature demon would code the **number** of vertical lines in the pattern, regardless of the length, intensity or "goodness" of each line. Similarly, a general feature demon for horizontal lines and for diagonal lines could be made by connecting up the appropriate neural detectors. The same could be done with angle information: One feature demon could specify the number of right angles in the pattern; another the number of acute angles. Finally, there ought to be some information related to curves. For the present purposes, we can invent two curve demons that would be useful in a pattern recognition system: One that responds to the number of continuous curves (such as in O and Q), and one that responds to the number of discontinuous curves (D and C). After making the appropriate connections, the resulting system would look like Figure 3-2.

1) connection of cells making a detectors for general extraction

Table 3-1

Here the sensory information has been analyzed for seven general types of features. Each feature demon reports the number of a certain type of features that are contained in the pattern. The cognitive demons look for the particular values of the features that describe their pattern, and the vigor of their response is determined by the number of such features found. The proper pattern is finally selected by the decision demon, who reacts to the cognitive demon who is responding most vigorously.

One more problem must be overcome before this system can function. Some letters differ from others only in that they have **additional** features. For example, F has a vertical line, two horizontal lines, and three right angles. The letter P has all those features plus a discontinuous curve. If P is presented to the system, there is no problem: The P demon responds more than the F. But if F is presented, both the F and P demons yell equally: The decision demon will be unable to chose between them. The same problem arises between P and R, V and Y, O and Q, etc.

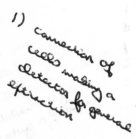

2) maximum response cell are responding only when everything the cell is quiet to respond to is present

One way to solve this problem is to set up a standard maximum response level for all demons. A demon responds at his maximum rate only when **all** those features it is looking for are present. Both the absence of a looked-for feature and the presence of an unsought feature inhibit the demon from yelling at full capacity.

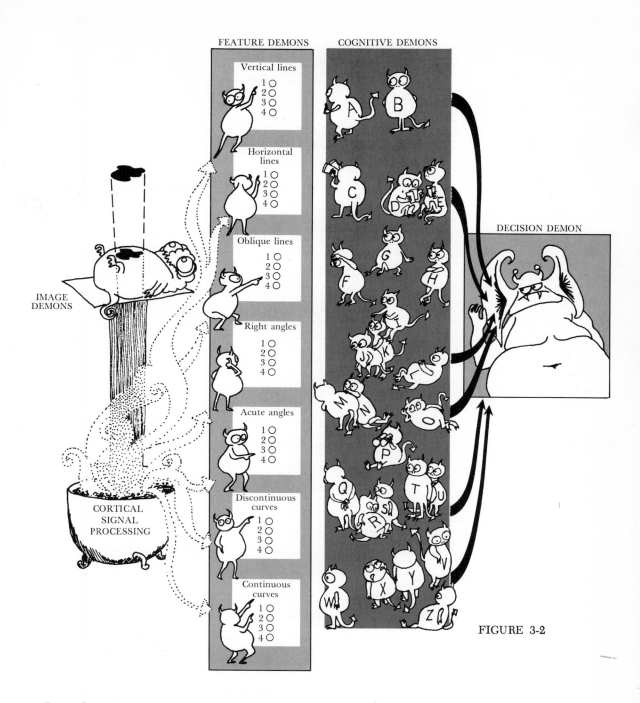

FEATURE DEMONS

COGNITIVE DEMONS

Vertical lines
1 ○
2 ○
3 ○
4 ○

Horizontal
lines
1 ○
2 ○
3 ○
4 ○

Oblique lines
1 ○
2 ○
3 ○
4 ○

Right angles
1 ○
2 ○
3 ○
4 ○

Acute angles
1 ○
2 ○
3 ○
4 ○

Discontinuous
curves
1 ○
2 ○
3 ○
4 ○

Continuous
curves
1 ○
2 ○
3 ○
4 ○

IMAGE
DEMONS

CORTICAL
SIGNAL
PROCESSING

DECISION DEMON

FIGURE 3-2

In outline, this is a prescription for a specific feature-recognition system. Will it work? The only way to find out is to test it and see how it behaves. Watch what happens when a letter is presented—say, the letter R.

Figure 3-3

	Vertical lines	Horizontal lines	Oblique lines	Right angles	Acute angles	Continuous curves	Discontinuous curves
A		1	2		3		
B	1	3		4			2
C							1
D	1	2		2			1
E	1	3		4			
F	1	2		3			
G	1	1		1			1
H	2	1		4			
I	1	2		4			
J	1						1
K	1		2	1	2		
L	1	1		1			
M	2		2		3		
N	2		1		2		
O						1	
P	1	2		3			1
Q			1		2	1	
R	1	2	1	3			1
S							2
T	1	1		2			
U	2						1
V			2		1		
W			4		3		
X			2		2		
Y	1		2		1		
Z		2	1		2		

TABLE 3-1

First, the R is encoded by the image demons, and the information is sent on for further processing. Now the feature demons begin responding. The first feature demon records the presence of a vertical line. This is not much help in classifying the pattern. The diagram shows the cognitive demons that are activated by the presence of a single

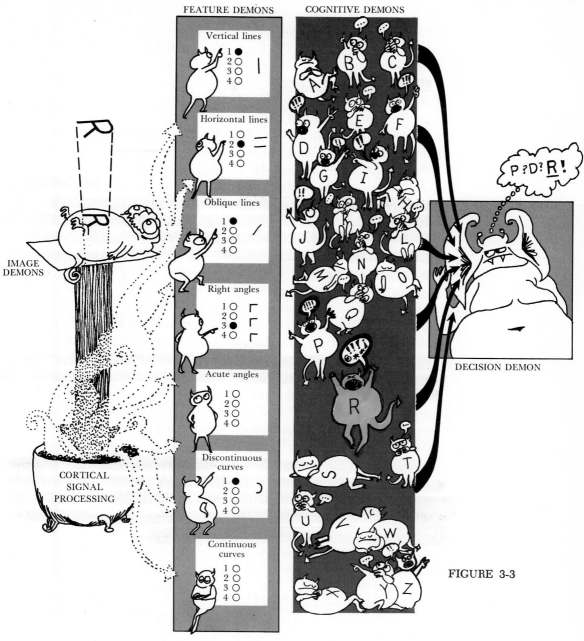

FEATURE DEMONS

COGNITIVE DEMONS

Vertical lines

Horizontal lines

Oblique lines

Right angles

Acute angles

Discontinuous curves

Continuous curves

IMAGE DEMONS

CORTICAL SIGNAL PROCESSING

DECISION DEMON

P ?D? R!

FIGURE 3-3

vertical line. Of the 26 possible letters of the alphabet, 13 have a single vertical line, 6 have two horizontal lines. As we follow down through the list, we see that different features activate different sets of cognitive demons. In this case, the decision demon has an easy choice, since R is clearly the most active responder. The next most likely pattern would be a P, which appears on four of the seven lists, and the third most active demon would be the D, which is matched by three out of the seven features.

The importance of errors. Notice some of the important characteristics of the behavior expected from this type of pattern recognition system. To recognize the R, for example, not all seven feature demons are needed. It suffices to note that there is an acute angle and a closed contour. The same would be true if the angle information was extracted from the pattern—the presence of the three right angles and the one acute angle uniquely characterizes the pattern as an R. For any given letter, then, the seven feature demons are supplying more information than is required. This means that some of the feature demons can fail, and the pattern recognition system would still operate correctly for some signals. All seven features are needed only when all the possible patterns are considered together. That is, if we write down the values for the features associated with each letter, we need seven different features in order to have a unique string of numbers for every letter. If more patterns are added, more features must be used, and the nature of the features will depend on the characteristics of the additional patterns.

A second point to notice is that the particular set of features selected for the recognizing of patterns will determine the kinds of recognition errors that are made. On the average, if there is trouble identifying an R, we might expect the P to be a likely alternative choice. When the incoming signal is transformed into the feature set, P is the pattern most similar to R.

One test for the theory, then, would be to present people with the various letters under conditions where they are difficult to identify, to see what kinds of errors are made. The results of such an experiment produce a *confusion matrix* which describes the patterns of errors subjects make when trying to identify the letters. Figure 3-4 shows an example of a confusion matrix produced by flashing the various letters shown in Figure 3-5 briefly on a screen and asking people to report what they saw. (These data come from an experiment by Kinney, Marsetta, and Showman, 1966.)

Vertically, along the left, are the letters that were actually displayed. Horizontally, along the top, are the letters which the subjects reported they saw. If we follow down the left column until we come to R, then the corresponding horizontal row gives the responses made when the subjects attempted to identify this letter. Moving across that row, we find that the observers made a total of six mistakes in identifying R: Four out of those six times, they reported they saw a P.

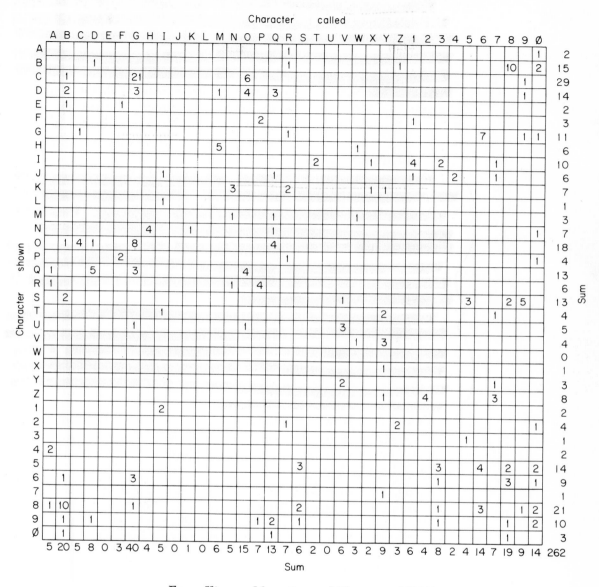

From Kinney, Marsetta, and Showman (1966).   FIGURE 3-4

A B C D E F G H I J K L M N O P Q R

FIGURE 3-5

S T U V W X Y Z 1 2 3 4 5 6 7 8 9 Ø

A third point to notice about a feature recognition scheme is that the errors in identifying letters need not be symmetrical. Take the letter C, for example. If this letter were presented, only the open contour (discontinuous curve) demon would respond. Thus, when C occurs, the decision demon should have trouble in deciding whether it was a C or a G. Note the errors made in recognizing C in the confusion matrix. Subjects had more difficulty in identifying C than any other letter: 21 times they reported they saw a G when a C was actually presented. The letter C, however, will not necessarily be a frequent response when G is presented.

Responses to distorted patterns. Now that we have explored some of the characteristics of pandemonium, let us return to consider the problems produced by distortions in the external pattern: Changes in the size of the characters do not present any problem for this feature-extraction scheme. The feature demons collect information from line detectors which are themselves insensitive to the length of the lines. Right angles are still right angles, and acute angles are still acute angles, regardless of the size of the letter.

Orientation is a different story. Laying an F on its side would be very confusing to these particular demons, since it creates a pattern with two vertical and one horizontal line plus three right angles. Turning F completely upside down, however, would not disturb this particular pattern-recognition system: The horizontal and vertical line demons would make exactly the same response.

Obviously, one way to correct the system's sensitivity to orientation is to build even more general feature demons. Connect together all the demons responding to straight lines to produce an overall line demon that responds regardless of orientation.

Figure 3-6

So long as we are talking about theories, this is simple to do. But would the recognition system still be able to identify all the letters with this more general set of features? Not quite. The letters M and W are confused, since each has four lines and three acute angles. Similarly, N and Z are confused: These two letters both have three lines and two acute angles.

Figure 3-7

Normally, adults do not confuse these two sets of letters, although sometimes children do. Clearly, this latter combination of features is not an appropriate description of the feature analysis performed by humans.

Features for recognizing speech It is not too difficult to see how a feature-extraction scheme might provide a reasonable start toward a system for recognizing letters. Even a very simple set of features appears to work reasonably well for letter patterns. The story is not nearly so simple with speech. Here, the very

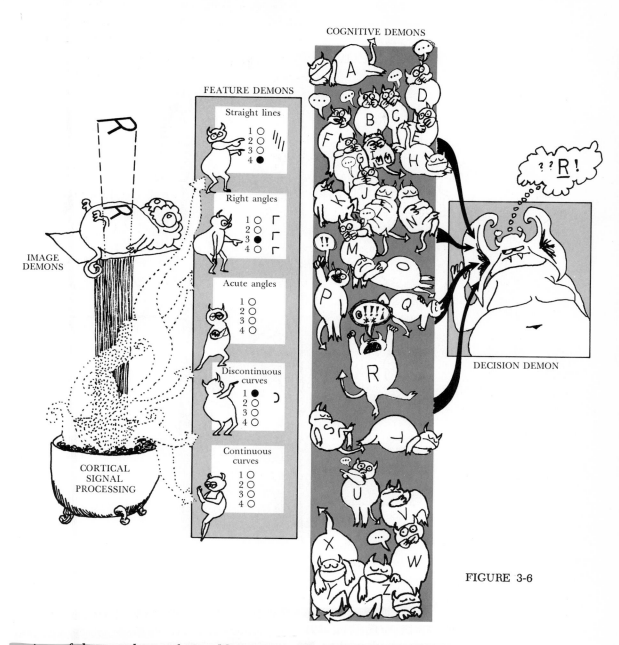

FIGURE 3-6

nature of the speech waveform adds immense difficulties to the analysis. Despite large expenditures of money and effort, no one has yet succeeded in devising a speech recognition system that has more than a very limited ability to recognize words, and then usually only when the words are clearly and carefully spoken by one of a small number of people.

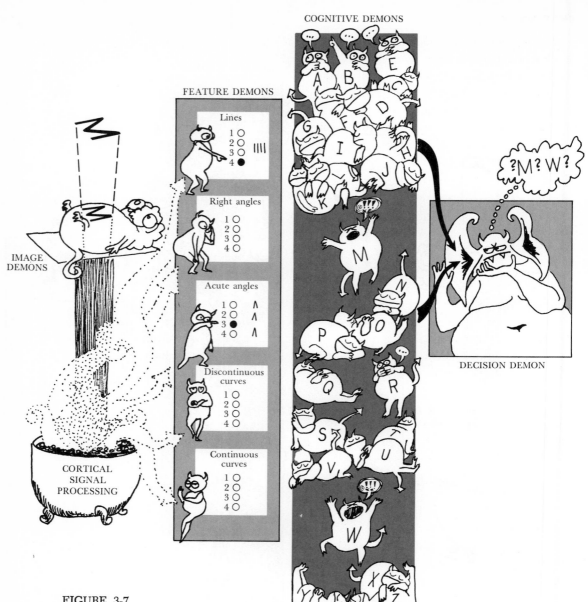

IMAGE DEMONS

CORTICAL SIGNAL PROCESSING

FEATURE DEMONS

Lines
1 ○
2 ○
3 ○
4 ●

Right angles
1 ○
2 ○
3 ○
4 ○

Acute angles
1 ○
2 ○
3 ●
4 ○

Discontinuous curves
1 ○
2 ○
3 ○
4 ○

Continuous curves
1 ○
2 ○
3 ○
4 ○

COGNITIVE DEMONS

DECISION DEMON

FIGURE 3-7

There are three major difficulties with the recognition of speech. First, there is the problem of segmentation: The units to be recognized are not clearly demarked. Second, there is enormous variability in the physical waveforms when different people speak the same word, or the same person speaks a given word in different contexts. Finally, there is little agreement about the identity of the basic features that could be used to recognize speech, if indeed there are any.

The segmentation problem. In the analysis of printed text, each letter is clearly separated from its neighbors by a fixed amount of space, and each word is separated from neighboring words by an even greater amount of space. Thus, it is a simple matter to determine the boundaries between letters, words, and sentences—not so with speech.

When you listen to someone speaking, his words sound distinct and usually reasonably well articulated. There appears to be a well-defined separation between most words. All this is an illusion. The clear distinctions that are so easily perceived are not present in the physical signal but are a result of the pattern recognition process: They are put in by the analysis. In fact, the spoken waveform is a peculiar combination of inarticulate sounds, ill-pronounced segments, deletions, and contractions. Worst of all, there is no apparent connection between the breaks in the speech waveform and the boundaries between words.

The easiest way to become convinced of this is to listen to someone speaking a foreign language. If you do not understand the language, the speech seems to come in a continuous stream at a rapid rate. Even the beginning student who has painstakingly learned the vocabulary of a language discovers he has a great deal of difficulty finding the words he knows in the apparently continuous utterances of the native speaker. In fact, the seeming rapidity of foreign languages is, in most cases, an illusion. The differences in our perceptions are due to the operation of a pattern recognition system. In the one case, the sounds can be meaningfully interpreted and the words stand out as discrete entities; in the other case, the recognition system is inappropriate, and the sounds appear as unorganized, meaningless nonsense.

There are some properties in the physical waveform that are of some use in segmenting the verbal message. None of the physical characteristics so far studied, however, provides entirely reliable clues to the boundaries between words. And in many cases it seems that the analysis system must know what the word is before it can find the proper boundaries. How can the sound pattern *ai-s-k-r-ee-m* be segmented appropriately until it is known whether the words are associated with the phrase, **When I see a snake** . . . or the phrase, **buy me some** . . . . The solution to this circularity in the analysis of speech waveforms is a more sophisticated pattern-recognition system, which will be discussed in the next section.

Phonemes. Linguists have long tried to characterize the sound components in speech. It is clear that in printed English the syllable and the individual letter represent elementary units of a word. In the spoken

Feature detectors for speech

speech, the basic units are not so easy to discern. But to the trained ear, there appears to be a small vocabulary of basic sounds from which all words are formed. A particular sound qualifies as a basic unit if it serves some functional purpose in the language. Consider the words **bat, pat,** and **vat.** Each of these words has a different meaning. The difference is signaled entirely by a change in only one sound, in this case the initial sounds "b," "p," and "v." A sound that, by itself, can change the meaning of a word is called a *phoneme.* The sounds "a," "e," "i," "u" (as in cup), and "oo" are also phonemes. When they are systematically substituted for the middle of **bat,** for example, they each produce a new meaningful word.

Note that every letter does not necessarily correspond to a phoneme. Moreover, the number and nature of phonemes differ from dialect to dialect in the English language. In some parts of the country, the three words **merry, marry,** and **Mary** are pronounced identically. In other parts of the United States, however, the three words are spoken quite differently.

Differences in sound that do not signal differences in meaning tend to go unnoticed. The phoneme "d" is pronounced rather differently when it appears in **dance** from when it appears in **handle,** yet the normal speaker is seldom aware of these differences.

Table 3-2   The Phonemes of General American English[a,b]

Vowels	Consonants	
ee as in h*ea*t	*t* as in *t*ee	*s* as in *s*ee
I as in h*i*t	*p* as in *p*ea	*sh* as in *sh*ell
e as in h*ea*d	*k* as in *k*ey	*h* as in *h*e
ae as in h*a*d	*b* as in *b*ee	*v* as in *v*iew
ah as in f*a*ther	*d* as in *d*awn	*th* as in *th*en
aw as in c*a*ll	*g* as in *g*o	*z* as in *z*oo
U as in p*u*t	*m* as in *m*e	*zh* as in ga*r*age
oo as in c*oo*l	*n* as in *n*o	*l* as in *l*aw
ʌ as in t*o*n	*ng* as in si*ng*	*r* as in *r*ed
uh as in th*e*	*f* as in *f*ee	*y* as in *y*ou
er as in b*ir*d	*θ* as in *th*in	*w* as in *w*e
oi as in t*oi*l		
au as in sh*ou*t		
ei as in t*a*ke		
ou as in t*o*ne		
ai as in m*i*ght		

[a] General American is the dialect of English spoken in midwestern and western areas of the United States and influences an increasing number of Americans. Certain phonemes of other regional dialects (e.g., Southern, British, etc.) can be different.

[b] From Denes and Pinson (1963).

If phonemes are the basic building blocks for words, have we found the features for a pandemonium system of speech recognition? Probably not. Equating phonemes with features is not very helpful. Unlike the line and angle detectors of the visual system, there is no known way of actually analyzing and extracting the phonemes from a speech waveform. So far, only the human can recognize a phoneme in the speech wave.

Distinctive features. The difficulties in identifying phonemes has led to other schemes for classifying speech sounds. One method is to examine how speech is produced to see whether the waveform can be described in terms of the various operations involved in generating the sounds. Speech sounds result from the complex interaction of a number of parts of the vocal apparatus. The diaphragm forces air up through the trachea. The soft palate opens and closes the nasal passages to the flow of air. The tongue, teeth, and lips all move in synchrony to determine the harmonic and temporal structure of the sound patterns produced.

Sounds can be classified according to the operation of these various components. If the air passing through the trachea vibrates the vocal chords, it produces a *voiced* sound, such as "a" or "z." When the vocal chords do not vibrate during the sound production, an *unvoiced* sound is produced, such as the "s" sound of **hiss.** Note that the only distinction between the way "z" and "s" are produced is in the voicing. Another distinctive feature is formed by the possibility of restricting the air passage somewhere in the mouth to produce the hissing, turbulent sound of a *fricative*—"sh," "s," "f," "v," "th." In other sounds the flow of air is completely interrupted for a short period of time, then released explosively to produce a *plosive* or *stop*—"t" and "d" are examples. Stops produce a definite break in the wave pattern, but unfortunately these breaks are not related to word boundaries. When we produce the word **standard,** for example, there are three distinct breaks in the speech flow: one after the "s," one after the "n," and one after the "r." There are also only these same three breaks in the phrase, **he uses standard oil.**

Thus, we can recode speech sounds into the distinctive features associated with their production: Each produces a unique characteristic in the resulting sound. Here is a table listing one possible classification of the distinctive features for each of the phonemes in the English language.

Table 3-3

Like phonemes, distinctive features are difficult to identify in a continuous waveform. The character of the sounds changes substantially when they appear in different contexts. As a result, at the moment, we have a variety of possible ways of classifying sounds, none of which

Table 3-3   One Version of Distinctive Features for English Phonemes[a]

Phoneme	Strident/ Mellow	Continuant/ Interrupted	Tense/ Lax	Nasal/ Oral	Flat/ Plain	Grave/ Acute	Compact/ Diffuse	Consonantal/ Nonconsonantal	Vocalic/ Nonvocalic
o (as in pot)					+	+	+	−	+
a (as in pat)					−	+	+	−	+
e (as in pet)						−	+	−	+
u (as in put)					+	+	−	−	+
ə (as in putt)					−	+	−	−	+
i (as in pit)						−	−	−	+
l (as in lull)								+	+
ŋ (as in lung)				+			+	+	−
ʃ (as in ship)	+	+	+	−			+	+	−
f̂ (as in chip)	−	−	+	−			+	+	−
k (as in kip)		−	+	−			+	+	−
ʒ (as in azure)	+	+	−	−			+	+	−
ĵ (as in juice)	−	−	−	−			+	+	−
g (as in goose)		−	−	−			+	+	−
m (as in mill)				+		+	−	+	−
f (as in fill)		+	+	−		+	−	+	−
p (as in pill)		−	+	−		+	−	+	−
v (as in vim)		+	−	−		+	−	+	−
b (as in bill)		−	−	−	−	+	−	+	−
n (as in nil)				+		−	−	+	−
s (as in sil)	+	+	+	−		−	−	+	−
θ (as in thill)	−	+	+	−		−	−	+	−
t (as in till)		−	+	−		−	−	+	−
z (as in zip)	+	+	−	−		−	−	+	−
ð (as in this)	−	+	−	−		−	−	+	−
d (as in dill)		−	−	−		−	−	+	−
h (as in hill)				−			−	−	−
# (as in ___ill)				−				−	−

[a] After Jakobson, Fant, and Halle (1951).

works completely satisfactorily. Some authorities prefer classification schemes based on the production of speech; others emphasize the perceptions of the listeners; some attempt to combine the two approaches. To date, we have been unsuccessful in devising a scheme that can enable a machine to recognize speech, well, with fluency, and when several different speakers are involved.

We have given you enough to get you started in thinking about the way in which a pattern-recognition system is built up on the basis of a feature analysis. The discussion illustrates how theories of pattern recognition are constructed and tested. For any theory, the first decision is whether, in fact, it will work. Do the selected features really classify and identify all of the patterns? If we are building a machine to read letter addresses and sort the mail, then, if possible, we do not want any errors at all. But humans do make errors. If we are attempting to model human pattern-recognition, then our system must make the same errors that a person would make. Analysis of errors turns out to be one of the most important ways in which we can obtain information about the operation of human pattern-recognition.

Summary of feature analysis

This general approach to pattern recognition seems to be on the right track, but the details are undoubtedly wrong. One important discussion concerns the different possible levels of abstraction of the feature extraction system. At one level, the system could respond to the number of vertical, horizontal and acute lines in a region. A different level might only examine the total number of lines of any orientation. It might be preferable to have intermediate steps or even more general feature analyzers. For humans, it is probably safest to assume that a pattern is classified simultaneously at varying levels of generality. At the highest level, the system may only respond that an A is present. Lower levels may report that the A is lying on its side, for example. Other parts of the system probably are aware of the details of the input, the various kinds of squiggly lines and extra dots that have been filtered out at higher stages of processing. For some tasks, it may be sufficient to attend only to the very general features of the pattern—its overall linearity or curvature. For others, a detailed analysis of the input may be necessary. In the effort to devise general schemes for recognizing patterns despite distortions, it is important not to discard the possibility of noticing that these distortions are in fact present in the incoming signal.

Feature extraction schemes break down in a number of situations that humans deal with routinely. How can analysis of features tell us whether the sounds *noo-dis-plaee* represent the words **new display** or the words

ANALYSIS BY SYNTHESIS

nudist play? What features tell us that the symbols I3 are numbers when they appear in the context of I3 579 but are letters when they appear in the context I3 O Y ? What does a feature recognition system do with this pattern—what features describe the cathedral?

FIGURE 3-8   *Roy Lichtenstein, "Cathedral #5." Lithograph, $48\frac{1}{2} \times 32\frac{1}{2}$ inches. Copyright © 1969, Gemini G. E. L.*

The demons of pandemonium are really not enough. More information must be included in the pattern-recognition process to explain the tremendous power of the human recognition-system. What else is there, though, when templates and features fail?

A large part of the interpretation of sensory data is provided by the knowledge of what the signal must be, rather than from information contained in the signal itself. This extra information comes from the *context* of the sensory event. Context is the overall environment in which experiences are embedded. You know many things about the material you are reading, in addition to the actual patterns of letters on this page. You know that it is written in English, that it is discussing psychology in general, and the psychology of pattern recognition in particular. Moreover, you have probably learned quite a bit about the style of writing, thus, as your eyes travel over the page, you are able to make good prediction the words which you expect to see. These predictions are good enough so that you automatically fill in the missing "about" or "of" in the previous sentence,[1] or, equivalently, not even notice its absence. The enormous amount of information that is accumulated and routinely used to understand the events, we call the context of those events. The ability to use context makes the human perceptual system far superior and more flexible than any electronic pattern-recognition system so far invented.

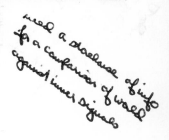

A matter of context

The effects of context are easy to document. Figures are perceived more quickly and easily if they are meaningful than if they are simply decorative. The ability to read and remember letters is much more difficult if they are laid out haphazardly in a meaningless string—sgtooeurua— than if the same letters appear in a meaningful order—**outrageous.** Even when the letters do make meaningful words—

Wet socks

inm
ycr
aft
ors
ull
ena
rt

—they are difficult to perceive unless they are in a format consistent with the normal mode of dealing with them.

[1] A good example of this is the fact that our typist, when originally typing the manuscript from a tape recording, automatically put in the missing "of."

A number of experimental techniques have been used to demonstrate the effects of context on the preceptual analysis of incoming signals. In one example (an experiment performed by Miller, 1962a), subjects listened to a string of words like **socks, some, brought, wet, who.** The words were mixed with noise so that each individual word could be correctly identified only about 50% of the time. In a second test, the words were then rearranged, so they appeared in a meaningful order— **who, brought, some, wet, socks,** and again the subjects attempted to identify them. When the words were spoken in a grammatical order, the recognition performance of the subjects improved dramatically. In fact, the contextual cues improved recognition an amount equivalent to decreasing the noise intensity to 50% of its previous value. The physical information is the same in both cases. It was the context that produced such a dramatically improved accuracy in the perception of an identical physical signal.

Consider what happens when a word is heard without any context, such as the **brought** in **socks, some, brought, wet, who.** It sounds like a hissing gurgle in the background of noise. Perhaps a few features are extracted. Perhaps the "b" sound is recognized and it is noted that the word is one syllable long. The two features are sufficient to rule out words such as **hospital, Mississippi, bananas,** and **boondocks,** but there are still a large number of possibilities left—words such as **brought, boy, brings, brags, buys, bought, bit, bones.** Let us use these eight words as our best possible selections. Without additional information, no decision can be reached. A guess at this point would be correct about 1 out of 8 times, $12\frac{1}{2}$%.

Now, suppose the same word is embedded in the phrase, **who b_____ some wet socks,** the second condition in Miller's experiment. The context allows the possible alternatives to be reduced considerably. The unknown word is probably a verb, so out go **boys** and **bones** as possible alternatives. It must be able to take an object: You cannot "brag" socks, so another possibility is eliminated. It must have some plausible meaning. "Who bit the wet socks" is an improbable statement, so out goes **bit.** Now there are perhaps four alternatives left: **brought, brings, buys,** and **bought.** With just a little extra information about feature, we can narrow down the choices even more. Was there a hissing sound of "s?" If not, the word is either **brought** or **bought:** only two possibilities. Even by guessing, there is now a 50% chance of being right, a great improvement over the $12\frac{1}{2}$% guessing chances without the aid of contextual information.

The power of context is clear. Rules can be used to reduce the number of possible alternatives that are to be considered at any moment. This does not imply, of course, that perception requires a conscious trial-and-error approach to determine the alternative that best fits the contextual information. We do not know exactly what mechanisms underly the use of contextual information, but we do know that context plays a major role in our perceptions. It supplies the rules underlying the construction of our perceptual world, tells us what to expect, and gives plausible interpretations of what we are perceiving.

Note that to take full use of contextual information, perception must lag behind the information received by the sensory systems. The perception of the word **brought** was aided not only by words appearing before it (**who**), but also by words that appeared after (**socks**). This lag between the intake of sensory information and the final interpretation of a message is an important part of the structure of our perceptual analysis. When reading aloud, for example, the eyes scan the words well ahead of the part of the text being spoken. When a skilled typist copies a manuscript, he reads the text far ahead of the place being typed. We move forward to gather as much contextual information as possible before actually executing the responses required by the task we are performing. The more we know about what is to come, the easier it is to perceive what is at hand.

The structure of language seems to be designed to complement the ability of the human to piece together the meaning of a communication from a few isolated fragments. English is highly redundant. We say and write much more than is necessary to be understood. Omit much words make text shorter. You not have trouble understanding. One scheme for estimating redundancy in the language is to mutilate the text in systematic ways and ask a person to reconstruct the missing sections. The ease with which this task can be done gives a measure of redundancy of the language. Thxs, wx cax drxp oxt exerx thxrd xetxer, xnd xou xtixl maxagx prxttx wexl. Thng ge a ltte tuger f w alo lav ou th spce.

The importance of redundancy

If the language were more efficient, or if humans were less able to use contextual information to guide their perceptions, then communication would be a painful and hazardous process. We would have to attend very carefully to every word spoken: one word missed, one distorted syllable, and the whole meaning of a sentence might be lost or misperceived. We could not afford to relax for an instant. Even the slightest noise could lead to disaster. The redundancy of the language, then, allows us to attend selectively to bits and pieces of a communication, to anticipate what will come next, and to look selectively for the key words and phrases that convey the basic meaning of the message. As a result, we can relax, confident that we can miss much of the details of speech or print, yet not miss the intended meaning.

SYNTHESIZING A SENSORY MESSAGE

It is much easier to demonstrate the effects of context than to work out the actual mechanisms underlying the use of contextual information in interpreting sensory signals. We just do not know enough about human cognitive processes and memory structures to construct a completely adequate model. Nevertheless, we can make a start on the problem to give you the flavor of the approach.

The discussion so far suggests that at one end, sensory systems respond to the external events and transform the sensory message into specific types of features. At the other end, a memory system contains a record of past experiences—the data and theories needed to interpret sensory signals. Somehow, these two sources of information must converge. The sensory evidence must be matched with stored information in order to recognize the signal. But the matching process cannot be arbitrary. It is not possible just to select any item from memory and hope that, somehow, it is related to the current sensory input. If a memory item were selected randomly, it would take a long time to identify even very familiar objects such as tables and chairs.

This is where the considerations of context must come in. The memory system holds not only the key to recognition, but also knowledge of the sensory events that have just been interpreted. There are **expectations** about what the next sensory event will be, based on what has just been perceived. Moreover, these expectations about what comes next are continuously changing as the signal processing proceeds. We call the construction and revision of expectations during the interpretation of a message an *active synthesizing process*.

Figure 3-9

In the diagram, most of the pandemonium model presented earlier is included in the "feature analysis" box. The decision demon is now in the box labeled "active synthesizing process," but he now has memory to work with, as well as sensory data. The job of the active synthesizing process is to put together a logical story consistent with both sources of information. At present, the box is empty. Now let us picture what is going on inside: Let us capture the synthesizing process in the middle of interpreting a message.

Figure 3-10

In Figure 3-10, we have stopped the action in the middle of reading the sentence, **THE BOY WORRIED HIS FATHER.** The sensory analysis system is shown working on the letter **R:** It has just found two

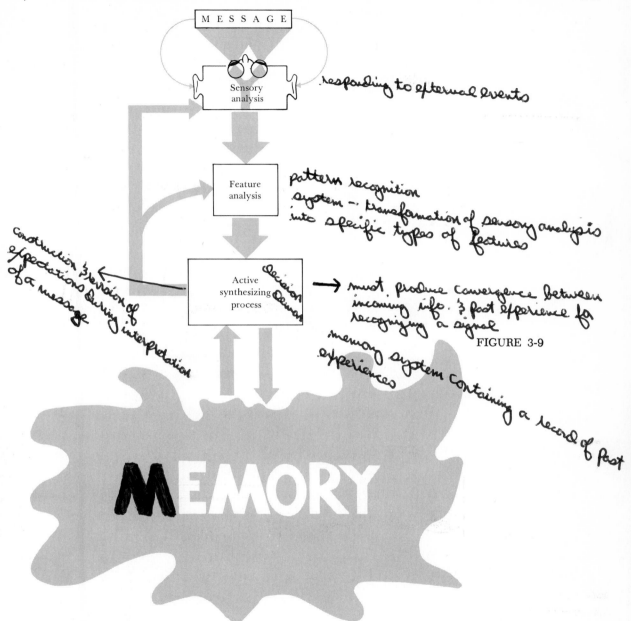

MESSAGE

Sensory analysis

responding to external events

Feature analysis

pattern recognition system – transformation of sensory analysis into specific types of features

Active synthesizing process

decision criterion

construction & revision of expectations during interpretation of a message

→ *must produce convergence between incoming info. & past experience for recognizing a signal*

FIGURE 3-9

memory system containing a record of past experiences

MEMORY

of the straight line features shown in the feature analysis box. Simultaneously, the memory system contains the portion of the message that has already been interpreted: **THE BOY WOR——**. In the middle, between sensory analysis and memory, the active synthesizing process is shown trying to match up expectations with the current sensory evidence.

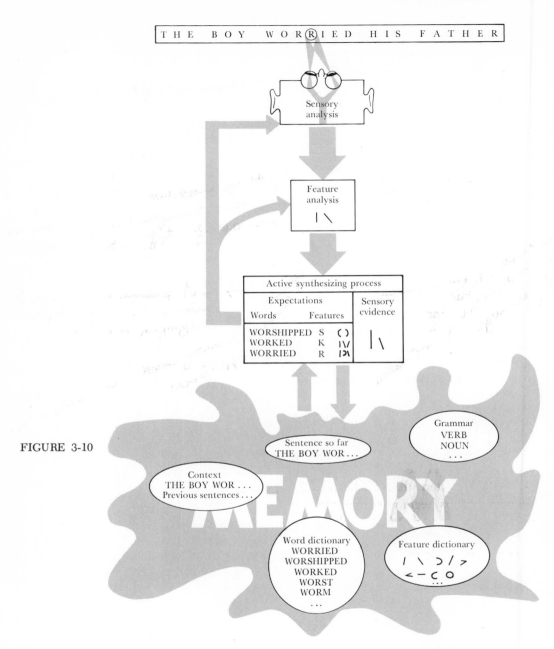

FIGURE 3-10

Look at the expectations. The word currently being analyzed starts out as **WOR**——. Suppose the possible words that are under consideration are **WORSHIPPED, WORKED,** and **WORRIED.** Let these be the only words known to the system consistent with all of the evidence to date. These words are being considered because they begin with **WOR,** and are verbs that can take a person as subject. Undoubtedly, the analysis of the word began with a much larger list of possibilities. As the interpretation proceeded, the set of expectations was continuously changed until these three possibilities were left.

As the synthesis process finishes each segment of the message, it can move on to the next part. The contextual information may tell it that the next important part of the message is the object of the verb, perhaps also a family term, since the preceding sentence has discussed the boy's relationship to his family. As the detailed analysis of the next word proceeds, new expectations will be generated and tested against the sensory evidence.

Figure 3-11

Here we have a pattern recognition scheme that continuously constructs and revises expectations about what it is perceiving as it proceeds to interpret a sensory message. It does not rely exclusively either on its own internal models or on the evidence of its senses, But the two sources of information must match before it concludes it has successfully interpreted the incoming signal.

This type of pattern-recognition system requires the ability to construct and test hypotheses simultaneously at several different levels. The rules embedded in the grammar and meaning of the language lead to the expectation of a verb, the expectation that the information yet to come should include an object of that verb, perhaps a modifier, and probably that the words have something to do with the boy's family relationships. Within this general context, a small set of specific words match both the context and the sensory evidence that has been interpreted so far. These expectations in turn generate predictions about the specific pattern that is currently being deciphered. As soon as the contour demons begin reporting, the whole complex of expectations will be simultaneously matched, and the system can move on to the next segment.

At the other end, the sensory system must supply a number of different levels of sensory evidence. Sensory data regarding the general length and shape of the word is combined with the contextual information to narrow down the set of alternative possibilities. Information about the approximate sizes and shapes and number of surrounding words is probably used to decide on what to interpret next. In addition to these general features, a small part of the message is being simultaneously analyzed in detail.

The great virtue of an active synthesizing process is that it allows a selective sampling of environmental information, so that only the

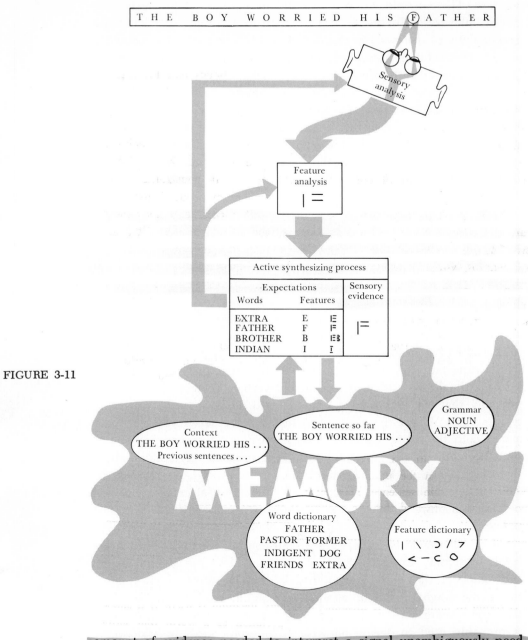

FIGURE 3-11

amount of evidence needed to interpret a signal unambiguously need be collected. The synthesizing process guides attention to the most pertinent parts of the message and, within the focus of attention, to the most pertinent features in the pattern. It can form incorrect hypotheses and make errors in predicting the sensory events, but it has many built-in safeguards. Suppose that when all of the evidence is in, the sensory data fail to match one of the expected letters. The smooth flow of processing must be temporarily interrupted until the ambiguity can be resolved. But consider the options for such a system in detecting and correcting errors. Letters can be skipped; spot checks can be made. Do the new sensory data fit with current expectations? If there is a successful match now, the previous mismatch could be due to a mis-formed or improperly detected input. When this happens, the system can still carry on. If it does fail, then it must go back and recheck to see if it began on the wrong track. Maybe houseboat a word has appeared entirely out of context, so that contextual constraints must be relaxed to let the sensory information play a more dominant role in guiding the interpretations. A word that is out of context in a sentence can be understood, although it may cause the system to do a "double take." Even words never seen before can be analyzed, although obviously no meaning will be found for such a malidrotful input.

THE SEQUENCE OF OPERATIONS

Two points have been simplified in the preceding examples. First, in the discussion of the effects of context, it was assumed that all the words in the sentence could be perceived clearly except for the word being analyzed. Thus, we suggested that noisy words could be understood because the con-textual information provided by those other words helped narrow down the set of possibilities. In Miller's experiment, described earlier, the other words are also noisy. How can one set of imperfectly perceived words help the deciphering of another imperfectly perceived one? A different, but related assumption was in the example just discussed: The analysis of the word **WORRIED** in the sentence **THE BOY WORRIED HIS FATHER.** Here the description assumed that the analysis of the sentence proceeded letter-by-letter, with the partial interpretation of the word **WOR**——leading to expecta-tions of the next sounds that might be present.

Neither of these statements is incorrect, but they are oversimplified. The important point about the analysis-by-synthesis procedure is that it is capable of using every source of information available about the nature of the input it is trying to understand. If meaning will help, meaning is used. If a single letter must be analyzed to finish the interpretation of a word, that letter will be analyzed. And if a whole segment of sound—perhaps even a full word—simply does not appear to be necessary to the understanding of the sensory events, then that whole segment may be ignored. Moreover, the process need not occur segment-by-segment, letter-by-letter. It could take place in a different order, or even whole segments simultaneously. It is natural to

FIGURE 3-12

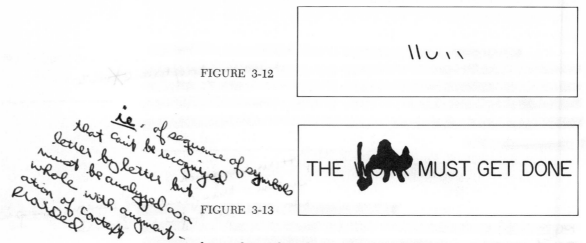

FIGURE 3-13

Handwritten margin note: ie. of sequence of symbols that can't be recognised letter by letter but must be analysed as a whole with augmentation of context provided.

presume that analysis takes place as the individual sensory signals are received, but although this is a convenience (and although this is the sequence we used as an example), it is certainly not a necessity.

Consider how the sequence of symbols shown in Figure 3-12 might get analyzed. Not one single letter can be identified. Yet, if that sequence is presented in the proper way, embedded within the sentence shown in Figure 3-13, then it can usually be deciphered. In Figure 3-13 we have an apparent ink spot overlaying the exact same symbols seen in Figure 3-12, yet now it is but a simple matter to read off the sentence **THE WORK MUST GET DONE.** Note that this illustration hits both our problem points. First, the perception of the noisy segments of the **W** now seems to help us perceive the **R**, just as the perception of the noisy parts of the **R** helps us perceive the **W**. Each part of that sequence of symbols helps the perception of the other parts. Even though no single segment can be seen clearly, the whole word is reasonably easy to read. Here then, is an example of a sequence of symbols that cannot be analyzed letter-by-letter, but must be analyzed as a whole. Moreover, the perception of each part is helped by the context provided by the other three parts—again, even though no single part is clearly perceived.

FEATURES VERSUS EXPECTATIONS

Two things are used in the analysis of perceptual information: the sensory features and expectations. Within most normal experiences the features and expectations match nicely to produce a simple, unambiguous perception. In certain situations, however, one source of information is missing, so the entire picture must be interpreted from the other. Look back at some of the illustrations used in the earlier chapter of this book. There we see explicitly the interplay between the information provided by features and that provided by context and expectations.

Here is a picture that is easily interpreted: Both features and expectations mesh.

Robert Glasheen (photographer), "La Jolla." Copyright 1966, Glasheen   FIGURE 3-14
Graphics.

But now look at this, the simple line drawing. The features are present, the expectations are almost met—but not quite. As a result, our perception of the image fluctuates as we try to force one or another set of rules onto the interpretation.

Figure 3-15

If there are only features, with no expectations, then the whole perception fluctuates radically, unable to form a stable interpretation. In Figure 3-16, there are distinct features present, but no constraints on the interpretations, so that it is possible to view the scene as patches of shifting,

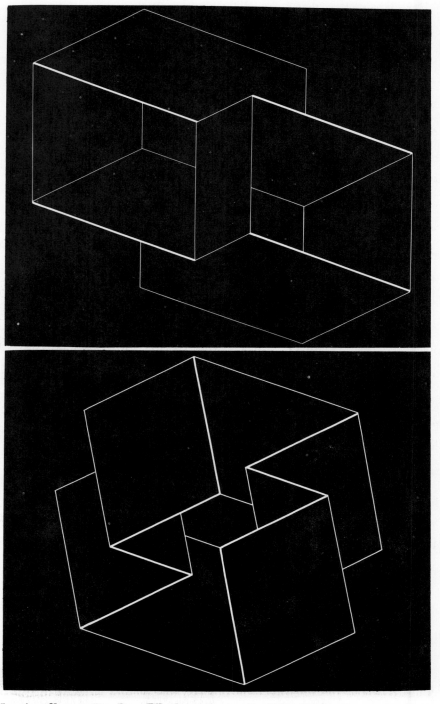

FIGURE 3-15   *Josef Albers, "Structural Constellations" 1953–1958. From Despite Straight Lines, pp. 63, 79. Courtesy of the artist.*

triangular networks, as rectangular tubes extending in depth either vertically or horizontally, or as other variants.

FIGURE 3-16

From Carraher and Thurston (1968).

Finally, recall the picture of the dalmation dog (Figure 3-17). Here there are no features to speak of, only interpretation. Once given the basic framework of the dog, however, the synthesizing process matches the specks of light and dark in the picture to that of the image of the dalmation dog, unambiguously and correctly identifying the photograph. Without the interpretation process, this picture is unintelligible.

FIGURE 3-17 *R. C. James (photographer). Courtesy of the photographer.*

w/o interpretation process picture is unintelligible

With the interpretation process, the dog stands out distinctly and clearly.

To understand the process of pattern recognition, we must understand many different steps in the analysis of information. The patterns of energy that strike the sensory organs can be interpreted as meaningful signals only through the combination of sensory analysis, memory processes, and thought.

analysis by synthesis

Analysis by synthesis is a pattern-recognition scheme that works at the task from all possible angles. It attempts to convert the sensory evidence into an interpretation consistent with our knowledge about the world. It is continuously constructing, testing, and revising hypotheses about what is being perceived. When the predictions fail or the context is lacking, it proceeds slowly, relying heavily on the sensory data. When operating in a familiar and highly predictable world, it

can move quickly and efficiently, sampling only enough data to confirm current expectations and reconstructing what it does not see according to the rules of its internal model. Moreover, the prescription for an active synthesizing process imposes some interesting demands on memories and on cognitive functions. There must be a temporary memory to record the results of the analysis to date. It must be able to retrieve the pertinent information from the permanent memory structures rapidly and efficiently. It must be able to work with different types of information at different levels of analysis at the same time, to integrate smoothly sensory, cognitive, and memory processes. It is a complicated mechanism, but so is the human brain. Every bit of its complexity is needed to explain human pattern-recognition.

SUGGESTED READINGS

Pattern recognition is not well covered in the psychological literature, although this will probably change in the future. One book has come out recently (Dodwell, 1970) that treats much of the material covered in this chapter. Neisser gives perhaps the best existing treatment of template and other schemes in his book, *Cognitive Psychology* (1967) and in the *Scientific American* article "Pattern Recognition by Machine" (Selfridge & Neisser, 1960). His *Scientific American* article, "Visual Search" (1964) is also relevant here.

The example of "wet socks" comes from the work of Miller, perhaps most easily accessible and interpreted in the book by Norman (1969a: paperback), especially Chapter 3. Uhr has collected a set of readings on the topic (1966: paperback), but the best literature comes from the engineering and computer sciences, and most of this is rather technical. A good introduction to the technical material is the book by Grasselli (1969), from which we took the example shown in Chapter 1 of detecting the interrelated blocks (from the chapter by Guzmán). The pandemonium model comes from the work of Selfridge (1959).

An excellent introduction to the problems of pattern recognition comes from the book on *The Psychology and Pedagogy of Reading* by Huey, even though it was written in 1908 (reprinted in paperback by the MIT Press in 1968). Kolers treats the problem with a number of insightful discussions both in his introduction to the MIT Press reprint of Huey and in *Recognizing Patterns: Studies in Living and Automatic Systems* (Kolers & Eden, 1968).

A very fine elementary introduction to speech analysis can be found in Denes and Pinson's *The Speech Chain* (1963: available by calling the local office of the telephone company). More advanced material can be found in the linguistics and acoustics literature, some starting points being Chomsky and Halle's book, *The Sound Pattern of English* (1968) and Liberman's paper on speech (1970), which lists numerous references on the analysis-by-synthesis literature—also called the "motor" theory of speech perception. These papers should lead you to other literature, as well as pointing out the journals in which the major work is published. Norman (1969a) provides an easy introduction to the analysis-by-synthesis literature,

A good review of the machine recognition of human language is serialized in three issues of the *IEEE Spectrum,* by Lindgren (1965). A number of interesting papers are collected together by Wathen-Dunn (1967), from the proceedings of a symposium on the perception of speech and visual form. In his book, *Models of the Nervous System,* Deutsch (1967) discusses some of the problems of doing pattern recognition.

An interesting article on the difficulties of analyzing even a reasonably simple part of the speech signal, the problem of recognizing the voice of the speaker, can be found in the article "Identification of a Speaker by Speech Spectrograms" (Bolt, Cooper, David, Denes, Pickett, & Stevens, 1969).

4

The visual system

Light enters the eye and passes through the various parts—the cornea, the aqueous humor, the iris, the lens, and the vitreous body—until finally it reaches the retina. Each part performs a simple task, but each appears to have flaws. In many respects, the eye is a rather peculiar kind of optical instrument. Certainly, were an optical specialist to try to design an eye, he would avoid some of the flaws found in the human eye: flaws that should make it an unwieldy and imperfect instrument. As is usual with the parts of the body, however, the eye ends up as a beautiful instrument, exquisitely tailored to the function it must perform, more sensitive, more flexible, and more reliable by far than any device made by man.

Light is described primarily by its frequency and intensity. The *frequency* of the light wave is the primary factor in determining the color (hue) that is perceived. The *intensity* is the primary factor in determining brightness. Light waves are part of the electromagnetic spectrum.

The frequencies of the visible part of the spectrum are just above those of microwave radio transmissions and infrared and below those of ultraviolet energy and X rays (see color plate, Figure 4-1, on page 216b). Because light frequencies are so high, frequency is not specified directly (the numbers range around 10^{15} cycles per second[2]), but rather light is described by its *wavelength,* the distance traveled during the time it takes to complete one cycle. Wavelengths of visible light range from about 400 (seen as violet) to about 700 *nanometers* (seen as a red).[3]

The specification of the units of light amplitude, intensity, and energy is always a very complicated business. Because these specifications are not important for our use here, we will not use physical units. The range of light intensities that stimulate the eye is enormous: The most intense light that can be seen without pain is roughly a million billion times more intense than the weakest visible light (a range of approxi-

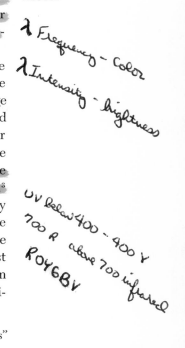

LIGHT[1]

---

[1] We recommend reading the first section of "Measuring Psychological Variables" (Appendix A) before starting this section.

[2] One *cycle per second* is called one *hertz* (abbreviated *Hz*). The unit is named after the German physicist, Heinrich R. Hertz (1857–1894), who produced and studied electromagnetic waves. We will be using the unit hertz quite often in Chapter 6, where we take up the auditory system.

[3] A *nanometer* (*nm*) is one billionth of a meter (10^{-9} meter). Sometimes, in older books, wavelength is specified in *millimicrons* (mμ), *angstroms* (Å), or even *inches*. One *nanometer* equals one *millimicron,* 10 *angstrom units,* or 40×10^{-9} inches.

mately 10^{16}). To describe this enormous range of intensities, it is convenient simply to discuss in powers of 10 how much greater one light is than another. That is, we describe the relationship between two light intensities as the logarithm of the ratio of the two intensities. This procedure was actually first used by acoustic engineers in the specification of sound intensity, so the unit used to specify the logarithm of one intensity to another is named after Alexander Graham Bell—the *bel*. A bel is too large a unit, so intensity ratios are usually expressed in the number of tenths of bels that they contain—the number of *decibels* (*dB*). The number of decibels that separates two light intensities I and I_0 is given by $10 \log(I/I_0)$.

Table 4-1A

"logarithms" & "decibels" used for simplification of Hecht's

Intensity (dB)	Psychological Correlate
200	
180	
160	Pain threshold
140	
	Sun
120	
100	
80	
	White paper in average reading light
60	TV screen
40	
	Lower light for color vision
20	
0	Threshold of vision of dark-adapted eye

Table 4-1B

Wavelength (nm)	Psychological Correlate
400	violet
450	blue
500	green
550	yellow-green
600	orange
650	
700	red

DECIBELS

1. Doubling (or halving) the ratio of signal intensities adds (subtracts) 3 dB.
2. Multiplying (or dividing) the ratio of signal intensities by 10 adds (subtracts) 10 dB.
3. If two lights are separated by $10n$ dB, their intensity ratio is 10^n. For example, a 60-dB difference in the intensities of two lights means that one light is 10^6 (1 million) times more intense than the other.
4. Since decibels refer to the ratio of two intensities, to say that a signal has a level of 65 dB is completely meaningless unless the comparison level is known. Generally, whenever you see statements of this form, it means that the signal is 65 dB more intense than the standard reference level: 10^{-10} *lamberts* is the figure used in this book as a standard. This standard is a very low intensity of light. It is, approximately, the minimum intensity of light that can be detected by a human observer.

Decibels

Number of dB $= 10 \log(I/I_0)$

I/I_0	dB	I/I_0	dB
0.0001	−40	10000.0	40
0.001	−30	1000.0	30
0.010	−20	100.0	20
0.032	−15	31.6	15
0.10	−10	10.0	10
0.13	−9	7.9	9
0.16	−8	6.3	8
0.20	−7	5.0	7
0.25	−6	2.0	6
0.32	−5	3.2	5
0.40	−4	2.5	4
0.50	−3	2.0	3
0.63	−2	1.6	2
0.79	−1	1.3	1
1.00	0	1.0	0

When light falls upon the eye, it first encounters the outside protective window, the *cornea* (see Figure 4-2). Most of the focusing of the image is actually accomplished by the bending of light at the corneal surface. Next, the light transverses a jelly-like substance, the *aqueous humor*; it then goes through the opening in the iris (the *pupil*).

lt. cornea, first hits of an object, most focusing bending lt. at cornea surfce

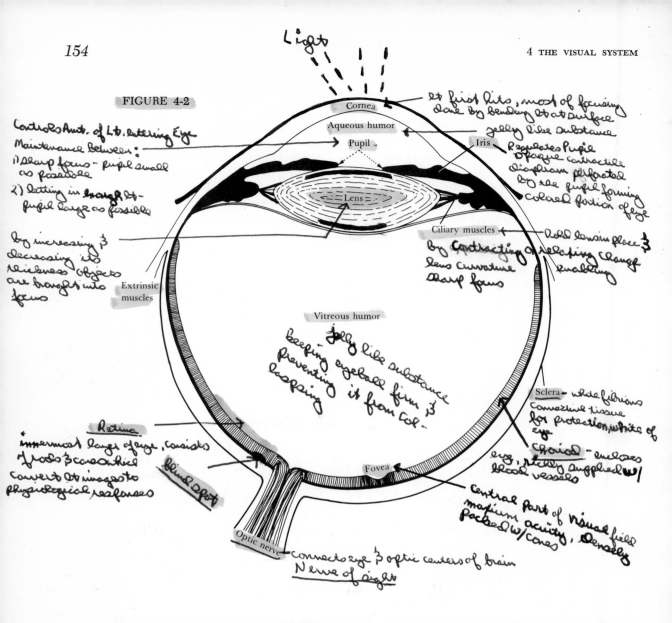

FIGURE 4-2

Light

Cornea
Aqueous humor
Pupil
Iris
Lens
Ciliary muscles
Extrinsic muscles
Vitreous humor
Sclera
Choroid
Retina
Blind spot
Fovea
Optic nerve

Handwritten annotations:

Controls Amt. of Lt. entering Eye
Maintenance between:
1) Sharp focus — pupil small as possible
2) letting in enough Lt. — pupil large as possible

by increasing its thickness objects are brought into focus / decreasing it

at first hits, most of focusing done by bending Lt at surface

Jelly like substance

Regulates pupil opaque contractile diaphram perforated by the pupil forming colored portion of eye

hold lens in place

by contracting & relaxing change lens curvature enabling sharp focus

Jelly like substance keeping eyeball firm & preventing it from collapsing

Sclera — white fibrous connective tissue for protection, white of eye

Choroid — encloses eye, richly supplied w/ blood vessels

innermost layer of eye, consists of rods & cones which convert Lt images to physiological responses

Central part of visual field maximum acuity, densely packed w/ cones

connects eye & optic centers of brain Nerve of sight

The pupil   In principle, the pupil controls the amount of light entering the eye. It becomes smaller in very bright situations (to protect the eye from excess light) and bigger when it is dim (to let in as much light as possible). But consider this: The most intense lights encountered without pain are many billion times as intense as the weakest lights detectable. Given this wide range of intensities, changes in pupil size make very little difference. The widest the human pupil ever gets is about 7 or 8 millimeters (mm) in diameter; the narrowest is about 2 or 3 mm. The total change in area is not great. At its tightest constriction, the pupil lets in about $\frac{1}{16}$ the amount of light that enters when it is wide open. Changes in pupil size only reduce the intensities of signals passing through the eye by a factor of 16 (or about 12 dB). Thus, the wide range of intensities to which the eye is exposed is not much reduced. A 10 billion to 1 range (100 dB) gets reduced to a .6 billion to 1 range (88 dB): hardly enough to make much difference.

Adjustments in pupil size are not very fast. When going from dim to bright light, the pupil takes about 5 sec to contract fully and about 1.5 sec to contract to $\frac{2}{3}$ its full size. When going from bright to dim light, it takes 10 sec to dilate to $\frac{2}{3}$ its full amount, and a full 5 min to open up completely. Clearly, the pupil does not control light intensity. Its primary function may be to restrict the light to the central regions of the lens where focusing is most precise. It also helps to maintain a good depth of field by keeping the opening as small as possible under a given lighting condition. The pupil adjusts its size to maintain a balance between sharpness of focus (for which it should be as small as possible) and letting in sufficient light to the retina (for which it should be as large as possible).

In addition to being responsive to changing light intensities, pupil size seems to monitor the states of the nervous system. Thus, the size changes with emotional factors and even with thinking and problem solving. Some use has been made of measurements of pupil size as a way of monitoring a person's progress during the attempt to solve difficult problems, and also of his emotional responses.

Next in the path of light is the lens. The primary function of the lens, of course, is to focus the light coming from an object onto the light-sensitive receptors at the back of the eye. In terms of overall performance, however, biological lenses are not of particularly good quality.

The lens is composed of many thin layers of crystalline tissue wrapped together, much like the skin of an onion. The lens focuses by increasing and decreasing its thickness (that is, by changing its focal length). This is accomplished by enclosing the lens in a membrane to which the muscles that control focus are attached. The lens produces a number of distortions. Light striking the edges is not focused on the same plane as that of light striking the center of the lens, producing a distortion called *spherical aberration*. Differently colored lights are focused differently, producing a distortion called *chromatic aberration*.

In addition to these problems, the lens is continually dying, a result of a compromise in its design. All living cells need a continual supply of nutrient substances, usually carried by the bloodstream. But, obviously one does not want blood vessels running through the lens, for this would severely impair its optical quality. Thus, for its nutrients,

the lens must rely on the surrounding liquids, an arrangement that is not optimal. The inner layers of the lens have difficulty getting an adequate food supply, and during the lifetime of the organism they gradually die. As the organism ages, these dead cells hamper lens functioning, in particular, focusing.

Focusing and convergence. To get a feeling for the focusing action, hold a pencil out at arm's length and focus on it. Now bring it slowly toward your nose, keeping it in focus. As the pencil comes to within a few inches of your eyes, notice that the image gets blurry and you feel a distinct "pull." As you move the pencil, two things are happening. One set of eye muscles is continuously adjusting the orientation of the eyes to keep them both pointed at (converged on) the approaching object. A second set of muscles is continuously increasing the thickness of the lens, thus bending the light rays to maintain proper focus on the retinal plane at the back of the eye.

Figure 4-3

When the pencil is moved far away from the eye, both sets of muscles relax, the lens returns to its normal elongated shape, and the two eyes point straight ahead. With this muscle action, the lens of a young person is capable of focusing on objects ranging from as close as a few inches to as far away as the stars. With age, however, the ability to increase the thickness of the lens is reduced so much that an external lens (eyeglasses) is often needed for focusing on nearby objects.

Another way to feel the muscle action is to hold a finger up in front of the eyes at a distance of about 6 inches. Then, without moving the finger, concentrate first upon the finger and then upon whatever object is just above the finger (the further away, the better). You can feel the difference between changing the focus from far to near (an active contraction of the muscles of focusing and accommodation), and changing it from near to far (a passive relaxation of the muscles).

The lens in the human changes focus by changing its thickness; in optical terms, it is a variable focal length lens. In cameras and other man-made instruments and, indeed, in some species of animals such as fish, focusing is usually accomplished by keeping the lens fixed and changing the distance between the lens and the light-sensitive elements.

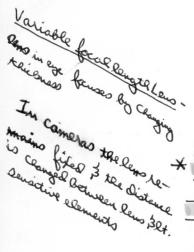

One of the unsolved operations of the eye is the way it maintains focus. Just how an object is brought into sharp focus is not known. One suspicion is that the focusing system tries to maintain a maximum sharpness by maintaining greatest contrast in the image. The neural cells that are sensitive to contours (edge, slit, and line detectors) have maximum output for a sharply focused image. Although focusing typically is done automatically and unconsciously, it is possible to change focus consciously. It is even possible to defocus the eyes so that no

FIGURE 4-3

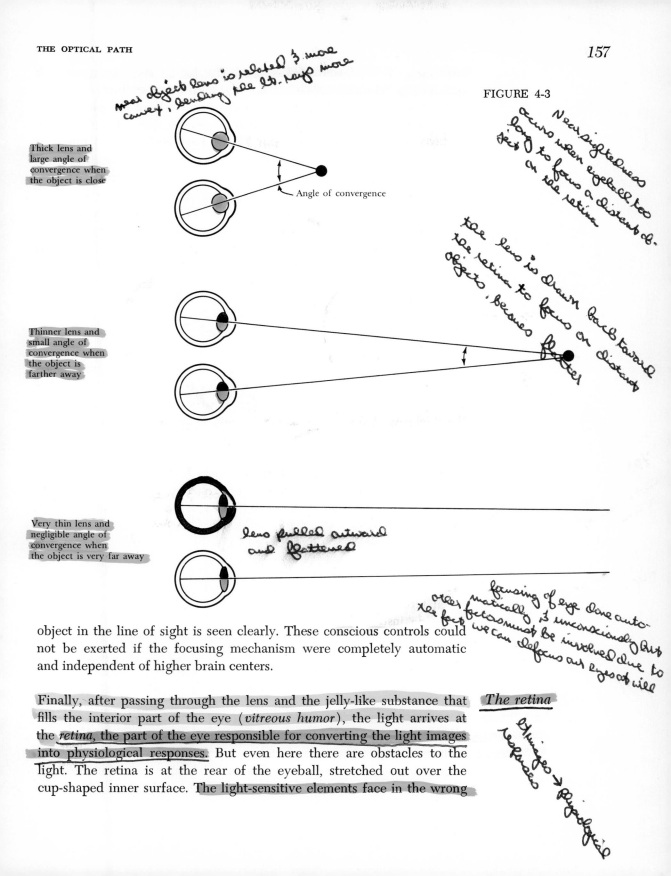

Handwritten annotation (top): Near object lens is rotated 3 more convex, bending the lt. rays more

Handwritten annotation (right): Nearsightedness occurs when eyeball too long to focus a distant ob. it to the retina

Thick lens and
large angle of
convergence when
the object is close

Angle of convergence

Handwritten annotation (right): the lens is drawn back toward the retina to focus on distant objects, becomes flatter

Thinner lens and
small angle of
convergence when
the object is
farther away

Very thin lens and
negligible angle of
convergence when
the object is very far away

Handwritten annotation: lens pulled outward and flattened

object in the line of sight is seen clearly. These conscious controls could
not be exerted if the focusing mechanism were completely automatic
and independent of higher brain centers.

Handwritten annotation: focusing of eye done automatically is unconsciously but the focus must be involved due to we can defocus our eyes at will

Finally, after passing through the lens and the jelly-like substance that
fills the interior part of the eye (*vitreous humor*), the light arrives at
the *retina*, the part of the eye responsible for converting the light images
into physiological responses. But even here there are obstacles to the
light. The retina is at the rear of the eyeball, stretched out over the
cup-shaped inner surface. The light-sensitive elements face in the wrong

The retina

Handwritten annotation: light → physiological responses

direction: They point inward, toward the brain, rather than outward, toward the light (see Figure 4-4). As a result, the nerve fibers connected to the light receptors lie in a tangled web directly in the path of the incoming light. Moreover, these nerve fibers are inside the eye, so to get out there must be an opening in the back surface. This produces a blind spot in each eye.

FIGURE 4-4

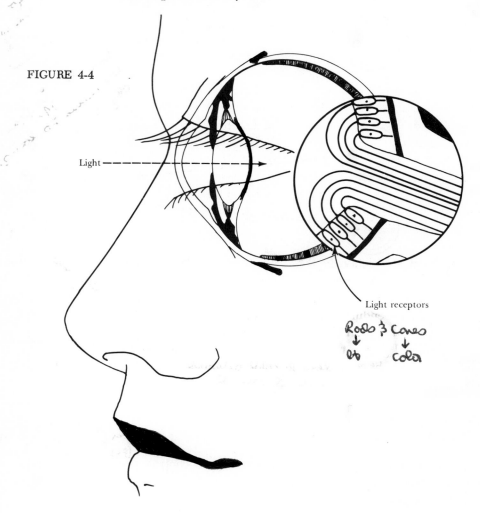

Light

Light receptors

CHEMICAL RESPONSES TO LIGHT One of the first and most dramatic demonstrations of the eye's photochemical response to light was the creation of an "optigram." An animal, such as a frog, is kept completely away from light for several hours. Then the visual environment is illuminated briefly by an intense light. The frog is killed and its retinas detached and placed in a chemical solution. Afterward, the result of the light's photochemical reaction on the cells of the retina can be seen: The visual environment has been painted in vivid yellow and red onto the retina of the frog. This technique has captured the imagination of some novelists, who write of murderers identified from the optigrams in their victim's eyes.

Photochemical processes are responsible for the eye's initial response to a visual signal. When the retina has not been exposed to light, it is reddish-purple in color. This characteristic color gives the chemical its name: *visual purple*. In response to light the retinal color changes, from reddish purple, to pale yellow, and finally it *bleaches* to be transparent and colorless.

Nocturnal birds and animals tend to have relatively high concentrations of visual purple, perhaps accounting for their excellent night vision. Reptiles, diurnal birds, and various species of fish have photochemical substances that bleach in the presence of light, but differ somewhat from visual purple in their sensitivity to lights of different colors. The basic method for describing these chemical reactions is to determine how much bleaching occurs for lights with constant intensity as wavelength varies. The resulting set of measurements is called the *absorption spectrum* of the photochemical substance.

The exact photochemical reaction in the eye is now well known. With no light present, there is a high concentration of *rhodopsin* (the chemical name for visual purple). When a light is turned on, a succession of changes take place, finally ending with a substance called *retinene,* which is finally reduced to *vitamin A.* The retinene gives the yellow color of the partially bleached pigment. The predominance of vitamin A after prolonged exposure to light produces the colorless appearance of the completely bleached retina.

Logic dictates that there must be some mechanisms for manufacturing or regenerating the photosensitive materials in the eye. The regeneration seems to be carried on by two separate chemical reactions. One provides a relatively fast restoration of rhodopsin levels by recombining the partially bleached products of retinene and opsin to make rhodopsin. A second, much more sluggish process produces rhodopsin from the fully bleached products, such as vitamin A.[4]

---

[4] The role of vitamin A in the photochemical process leads to the notion that eating carrots (rich in vitamin A) is good for your eyes. In World War II, during the battle of Britain, rumors were circulated that the British fliers were being given special vitamin extracts to give them extraordinarily good night vision. The rumor was encouraged as part of the attempt to cover up the invention of radar.

In fact, vitamin A in excess of the rather small amount needed daily by the body serves no useful purpose. It most certainly does not improve vision.

Chemical reactions play a role in determining the general characteristics of visual sensitivity. Unfortunately, there does not appear to be a simple relationship between visual sensitivity and the photochemical reactions in retinal receptors. Under ordinary lighting conditions, only a very small percentage of the available rhodopsin is actually bleached. Moreover, bleaching only 2% of the rhodopsin concentration may change sensitivity by fifty-fold.

Despite considerable effort, the exact nature of the link between the photochemical response and the initiation of electrical impulses in the nerve fibers has not been discovered. The question of how the chemical reactions actually generate the neural impulses that carry the visual signal to the brain has yet to be answered.

THE NEUROANATOMY OF VISION

The retina is not a continuous surface of light-sensitive material. It is composed of a very large number of individual light-sensitive elements, or receptors, each element making an independent response to the light energy falling upon it. In animals such as monkeys and men, there are two different types of light-sensitive elements, one called *rods*, the other *cones*.

Figure 4-5

Other animals have one or the other but not both. Pigeons have only cones, while the retina of the cat is made up mostly of rods.

Apart from the distinctive anatomy which first led to their discovery, the rods and cones have some definite functional differences. They are really two separate visual systems housed within the same eye. Each system has its own special response characteristics. Visual purple, rhodopsin, is found only in the tips of rods—not in cones. The cones contain a variety of photochemical substances necessary for color vision. A rod is about 500 times more sensitive to light than a cone, but provides no color information. In addition to all these functional differences, there are also differences in the neural arrangement that transfers the information in the two systems out of the retina to the brain.

In man, each eye has approximately 6 million cones and about 120 million rods: about 125 million receptors in all. This is an extraordinarily rich density of receptor cells. The picture on a television screen, for example, has only around 250,000 independent elements. Overall, the density of packing of the light-sensitive elements is highest in the center of the eye and decreases in the peripheral regions.

Figure 4-6

Distribution of receptors on the retina is different for rods and for cones. Rods are more prevalent in the periphery, cones in the center. At the very center of the eye, there is a tiny depressed region with no rods at all, only cones. This region, called the *fovea*, has a very

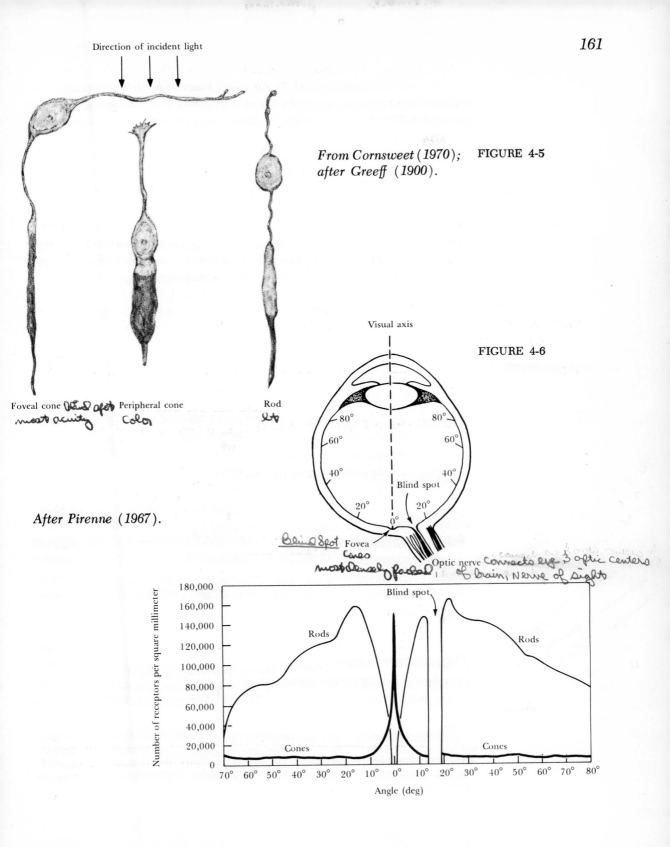

Direction of incident light

From Cornsweet (1970); FIGURE 4-5
after Greeff (1900).

Foveal cone *blind spot* Peripheral cone   Rod
most acuity   *color*   *eat*

Visual axis

FIGURE 4-6

80°   80°
60°   60°
40°   40°
20°   20°
0°

Blind spot

After Pirenne (1967).

Blind Spot Fovea
          Cones
most densely packed Optic nerve *connects eye + optic centers of brain, nerve of sight*

Number of receptors per square millimeter

180,000
160,000
140,000
120,000
100,000
80,000
60,000
40,000
20,000
0

Rods   Blind spot   Rods

Cones   Cones

70° 60° 50° 40° 30° 20° 10° 0° 10° 20° 30° 40° 50° 60° 70° 80°

Angle (deg)

high density of receptors—approximately 150,000 cones per square millimeter. It is optimally located so that it receives the central parts of the image around the point at which the eye is fixating. The fovea is also the region of maximum acuity. Although most receptor elements do not connect directly to the brain, individual foveal elements tend to have their own private communication line to higher brain centers.[5]

The two eyes, then, collect information from the visual environment with a total of about 250 million individual receptors and send the information to the brain over about 1.6 million nerve fibers. The two different types of receptor systems complement one another. The cone system is a high resolution system capable of sending color information, but its sensitivity is limited. The rod system is very sensitive to light, but its resolution is limited and it is insensitive to color. Working together, the two systems provide an extraordinarily flexible and powerful system for carrying out the initial visual reactions to light signals occurring in the environment.

The retinal network

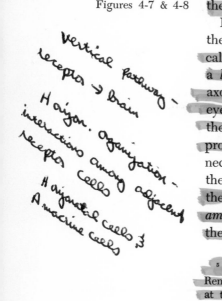

Figures 4-7 & 4-8

While still at the retina, the neurological responses of the receptors go through the initial stages of processing. In Chapter 2, we investigated some of the operations that take place in this retinal network. Anatomically, two types of organizations of the neural pathways can be specified: a *vertical organization*, which carries the signal from the receptors toward the brain, and a *horizontal organization*, which is responsible for the various interactions among adjacent receptor cells.

Different types of neural cells are involved in passing the signal from the rods and cones to the brain. Signals from the receptor cells go vertically up through two synapses, first between the *receptor* itself and a *bipolar cell*, then between the bipolar cell and a *ganglion cell*. The axons of the ganglion cells make up the *optic nerve* that leaves the eye. At the same time, the analysis of the signals are performed by the horizontal organization of the retina—primarily by cells named, appropriately enough, *horizontal cells*. These horizontal cells make connections among the receptors themselves, modifying the activity at the junction between the receptors and the bipolar cells. In addition, there is a second level of horizontal processing performed by the *amacrine cells* at a slightly higher level. These amacrine cells modify the activity at the junction between bipolar cells and ganglion cells. These

---

[5] Most people have difficulty in remembering which cells—rods or cones—do what. Remember it this way. The **fovea** is the central part of the visual field: The *fovea* is at the *focus* of attention. This is the spot where you want to see things in color. **Cones**, in the *center* of the eye, are sensitive to *color*. The *rods* are in the periphery—toward the *rear*.

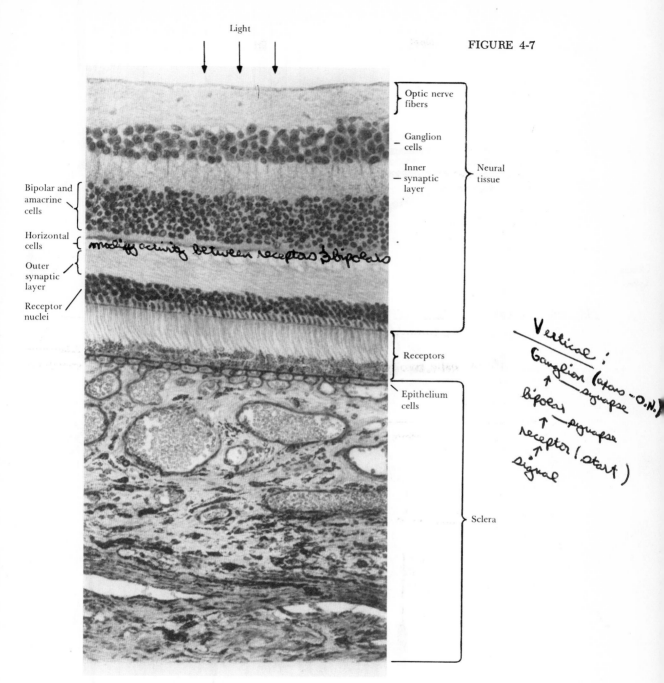

FIGURE 4-7

Cross section through the back of the human retina. Magnification approximately ×150. From Polyak (1957).

LIGHT

FIGURE 4-8

From Cornsweet
(1970).

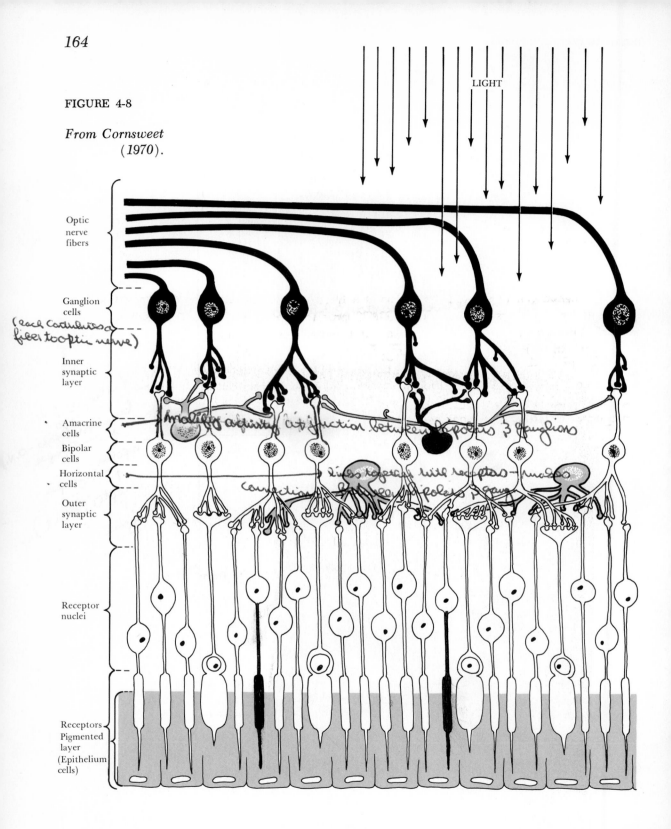

Optic
nerve
fibers

Ganglion
cells

(each constitutes a
fiber to optic nerve)

Inner
synaptic
layer

Amacrine
cells

modify activity at junction between bipolars & ganglions

Bipolar
cells

Horizontal
cells

lines together with receptors — makes

connection between bipolars & ?

Outer
synaptic
layer

Receptor
nuclei

Receptors
Pigmented
layer
(Epithelium
cells)

two layers of horizontal connections are the anatomical basis for the neural circuits of the retinal network.

The density of interconnections varies in different parts of the retina. In the periphery, a single ganglion cell may receive information from thousands of rods. At the central foveal region of the retina, an individual cone may connect directly through a single bipolar cell to an individual ganglion cell, with no interactions among neighboring units. Direct connections of this type are usually made by smaller cells, *midget bipolar* and *midget ganglion* cells. Typically, a given ganglion cell is connected only to rods or to cones, although some exceptions to this rule have been found.

Each ganglion cell of the retina contributes a fiber to the optic nerve. All together, the fibers number about 800,000, producing a cable about the thickness of a pencil. In the human and most higher mammals, the nerve fibers leaving each eye cross at a location called the *optic chiasma*. [The chiasma is similar in appearance to the Greek letter χ (chi), hence the name.] All the fibers from the left half of each retina go to the left hemisphere of the brain; all the fibers from the right half of each retina group together and travel to the right hemisphere of the brain.

There is no interruption in the nerve fibers at the optic chiasma: no new synaptic connections are made. As shown in Figures 4-9, 4-10, and 4-11, this regrouping at the optic chiasma splits the visual scene into two halves. The parts of the visual scene to the left half of the fovea end up at the right half of the brain; everything to the right of the fixation point ends up at the left half of the brain. (The lens reverses the visual image: Thus, an object on the left is focused on the right half of the retina and, as a result, the neural signals from that part of the image get sent to the right hemisphere of the brain.)

The primary emphasis in the processing of the visual image is concentrated upon the central part of the visual field, especially the part that falls upon the fovea. As shown in Figure 4-6, most of the cones are in the fovea. In the visual cortex, more than 50% of the neurons appear to be concerned with the analysis of the central 10% of the visual field.

The periphery of the eye is more sensitive to light than is the center, but it is not as responsive to the fine details of the scene or to color information as the fovea.

THE PATHWAY TO
THE BRAIN

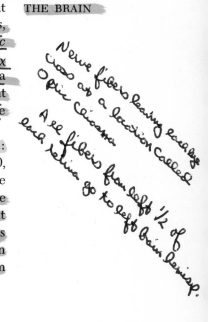

SAMPLING VISUAL
INFORMATION

Blind spot for
the left eye

Fixation point

This area will just
fill the fovea at a
distance of 8 inches

Blind spot for
the right eye

Everything seen on
this side goes to
the right side of the
retina and the right
half of the brain

Everything seen on
this side goes to
the left side of the
retina and the left
half of the brain

8 inches

FIGURE 4-9   Instructions: *Close your right eye. Hold the page about 8 inches in front of you (see scale on left). Hold the page very straight, without tilting it. Stare at the fixation point. Adjust the angle and distance of the paper until left-eye blind spot disappears.*

- *Open your right eye—blind spot reappears (keep staring at the fixation point).*
- *Close your left eye—right-eye blind spot should disappear (you may have to adjust the paper again).*
- *When you find the blind spot, push a pencil along the paper toward it. Watch the end of the pencil disappear. (Remember to keep one eye closed.)*

The organization scheme of the retina has some obvious advantages. But, because only a small portion of the visual scene is analyzed in great detail, the pattern-recognition system must have a way of guiding the eye to specific parts of the visual field.

Eye movements   The eyes move frequently, successively sampling different regions of the scene. The pattern of eye movements consists of series of discrete jumps or *saccades* from one part of the scene to another. These may occur four or five times per second. This saccadic movement is a result

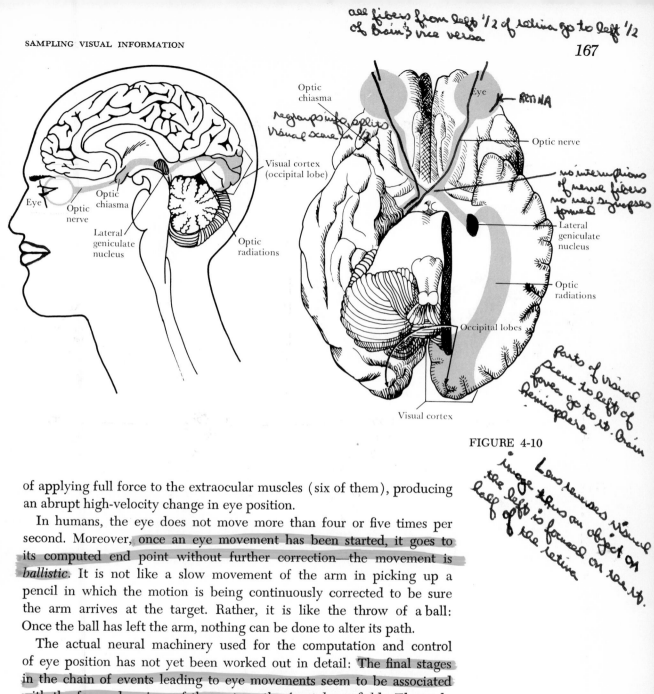

all fibers from left 1/2 of retina go to left 1/2 of brain & vice versa

regions info splits visual scene in 1/2

no interruptions of nerve fibers no new synapses formed

RETINA

Parts of visual scene to left of fovea go to rt. brain hemisphere

Lens reverses visual image thus an object on the left of off is focused on rt. half of the retina

FIGURE 4-10

of applying full force to the extraocular muscles (six of them), producing an abrupt high-velocity change in eye position.

In humans, the eye does not move more than four or five times per second. Moreover, once an eye movement has been started, it goes to its computed end point without further correction—the movement is *ballistic*. It is not like a slow movement of the arm in picking up a pencil in which the motion is being continuously corrected to be sure the arm arrives at the target. Rather, it is like the throw of a ball: Once the ball has left the arm, nothing can be done to alter its path.

The actual neural machinery used for the computation and control of eye position has not yet been worked out in detail: The final stages in the chain of events leading to eye movements seem to be associated with the forward regions of the cortex—the *frontal eye fields*. Electrode stimulation in these regions initiates saccadic movements, with the direction and extent of movement depending on the particular location of the stimulating electrode. Generally, stimulation of the left hemisphere initiates saccadic movements to the right and stimulation in the right hemisphere produces left saccades. When both hemispheres are stimu-

FIGURE 4-11

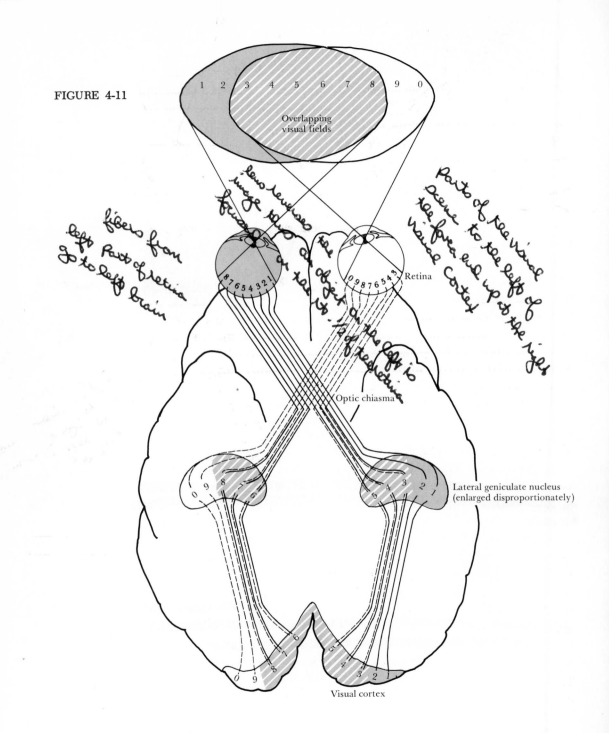

Overlapping visual fields

Retina

Optic chiasma

Lateral geniculate nucleus (enlarged disproportionately)

Visual cortex

lated simultaneously, a compromise results: The direction and extent of the movement depends on the relative intensity of the stimulation in the two hemispheres.

But the mechanisms responsible for computing the direction and extent of movement from an analysis of the visual image are unknown. Some saccades seem to be relatively automatic. A movement in the peripheral parts of the visual field, for example, frequently triggers an involuntary saccade aimed at the source of the movement. For the most part, however, eye movement patterns appear to reflect a systematic sampling of environmental information based on a meaningful interpretation of the incoming sensory data. Saccades even occur during sleep. For many years now, saccadic eye movements have been the major index of dream periods (rapid-eye-movement sleep, or REM sleep) in the study of sleep.

Although the process involved in computing the location of targets from the visual image are not well understood, recent evidence suggests that they may be carried out by a neural channel separate from the one involved in normal pattern-recognition. This might be expected. Ordinarily, the operations associated with localizing an object in the environment and those involved in recognizing it are smoothly coordinated. But an analysis designed to determine **where** things are is, to some extent, incompatible with an analysis to determine **what** things are.

In **identifying** an object in the visual image—a person or a chair—exact orientation, distance, or its location in the visual field is not important. Ideally, the pattern-recognition system should ignore all these properties and concentrate only on the characteristics that are important for actually identifying the object as a chair (or person). In **locating** an object, however, identification of the objects is not important. The only relevant data are position and orientation.

Are there two independent neural channels involved in these two distinct types of analysis? The anatomy of the visual system suggests that there may be. One set of nerve fibers traveling from the eye to the brain breaks away from its neighbors and, rather than going to the *lateral geniculate nucleus* with the rest, ends up at a brain center called the *superior colliculus*.

Like the lateral geniculate and the visual cortex, fibers leaving adjacent regions in the retina end up in adjacent regions in the superior colliculus. That is, the spatial organization of the retina is preserved. Unlike the visual cortex, however, the foveal region of the eye does not seem to be given any special treatment. The fibers leaving the colliculus appear to connect with the motor control system for eye movements, head orien-

The localizing channel

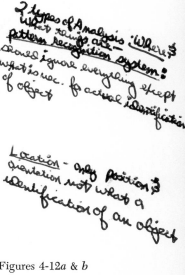

2 types of Analysis: Where things are — pattern recognition system: Should ignore everything except what is nec. for actual identification of object

Location — only position & orientation not what a identification of an object

Figures 4-12a & b

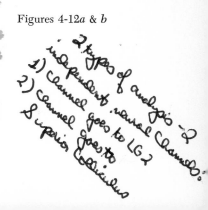

*2 types of independent neural analysis —
1) Channel goes to LG?
2) Channel goes to Superior Colliculus*

FIGURE 4-12a

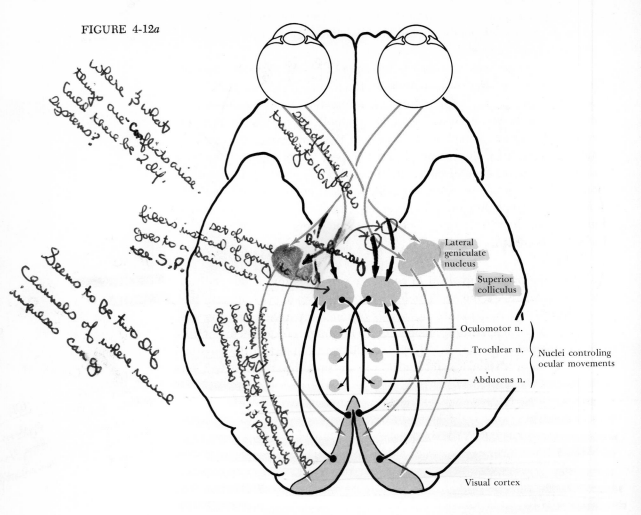

[handwritten marginal notes:]

Where is what things are "conflicts arise. Could there be 2 dif. systems?

Seems to be two dif channels of where neural impulses can go

fibers instead of going to LGN goes to a brain center see S.P.

set of nerve goes to a brain center

Breakaway

2 set of optic fibers traveling to LGN

Lateral geniculate nucleus

Superior colliculus

Oculomotor n.

Trochlear n.

Abducens n.

Nuclei controling ocular movements

connections to motor control system for eye movements head orientation & postural adjustments

Visual cortex

tation, and postural adjustments. Finally, there is some evidence for inputs into this collicular structure from the visual receiving areas of the cortex.

The anatomical organization of this collicular pathway makes it a prime candidate for a neural channel specifically concerned with localizing objects in the environment. But there is more persuasive evidence than anatomy. When neurons in this channel are activated by electrodes in an awake animal, some head movements and postural adjustments result. When neurons associated with a particular part of the visual field are stimulated, the animal orients in the appropriate direction,

FIGURE 4-12*b*

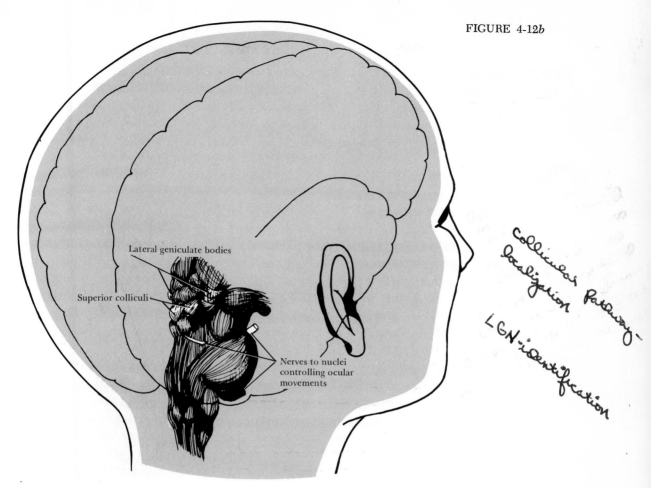

Lateral geniculate bodies

Superior colliculi

Nerves to nuclei
controlling ocular
movements

*colliculer
localization Pathway -*

LGN - identification

pointing to where the object would have been, had the activity been produced by normal visual conditions.[6]

Whenever a neural structure associated with a particular function is identified, it opens up new experimental opportunities. What happens to vision if one or another of these two main visual channels is disrupted?

[6] Some very recent evidence suggests that the colliculus combines information about both movement and location. Moreover, some cells sensitive to *auditory* stimulation have just been discovered in the *visual* colliculus. It makes good sense for a localization center to combine information about position gathered from all sensory modalities. Information about movement is closely related to information about location, so, here too, the colliculus would appear to be a reasonable place to combine the analyses.

Consider first the results of disrupting the channel assumed to be primarily involved in recognizing patterns.

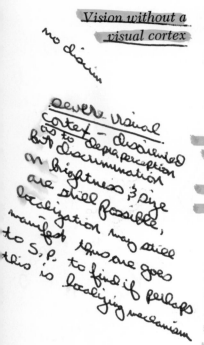

Vision without a visual cortex

The neural channel associated with pattern recognition can be disrupted by surgically removing the visual cortex (*cortical ablation*). In cats and monkeys, ablation of the visual cortex at first appears to produce total blindness. The animals show no ability to see objects in the environment, to carry on normal visual–motor coordination, or to learn any task requiring discrimination among visual signals. Careful testing, however, demonstrates some residual visual capacities. The animal without a visual cortex can learn to make discriminations based on brightness and perhaps size.

Recently, it has been demonstrated that monkeys without a visual cortex also have some success in localizing objects. Movement seems to be important. When the experimenter holds out a choice morsel of food such as a nut, at first the monkey does not appear to notice it, but if the experimenter moves his hand, the monkey will reach out in the appropriate direction. He makes errors in estimating depth, however. The animal is never able to learn tasks that require discrimination among visual patterns.

Some degree of localization seems possible when the channel carrying pattern information is disrupted. Since the operation does not interfere with the superior colliculus, it might be suspected that this neural channel handles information about position. To prove the case, the collicular channel should be disrupted and the animal's localization ability tested. If the two channels function independently, then pattern recognition should remain intact and localization should be severely impaired.

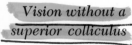
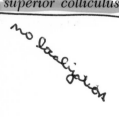

Vision without a superior colliculus

The experimental animal in this case is the golden hamster, whose collicular and cortical channels are particularly well separated, making it convenient for surgery. When the collicular structures are disrupted, the hamster loses all ability to localize. When offered a food (such as sunflower seeds), he is unable to perform the appropriate orientation and reaching responses. But the apparent inability to localize could really be a deficiency in pattern recognition. Maybe he simply does not recognize the food offered to him.

There is a tricky experimental problem here. If a standard experimental test is used, the hamster appears unable to learn to discriminate simple visual patterns. For example, if he must choose between two patterns located at the ends of two alleys, he never learns to select the right one in order to obtain food. Normal hamsters have no trouble

Experiment to test localization & discrimination

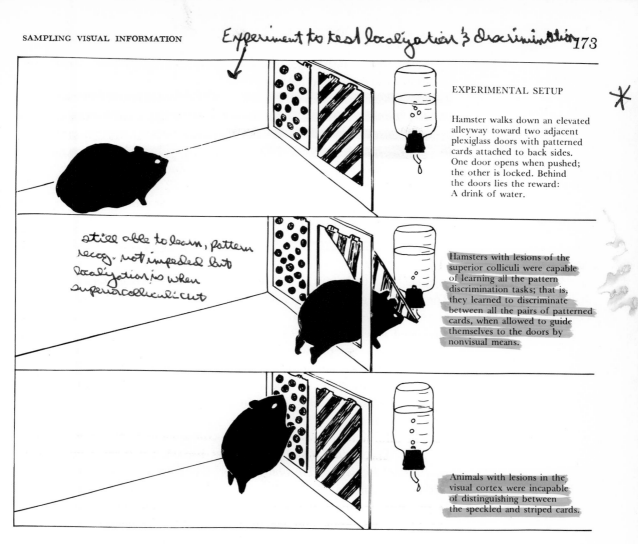

EXPERIMENTAL SETUP

Hamster walks down an elevated
alleyway toward two adjacent
plexiglass doors with patterned
cards attached to back sides.
One door opens when pushed;
the other is locked. Behind
the doors lies the reward:
A drink of water.

*still able to learn, pattern
recog. not impeded but
localization is when
superior colliculi cut*

Hamsters with lesions of the
superior colliculi were capable
of learning all the pattern
discrimination tasks; that is,
they learned to discriminate
between all the pairs of patterned
cards, when allowed to guide
themselves to the doors by
nonvisual means.

Animals with lesions in the
visual cortex were incapable
of distinguishing between
the speckled and striped cards.

FIGURE 4-13

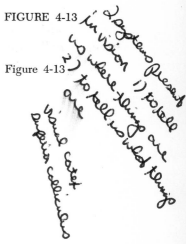

with this task: They soon learn to identify the appropriate pattern and
are successful at obtaining the food reward each time they are placed
in the box.

But think about the task. To do this task the animal must both recognize the correct pattern and must localize it properly; but if we design
the task so that no localization is required, things change. Without the
requirement of localization, the hamster's behavior changes rather
dramatically. He shuffles along one side of the box, and eventually he
arrives at one of the patterned doors. Here he rises up on his hind
paws and appears to inspect the pattern. He then either enters the
door or continues shuffling along the wall until he comes to the next
door, where the performance is repeated. If he does not enter the second
door, he may follow the edge around the entire box until he returns

to the first door and begins the whole sequence again. This experiment illustrates the difference between localization and recognition.[7]

The experimental work in this area is in its early stages, and the details of the localization system have not yet been worked out. The results so far are consistent in indicating that there are two separate systems operating: one to tell us where things are; one to tell us what they are. But ordinarily two systems cannot work independently, since how could objects be matched up to their proper location? Together the two channels provide a powerful and sophisticated apparatus for sampling and analyzing the visual environment.

SUGGESTED READINGS

A good spot to begin is with Gregory's book, *The Eye and the Brain: The Psychology of Seeing* (1966). Then go either to LeGrand or to Cornsweet. LeGrand (1957) treats various visual phenomena at a more advanced level. Cornsweet's book (1970) is excellent, and covers many of the same concepts we do (as well as some more advanced ones) with a somewhat similar style. Advanced treatments of these topics can be found in the series of books edited by Davson (1962), in the book edited by Graham (1965), and in Pirenne's book, *Vision and the Eye* (1967).

A review of the role of the visual cortex can be found in Teuber's chapter, "Perception" (1960). Excellent sources for reviews come from the *Annual Review of Physiology* articles by Bishop (1967) and Creutzfeldt and Sakmann (1969). Bishop and Henry's article, "Spatial Vision" in the *Annual Review of Psychology* (1971) is also very useful.

An excellent review of the neurological system for controlling eye movements is given by Robinson's article on the topic in *Science* magazine (1968).

The distinctions between localization and pattern recognition (and the implication that one is done in the colliculus and the other in the visual cortex) come from several recent sources. The experiment on the hamster, plus a considerable amount of supporting evidence, is reported by G. E. Schneider in a *Science* article, "Two Visual Systems" (1969). A number of relevant articles are collected in an issue of the German journal, *Psychologische Forschung* (1967 and 1968, Volume 31). (The relevant articles are printed in English.) Some of the important articles you might wish to look at are those by Held (pp. 338–348), Ingle (pp. 44–51), G. E. Schneider (pp. 52–62), and Trevarthen (pp. 299–337). In addition, some of the articles in the *Neurosciences: Second*

[7] See G. E. Schneider (1969) for details of the original experiment.

Study Program, New York: Rockefeller University Press, in press, promise to be important in reviewing these areas. Some of the physiological studies of the colliculus in a manner similar to that used to study the simple, complex, and hypercomplex cells of the visual cortex are reported in the articles by Wickelgren and Sterling (1969; Sterling & Wickelgren, 1969). We have found the *Annual Review of Psychology* article by Bishop and Henry, "Spatial Vision" (1971), exceedingly useful in finding references to these areas.

5

The dimensions of vision

The visual image present at one part of the retina affects the perception of an image seen in neighboring locations. Horizontal neural connections (the horizontal and amacrine cells) interlinking the retinal receptors cause interactions among neighboring regions in the retina as the information passes through the eye. This interaction plays a major role in the processing of visual inputs and accounts for some basic perceptual phenomena. The neural machinery involved was discussed in some detail in earlier chapters. At this point, we concentrate on some of the psychological experiences that are produced by these underlying interaction networks.

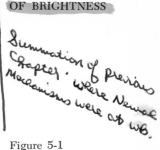

Summation of previous Chapter. Where Neural Mechanisms were at wb.

Figure 5-1

One of the most interesting effects of spatial interactions is a phenomenon of brightness contrast named after the Austrian scientist Ernst Mach. In his early investigations into sensory physiology (in the 1860's), Mach noted that he could see bands of darkness and brightness where there were no corresponding physical changes in the intensity of the light. The phenomenon is as follows. A gradation in a visual image from a dimly illuminated area to a more intensely illuminated area (as shown in Figures 5-2 and 5-3) is perceived as a much sharper change in light intensity than actually exists. In fact, dark and light bands can be seen on either side of the gradation; these are *Mach bands*.

Mach bands

Percieve Bands of Lt. & Dark where in fact there were no Physical changes in lt intensity

The figures show two ways of producing the gradient in illumination. In one method, a wheel, colored black and white, is rotated in the fashion shown, rapidly enough so that the black and white portions merge, producing uniform, nonflickering grays. (The rotation speed has to be faster than 30 revolutions per second, or 1800 rpm.) With the other method, a diffuse shadow is produced by placing a sharp edge in the path of a nondistinct source of illumination. In either case, there is the steady change in illumination as shown in the diagram, starting from a more intense region labeled α, to a less intense region labeled δ, with the transitions in intensity starting at the point β and ending at the point γ. This is a description of the actual light reflected from the surface. It does not describe what is seen. The perception is not a smooth transition in brightness. Rather, a bright line appears to be at β and a dark one at γ. Figure 5-4 shows both the actual intensity pattern (dashed line) and its perceived brightness (solid line). What is being seen here is the effect of the lighting pattern at one section of the visual image interacting with the perception of the lighting pattern at another section. This is exactly the phenomenon illustrated in Figure 5-5 (see the discussion in Chapter 2, around page 72).

These interactions are also responsible for the way in which the vertical bands of Figure 5-6 are perceived. Although each band has constant

FIGURE 5-1

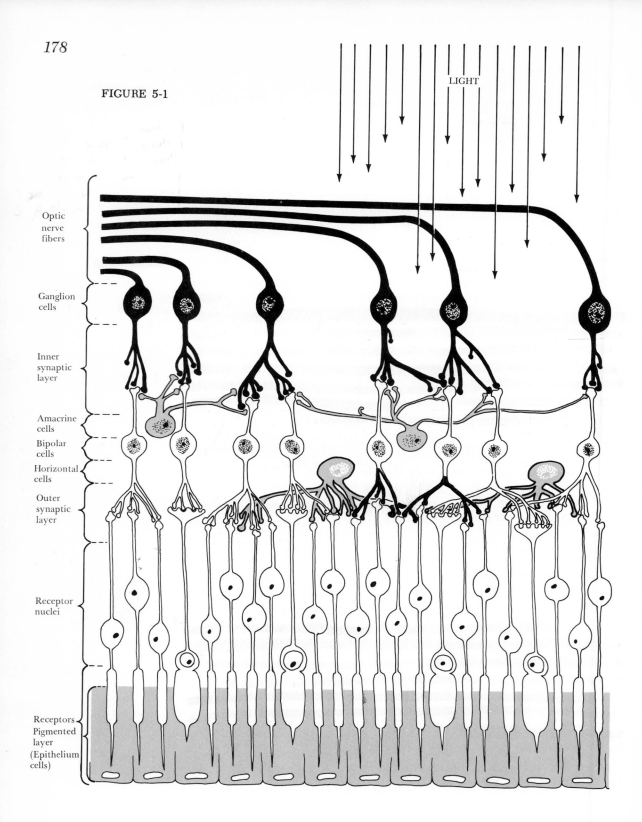

LIGHT

Optic
nerve
fibers

Ganglion
cells

Inner
synaptic
layer

Amacrine
cells

Bipolar
cells

Horizontal
cells

Outer
synaptic
layer

Receptor
nuclei

Receptors
Pigmented
layer
(Epithelium
cells)

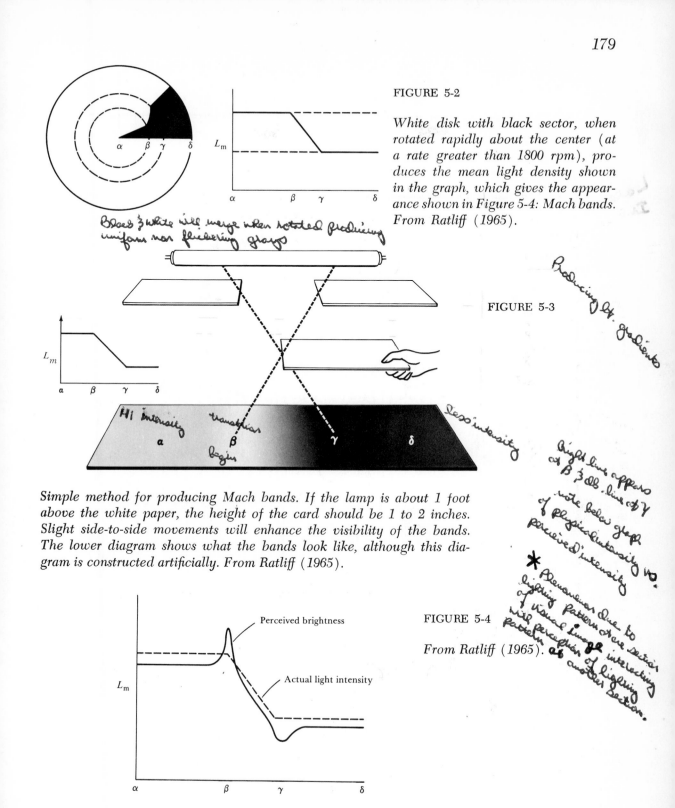

FIGURE 5-2

White disk with black sector, when rotated rapidly about the center (at a rate greater than 1800 rpm), produces the mean light density shown in the graph, which gives the appearance shown in Figure 5-4: Mach bands. From Ratliff (1965).

FIGURE 5-3

Simple method for producing Mach bands. If the lamp is about 1 foot above the white paper, the height of the card should be 1 to 2 inches. Slight side-to-side movements will enhance the visibility of the bands. The lower diagram shows what the bands look like, although this diagram is constructed artificially. From Ratliff (1965).

FIGURE 5-4

From Ratliff (1965).

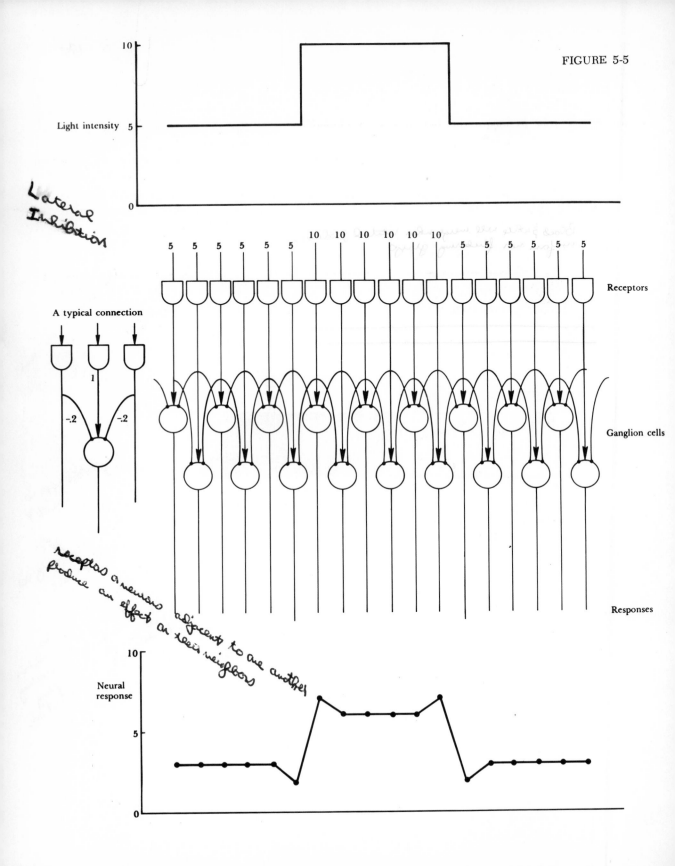

FIGURE 5-5

Light intensity

Lateral Inhibition

Receptors

A typical connection

Ganglion cells

Responses

receptors a neurons adjacent to one another produce an effect on their neighbors

Neural response

intensity, they are not seen as such. Rather, the perception is of nonuniform brightness.

It is easy to think of a good reason for these interactions. It is important to be able to locate the boundaries of objects, even if there is not much actual difference in light intensities between the object and the things surrounding it. The enhancement in the differences in the

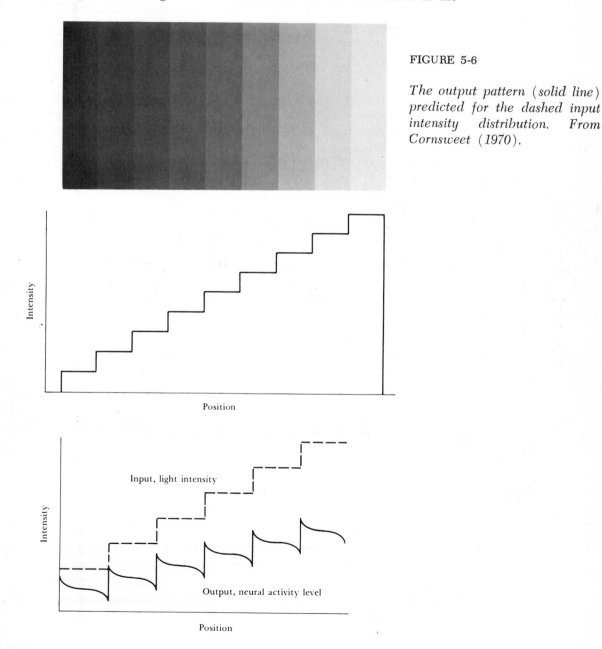

FIGURE 5-6

The output pattern (solid line) predicted for the dashed input intensity distribution. From Cornsweet (1970).

Intensity

Position

Intensity

Input, light intensity

Output, neural activity level

Position

neural firing rates of receptors located at either side of the border should help the processes of pattern recognition, which must pick out those borders in order to identify the objects viewed.

The neural interactions responsible for these visual experiences are very similar to the mechanisms found in other sensory modalities. In fact, this same type of neural sharpening is found almost anywhere that individual sensory receptors are lined up next to one another—in vision, hearing, taste, touch, and smell. The interaction patterns seem to be critically important during the first stages of analysis in all sensory systems.

Brightness contrast   Examine the interior squares in the illustration shown in Figure 5-7. All of the inner squares are printed identically: The same amount of light comes from each. Yet the perceived brightness of the inner squares varies depending upon what surrounds them. The inner square on the far left appears brighter than the one on the far right.

FIGURE 5-7

From Cornsweet (1970).

Normally, one expects that as physical intensity increases, so too will the psychological perception increase. Thus, the brightness of an object ought to increase whenever more light is reflected from it, just as the loudness of a sound increases whenever the intensity of that sound increases. But the brightness of a target depends on the surrounding field. As the intensity of the light falling on a surface is increased, the perceived changes in brightness depend on what else is present. Look at the left pair of squares in Figure 5-7. Call the inner square the *target* and the outer area the *surround*. If the overall illumination is increased, the intensity of both the target and the surround will increase proportionally and the physical contrast between the two will remain exactly the same. The brightness of the target, however, does not necessarily increase when the illumination is raised. It may get brighter, or it may remain the same, or it may even appear to decrease in brightness. It all depends on the relative intensities of the center and surround.

The way that the brightness of the target changes with increased illumination is shown in Figure 5-8 for different ratios of contrast between

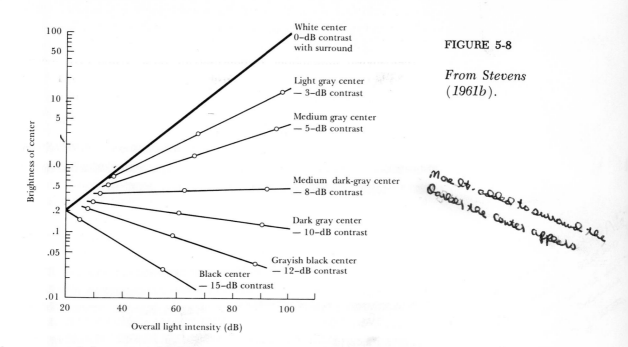

FIGURE 5-8

*From Stevens
(1961b).*

*[handwritten note:] Moe lt. added to surround the
Darker the center appears*

the center and the surround (the contrast ratio is specified in decibels).[1]
When the center is the same as the surround (a 0-dB difference in contrast), then the judgments of the center brightness increase smoothly
and consistently with light intensity, as shown in the upper heavy line.
As the contrast between center and surround increases, the brightness
of the center does not increase as rapidly as the overall light level. With
a medium dark-gray center (a contrast difference of around 8 dB), there
is perfect brightness constancy: The perceived brightness of the center
remains the same even though the illumination levels are increasing.
With higher contrast, an interesting effect takes place: The more light
added, the **darker** the center appears.

It is possible for you to try this experiment yourself, using the squares
in Figure 5-7. To do this, you need a dark room with some way of
varying the light intensity without also varying the color of the light.
In the normal living quarters there are only two ways to do this. One
method is to go into a closet, shut the door, and then slowly open
the door. The amount of light entering the closet can be controlled
by how far the door has been opened. (Careful, if the outside room
is reasonably well lit, you need open the closet door only a fraction
of an inch to get sufficient light.) A second method is to use a television

[1] These brightness measurements were done using the technique of magnitude
estimation as described in Appendix A of this book. The experiment was reported
by S. S. Stevens (1961b).

set as a light source. Turn on the television set in an otherwise dark room and tune it to an unused channel. The brightness control of the set now acts as a way of controlling the room light. (You may wish to have the contrast control set at minimum to avoid the random dots that would normally appear on the screen.)

Now look at the squares. As you increase the room illumination from its lowest value, the right target square will get darker and darker. When you try the same thing while looking at the target on the left, it will get lighter as the room light gets brighter. Remember that all the target squares are identical: The differences in the way you perceive their brightness come from the differences in the surround. (**Note:** Do **not** try to vary illumination using a light dimmer: The color of the illumination will change.)

Although at first the fact that a target appears to become darker as the illumination is increased seems strange, it is quite apparent that it must be true. In conditions of minimum illumination, when there is absolutely no light falling upon the eyes, the resultant perception is of gray, not black. The neutral state of the perception of brightness appears to be given by the background rate of firing of the neurons: Thus it is gray. When some light is present, then we are able to see blacks, but only if there are some brighter surfaces to inhibit the black-appearing areas.

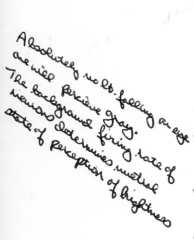

Consider the neural circuit of Figure 5-9. When there is no light presented to any of the three receptors, each responds at its background rate—50. When a weak light is presented—two areas of intensity 20 surrounding a region of intensity 10—then the neural responses for the two outside areas A and C increase with the increased intensity, whereas the responses for the central area B are reduced, even though more light is now falling on B than before. In doing the computation, assume that the region of greatest light intensity extends indefinitely to the left and right.) When the light signal is increased in intensity by a factor of 4 so that the more intense outer region becomes 80 and the weaker inner region increases to 40, then the phenomenon still holds. The neural responses to A and B increase with the increased illuminations, whereas the responses to the central region **decrease** still more.

A simple example of this phenomenon comes from considering the screen of a television set. When the set is turned off the screen is a neutral gray in brightness. If the set is turned on, some areas on the screen show intense blacks, much darker than the gray of the screen when the set was off. Yet the television set can only intensify the screen: The electron beam that impinges upon the phosphor face of the tube can only cause light to be emitted, it cannot absorb light. The apparent darkening of the screen comes about as a result of the simultaneous contrast mechanisms of the eye.

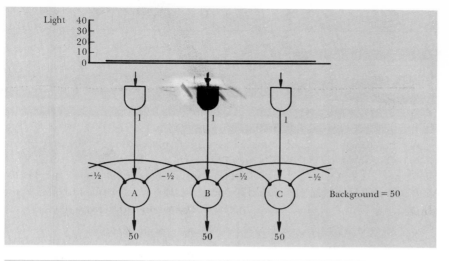

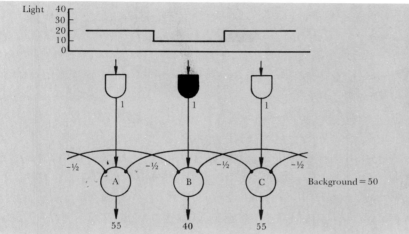

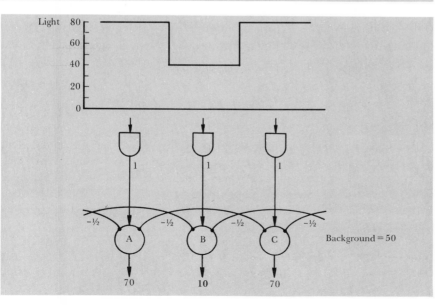

lateral inhib.
to emphasize or deemphasize
brightness

intensity becomes larger
center fires slower & slower

FIGURE 5-9

BRIGHTNESS AND DEPTH

A simple computation of brightness does not always explain our perceptions. Consider this experiment, which demonstrates how both brightness and depth information interact to produce a perception that takes a number of different factors into account (Hochberg & Beck, 1954).

A room is arranged with some white objects placed on a table (see Figure 5-10). The observer views the room through a hole cut in the wall. Since he cannot shift his head, everything must be seen from a fixed angle. He sees a number of objects sitting on a table lit by an overhead light. Some of the surfaces are illuminated directly, others are in shadow (see Figure 5-11).

FIGURE 5-10

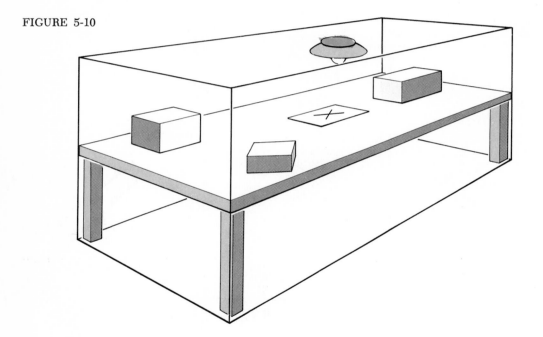

Although the amount of light reflected by the various surfaces is different, all of the surfaces are perceived to have the same color: white. Why? The observer perceives the objects in three dimensions. Thus, some surfaces are lying directly under the light, while others are in shadows. Their orientation in space accounts for the varying degrees of reflected light and brightnesses are therefore perceived to be constant.

Suppose the piece of paper marked × is raised to stand in front of the overhead light, as shown in Figure 5-12. The paper is now in shadow and

FIGURE 5-11

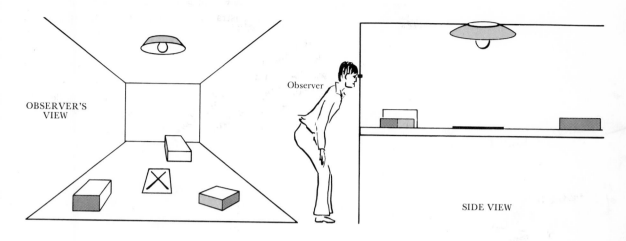

OBSERVER'S
VIEW

Observer

SIDE VIEW

FIGURE 5-12

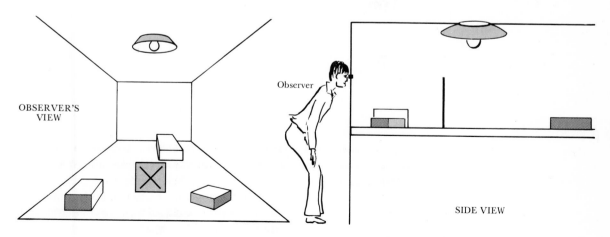

OBSERVER'S
VIEW

Observer

SIDE VIEW

the amount of light it reflects is drastically reduced. Nevertheless it still appears just as white as the other objects. Again its perceived orientation in space is consistent with the light being reflected from it.

To change the perceived brightness, the edges of the paper can be cut to shape it like a trapezoid (Figure 5-13). When it is placed vertically in

FIGURE 5-13

[handwritten: a plane figure w/4 sides, having any 0 2 sides, parallel]

[handwritten: Better Know !]

front of the light, the sides appear to be converging and the observer perceives the upright trapezoid as a rectangle lying flat under the light (Figure 5-14). Now, however, the paper is in fact in shadow and does not reflect

[handwritten: Perception of brightness is result of our fig. Perception]

FIGURE 5-14

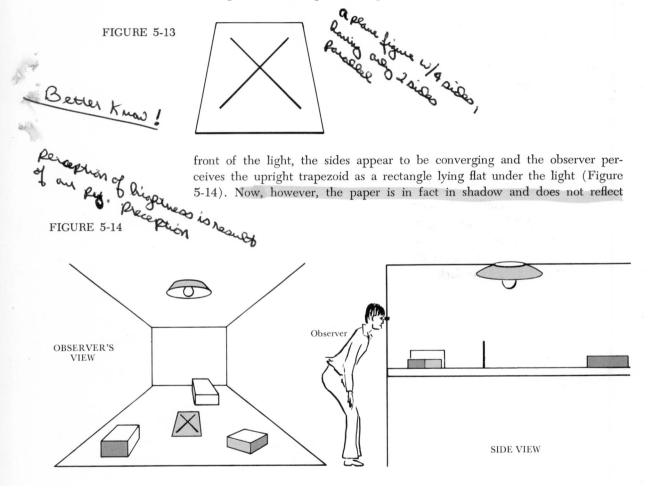

OBSERVER'S VIEW

Observer

SIDE VIEW

[handwritten: brightness can alter our Perceptions]

the amount of light appropriate to a horizontal object. Its perceived brightness therefore changes, and the paper looks much grayer than the other objects on the table. If a stick is then placed behind the paper, the depth interpretation is no longer tenable, the object is once again perceived as vertical, and it reverts to its normal brightness. In the perception of brightness, the very same visual scene can be interpreted in different ways depending upon the overall interpretation of the visual inputs.

If you actually brought someone in off the street in order to measure his visual sensitivity, the process would not go smoothly. In fact, you would probably find his behavior to be frustrating. Suppose you wished to find his *threshold:* The minimum light intensity he can see. A convenient way to start is to show him a reasonably intense test light and then gradually reduce the intensity until he says that he no longer sees it. This is a rough approximation to the threshold value. Just as you are about to record the threshold value, however, he would probably interrupt you to say that he could now see the light. You try reducing the intensity again, and the same thing would happen. First he would report that the light has disappeared, then a few seconds later he would change his mind and report that he could see it again. You would be trapped by the process of *visual adaptation—the ability of the eye to adjust its sensitivity to changing illuminations.*

To follow this process more precisely, the subject should first be exposed to an intense source of light (so that we know where he starts out) and then he should be enclosed in a lightproof room. Visual sensitivity is measured by presenting him with weaker and weaker test lights. With the passage of time, he becomes increasingly sensitive to light. Figure 5-15 shows the typical changes in sensitivity as a function of time in the dark room, the *dark-adaptation curve.*

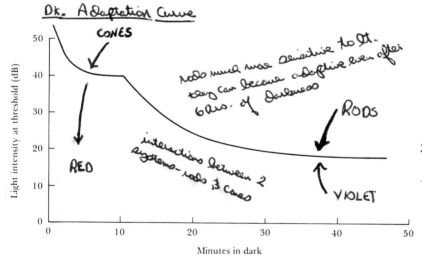

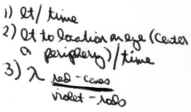

FIGURE 5-15

After Chapanis (1947).

Even a casual inspection of this curve indicates that something peculiar is happening around the 10-min mark. When faced with a bumpy curve such as this, one suspects that more than a single mechanism is producing the behavior. In the case of vision, of course, there are good grounds for this suspicion. There are two separate receptor systems operating in the eye: rods and cones. It would be nice to demonstrate that the bump in the curve results from an interaction in the behavior of these two systems.

The anatomical and functional differences between the two systems can be used to break up the dark-adaptation curve into its separate components. The rods are most dense in the periphery, the cones in the center. Restricting the test light to the periphery should produce a *rod-adaptation* curve; restricting it to the center should produce a curve based mainly on changes in cone sensitivity. Moreover, rods and cones are differentially sensitive to light of different wavelengths (as shown in Figure 5-16). Hence, the appearance of the dark-adaptation curve

FIGURE 5-16

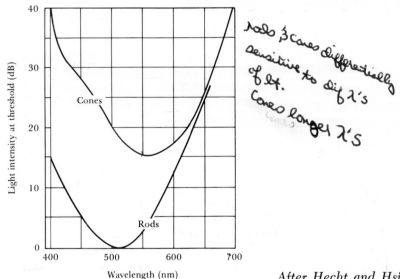

Wavelength (nm)

After Hecht and Hsia (1945).

should depend on the wavelength of the test light. Thus, we should be able to get a rod- or a cone-adaptation curve at will. Testing at the periphery or with violet light (less than 450 nm) should yield a relatively pure rod-adaptation curve. Testing at the center of the eye or with red light (greater than 650 nm) should yield an adaptation curve based primarily on cone vision.

Indeed, all these predictions show up. For example, in Figure 5-17, a set of dark-adaptation curves is shown. The only difference among them is the color of the test light. For red test lights of very long wavelengths (above 680 nm), the dark-adaptation curve shows no sign of the kink: It is a pure cone-sensitivity curve. As wavelength decreases, the bump begins to appear and the curve for a green light (485–570 nm) is almost identical to the curve for white light. Finally, the maximum sensitivity and the greatest degree of adaptations are found with the shortest visible wavelengths, a violet test light (less than 485 nm) where the rod system is carrying the main burden in responding to the visual signal. A similar set of curves results if the test light is moved from the center of the visual field toward the periphery:

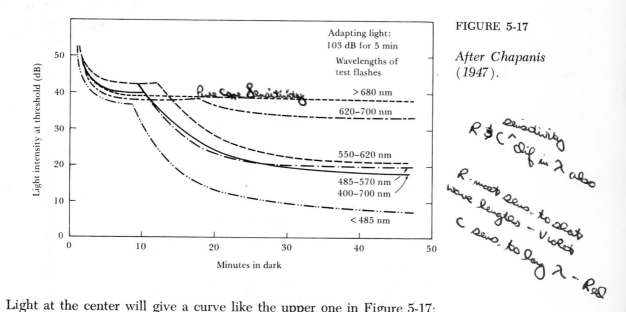

FIGURE 5-17

After Chapanis (1947).

Light at the center will give a curve like the upper one in Figure 5-17; light at the periphery will give a curve like the lowest one.

There is another way to see the effects of dark adaptation. As wavelength of a test light varies, so too will its brightness. The *equibrightness contour* shows the light intensity required to maintain a constant brightness as the test light varies in wavelength. These curves are analogous to the *equiloudness contours* for hearing. The set of equibrightness contours in Figure 5-18 shows how the curves change at different stages of dark adaptation. As the adaptation level changes, the equal brightness curves shift the wavelength at which they are maximally sensitive. This shift results from the different amounts of rod and cone activity present at each level of adaptation. With little adaptation (top curve), cone vision plays the major role and longer wavelengths appear brightest. With a large amount of adaptation, vision depends mostly on rods and the maximum sensitivity shifts down towards the shorter wavelengths. This was first noticed by the Bohemian physiologist, Johannes Purkinje and,

Equibrightness contours

FIGURE 5-18

[handwritten margin note: With little adaptation cone vision playing major role w. longer λ's appearing brightest]

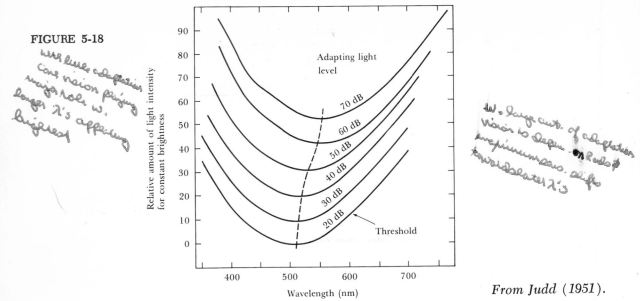

[handwritten margin note: W. large amt. of adaptation vision is deper maximums rods towards later λ's]

From Judd (1951).

in fact, was one of the earliest sets of behavioral observations used to establish the difference between the rod and cone systems.

The change in sensitivity has a practical result. In bright light, reds appear brighter than blues. In dim light, the reverse is true. Visual signals designed for night use must take this shift in sensitivity into account. (See color plate on the Purkinje shift, Figure 5-19, on page 216c.)

If someone needs to keep his eyes dark-adapted, yet also has to work occasionally in well-lit rooms, then it is necessary to be sure not to interfere with the adaptation level of his rod vision. This can be done by controlling the wavelength of light to which he is exposed. Wearing goggles which only allow red light through to the eyes will protect the rod system against bright lights. With red goggles, even in a well-lit environment only the cones will be exposed to light and the adaptation level of the rods is not affected. In the dim environment, when the goggles are removed, the rods will be found to have maintained their high sensitivity; even though the cones are now light-adapted, they will not affect the vision. This is the principle behind the use of red goggles or rooms illuminated only with red lights for people such as radar observers who keep their eyes dark-adapted, even during rest breaks when they want to move about in normally lit rooms.

Figure 5-20 How long does it take to become dark-adapted? The curve in Figure 5-17 shows that the most rapid changes in sensitivity take place during

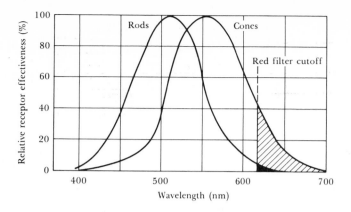

The shaded area indicates the region where the red filter allows light to
pass. Thus, almost no light excites the cones. The vertical line indicates
the place at which a common red filter cuts off. It transmits $\frac{1}{10}$ of the
light involved in the cone curve, and $\frac{1}{100}$ of that in the rod curve. From
Hecht and Hsia (1945).

FIGURE 5-20

the first 10 to 20 min. For most practical purposes, 30 min is sufficient
for close to maximum adaptation, but careful measurements show the
sensitivity continues to change very slowly for as long as 6 hours. Remember, however, that the 20 to 30 min is for a situation where the
subjects are first exposed to extremely bright lights (such as a flash
bulb going off in front of their eyes). With much dimmer illumination—
say, the level in a fairly large room lit by several 50-watt incandescent
bulbs—it may only take 5 min to become adapted to the dark. Moreover,
once the eye is dark-adapted, turning on a dim light for 10 sec or
so does not change the adaptation level very much; only 60 sec are
then required to return to the original state. Were this not true, night
driving would lead to considerable difficulties, since the lights from
an oncoming car would interfere with dark adaptation, severly hamper-
ing the ability to see objects. Yet such lights have little noticeable effect
on visual sensitivity.

Vision is not instantaneous. It takes time for the reaction to a visual
image to be established and, then, once established, the reaction persists for awhile, even if the image is taken away. The chemical reactions
appear to require some time to translate the light source into a neural-
electric response. The retinal image fades away gradually, so the persistence can be seen for several tenths of a second (see the discussion
of the visual short-term store in Chapter 9).

TEMPORAL
CHARACTERISTICS
OF VISION

Integration time

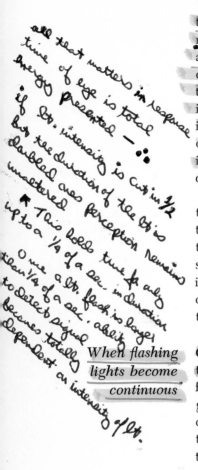

It is possible to perform a trade between the intensity of light and the duration that it is on. Within the response time of the eye, all that matters is the total energy presented. Thus, if the light intensity is halved and the duration doubled, a person's ability to detect a signal is unchanged. The time–intensity trade works rather well for durations up to about 20 msec. For flashes longer than 20 msec, a reduction in light intensity cannot quite be compensated for by a corresponding increase in signal duration. Once the signal flash is longer than about a quarter of a second (250 msec), the ability to detect the signal becomes totally independent of the duration, and is determined solely by the intensity of the light.

This interchange between time and intensity is, of course, not unique to the visual system. It is common to photochemical processes of all types. Suitable exposure for photographic film, for example, can be obtained with a large number of combinations of integration times (shutter speed) and intensities (aperture opening). Cameras typically provide integration times from 0.001 to 1.0 sec—a much wider range than that of the human eye. But the visual system is far more sensitive to light than the average camera film.

When flashing lights become continuous

Once initiated, the visual perception persists for a brief period after the light itself is turned off. The persistence of the visual image was first measured by an ingenious investigator in the 1700s who tied a glowing ember to a string and whirled it around in the dark. You can do the same thing with a flashlight. The speed of rotation at which the moving light appears to form a continuous circle gives the information necessary to compute the persistence of the image. The experiment gives the same result whether done with a sophisticated electronic measuring apparatus or with a flashlight or glowing ember: The estimate is about 150 msec. This value is very close to the duration of the electrical activity in the retina that is produced in response to a brief flash of light. The fact that the light pattern seems to be retained by the visual system for about 150–250 msec will turn out to be very important to our study of memory (Chapters 8 and 9).

Critical flicker

By timing things just right, it should be possible to make lights which are actually flashing appear to be on continuously. Suppose a light is flashed. The visual response builds up and persists over some 100 msec. If a second flash is added soon enough, the response to it will build up before the reaction to the first has died away. A third flash can be added before the visual reaction to the second flash dies away. The flashing lights then, produce a continuous reaction in the visual system that is perceived as continuous light. The rate at which a flickering light appears to be continuous is called the *critical flicker frequency* (*CFF*).[2]

Any factor which alters the speed of integration and persistence in the visual system also alters the rate at which flashing lights are perceived as continuous. Intense flashes produce short integration periods and, thus, must be presented at much higher rates before they fuse and become continuous. Weak flashes fuse at slow rates. The rod system, which works best at low levels of illumination, has a lower critical flicker frequency than the cone system.

The apparent brightness of a flickering light that has fused is predictable from the integration mechanism that produces the fusion. A light flashing on and off for equal times at a rate greater than its fusion frequency appears to have the same brightness as a light that is on continuously, but only half as intense (this is called *Talbot's Law*). The visual system averages the intensity throughout the integration period, and the perception follows accordingly.

These integrational aspects of visual information-processing clearly limit the speeds at which the eye can detect and track changes in the pattern of stimulation falling on the retina. The averaging process merges one image into the next, creating a smoothly flowing, continuous visual perception. It converts the succession of discrete pictures that are flashed on a television set or movie projection screen into the illusion of a steady, continuous visual environment.

The images on the television set or movie screen would actually flicker somewhat were not clever strategies used. Professional motion pictures are projected at the rate of 24 frames per second (sometimes 30). The light projected to the screen is interrupted during the time it takes to advance the film from one frame to the next. If this were projected normally, flicker would be seen. To avoid flicker, each frame of film is projected on the screen several times. That is, instead of a steady projection of each frame, the light is interrupted one or more times. Thus, even though only 24 frames are shown each second, the eye receives a frequency of at least 48 flashes per second, a sufficiently high rate to avoid flicker. (Some projectors interrupt the light beam twice during each frame, producing a frequency of 72 flashes per second.)

---

[2] Those of you familiar with electronic circuits will note that the temporal characteristics of the eye approximate those of a bandpass filter with an upper cutoff between 10 and 50 Hz, depending upon intensity, and with little or no direct-current response. [See Cornsweet (1970) for a discussion of the bandpass filter method of analysis.]

Television faces a similar problem. A television image is painted upon the screen dot-by-dot, with the image consisting of some 525 lines, each line having a theoretical resolution of approximately 500 dots. The complete image is presented 30 times each second. If the image were painted consecutively, starting at the top left corner and working across the rows and down to the bottom right, there would be flicker because the presentation of each dot is for such a brief percentage of the time taken to present the entire picture. This is not true of a motion picture, where each element in the picture is exposed whenever the scene is illuminated.

To avoid flicker, the picture is split in half by presenting every other line of the image. This takes $\frac{1}{60}$ sec. Then, the electron beam goes back and fills in the missing lines. Thus, although the entire picture still takes $\frac{1}{30}$ sec to be presented, every area of the screen has some part of the picture presented to it every $\frac{1}{60}$ sec. This interlacing effectively eliminates flicker.

Recently, the entertainment industry has deliberately reintroduced flicker, providing us a chance to see what the environment would look like if our visual system did not have these integration mechanisms. The stroboscopic lights sometimes used in light shows provide a series of discrete snapshots with enough time between each that the image from one flash decays before the next appears. At these high intensities and low flashing rates, the visual system no longer merges one image into the next, and perception takes on an unreal, disconnected quality.

COLOR

The start of modern theories of color vision must be credited to Isaac Newton and his observations that a prism could split the light from the sun into a full spectrum of colors. From that simple fact comes the first simple theory: The color that is seen depends upon the wavelength of the light striking the eye. Like many theories, the facts are true but the theory is not (see color plate, Figure 4-1, page 216b).

A prism (or the equivalent in nature, a rainbow) separates out the different wavelengths contained in white light and lays them neatly in a row, from long wavelengths to short. We perceive the spectrum as different colors laid out neatly in a row from reds to violets. Perhaps this is all there is to color vision. Maybe there is a different kind of receptor responding to each different wavelength of light (*monochromatic* light), just as there are different neurons in the auditory system that respond to different frequencies of sound.

A careful examination of color perception shows that this theory is too simple. In the spectrum of pure lights produced by a prism, some colors are absent. There is no brown or purple or pink. These colors

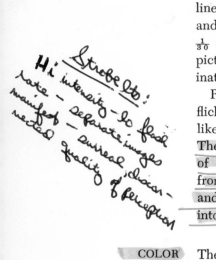

must be created by something other than a simple monochromatic light.

When two different wavelengths of light are mixed together, we do not see two colors. Rather, we see one new color formed from the mixture. Once the lights are combined, it is absolutely impossible for the human to determine the original set of colors that went into the mixture. This is quite unlike the situation in hearing where the individual tones that make up a chord can be identified by the listener. Moreover, in color vision, mixing certain wavelengths seems to cancel out the color altogether. For example, if a bluish-green monochromatic light (with a wavelength of 490 nm) is mixed with a yellow-red monochromatic light (with a wavelength of 600 nm), and the relative amounts of the two lights are adjusted just right, the colors cancel, leaving a colorless gray. Such mixtures of lights are called *complementary* pairs.

Complementary pairs provide a clue to a useful description of human color vision. The first thing that is needed is some way of expressing the relationships that hold among all the possible perceptions of lights and colors. Ideally, it should be possible to find a descriptive system that predicts the perceived color of any mixture of lights. This is usually done by drawing a diagram in which the different possible colors and mixtures are represented, with a set of rules that describes how one predicts the results of combinations of lights. Such a diagram (and its equivalent mathematical representation) is a *color space*. Color spaces can take many forms, from a simple circle to a rather complex three-dimensional space.

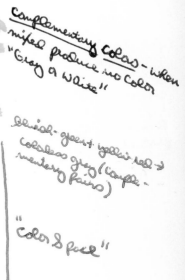

We can use the sets of complementary colors to give us the first system for describing color mixtures. The layout of colors produced by a prism describes reasonably well the perceptions caused by single, monochromatic light. It would be useful to take advantage of this description. To do so, notice two things: first, the fact that some colors are "opposites" or complements of one another; second, the two ends of the spectrum look reasonably similar—deep blue or violet at the short-wavelength end, purple at the long-wavelength end. Combining these two observations leads to a simple solution: take the line of colors given by the spectrum and draw it as a circle, putting complementary colors directly opposite each other across the diameter of the circle. Surprisingly enough, this simple scheme for representing color works. It describes much more than might be expected from the simple rationale behind its construction. Note that so far there is no hint of a theory of how humans perceive color, only an attempt to describe the relationships among the colors that are perceived.

MIXING COLORS

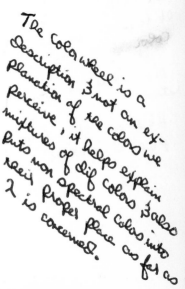

The color wheel

Figure 5-21 shows a possible color wheel. Along the circumference of the circle are the color names and the approximate locations for the wavelengths of light that produce those colors when viewed in the spectrum (see Figure 4-1 for a different representation). Complementary color pairs may be found by lining up opposite tic marks (The region marked "purple" cannot be produced by monochromatic light. It will be discussed later.)

FIGURE 5-21

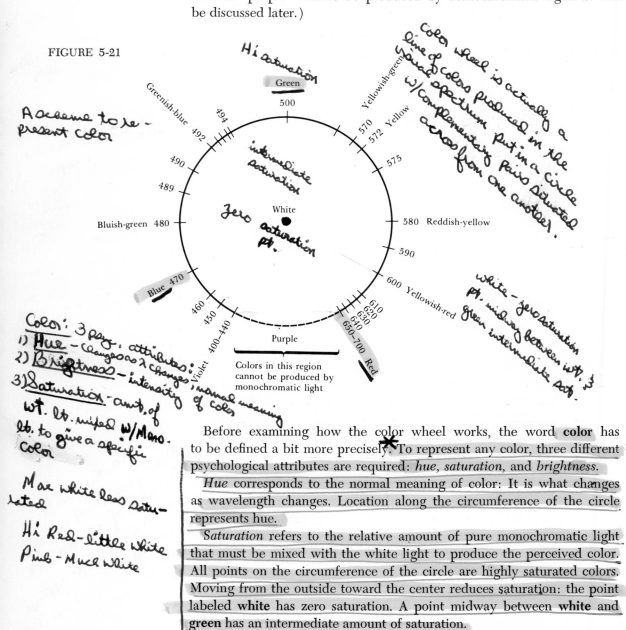

Colors in this region cannot be produced by monochromatic light

Handwritten annotations on figure:
Hi saturation
Color wheel is actually a line of colors produced in the visual spectrum put in a circle w/complementary pairs situated across from one another.
intermediate saturation
Zero saturation pt.
A scheme to represent color
white — zero saturation pt. midway between wt. & green intermediate sat.

Before examining how the color wheel works, the word **color** has to be defined a bit more precisely. To represent any color, three different psychological attributes are required: *hue, saturation,* and *brightness.*

Hue corresponds to the normal meaning of color: It is what changes as wavelength changes. Location along the circumference of the circle represents hue.

Saturation refers to the relative amount of pure monochromatic light that must be mixed with the white light to produce the perceived color. All points on the circumference of the circle are highly saturated colors. Moving from the outside toward the center reduces saturation: the point labeled **white** has zero saturation. A point midway between **white** and **green** has an intermediate amount of saturation.

Handwritten annotations in left margin:
Color: 3 psy. attributes:
1) Hue — changes as λ changes
2) Brightness — intensity of color
3) Saturation — amt. of wt. lt. mixed w/mono. color lt. to give a specific color

More white less saturated

Hi Red — little white
Pink — Much white

Brightness is used exactly as it was in the earlier sections of this chapter. The brightness dimension does **not** show up on the color circle. The most direct physical correlate of brightness is light intensity (with the same restrictions discussed previously).

Mixing two lights. To see how two colors combine to form a third, the first step is to locate the individual colors on circumferences of the circle, then connect the two points by a straight line. Any mixture of the two individual colors will produce a third color that lies somewhere on that line: The exact location depends on the exact amounts (intensities) of the two individual colors present in the mixture.

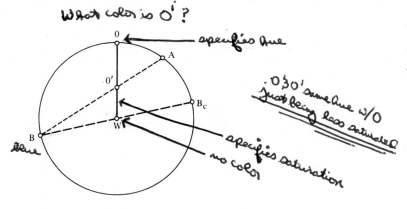

FIGURE 5-22

Suppose we mix together two monochromatic complementary colors: call them B and B_e. These two are shown on the color circle of Figure 5-22 by two points along the circumference that lie on opposite ends of a diameter. Let the mixture of B and B_e that exactly cancels be given by the point midway between the two: The center of the circle. Thus, the center represents a point with no color, a white (W). [In this scheme, all perceptions that do not have a color (hue) are called **white**, regardless of brightness. White, therefore, refers to the general class of perceptions that range from black (very low brightness), through the grays (intermediate amounts of brightness) to white (high brightness). For purposes of describing color, all these are alike.]

Suppose two colors that are not complementary are mixed, say A and B. The result is some new color 0′, as shown in Figure 5-22. What color is 0′? The easiest way to start is to consider the changes in perception that occur as we move from point B on the circumference of the color wheel toward W. At B, there is a spectral color, one produced by a pure monochromatic light. Suppose that point B is **blue**. To move from B to W, we simply combine together two lights, one of which is white, the other monochromatic blue. As the relative proportion of the two lights changes, we go from point B (all blue light, no white) through some point that represents equal amounts of both lights, to W (all white light, no blue). Looking at the resulting color sensations, the essential attribute that most people regard as **color** would not be changed by the addition of white, rather it is the saturation—the "lightness" or "whiteness"—that would change. To prove that, take any point along the line BW (except for B and W) and ask an observer to look at the spectral colors and pick out the one that matches that point most closely: He will choose the spectral color corresponding to B.

Now, back to the original question: What color does 0′ in Figure 5-22 have? A radius drawn from the center of the circle (W) through 0′ to the circumference, point 0 on the figure, specifies the hue. The distance along the radius from W to 0′ specifies the saturation. The points 0 and 0′ have the same hue, but 0 is more saturated. We see that mixing A and B together produced 0′, a color with the hue of 0, but less saturated.

If we wish to match 0 by mixing together A and B we would fail, for the only possible results of the mixture lie on the straight line AB; the exact location depends upon the relative intensities of A and B. The more intense A is, the closer to A the resulting mixture. In attempting to match 0 by mixing together A and B, the closest that it is possible to come is 0′: The same hue, but reduced saturation.

Mixing three lights. Three monochromatic colors—call them A, B, and C—mixed together can produce any color that lies inside the triangle formed by the three points. To see why, consider how to mix together A, B, and C to get the color Z.

First, in Figure 5-23, it is clear that if any two colors are mixed together (A with B, B with C, or A with C), the colors resulting from the mixtures are specified by the straight (dotted) lines joining those colors. The color that is to be matched, Z, does not lie on any of these lines. This does not mean, however, that Z cannot be matched. Look what happens if A and B are combined to form D. Now, although D is actually produced by a mixture of two monochromatic lights, so far as the color circle is concerned, it acts just as if it were a pure light. Thus, if C is mixed with D, the result is any color lying on the line joining C with D. So, to match Z, simply mix A and B in just the proper amount so that the D formed lies on the line connecting C and Z. Then, mix C with D until it yields the color that matches Z. By this same argument, it is always possible to find the right combination of mixtures of A, B, and C to match any point that lies within the triangle formed by the lines connecting A, B, and C.

Are there three monochromatic lights that, when mixed, will produce all possible colors that can be perceived? Call these three basic lights

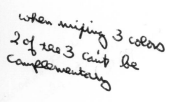

when mixing 3 colors
2 of the 3 can't be
complementary

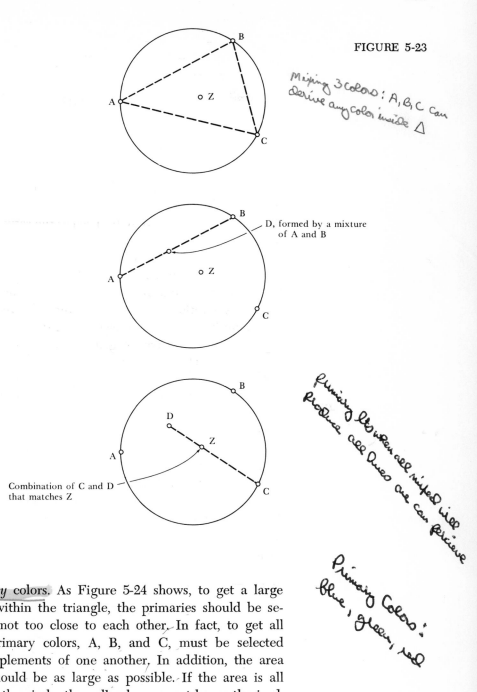

FIGURE 5-23

D, formed by a mixture
of A and B

Combination of C and D —
that matches Z

Mixing 3 colors: A, B, C can
derive any color inside △

Primary lts when all mixed will
produce all hues are can relieve

Primary Colors:
Blue, Green, red

primary lights or primary colors. As Figure 5-24 shows, to get a large
range of colors falling within the triangle, the primaries should be selected so that they are not too close to each other. In fact, to get all
the colors, the three primary colors, A, B, and C, must be selected
so that no two are complements of one another. In addition, the area
covered by the three should be as large as possible. If the area is all
one side of the center of the circle, then all colors cannot be synthesized.
The triangle must include the center of the circle within its interior.
A formal way of stating this requirement is that the three primaries

refers to above

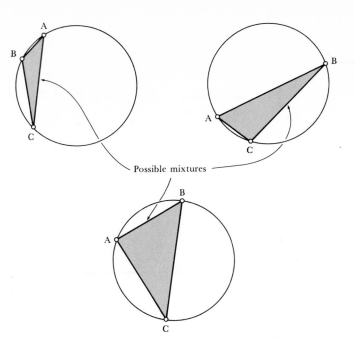

Possible mixtures

FIGURE 5-24

shall be chosen so that no two are complements of one another, and no one can be matched by a mixture of the other two.

The ideal set of primaries is shown in Figure 5-25: a large equilateral triangle that completely envelops the circle. Unfortunately, although this is the set of primaries needed to produce every color within the circle, the primaries A, B, and C are outside the circle. Therefore, they cannot be produced by any monochromatic lights. The best that can be done with real lights is the equilateral triangle contained within the circle shown in Figure 5-26.

The color circle summarizes a good deal of the phenomena of color perception. But it is a description, not an explanation. It demonstrates

FIGURE 5-25

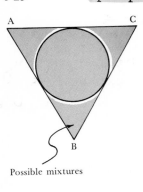

Possible mixtures

Possible mixtures

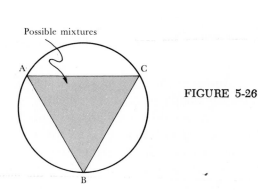

FIGURE 5-26

how these primary colors mixed together can produce all of the hues we perceive. So far as the color wheel is concerned, however, any three would do (provided, of course, they met the restrictions just described). We still have not discussed what are the actual primary colors of the visual system.

PAINTS AND LIGHTS

The color circle applies to mixtures of lights, not mixtures of paints. To determine how paints mix together, we need to consider the fact that they produce their color by absorbing light of all wavelengths except those which cause the color. The wavelengths causing the color are reflected. To see how two paints add together, it is necessary to examine the wavelengths that the new combination absorbs. Because the absorption of colors is the most important attribute of paint, these mixtures are called *subtractive*. Mixture of lights is called *additive*.

The mixture of red and green light can produce yellow. The mixture of blue and yellow light can produce gray. (Look back at Figure 5-21.) These are the facts of color mixture, but they are contrary to all that most people learn about the mixing of colors from art classes. Why the difference? The answer has to do with the differences between the ways that two lights and two paints add together. To make a prediction of the color that results from a mixture, we should not ask what colors have been added together: That has little to do with it. The important question to ask is, what colors get to the eye?

Consider the mixture of lights. Examine Figure 5-27. Shine a blue light onto a piece of paper: Blue reflects from the paper into the eye and the paper looks blue.

Shine a yellow light onto a piece of paper. Yellow reflects and the paper looks yellow.

Shine both blue and yellow onto the paper. Both blue and yellow bounce off, and both are seen. The resulting color that is perceived is given by the mixture: gray.

Consider the mixture of paints. Paint paper blue. White light shines on the paper. The paint absorbs long wavelengths, allowing only greens, blues, and violets to reflect. The eye sees a combination of green, blue, and violet. The paper looks blue.

Paint paper yellow. White light shines on the paper. The paint absorbs short wavelengths so that only greens, yellows, oranges, and reds reflect. The eye sees these mixed together. The paper looks yellow.

Paint paper with a mixture of blue and yellow. White light shines on the paper. The blue paint absorbs long wavelengths (yellows, oranges, and reds) while the yellow absorbs the short wavelengths (blues and violets). All that is left is intermediate wavelengths: greens. Hence, the mixture of blue paint and yellow paint looks green.

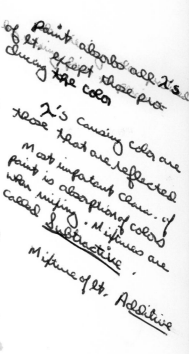

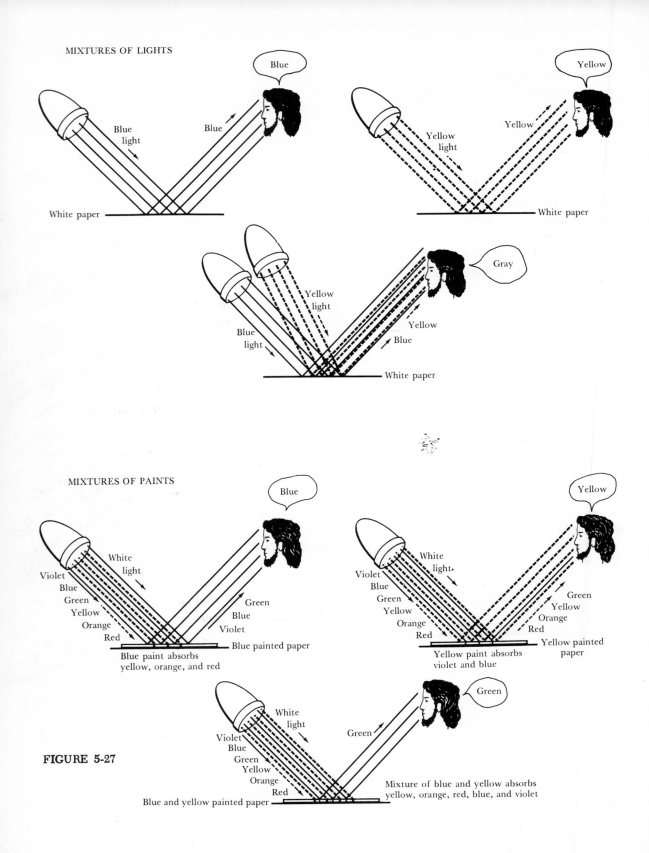

FIGURE 5-27

The principles of color mixture learned from lights can also apply to paints. To do this, some care is needed in mixing the paints together. Suppose we wish to create a yellow by mixing red and green paints. Were we simply to mix the paints together and apply them to the paper, we would end up with some dark combination, probably reddish. This is because the paints were mixed together so that their effects on light interfered with each other. But suppose the red were painted as many small dots of paint. From a distance, it would look like a solid red. Similarly, the green could be painted as many small dots, carefully located so that the green and red dots filled the entire paper, never overlapping one another. From up close the many small red and green dots would be visible. From a distance, far enough back so that the individual dots could not be seen, the eye would receive a mixture of red and green light. The light would look yellow.

This is the principle used by a color television set to mix together its color. If you examine the screen from close up, the individual dots of color become visible. Long before the age of color television, the impressionist painter George Seurat (1859–1891) experimented with additive color mixtures by forming his paintings with many small individual dots of color. When viewed from a distance, the mixture of lights formed the desired colors.

Making paints mix as lights

use dots of dif. colors carefully located so entire surface filled

---

Stare at the color patch of Figure 1-49 on page 216a for awhile without moving your eyes until the patch starts to "glow" slightly. Then look at a white surface; you will see an afterimage of the color patch. The color of an afterimage is almost exactly the complementary color of the image. Thus, the color circle describes afterimage colors: The color of the afterimage is directly across the circle from the color stared at. (There is a small error in the predicted color of an afterimage which has not been fully explained yet, but the best hypothesis is that it is due to an error introduced by the slight coloration of the interior of the eye.)

Afterimages are reciprocal. That is, if a blue produces a yellow afterimage, then a light of that same yellow color will produce a blue afterimage. Some greens, however, produce purple afterimages, yet there is no single wavelength of light that can produce purple by itself. Purple and related colors are *nonspectral* colors, because they cannot be produced by a single wavelength from the visual spectrum. These colors can be placed on the color circle, however, by knowing their complements. They are specified by the wavelengths of their complements. If you look again at the color circle, however, you can see that mixtures of lights will produce purple. A violet of 400 nm mixed with a red of 700 nm will produce an intense purple. Thus, the color circle not only helps explain mixtures, it also puts nonspectral colors into their rightful place.

Afterimages

Color of an afterimage is complementary color of the image. Affects of fatigued receptors influencing adjacent cells.

Nonspectral colors can't be produced by single λ from an its spectrum "Purple is"

color circle explains colors of mixtures of & puts nonspectral colors in their proper place

The explanation of afterimages is simple. Prolonged viewing of a scene fatigues the receptors, allowing the opponent system to take over when the gaze is shifted to a neutral stimulation. Thus, as with induced color, it is possible to produce "unnatural" colors with this procedure. First view a saturated green for awhile, and then switch to a saturated red:

FIGURE 5-28

From Wald (1964).

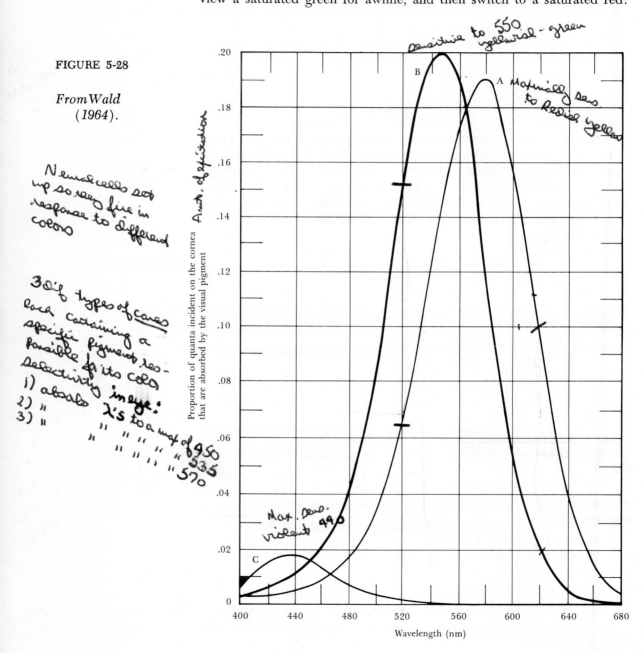

You will perceive a red of supersaturation. The green receptors will be fatigued. They no longer operate to mix with the red and desaturate it. Thus, the resulting red is more brilliant than any that can be produced simply by monochromatic light.

The effect can be enhanced by adding induced colors. Look at a deep red surrounded by deep green. Then switch to deep green surrounded by deep red. You can create this easily yourself by having color slides made that are both positives and negatives of the original scene (this is easily done by your local film processor because several different color films— such as **Kodacolor**—yield color negatives which are complementary in color to the original). Project them alternately upon a screen so that they overlap. A rapid alternation is extremely effective.

By direct measurement of the color sensitivity of the cones in the human retina, three different types of cones have been discovered, each of which contains a specific pigment that is responsible for its color selectivity. The different pigments absorb light differently, each being selective to a special set of light wavelengths. One absorbs wavelengths of 445 to 450 nm best, the second has maximum absorption around 525 to 535 nm, and the last has a maximum in the region 555 to 570 nm. The overall absorption properties of the different pigments are very much like that shown in Figure 5-28. These are the three primary color receptors that control normal color vision.

From the description of the sensitivity of the primary receptors, it is possible to work out most of the phenomena of color vision. For example, the color wheel suggests that mixture of a green (at 520 nm) and a red at 620 nm should match a yellow of 564 nm. How is that related to the cone sensitivities of Figure 5-28?

Let the vertical axis of the graph represent the amount of excitation given to each of the color receptors for a light of intensity 100 at a wavelength specified by the horizontal axis. Now consider what happens when 100 units of 620 nm is mixed with 100 units of 520 nm.

Amount of Excitation of Color Receptors

	A	B	C
Red (620 nm)	10	2	.0
Green (520 nm)	7	15	.2
Total:	17	17	.2

The total gives us the excitation that each receptor receives when excited by 200 light units: 100 from the red and 100 from the green. To use these curves, the values have to be rescaled. There is a total of 34.2 units of neural excitation. Of this, A is 17/34.2 or 50% of the total; B is 17/34.2 or 50%; C is 1%. Now go back to the curves of Figure 5-28 and find a wavelength which excites A, B, and C in these relative percentages. In this case, it is easy to find. About the only place where receptor A is excited about the same as B and excitation of C is negligible is in the region between 560 and 565 nm. The mixture will be perceived as yellow. The color circle gives the same answer.

It is clear from the computations that it is a straightforward, if tedious, matter to compute for any combination of lights the relative amounts of stimulation that will occur in the three color-receptors and thus determine what other combinations of lights (or monochromatic light) will match that relative excitation. Obviously, if the color circle works, it provides a much more reasonable computational method to use.

Still remaining in the description of the color process is how the signals from the primary receptors are actually combined by the visual system. There has been a long and vigorous debate about the matter. The disagreement involves whether the information provided by the basic receptors is interpreted directly by higher brain centers, or whether some intermediate stages are involved.

Opponent-process color theory

When a patch of gray is located inside a red surround, it takes on the shade of the complementary color to red—green. The appearance of colors is strongly affected by the context of surrounding colors. These phenomena, as well as the data on complementary colors and color blindnesses, suggest opposing processes underlying color perception. As early as 1878, Ewold Hering proposed an *opponent-process theory* of color vision. In his system, colors are mixed in the complementary pairs: blue with yellow, red with green, and black with white. The judgment of brightness is based on the response of the black–white mechanism. Colors result from combining blue–yellow and red–green activity.

In the opponent-process system, the three basic color receptors, the ones labeled A, B, and C in Figure 5-29, enter into various combinations. Exactly how this is done is not yet known, but there are several possibilities. For example, one scheme for combining the three receptors to form a **red–green**, a **black–white**, and a **blue–yellow** pair is shown in the figure. Here, the three receptors are connected to three neural cells. There are several other possible interconnections: Presumably physiological investigations in the next few years will decide on the correct one.

Although the exact details are not known, the fact that receptors com-

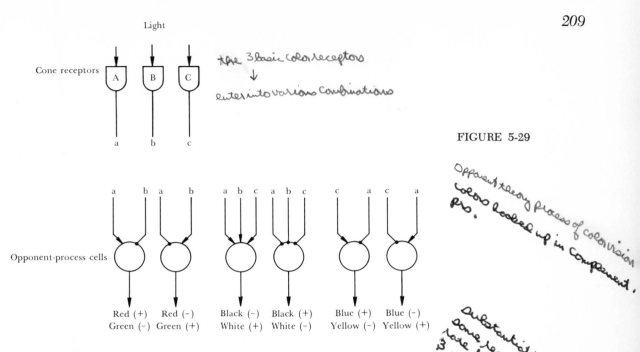

FIGURE 5-29

Physiological network based on DeValois and Jacobs (1968).

[handwritten: the 3 basic color receptors ↓ enter into various combinations]

[handwritten: Opponent theory. Process of color vision colors looked up in Complement pro.]

[handwritten: Substantiation of OPT Some receptors increased response rate for green & decrease it for red vice versa in monkeys]

bine in some fashion like that shown in Figure 5-29 is well established by other behavioral and physiological investigations. For example, physiological studies of the fibers in the lateral geniculate nucleus of monkeys show receptors that increase their response rate for red lights but decrease it for green lights: exactly the type of opponent process postulated by the theory. Other receptors do just the opposite, increasing their response rate for green and decreasing it for red.

Figures 5-30a, b, & c

Blue–yellow pairings have also been found, although with far less frequency than the red–green pairs (at least in the monkeys studied to date). This is consistent with the fact that the blue–yellow system is less sensitive than the red–green one.

With color, much as with black-and-white, what is seen at one point affects the perception of neighboring points. This is caused by lateral inhibition: The same phenomenon responsible for increasing contrasts and for brightness constancies. Looking at a blue patch at one location reduces the sensitivity to blue in the neighboring areas; hence, more sensitivity to yellow. Looking at black increases the sensitivity to white in the neighborhood. Looking at red increases the sensitivity to green. These contrast effects are called *spatial contrast* or *induced contrast:* A color induces its complement onto neighboring regions.

[handwritten: Induced contrast a SPATIAL CONTRAST a color induces its compl. onto neighboring regions

again Lat. Inb. at work Median.]

FIGURE 5-30a

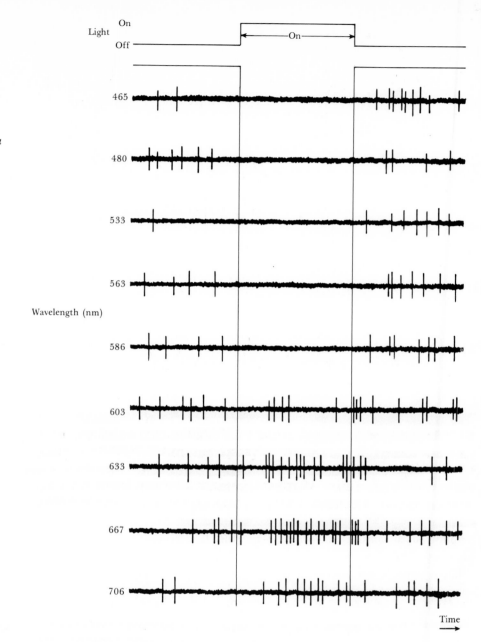

(a) Responses recorded from a single microelectrode in the lateral geniculate nucleus of a monkey showing an opponent process cell; (+): responses to long wavelengths (red); (−): responses to shorter wavelengths. (b, c) Average responses of various classes of spectrally opponent cells in the brain of the monkey. The three curves in each plot are three different intensity (energy) levels, in arbitrary units. From unpublished data of DeValois and DeValois, Abromov, and Jacobs (1966).

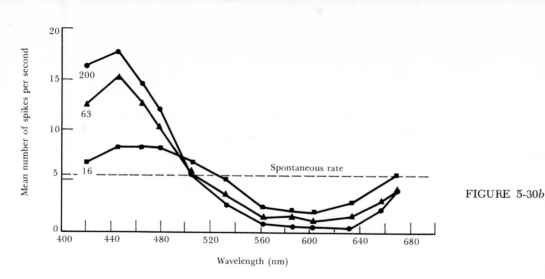

FIGURE 5-30*b*

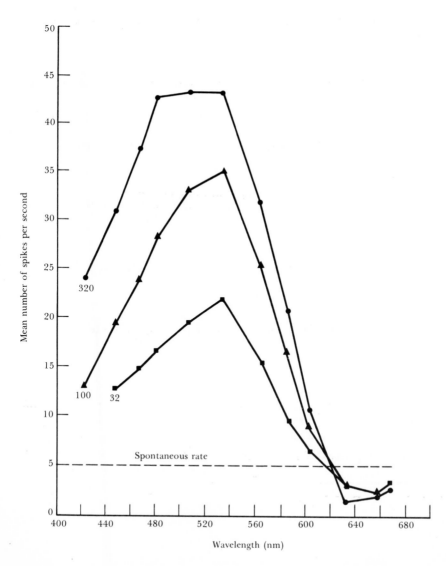

FIGURE 5-30c

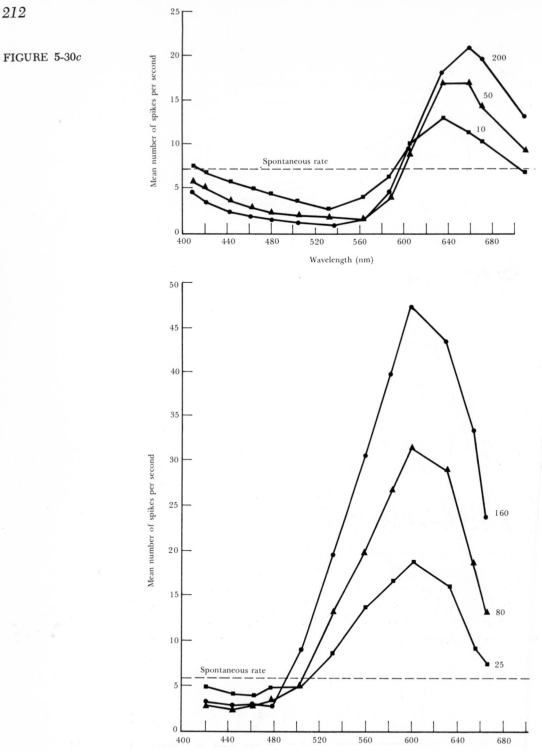

To explain these statements, it is necessary to assume that one basic neuron, when excited, inhibits all surrounding neurons of the same class. That is, each of the three basic color-receptors A, B, and C inhibits surrounding A, B, and C receptors. Because of the way that these receptors are paired to create the opponent-process system, inhibiting one receptor is equivalent to making the opponent receptor more sensitive. Hence, color contrasts. The biggest effect of contrasts will occur with complementary pairs. In fact, complementary pairs of colors can be very disturbing to look at. For one thing, the induced color caused by the spatial interactions can make a color look more intense, more saturated than it has any right to be (see Figure 5-31, page 216d).

Examine the green hearts in Figure 1-49, page 216a. Fixate on the black dot to form an afterimage—fixate until the colors shimmer a bit. Now look at the white surface. Yes, you see afterimages of pink hearts, but why is there any green present? It is induced.

Incidentally, now you know why the shimmering of colors occurs when you stare for a long time at a scene. The shimmering occurs at the boundaries in the picture. The small, unavoidable eye movements cause this part of the picture to oscillate back and forth so that the retinal image is not stationary: It fluctuates between the two colors on either side of the boundary. Thus, as some receptors are fatigued by the steady gazing, the receptors corresponding to the boundaries are not nearly so fatigued and are more subject to contrast effects. The result is that the borders adapt differently, producing shimmering perceptions.

Induced color is so powerful that at least one experimenter, Edwin Land of the Polaroid Corporation, has demonstrated that nearly the full range of perceived colors can be created by a *two*-color mixture. For a while, Land's demonstrations of color vision created by only two primaries caused some concern to the proponents of three-color theories. But it now appears that the effects result from sophisticated applications of the principles of opponent-color systems and spatial-contrast effects. The two colors Land uses are not monochromatic wavelengths; rather, they are bands of light: one band of long wavelengths and one band of short wavelengths. With two monochromatic lights, the full color-spectrum is not perceived. More important, the Land colors require a large mixture of objects, a requirement designed to maximize the effect of induced colors. With simple, homogeneous projections of lights, Land's colors are identical to those expected from the color wheel.

The beginning part of this chapter concentrates on the role of lateral inhibition and the resulting interactions of excitation at different spots

Induced Contrast

Biggest effects of contrast occur in comp. prs.

inhibit 1 receptor = more sensitive opponent receptor hence "Color Contrast"

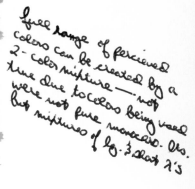

full range of perceived colors can be created by a 2-color mixture — not true due to colors being used were not pure monochro. clrs. but mixtures of lg. & short λ's

in the visual field with each other. For this topic, three books are essential reading. One, Ratliff's book *Mach Bands* (1965) is an excellent introduction to lateral inhibition, to the collection of psychological data relevant to its analysis, and to a wide assortment of interesting psychological, physiological issues that result from the study of this phenomenon. Second, Georg von Békésy's book *Sensory Inhibition* (1967) expands the phenomena of lateral inhibition to cover a wide variety of sensory systems, including taste and smell. This, too, is a fascinating book, interlaced with observations about the way a scientist ought to proceed in the study of his field. If it sounds like we are going overboard in our recommendations of the books by Ratliff and Békésy, you are probably correct, but it is for good reasons.

Finally, the book *Visual Perception* by Cornsweet (1970) shows how to apply the mechanisms of lateral inhibition to the phenomena encountered in visual perception. Cornsweet's book is the best treatment we have yet seen on the operation of the eye at the level of the retinal processes. Moreover, he presents in very thorough and intelligible form the results of the most recent concepts of spatial Fourier analysis to the understanding of such issues as brightness constancy and critical flicker fusion. These are important issues, and the more advanced student would do well to study the latter sections of Cornsweet's book with care. (Cornsweet also provides a unique, highly intelligible treatment of color vision. It might be best, however, not to try to read both his and ours at the same time. We both use different systems to discuss this phenomenon. Although the experienced reader will be able to follow both discussions, the beginning reader will probably get confused.)

The basic references for technical, overall discussions of vision and visual perception at an advanced level are the several relevant chapters in *The Handbook of Experimental Psychology* edited by Stevens (1951), and in the book *Experimental Psychology* by Woodworth and Schlosberg (1954). The entire book edited by Graham (1965) is relevant to vision. These are advanced books, a little bit old, but very thorough.

The experiment on the effects of depth cues on brightness originally was performed by Hochberg and Beck (1954). A more recent examination of this phenomenon can be found in the article by Flock and Freedberg (1970), and although the paper is rather technical, it is worth the effort, since it presents several alternative theories (as well as numerous references).

There are a number of fascinating studies on brightness contrast. A particularly intriguing result is given in Coren (1969), who shows how brightness contrast can change depending upon how a figure is viewed: That is, if an ambiguous figure is given another interpretation, brightness contrasts may be altered. A review of this entire phenomenon can be found in the article by Festinger, Coren, and Rivers (1970). Another important article on a phenomenon commonly known as the Gelb Effect is the analysis by Mershon and Gogel (1970). An excellent book on brightness constancy is the one by Hurvich and Jameson (1966).

Some important visual phenomena not covered in this book are discussed in Hochberg's book *Perception* (1964). In addition, the review article by Harris (1965) discussed the recovery of vision after viewing the world through distorting prisms. This is a particularly intriguing topic, and Harris not only gives a good review, but also provides relevant literature references. The work by Julesz (1960, 1964) provides a particularly novel and important introduction to some of the problems of three-dimensional space perception. His book is especially important (Julesz, 1971) and, moreover, it is thoroughly enjoyable, especially when his three-dimensional images are viewed through the colored lenses that come with the book. Enright's (1970) article on the illusion known as the "Pulfrich Pendulum" is also important here, combining as it does the discussion of a visual illusion, discussion of the perception of depth, and computations on the rate of response of the retina to visual signals. As usual, the *Annual Review of Psychology* provides a good access into material on this topic: the article by Bishop and Henry "Spatial Vision" (1971) is relevant.

Color vision

Color vision is an enigma. Although it clearly is a very important topic, books which treat this in an intelligible manner are difficult or impossible to find. Cornsweet (1970) comes close, but his treatment should not be mixed with ours, as we have already noted. Graham's book (1965) contains most of the important information, but it will take a lot of hard work to understand it. Perhaps the best treatment is that by LeGrand (1957). Unfortunately, he does not include much of the modern work. But perhaps the best thing to do is to start with LeGrand and then work your way through the literature from there.

A good review of the literature can be found in the *Annual Review of Psychology* article, "Color Vision" by Ripps and Weale (1969). The book by Wyszecki and Stiles (1967) contains a good compilation of the facts of color vision. Some representative papers are by DeValois and Jacobs on primate color vision (1968), and Jameson and Hurvich on opponent color-processes (1962).

FIGURE 1-46 *If you stare at the center of this picture from a distance of approximately 6 inches* without moving your eyes, *the circles will fade away. For an explanation, see Figure 1-47. (Peter Sedgley, Looking Glass Suite, No. 9, Lithograph. Collection: D. A. Norman.)*

FIGURE 1-49 *Stare at the black dot in the left panel with head and eyes steady until the whole figure starts to shimmer. Then look at the right black dot, the one in the white area. You will see pink hearts on a greenish background. (It helps to blink a few times to get the afterimage started.) The pink is an afterimage. The green is "induced." (Modified from The Color Tree, Interchemical Corp., New York, 1965.)*

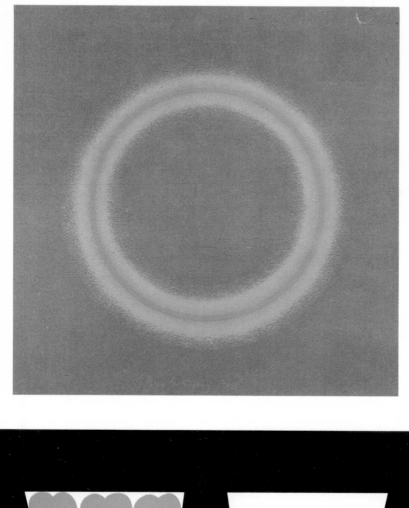

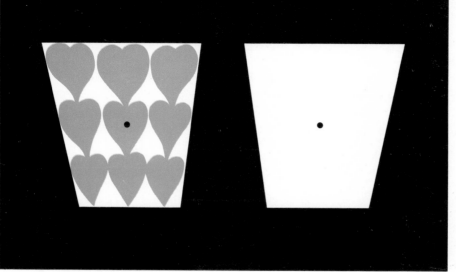

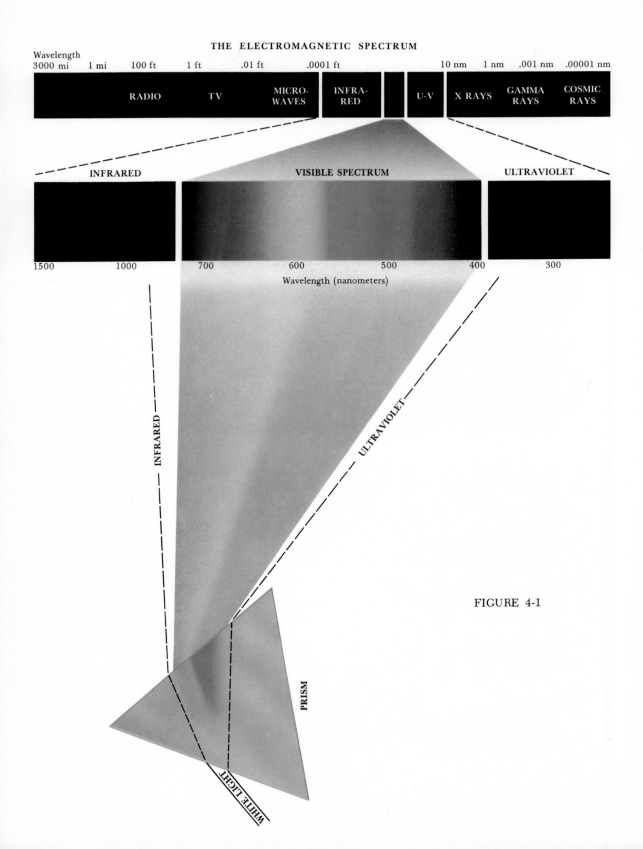

THE ELECTROMAGNETIC SPECTRUM

FIGURE 4-1

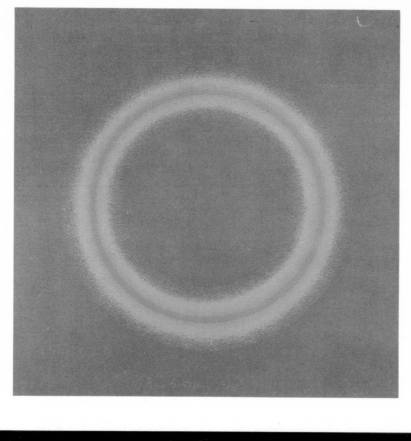

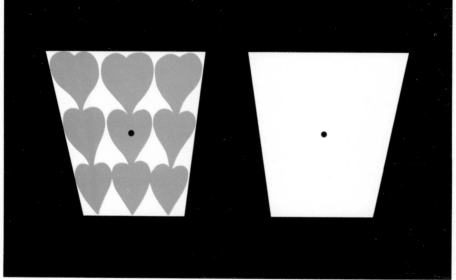

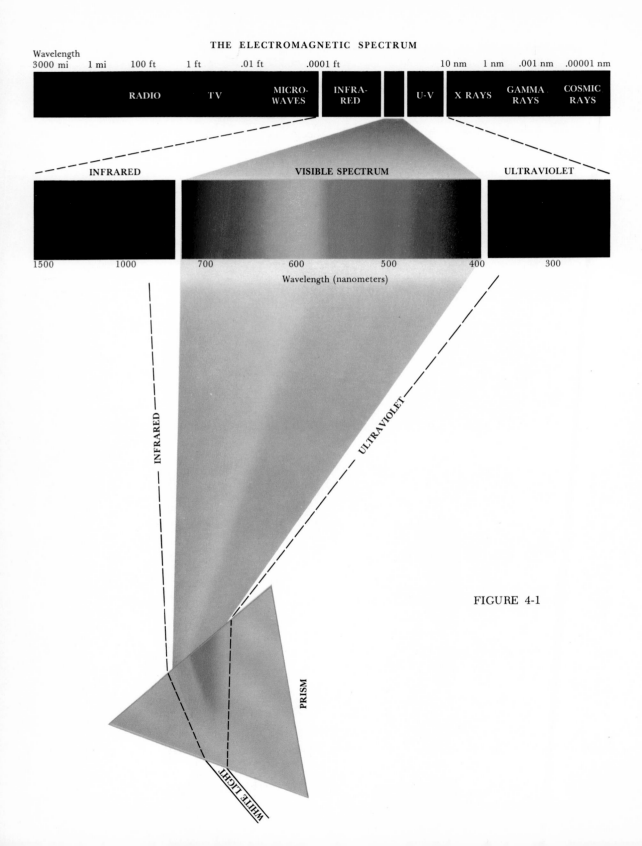

THE ELECTROMAGNETIC SPECTRUM

FIGURE 4-1

Purkinje Shift: *The difference between night and day visual sensitivity* FIGURE 5-19
(red and cone vision). Normally, the red and blue flowers are equally
visible, with the red appearing brighter than the blue. The two are
seen with cone vision. After about 5 min of viewing the picture in
very dim light, the red flower will no longer be visible: only the blue
will be seen. If the light is dim enough, only rod vision will be involved.

   The effect can be speeded by viewing the flowers out of the corner
of the visual field by fixating on the center of the red flower. In this way,
the red falls upon the area of the retina with increased density of cones
and the blue falls upon the area with increased density of rods. (Modi-
fied from The Color Tree, Interchemical Corp., New York, 1965.)

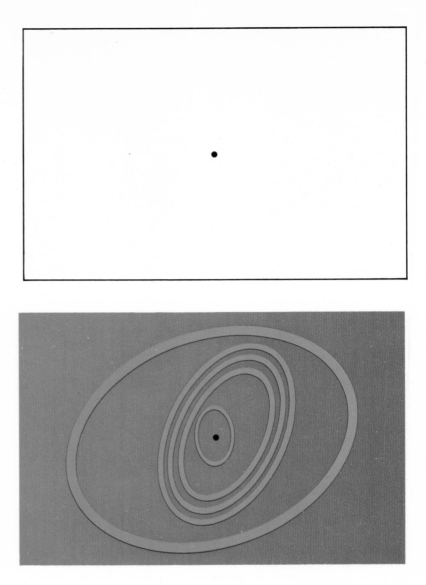

FIGURE 5-31 *Stare at the fixation point in the middle of the bottom picture. The figure will shimmer and parts will disappear. Now look at the fixation point in the rectangle above. The rings and background will be seen in complementary colors. (Modified from The Color Tree, Interchemical Corp., New York, 1965.)*

The auditory system

The human ear is surprisingly complicated. From outward appearances, it consists mainly of a tube between the outside world and a small internal membrane, the eardrum. Vibrations in the air cause the eardrum to vibrate. These outermost parts of the ear, the ear flap, the ear canal, and the eardrum, however, are the least important components for the ear's successful operation. The vibration of the eardrum in response to changing air pressure is only the beginning of a long chain of events, which ultimately produces our perception of sound.

The process of getting the sound through the ear to create neurological signals involves a rather intricately detailed set of steps. Examine Figures 6-1 and 6-2. First, the sound wave arriving at the ear travels down the auditory canal and causes the membrane at the end—*the eardrum*— to vibrate. This vibration is transmitted through the three small bones *(tympanic membrane)* of the middle ear to another membrane, the *oval window*. This window *(hammer & anvil to the stirrup)* is the opening into the bony, spiral shaped structure of the inner ear, *the cochlea*. Fluids in the cochlea are set into motion by the movements of the oval window and, in turn, cause a membrane that lies along *→ The Basilar Membrane* the spiral inside the cochlea to vibrate. The vibration pattern of this last membrane, *the basilar membrane*, is sensed by several rows of hairs *organ of Corti* that line the membrane, causing the cells to which they are connected to create the neural impulses that carry the acoustic information to the brain. Each component in this strange path has a good reason for its presence. Our task is to discover how each of these components contributes to the development of the neural message sent along the auditory nerve to the brain and then, how that message is decoded into the psychological experiences of sound, of music, and of speech.

Sound consists of pressure variations. When an object "makes a sound" it causes pressure waves to propagate out through the surrounding medium. The sound pressures measured some distance away from the sound source create an imperfect image of the sound pressures initially generated. In part this is because the wave has been attenuated by its travel through the air and, in part, because of various types of reflections and refractions caused by objects encountered in the path of the wave.

Pressure variations: sound

The frequency of sound

For the simplest kind of sound, the pressure variations in the air over time produce a waveform that looks like that in Figure 6-3. To describe this waveform (a *sine wave*) three things must be specified: how rapidly it is varying (its *frequency*); how great a pressure it produces (its *amplitude*); when it starts (its *phase*). In general (with exceptions that will be described later), the larger the amplitude of the sine wave,

FIGURE 6-1

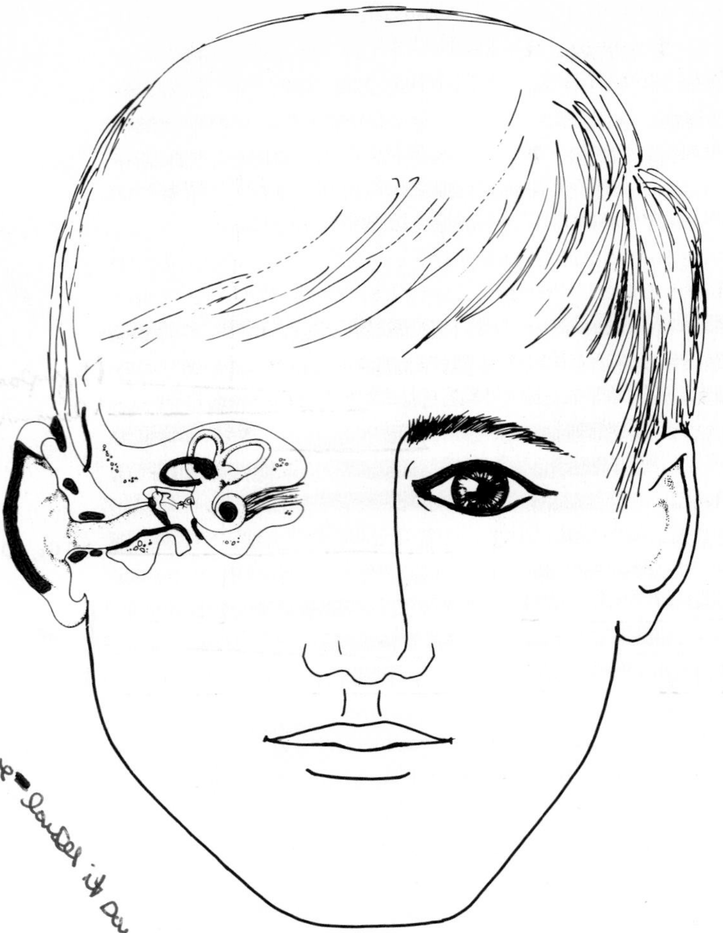

[handwritten marginalia:] Hier Amplitude of Sin Wave = Louder it Sounds
Hier Frequency = Hier Pitch
Hz cycles P/sec. - frequency

the louder it sounds; the higher the frequency, the higher the pitch. A sine wave with a frequency of 261.63 cycles per second, for example, has a pitch of middle C on the musical scale. One *cycle per second* is called one *Hertz* (Hz).[1]

Although the description of the variations in sound pressure with time produce a complete description of the sound, it is often more convenient to describe the wave in an entirely different fashion. Look at the sound pressure patterns shown in Figures 6-4 and 6-5. These complex

[1] The unit of frequency comes from the name of the German physicist, Heinrich R. Hertz (1857–1894). Frequency is often specified in *kilohertz* (*kHz*), where 1 kHz is equal to 1000 Hz.

The true sense organs of the ear are the Cochlea (Hearing) & Semicircular Canals (Sense of Balance). Other parts transmit waves to Cochlea. The Semicircular canals are filled w/ fluid & contain hair cells that are stimulated by movements of the fluid & convey info. about movements of the head.

FIGURE 6-2

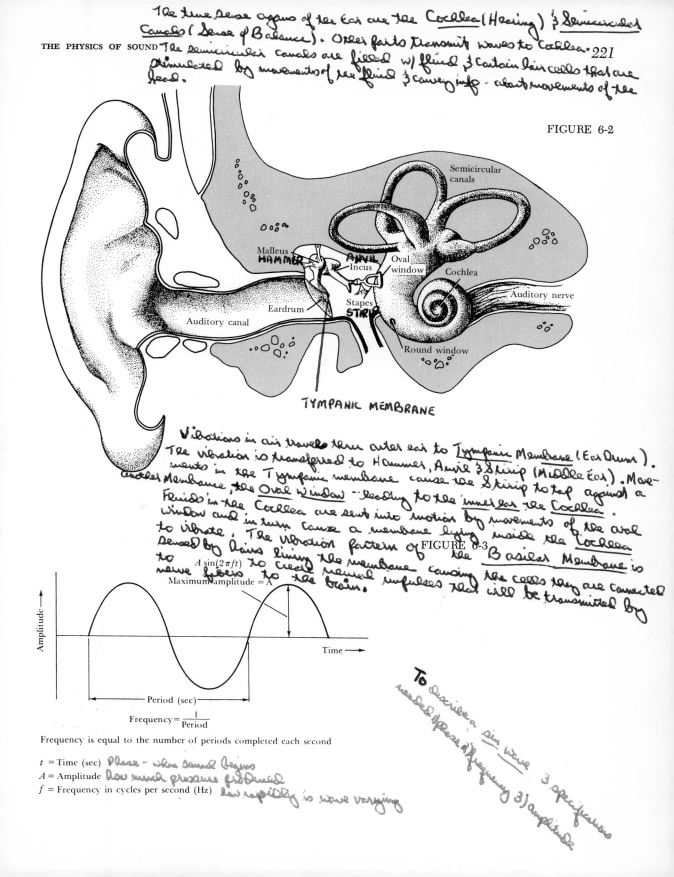

Semicircular canals

Malleus
HAMMER
Incus
ANVIL
Oval window
Cochlea

Stapes
STIRUP

Auditory nerve

Eardrum

Auditory canal

Round window

TYMPANIC MEMBRANE

Vibrations in air travels thru outer ear to Tympanic Membrane (Ear Drum). The vibration is transferred to Hammer, Anvil & Stirrup (Middle Ear). Movements in the Tympanic membrane cause the Stirrup to tap against another Membrane, the Oval Window — leading to the inner ear the Cochlea. Fluids in the Cochlea are sent into motion by movements of the oval window and in turn cause a membrane lying inside the Cochlea to vibrate. The vibration pattern of the Basilar Membrane is sensed by hairs lining the membrane causing the cells they are connected to to create neural impulses that will be transmitted by nerve fibers to the brain.

FIGURE 6-3

$A \sin(2\pi ft)$

Maximum amplitude = A

Amplitude →

Time →

Period (sec)

$$\text{Frequency} = \frac{1}{\text{Period}}$$

Frequency is equal to the number of periods completed each second

t = Time (sec) Phase — when sound begins

A = Amplitude how much pressure produced

f = Frequency in cycles per second (Hz) how rapidly is wave varying

To describe a sin wave is needed 1) Phase 2) frequency 3) amplitude

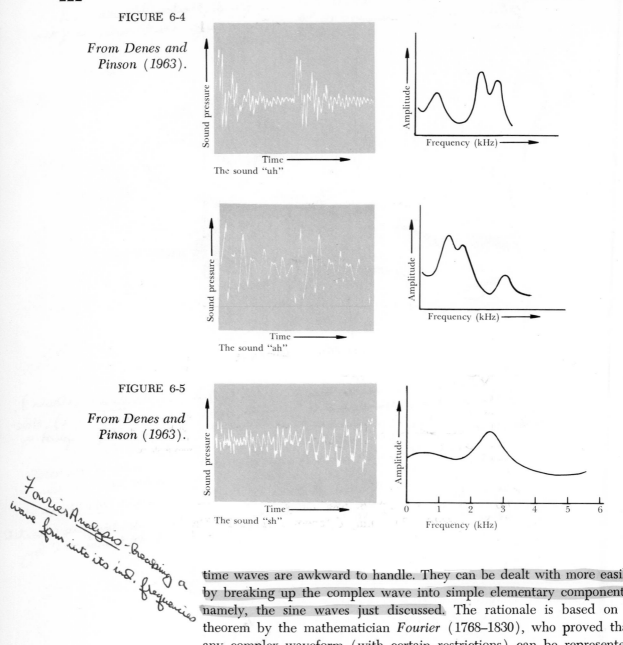

FIGURE 6-4

*From Denes and
Pinson (1963).*

The sound "uh"

The sound "ah"

FIGURE 6-5

*From Denes and
Pinson (1963).*

The sound "sh"

*Fourier Analysis – breaking a
wave form into its ind. frequencies*

time waves are awkward to handle. They can be dealt with more easily
by breaking up the complex wave into simple elementary components,
namely, the sine waves just discussed. The rationale is based on a
theorem by the mathematician *Fourier* (1768–1830), who proved that
any complex waveform (with certain restrictions) can be represented
by a combination of sinusoidal waves of specific frequencies and intensities: The decomposition of a waveform into its individual component
Figure 6-6   frequencies is called *Fourier analysis*.

Representing complex waves by their sinusoidal components seems also
to be most compatible with the way the ear actually deals with sounds.

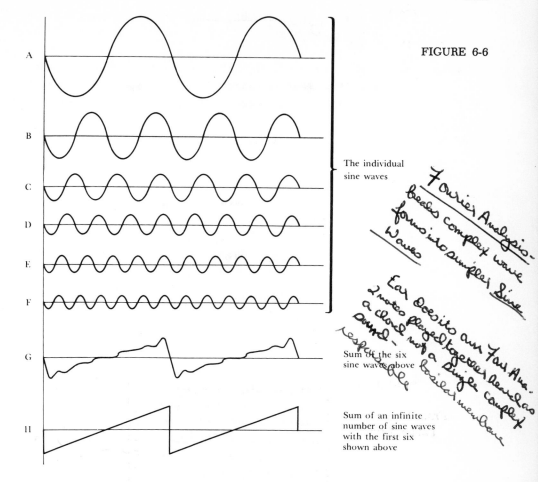

A

B

The individual
sine waves

C

D

E

F

G

Sum of the six
sine waves above

H

Sum of an infinite
number of sine waves
with the first six
shown above

FIGURE 6-6

*Fourier Analysis -
breaks complex wave
forms into simpler Sine
Waves*

*Ear does/to an Fou Ana -
2 notes played together heard as
a chord, not a single complex
sound - basilar membrane
responsible*

In fact, the ear appears to do a rough Fourier analysis on its own. If a 440-Hz tone (A above middle C) is played together with a 698-Hz tone (an F), the combination is heard as two notes played together as a chord, not as a single complicated sound. This fact first impressed the German physicist Georg Ohm (1787–1854), and the correspondence between what is heard and the representation of sounds in terms of its separate frequency components has come to be known as Ohm's Law. (This is the Ohm who proclaimed the Ohm's Law of electricity; same Ohm, different law.) Things are quite different with light. When a light of a frequency that looks red (a wavelength of 671 nm) is mixed with a light of a frequency that looks green (a wavelength of 536 nm), the resulting mixture is a light that looks yellow (a wavelength of 589 nm). Unlike the auditory system, the visual system does not keep separate the different frequencies impinging upon it: Visual wave-

*Ohms Law - corespondence
between whats heard & the representation of sounds in terms of
separate frequency components / its*

forms are combined by the eye, leaving no trace of the individual components.

The intensity of sound As is true with light intensities, the difference in sound intensity between the weakest sound that can be heard and a sound producing physical pain is immense. At 2000 Hz, for example, the most intense sound that

Table 6-1

Sound	Intensity (dB)
	200
Manned spacecraft launch (from 150 feet)	• 180
	160
Pain threshold	•
	140
Loud thunder: rock band	•
	120
Shouting	• 100
Conversation	• 80
	60
	40
Soft whisper	•
	20
Threshold of hearing at 1000 Hz	• 0

Sound	Frequency (Hz)
Lowest note on piano	27.5
Lowest note of bass singer	100
Lowest note on clarinet	104.8
Middle C on piano	261.6
Standard tuning pitch (A above middle C)	440
Upper range of soprano	1,000
Highest note on piano	4,180
Harmonics of musical instruments	10,000
Limit of hearing for older persons	12,000
Limit of hearing	16,000–20,000

is tolerable is about one thousand billion times more intense than the weakest detectable sound. This enormous range of intensities makes it inconvenient to describe sound intensities directly. The range is compressed by describing sound intensities in *decibels*.

Table 6-1

DECIBELS

1. Doubling (or halving) the ratio of signal intensities adds (subtracts) 3 dB.
2. Multiplying (or dividing) the ratio of signal intensities by 10 adds (subtracts) 10 dB.
3. If two sounds are separated by $10n$ dB, their intensity ratio is 10^n. For example, a 60-dB difference in the intensities of two sounds means that one sound is 10^6 (1 million) times more intense than the other.
4. Since decibels refer to the ratio of two intensities, to say that a sound has a level of 65 dB is completely meaningless unless the comparison sound is known. Generally, whenever you see statements of this form, it means that the sound is 65 dB more intense than the international standard reference level of .0002 dynes cm^{-2}. This standard is a very low intensity of sound. It is, approximately, the minimum intensity of sound that can be detected by a human listener for a sound of 1000 Hz.

Decibels

Number of dB = $10 \log (I/I_0)$

I/I_0	dB	I/I_0	dB
0.0001	−40	10000.0	40
0.001	−30	1000.0	30
0.010	−20	100.0	20
0.032	−15	31.6	15
0.10	−10	10.0	10
0.13	−9	7.9	9
0.16	−8	6.3	8
0.20	−7	5.0	7
0.25	−6	4.0	6
0.32	−5	3.2	5
0.40	−4	2.5	4
0.50	−3	2.0	3
0.63	−2	1.6	2
0.79	−1	1.3	1
1.00	0	1.0	0

Decibels — measurements used to compress huge range of intensities in frequency the ear can pick up

dB's refer to ratio of 2 intensities

THE MECHANICS OF THE EAR

The inner ear

To the psychologist, the most important part of the ear is the tiny snail-shaped bony structure in the inner ear called the *cochlea.* The cochlea is a tube, coiled up $2\frac{1}{2}$ times (in man) and filled with a saline solution. In man, the cochlea is about the size of a sugar cube—about .2 inches long and .4 inches wide.

There are two openings in the bone that encloses the cochlea. One, a small membrane called the *oval window* is connected to the last bone in the lever chain of the middle ear. Vibrations from the eardrum via the middle ear bones pass into the cochlea through this membrane. Because the cochlea is filled with an incompressible fluid, some means must be found for relieving the pressures generated at the oval window. This is done with another small opening in the bone structure, also covered by a thin membrane. This is the opening at the rear of the cochlea—the *round window.* [You can remember which window is which by a simple mnemonic device: The *O*pening into the cochlea is the *O*val window (**O**); the window at the *R*ear is the *R*ound window (**R**).]

Figures 6-7 & 6-8

Inside the cochlea is a highly sophisticated mechanism for converting the incoming pressure variations into the electrical signal of the auditory nerve. It is easier to examine this mechanism if we unwind the cochlea

Cochlea - saline solution inside an incompressible fluid, needing a means for relieving pressures generated at oval window we come to the round window the opening at the rear of the Cochlea.
Oval Window & Round Window enclose Cochlea

FIGURE 6-7

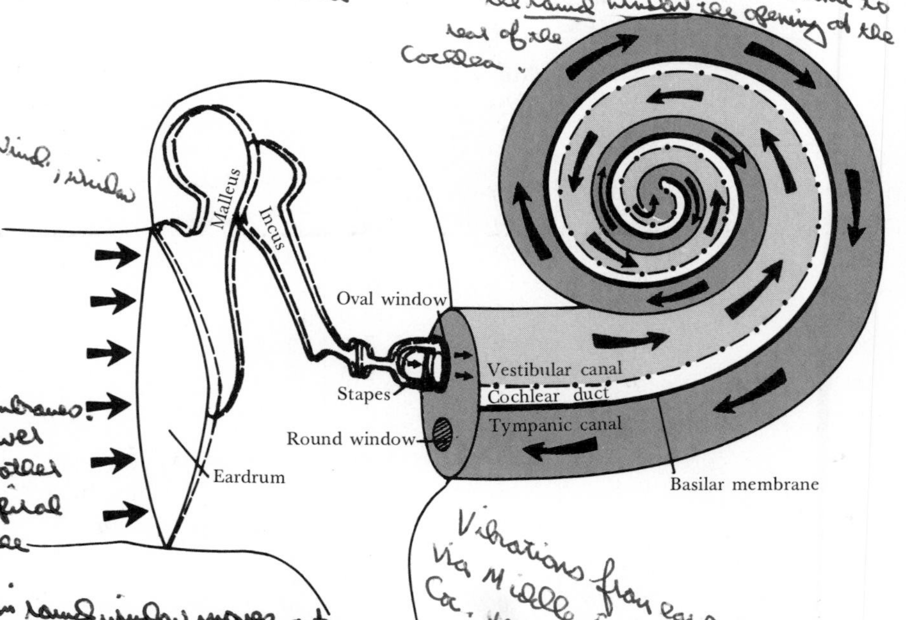

Opening to Co. Oval Wind., window at Rear is Round

Cochlea: 3 fluid filled canals separated by membranes. At base of the upper & lower canals connected w/ each other at the far end of the spiral are membranes called the oval & round windows.

As oval window moves in round window moves out keeping pressure equal. Hearing really depends on movements of fluid stimulating hearing cells.

The central canal contains organ of Corti which rests on the basilar memb. The movement of fluid along outer surface of central canal causes vibrations in the basilar memb. which in turn stimulate ind. sensory cells, hair cells, w/in O. of C.

Vibrations from eardrum via Middle Ear Bones pass into Co. thru Oval Window

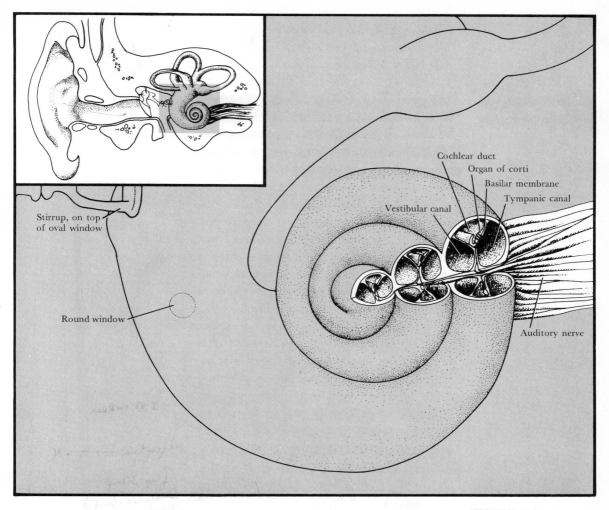

Cochlear duct
Organ of corti
Basilar membrane
Tympanic canal
Vestibular canal
Stirrup, on top
of oval window
Round window
Auditory nerve

FIGURE 6-8

(which is possible artistically, but not physically) so that you can see
inside, as is done in Figure 6-9.

The two membranes running the length of the cochlea divide it into
three different regions, each of which is filled with fluid. The membrane
that has most importance for our discussion is the *basilar membrane*.
This membrane extends all the way from the start of the cochlea (the
base), where the middle ear bone vibrates the oval window, to very
near the end of the inner tip (the *apex*) of the coil. At the apex there
is a small space between the membrane and the walls of the cochlea.

Figure 6-10

When stretched out, the basilar membrane is about 1.4 inches long, with a width that increases from the oval window to the apex. This increase in width plays an important role in its operation.

Movements of the basilar membrane

Pressure exerted inward at the oval window produces a pressure in the fluids above the basilar membrane that is applied, essentially, instantaneously across the whole length of the membrane. (The pressure wave requires only about 20 millionths of a second to travel the length of the cochlea.) Thus, the pattern of activity produced in the basilar membrane does not depend upon which end of the cochlea is stimulated. If the system were set into motion at the apex rather than the oval window it would work just as well.

The basilar membrane itself does not react immediately to the pressure that is applied to it. As one watches the membrane where the oval window begins vibrating there appears to be a traveling wave: First it bulges at the end by the oval window, then the bulge gradually travels up the membrane toward the apex. It takes several milliseconds for the bulge to go from one end of the basilar membrane to the other. The distance it travels and the speed at which it moves depend upon the frequency of the sound wave.

The traveling bulge results from the elastic properties of the membrane. Remember that the membrane increases in width as it goes from the oval window toward the apex. It also increases in stiffness, being some 100 times stiffer at the apex than at the oval window. These factors, combined with the geometry of the cochlea itself, cause the size of the bulge produced by a sound wave to increase gradually as

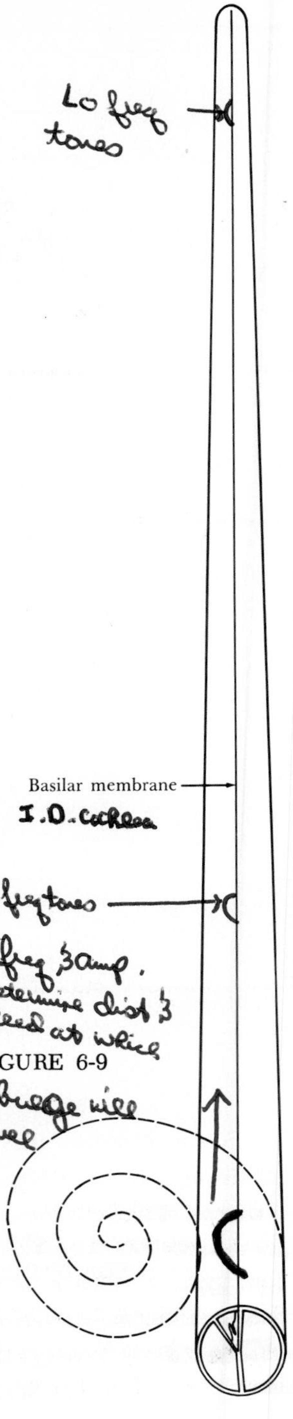

Lo freq tones

Basilar membrane

I.O. cochlea

Hi freq tones

freq 3 amp.
Determine dist 3
speed at which
the bulge will
travel

FIGURE 6-9

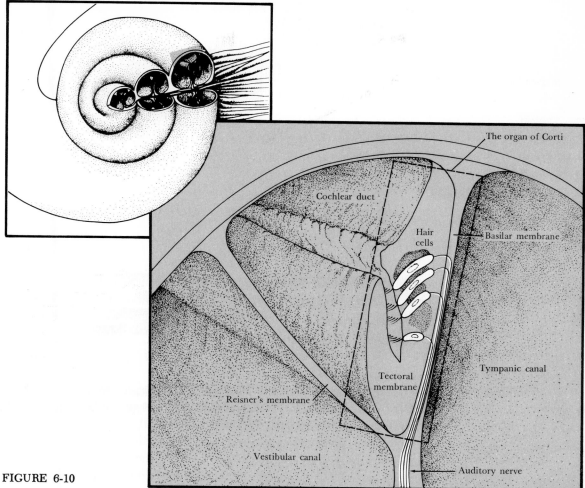

The organ of Corti

Cochlear duct

Hair cells

Basilar membrane

Tympanic canal

Tectoral membrane

Reisner's membrane

Vestibular canal

Auditory nerve

FIGURE 6-10

the wave moves out from the round window. The point along the membrane at which it reaches its maximum size depends on the frequency of the sound. The displacement then drops off rapidly as the wave continues on to the end of the membrane. For high-frequency tones, the maximum displacement of the basilar membrane occurs near the oval window, and there is very little activity in the remainder of the membrane. For low-frequency tones, the bulge travels all the way to the apex, reaching its peak just before the end of the membrane.

Figures 6-11 & 6-12

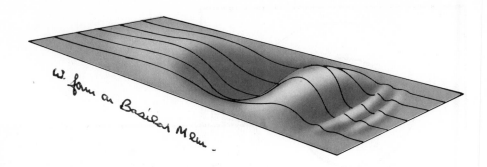

W. form on Basilar Mem.

FIGURE 6-11   *After Rasmussen and Windle (1960).*

The vibration pattern converts different sound frequencies into activity at different locations along the basilar membrane. This recoding of the frequency of an acoustic signal into a particular place of vibration along the basilar membrane is what is meant by the statement, "The ear performs a Fourier analysis of the incoming signal."

The hair cells

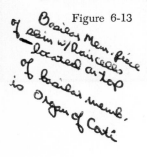

Basilar Mem. piece of skin w/ hair cells located on top of basilar memb, is Organ of Corti

Figure 6-13

The basilar membrane is really a piece of skin and, like skin, it has hair cells attached to it. These hair cells are part of a complex structure called the *organ of Corti,* located along the top of the membrane. In the human, there are approximately 25,000 of these hair cells arranged into two subdivisions, divided by an arch. The cells on the side of the arch closest to the outside of the cochlea are called *outer hair cells* and are arranged in rows three to five abreast. The hair cells on the other side of the arch are called *inner hair cells.* They are usually in a single row. There are some 25,000 outer cells, and any given cell may have as many as a hundred hairs protruding from it. There are only about 3500 inner hair cells.

As you can see from the way they are sandwiched between the two membranes in the organ of Corti, any movement in the basilar membrane causes the hair cells to twist and bend. Moreover, since the membranes are anchored, there will be more movement associated with the outer hair cells than with the inner cells. The stresses and strains exerted on the hair cells initiates neural activity in the fibers connected to them, starting the flow of electrical impulses up the auditory nerve.

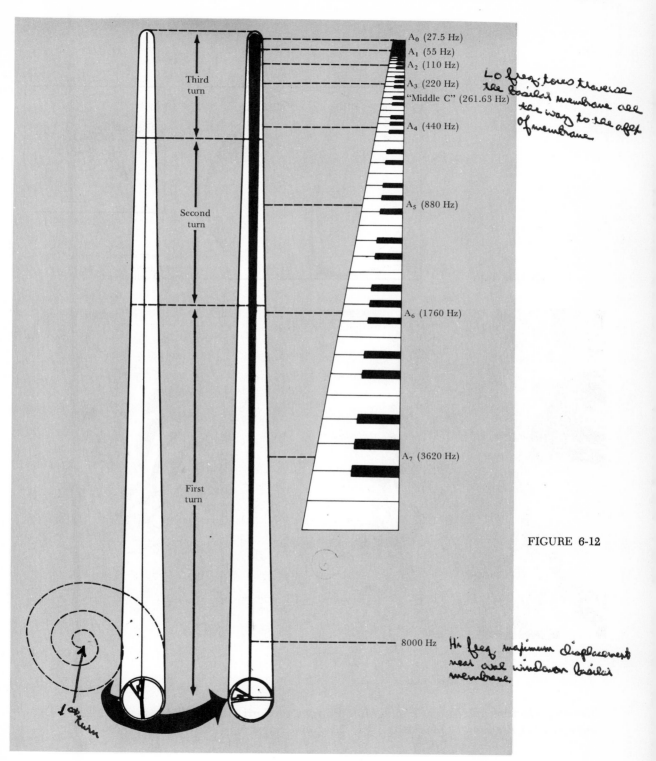

FIGURE 6-12

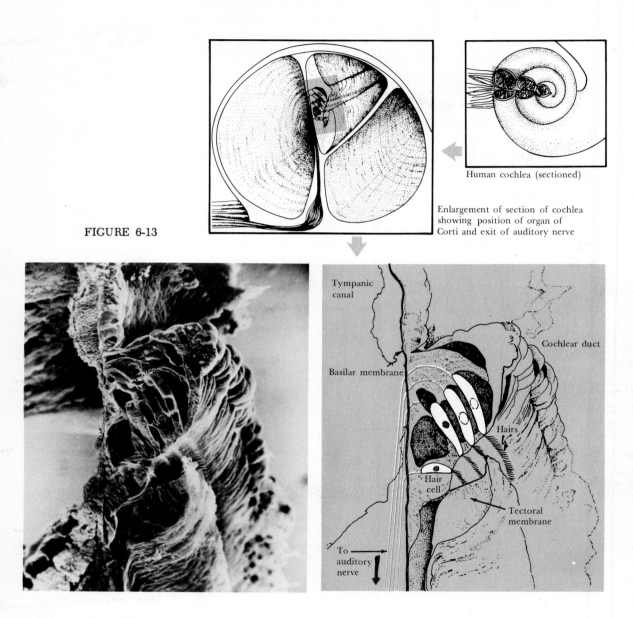

FIGURE 6-13

Human cochlea (sectioned)

Enlargement of section of cochlea
showing position of organ of
Corti and exit of auditory nerve

Tympanic
canal

Basilar membrane

Cochlear duct

Hairs

Hair
cell

Tectoral
membrane

To
auditory
nerve

Scanning electron microscope photograph of organ of Corti. ×370. Photograph from Bredberg, Lindeman, Ades, West, and Engström (1970).

No matter how elegant the mechanical responses of the ear, they would be of no value unless there were some way of converting this activity into signals that can be used by the nervous system. The mechanical responses convert auditory frequency and intensity into vibration patterns along the basilar membrane. This information must now be analyzed by the nerve cells, which carry the signal along the pathway to the brain.

ELECTRICAL RESPONSES TO SOUND

With a careful surgical preparation, a tiny electrode can be inserted into the auditory nerve so that it records the impulses flowing down a single auditory fiber. The first thing that is noticed is that this fiber is not quiet. Even when no sounds are presented it responds sporadically at anywhere up to 150 impulses per second. This *background* or *spontaneous* firing in the absence of any external signal is a characteristic of almost all types of sensory neurons.

Tuning curves

The first step in investigating the neuron is to determine what kind of signal makes it respond. We start by presenting a pure tone of moderate intensity and some high frequency, say 10,000 Hz, and then we slowly lower the frequency. At first, the neuron does not seem to notice the tone at all; it continues firing at its spontaneous rate. As the frequency comes within a certain critical range, the neuron's response will increase, reaching a peak at a particular signal frequency called the *critical frequency*. As we continue to lower the frequency, the activity of the neuron again becomes less vigorous, until it finally goes back to its spontaneous background rate. The response of the unit to different frequencies looks like this:

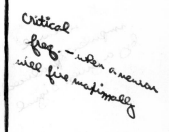

Critical freq. – when a neuron will fire maximally

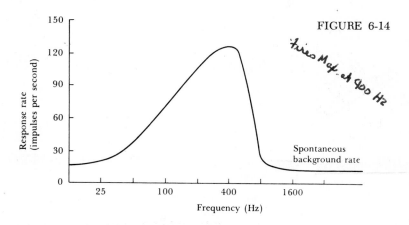

FIGURE 6-14

fires Max. at 400 Hz

This particular unit appears to be most sensitive to a tone whose frequency is 400 Hz. For frequencies higher than 400 Hz, its response rate drops off rather rapidly. For lower frequencies, the response rate changes more slowly with changing frequencies.

This is exactly the response pattern we expect if the neuron being monitored is reacting directly to the amount of activity in a local region of the basilar membrane. Suppose that the neuron is recording the responses of hair cells in a region about 24 mm from the oval window. The maximum vibration of the membrane occurs at this point where a 400-Hz tone is presented. But there will be some activity at this point when frequencies other than 400 Hz are presented. Here is a diagram of the amplitude of the vibration for frequencies ranging from 25 to 1600 Hz. On the right, the amplitude on the membrane is shown as a function of frequency.

FIGURE 6-15

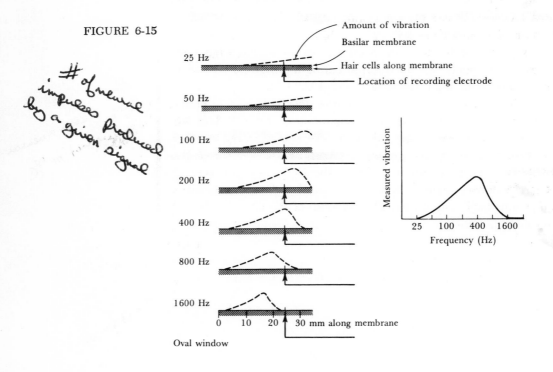

# of neural impulses produced by a given signal

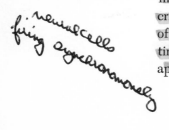

Temporal coding in
neural responses

neural cells firing synchronously

So far, we have been concerned only with the number of neural impulses produced by a given signal. The temporal patterns in the activity of individual neurons are also important. Consider a neural cell with a critical frequency of 500 Hz. This signal goes through a complete cycle of sound pressures in 2 msec. The impulses from the cell mirror the time properties of the critical frequency: The interval between pulses is approximately 2 msec: The cell fires in synchrony with its signal. Sometimes a pulse will fail to appear at the right time, but when it does reappear, it will again be in synchrony with the repeated cycles of the external signal. In short, a 500-Hz tone tends to produce a regular response of 500 impulses per second.

Even if the cell cannot fire as rapidly as its critical frequency, it still maintains synchrony. Suppose a cell with critical frequency of 500 Hz can only manage a maximum of 250 or 125 impulses per second. It will respond at some frequency that is a rational divisor of the signal frequency, say at 250, 125, or even 67.5 impulses per second. It will not respond to a 500-Hz tone at 73 or 187 impulses per second.

This synchronized firing might be expected from a consideration of the vibration pattern of the basilar membrane. When the membrane is moving up in response to a pressure change, it bends the hair cells sandwiched between it and the membrane above, initiating the neural impulse. No response occurs when the membrane moves down. Upward movement is produced when the pressure in the fluids above the membrane is reduced, which happens as the oval window is pulled out by the low-pressure (rarefaction) phase of the signals.

The ability of individual neurons to follow the pressure changes of an incoming signal suggests a way of coding frequency. Signal frequency can be determined directly from the impulse rate or from the average interval between pulses. The fact that individual fibers may not be able to keep up with the pressure changes in a given signal (particularly at higher frequencies) is no problem. A large number of fibers are involved in monitoring any given region of the basilar membrane. An individual nerve may miss a few cycles, but its neighbors that are responding to the same frequency will probably respond to these missing components. When the responses of all the units are considered together, there should be a burst of impulses for every rarefaction phase of the signal.

This is precisely what is seen in physiological recordings. The activity rises and falls regularly and in synchrony with the pressure changes in the signal. The auditory nerve seems to be able to follow signals with frequencies as high as 3000–4000 Hz; such frequencies are well above the response rate that can be achieved by any individual unit. Beyond 4000 Hz, the regular cyclic response in the auditory nerve breaks down into a disorganized, continuous impulse flow.

Responses of neurons in the acoustic nerve to changing intensities are much less complex than their response patterns to changing frequency. Basically, if the frequency is held constant while intensity increases, the response rate of the units goes up. Of course, it cannot go up in-

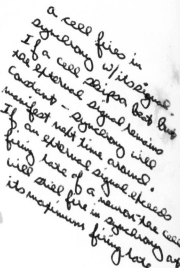

a cell fires in synchrony w/ its signal. If a cell skips a beat but the external signal remains constant — synchrony will manifest next time around. If an external signal exceeds an external signal exceeds firing rate of a neuron the cell will still fire in synchrony at its maximum firing rate

"Volley Theory"

Figure 6-16

Coding of intensity information

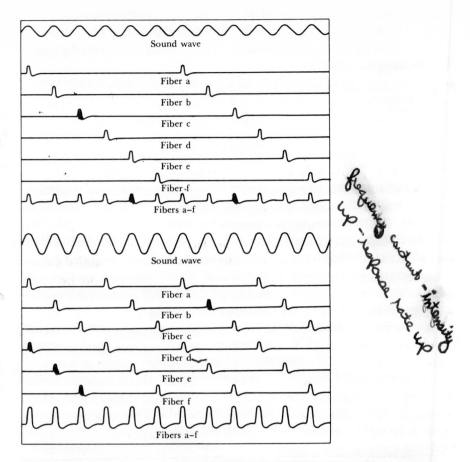

FIGURE 6-16   *The "volley" theory. Each cycle of the sound wave elicits a response in at least one fiber in the array, so that the stimulus frequency is represented in the combined pattern. At higher stimulus intensities (below), more than one fiber responds at a given cycle. From Wever (1970).*

definitely. In fact, an individual cell may start off at a spontaneous level of some 200 responses per second, increase its rate to, say, 300 responses per second when the intensity is changed by 10 dB, but show no further increases in rate with additional increases in intensity. Thus, the range over which most cells code intensity in the signal is relatively small compared to the total range of hearing. Moreover, there is an enormous variability in both the baseline rates and the reactions of individual cells to increases in the intensity of the signal.

Of course, a cell's increase in its firing rate must still maintain synchrony with the sound wave. Thus, if an individual cell has a spontaneous firing rate of 200 impulses per second, it will react to a sound first by changing the spontaneous, random firing into one synchronized with the signal, and then by increasing the number of neural impulses it produces to the sound—always, however, maintaining synchrony.

When the basic frequency and intensity information has been encoded by the auditory nerves, the signal is finally on its way to the brain. Several different things are done as the signal makes its way up. Specific auditory information is extracted, localization of the sound source takes place, and a rough determination of the sound's loudness and pitch components are extracted.

As the previous chapters have shown, neurons in the visual system react to significant features in the visual signal. They detect lines and angles, movement, and color. There is a heirarchy of specialized neural detectors, from center–surround units, through simple, complex, and hypercomplex cells. But what of the auditory system? What happens to the auditory message as it makes its way from the ear to the brain?

The answer is disappointing, for very little is known of the nature of auditory neural processing. In some sense, our lack of knowledge reflects our lack of understanding of the analysis of auditory patterns. With visual signals, it is quite obvious that lines and contours, angles, and movement must play an important role in pattern recognition. But what are the analogous features for auditory patterns? Are they pure tones or complex ones, steady sounds or changing ones? We just do not know.

The nature of human speech makes it appear reasonably definite that there are specialized sound detectors for dealing with it. The whole nature of speech seems geared to the peculiarities of the vocal and hearing apparatus, but just how speech features might be extracted by auditory mechanisms is not known. True, most physiological experiments in hearing are performed on cats and monkeys, but even though these animals do not have speech, presumably their auditory mechanisms should show some unique features of their pattern-recognition system.

It is quite clear that some sort of complex analysis must take place by neurons in the auditory cortex. Evidence of a sort comes from the fact that about 40% of the neurons there will not respond to pure tones at all, but only to more complex sounds such as bursts of noise or clicks (Whitfield, 1967). It may be that these neural units are actually designed to respond only to special, unique sounds, but the closest that we have so far been able to approach the proper sound is simply a click or noise burst.

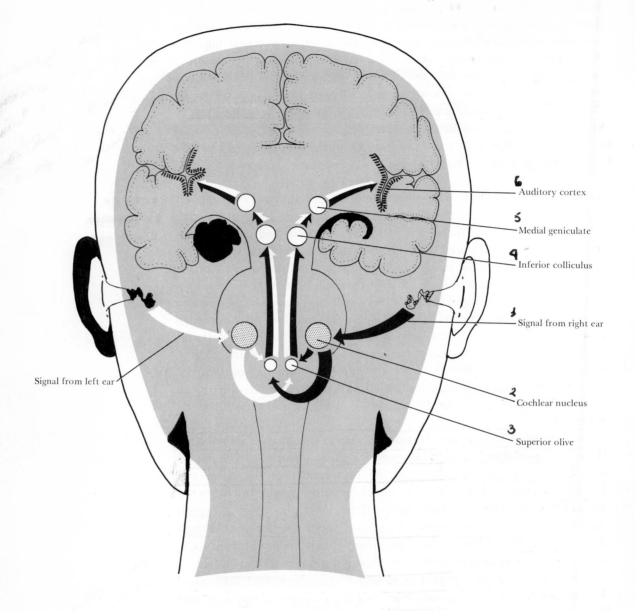

FIGURE 6-17   (a) Above: Pathway to auditory cortex from ear. Backview of brain
with cerebrum sectioned.
(b) Right: View of brainstem, showing locations depicted in (a).

Even the 60% of the neural units that respond to pure tones do not do so in simple ways. Some increase their rate of firing when a tone is presented (an *excitatory* response). Others decrease the rate of firing (an *inhibitory* response). Some respond only when the tone is turned on (an *on* response), others only when the tone is turned off (an *off* response), and still others both when the tone is turned on and again when it is turned off (an *on-off* response) (see Figure 6-18). These responses, of course, are similar to those found in the visual system.

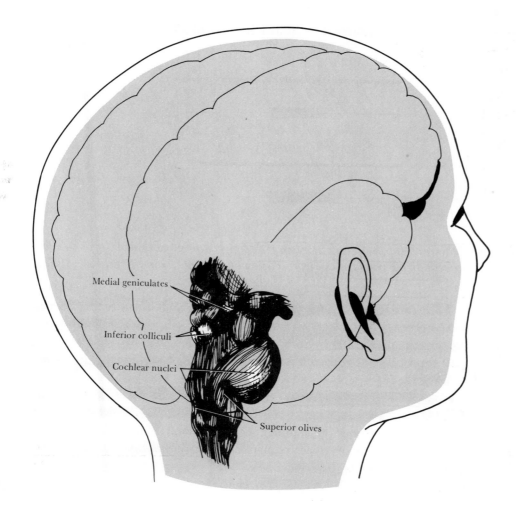

Medial geniculates

Inferior colliculi

Cochlear nuclei

Superior olives

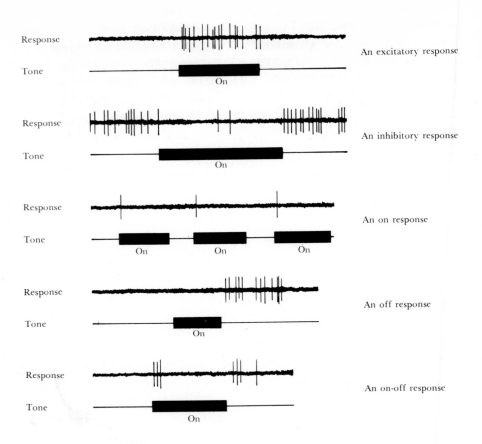

Response — An excitatory response

Tone — On

Response — An inhibitory response

Tone — On

Response — An on response

Tone — On   On   On

Response — An off response

Tone — On

Response — An on-off response

Tone — On

FIGURE 6-18   *Different types of unit response to tonal stimuli obtained from the unanesthetized primary auditory cortex of the cat. From Whitfield (1967).*

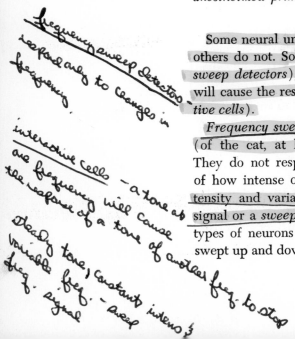

Some neural units in the auditory cortex maintain sharp tuning curves, others do not. Some respond only to changes in frequencies (*frequency sweep detectors*), others have regions wherein a tone at one frequency will cause the response to a tone of another frequency to cease (*interactive cells*).

Frequency sweep detectors.   A number of cells in the auditory cortex (of the cat, at least) seem sensitive only to **changes** in frequencies. They do not respond to a pure tone of constant frequency, regardless of how intense or of what frequency. A steady tone with constant intensity and variable frequency is called either a *frequency modulated* signal or a *sweep frequency* signal. Here is a typical response of specific types of neurons to a sweep frequency signal (the frequency has been swept up and down in a sinewave pattern).

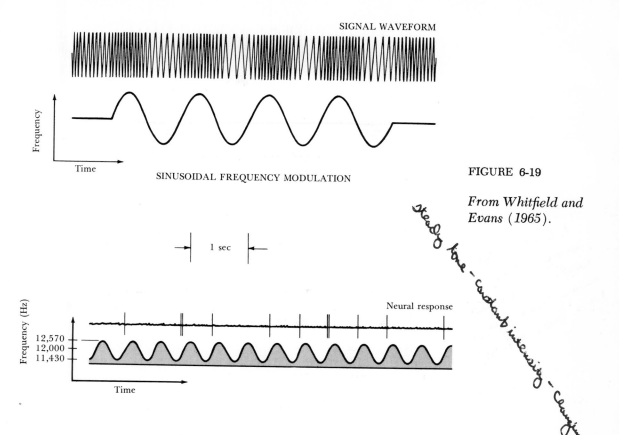

SIGNAL WAVEFORM

SINUSOIDAL FREQUENCY MODULATION

FIGURE 6-19

From Whitfield and Evans (1965).

steady tone - constant intensity - changing freq.

Linear changes in signal frequency produce something that looks like a ramp: a *ramp modulated signal*. A typical signal and the corresponding neural response looks like that in Figure 6-20.

Notice that the particular neural units shown here respond only to changes in frequency in particular directions. With the sinusoidal modulation, the unit shown appears to respond only to increases in signal frequency. With the ramp modulation, two different types of units are shown, one that responds only to increases in frequency, and one that responds only to decreases.

What might the neural circuit look like for these sweep frequency detectors? From a consideration of the pattern that a changing frequency makes on the basilar membrane, we see that a change in frequency creates a movement in the location of maximum stimulation along the membrane. Hence, if we were to build a movement detector for activity along the membrane, connecting together the basic characteristic frequency cells in exactly the same manner as we connected the center–sur-

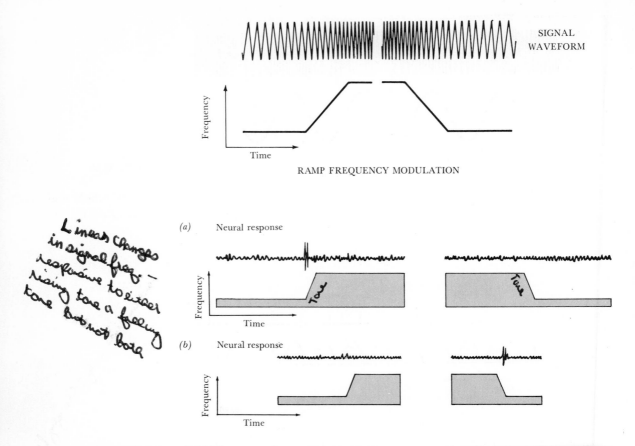

SIGNAL
WAVEFORM

RAMP FREQUENCY MODULATION

(handwritten note in left margin) Linear changes in signal freq — responsive to either rising tone a falling tone But not both

FIGURE 6-20   *(a) The unit fires in response to a rising tone, but not to one falling through the same frequency range, (b) the unit fires in response to a falling tone, but not to a rising one. From Whitfield and Evans (1965).*

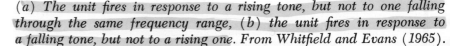

round units in Chapter 2, we would have a frequency sweep detector. Just as the movement detectors were sensitive only to movement in a single direction, so should the frequency sweep detector be sensitive to only increases or decreases in frequency, not both.

Three different types of frequency modulated units have been found in the cat (Whitfield, 1967). They all seem to be sensitive only to frequencies within a certain region, much like the tuning curve characteristics discussed earlier. But rather than responding to any tone within a tuning curve, they respond only to tones such that the direction of frequency change is always either:

1. increasing in frequency;
2. decreasing in frequency;
3. upward in the low-frequency part of the response and downward in the high-frequency part.

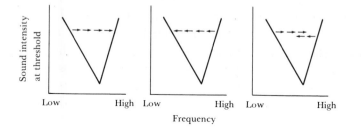

Left: Units responding only to rising tones anywhere within its response area. Center: units responding only to falling tones anywhere within its response area. Right: Units responding to rising tones in low-frequency half of response area and to falling tones in a high-frequency half. From Whitfield and Evans (1965).

FIGURE 6-21

What does the cat do with these sweep frequency detectors? We do not know. We know that bats have an extraordinarily large number of sweep frequency detectors. They appear to be essential to the bat's ability to navigate by echo location: By sending out acoustic signals and analyzing the echos to determine the distance and direction of the objects in the environment. Do humans have and use sweep frequency detectors? Again we do not know. It is possible that such information would be useful for the very complex sound patterns that must be dealt with in order to analyze speech.

The best modern reference for the physiological operation of the auditory system is Whitfield's *The Auditory Pathway* (1967). Kiang's book (1965) is also good, but it is really suitable only for the advanced student of physiological processes. A good introduction to hearing is the text by Stevens and Davis (1938). Even though this book is very old, it has aged well, and many of the basic facts are in it. Similarly, the

SUGGESTED READINGS

Handbook of Experimental Psychology edited by Stevens (1951) is excellent, but both old and more advanced. Much of this chapter has been derived around the work of Whitfield and the chapters in the handbook edited by Stevens. A summary, with emphasis on physiological processing, is given in the book by Gulick (1971).

The works of Georg von Békésy won him a Nobel Prize for his studies of the operation of the inner ear. Anyone who intends to do work in the field of hearing will sooner or later come upon his material. Most of his important articles on hearing are reprinted in Békésy's *Experiments in Hearing* (1960). Békésy's papers are delightful to read because he never sticks to a simple topic, but rather delights in demonstrating how the topic he is discussing relates to a wide variety of other phenomena. His second book, *Sensory Inhibition* (1967), has already been recommended as an essential reference for those interested in the phenomenon of lateral inhibition.

Also see the Suggested Readings for Chapter 7.

7

The dimensions of sound

LOUDNESS

Equiloudness contours
Listening to music
   Loudness compensators
Masking
   The masking experiment
   The mechanism of masking
   Masking of music
The measurement of loudness
   Sones

PITCH

The musical scale
The mel scale
Place theory: position on the basilar membrane
Periodicity pitch
   Loudness and pitch
   The case of the missing fundamental
   Evidence against nonlinearities
Masking the missing fundamental
   The place theory explanation
   The periodicity pitch explanation
     PITCH DISCRIMINATION WITHOUT A BASILAR MEMBRANE
Evidence against the periodicity pitch theory
The duplicity theory of pitch perception

THE CRITICAL BAND
AUDITORY SPACE PERCEPTION

Localization
Binaural interactions
Importance of binaural listening
   Localization
   Masking level difference
   Masking
Recordings
The precedence effect

SUGGESTED READINGS

An orchestra creates a rich auditory experience. Rock groups, music synthesizers, electronic sounds are all combined in experimental works that stimulate the listener. New recording and playback techniques provide the means of recreating for the listener the experiences of the original event, be it a conference, a speech, a musical performance, or even the special effects imagined by creative composers that cannot exist, except through recordings.

Meanwhile, noise sources pollute the environment. The noises from aircraft annoy and disturb, sometimes being simply a tolerable nuisance, other times disrupting ongoing events, sometimes even causing physical damage and mental fatigue.

All these characteristics of sound are within the domain of the psychologist. From a knowledge of the mechanics of the ear, his understanding of the psychological dimensions of pitch and loudness, and his study of the phenomena of masking and auditory space perception he can talk about, explain, and predict many of the attributes of the auditory experience.

In this chapter, we examine some of the rich auditory experiences produced by sounds. We explore in turn four topics: loudness, pitch, the critical band, and auditory spatial perception. With each topic we introduce what has been learned from science and then deduce the practical implications. We examine the role of the four factors on the perceptions of music, speech, and noise. In addition, some of the more technical aspects of sound measurement are described in Appendix A.

The loudness of a tone depends upon both its intensity and its frequency. When frequency is constant, intense sounds appear louder than weak sounds. But when intensity is held constant, very high and very low frequency sounds seem much softer than sounds of intermediate frequency. In the extreme cases, this obviously must be true. Consider a whistle of intermediate frequency at a medium intensity level. Keep the intensity of the whistle constant but change the frequency so that it goes below 20 Hz or above 20,000 Hz (you have to do this electronically—you cannot do it by whistling). At these extreme frequencies, the sound becomes inaudible. Loudness, then, depends upon frequency, if for no other reason than the simple fact that there are limits in the ranges of frequencies to which the ear can respond. But loudness also depends on frequency within the normal hearing range.

LOUDNESS depends on intensity & frequency

freq.-limits

The interaction between frequency and intensity in the perception of loudness can be determined by asking people to compare two tones

Equiloudness contours

that have differing frequencies and intensities. Let one tone be the *standard* and give it a fixed frequency, intensity, and duration: for example, let the standard be a 1000-Hz tone with an intensity of 40 dB presented for .5 sec. Let the second tone be the *comparison* tone. Make it .5-sec long also, but with a frequency different from that of the standard, say 3000 Hz. Now, the task of the listener is to listen alternately to the standard and the comparison tones, adjusting intensity of the comparison until it sounds exactly as loud as the standard. When that is done, set the comparison tone to a different frequency and repeat the whole procedure. The typical result is shown in Figure 7-1: a curve describing the intensity at which tones of various frequencies have the same perceived loudness as the standard. This curve is called an *equiloudness contour*. The level of the standard tone can be called the

FIGURE 7-1

Equiloudness contours from data of Robinson and Dadson (1956).

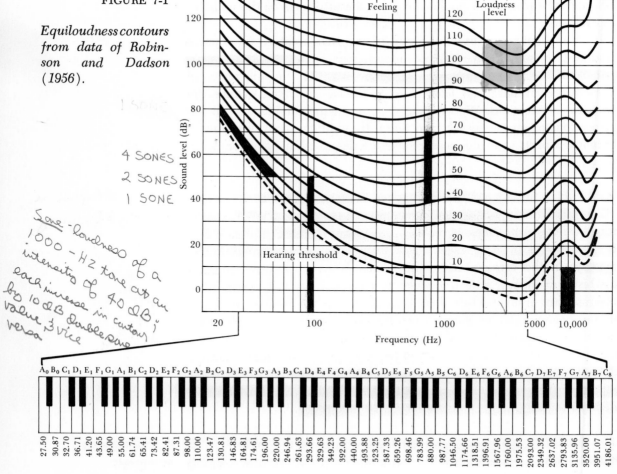

loudness level of the entire curve because it has been constructed by varying the comparison-tone frequency systematically while keeping the loudness of the comparison equal to the loudness of the standard.

Figure 7-1 shows the results of an experiment using many different standards. For each curve, the standard tone was always at a frequency of 1000 Hz, but with different intensities. The curve labeled 40 corresponds to the example just discussed: The standard tone had an intensity of 40 dB and a frequency of 1000 Hz. The curve labeled 100 is an equiloudness contour obtained when different frequencies are compared against a standard tone with an intensity of 100 dB, but still with a frequency of 1000 Hz.

The bottommost contour (the dashed line) shows the absolute sensitivity of the ear to different frequencies. Sounds below this line cannot be heard. Sounds on the line are just barely detectable (and are thus also assumed to be equal in loudness). At the other extreme, the topmost contour, very intense sounds lead, first, to a sensation of "tickling" in the ear and then, as intensity is increased further, to pain. Sounds in these regions can lead to ear damage. (Damage can also occur from sounds of weaker intensity if there is prolonged exposure.) Note that the equiloudness contour at the threshold of pain is much flatter than the contour at the threshold of hearing. If sounds are intense enough, they tend to sound equally loud, regardless of frequency.

Threshold

It may come as a surprise to see where the sounds of the instruments of an orchestra lie on the equiloudness contours. The piano has the widest range of frequencies, going from about 30 to about 4000 Hz. Middle C (C_4)[1] on the piano is about 260 Hz (261.63, to be exact).

Listening to music

To help you see where these frequencies lie on the equiloudness contours, we show a piano keyboard in Figure 7-1 and indicate what region it covers on the curves. Figure 7-2 shows the frequency range of a number of different musical instruments. Thus, most of the sounds of musical instruments lie in the region where the perception of loudness is most sensitive to changes in frequency. This has two results: One, unless you listen to the orchestra at reasonable intensity levels, you will not hear many of the frequencies emitted by the instruments; second,

[1] Subscripts indicate which octave of the note is referred to. The notation is the standard used by acousticians, but not always by musicians. The first C on the piano keyboard is named C_1. All notes within the octave immediately above it are given the subscript 1: D_1, E_1, . . . , B_1. The second C on the keyboard, and all the notes within the octave above it, are subscripted 2: C_2, . . . , B_2. By this scheme, the middle C on the piano keyboard is C_4; the note on which the instruments of an orchestra tune is A_4. The highest note on the piano is C_8; the lowest is A_0 (see Backus, 1968).

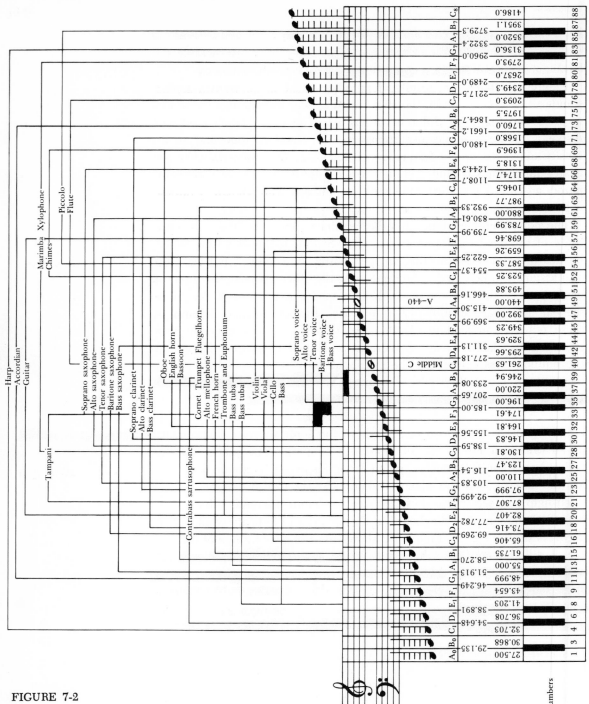

FIGURE 7-2

From C. G. Conn, Ltd.

the loudness relations among the instruments, so carefully worked out and controlled by the conductor, depend upon your listening to the music at the same intensity that the conductor expected for his audience. When listening to recordings of symphonic music at home, you are not likely to turn up the level on your audio equipment to recreate the intensities originally present in the hall. You hear the music on a different set of loudness contours than the conductor planned for, so that you hear a different piece of music than the conductor intended.

The problems of playing back music so that it sounds the same in the home as it did when it was recorded are well known. Consider a segment of a symphony piece which is being played so that the overall sound intensity is approximately the same at different frequencies, as shown in Figure 7-3. When a recording is played back at home, the overall picture looks similar but the intensity is reduced. Now some of the sound levels fall below the threshold of hearing. Lower frequencies that were perfectly audible at the concert can no longer be heard. Moreover, as the levels change, the relative loudness at different frequencies also changes. If an organ plays a scale at very high intensity going from low notes to high ones, in the actual auditorium all the notes would be perceived to have approximately the same loudness (at high intensities, the equiloudness contours are relatively flat). At home, however, when the scale is played back at a reasonable listening level, not only would some of the lower frequencies be inaudible, but they

FIGURE 7-3

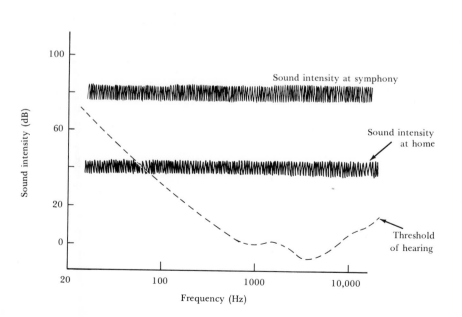

would now fall in the region where frequency is affecting loudness: The notes would appear to get louder and louder up to about two or three octaves above middle C, where they would start decreasing in loudness. (Note from Figure 7-1 that as frequencies decrease below 1000 Hz, they must be increased in intensity to be perceived as equally loud; thus, when intensity is constant, as frequency decreases the notes are perceived as getting softer.)

Loudness compensators. Most high-quality audio amplifiers now come with circuits that compensate for these psychological mechanisms. The control labeled *loudness compensator,* or sometimes simply *loudness,* makes the audio set overemphasize very low- and very high-frequency sounds when it is playing at low sound-levels. At high sound-levels, the loudness compensator should automatically be disconnected so that it no longer has any effect. With good playback equipment, the effect of loudness compensation on the sound levels is shown in Figure 7-4.

FIGURE 7-4

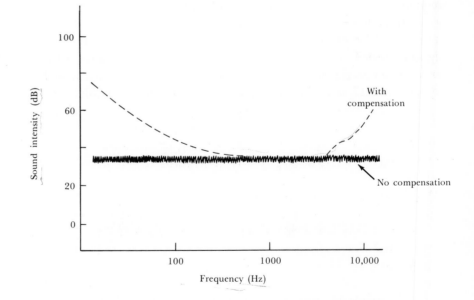

This results in a perceived loudness that looks like that shown in Figure 7-5. Actually, this compensation can work only if everything is done just right. The compensatory mechanism must take into account the peculiarities of the acoustics of the room where the speakers are located, as well as the particular sound equipment being used.

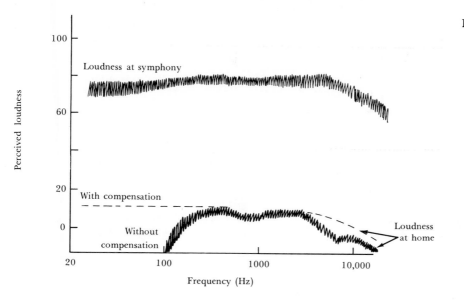

FIGURE 7-5

The loudness of a sound depends not only on its own intensity but *Masking* also on other sounds present at the same time. Sounds *mask* one another: The presence of one sound makes another more difficult to hear. Rustling of papers, clapping of hands, coughing—all these tend to mask speech or music. To determine the effect of a masking, it is necessary to measure how much more intense a *test sound* must be in order to be heard in the presence of a *masking sound*. The procedure is basically similar to the one used for obtaining equiloudness contours.

The masking experiment. One way of doing the experiment goes something like this: Two tones are presented to an observer; one is called the *test tone,* the other the *masker.* The masker is set at some fixed intensity and frequency. Then the test tone is set to some fixed frequency and the intensity value adjusted until the test tone can just barely be detected. This procedure is repeated for different values of frequency of the test tone until an entire *masking curve* has been traced out, showing exactly how intense the test tone must be at different frequencies in order that it can be detected in the presence of the masker. Once the masking curve has been determined for one particular masker, the masker itself might be changed in either frequency or intensity and a new masking curve determined.

A typical result of this experiment is shown in Figure 7-6. In this

FIGURE 7-6

From Zwicker and Scharf (1965).

tones below maskers freq. are little affected / tones about maskers freq. of 1200 Hz are much harder to hear

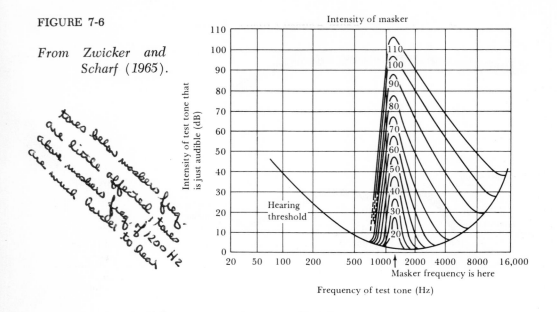

Frequency of test tone (Hz)

case, the frequency of the masker[2] was held fixed at 1200 Hz and the intensity was varied from 20 to 110 dB in steps of 10 dB to give 10 different masking curves.

The most striking feature of these data is the asymmetry. The masker has relatively little effect on tones below its own frequency of about 1200 Hz, but tones above this frequency are made much more difficult to hear by the presence of the masker.

The mechanism of masking. One of the explanations for this asymmetry comes from an examination of the vibration patterns of the basilar membrane. Remember the patterns shown in Figure 7-7: Low-frequency sounds tend to produce activity over much of the membrane, whereas high frequencies affect a more restricted region. If we examine these effects in more detail, as in Figure 7-8, we can compare the vibration

---

[2] Actually, the masker was not a pure tone, but rather a narrow band of noise. Noise gives smoother results than does a tone. Other than this, the differences between the masking produced by a pure tone and by narrow-band noise are slight, and only of technical importance.

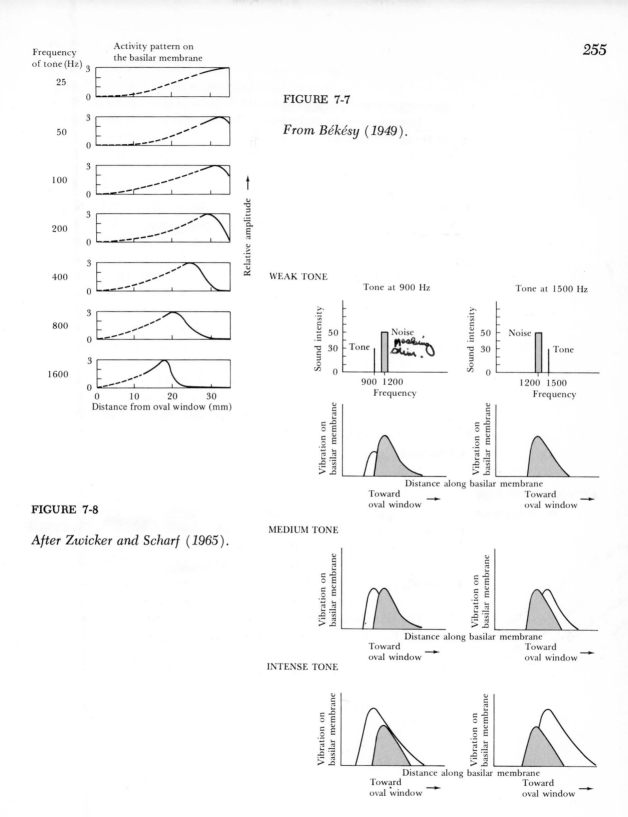

Frequency of tone (Hz) — Activity pattern on the basilar membrane

FIGURE 7-7

From Békésy (1949).

FIGURE 7-8

After Zwicker and Scharf (1965).

WEAK TONE

Tone at 900 Hz — Tone at 1500 Hz

MEDIUM TONE

INTENSE TONE

patterns on the basilar membrane produced by the masker with those produced by the test tones. When the tone is weak and slightly higher in frequency than the masker, no part of the activity pattern produced by the tone manages to make itself felt above the pattern already caused by the masking noise. But the same weak tone at a frequency lower than the masker produces new activity in a separate nonoverlapping region. It does manage to be heard. Note that as the signal level is increased, the roles of the test signal and masker are reversed. A low frequency, relatively high-intensity test tone will mask the masker.

Masking of music. Masking adds another factor to the perception of loudness and of music. Intense, lower-frequency instruments mask the sounds of weak, higher-frequency instruments. The violas mask the violins; the timpani mask the violas; the brass mask the woodwinds. But when the sounds are played back in the home, the intensity is less than when they were recorded. As a result, the masking patterns are changed. Suddenly you can follow the fine fingerings of the violin or guitar, for the sounds of the basses are much reduced in level. Is this a virtue? Not necessarily. The composer, conductor, and the players did not have this in mind; their musical intuitions took into account the effect of masking and used it assuming it would be present for the listener. To eliminate the masking effect is to eliminate the sound balance among the instruments so carefully planned according to the grouping.

The measurement of loudness

Loudness measurements are of great importance for many practical problems. Since our psychological perception of loudness does not correspond directly to measures of physical intensity, it is essential to have methods that take these differences into account.

Sones. One such procedure is based on the method of *magnitude estimation.* We present a person with two tones, both, say, at 1000 Hz, and ask him how many times louder one sound appears to be over the other. The question is a peculiar one, but people can and do answer it sensibly. (For more information and some examples you can try yourself, see Appendix A.)

The results of the magnitude estimation procedure show that loudness increases as the cube root of sound intensity. That is, the psychological judgment of loudness, *J*, is related to the physical Intensity of the sound, *I*, by a power law of the form

$$J = kI^{0.3}.$$

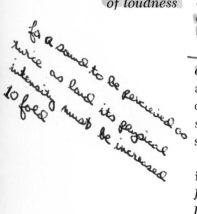

for a sound to be perceived as twice as loud its physical intensity must be increased 10 fold

This value of exponent (0.3) is very convenient. It works out that if the sound intensity is specified in decibels, a 10 dB increase always changes loudness by a factor of 2. Every time the physical intensity is multiplied by 10, psychological loudness is multiplied by 2, as shown in Figure 7-9.

This measurement procedure has been standardized by the International Standards Organization. The unit of loudness is the *sone*. By definition, the loudness of a 1000-Hz tone at an intensity of 40 dB is equal to 1 sone.

To get the loudness of tones at other frequencies, the equiloudness contours can be used. All tones on the equiloudness contour in Figure 7-1 marked 40 have a loudness of 1 sone. Those on the contour marked

Sone – unit of loudness

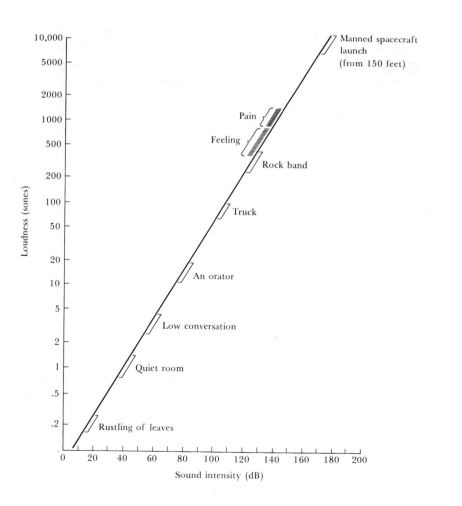

FIGURE 7-9

50 have a loudness of 2 sones, and on the contour marked 60 have a loudness of 4 sones. Each increase in contour by 10 dB doubles the sone value: Each decrease of 10 dB halves the number of sones. ✱ The sone measurement describes the perceived loudness of pure tones. With complex sounds that contain many frequency components, such as voices, orchestras, or aircraft and automobile sounds, the loudness is determined by comparing them with a 1000-Hz standard. The sone value at which the 1000-Hz tone appears as loud as the complex sound is the sone level for that complex sound. The sone values for some typical sounds are shown in Figure 7-9.

PITCH

The musical scale

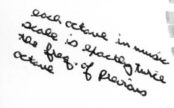

The musical scale of pitch is logarithmically related to sound frequency. Each octave in the standard musical scale is exactly twice the frequency of the previous octave. The note that orchestras use to tune their instruments, A_4 (the A above middle C), has a frequency of 440 Hz. The A's one and two octaves above that, A_5 and A_6, have frequencies of 880 and 1760 Hz, respectively. Similarly, the A's one and two octaves below have frequencies of 220 and 110 Hz, respectively. In an even-tempered musical scale, then, increasing the note by an octave doubles its frequency. Moreover, there are 12 equally spaced notes in an octave (counting all the whole and half notes). In order to divide the frequency range spanned by an octave into 12 equal intervals, each note is exactly $2^{1/12}$ times the frequency of the one before it.

The mel scale

Is the note of one octave perceived to be twice the pitch of the same note in the preceding octave? Our intuitions suggest yes, but experimental data indicate the answer is no. When subjects are presented with different notes and asked to judge the pitch relations among them, their perceived pitch does not follow the musical scale. Doubling or halving the frequency of the note does not double or halve its perceived pitch. (This result comes from use of the magnitude estimation procedure, described in Appendix A.) The actual relationship is shown in Figure 7-10. The unit of pitch in this diagram is called the *mel*. By definition, a tone of 1000 Hz (at 60 dB) has a pitch of 1000 mels.

Although this result may be incompatible with our intuition about pitch, it is highly compatible with some of the concepts in music composition. Musicians frequently debate the consequences of transposing a piece from one key to another. If a piece is written in C major and then transposed to A major, should it matter? If the change from one note to another always has the same psychological magnitude, regardless of the notes involved (equivalently, that raising a note an octave doubles

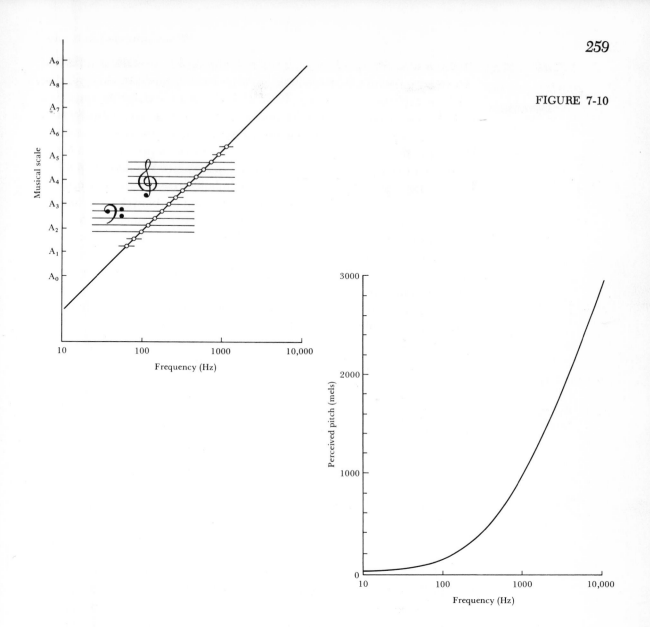

FIGURE 7-10

the pitch), then why should it matter if the piece is transposed? The psychological distances between the notes will be the same, regardless of the key the piece is played in. But most musicians argue that transposition changes the character of the piece. The effect is subtle, but it is there. This argument is compatible with the psychological judgments of pitch relations. The change in perceived pitch involved in going from a C_4 to a D_4 is different from that involved in going from an F_4 to a G_4 or, for that matter, going from C_5 to D_5, an octave up.

Place theory:
position on the
basilar membrane

To consider the question of what determines our perception of pitch, let us again return to the vibration pattern along the basilar membrane. Different frequencies set up different patterns of activity on the membrane. The location of the maximum vibration moves systematically from the oval window end of the membrane toward the apex as the frequency goes from high to low. As early as 1863, the German physicist Helmholtz proposed that pitch is determined by the position of the maximum vibration along the membrane. Although Helmholtz' reasons were inaccurate, his conclusion was sound. Psychological distance between the pitches of two tones seems to be related to the physical distance between the position of the peak activity produced by the tones. The two functions are shown in Figure 7-11. Here, location of the maximum of the vibration patterns produced by tones of different frequencies is plotted in terms of its distance from the far end (the apex) of the membrane. Perceived pitch as measured by the mel scale is also shown. The two functions are similar, not identical.

FIGURE 7-11

From Zwislocki
(1965).

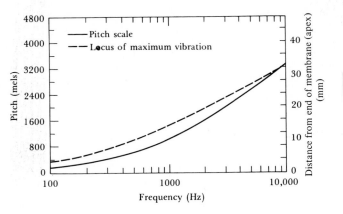

Why should distance be the critical feature? It is of no intrinsic value to the nervous system unless there are neural mechanisms to take advantage of it. The way the 30,000 fibers of the acoustic nerve distribute themselves along the membrane suggests such a mechanism. Near the oval window and for the first few turns of the cochlea, the density of the neurons appears to be constant at approximately 1150 ganglion cell neurons per millimeter. But the density of neurons decreases toward the apex. If a higher density of neurons provides more precise position information, then this distribution suggests there should be less sensitivity to changes in activity patterns in the low-frequency region—the points nearer the apex. When the curve is corrected for the relative density of the neurons, there is very good agreement: Each unit change in pitch on the mel scale is approximately equal to a movement of the vibration pattern along the membrane by 12 neurons.

The exact sensitivity of the ear to changes in frequency can be measured directly by successively presenting pairs of tones to an observer and asking him to decide whether they have the same or different pitches. We obtain a measurement of the *just noticeable difference* (the *jnd*) between pitches. The ability to make such discriminations varies with frequency. At 100 Hz, a 3% change in frequency (3 Hz) is necessary before the pitch becomes noticeably different. This percentage value steadily decreases until it reaches a minimum of around .2 or .3% at 1000 Hz. For low frequencies, the jnd for pitch is approximately constant in absolute value. Thereafter, the percentage change required to make the discrimination remains reasonably constant at about .3%.[3]

If the jnd for pitch is compared with the distance between the peaks in activity along the basilar membrane produced by the two frequencies being discriminated, there is good agreement in high-frequency regions but disagreement at low frequencies (Figure 7-12). But, as before, we should really take into account the way that the hair cells are spread out along the membrane. When the curve is corrected for the relative density of neurons, the match is improved: We can discriminate the difference between two frequencies whenever their peak activity is separated along the membrane by about 52 neurons.

An examination of the location of maximum vibration along the membrane, coupled with a consideration of the neural distribution, describes

---

[3] This pattern of changing discriminability is common to a number of different signal dimensions in different sensory systems. The discriminability between the intensities of an auditory signal, for example, shows a similar pattern with the jnd being approximately constant in absolute value for low intensity signals and then having an approximately constant **percentage** value as the intensities move into the middle regions of the hearing range. A constant percentage associated with discrimination is typical of many types of measuring instruments. It results from the fact that the variability in the measures being taken often depends on the level being measured, and increases with increasing levels. Consequently, the absolute size of the signal change needed for reliable discrimination will also increase. When these size increases result in a constant percentage change, the system is said to be following Weber's Law, named after the physiologist Weber (1795–1878), a contemporary of Helmholtz. If we let ΔI stand for the size of the jnd, the change in intensity that a signal must make in order for that change to be just noticeable, and I for the signal intensity, Weber's Law states that

$$\Delta I = kI,$$

where k is the relative change ($100k$ is the percent change).

FIGURE 7-12

*From Zwislocki
(1965).*

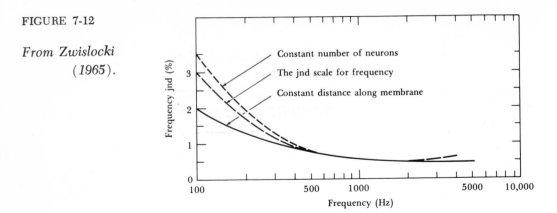

both the subjective perception of pitch and the ears' sensitivity to changes in frequency:

- 1 jnd is approximately 52 neurons;

- 1 mel is approximately 12 neurons.

Note that a pitch change of 1 mel is less than one jnd: It cannot be detected. Pitch must change by 4 or 5 mels before an observer can detect the change. At higher frequencies (above 500 or 1000 Hz), where the density of neurons is reasonably constant along the membrane, the jnd represents a constant distance—about 0.05 mm or about .002 inches—along the membrane.

Periodicity pitch

The analysis of the patterns of vibrations along the basilar membrane describes a number of the phenomena associated with our perception of pitch. But some puzzles remain.

Loudness and pitch. The ear is not very sensitive to low-frequency sounds, yet many musical instruments produce sound frequencies in this insensitive region. Thus, a note played softly will have much of its energy lying below the threshold of hearing. What happens to our perceptions? Obviously a note played more and more softly sounds much the same, but why? Shouldn't the same piano note keep changing in pitch as it gets softer and softer and as more and more of its low-frequency components become inaudible?

Consider the piano note C_3, the C below middle C—not a particularly low note. It has the same pitch as a tone of 131 Hz (actually 130.9 Hz). But the piano note is not a simple tone. Look at the spectrum shown in Figure 7-13. Although there is more energy at 131 Hz than at other

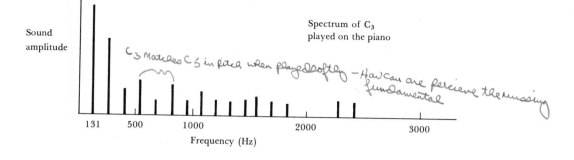

FIGURE 7-13

Sound amplitude

Spectrum of C₃
played on the piano

C₃ Matches C₅ in pitch when played softly — How can are percieve the missing fundamental

| | | | |
131 500 1000 2000 3000

Frequency (Hz)

frequencies, there actually is some energy over a wide range of frequencies. As the note is played more and more softly, these low-frequency components will drop in intensity below the level that can be heard. Thus, the lowest frequency present will change from 131 Hz, when the note is played at a comfortable level, to 262, to 393, and finally to 524 Hz, when the note is played reasonably softly. A pure tone with a frequency of 524 Hz matches C_5 in pitch. This is a reasonably high pitched note—it is one octave above middle C. But quite clearly, there is something peculiar going on here. A musical note simply does not appear to change in pitch in this manner as it gets softer. If pitch is determined by the location along the basilar membrane, why does the pitch of a complex tone, such as a piano note, appear to remain constant even though its frequency structure is changing? How can the piano note continue to have the pitch of its fundamental frequency of 131 Hz when the lowest frequency that is audible is 524 Hz? How do we hear the missing fundamental?

Figure 7-14

The case of the missing fundamental. To answer the question, consider a simpler situation, shown in Figure 7-15. Two pure tones, 1000 Hz (upper row) and 1100 Hz (middle row) are added to produce a complex waveform (lower row). Note that even though the only sound energy present in the system is at the two frequencies 1000 and 1100 Hz, the resulting wave pattern appears to vary at an overall rate of 100 Hz. The phenomenon in the diagram is called a *beat.* Two sinusoidal waves played together produce a beat pattern, a regular rise and fall in the sound energy at a rate equal to the difference of the frequencies of the component sine waves. On the basilar membrane, however, this beat component should not be present. There are no physical frequencies in the wave corresponding to the beat frequency. Maximums in the activity pattern should be produced only at the locations corresponding

FIGURE 7-14

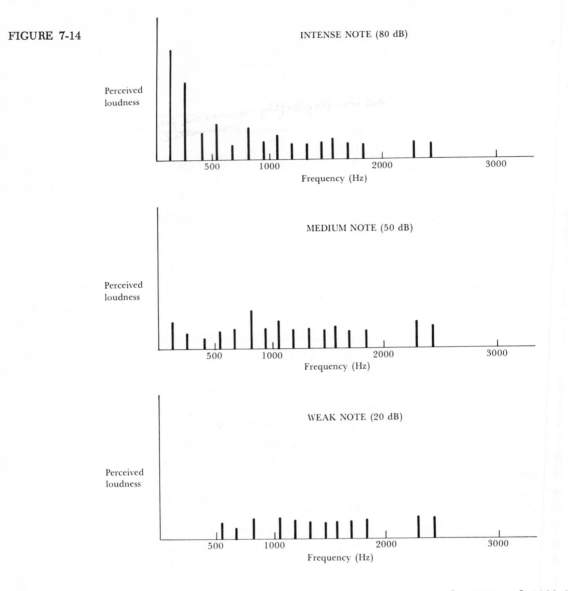

to the actual physical components of the sound—1000 and 1100 Hz. Thus, if we perceive pitch by noting the points of maximum vibration, we should perceive the 1000 and 1100 components, but not the 100-Hz beat frequency. In fact, we do hear the beat.

There are two possible theories to explain this phenomenon. One proposes that the perception of the beat frequency results from the fact that the ear is an imperfect transmitter of sound: It has *non-*

why the "Beat" is heard

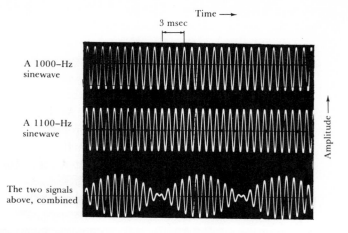

FIGURE 7-15

Beats. The fluctuation in overall sound pressure which results when two sine waves of different frequencies are added together. The resulting pattern fluctuates ("beats") with a frequency given by the difference between the frequencies of the components. In this illustration, the 1000-Hz sine wave is mixed with a 1100-Hz sine wave to give a beat frequency of 100 Hz. Thus, the beat pattern repeats itself every 10 msec. Note that there is no sound energy present at a frequency of 100 Hz. We did not create a new sine wave by adding together the 1000- and 1100-Hz signals: Simply the overall envelope of sound pressures varies at the beat frequency.

linearities. The mechanical structure in the ear (mainly the middle ear) actually adds extra frequencies to the incoming acoustic signal. In particular, the beat frequency is added, and thus the basilar membrane is activated in this frequency region. This explanation is compatible with the notion that a particular pitch is only perceived when there is a corresponding maximum in the vibration pattern on the membrane: the *place theory* of pitch perception.

The second theory emphasizes the importance of the synchronized firing of neurons to the changing pressures in the acoustic wave. The nerve cells reacting to the activity patterns on the basilar membrane fire in synchrony with the regular rise and fall of the beat frequency. This synchronization in the neural responses is at the basis of the perceived pitch: the *periodicity theory* of pitch perception. These are the two major explanations of pitch perception and the study of the missing fundamental is the key to evaluating them.

Evidence against nonlinearities. The introduction of nonlinearities during the transmission of sounds is typical of most mechanical systems, and the ear is no exception. But there are two sources of evidence against this explanation as a complete account of the missing fundamental. First, the ear is not really very nonlinear, especially at low-intensity sounds. At high intensities—sound levels greater than 80 dB—the ear is indeed nonlinear, and the reasons for hearing the beat frequency just described are correct. At higher intensity levels, the middle ear bones and muscles act to protect the inner ear by reducing the signal that gets through. This protective mechanism also introduces distortion into the signal being transmitted. Numerous studies have confirmed that high intensity signals do result in nonlinearities and the addition of just those tones required by the theory.

But what about the piano note with a sound intensity of only 30 dB? Nonlinearities are not much in evidence at these low intensities, at least not to an extent sufficient to explain why the pitch of the G_1 is that of the fundamental, even though the fundamental is below the threshold of audibility.

Masking the missing fundamental   Consider a complex sound made up of the following frequencies:

1000 Hz   1200 Hz   1400 Hz   1600 Hz
1800 Hz   2000 Hz   2200 Hz

A subject is asked to adjust an oscillator so that its pitch is the same as that of the complex sound.[4] He will set the oscillator to 200 Hz. Both theories of pitch perception can explain this simple phenomenon.

The place theory explanation. The ear is nonlinear. It produces difference frequencies: The seven tones presented give six opportunities for a 200-Hz difference frequency to be added by the distortion introduced during transmission. This difference frequency, then, is a prominent contributor to the perception of the pitch of the sound.

The periodicity pitch explanation. The overall impulse flow in the auditory nerve is following the beat pattern of the sounds. There are nonlinearities. But neural activity is rising and falling regularly 200 times per second, and it is this activity pattern which is at the basis of the perceived pitch of the sound.

The critical difference, then, is whether the membrane is actually being activated in the 200-Hz region. The place theorist thinks the basilar membrane is vibrating at the 200-Hz location, and the subject perceives this. The periodicity pitch theorist believes that the membrane is only vibrating in the high-frequency region between 1000 and 2200 Hz, but

---

[4] The experiment described in this section was performed by Patterson (1969).

the nerve firings at these locations are synchronized to 200 Hz. What is the critical experiment? Disrupt the membrane in the location around 200 Hz and find out if the subject can still hear the associated pitch.

It is rather easy to disrupt the membrane in this way. One way is to add low-frequency noise to the signal—a sound that contains energy at all frequencies below some value. To be sure the noise will mask out any low-frequency activity on the membrane, add noise that contains all frequency components up to 500 Hz. How intense should the noise be?—intense enough to disrupt a real tone, if one were there. To determine this value, first present a real 200-Hz tone to the subject and have him adjust its intensity so that it sounds exactly as loud as the 200-Hz tone he hears in the complex sound. Then add low-frequency noise in an amount sufficient to mask completely the real 200-Hz tone. This noise level should be sufficient to mask any activity produced by nonlinearities. Once again, the complex tone is turned on. This time the masking noise is added. Will the 200-Hz component still be audible? The periodicity theorist is correct: The missing fundamental is still heard when all activity in its frequency region is being physically masked by noise. Moreover, to prove that the noise does have the proper masking

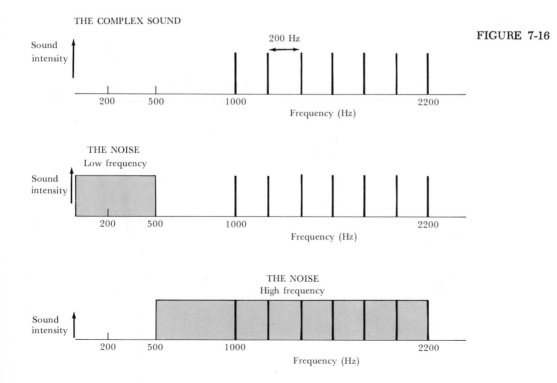

THE COMPLEX SOUND

FIGURE 7-16

effect when placed appropriately, a high-frequency noise can be tested
—a noise containing all frequencies above 500 Hz. Now the place
theorist should say that the 200-Hz pitch will still be heard, since the
associated location on the membrane is not disturbed by the high-frequency noise. The periodicity theorist argues the opposite: The neural
response pattern will be disrupted by the high-frequency noise, and the
missing fundamental will no longer be heard. The result? With high-
frequency noise presented, the missing fundamental is no longer audible.

Figure 7-16

PITCH DISCRIMINATION WITHOUT A BASILAR MEMBRANE[5]

One way to test for the workability of a periodicity theory is to study
an animal that has no basilar membrane: Can it discriminate different audio
frequencies? According to place theory, if there is no basilar membrane, there
can be no encoding of pitch. According to periodicity theory, pitch discrimination should be reasonably good, at least up to the point where the neural
firing can no longer keep up with the signal.

The goldfish is such an animal. It has hair cells, but no membrane. The
ears of most fish are rather different from those of mammals—for good reason.
Not only are they evolutionarily less advanced, but the water makes a peculiar
medium for sound. Water is more dense than air: Sound travels five times
as fast in water as in air. Moreover, the density of the water does not differ
much from the density of the body tissues and fluids. This means that the
entire outer ear and middle ear are unnecessary, perhaps even harmful. Sound
tends to travel right through fish, with no diminution in intensity. The ears
of fish are located at the air bladders, and the distinctions found among
the ears of fish seem related to the distinctions in the way their air bladders
are located. What is most important, of course, is that fish—and the goldfish
in particular—do have hair cells and acoustic nerves, but no basilar membrane.
How, then, can they discriminate frequency?

Figure 7-17

When the goldfish is properly trained, it can indeed tell one frequency
from another. The test is to hold the fish securely in a cheesecloth-padded
harness and continually pair the presentation of a tone with an electric shock.
The fish is presented with a series of tones of the same frequency. Then
one tone is changed in frequency, and a shock follows. The fish soon learns
to anticipate shock whenever the frequency changes: It shows this anticipation
by momentarily stopping its breathing.

The data so obtained are shown in Figure 7-18. Note that the minimum
frequency change that can be detected by the goldfish is about ten times

---

[5] The experiments on goldfish were reported by Fay (1970) and Fay and MacKinnon (1969).

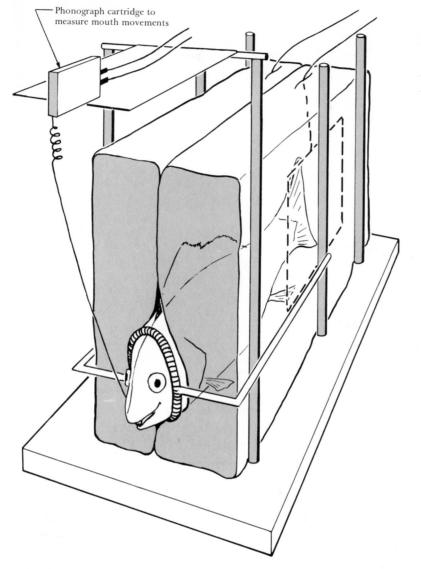

Phonograph cartridge to
measure mouth movements

FIGURE 7-17

*From Fay and Mac-
Kinnon (1969).*

larger than the minimum amount that can be detected by humans. Although
the fish is much less sensitive in absolute terms, the way its sensitivity varies
with frequency is similar to the corresponding human discriminability function.
The ability of the goldfish to discriminate among frequencies disappears around
1000 to 2000 Hz, exactly what one would suspect from periodicity theory:
At these levels, the nerves should no longer be able to fire in synchrony
to the auditory signal.

FIGURE 7-18

From Fay (1970).

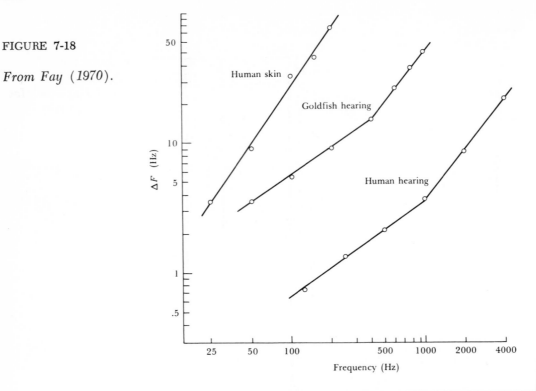

Evidence against Although the periodicity theory seems to fare pretty well in these mask-
the periodicity ing experiments, there are two phenomena that give trouble to the peri-
pitch theory odicity account of pitch perception.[1] One is that an individual nerve
cannot respond more rapidly than about 300 to 400 times each second.
How, then, can it be the basis for perceiving pitches corresponding
to 4000-Hz signals?[2] A second problem is the interesting anomaly of
hearing called *diplacusis,* in which the same tone is perceived to have
a different pitch with each ear. How could this be if the nerves simply
fired at the rate at which the membrane was vibrating?

   To answer the first criticism, periodicity theorists rely heavily on the
volley principle (see page 235). Neurons fire in patterns, with a group
of nerve fibers able to follow together a frequency that no single one
of them could. If one nerve fires at a rate of only 300 Hz, a group
of four neurons is capable of firing at a combined rate of 1200 Hz,
given that everything is synchronized properly. Even so, there is no
evidence that nerves, whether singly or in groups, can follow patterns
of auditory frequencies greater than 2000 or perhaps 3000 Hz.

   One of the strongest pieces of evidence against periodicity theory as a complete explanation is the anomaly of diplacusis, an ailment which lends credence to the theory that pitch is determined by the location of the maximum vibration on the membrane. Someone who suffers from a severe case of diplacusis will hear two different pitches when the same tone is played to each ear. Actually, everyone perceives some small differences in the pitch of a tone heard at the two ears, especially at high frequencies. The simplest explanation is that there is not a perfect match of positions along the basilar membrane. In fact, if you consider the precision of neural wiring that would be necessary to make each pair of locations on the two membranes correspond exactly, it is surprising that this phenomenon is not more prominent. It would be surprising even if the two membranes were exactly the same size, let alone matched neuron for neuron. Moreover, as one follows the neural processing up toward the brain, it is clear that there are many places where there might be a slight mismatch between the locations of neural fibers and the critical frequencies for which they are most sensitive (see van den Brink, 1970).

The complete account of pitch perception would appear to require an amalgamation of the two theoretical positions. Certainly, place along the basilar membrane is an extremely important part of the extraction of pitch information in a signal: The evidence in favor of this view is overwhelming. But it would also appear that the firing pattern in the neurons provides additional pitch information, particularly for frequencies below 1000–2000 Hz. The case of the missing fundamental is difficult to explain otherwise. But there is no reason why both theories cannot be correct: They supplement each other nicely.

The duplicity theory of pitch perception

The location at which the maximum vibration occurs on the basilar membrane, then, would appear to be a primary determinant of pitch, supplemented by information carried by the rate at which the fibers of the acoustic nerve respond. If the fibers located at the 1000-Hz location respond at a firing rate of 1000 Hz, everything is consistent. The perception is of a pitch given by a 1000-Hz tone. If the fibers at the 1000-Hz location respond in patterns of 100 Hz, then the perception is of a complex sound, with a fundamental pitch equal to that of a tone of 100 Hz, but with a harmonic structure in the 1000-Hz region. In this case, the firing rate helps determine the pitch: The location at which the membrane is responding determines the sound quality or *timbre*. Stimulation of a location along the basilar membrane is always accompanied by a firing rate appropriate to the location. Firing rates, however, are not always accompanied by stimulation of the appropriate membrane location.

This duplicity of operation is assumed to operate only at frequencies below 1000 or 2000 Hz. Above that point, it is unlikely that neural firings can be synchronized with vibration rates. (Note that some investigators believe that the periodicity pitch caused by firing rate can go as high as 4000 Hz.) Thus, for frequencies between 1000 or 4000 Hz and 20,000 Hz, the place mechanism must be solely responsible for pitch perception. But most natural sounds used by humans for communication or for recreation occur at the lower frequencies, where both mechanisms might be operating. The highest note of a soprano vocalist has a fundamental frequency of around 1400 Hz.

THE CRITICAL BAND

Suppose two pure tones are presented to a subject who is to judge the loudness of the resulting sound. As the two tones move farther apart in frequency (keeping their average frequency constant), the combined sound does not change loudness until a critical frequency separation is exceeded. Beyond this, the loudness of the tone pair increases with increased frequency separation.

FIGURE 7-19

From Scharf (1970).

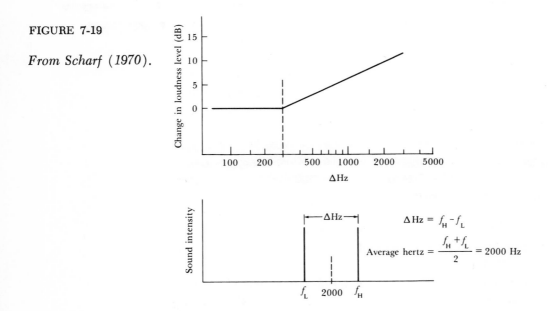

In a similar fashion, a sound containing components of all frequencies between some lower frequency f_L and a higher one f_H appears to have a constant loudness as the distance between f_L and f_H is increased, until, again, a critical value of separation is reached. From that point, the loudness of the sound increases as more and more frequencies are added.[6]

Consider a third example, a subject trying to detect a pure tone that is masked by bandpass noise centered around the frequency of the tone. As the distance between f_L and f_H is increased, detection becomes more and more difficult until a critical separation is reached. Beyond that point, detection is no longer affected by further increases in the width of the noise band.

All three of these examples indicate that within some critical region of frequency, sound energies are interacting with one another. As we move outside the critical region, sound energies no longer interact, although psychological attributes do add. The critical region is called the *critical band*. Its size depends upon its center frequency.

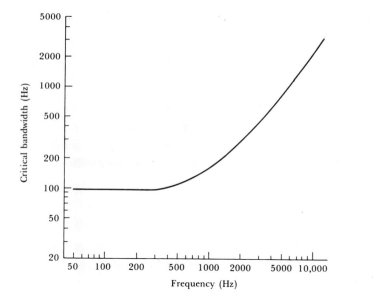

FIGURE 7-20

From Scharf (1970).

If one looks at the pattern of excitation along the basilar membrane, it is surprisingly simple to find a correlate for the critical band similar

---

[6] Note that constant energy must be maintained in the sound (called *bandpass noise*, where the bandpass refers to the frequencies between f_L and f_H). To see how this is done, consider a simpler case in which a complex sound composed of separate tones is presented to a subject. If more tones are added, it is important for this task that constant total energy of the sound be maintained. Thus, if the number of tones is doubled, the energy of each tone presented must be halved to keep total energy constant. So it is with noise: The energy level at each frequency is kept proportional to $1/(f_H - f_L)$.

to the correlates found for the jnd and mel scale for pitch. Here is a diagram of the activity patterns produced by two tones separated by 300 Hz.

FIGURE 7-21

From Zwislocki (1965).

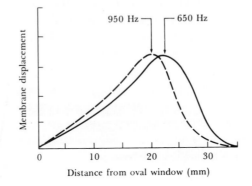

A jnd for frequency differences in this region would be about $\frac{1}{50}$ of the separation shown here. Thus, even though there is a large overlap in the patterns produced by the tones, the sounds are easily discriminated by the human. In fact, these tones are separated by two critical bands, placing them well beyond the region where they even interact in our psychological perceptions. By comparing Figure 7-21 with the properties of the basilar membrane and the mel and jnd scales, the relationship among these factors can be nicely summarized:

- 1 mel is approximately 12 neurons, 0.23 jnd, and 0.009 critical bands;
- 1 jnd is approximately 52 neurons, 4.3 mels, and 0.04 critical bands;
- 1 critical band is approximately 1300 neurons, 108 mels, and 25 jnd's.

The critical band has many important properties. Beats between different tones appear to be noticeable only if the tones involved fall within the same critical band. Thus, the periodicity pitch phenomenon requires that the components which give rise to a missing fundamental must lie close enough together—namely, within a critical bandwidth. The critical band has also been suggested as the mechanism responsible for the dissonance associated with some combinations of tones. Dissonance, it is argued, results from beats caused by two tones whose frequencies lie within a critical bandwidth of one another. Musical instruments produce complex tones, containing many harmonic frequencies. Two notes may be dissonant if any pair of their harmonics falls within the same critical band. The more audible these harmonics, the more dissonant the sound.

We have two ears, but we hear one acoustic world. With differences in information received by listening with two ears (*binaural*) rather than with one (*monaural*), we determine the locations of sound sources, an important factor both in adding to the enjoyment of our perceptions and in making acoustic messages more intelligible. It is difficult to appreciate the importance of sound localization because it is so seldom that we are without it: It is so common a phenomenon that we take it for granted.

With modern audio sets, however, the importance of sound localization is easy to demonstrate. Listen to a good, high-quality stereophonic recording over earphones.[7] Now, simply switch between monophonic and stereophonic reproduction. Listen to the difference. Stereophonic reproduction not only allows the sounds to be perceived as originating from different locations in the imaginary space around you, but also gives a richer sensation of sound—one in which the various sounds are more distinct and easier to listen to.

The cues used to localize a sound source are the exact time and intensity at which the tones arrive at the two ears. Sounds arrive first at the ear closest to the source and with greater intensity. The head tends to cast an acoustic shadow between the source and the ear on the far side.

Localization

With some simple calculations, it is possible to determine the approximate maximum possible time delay between signals arriving at the two ears. The width of the human head is approximately 7 inches. If a sound source is located directly to one side, the sound hits one ear directly but has to travel around the circumference of the head to get to the other ear. If the head is assumed to be a sphere with a radius of 3.5 inches, the extra path length is 3.5π, or 11 inches. Since sound travels at approximately 1100 feet sec^{-1} in air, it takes 76 μsec to travel an inch. For a sound to travel from one ear to the other takes around 840 μsec.

Figure 7-22

This time difference, of course, depends exactly on where the sound is located. When the sound is straight ahead, it reaches both ears at the same time. When the sound is 3° to the right, it arrives at the right ear 30 μsec before arriving at the left. This slight change—30 μsec of

---

[7] Speakers will not give so dramatic an effect, unless you sit so that one speaker is directly to your left and one directly to your right. The recording must be one that was recorded in the studio for stereophonic reproduction—old records or budget productions may not be very good for this. Most good rock groups or modern symphony recordings are excellent.

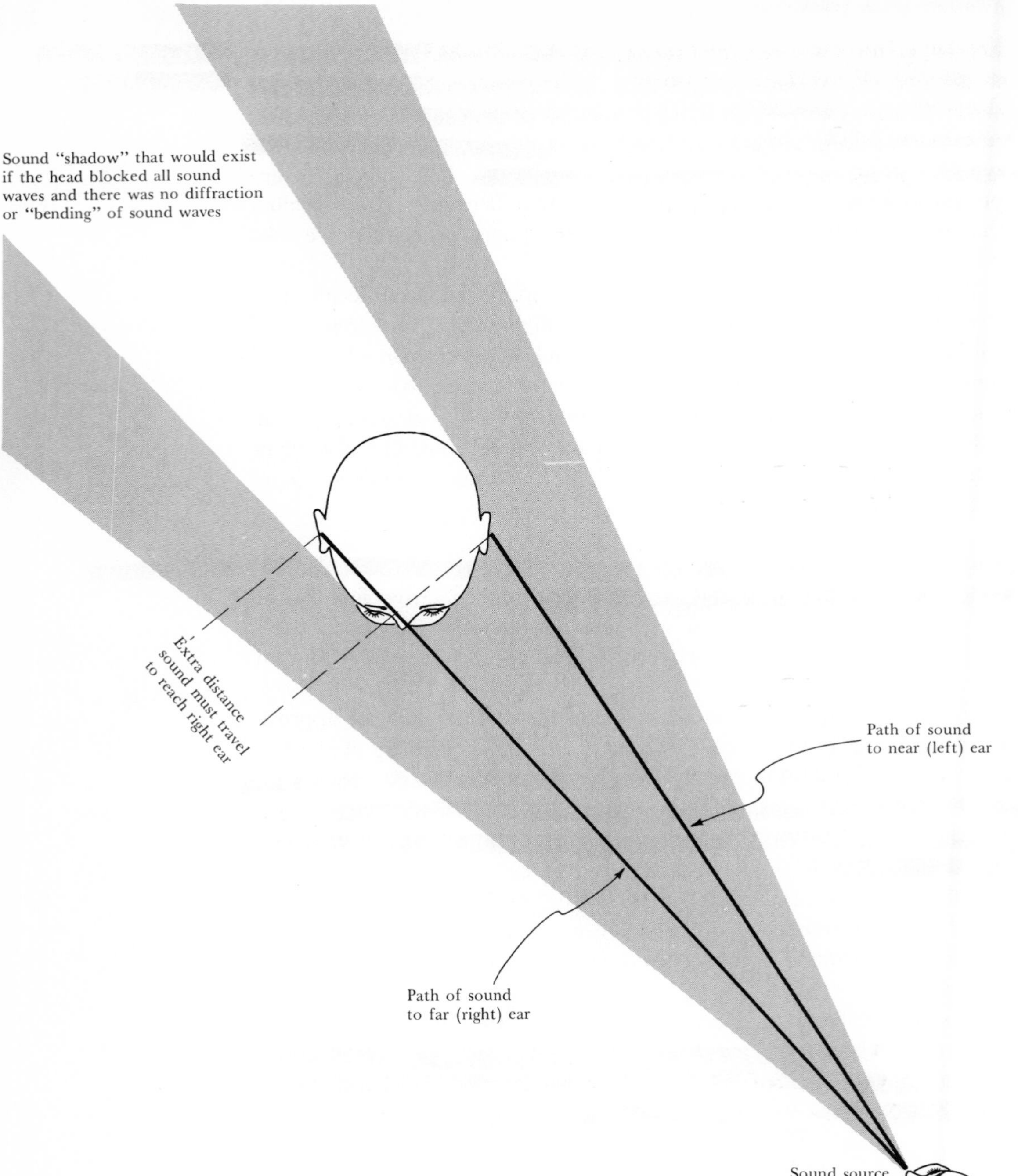

Sound "shadow" that would exist if the head blocked all sound waves and there was no diffraction or "bending" of sound waves

Extra distance sound must travel to reach right ear

Path of sound to near (left) ear

Path of sound to far (right) ear

Sound source

FIGURE 7-22

time difference—is detectable. It is all the change needed for an observer to detect a change in the location of the sound source. This is amazing performance, especially since the signals at the two ears must be compared with each other in order to localize the sound. The nervous system must be preserving information about the time at which a signal arrives at an ear within an accuracy of 30 μsec.

Approximate computation of binaural difference in path length for a distant sound source.   FIGURE 7-23

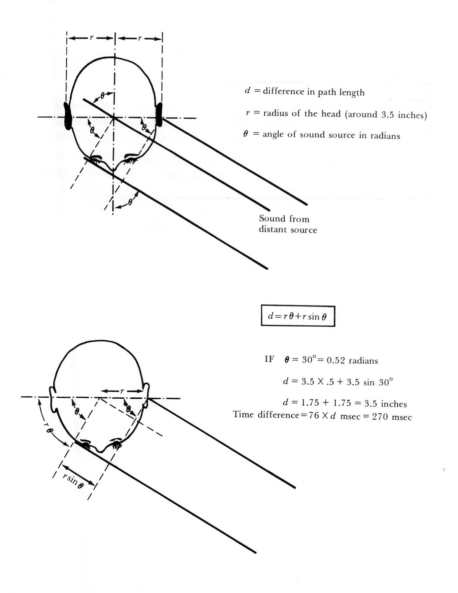

$d =$ difference in path length

$r =$ radius of the head (around 3.5 inches)

$\theta =$ angle of sound source in radians

Sound from distant source

$$d = r\theta + r\sin\theta$$

IF $\theta = 30° = 0.52$ radians

$d = 3.5 \times .5 + 3.5 \sin 30°$

$d = 1.75 + 1.75 = 3.5$ inches

Time difference $= 76 \times d$ msec $= 270$ msec

The difference in the arrival time of a signal at the two ears results in a phase difference between the signals: One lags behind the other. For high-frequency signals, this time lag is ambiguous and cannot be used as a cue for localization. To see this, consider a 10,000-Hz signal. It completes a cycle of sound pressure variation every 100 μsec. When a 10,000-Hz signal is in front and to the right at an angle of 55°, the sound will arrive at the left ear some 450 μsec after it arrives at the right ear. The waveform heard at the right ear, then, is $4\frac{1}{2}$ cycles ahead of the waveform at the left. But how can one tell whether two tones differ by $4\frac{1}{2}$ cycles, $3\frac{1}{2}$, $2\frac{1}{2}$, $1\frac{1}{2}$, or even $\frac{1}{2}$ cycle? Alternatively, how can one tell if the source is 55° to the right or 40°, 27°, 17°, or 6°? There is no way. The longest time delay between the ears is around 840 μsec, and any sound frequency that takes less time than this to complete a cycle starts to give ambiguous location information. Time differences only provide good clues to location for sounds with frequency components less than about 1300 Hz.

Actually, localization is ambiguous even at low frequencies, since if the head is perfectly stationary, time difference alone cannot distinguish whether a sound comes from above or below, or even from front or rear. A sound in front and to one side has the same delay pattern as one in the rear in the same relative position. In real situations, these ambiguities can be removed by head movements, by visual cues, and by differences in sound quality caused by the way different frequencies are reflected and refracted by the head and outer ear.

A second cue to sound localization is the sound shadow cast by the head. With low-frequency sounds, the sound wave is diffracted and "bends" around the head, causing little or no shadow. But at high frequencies—when the wavelength is short compared with the dimensions of the head—diffraction does not take place to any significant degree. For example, a 100-Hz sound has a wavelength of 11 feet. Thus, it bends easily around the head. But a 10,000-Hz sound has a wavelength of only .11 feet (1.3 inches) so that it is reflected by the head, thus casting a shadow. With a source of sound at a 15° angle, the effects of the sound shadow can be measured:

Frequency	Ratio of Sound Intensities at the Two Ears
300 Hz	1 dB
1,100 Hz	4 dB
4,200 Hz	5 dB
10,000 Hz	6 dB
15,000 Hz	10 dB

Starting about 3000–4000 Hz, the intensity difference is great enough to be reliably discriminated, and thus provides a useful cue to localization.

Sound localization is carried out by a dual system: time differences for low frequencies and intensity differences for high frequencies. The switch between the two systems occurs in the frequency range of 1000–5000 Hz—the range of sound frequencies characterized by the largest amount of error in localization.

To account for the precision with which sounds are localized, the auditory system must be able to detect time differences on the order of a 10- or 20-μsec difference. Its anatomical design seems to be well suited for preserving the timing information contained in primary auditory neurons.[8] Earlier, it was noted that the neural signals leaving the ear travel only a very short distance before they arrive at the point where messages from the two ears are combined: the *superior olive*. In the superior olive, excitatory and inhibitory interactions take place between the signals arriving from the two ears—just the sort of mechanism required for binaural localization. Here in Figure 7-24, for example, is a schematic of the general types of interconnections occurring in the superior olive (E stands for excitatory, I for inhibitory). (The exact anatomy has not yet been fully worked out.) Many individual neurons in the superior olive respond differently, depending on which ear receives the signal first. If the signal occurs first in one ear, the response rate of the unit is higher than if the signal occurs first at the other ear. Different neurons seem to have different preferred sides. Moreover, in the cat, the range of time differences for which this effect is observed is about 250 μsec, approximately the time it takes a sound to go from one side of a cat's head to the other. A similar relationship is found with differences in sound intensity. The results of both these variables combine to give remarkably strong evidence that this nerve station is supplying the information that is important for the localization of sounds in the environment.

Binaural interactions

Some higher levels in the auditory system also seem to be involved

[8] *An interesting aside:* Since the time resolution required for precise localization is the same for all animals, how does a large animal manage? The elephant has perhaps the biggest head of all land-dwelling mammals. But the various components of its auditory system are not simply scaled up proportionally in size. Rather, it has an extraordinarily long ear canal—almost 4.5 inches long. This puts the inner ears 9 or 10 inches closer together than the size of the head would imply. Without these long ear canals, the elephant would need relatively long neural cables connecting the two ears, which might increase the risk of losing the precise timing information needed for localization.

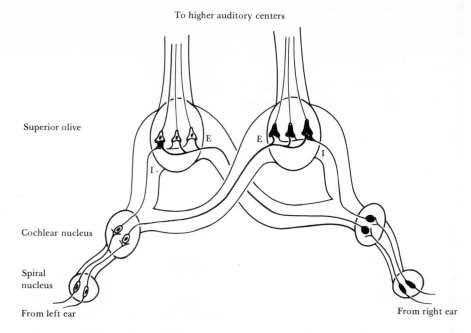

To higher auditory centers

Superior olive

Cochlear nucleus

Spiral
nucleus

From left ear

From right ear

FIGURE 7-24   *From van Bergeijk (1962).*

in comparing the signals arriving at the two ears—for example, the *inferior colliculus.* Many units in the inferior colliculus can be activated by sounds from either ear. Some units are excitatory, some inhibitory, and some produce just the sorts of interactions needed for localization. The response patterns are similar to those found in the superior olive. Also, the colliculus is organized so that different auditory frequencies are represented in very orderly patterns. This may help in both tonal judgments and in the separation and localization of different sound frequencies.

Although we are beginning to discover some of the neural mechanisms involved in comparing and combining signals from the two ears, the problem of explaining localization is far from solved. What are the neural mechanisms that tell us that something is 37° to the right and slightly elevated? How are complicated sound patterns like several people talking at once separated out and localized? These questions lie beyond our current level of understanding.

Importance of binaural listening   In addition to adding a spatial dimension to the perception of sound, binaural presentation also adds clarity. This is a consequence of three different mechanisms: localization, an apparent reduction in interference, and the minimization of masking.

Localization.   Localization allows us to spread out in space many of the sounds that are heard. Suppose we are stuck with some boring people at a party. We can keep nodding and agreeing while actually attending to a neighboring conversation. Localization makes this possible. We can choose the frequency, intensity, or spatial location to which we want to listen.

When tape-recording a conversation, the result is often very difficult to understand. There are echoes and noises. The sounds of people coughing and moving about drown out the desired voice. In the real situation, we are not aware of these noises, even though they are present. Localization cues let us attend selectively only to the auditory signals of interests. A dramatic improvement in clarity comes by adding a second microphone—making a stereophonic recording. Suddenly, one can listen to **where** the voice is, tuning out the distractions. All that is needed are two microphones differentially sensitive to sound direction. They are set up properly if one is primarily sensitive to sounds coming from the right, while the other mostly picks up sounds from the left. When a person speaks from between the two microphones, he should be picked up equally on both of them. If he stands to one side, he will come through more on one than on the other.

The problems encountered in listening to a single-channel, monaural tape recorder dramatically illustrate the problems that must be encountered by individuals who are deaf in one ear. The difficulty is caused not so much by decreased sensitivity to sound, but by the reduced ability to localize sounds. If a hearing aid is used, where is the microphone to be placed? If the hearing aid microphone is worn in a shirt pocket, normal localization will not be possible. The microphone should be as close as possible to the ear. In fact, it might be best to use two hearing aids, one for each ear (even if one ear is normal), in order to recover the ability to localize sounds.

Masking level difference. The second way in which binaural reception improves clarity is by means of a phenomenon called *the masking level difference.* When trying to hear a weak voice mixed with noise presented to one ear, the addition of the same noise to the other ear will significantly improve the clarity. One ear has both signal and noise; the other ear has noise alone. One way of looking at this is to imagine the inputs to the two ears being subtracted from one another, causing the noise to be cancelled. Thus, putting the same signal and noise in both ears would do no good: Subtracting the inputs to the two ears leaves nothing. An alternative way to view this is to notice that the noise being presented to both ears is lateralized in the center of the head, whereas the signal is heard only at one ear. The difference in spatial location leads to the improvement in intelligibility.

Masking. There is a third way in which binaural reception can improve clarity. Imagine listening to an orchestra with a big bass drum banging away while a clarinet plays in the low registers. If this is recorded monaurally, the very low frequencies of the drum will mask the low frequencies of the clarinet. This results from the overlap of excitation along the basilar membrane. However, if the clarinet and drum are heard in opposite ears, there can be no interaction along the membrane: Masking should not occur. Obviously, in an actual concert, sounds from the clarinet and drum will get to both ears, but if the listener moves his head about, he can adjust things so that most of the sound of one instrument goes to one ear and that of the other instrument goes to the other. This elimination of masking makes the sounds clearer and more distinct in a binaural than in a monaural recording.

Recordings

To get a recording of an event that really sounds as if you were sitting in the auditorium, it is necessary to make a *binaural* recording. To do this properly requires that a dummy of a head be placed in a seat in the auditorium, with microphones in each of the dummy's ears. When played back over earphones, binaural recording gives beautiful fidelity.

Binaural recording is very different from the **stereophonic** recordings which are used for most records and tapes. In stereophonic recording, the object is to try to slice across the wavefront as it crosses some point in the auditorium and reproduce it in the listener's home. There is no way that this can actually be done accurately with only two microphones and two speakers. For this reason, three- and four-channel recorders are now being tested for home use. Ideally, with two speakers there should be two microphones spaced the same distance apart as the speakers will be. This isn't very good, since it demands too much in the way of control of the playback conditions. As a result, recording engineers have learned to combine many microphones, mostly by trial and error. Pleasing results can be obtained in this manner, so that is the way recordings are currently being done. Generally, when someone wants to make a really good recording he uses many microphones scattered over the auditorium: The recording engineers determine how to combine them into two channels to give the proper effect. Psychological acoustics does not help much here. The best way to combine channels probably differs for every auditorium, for different numbers of people in the audience, and even for the way the audience is dressed.

Figure 7-25

The precedence effect

In theory, localization is performed simply by using differences in the sounds arriving at the two ears. Usually, however, the initial signal

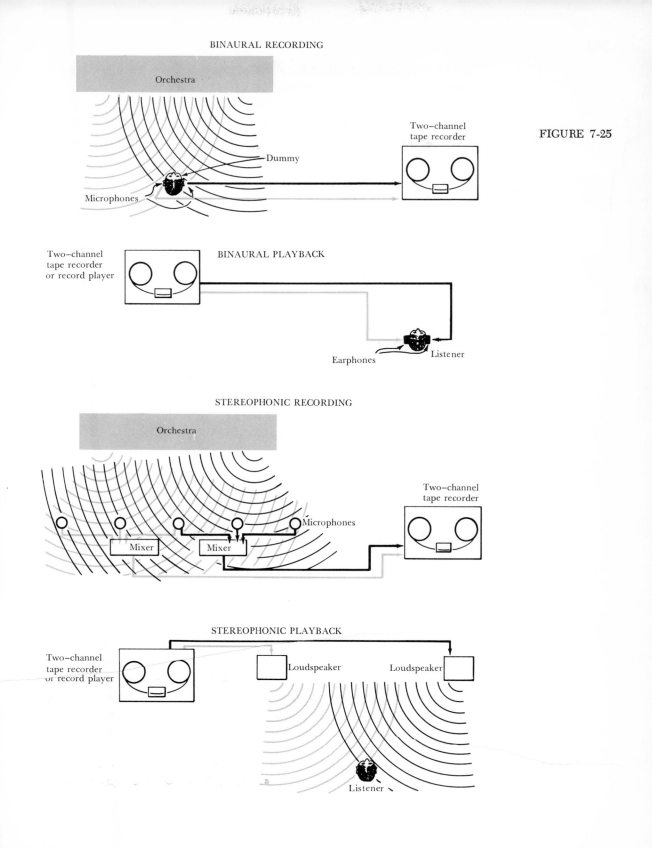

BINAURAL RECORDING

Orchestra

Dummy

Two–channel
tape recorder

Microphones

FIGURE 7-25

Two–channel
tape recorder
or record player

BINAURAL PLAYBACK

Earphones

Listener

STEREOPHONIC RECORDING

Orchestra

Mixer

Mixer

Microphones

Two–channel
tape recorder

STEREOPHONIC PLAYBACK

Two–channel
tape recorder
or record player

Loudspeaker

Loudspeaker

Listener

is immediately followed by numerous echoes. Once all the echoes are accounted for, even a simple click can be very complicated. First the click arrives at one ear, then the other, and then parts which have bounced off the walls and ceiling of the room start arriving at the ears. The two ears hear a rapid succession of sounds. How can one make use of all that to localize?

FIGURE 7-26

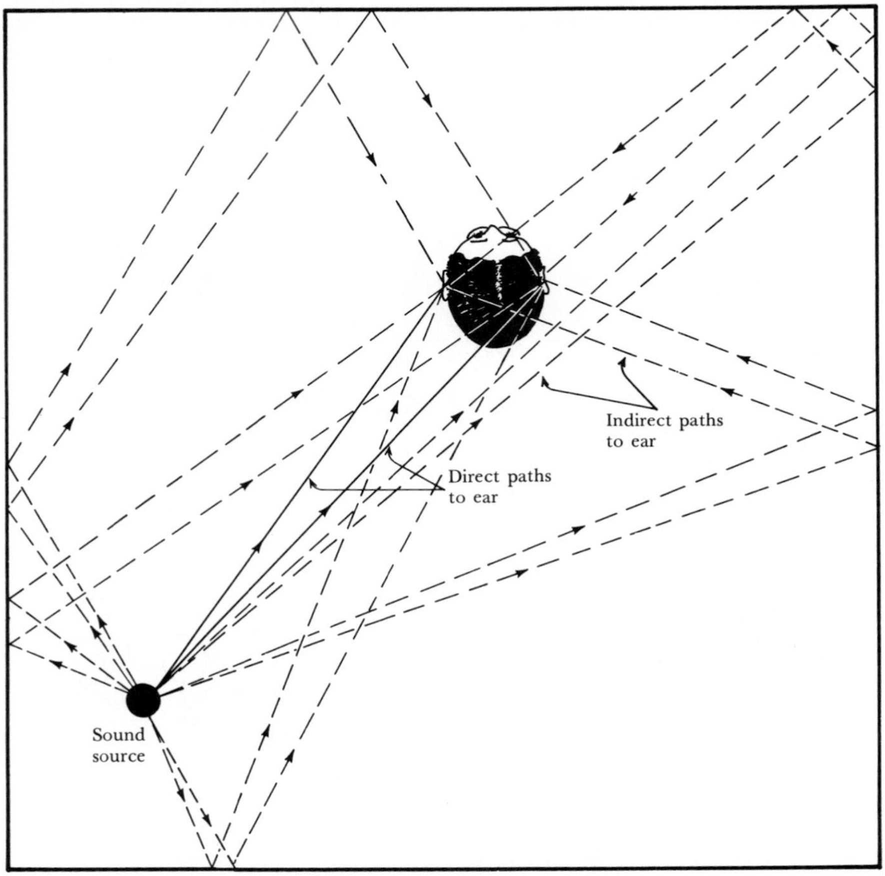

Fortunately, only the first sound to arrive appears to be used. This is called the *precedence effect*. It is not completely understood. Echoes play almost no part in the psychological interpretation of the sound. Not that they are not heard. If we record various sounds, some followed by echoes and some not, it is easy to tell the difference between them. Thus, the sound information is heard, but fortunately, it is ignored by the mechanism responsible for localization.

In addition to the readings suggested for Chapter 6, there really is not too much material easily available to study the dimensions of hearing. The chapter by Zwislocki (1965) in the *Handbook of Mathematical Psychology* (Volume III) is excellent, although a bit advanced. Do not be too dismayed by all the equations in the first part of the chapter. We have found that introductory students can get much meat out of this chapter if they simply skim quickly over the first few sections. The latter part of the chapter is especially valuable in discussing the relationships between the anatomy and physiology of the ear and the perception of loudness, pitch, and masking.

The books *Foundations of Modern Auditory Theory* (Volumes I and II) edited by Tobias (1970, in preparation) include several important chapters, especially on the measurement of loudness and on different theories of pitch perception.

The book by Kryter (1970) covers in detail *The Effect of Noise on Man* (which is also the title). Unfortunately, although the material covered by the book is of utmost importance, the level of writing makes it very difficult for the reader.

8

Neural basis of memory

It is a mistake to think of human memory as a unitary thing. Many THE MEMORY SYSTEMS
different kinds of processes are involved. Moreover, there are at least
three distinctly different types of memory: a *sensory information storage,*
a *short-term memory,* and a *long-term memory.* There may be others
as well, but if so, their properties are still not known to experimental
psychologists. Let us start the study of memory by a brief tour of the
memory systems. Then, with the overall structure in mind, we can return
to the detailed examination of each.

FIGURE 8-1

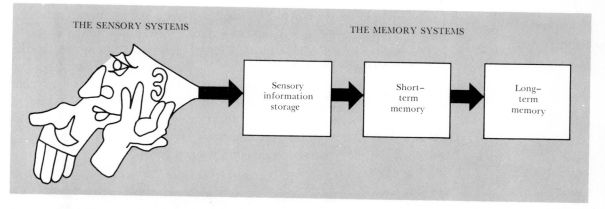

This system maintains a rather accurate and complete picture of the
world as it is received by the sensory system. Its duration is short—perhaps .1 to .5 sec.

Sensory information storage system

- Tap four fingers against your arm. Feel the immediate sensations—
  note how they fade away so that at first you still retain the actual
  feeling of the tapping, but later on only the recollection that you
  were tapped.
- Close your eyes, then open them for as short an interval of time as
  possible before you close them again. Note how the sharp, clear image
  that you picked up stays for awhile and then slowly dies away.
- Listen to some sounds, say the tapping of your fingers or a few
  whistled notes. Notice how the distinctness of the image in your
  mind fades away.
- Hold your clenched fist out in front of you. Rapidly open your hand,
  extending two fingers, and then close your fist again. But see the
  shadowy trace of the fingers remain for awhile even after your fingers
  have again formed a fist.

- Wave a pencil (or even your finger) back and forth in front of your eyes while you stare straight ahead. See the shadowy image that trails behind the moving object.

This last demonstration is the most important, for with it you can estimate how long the image lasts. Change the rate at which you wave the object back and forth. Note that if you go too slowly, you lose the continuity of the image between the endpoints of the movement. At what rate does the shadowy image just barely maintain its continuity? You should discover that it takes about 10 cycles every 5 sec to maintain the continuity of the afterimage. This means that the moving object passes in front of your eyes 20 times in 5 sec, or four times each second—the visual trace lasts about .25 sec (250 msec).

The characteristics of the visual sensory-information store are closely linked with the characteristics of the response time of the visual system studied in Chapter 5. There we suggested that the duration of the system could be measured by watching a flashlight rotate in a circle: The rate of rotation that allows the trail of a full circle to be seen gives an estimate of visual response time. Does this estimate agree with the one from the "shadowy image of a waving pencil"?

Short-term memory

The *short-term memory* system holds a different form of material than the sensory information store. Here the information retained is not a complete image of the events that have taken place at the sensory level. Rather, short-term memory seems to retain the immediate **interpretation** of those events. If a sentence has been spoken, you do not so much hear the sounds that made up the sentence as you remember the words. There is a distinct difference here between remembering an image of the events and remembering the interpretation of those events, a difference to be described in more detail later.

Things like the last few words of the sentence you have just heard or seen, a telephone number, or a person's name can be retained in short-term memory, but capacity of this memory is limited. Only about the last five or six items that have been presented can be retained. By conscious effort, by repeating the material to yourself over and over again, you can maintain the material that is in short-term memory for an indefinite amount of time. The ability to keep things active in short-term memory by this **rehearsal** of the items is one of the most important characteristics of the memory system. Information in the sensory information store cannot be rehearsed. It lasts only a few tenths of a second and there is no way to prolong it. In short-term memory, a small amount of material can be retained indefinitely by the act of rehearsal.

There is a clear and compelling difference between the memory for events that have just occurred and the memory for events long past. The one is direct and immediate; the other is tortured and slow. Events that have just occurred are still present in the mind—they have never left consciousness. Time and effort is required to insert new material into long-term memory. Past events have to be dredged up with effort. Short-term memory is immediate and direct; long-term memory is labored and strained. From short-term memory:

What were the first few words of this sentence?

From long-term memory:

What did you eat for dinner last Sunday?

Long-term memory is the most important of the memory systems, and it is also the most complex. The capacity of the sensory information store and short-term memory systems is very limited—one by a few tenths of a second, and the other by a few items, but there appears to be no practical limit on the capacity of long-term memory.[1] Everything that is retained for more than a few minutes at a time obviously must reside in the long-term memory system. All learned experiences, including the rules of language, must be a part of long-term memory. In fact, much of experimental psychology can be considered to be concerned with the problems of getting material into long-term memory, keeping it there, retrieving it, and interpreting it properly.

L.T.M. unlimited

The real difficulties associated with long-term memory stem mainly from one source: retrieval. The amount of information contained in the memory is so large that it should be a major problem to find anything. Yet things can be found rapidly; even in so prosaic an act as reading, the meanings of the symbols on the printed page must be interpreted through direct and immediate access to long-term memory. The problems associated with being able to get to the one correct item from among the millions or billions that are stored dictate much of the overall structure of all the stages of the memory system. We devote all of Chapters 10 and 11 to the study of the organization of long-term memory.

These are the memory systems. We begin the study of memory by

---

[1] Obviously, there has to be some limit: The brain is a finite device. But there are approximately ten billion (10^{10}) neurons in the brain, each capable of storing a reasonable amount of information. There are also many giant molecules—such as RNA—which individually can store vast amounts of information (see the section on "The Chemistry of Memory"). For all practical purposes, then, we can consider that the memory capacity of the human brain is unlimited.

examining the neural machinery. We look at the brain structures involved in the storage and retrieval of information and at the psychological processes of human memory.

STORING INFORMATION

Despite years of research, much of the brain remains a mystery. An anatomical examination of the brain shows that it is divided into a number of distinct regions. Seen from the top, the human brain appears as two masses of convoluted tissue split down the middle. The two halves are called the *hemispheres, left* and *right. Together they form the *cortex*, the most advanced part of the brain (sometimes called the *cerebral cortex*).

FIGURE 8-2

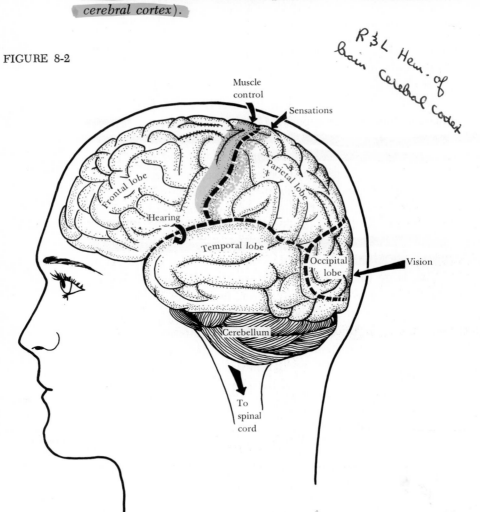

Muscle control

Sensations

Frontal lobe

Parietal lobe

Hearing

Temporal lobe

Occipital lobe

Vision

Cerebellum

To spinal cord

The different sections do differ anatomically, so they have been given different names. The front parts are called the *frontal lobes*, on the sides are the *parietal* and the *temporal lobes* (actually tucked under somewhat), and to the rear are the *occipital lobes*. The brain is symmetric: There are two each of these lobes—one on the left hemisphere, one on the right. (As with the rest of the body, the symmetry is not exact. The left half of the brain is usually slightly larger than the right, just as the right hands and feet are often slightly larger than their mates.)

Some structural or chemical changes in the brain must occur as a result of the acquisition of new knowledge. Somehow, cortical neurons alter their reaction patterns to the external events the organism comes to recognize and remember. There are a number of popular theories of how this comes about, all of them highly speculative. We are a long way from having a truly accurate or complete description of the way in which the nervous system stores information. The theories are important, even if incomplete, for they serve as useful guideposts as we follow the trail of the memory system.

There is reasonably good agreement that permanent storage of information takes place either through chemical or structural changes in the brain. There is little or no disagreement that the immediate, ongoing activities of thought, conscious processes, and the immediate memories—sensory information store and short-term memory—are mediated through electrical activity. This means that the two processes must make contact with one another: Somehow the chemical or structural changes in the brain must affect the electrical activity. Moreover, if the immediate memory systems are the result of electrical activity, then we should be able to show that neural circuits can indeed be constructed that have the capability of acting as a memory. Let us start the study of the memory systems with this problem: Devise the circuits that remember.

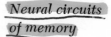
Neural circuits of memory

The main requirement of a memory circuit is that the effects of an input persist after the input has ceased, since this is the definition of memory. But more is required. A memory circuit must be selective. It should show a preferential response to a certain pattern of inputs and little or no response to other patterns. We begin by putting together some simple circuits that can qualify as memory. But first, for those readers who have not worked through Chapter 2, a brief review of neural circuits.

A review of neural circuits. The electrical impulse conveyed by the *neuron* travels from the *cell body* through the *axon* to the next cell

Figure 8-3

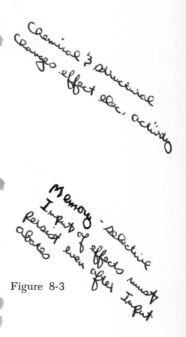

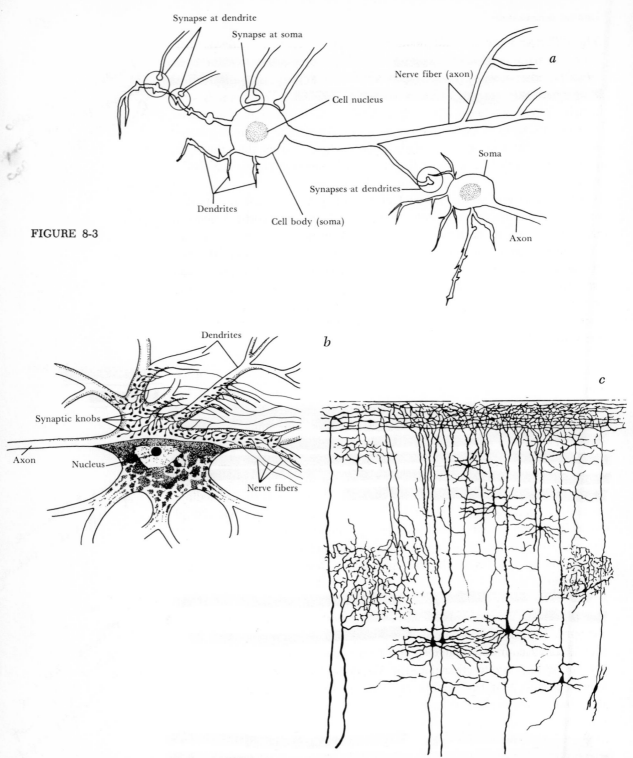

FIGURE 8-3

a

Synapse at dendrite
Synapse at soma
Nerve fiber (axon)
Cell nucleus
Dendrites
Cell body (soma)
Synapses at dendrites
Soma
Axon

b

Dendrites
Synaptic knobs
Axon
Nucleus
Nerve fibers

c

These figures are after Eccles (1965).

body. The place where the neural axon makes contact with the cell body is called a *synaptic junction*. There may be many thousands of synaptic junctions on a single cell body. In diagrams, the basic neuron is represented by a circle and a line. The circle is the cell body, the line an axon connecting the neuron to others. There are basically two kinds of synaptic connections, *excitatory* and *inhibitory*. An excitatory connection means that if a signal (neural impulse) comes along an axon to an excitatory connection, it tends to make the neuron on the other side of that synapse respond with its own neural impulse. That is, an excitatory connection tends to make the new neuron *fire*. An inhibitory connection tends to prevent firing. In the nervous system, a rather large number of impulses arriving at excitatory connections may be required to make a cell body fire: One is seldom sufficient. For the present analysis, however, we shall suppose that a single neural response arriving at an excitatory synaptic connection can make the new cell respond. Although this is inaccurate, it is only wrong in terms of numbers. The logic is sound and the story is easier to follow in terms of single neural impulses.

FIGURE 8-4

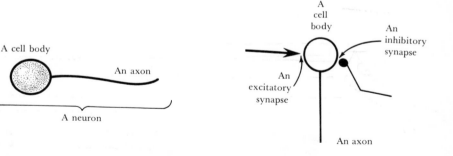

Consider the problem of maintaining a memory for a sensory input. Suppose that the printed capital letter **A** has been presented, that the various stages of pattern recognition have taken place, and that the **A** has been recognized. There are at least three different ways in which the nervous system could respond to the presence of the **A**.

There could be a *unique cell* that encodes the presence of each item, so that whenever the pattern recognition system discovers the presence of **A**, the unique "A" cell responds.

There could be a *unique pattern* of cells that responds to each item, so that the presence of an **A** is designated by the unique configuration of neural cells that respond.

There could be a *unique code* for each item, so that the letter **A** is specified by a special pattern of neural firings.

Whichever of these possible codes is present, there still must be some way of **remembering** that the **A** occurred. Let us examine one simple scheme for constructing a memory.

FIGURE 8-5

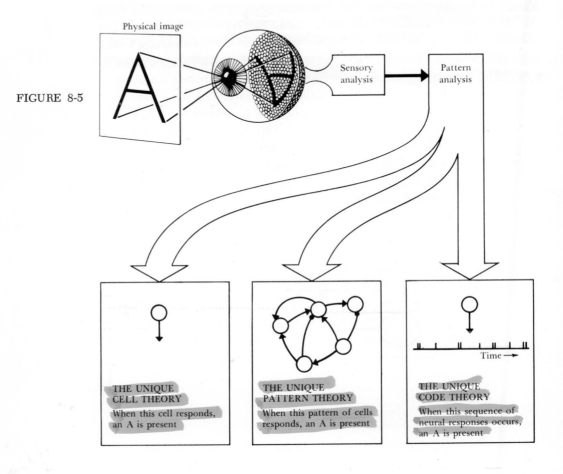

Physical image

Sensory analysis

Pattern analysis

THE UNIQUE CELL THEORY

When this cell responds, an A is present

THE UNIQUE PATTERN THEORY

When this pattern of cells responds, an A is present

THE UNIQUE CODE THEORY

When this sequence of neural responses occurs, an A is present

Time ⟶

Reverberating circuits. The simplest circuit that qualifies as a memory circuit is a closed loop. Suppose that in Figure 8-6 cell groups A and B are in the cortex. Assume that some sensory signal has just been presented and nerve fibers X and Y come from the pattern-recognition system. Thus, responses in these fibers might represent any of the three possible codes just discussed. The exact type of information arriving on the input lines in this example is not crucial to the analysis of the memory circuit.

INPUT MEMORY CELLS

FIGURE 8-6

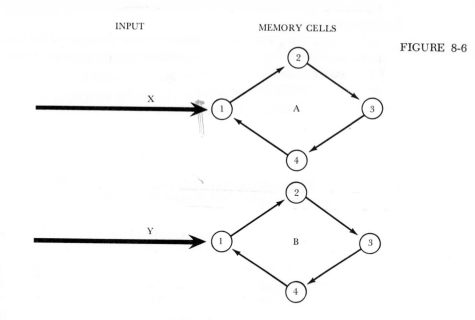

In the circuits of Figure 8-6, a signal arriving at X starts a chain of events in cell group A. Cell A1 responds to the activity in X, causing cell A2 to respond. Impulses start around the loop, firing each neuron in turn, with the sequence coming to a full circle and then starting all over again. The circuit **reverberates**: An incoming sensory signal initiates a sequence of electrical events that persists indefinitely, long after the signal stops. Reverberation in the loop A represents an electrical memory of the fact that activity has occurred along fiber X. Similarly, any activity in loop B represents an electrical memory for event B.

The reverberating activity set off by an event should not really continue indefinitely, for that is not how short-term memory operates. What stops the reverberations? There are several possibilities. One arises from the fact that an actual reverberating circuit would be much more complex. The cell groups (such as A and B) would actually involve large numbers of neurons arranged in complex patterns. All the background activity in these neurons, as well as the firing pattern (both excitatory and inhibitory) from the many extraneous inputs to the loop would probably eventually disrupt the circulating patterns. A second possibility is that the occurrence of new events might actively inhibit previous reverberating activity. A third possibility is that the neural circuits themselves may be somewhat unreliable. An impulse in one link of the chain may not always be able to initiate activity in the next link, so that eventually the impulse flow would die down. Finally, the reverberations

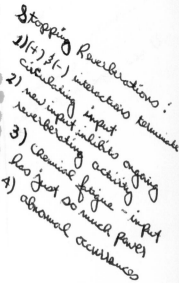

Stopping Reverberations:
1)(+)&(-) interactions terminate
circulating input
2) new input inhibits ongoing
reverberating activity
3) chemical fatigue - input
has just so much power
4) abnormal occurrences

might stop through some kind of chemical "fatigue" in the neurons or at the synapses.

Besides these built-in structural possibilities, abnormal events can occur that completely disrupt all neural activity. The abnormal event might be the concussion resulting from an accidental blow to the head which can disrupt neural activity temporarily, causing amnesia for all events still electrically encoded. Also, deliberate or accidental administration of massive electric shocks to the brain (as in electroshock treatment of psychiatric patients) can obviously disorganize the activity in memory circuits.

The selective electrical activation of a particular neural loop provides a short-term memory, one that persists only briefly. How is long-term memory represented in such a scheme?

Consolidation. In the configurations required for reverberating circuits, the memory is stored permanently by the interconnections among the neurons. One popular theory of how this comes about is that repeated electrical activity in the neural circuits can cause chemical or structural alterations in the neurons themselves, leading to the development of new neural circuits. The process of altering a circuit so that it encodes a new memory is called *consolidation*. Consolidation of a memory presumably occurs over a prolonged period of time. By this theory, specific neural circuits are built up for specific memories. Electrical activity through the circuits represents a temporary activation of them. This temporary electrical activity is what is called short-term memory. Long-term memory is represented by the permanent structure of the neural circuits. Thus, short-term and long-term memory might actually represent the very same neural tissues, with short-term memory being the temporary electrical activity in the neurons and long-term memory the permanent structure of the same neurons.

Now, by what mechanisms does the consolidation of a memory circuit operate? To answer that requires some more knowledge about how the permanent structure of the memory is represented. There are two possibilities most frequently considered: a chemical encoding, or a growth of new synaptic junctions. Let us consider these two possibilities.

Suppose long-term memory resides in the structure of protein molecules at each synapse. How could that chemical information affect the neural transmission across synapses? One way is that the protein affects the transmission of information across the gap separating the axon from the cell body. Neural information bridges this gap by chemical means: The arrival of a neural impulse at the synapse releases a *transmitter* substance which bridges the gap and affects the excitability of the cell body. Were the memory to be stored chemically, either in the synaptic

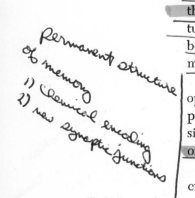

L.T.M.

Permanent structure
of memory
1) Chemical encoding
2) new synaptic junctions

junction or somewhere in the structure involved in releasing the transmitter chemicals, then it could easily control the operation of the synaptic junction.

Alternatively, long-term memory could be the result of the growth of new synapses. If this theory is true, then the brain actually changes physically whenever new concepts are learned. In principle at least, such changes should be visible: They could be seen by microscopic examination of the neurons. In practice, of course, such changes have been impossible to observe, primarily because of the extreme difficulty in viewing live neural cells through a microscope while they are responding to neural activity.

Whichever system operates to encode memory permanently—chemical changes or new neural growth—the result is that the synapse is where the effects are felt. Thus, either of these systems easily handles the encoding of memory by the *unique cell* method: The synapse now becomes such that the cell responds only when the specific information that it represents is present. If the memory is represented by a *unique pattern* of cells, this requires that a number of different synaptic junctions be affected. For a new memory to be encoded in this manner, changes in the synapses of different cells must all occur at approximately the same time. Finally, if the memory is encoded as a *unique code* of neural firings, then there must be some means of decoding the temporal information. For example, a cell might respond only if it is stimulated by two impulses in rapid succession followed by a pause of specified duration and then a single neural impulse (something like Morse code). For either a single cell or a group of cells to be sensitive only to this pattern, either there must exist timing circuits in the neural structure or a new kind of synaptic substance would be required. It is possible, for example, to have molecular structures that are inhibitory except when triggered by just the proper sequence of neural impulses, at which point they become excitatory.

Whatever the exact encoding procedure, one point does appear certain: Short-term memory is electrical in operation. The immediate memory for events is maintained by an electrical response to that event.

When the chemical processes of genetics began to be understood, it was natural to consider the possibility that the same machinery was involved in memory processes. The unique genetic information for each organism is stored in its giant molecules, *deoxyribonucleic acid* (*DNA*); the information is transferred from DNA by a second molecule, *ribonucleic acid* (*RNA*), and carried into the surrounding protoplasm. Be-

THE CHEMISTRY
OF MEMORY

cause DNA contains the genetic memory for each individual organism, it is logical to consider the possibility that it, or the RNA, could also transmit acquired knowledge. We know that proteins are involved in the operation of neurons, and that RNA is involved in the synthesis of new proteins. Might not this synthesis also be involved in the memory process?

RNA changes and learning

The recipe for protein synthesis carried by an RNA molecule is found in the specific sequence of the organic bases that are attached to the molecular chain. These bases act as templates in the construction of proteins. A different sequence of RNA bases yields a different protein. It is conceivable that the sequence of the bases, and even their relative concentrations, can be altered by an animal's experience in a learning situation.

learning may alter base sequence in RNA

In one typical experiment, a group of rats were trained to climb a wire in order to reach food on a raised platform. To control for the sheer stimulation produced during such a balancing act, a second group of rats was rotated back and forth, up and down, in a special apparatus designed to match the activity of the experimental rats. When the first group of rats had mastered the learning task a biochemical assay was taken of the RNA reservoirs of the orientation system in the brains (vestibular system) of the two groups. Both groups had higher than normal RNA concentrations. For the group subjected to the learning task, however, the relative concentrations of **bases** had also changed (Hydén & Egyházi, 1964).

Both repeated neural activation and learning experiences do have measurable effects on RNA chemistry. The kinds of changes that have been detected so far, however, are rather gross. This is due, in part, to the technical difficulties of performing the necessary experiments and biochemical assays.

Learning after alterations in the available RNA

Does the alteration in RNA after a learning experience contain information about the task? One way to test this notion is to train an animal on a specific task, extract RNA from the relevant parts of his nervous system, and then try to use this RNA to transfer some or all of that knowledge to other animals. This is a big step: The path is fraught with difficulty. But several fascinating (and highly controversial) results have been reported.

The planarian studies. The first studies began modestly. The animal studied was a rather peculiar one, the worm *Planarian* (flatworm). The attractive aspect of this worm is simply that when cut into two parts, each half regenerates to form a completely new worm. The planarian provides the ideal control condition for an experimenter: When two different tests are needed on the same animal, simply cut one in half and there you are—two identical organisms.

The experiment, then, is simple and direct. First, teach the animal some task. Then, cut the animal in half, producing two. When both halves have regenerated fully, test. If memory is encoded chemically, maybe the task will be retained by both new halves. If memory is retained in special neural connections in the head, then the animal that regenerates from the tail section may be genetically identical to its twin, but it should not contain any knowledge of learned events.

FIGURE 8-7

① The experimental animal: A planarian, with the ability to regenerate two bodies when cut in half

② Planarian tenses when given electrical shock. Shock is preceded by a bright flash of light

③ After period of training, planarian tenses when light appears

④ The trained planarian is cut in half

⑤ Result: Two complete planaria

⑥ Both animals tense when light appears, showing that learning has been retained.

A planarian normally tenses up reflexively when it is shocked. If a shock is presented to it frequently, with the shock always preceded by a bright light, the tensing motion becomes conditioned to the light, so the animal tenses whenever the light comes on, even if the shock does not follow. After training in the light–shock pairing, the animals are cut in half and the two halves allowed to regenerate. Both animals— the one grown from the tail and the one from the head—appear to remember the task (McConnell, Jacobson, & Kimble, 1959).

This, by itself, is puzzling. Normally we expect information to be stored in the brain. How is it that the planarian regenerated from the tail section remembers the connection between light and shock? Even if this information is stored in RNA molecules, how does it get to the tail? Of course, the planarian is a rather strange organism, capable of regenerating a whole new body from just a segment. Obviously, an animal that has that capability might very well have to spread out its memory throughout its body.

The reliability of the RNA interpretation is strengthened by the finding that if a trained planarian was cut in two and each half allowed to regenerate in a solution containing ribonuclease, a chemical that destroys RNA, the animal that regenerated from the old head retained the learned information as before. But the new animal that regenerated from the tail did not appear to remember the prior learning experiences (Corning & John, 1961). There are several possible interpretations of this result, the one most relevant to our purposes being that the RNA containing the information of the learned reflex was not transferred to the new body part during regeneration in a ribonuclease solution. This implies that even if RNA containing the stored information is present all throughout the body (in the worm, at least), it can only be used by the head.

Figure 8-8

Chemical studies. There are other forms of chemical studies. Many drugs have been used on a variety of animals (including humans) in a number of learning situations. The drugs most frequently used for these studies can be classed as those that **promote** protein synthesis and those that **interfere** with it. The ones that help protein synthesis usually do so by increasing the availability or the effectiveness of RNA; those that inhibit or interfere with protein synthesis usually do so by reducing the RNA availability or by competing for the constituents used for protein synthesis. Other drugs affect the transmission of neural messages across a synapse.

These studies suggest some novel aspects about memory function. The memory appears to be most vulnerable to interfering drugs soon after learning. The longer the delay between the learning experience and the administration of the drug, the larger the dosage needed to erase the memory. Does this mean that the memories become stronger simply with the passage of time?

There are, of course, many difficulties with these experiments. The debate over their interpretation has been vigorous. The fact that memory can be disrupted or impaired by chemical injections does not mean that the memory itself is based on a chemical code. Proper neural functioning depends critically on a delicately balanced and closely controlled chemical environment. This environment can be easily upset by a wide range of factors and chemicals, such as poisons, lack of oxygen, alcohol, and hallucinatory drugs, in addition to those substances specifically associated with protein synthesis and synaptic transmission. These difficulties mean that firm conclusions cannot yet be drawn.

The most dramatic psychological experiments in recent years have come from the attempts to transfer the memories of one animal to another. In addition to their ability to grow brand new bodies from partial sections, *planaria* also are cannibals—they eat one another readily: If a

Memory transfer

FIGURE 8-8

① Planarian trained to respond to light as in the previous experiment

② The trained planarian is cut in half and placed in medium containing ribonuclease

③ Ribonuclease alters formation of RNA in new half of body

④ Planarian generated from head-part responds to light; planarian generated from tail-part does not

∴ RNA is responsible for memory

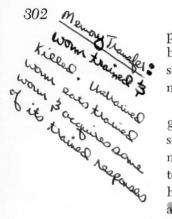

Memory Transfer:
worm trained &
killed. Untrained
worm eats trained
worm & acquires some
of its trained responses

planarian is trained at a task (taught that a shock is always preceded by a light) and then killed, mashed up, and fed to another planarian, some of the knowledge appears to be transferred to the eater (McConnell, 1962, 1964).

As might be expected, the studies of memory transfer were met with great excitement by the public and an equally great skepticism by the scientific community. Most early attempts to replicate the experiments met with failure. There appeared to be many different possible reasons to explain the apparent success of the first experiments, none of which had anything to do with memory. But even if memory were involved, a planarian is a relatively crude organism. It may have idiosyncratic learning mechanisms that are completely irrelevant to our understanding of the memory of higher organisms.

In the midst of the debate, a similar form of memory transfer was reported for rats and mice (Ungar, 1966; Ungar & Oceguera-Navarro, 1965). Rats (and people) normally jump when a very loud tone is presented. In the preliminary experiment, rats were repeatedly presented with loud tones until they became habituated to them, and no longer gave a startle response when one was presented. This habituation takes about 9 days. Dialyzed brain homogenate from the trained donors was then injected into naive mice, who were then tested for their startle reactions to a tone. The injected mice took only an average of 1.2 days to suppress their startle response: a dramatic improvement, augmented even further by the fact that an uninjected mouse takes longer than a rat to supress its startle response. Mice injected with dialyzed homogenate from untrained rats took 11 days to habituate to the tone, a rate comparable to uninjected animals.

These results are impressive, but was it actual information being transferred from animal to animal, or simply a general depressive effect? The second experiment showed that the effect of the injection was indeed specific.

One group was habituated to the tone, another to a puff of air (which normally also causes a startle reaction). When naive animals were injected, they showed a memory transfer only for the specific habituation acquired by their donor. A recipient of brain homogenate from a rat previously habituated to suppress the startle response to an air puff showed a suppressed response only for the air. This same recipient showed no reduction in the startle reaction to a tone, a task which his donor had not previously experienced.

Figure 8-9

What can be made from all this? As yet, the final answers are not in. Many scientists are rather skeptical of the whole business. If stored information can be transferred, it poses some interesting puzzles about the nature of memory. It would mean that specific memories are encoded in chemicals, that the chemicals can be moved about rather freely in the body and, indeed, from one animal to another, and even from rats to mice. How could we explain the neural encoding with all this portability? There are no clues whatsoever as to what mechanisms might allow such a system to work. We will have to await more results before we can begin to decide on its implications for the process involved in storing and retrieving information.

Evidently, the short-term memory is necessary to hold information for the time period required for consolidation. During the period of electrical activity after the occurrence of an event, the memory for it becomes consolidated into long-term storage. Thus, it should be possible to interfere with the permanent memory of events by interfering with this electrical activity. This turns out to be true. The application of large amounts of electrical current to the living brain disrupts short-term memory.

As the name implies, *electroconvulsive shock* (*ECS*) consists of applying an electrical voltage of such a magnitude as to induce convulsions. In a typical animal experiment, a rat is placed on a raised pedestal that is too small for comfort. The grid below the pedestal is electrified. When the rat steps down, his natural reaction, he is given a mildly unpleasant shock to the legs. Under normal conditions, a rat exposed to this condition learns very quickly, usually on a single trial, to remain perched on the pedestal as long as possible. But if an ECS is applied to the rat on each trial immediately after he steps down, he will continue to behave like a naive animal and step down off his perch and receive small shocks, trial after trial. The longer the delay between the response and the administration of ECS, the less likely it is that the animal will step down.[2]

The pedestal experiment avoids several problems. Suppose a different task were studied: Suppose the animal were trained simply to go down a particular alley of a maze in order to obtain food, and suppose he were given ECS after each learning trial. He might very well avoid the alley containing the food because of the unpleasant experience of the shock. That is, it would not be possible to distinguish between his inability to remember where the food was and his attempts to avoid

DISORDERS OF
MEMORY

*time is needed for STM.
to be consolidated so it
can then become incorporated
into L.T.M.*

*Electroconvulsive
shock*

*ECS: impeded rats
memory process*

Figure 8-10

[2] There have been many studies of the relation of electroconvulsive shock to retrograde amnesia. A critical review and bibliography of these experiments can be found in the paper by Deutsch (1969).

FIGURE 8-9

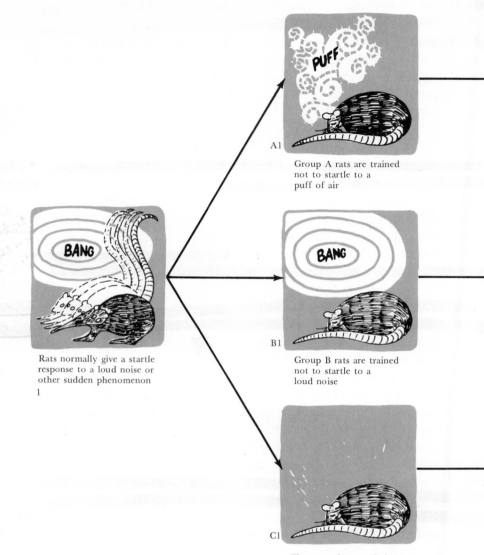

A1

Group A rats are trained
not to startle to a
puff of air

B1

Group B rats are trained
not to startle to a
loud noise

C1

The control group C, is not
trained in any way

Rats normally give a startle
response to a loud noise or
other sudden phenomenon
1

the ECS shock. In the pedestal experiment, however, he continues to
make a response which results both in a foot shock and ECS. If he
remembered any unpleasantness due to the ECS he should show an
increased reluctance to step off the pedestal. This does not happen,
so the animal appears to forget both the unpleasantness of the shock
to his feet as well as the unpleasantness of the ECS.

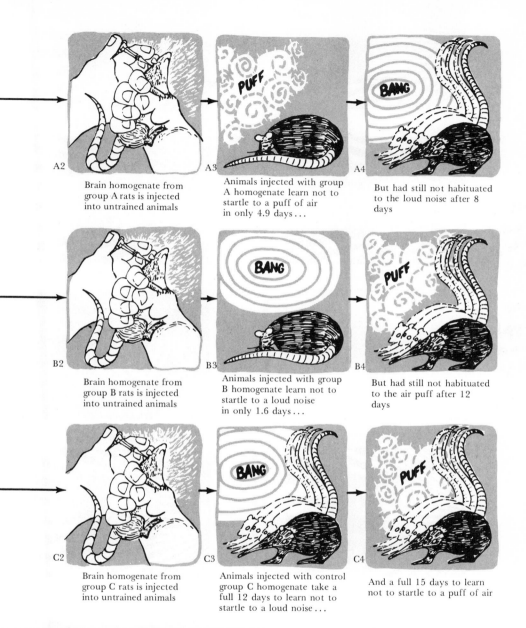

A2 — Brain homogenate from group A rats is injected into untrained animals

A3 — Animals injected with group A homogenate learn not to startle to a puff of air in only 4.9 days...

A4 — But had still not habituated to the loud noise after 8 days

B2 — Brain homogenate from group B rats is injected into untrained animals

B3 — Animals injected with group B homogenate learn not to startle to a loud noise in only 1.6 days...

B4 — But had still not habituated to the air puff after 12 days

C2 — Brain homogenate from group C rats is injected into untrained animals

C3 — Animals injected with control group C homogenate take a full 12 days to learn not to startle to a loud noise...

C4 — And a full 15 days to learn not to startle to a puff of air

Clearly, then, ECS affects an animal's memory. Since ECS has also been used as a therapeutic technique for treating human psychiatric disorders, there have been some attempts to study the effects of it on the patient's memory. The results, however, are not very convincing. If patients are required to learn a list of words just before an ECS treatment and then tested after the treatment, there does appear to

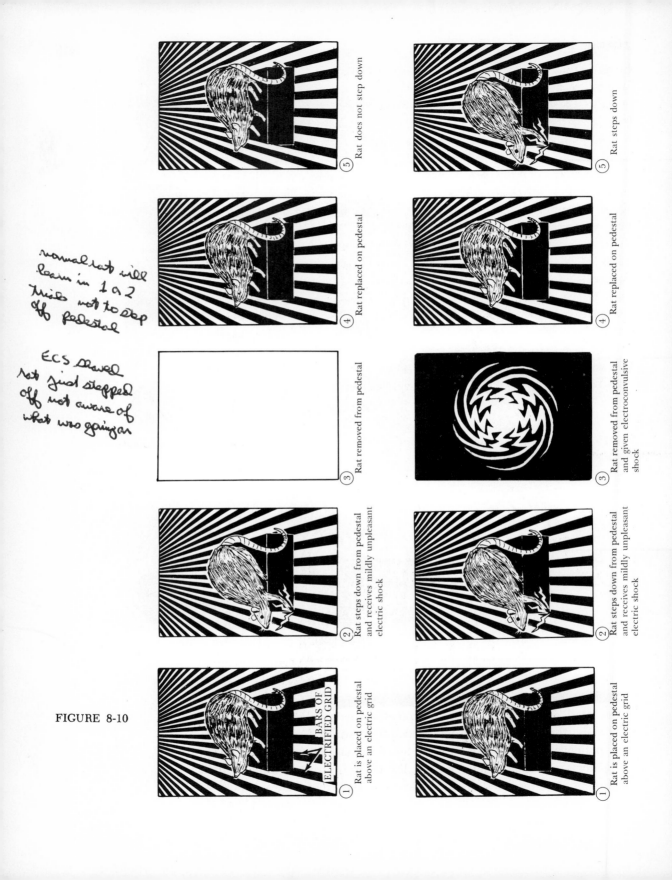

FIGURE 8-10

normal rat will learn in 1 a 2 trials not to step off pedestal

ECS slowed rat just stepped off not aware of what was going on

① Rat is placed on pedestal above an electric grid

② Rat steps down from pedestal and receives mildly unpleasant electric shock

③ Rat removed from pedestal

④ Rat replaced on pedestal

⑤ Rat does not step down

① Rat is placed on pedestal above an electric grid

② Rat steps down from pedestal and receives mildly unpleasant electric shock

③ Rat removed from pedestal and given electroconvulsive shock

④ Rat replaced on pedestal

⑤ Rat steps down

BARS OF ELECTRIFIED GRID

be more than normal forgetting of the word list. But many motivational factors are also involved—the patients have some psychological disturbances to begin with, they are normally very anxious about the impending shock treatment, and they usually do not have much interest in learning a group of unrelated words (but see Williams, 1966).

Electroconvulsive shock can disrupt learning in animals, and may create an amnesia in humans, at least for very recent events. These amnesiac effects are interesting in themselves and offer some guidelines for the study of memory. A common form of amnesia is called *retrograde amnesia*. It usually is brought about from some severe jolt to the brain, either by a fall, a crash, by being hit on the head or, of course, by electric shock. The victim of retrograde amnesia appears to forget events prior to the accident. Strangely enough, however, he does not forget events that occurred far in the past. Rather, it is as if there were a simple line in the memory extending in time. When the accident occurs, the line is erased, starting with the time of the accident and extending backward for a duration proportional to the severity of the wound.

    As the patient recovers, old memories return first.

Amnesias

Hypothetical recovery phase after retrograde amnesia. After data of Barbizet (1970).   FIGURE 8-11

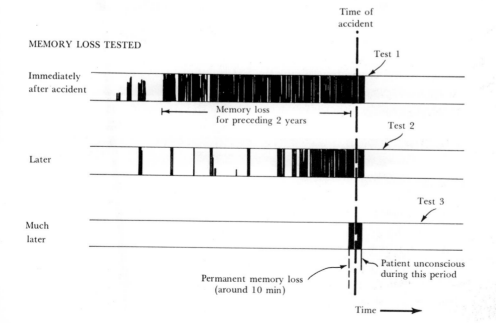

Thus, memories were not really erased: Rather, they were simply covered over. The process of recovery appears to be that of uncovering the memory line, starting with the very distant past and working its way forward to the present. How much is eventually recovered depends upon many factors, but almost everyone recovers. (The scenes you see in the movies in which memory is lost for years and years seldom happen, and when they do, they are likely to be caused by psychological factors rather than by physical brain damage. That is, the patient is deliberately—albeit, unconsciously—suppressing certain memories. They can all be retrieved after sufficient psychiatric treatment.) The last few minutes prior to the accident never seem to be recalled. It is as if these events were only in short-term memory at the time of the accident and never made it to long-term memory. This fact is often used as support of the time period required for the consolidation of a memory.

The pattern of forgetting and recovery in retrograde anmesia has some important implications concerning the way memories function. First, notice that only the memory for events that have occurred in the past is affected. Other kinds of stored information—information about the comprehension and use of language—remains intact. We will see later that some kinds of brain damage appear to affect only language functions without disrupting the memory for the past.

Because the memory does gradually recover after the traumatic experience, the information cannot have been wiped out by the shock, but simply made inaccessible. Thus the actual storage of information must be separate from the processes that retrieve stored memories.

Consider again the strange pattern of recovery from amnesia. Older memories are both the least likely to be lost and also the first to come back. The recovery proceeds in time from the distant past to the present. This suggests two things about the nature of memory. For one, information about when an event occurs must be an important cue to its subsequent retrieval. Otherwise, why would the recovery pattern be so closely connected to the time an event happened? Second, this patterning would tend to imply that older memories are stronger than newer ones: Memory may somehow be automatically strengthened simply with the passage of time. Otherwise, why should the oldest memories be most resistant to the effects of traumatic shock and the recent memories the most vulnerable? But this interpretation also goes against all common sense. Certainly, we have greatest trouble in retrieving old memories; if they are the strongest, should they not also be the easiest to use?

The very difficulty of getting to older memories may be the clue to their apparent resistance to amnesias. Maybe the event only affects stronger and more accessible memories. Maybe the trauma spreads from

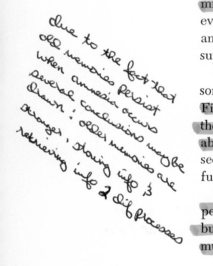

due to the fact that old memories persist when amnesia occurs several conclusions may be drawn: older memories are stronger; storing info & retrieving info 2 dif processes

the present—certainly the most available of our memory experiences—to the past through the trail of the long-term memory structure. If so, then actually we need to reassess some of the studies on the chemical basis of memory. If you remember from that section, it was found that the longer the delay between training on a task and administration of the memory-erasing drug, the larger the dosage needed to have the effect. Was this because older memories are stronger (as was suggested there), or simply because older memories are not as immediately accessible as new memories and, therefore, are harder to destroy? How does one tell?

The fact that the events of the last few minutes before the brain injury are never recovered is consistent with the earlier results concerning the effects of ECS.[3] Disruption of short-term memory seems to interfere with the storage of the events in long-term memory. This does not mean that so long as short-term memory is functioning properly, the information will be automatically recorded in long-term memory. We remember the events that just happened for a brief period of time, apparently without effort. But to record a more permanent memory of the events seems to require active effort. Something more than short-term electrical reverberation seems to be necessary in order for the storage of long-term information to take place.

Consider the memory disorder suffered by a patient whom we shall call N.A. He was stationed at a rather boring military base, so, to pass the time, he used to fence. One day the protective tip of the foil used by his opponent came off, and N.A. was wounded; the tip of the weapon passed through the rather weak bone structure of the nostril and penetrated slightly into the brain. Several months after the incident, to the casual observer, N.A. appeared to be fully recovered. He walked about and acted normally. He could hold normal conversations. There was one striking feature about his behavior: He did not appear to be able to retain any new knowledge for more than a very short time.

A good illustration of his difficulties comes from this anecdote.

One of the psychologists studying N.A's memory difficulties was Dr.

The cases of H.M. and N.A.

[3] There is a disconcerting discrepancy here between the times associated with short-term memory in animals and in humans. The ECS work with animals suggests that short-term memory lasts for as long as an hour. In some animal studies, anything retained during the first 24 hours after an event is considered to come from short-term memory. With humans, short-term memory typically refers to time measured in seconds. In the next chapter, we see that human short-term memory may persist only for a period of some 20 to 30 sec.

Wayne Wickelgren, then at the Massachusetts Institute of Technology. As Professor Wickelgren tells the story:

> I was introduced to N.A. in a small coffee room in the Psychology Department at M.I.T. The introduction went approximately as follows. N.A. heard my name and he said,
>
> "Wickelgren, that's a German name, isn't it?"
>
> I said, "No."
>
> "Irish?"
>
> "No."
>
> "Scandinavian?"
>
> "Yes, it's Scandinavian."
>
> After having about a five minute conversation with him, I left to go to my office for perhaps another five minutes. When I returned, he looked at me as if he had never seen me before in his life, and I was introduced to him again. Whereupon he said:
>
> "Wickelgren, that's a German name, isn't it?"
>
> "No."
>
> "Irish?"
>
> "No."
>
> "Scandinavian?"
>
> "Yes."
>
> Exactly the same sequence as before. [Wickelgren, personal communication]

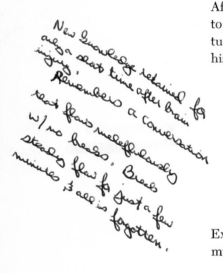

New knowledge is retained for only a short time after brain injury. Remembers a conversation, that flows meticulously w/ no break. Breaks steady flow for just a few minutes & all is forgotten.

Although each conversation with N.A. appeared to be perfectly normal, whenever anything occurred to break the continuity of the session, then things started all over again as if they had never occurred before.[4]

---

[4] Incidentally, this makes it very difficult to do experiments with these patients. One of us had been working with Professor Wickelgren studying short-term memory in Harvard and M.I.T. students. On one of N.A.'s visits to M.I.T., we thought it would be valuable to test N.A. on our experiments, since this would allow us to compare N.A.'s memory with that of our other subjects. We were never able to get beyond the instructions. N.A. would listen to our explanation of the experiment, nod his head and say, "Fine, let's go." Then we would turn around to start the tape recorder and other apparatus. Just as the first experimental material was to be presented, we would say, "Are you ready?" Invariably, the reply would

What is life like for someone with this impairment? Another patient who has been studied extensively is H.M., who had severe epileptic seizures. When he was 27 years old, he was no longer able to work, and because of his desperate condition, both of his medial temporal lobes were surgically removed. (These are the lower side lobes of the brain.) Afterward, his severe epileptic seizures disappeared, his IQ measured at 118 (compared with 104 before the operation), but he could not learn new things. Here is how some of the scientists who have studied H.M. describe his life:

> During three of the nights at the Clinical Research Center, the patient rang for the night nurse, asking her, with many apologies, if she would tell him where he was and how he came to be there. He clearly recognized that he was in a hospital but seemed unable to reconstruct any of the events of the previous day. On another occasion, he remarked, "Every day is alone in itself, whatever enjoyment I've had, and whatever sorrow I've had." He often volunteers stereotyped descriptions of his own state by saying it is "like waking from a dream." His experience seems to be that of a person who is just becoming aware of his surroundings without fully comprehending the situation, because he does not remember what went before. [Milner, Corkin, & Teuber (1968)]

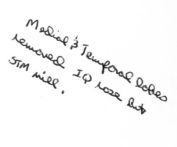

Once again, the type of impairment suffered by these patients poses some interesting implications about memory. Their memory systems appear to work properly in every respect but one: Entry into long-term memory. The entry and retrieval of information from short-term memory seems to be unimpaired. The patients can hold a conversation and thus must be able to retrieve word meanings from their permanent memory. They are capable of using the system—they simply cannot put anything new into it.

---

be something like, "Ready for what? Do you want me to do something?" Later on, Wickelgren was more successful, but our initial difficulties illustrate the fact that, although such patients appear to provide extremely useful information about memory, it is extremely difficult to obtain the necessary data. In addition, they suffer from other problems caused by the neurological deficit, problems which are unrelated to memory but which also cause motivational and emotional difficulties in doing these studies.

For a more complete description of the tests one performs on such patients, see the series of six papers which appeared in *Neuropsychologia*, 1968, **6**, pp. 211–282 (described in more detail in "Suggested Readings"), which discusses the two individuals, N.A. and H.M.

This is an important distinction. How can a patient carry out the complex retrieval processes needed to comprehend and use language, yet be unable to enter new material into the memory system? Even H.M., the patient most severely affected by his disorders, had undisturbed comprehension of language: "He can repeat and transform sentences with complex syntax, and he gets the points of jokes, including those turning on semantic ambiguity." [Milner *et al.* (1968).]

Previously we found it was important to distinguish between the information that already resides in memory and the processes responsible for retrieving it. Evidently it is also important to distinguish between those procedures which access long-term storage and those responsible for entering new information into long-term memory. These patients can set up temporary memories—both the normal short-term memory and whatever "working memories" are required to keep track of the information as it is retrieved from long-term memory. But the processes responsible for making this temporary material permanent have been selectively disturbed.

What can these patients learn? The answer to this question is not easy to obtain. It is clear that some things can be learned: H.M. could not describe his job in the state rehabilitation center (mounting cigarette lighters on cardboard frames for display), even after 6 months of daily exposure. But he did become "dimly aware" of some things—his father's death, the assassination of President Kennedy. Does this slight residual memory capacity tell us something of the nature of the memory processes, or is it simply an indication that the neurological deficit is not complete? Patient N.A., for example, did continue to improve his memory ability slightly during the period following his accident, so that when one of us tested him at the University of California (some 5 years after the incidents described earlier), he had improved somewhat in his ability to learn things. However, attempts to try to improve his memory still further through training in mnemonic techniques met with dismal failure. H.M. has not improved in his memory skills with time.

The ability to acquire new material may depend on the type of information involved. For many patients suffering from memory deficits, there is a distinction between their ability to learn verbal material and to learn nonverbal things.

Mechanisms of memory Some of the general characteristics of memory begin to emerge as we study the types of memory impairments resulting from neurological disorders. For a brief time after their occurrence, events seem to persist in a short-term memory. Disrupting this memory disrupts the ability to form a more permanent record of the incoming information. But short-term persistence is not enough for long-term storage. An individual may not be able to acquire new information even though his short-term memory seems to be operating properly. Moreover, there seem to be separate processes related to retention of old information and the acquisition of new: We can have the one without the other. Furthermore, retrieval mechanisms must be considered separately from those mechanisms which actually store information. Retrieval can be disturbed without affecting storage, and disruptions in retrieval may be only for specific classes of information.

As these general characteristics of memory begin to take shape, a natural question comes up: Where are these various functions located in the brain? Are specific parts of the brain responsible for carrying out specific aspects of storage and retrieval? If the locus of these memory functions can be discovered, then we can start to work out the details of their operation.

The first information regarding localization of brain function came from very gross observations of patients with brain injuries. Thus, it was quickly noted that destruction of the areas to the rear of the skull caused visual deficits, while destruction of parts of the frontal areas tended to produce emotional and motivational deficits. In addition, destruction of the left half of the brain affected speech, especially for right-handed individuals. Hence the first general statements of localization of function.

THE SEARCH FOR LONG-TERM MEMORY

But there is a complication. To the surprise of everyone, both people and animals can sustain huge injuries that destroy large portions of the brain without any apparent disruption in their memories. In fact, it seems to be almost impossible to eradicate specific memories absolutely once they have been established. About the only rule that emerges is a very general one: The greater the damage to the brain, the more it affects the patient.

can't eradicate memories once they've been established

This last statement, known as the *Law of Mass Action,* originates with the pioneering work of the psychologist Lashley (1931, 1950). Lashley sought the *engram,* the neural trace of a specific memory. He taught various tasks to his experimental animals, and then surgically destroyed parts of their brains, hoping to discover just which part contained the memory for the task. Lashley failed to find any evidence whatsoever that a specific memory is stored in a specific part of the brain. Instead, he found that the memory for the task was disrupted in a manner roughly proportional to the amount (weight) of the brain tissue destroyed—the Law of Mass Action.

Mass Action

This same result is mirrored by the types of memory losses typically encountered in patients who suffer from neurological damage, whether by accident or by surgery. It has never been possible to show that specific memories are destroyed. It is possible to lose memories of a restricted time period, as in amnesias, but a specific memory for a specific event, once well established, cannot be surgically erased. Granted, a patient may not be able to recall specific events, he may have great difficulties with his memory, being unable to distinguish new events from old ones, but there is no evidence that this is any more than damage to certain retrieval functions, making old recollections difficult to get at.

What is the general conclusion from this? One possibility is that memories are not stored in specific locations, but rather they are scattered about as patterns throughout the brain. In this case, any specific memory would involve large sections of the brain, with no one section being absolutely necessary, but the more sections that join in, the clearer the recollection. Thus, some scientists suggest that incoming events are impressed upon the continuing activity over much of the brain, and memory consists in an alteration of this complex diffuse pattern of ongoing activity.[5]

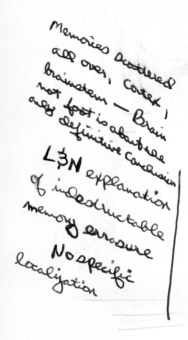

Memories scattered all over, Cortex brainstem — Brain not lost is about the only definitive conclusion

LBN explanation of indestructable memory errosure

No specific localization

ONE BRAIN OR TWO

The body is symmetrical. We have two arms, two legs, two eyes, and two ears. We also have two brains, or at least two halves that are almost exact duplicates of one another. Each half has its own centers for receiving auditory, visual, and tactile information and for control of muscle movements. The two cortical halves of the brain communicate with each other by means of a massive set of nerve fibers called the *corpus callosum*.

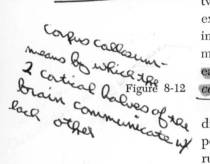

Corpus callosum — means by which the 2 cortical halves of the brain communicate w/ each other

Figure 8-12

The symmetry in the anatomy of the two halves of the brain immediately raises the question of whether or not they could work independently of one another. Certainly, the anatomical evidence does not rule out such a possibility. Each sensory organ sends its information to both halves of the brain. But are there two separate memory systems? Does each half of the brain store the same information, providing redundancy in case of breakdown? Or do they divide the load, with one

---

[5] Those of you who know about the way that a visual image is recorded on a *hologram* will immediately recognize the analogy. Unfortunately, the analogy is too simple. There are many more facts about human memory that must be explained than simply the Law of Mass Action. Hologram models have not yet been applied to sufficient numbers of problems of human memory to allow them to be evaluated.

FIGURE 8-12

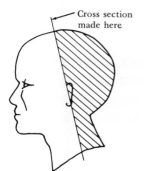

Cross section
made here

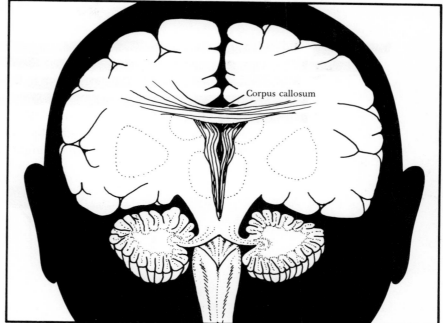

Corpus callosum

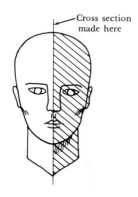

Cross section
made here

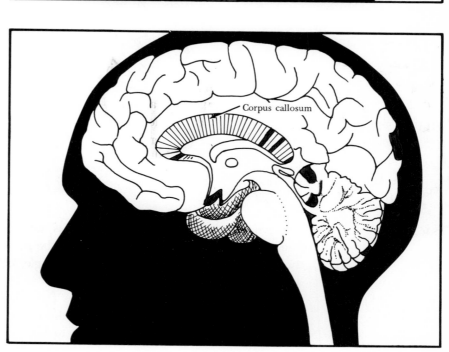

Corpus callosum

half doing some things and the other half others? Or, possibly, does one half loaf, doing little or no work, being completely superceded by the other, functional half? The answers to all these questions appear to be yes: a cautious and guarded yes, with if's, but's, and maybe's, but yes.

Split brains | The visual system provides the best test of the function of the two
in animals | hemispheres. With the visual system, everything at the left half of the retina gets sent to the left half of the brain. Everything on the right half of the retina gets sent to the right half of the brain. This is true of both eyes. (Remember that the lens of the eye reverses the image, so that when you look straight ahead, objects to the left end up on the right half of the retina and, thus, at the right half of the brain.)

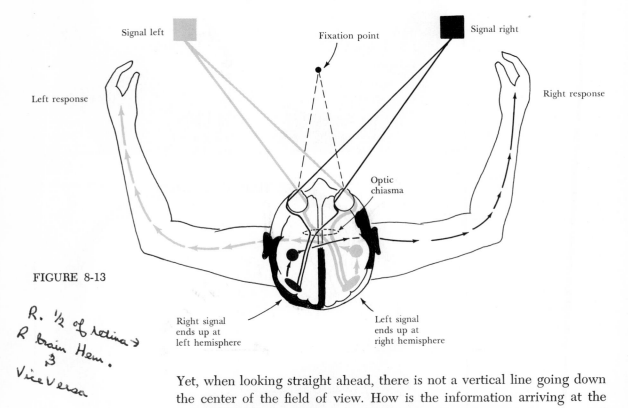

FIGURE 8-13

R. ½ of retina →
R brain Hem.
3
Vice Versa

Yet, when looking straight ahead, there is not a vertical line going down the center of the field of view. How is the information arriving at the two hemispheres coordinated to give a single, coherent perception and memory?

The first question, then, is how does the information arriving at one side of the brain interact with the information arriving at the other side? One way to get at this issue is to train an animal on some task where only one side of his brain receives the sensory information. Then test him under conditions where only the opposite side, the untrained hemisphere, can see the test stimulus. Can the animal perform the task properly?

Figure 8-13 shows the optic fibers going from the eyes to the brain, meeting and crossing over at the location called the *optic chiasma* (see Chapter 4). If a surgical cut is made through the middle of this structure, then the left half of the brain receives information only from the left eye and the right hemisphere receives information only from the right eye. This is the first test. With the optic chiasma cut, the animal is trained with his left eye open and a patch over his right eye. After he has learned the task he is tested with the patch over his left eye and his right eye open. Does the right half of his brain know what the left half learned? The answer is yes. The animal is perfectly able to perform the task even though his right hemisphere has had no direct experience with the information before.

The left and right halves of the brain seem to be aware of what each is doing. How does this happen? Two reasons come to mind. One, each hemisphere sends incoming information it receives to the other side as soon as it comes in and this duplicates memory records in both hemispheres. Since both halves of the brain are remembering the information, it doesn't matter which is subsequently tested on the learning task. Two, the material presented to the left hemisphere is stored only in that hemisphere. During testing, the right hemisphere may simply have complete access to the information stored in the left. Again, obviously, this system would be able to perform the experiment just tried.

Clearly, the key is the communication channel between the two halves of the brain. Suppose an experiment starts out exactly as before with the optic chiasma cut and the animal trained on a task using only his left eye. This time, after training but before testing, a cut is also made through the corpus callosum, severing the communication lines between the two hemispheres. The animal is then tested with his right eye. Now his right hemisphere no longer has access to the left and can't use any information that might be stored there. Unless duplicate memories have been built up, the animal should be unable to perform the task. The task can sometimes be done just as well with the right eye as with the left. Apparently both hemispheres have stored information relevant to the learning experience.[6]

---

[6] There is actually a good deal of debate on this point. Some researchers believe that only "simple" tasks get stored in both hemispheres, with "complex" tasks residing primarily in one (see Myers, 1962). See Chapter 5 of Gazzaniga's book *The Bisected Brain* (1970) for a more complete discussion of this issue.

Just when are those duplicate memories formed? Are they automatically built up as the animal learns the task? Or are they first recorded in the half of the brain receiving the sensory information, then subsequently transferred over the corpus collosum to the other half? Cuts of the corpus callosum cannot answer this question, since they can only be made sometime after the learning experiences, time during which the memory could be transferred. Some method is needed of temporarily stopping the activities of one hemisphere, then later testing it when it is operating normally—a reversible lesion.

This can be done by chemical means. Puromycin and potassium chloride are two chemicals that temporarily suppress the electrical activity in the cortex. With the whole cortex suppressed, the animal is unable to learn even simple discrimination tasks. The application of these chemicals, then, provides a technique for temporarily deactivating one of the hemispheres. It provides a substitute for surgical cuts of the optic chiasma and corpus callosum.

Now for the test: Train the animal with his right hemisphere suppressed. Let the chemicals wear off and allow time for the memories to transfer, if that is what is going on. Then test him with the left hemisphere suppressed. When this is done, it turns out that the animal cannot perform the task: He acts as though he has never been exposed to the situation before. Duplicate memories must be formed at the time the task is being learned.[7]

Split brains in humans Unlike animal brains, the two hemispheres in the human brain seem to be specialized in the kinds of information they store. The left hemisphere usually contains the information necessary for processing language symbols. This raises some interesting questions: What memory functions can be performed by the mute half of the brain? Can it recognize anything? Can it memorize?

Consider the typical behavior of a patient who has undergone split-brain surgery to arrest epileptic symptoms. The operation is similar to the one for animals. The corpus callosum is sectioned, severing cortical communication between the two halves of the brain.

From casual observation, the patient appears to be perfectly normal after the operation. (In fact, some people have been born with this split and lived for many years without problems.) Careful experimental procedures are needed to detect any peculiarities in behavior. The key is to test the patient when the sensory input is restricted to a single

[7] For studies of hemispheric depression, see Bureš and Burešová, 1960. A critical summary of studies of hemisphere depression (with the intent of *disproving* the whole memory interpretation) occurs in the paper by Deutsch (1969).

hemisphere of the brain. By controlling which hemisphere receives the sensory information and asking some questions, we can probe the memory capabilities of each half of the brain.

First of all, the patient responds normally to any object presented to his right hand or to his right visual field. That is, if he is shown or handed a pair of scissors on his right side, he will say, "That is scissors."

This is to be expected, since the sensory input in this case reaches the left hemisphere and therefore makes normal contact with the language centers. Objects presented to the left visual field or to the left hand have an entirely different effect. If the patient is asked what he is holding in his left hand, he answers that his left hand feels numb. If a visual image is presented to the left visual field, he states that he sees a flash but cannot make out any details.

What is the problem here? At first, it appears that he cannot recognize anything with the right hemisphere. But if an object is first put into his left hand, then removed and put in a bag with other objects, the patient is quite capable of retrieving the correct object with his left hand when asked to do so. Moreover, if after an object is presented to his left hand, a series of pictures is flashed to the left visual field, he can point to the appropriate picture, but only with his left hand. In addition, although he cannot **describe** the object, he can show by gestures the **function** of the object. For example, if shown a knife, he might make cutting gestures. If shown a key, he might place it in an imaginary keyhole. Finally, he can draw with his left hand a picture of what he has seen in his left visual field. In all of these cases, he is totally incapable of describing the object verbally.

Even after a patient has successfully retrieved an object from a bag or has pointed it out in a picture, or has demonstrated its use, he will be unable to name it properly. If he is asked what he has drawn with his left hand, his answer will be wrong. For example, if a picture of "$" is presented to his left visual field and "?" to his right visual field, he will draw "$" with his left hand, and "?" with his right. If the word "key" is presented to his left visual field and "case" to his right, he will say he does not know what he saw, but he nevertheless can search with his left hand and find a key. When asked what he is holding, he may say that it is a case of some sort, such as "a case of beer" (Sperry, 1968).

What do these phenomena indicate? They suggest that when communication has been cut between the two hemispheres of the brain, the person begins to act as if he were two separate people; the left hand truly does not know what the right hand is doing. Since the left half

Figure 8-14

*L.B. lang.
responses w/in rt.
visual field normal after
operation – sectioning the
C.C.
responses w/in lft.
visual field impeded.
Can't describe objects
Can gesticulate
of object function*

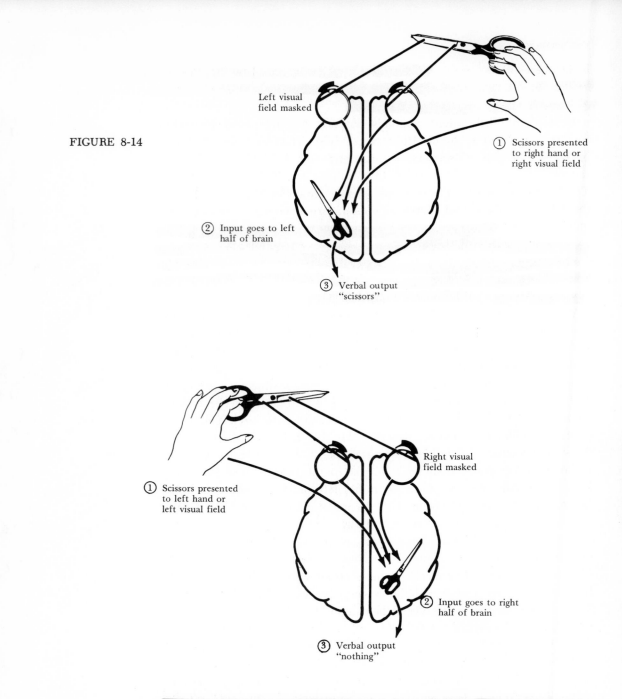

FIGURE 8-14

Left visual
field masked

① Scissors presented
to right hand or
right visual field

② Input goes to left
half of brain

③ Verbal output
"scissors"

Right visual
field masked

① Scissors presented
to left hand or
left visual field

② Input goes to right
half of brain

③ Verbal output
"nothing"

of the brain is the only one that can use language, the person is incapable of verbalizing or writing about anything the right half of the brain is monitoring. But the right half of the brain is still capable of object recognition and memory as well, for it can search for and find an object that was presented and then removed. Furthermore, it is evident that the classification of information in the right half of his brain involves

rather sophisticated conceptualization. Suppose he is presented with a
picture of a clock in his right visual field and asked to pick it out
from a pile of objects with his left hand. If there is no clock, but only
a wrist watch, he will select the wrist watch. The watch is functionally
the same as a clock. Moreover, he picks out the watch even though
there may be other objects in the pile which are physically more similar
to a clock. In other words, although the right half of the brain cannot
use language normally, it can use concepts. The right half of the brain,
then, while independent of language, is nevertheless still capable of
intellectual tasks.

One rather startling result is that while the right half of the brain
cannot speak, it can obey spoken commands and can recognize written
words. Thus, it is not quite accurate to say the right half of the brain
is working entirely without any language function.

The right half of the brain is incapable of language **production,** but
it is capable of language **recognition.** The left hand (controlled by the
right half of the brain) cannot write the name of an object flashed
into the left visual field (this is language production). Yet, the right
brain can recognize a written name of an object flashed in the left
visual field (this is language recognition). To demonstrate that recognition had indeed occurred, the patient is asked to push a button when
the specific name is presented or to use his right hand to pick out
an object from among many objects in a bag.

The right half of the brain is limited in its ability to recognize language. It is very good at comprehending concrete nouns, but somewhat
less good at comprehending verbs or nouns derived from verbs (such
as "locker," "clipping," or "fall") (Gazzaniga, 1970, p. 119). For example,
the patient is incapable of moving either hand appropriately to commands such as "knock," "squeeze," "point," when they are presented
to the right hemisphere. A simple control test demonstrates that this
inability to respond is due to problems of language comprehension rather
than of motor control. The patient is perfectly capable of using his
hand to perform the appropriate movement if a **picture** of the movement,
rather than a verbal command, is flashed to the right hemisphere.

The brain of higher organisms, then, seems to consist of two fully
equipped central processing systems, tied together by a massive set of
communication lines. Ordinarily, each system receives only part of the
sensory information arriving from the various sensory receptors. The
left half of the brain receives visual information from the right half
of the visual field, tactile information from touch receptors in the right
half of the body, and the bulk of the auditory information from the
right ear. The right half of the brain receives the complementary set

[Handwritten margin notes: Speaking of brain as 2 separate entities. rt. ½ of brain can use concepts even though it can't use lang. normally. rt. ½ brain capable of intellectual tasks]

of sensory data. The communicating fibers of the corpus callosum seem to be used to transfer the missing parts of the message to each cortex, so that each half of the brain has a complete representation of the environment. Normally, the two hemispheres appear to build up duplicate memories in a learning task, even when the sensory messages may be restricted to one half of the brain. When the two processing systems are disconnected, they are capable of functioning independently. Each half can acquire and store the information needed to perform a learning task. The fact that each hemisphere is receiving only part of the environmental information does not seem to be a serious handicap. Congenital brain damage affecting the corpus callosum in humans does not produce any serious impairment of perceptual or intellectual abilities.

The fact that the two halves of the brain in a split-brain patient function independently of each other does bring up certain problems in decision making, as the following excerpt from Gazzaniga's book illustrates.

> Case I . . . would sometimes find himself pulling his pants down with one hand and pulling them up with the other. Once, he grabbed his wife with his left hand and shook her violently, while with the right trying to come to his wife's aid in bringing the left belligerent hand under control. Once, while I was playing horseshoes with the patient in his backyard, he happened to pick up an axe leaning against the house with his left hand. Because it was entirely likely that the more aggressive right hemisphere might be in control, I discreetly left the scene—not wanting to be the victim for the test case of which half-brain does society punish or execute. [Gazzaniga (1970), p. 107]

Duplication of memories
coordinates the activity
of a 2 brain system
controlling the same
organism

Selective environ.
Pressures

Since there are two brains controlling the same organism, duplicating memories seems to be a straightforward way of coordinating the activity of the two systems. It avoids the possible conflicts that might arise if each half of the brain were learning different things. This duplication of memory, however, may be a luxury that can only be afforded by lower organisms for whom the demands of the environment seem unlikely to strain their learning and memory capabilities. In humans, the situation is not so simple. The extraordinary perceptual learning, memory, and motor demands imposed by the human's language system seem to have led to some degree of specialization in the functions performed by the two hemispheres. One of the hemispheres, usually the left, seems to develop most of the functions needed for language production. Only brain damage to this "dominant" hemisphere appears to affect a person's ability to cope with language.

In addition to raising problems in coordinating information, having two brains that can function independently has its advantages. First, it gives great flexibility to the operation. With two symmetrical halves of the brain, either can take over, should emergency arise. When children receive severe brain injury at an early enough age the other side of the brain can take over, compensating for the damage. Is the compensation complete? It is difficult to tell. To tell would require a control, some way of knowing how the person would have developed had the brain been normal. Whether or not it is complete, the compensation is amazingly good.

The brain does not retain this flexibility, however, as the organism grows older. The younger the child when the damage occurs, the greater the chance that the unimpaired hemisphere can take over the duties of the injured one. Whether the dependence upon age has to do with maturation or simply with the learning of language is not known, but certainly it seems safe to generalize and say that the more language has been developed, the harder it will be to have one hemisphere take over for the other. Language is a strange and complex behavior that requires an immense amount of storage and computational ability. Man may be unique in having a complex language, one in which the ordering of symbols determines their meaning and in which sentences can be transformed from one form to another without changing meaning. Although some animals have means of communication, none has yet shown that it has a language of anywhere near the complexity of man's. Certainly, the complexity of the language is related to the complexity of the brain structure.

Thus, when a language has been well started with a reasonably large vocabulary and reasonable comprehension of grammatical rules, then it makes sense that the brain structures have become organized around the language, whether by biological or chemical changes or simply by acquiring a large, complex data base of information. And with this complex organization, the ability to transfer to a new hemisphere should the old one become damaged is also lost. In fact, after puberty, should the language hemisphere become damaged, it is very unlikely that the other will be able to take over the function.

It is not known why the left hemisphere usually controls language. The two hemispheres seem to start off the same, and from appearances there is no reason why one should be better suited for dealing with language than the other. Yet, language usually develops in the left half,

Two brains: fixed or flexible

2 brains - flexibility

Figure 8-15

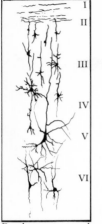

Development around
language area at birth

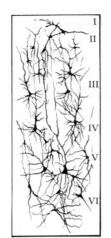

At 1 month

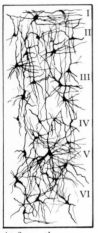

At 3 months

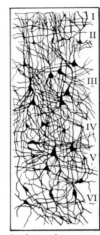

At 6 months

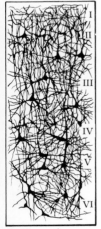

At 15 months

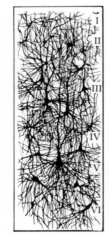

At 2 years

FIGURE 8-15

Neurons in the VI layers of the cerebral cortex as a function of age. After photographs of Conel (1939–1963) and graphs of Schadé and van Groenigen (1961) and Lenneberg (1967).

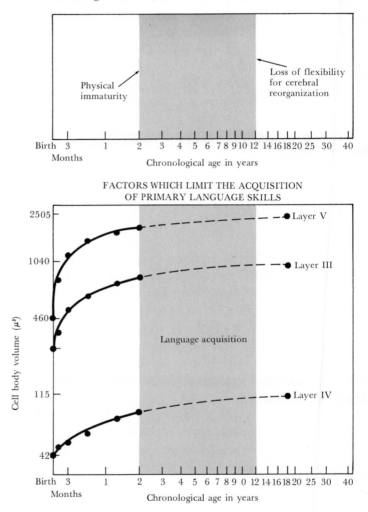

FACTORS WHICH LIMIT THE ACQUISITION
OF PRIMARY LANGUAGE SKILLS

nonverbal skills in the right. Most people are also right-handed, although there is no logical reason why this should be so: Why shouldn't 50% of the population be left-handed? It is thought that there is a connection between the left-hemisphere dominance of language and right-handed-ness. Indeed, it seems to be the case that left-handed people tend to use the right hemisphere for language. But this is not always true. It tends to be more true, the stronger the trait of left-handedness runs in the family. Thus, the son of a left-handed father, especially if some of his brothers and sisters are also left-handed, is likely to be right-hemisphered.

When we consider the attempts to locate the brain mechanisms responsi- **CONCLUSIONS** ble for learning and memory, it is clear that Nature has not been kind to us. She has not put our memory system in a specific box in the brain where it can be easily identified and studied. The brain appears as an enormously complex structure, many of the parts of which can be used interchangeably. This resilience in the learning mechanisms is perhaps the most remarkable feature. Unlike the machines we build to model it, the brain can sustain extensive damage without totally in-capacitating the organism. There seem to be no critical parts on which the whole system depends. Although our studies have not succeeded in discovering the locus of memory, they have given us a compelling picture of the plasticity of the neural mechanisms underlying the record-ing and storage of information.

An excellent introduction to the understanding of the chemical properties **SUGGESTED** of memory can be found in Gurowitz's book, *The Molecular Basis of* **READINGS** *Memory* (1969: paperback). In addition, you might look at the book by Gaito, *Macromolecules and Behavior,* first published in 1966, with a second edition now in press. An extremely influential discussion of possible neurological circuits was published by Hebb in 1949. The dis-cussion of reverberating circuits in this chapter was derived from his works.

Several *Annual Review* articles are relevant here, such as J. A. Deutsch's article in the *Annual Review of Psychology* (1969) and Glass-man's review article in the *Annual Review of Biochemistry* (1969).

Some discussion of neurological bases of memory can be found in Kimble's *The Anatomy of Memory* (1965). These are the proceedings of a conference on brain function. S. Deutsch (1967), an electrical engi-neer who has modeled memory structures, gives some interesting speculations. John's book, *Mechanisms of Memory* (1967) is also of general interest in presenting one theoretical framework of the mechanisms underlying memory storage.

The experiments on transfer of learning from one animal to another are highly controversial. Before believing too strongly the material presented here, you ought to read the letter to the editor published in *Science* magazine in 1966 (Byrne *et al.*, 1966), as well as the review by Jensen (1965).

A summary of the work on cannibalism may be found in John's *Mechanisms of Memory* (1967, see p. 110). An excellent discussion appears in Chapter VII of Gurowitz's book (1969). The original experiments were carried out by McConnell. See his two articles, "Memory Transfer through Cannibalism in Planarians" (1962) and "Cannibalism and Memory in Flatworms" (1964). There is a journal, *The Worm Runners Journal*, written mostly tongue-in-cheek, which might be of some interest and amusement for these issues.

There are a number of good books on amnesias and memory pathology. Talland (1965, 1968) covers mostly the Korsakov syndrome, patients who have memory deficits as a result of acute alcoholism. More general books are the articles collected by Talland and Waugh (1969) on general memory pathologies and some laboratory research, Barbizet's *Human Memory and Its Pathology* (1970), and the book, *Amnesia*, by Whitty and Zangwill (1966). (See especially the chapter by Williams on the effect of ECS with human patients.)

The studies of patients H.M. and N.A. were reported in a series of six papers which all appeared in the same issue of *Neuropsychologia*, 1968, **6**, pp. 211–282. A summary of the behavioral results of brain injury can be found in Rosner's *Annual Review of Psychology* (1970) article, "Brain Functions."

Lashley's work is of great importance in the study of the localization of specific memories, even though some recent experiments are shedding some doubt upon its generality. Three important papers by Lashley that ought to be examined are 1931, 1950, and perhaps most important, his famous and influential paper on the problem of serial order (1951). The best way to start is with the book, *The Neurophysiology of Lashley* edited by Beach *et al.* (1960). Lenneberg's book (1967), *Biological Foundations of Language* presents important information about memory disorders that affect the development of language, as well as a discussion of *aphasia*, a language-specific impairment that results from brain injury. A good summary article on aphasia is the article in *Science* by Geschwind (1970).

Some very recent studies carried out in England (reviewed in Warrington & Weiskrantz, to be published) indicate that there are alternative explanations to the problems suffered by some amnesic patients. It may not be that they are unable to enter new information into long-term memory; rather they may simply be unable to retrieve it properly from among all of the various items they have acquired since their deficit. In addition, the existence of a novel patient with a very much impaired short-term memory but with no apparent deficit in acquiring new material raises some interesting puzzles. It is too early for these results yet to be evaluated. The Warrington and Weiskrantz paper appears in a book entitled *Physiological Basis of Memory*, edited by J. A. Deutsch (to be published), which also contains other articles of further interest.

The literature on split brains and their general implications ought to be examined by starting first with the articles of Sperry (1961, 1968). The literature is reviewed very nicely in Gazzaniga's *The Bisected Brain* (1970), and the references contained in that book will send you to the rest of the literature. One additional source is Mountcastle's book on cerebral dominance (1962).

The bilateral symmetry of the brain has interesting implications for behavior, among them a possible explanation of the difficulty faced by children (and some adults) in distinguishing left from right. These issues are discussed in an article by Corballis and Beale (1970).

9

Transient memories[1]

[1] The introductory section to Chapter 8 ("The Memory Systems") should be read before starting this section. In addition, some of the concepts in Chapter 3 ("Pattern Recognition") are used in the discussions here.

Several transient memories exist in the sequence of stages involved in the processing and interpretation of information from the sensory systems. Each memory serves a different function, stores a different form of information, has different capacity limitations, and operates according to somewhat different principles. Let us consider how each of these transient memories functions.

The job of extracting the features of a sensory message in order to determine what that message represents may take time—more time than the duration of the actual signal allows. The *sensory information storage* system (SIS) plays the logical role of giving the feature extraction and pattern recognition systems time to work on the signals arriving at the sensory organs.

After a visual input, a visual image remains for several tenths of a second. This image is the visual sensory information store. This means that it is possible to work on a sensory event for a duration of time that is longer than the event itself. This storage is useful in situations where an image is exposed very briefly: in viewing motion pictures and television, in maintaining a continuity of perception during the time it takes to complete an eye movement or eye blink. In fact, for brief exposures to a signal, the duration of time for which the visual image is present is almost irrelevant: The controlling duration is the length of time material stays in the SIS.

*SIS
P.R. & feature extraction
systems time to work on — as necessary* — gives time for

Not only does the SIS seem to retain a good image of the sensory events that have occurred during the past few tenths of a second, but there is more information stored there than can be extracted. This discrepancy between the amount of information held in the sensory system and the amount that can be used by later stages of analysis is very important. It implies some sort of limit on the capacity of later stages, a limit that is not shared by the sensory stages themselves. The limitation shows up during the attempt to remember the material presented. The tremendous amount of information carried in a sensory image is usually of no importance for interpreting its meanings. In fact, for many purposes, too many details just make the job harder. Computer devices which attempt to read printed text, decode spoken speech waveforms, or even read printed music are easily thrown off the track by trivial details in the input that are never even noticed by the human doing the same task. Tiny dirt spots, or breaks in printed letters confuse the computers. But with the human, even gross errors such mispellings often go unnoticed.

SIS must maintain an accurate image of everything since it has no way of determining what is of value

The sensory system must maintain an accurate image of everything that arrives at the sense organs, since although most of that information will turn out to be useless, the sensory system has no way of determining what aspects of the input will be of value. Only the systems that recognize and interpret the signals can do that. The SIS would seem to be ideally suited for its purposes. It holds everything for a short duration of time, giving the processes of pattern recognition time to pick and choose.

THE TACHISTOSCOPE

The apparatus most frequently used in the study of human visual processes is the *tachistoscope*. Basically, this is simply a device to present visual images for very brief periods of time. It was invented in the 1880s, and although today the instruments are fully controlled by automatic electronic circuits (and even computers), the principles have not changed since about 1907.

The basic tachistoscope is a lightproof box, often simply a long, enclosed rectangular tube made out of some lightproof material. The subject looks in at one end. The object he is to see is placed at the other end (see Figure 9-1). Initially, however, everything is dark, so nothing can be seen. When a light is flashed inside the box, whatever is at the end of the tube can be seen. By using special lights, usually gas-filled bulbs that are ionized by the application of a high potential between electrodes, it is possible to control the light duration accurately to fractions of a millisecond.

FIGURE 9-1

Often, the experimenter wants to control the viewing of several different objects. This can be done by adding mirrors to the box. Special mirrors are used, with the surface of the glass only half-silvered, so that half the light hitting the mirror goes through it and half gets reflected. With the arrangement shown in Figure 9-2, the subject can see into three different locations. If only light A is on, all he sees is stimulus A. Similarly, light B allows him to see stimulus B, and light C controls stimulus C. Thus, information can be presented at any or all of three locations. All that is needed is to control accurately the times at which each of the three lights is on.

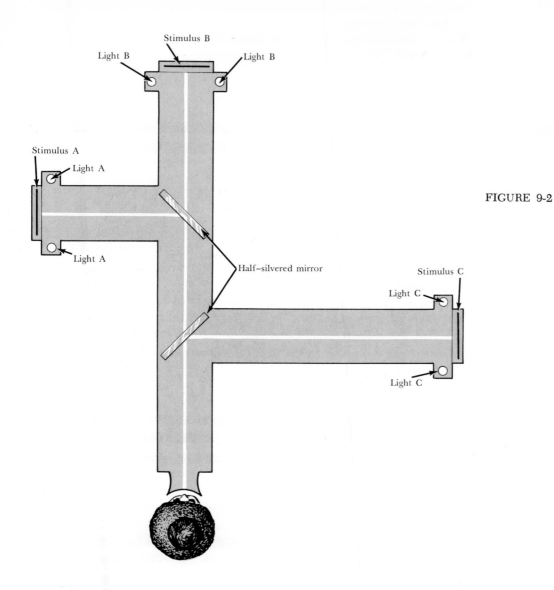

Stimulus B
Light B
Light B
Stimulus A
Light A
Light A
Half—silvered mirror
Stimulus C
Light C
Light C

FIGURE 9-2

This particular tachistoscope, called a *three-field tachistoscope*, is the type of instrument used in many of the experiments discussed in this chapter, with one modification. The quality of the image seen by the subject depends upon the number of mirrors the image has bounced off and gone through. In the instrument of Figure 9-2, more light can come from C (the path only involves one mirror) than from B or A (the path involves two mirrors). Thus, modern tachistoscopes add dummy mirrors and filters so that the images from each of the fields will (as much as possible):

1. Travel exactly the same distance in going from the location of the stimulus card to the subject;
2. Pass through the same number of mirrors;
3. Be reflected off of the same number of mirrors.

The capacity of SIS

It is easy to demonstrate that the SIS initially contains more information than the stages of analysis that follow are able to use. Suppose a complex visual image is presented briefly. The observer will only be able to extract a small amount of the information present in the image. He will claim that he did not have enough time to "see" it all. But if he is told to look at only one particular part of the image, he can concentrate his attention on that part and report on it with high accuracy. This basic phenomenon indicates that the restriction on our ability to deal with sensory inputs comes during the analysis process.

The experiment. It is important to examine this experiment with some care, since it is the central technique used in the study of sensory information storage systems. In one form of the basic experiment, the card of Figure 9-3, containing nine letters arranged in three rows of three letters each, is exposed in a tachistoscope for 50 msec. Typically, the subject will manage to read only four or five of the nine letters. Even if more letters are presented or the exposure duration varied, the

Figure 9-4   number of letters he reports remains nearly the same: about four or five.

To find out what the subject can actually see, we should not ask him to report everything. Maybe he sees them all, but then forgets some. To test this idea we can ask for a **partial report** of the letters presented. That is, present the group of nine letters as before, but mark off one of the letters from the rest with a marker and ask him simply to report the marked letter. The subject never knows which of the nine letters is going to be marked until **after** the exposure (see Figure 9-3).[2]

Now, if he can always report any randomly marked letter, he must really be able to see **all** nine letters in the flash, if he does not know which letter is to be marked until after the exposure, he must have all nine in his SIS, to be able to search for the marker, then report the letter.

The results of the experiment are shown in Figure 9-5: The subject almost always correctly identifies the marked letter. Thus, he does see

---

[2] These experiments were performed by Sperling (1959, 1960). Sperling actually signals the letters to be recalled with a tone, rather than with a bar marker. This leads to slightly different results than those shown here, but the difference *is* slight and the principle demonstrated here is correct.

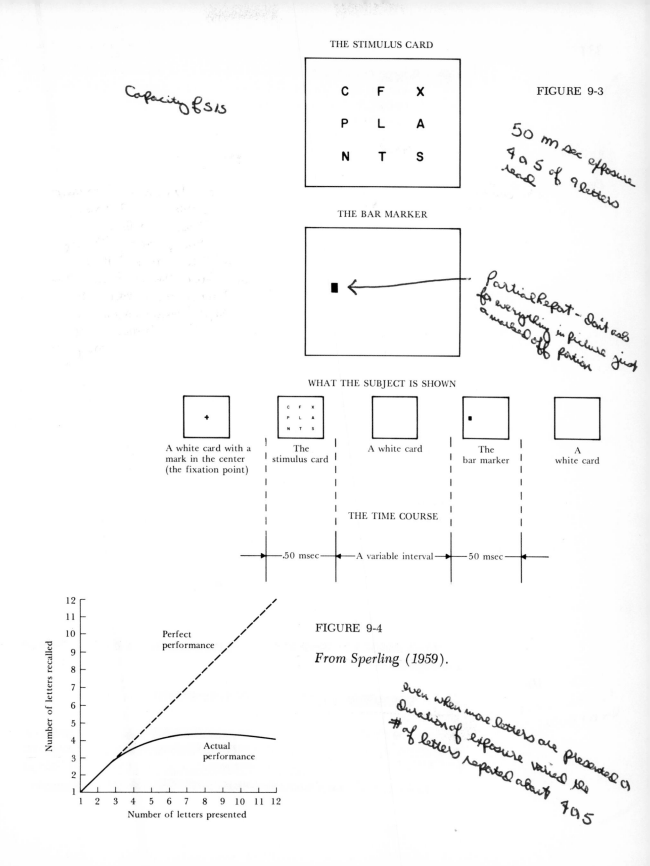

Capacity of SIS

THE STIMULUS CARD

C F X
P L A
N T S

FIGURE 9-3

50 m sec exposure
4 a 5 of 9 letters
read

THE BAR MARKER

Partial Report - don't ask
for everything in picture just
a marked off portion

WHAT THE SUBJECT IS SHOWN

| A white card with a mark in the center (the fixation point) | The stimulus card | A white card | The bar marker | A white card |

THE TIME COURSE

.50 msec — A variable interval — 50 msec

FIGURE 9-4

From Sperling (1959).

Even when more letters are presented (9)
Duration of exposure varies the
# of letters reported about
4 a 5

Perfect performance

Actual performance

Number of letters recalled (y-axis, 1–12)

Number of letters presented (x-axis, 1–12)

more than he can report. Evidently, in the original experiment, all the letters were in SIS, but by the time he had processed three or four of them, the others had faded away.

FIGURE 9-5

Data from Sperling (1959).

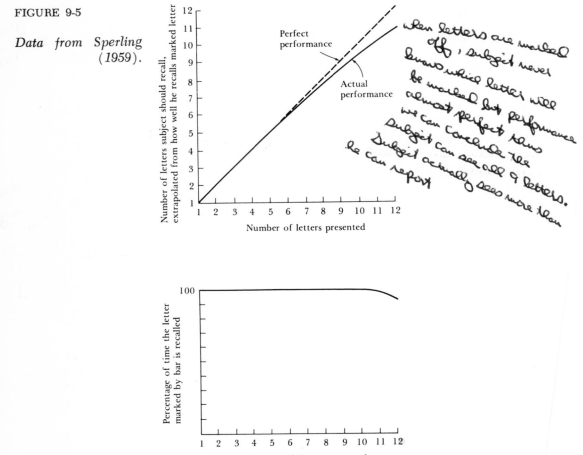

The bar-marker technique is a valuable procedure for the study of perception. The next important use of the technique is to delay the marker, make it so that it does not come on immediately with the other letters. This should tell us what the SIS looks like. The general results of this manipulation are easy to determine, even without doing the experiment. First of all, the subject normally can recall only about four or five of the letters presented to him if there is no marker. Second, he can get any of the marked letters if the marker appears at the same time as the letters. Thus, if the marker is delayed for a very long time—

long enough so that the visual image has completely faded away and the subject reports that he cannot "see" the letters any more—then according to Figure 9-4 the subject should remember only about half (four or five) of the nine letters. The chance that he will remember one particular letter of the nine, the one that is indicated by the marker, is therefore about 50%. As the delay in the marker is increased, then, the performance will range from about 100% correct to about 50% correct.

Typical results of the experiment are shown in Figure 9-6. The ability to report a randomly designated letter decreases smoothly as the marker is delayed more and more, with the performance leveling off after about 500 msec (.5 sec). It looks as if the SIS consists of an image of the signal that decays in time such that little remains of the image after about .5 sec. (Alternatively, the decay of the memory image looks like an exponential process with a time constant of approximately 150 msec.)

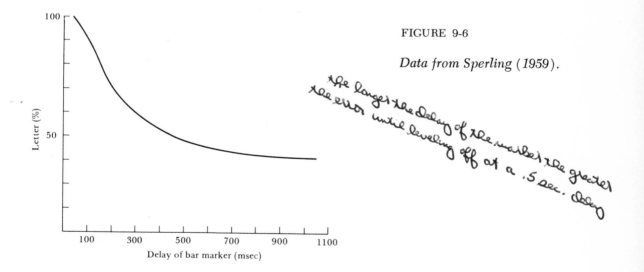

FIGURE 9-6

Data from Sperling (1959).

the larger the delay of the marker the greater the error until leveling off at a .5 sec. delay

A strange thing happens with certain types of markers. In the early studies of the visual information storage system, a circular marker was used and the subject's task was to report the letter that appeared within the circle. Unlike the situation with the bar marker, when the circle comes on shortly after the letter set, it seems to "erase" the letter that it surrounds.

Figure 9-7

This phenomenon of erasure is both intriguing and important. It is a potentially useful tool in controlling the duration that the SIS maintains the image.

Whenever one signal is presented after another, two different things

FIGURE 9-7

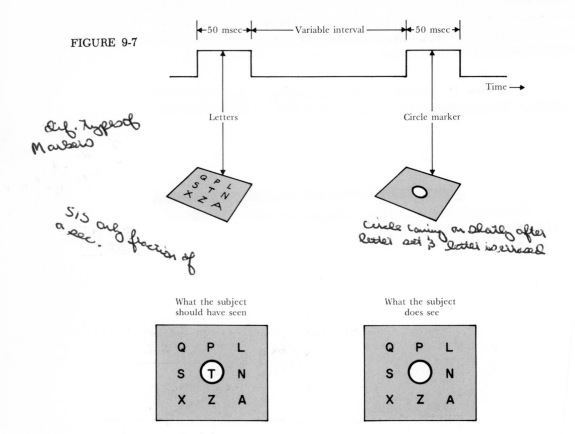

Handwritten margin notes: Dif. types of Markers

SIS only fraction of a sec.

Handwritten note near circle marker: Circle coming on shortly after letter set so letter is erased

Letters

Circle marker

What the subject should have seen

What the subject does see

seem to happen. First, there is a summation of the trace of one signal with the image of the other. This can lead to a reduction in the contrast or clarity of the fading image of the first figure, thus reducing the amount of processing on that figure. Second, there can be disruption in the processing of the first if a second image is presented before the first has been fully analyzed. Which of these two processes predominates depends on the particular image sequence presented: Both are always present, but sometimes one is more important than the other.

Regardless of how the phenomenon of erasure is explained, it is an important tool, for when the second stimulus (the masker) is presented, it effectively stops the processing of the first (the signal). Thus, even though the SIS lasts for some time after the signal has been presented, the time available for processing the signal can be precisely controlled by presenting a masker at the desired time.

To determine how fast each individual letter in a visual display can be processed, one experimental technique is to present the letters followed by the masker. The number of letters the subject can report in the processing time between the signal and the masker tells the speed of operation of the system. Can he process figural information such as faces faster than letters? How much faster? The same technique can be used.

It is now common practice that when material is to be exposed tachistoscopically to a subject, it is followed by a masking stimulus. Without the masker SIS maintains the image, so it is not possible to know exactly how long a period of time the subject spends processing the material. With the masker, the time is controlled precisely by the experimenter.

[margin note: w/o Masker SIS retains info. w/Masker time can be controlled by the experimenter]

In 1954 two psychologists at the University of Indiana, Lloyd Peterson and Margaret Peterson (1959), tried a very simple experiment, but with surprising results. They asked subjects to remember three letters and then, some 18 sec later, asked them to recall the three. The experiment sounds absolutely trivial. The interesting thing is that the subjects were not able to remember the three letters. What is the gimmick? Simple. Between the time the three letters had been presented and the time they were to be recalled, the subjects had to do some mental work. They had to count backward, by threes, at a rapid rate.[3]

[margin note: SHORT-TERM MEMORY]

This simple experiment illustrates the central property of the short-term memory system. But there is more, a change in the material that is to be remembered produces surprisingly little change in the memory, so long as the number of items is constant. Look at Figure 9-8. This shows the rate at which subjects forget things. The curve labeled "three consonants" is the experiment just described. In the figure, the horizontal axis tells the time in seconds between presenting the three letters (all were consonant letters) to the subjects and asking them to recall them. (Remember, all during this time the subjects are busy counting backward by threes.) The vertical axis shows the percentage of times that the subjects could recall the material when tested at any particular retention interval. Thus, if there is as little as 6 sec between presenting three consonants and testing for their recall, only 40% of the subjects can recall all three of the consonants.

---

[3] In "counting backward by threes" the subject starts at a randomly selected three-digit number, such as 487. He must then say aloud the sequence of numbers formed by subtracting three from each previous value, e.g., 487, 484, 481, 478, 475, ... The subject is required to do this counting at a rapid rate, either simply "rapidly," or in time to the clicks of a metronome. Try it yourself: The task is harder than it would seem.

FIGURE 9-8

*After Murdock
(1961).*

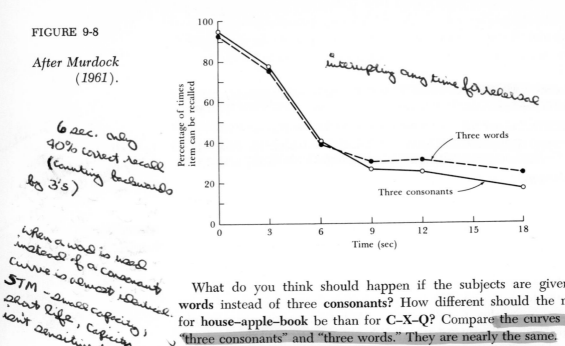

*6 sec. only
90% correct recall
(counting backwards
by 3's)*

*when a word is used
instead of a consonant
curve is almost identical.*

*STM - small capacity,
short life, capacity
isn't sensitive to length*

*STM here
only tested up to
20 sec. Hence is dif
from SIS but it is still
not long term Memory*

✗

What do you think should happen if the subjects are given three **words** instead of three **consonants**? How different should the memory for **house–apple–book** be than for **C–X–Q**? Compare the curves labeled "three consonants" and "three words." They are nearly the same.

What possible mechanisms could produce such a memory system? It is a memory that appears to have a very small capacity and a very short life. But the capacity is not too sensitive to the length of the items stored. Obviously, this is not the SIS of the previous section, since there, memory lasted only a fraction of a second; here it is described in terms of 20 sec. But neither is it the long-term memory system, since there, material is retained indefinitely. In this memory, material lasts only a short time: Hence, it is short-term memory.

*Errors in recall
from short-term
memory*

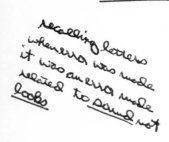

*recalling letters
whenever was made
it was an error made
related to sound not
looks*

Start with a sequence of **visually** presented material, such as letters of the alphabet. To test memory for these letters, ask the subject to **write** down as many of the letters as he can remember. When the subject makes an error trying to recall the letter **F**, he is much more likely to report it as an **X** than as an **E**. Although **F** and **E** share common visual features, **F** and **X** share a common initial sound. Similarly, a **C** is more likely to be recalled as a **T** than as an **O**. When the subject makes an error, it is most likely to be by producing a letter that **sounds** similar to the one he is attempting to recall, not one that **looks** similar.

For the pattern-recognition system in Chapter 3, exactly the opposite types of errors were made: **C** and **O** might be confused, certainly not **C** and **T**. This difference results from the fact that short-term memory is a later stage in the system. When the visual input is at the first stages of pattern recognition, then visual errors can occur. These errors indicate that in the process of encoding the visually presented information into short-term memory, it has gotten into an acoustic form. Yet nowhere in the experiment was a spoken representation required by the subject: He **saw** the letters when they were presented, and he was asked to **write** the answers.

Acoustic confusions. The whole concept has set off a plethora of experiments and theoretical interpretations. At first, the observations seemed natural and obvious. Most people can "hear" themselves saying the things they read. If you say things to yourself, isn't it natural that you should remember the sounds rather than the sights? But just what is this "saying?" Although you can hear yourself, it is a mentalized hearing that is involved—an inner, silent speech.

Is inner speech absolutely necessary for verbal processes? Must all visual words be recoded into inner speech? If so, what of someone who is born deaf? He does manage to read, yet clearly without the need to transform visual words into auditory ones.

And what about this: Are the confusions really among the **sounds** of the spoken words, or are they perhaps **articulatory** in nature? That is, so far we have implied that visually presented words are encoded by matching the letter patterns to the **sounds** made when those words are pronounced. This would lead to **acoustic** confusions. But it is also possible that the recoding is not into sounds, but rather into the sequence of muscle patterns necessary to speak the words. In this case, sounds that are **produced** in similar ways would be confused: *articulatory confusions.* Several of the theories on how humans recognize speech require one or the other of these modes. It would be valuable to be able to distinguish between the two, but no one yet knows how to do so. The problem is that any two patterns of speech that sound similar are also going to be produced in similar ways. With minor exceptions, the patterns of confusions of similar sounds are almost the same as the pattern of confusions from similar articulations.

On top of all these issues comes yet another question: Why is acoustical coding necessary at all? (From here on, the words "acoustical coding" are used to indicate that the visual representation is changed to something related to the sound or production of the words; no favoritism is implied for acoustical over articulatory theories.) Why can't people simply read a passage of printed text without transforming the word into some acoustical format? This is exactly what some speed reading courses promise to teach. And what about the memory for a visual scene? Certainly, we do not transform the visual image of the room before us into the sequence of words which describe that image.

It is patently obvious that everything seen does not need to be transformed into words. But there is good sense to the notion that material input to the system does get transformed into a common format. Some sort of commonality of the input must be recognized. Certainly, it would be silly to store the minute patterns of each individual input. It is not important whether a sentence is spoken slowly or in haste; whether the printed text is viewed from straight on or rotated at an angle. These are trivial physical variations: It is the meaning of the words, not their appearances that should be remembered. Similarly, a sentence means the same whether it is spoken or read—why should the differences be preserved? Doesn't it make sense that the same mechanisms that eliminate such trivial variations of the input as the angle at which letters are viewed might also eliminate other aspects?

The problem of determining the meaning of the sensory signals is very difficult, as the analysis of Chapter 3 has shown. But it is clear that thought processes must operate on some internal coding—a coding that reflects the meaning of the material being thought about, not its physical realization. In order to make most efficient contact with the storage of information in the long-term memory, it would be useful for all information to be transformed into the same common form.

Rehearsal

The importance of inner speech comes up in another place. Suppose you are given a list of names to learn or a telephone number to dial. In general, whenever it is necessary to retain information for more than a few seconds of time, some of the information is lost unless it is consciously repeated over and over again. This silent, mental repetition of the material that is to be retained is called *rehearsal*. Rehearsal appears to serve two primary functions. First, it allows material in short-term memory to be retained for an indefinite period of time. Second, it appears to aid in the transfer of material from short-term memory to its more permanent storage in long-term memory.

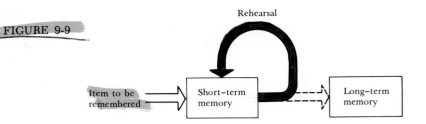

FIGURE 9-9

Retention of material in short-term memory through rehearsal can only come about if the amount to be retained is sufficiently small. Although rehearsal is capable of keeping material alive, it cannot increase

Handwritten margin notes:

Thought processes operate on internal coding. A coding that reflects the Meaning of Material being thought about not its Physical Realization

Transformation of info into Common form to make most efficient contact w/ LTM

the capacity of the memory system. It is as if the rehearsal process simply took the weak, decaying trace of the signal and refreshed it, thus effectively reentering it into short-term memory. Hence, the way of showing rehearsal in Figure 9-9: A loop leaving and entering short-term memory. If too many items are to be rehearsed, however, then the rehearsal of them all will not be completed in time. The last item will decay away before the rehearsal process can get to it.

How fast can rehearsal be done? Silent speech takes place at a rate very close to the rate of spoken speech. To measure the rate of silent speech, pick up a pencil and count mentally (and therefore silently) as rapidly as you can from 1 to 10. As soon as you reach 10, start over again, simultaneously making a mark on the paper. Do this for exactly 10 sec, and then count the marks. How far did you count? If you got to 82, then you rehearse 8.2 digits per second. You can confirm this by trying other material: Try the alphabet.[4]

How is material lost from short-term memory? There are two possible ways: Forgetting could result from interference from other material or simply as a result of the passage of time. Let us examine the implication of each possibility.

Forgetting by interference. In this mode of operation, the short-term memory is assumed to have a limited capacity for the number of items it can retain. There are several ways in which you can think of this. For example, short-term memory could be treated as though it were simply a set of slots somewhere in the brain. Whenever something is presented, it goes through the standard processing by the sensory system and is identified by the pattern-recognition stages. Then, the meaningful representation of the item presented is inserted into one of the empty short-term memory slots. If there is a limited number of slots—say, seven—then when the eighth new item comes in, one of the previous seven would have to go.

This basic formulation of a limited capacity short-term memory suggests that forgetting is caused by interference from newly presented items, because each new presentation causes one old item to be lost. (This, of course, only happens after short-term memory has become filled.) This particular version of the slot model is too simple to work well: It says, for example, that exactly seven items should always be

---

[4] It is instructive to try **visual** rehearsal: Go through the alphabet visually, as rapidly as possible, mentally imagining the image of each letter before going on to the next. You will discover that visual rehearsal is slower than acoustical rehearsal. To prevent yourself from cheating as you go through the letters, say aloud **yes** or **no** whether each capital letter has a horizontal line. Hence, the first five letters yield: **Yes, Yes, No, No, Yes.**

[Margin notes:]

Forgetting

interference
passage of time

STM – limited capacity
.. when saturated some-
thing has to go.

Overly simplified
because things are not
totally remembered or
totally forgotten

remembered, never more, never less; it also says that an item is either remembered perfectly or forgotten altogether. But it is not too difficult a task to modify the structure to take care of these objections.

One way is simply to realize that the memory need not be entirely present or absent: It can partially exist. Think of trying to understand a soft voice in the midst of other voices—the louder the voice, the easier it is to understand, the softer the voice, the more difficult, until it is so weak that it is not even possible to tell whether the voice being listened for is present or not. If the voice is the **signal** and the background voices the **noise,** then it is the ratio of signal level to noise level that determines the ability to understand the voice. So it could be with memory. The representation of an item in the memory is its *memory trace.* It is the **signal** we are trying to recall against the background of other memories, the **noise.** The stronger the memory trace, the easier it is to decipher; as the memory gets older it fades away, until finally its trace is so weak as to be undecipherable.

There is an analogy, then, between deciphering a weak signal in noise and remembering an old memory. Newly presented items have high strength; older items have weak strength. Just as there will be mistakes in interpreting a voice which has a low ratio of signal to noise levels, so too there will be errors in retrieving memories that have low trace strength. And, in retrieving from short-term memory, these errors will tend to be acoustically related to the words that were stored.

Now how do the memory traces get weaker? According to this theory, the strength of the memory depends on the number of items that have been presented. Suppose that initially when something is presented into memory it gets a trace strength of, say, A. Each time a new item is presented, it causes all the trace strengths of previous items to decrease by some constant percentage of their previous value. If the fraction of the memory trace strength is represented by the forgetting factor f (f is obviously a number between 0 and 1), then we can follow the fate of an item (call it the *critical item*) as more material is presented.

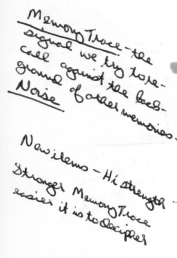

Figure 9-10

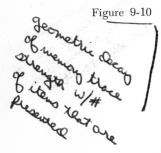

When the item is first presented, its trace strength becomes A.

When one more item is presented, the trace strength of the critical item drops to Af.

When a second new item is presented, the critical strength drops to $(Af)f$ or Af^2.

In fact, if i interfering items have been presented after the presentation of the critical item, the strength of the critical item is Af^i—a simple geometric decay of memory trace strength with the number of items that has been presented.

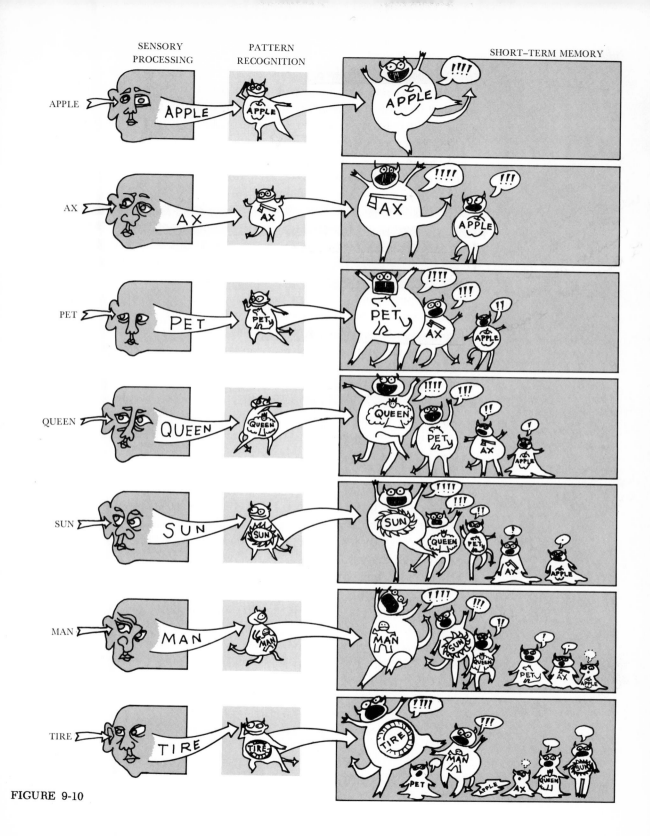

SENSORY PROCESSING   PATTERN RECOGNITION   SHORT–TERM MEMORY

FIGURE 9-10

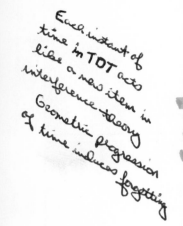

Forgetting by time decay. The second way by which the capacity of short-term memory might be limited is by a time-dependent process, one in which the longer an item stays in memory, the weaker is gets, until finally it disappears entirely. Here, time alone is sufficient for the disappearance of material from memory, much like the role that time plays in the loss of electrical charge from a capacitor or in the decay of radioactive substances. Aside from this, however, the description is very much like the one for item decay.

For the time theory, assume that each instant of time causes a reduction in the trace strength of previously acquired items. That is, each instant of time in the time-decay theory acts much as each presentation of a new item in the interference theory. Simply replace the *i* for the number of items with *t* for the amount of time. If *t* seconds have elapsed since the presentation of a critical item, its trace strength will have decayed from its original value of A to a value of Af^t.[5]

Forgetting: time or interference? The critical test of the two competing theories requires some way of first presenting material to the subject and then having him do nothing until he is tested for his memory of the material. The time decay theory predicts a loss of memory: The interference theory predicts no loss. The problem with this critical experiment lies in the difficulty of getting a subject to "do nothing." If he truly has nothing else to do, then he rehearses the material presented to him. A perfect memory in this experiment is equally well explained by the rehearsal or by the lack of interference: The experimental results prove nothing. If the rehearsal by the subject is prevented by giving him some other task to do, then that other task can cause interference, so a poor memory after this experiment also proves nothing: The loss in memory could be equally well explained by a time decay or by the effects of interference.

One way of doing the experiment is to devise a task so difficult that the subject is unable to rehearse the memory material, yet so different from the memory task that it should not add any interference. One such task is that of detecting a weak signal in noise. Thus, if the subject is first presented with a set of letters to learn, then with a difficult detection task for 30 sec, then he is tested on his memory for the letters; there is the possibility that neither rehearsal nor interference has taken place (Reitman, 1971).

[5] Those of you who think that exponential functions should be expressed by the value of e can translate this expression to its equivalent form:

$$Af^t = Ae^{-kt},$$

where $k = -\ln(f)$.

The results of such experiments indicate that some form of compromise must take place in the theoretical explanations. Thirty seconds after the material to be remembered has been presented, subjects recall it almost perfectly: There is no sign of time decay. At first, this result seems to imply that the interference theory is correct. But there is more to it. The memory after 30 sec is very fragile—even the slightest amount of interference destroys it. There appears to be some change in the memory strength after the lapse of 30 sec—not a change in the ability to recall the items, but a change in their susceptibility to interference. One explanation is that the memory has indeed decayed to a very weak level, but it still stands out above the background noise. Any interference, however, is sufficient either to lower the memory strength below the noise, or, equivalently, to raise the noise level to cover the memory (Atkinson and Shiffrin, 1971).

As is often the case when there are two competing theories to explain a phenomenon, the truth probably lies somewhere in between. Evidently, forgetting in short-term memory comes about through both a decay in time and through interference from the presentation of other material.

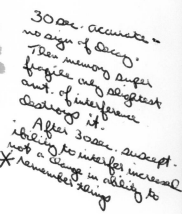

Now let us return to the question of the basic unit of storage. What is the nature of these memory traces in short-term memory? One previous datum yields quite a bit of information: the fact that acoustic confusions occur in short-term memory.

Consider the word **hose.** The goal is to determine just how this word is represented in the short-term memory. Suppose that it is **attributes that get stored, not words.** For example, assume for the moment that each sound is an attribute. This is, of course, a gross oversimplification of the truth, but it is sufficiently accurate to illustrate the concepts. Suppose the item **hose** is to be stored. It is not put away simply as a single unit. Rather, the single memory-unit contains the three basic attributes: the sounds of **h, o,** and **z.** Thus, each attribute of **hose** can be forgotten independently. Now, when the subject tries to recall the word presented to him, he examines the three attributes and attempts to reconstruct the word they must have represented.

- If the **h,** the **o,** and the **z** are remembered, then the word recalled will be **hose.**
- If only the **o** and **z** are remembered, then the word recalled might be **doze, rose,** or even **hose.**
- If only the **h** and **z** are remembered, then the word recalled might be **his, haze,** or even **hose.**
- If only the **h** and **o** are remembered, then the word recalled might be **hole,** or even **hose.**

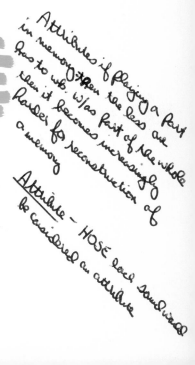

When a single attribute is lost, then the possible words that can be reconstructed from what remains (plus the knowledge that there are a total of three components) is rather limited. All, obviously, are acoustically similar to the original. Note that the correct item will be remembered a reasonable percentage of the time simply by lucky reconstruction from what is left. With two attributes lost—so that all that remains is the sound h, o, or z, then there are many more possible items that fit in with the information that is retained and a very small chance of being lucky enough to get the correct word. With all three attributes gone, nothing remains to guide the reconstructive process.

The reconstruction process of memory. Let us now examine the reconstructive nature of short-term memory. We have just seen how acoustic confusions are produced during the reconstruction of partial information. This is one positive piece of support for the idea that attributes are stored. If it is attributes that are stored, then clearly the longer the name of the item presented, the fewer the items that can be retained. Let us see how the nature of the items themselves determines how much can be recalled.

Suppose this list of letters is to be remembered:

L
B
X
K
F
M

The memory system retains the attributes, namely:

e,l
b,ee
e,ks
k,ai
e,f
e,m

We know that the capacity of short-term memory is limited. For the present example, assume that short-term memory can hold only six attributes. How many letter names can be remembered? It depends upon what six attributes were retained. If they had distributed themselves this way:

```
_____,l
b,_____
_____,ks
k,_____
_____,f
_____,m
```

probably all six of the letters could be recalled correctly, simply by reconstructing what must have been present. After all, what letter besides **X** ends in "ks"?

Suppose the memory for the six attributes was scattered, one attribute per letter, in this way:

```
e,_____
_____,ee
e,_____
_____,ai
e,_____
e,_____
```

Even then, the reconstructive process would still do reasonably well. Look at the four cases where the items are "e_____." How many possible letters are there that start off with "e"?

F, L, M, N, S, and **X.**

Six possible letters, and the reconstructive process must select four. Thus, anywhere from two to four of the letters starting with "e" would be recalled correctly just by chance alone.

Similarly, when the memory for the other attributes is considered, recall would always be reasonably accurate simply by guessing. On the average, three to four of the letters can be correctly recalled from any sequence of six attributes.

The important point of this demonstration is that there is more to the short-term memory process than simply counting up how many attributes are retained. There is also a reconstructive process that pieces together the information available into the most likely description of what has been presented. With skill and some luck, it is quite likely that with only six attributes in memory we could remember all six letters—a feat that would require all twelve attributes if there were no reconstruction of the possible letters from the information that had been retained.

The reconstructive process is not always so successful. It is possible

to create sequences of words that give the process difficulties. Consider the memory for the sequence:

BEE
SEE
PEE
LEE
MEE
FEE

Here, the attributes are

b,ee
s,ee
p,ee
l,ee
m,ee
f,ee

As before, suppose only six were remembered. With luck, all six items could be reconstructed:

b,_____
s,_____
p,_____
l,_____
m,_____
f,_____

The sounds of "ee" add absolutely nothing to the ability to remember the list, so if only the "ee" attributes were lost, no errors in memory would occur. But, with an equally likely choice of attributes, the reconstructive process would face severe difficulties:

_____,ee
_____,ee
_____,ee
_____,ee
_____,ee
_____,ee

From these six attributes, what were the original items? You cannot tell. In fact, on the average, fewer items could be recalled from this latter list than from the first one. In the first case, with the letters **L, B, X, K, F,** and **M,** we could always recall between three and six of them, depending upon which attributes had been retained. This is an average of four and a half letters. But when the items were BEE, SEE, PEE, LEE, MEE, FEE, between zero and six can be recalled, depending upon which attributes had been retained. This is an average of approximately three. Moreover, in the first case we would remember the correct **order** of the letters, but certainly not in the second case.

This discussion has made several different points. The number of attributes in memory does not immediately tell how many items can be recalled. To determine that, it is necessary to know something of the reconstruction process. Some material will be easier to reconstruct from the attributes that do remain in the memory than other material. In general, it is possible to recall more items that are **acoustically different** from one another than items that are **acoustically similar.**

Memory for very long words, words such as the names of states, does not pose any particular problems for this scheme. Suppose the memory list had been

> CONNECTICUT
> MASSACHUSETTS
> PENNSYLVANIA
> CALIFORNIA
> ALABAMA
> MISSISSIPPI

At first, it might seem that it should be more difficult to remember long names with such large numbers of attributes. Not necessarily so. Granted that it does take many attributes to encode CONNECTICUT— *k-uh-n-e-t-i-k-uh-t*—only a few of these attributes are needed to reconstruct it. After all, if the only attributes still in memory were "n," "e," "t," then these sounds plus the knowledge that the word is the name of a state is sufficient to reconstruct CONNECTICUT. Long words are often recalled better than short words, simply because there are fewer of them: If even part of the word can be remembered, there is a good chance of guessing the rest.

Suppose you look up a telephone number or meet a person at a party, you know the number or name for a few seconds, but then you lose track of it completely. The material gets stored perfectly in short-term memory, but it never seems to make it to long-term memory. The difference between the accurate memory for material that is still in short-term memory and the meager, impoverished memory for other material can easily be demonstrated.

FROM SHORT- TO LONG-TERM MEMORY

Table 9-1

	A	B	C	D	E	F
1.	REAM	TIME	CROW	IDES	CLOVE	SQUAB
2.	LATCH	STAB	BORE	TROOP	THUS	QUIP
3.	HOT	SOLVE	WILT	KEY	PLAY	SPREAD
4.	SKIRT	HOUSE	PLATE	HERS	COO	GRADE
5.	JAB	MUFF	JAZZ	STUB	SQUILL	RARE
6.	CLOG	DRAFT	DEAR	GOAD	CLOY	TRIED
7.	MARE	SAY	FAN	CHART	CLING	SHOAL
8.	ELSE	OFF	WRENCH	BATHE	MAID	HAT
9.	WAGE	BOIL	POLE	TEACH	PLATE	QUICK
10.	JOWL	COURT	HERB	BED	PRATE	SHOW
11.	CHAP	SLOT	LAUGH	SCALD	WALL	TRILL
12.	TROUT	HAND	FIT	CAPE	LET	PLAY
13.	BLOT	DIRT	GRILL	THRONE	RAW	SOP
14.	REEK	CLOT	SWIRL	GNAW	WOOD	SAGE
15.	TAPE	OUT	COAST	NET	SWARM	BLONDE
16.	DUSK	GREET	SNACK	SWAM	ELK	TELL
17.	LIST	PENT	SNOW	PRICE	HOWL	JADE
18.	SMUG	STALE	DRAPE	SWEPT	SHOP	IRE
19.	DUCK	STONE	SNAIL	BLANK	PEN	MOON
20.	BIG	DICE	RAGE	SPRAY	ROCK	SLEIGH

You are asked to learn a list of unrelated words. One at a time, each word that is to be learned appears before you, either flashed on a screen or spoken clearly and distinctly. You are allowed exactly 1 sec to attend to each word before the next is presented. Finally, after 20 words have been presented to you, you are asked to recall as many of them as possible. Try the experiment using 20 words from Table 9-1. It will help the discussion that follows if you try the task, giving yourself some feeling for what it is like to be in such an experiment.

When most people do this task they find it advantageous to recall the last words that were presented as quickly as they can, first, before trying to remember anything else. The last words are in a type of "echo box," a temporary memory from which the words can be recalled with ease only if nothing else happens to interfere with it. If there is some conversation, or if the person tries to recall other words first, then the contents of the "echo box" disappear. This "echo box" is, of course, the short-term memory. Most subjects quickly learn to empty their short-term memory immediately before going on to other things.

One way of examining the results is to number the words according to the position in which they were represented, and record the chance that a word will be recalled as a function of its position in the list. This analysis produces the *serial position curve* shown in Figure 9-11.

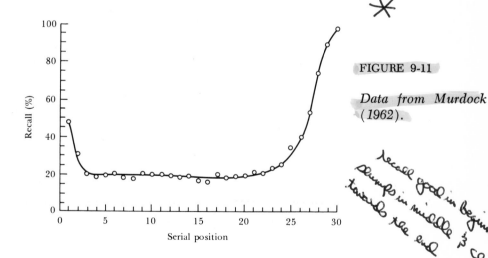

FIGURE 9-11

Data from Murdock (1962).

Here, the length of the list was 30 words, the percentage of times each word was recalled is shown for the words in each position of the list. This particular set of data comes from an experiment conducted by Bennet B. Murdock, Jr. in 1962. In this study, 19 subjects listened to a list of 30 unrelated words presented at the rate of one word each second.

At the end of each list, they were given 1.5 min to write down all the words they could remember in any order they wished. Five to 10 sec after they finished writing, a new list was presented. This same procedure was repeated 80 times (on four separate days, so only 20 lists were learned in any one session).

The serial position curve is an important tool of psychologists. But it is really not a single curve. It should be separated into the two parts shown in Figure 9-12. The last part of the list is remembered better

FIGURE 9-12

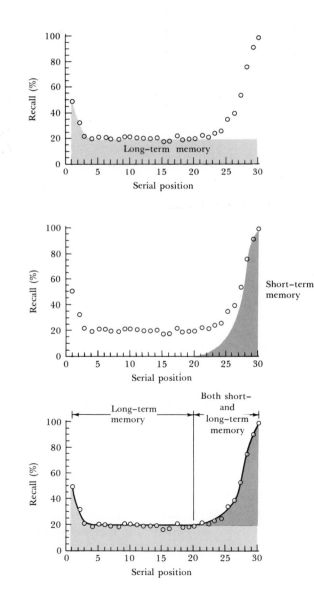

than the rest: The last item is recalled about 97% of the time. This later part of the curve represents recall from short-term memory. The rest of the curve reflects a different memory process—the retrieval of information from long-term storage.[6]

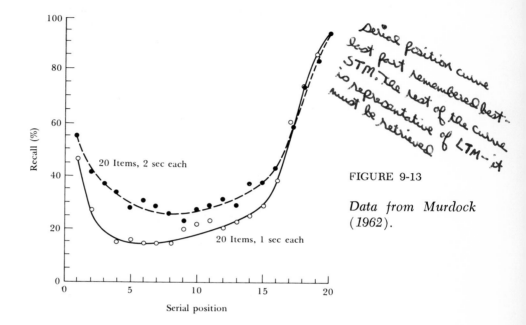

Serial position

Data from Murdock (1962).

FIGURE 9-13

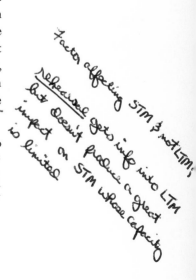

How do we know this? Well, for one thing, some operations affect one of the memories and not the other. For example, if presentation of the words is slowed up to allow 2 sec on each word rather than one, the results look like those shown in Figure 9-13. There is no change in the short-term memory portion of the curve. There is an improvement in long-term memory. (These data were also collected by Murdock, the only difference being that the lists were 20 items long and each item given for 2 sec.) Evidently, the added time gives subjects more

[6] In Figure 9-12, the percentages for long-term memory cannot simply be added to those from short-term memory to give total recall. Rather, we assume that an item is recalled **either** from long-term memory **or** from short-term memory, but not both. Thus the percentage recall is given by the sum of the **percentage** of words recalled from short-term memory plus the **percentage** of those words from long-term memory that were not already recalled from short-term memory. If R is percentage recall,

$$R = \text{STM} + \text{LTM}\left(1 - \frac{\text{STM}}{100}\right)$$

time to rehearse and work on the material, thus getting more information into long-term memory, but having no effect on short-term memory. In fact, varying both how many items are presented in the list as well as how fast they are presented produces a family of curves (Figure 9-14), which again show that the short-term memory component of each curve is the same for all, while the long-term memory sections differ.

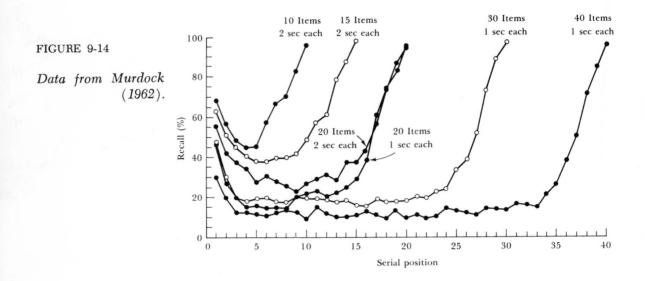

FIGURE 9-14

Data from Murdock (1962).

It is possible to show the opposite: factors that affect short-term memory and not long-term memory. One obvious way of doing this is to prevent subjects from immediately recalling the words from short-term memory at the end of the experiment. That is, we do exactly the same experiment as before, but this time, at the end of the presentation, the subjects are given a three-digit number and asked to count backward by threes—the task described earlier for the short-term memory experiments (see page 337). Short-term memory recall should disappear. And so it does (Postman & Phillips, 1965). The easiest way to convince yourself of this is to try it. Take 20 words from Table 9-1 and read them at the rate of one word per second. As soon as you get to the end of the list, start counting backward by threes from some arbitrary number, say 978. Count as rapidly as you can for approximately 20 sec. Your short-term memory will be wiped clean. The experimental results from an experiment just like this are shown in Figure 9-15. Notice that the last part of the curve is perfectly flat: no short-term memory.

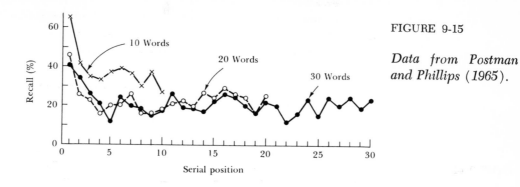

FIGURE 9-15

Data from Postman and Phillips (1965).

In these experiments, subjects have a difficult task. Presumably, they must attend carefully to each word presented, rehearse it, and exert conscious effort to the task of learning as many of the words as possible. In the absence of this effort, then, very little of the information presented is stored beyond the short-term memory. What happens when subjects do not exert any effort, when they pay little or no attention to the material presented to them? From what we have just said, it is possible that this would result in a lack of permanent memory—no learning would take place.

Obviously, attention processes occupy a key position during the interpretation of a message. It is important to examine these processes carefully. What are the limits and capabilities of attention? How does it operate during the storage and retrieval of information? To answer these questions we must backtrack a bit and pick up a line of research that has been concerned specifically with the attentional processes that go on during the processing of incoming messages.

Imagine yourself at a crowded, noisy party. You are standing with a group of people with other groups all around. To which conversation will you listen? Despite all the noise, you can decide which of the many conversations you wish to listen to—you could eavesdrop on the conversation behind you, or on the one to the right or left. But whichever conversation you listen to causes the loss of the others. This, then, is the selectivity of attention. It is possible to stand in the room and select which of the many conversations is to be attended. But it is not possible to take part in two or more different conversations simultaneously. Yes, several conversations can be monitored by following a few words from each and perhaps keeping track of who is where. But if the conversations are at all serious, the sense of each gets lost when you try to do too

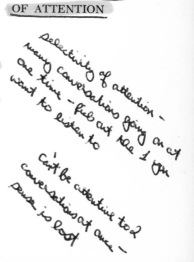

much. It is possible to be selective in extracting sense out of all the noise of the party; there is a limit on the ability to understand different conversations simultaneously.

Attention is somewhat of a two-edged sword. On the one side, it gives the desirable attribute of allowing us to follow the one set of events that may be of interest from among many going on simultaneously, even though each tends to obscure the others. Without this selective ability life would be chaotic, since we could make no sense out of the events of the world unless each occurred in isolation without competition or interference from others. But, on the other side, attention limits our ability to keep track of the all events that do occur. Often it is desirable to keep track of several things simultaneously. Even if only one set of events is of immediate interest, it is undesirable to follow it with such concentration so as to be unaware of the occurrence of other events that are potentially more important than the one on which we are concentrating. It is desirable to be able to concentrate on one event to the exclusion of others only so long as we will be interrupted from that concentration whenever something more important occurs. For this to happen, some way must be devised of monitoring even those events to which we are not attending, separating out the irrelevant aspects and interrupting our concentration for the pertinent aspects.

Selecting messages   Let us start with an experiment. In the passages that appear in the figures for this section, two different messages are printed together. Your job is to follow one message (a relevant message) and ignore the other (an irrelevant message). Read the shaded message aloud as rapidly as possible and ignore the other. Make sure you read as quickly as possible only the shaded message. Try it now with Figure 9-16 before reading on.

FIGURE 9-16   In performing an experiment like this one on man attention car it house is boy critically hat important shoe that candy the old material horse that tree is pen being phone read cow by book the hot subject tape for pin the stand relevant view task sky be read cohesive man and car gramatically house complete boy but hat without shoe either candy being horse so tree easy pen that phone full cow attention book is hot not tape required pin in stand order view to sky read red it nor too difficult.

Without looking back, what did you notice about the unshaded words? Do you remember any of them? Did you notice that each word appeared twice? Probably not.

This is the first piece of informal evidence about the cues used in selecting messages. You can be reasonably successful at limiting attention to a single, relevant passage. Physical characteristics of the message, shading in this case, can be used to separate the relevant message from the irrelevant one. It is as if you had some internal switch which allowed messages with the right physical properties to pass but rejected the rest.

Cues tell us what to pay attention to

But how far did you go in analyzing the irrelevant material? Did you really reject it solely on the basis that it wasn't shaded? If nothing is remembered about the rejected message, then perhaps the first theory of attention is that irrelevant material is only analyzed far enough to determine its general physical characteristics. Then the processing of irrelevant material is discontinued.

This initial hypothesis is clearly too simple. Consider the task illustrated in Figure 9-17. Once again read aloud the text that is shaded as fast as you can, just as before. Ignore the unshaded material.

It is important that the subject man be car pushed house slightly boy beyond hat his shoe normal candy limits horse of tree competence pen for be only in phone this cow way book can hot one tape be pin certain stand that snaps he with is his paying teeth attention in to the the empty relevant air task and hat minimal shoe attention candy to horse the tree second or peripheral task.

FIGURE 9-17

Notice what happened here. All of a sudden the shaded sentence dissolved into a series of unrelated words. The sentence itself continued in the unshaded print—the print you were supposed to ignore. Now, if you can reject irrelevant material solely on the basis of its general physical characteristics, then you should have had little difficulty in continuing to read the shaded words. In fact you should not even have noticed that the sentence was continued in unshaded print. Most people, however, will start to read the unshaded letters, thus following the meaning of the material rather than obeying instructions and processing only the information with the correct physical properties.

Physical cues are useful in separating relevant from irrelevant information. But more than physical cues must be involved in selecting which words to read, or there would be no tendency to switch to the unshaded words when they fit into context. The problem, then, is to figure out just what is being attended to and what is being ignored. It is obvious that to do this, we need a better way of controlling attention. Did you really attend only to the shaded message, or did you cheat a bit (inadvertently) and look at the other message to see what it said? If we want to find out the limits of the attention capacity, we must make sure that all attention is devoted to one task. Failing that, at the very least, we must be able to measure how much attention is applied to the relevant information. Only then can we start to discover how much can be extracted from irrelevant material.

Shadowing. To determine the type of information that gets extracted from an unattended message, we need an experimental task that allows us to tell whether the subject is truly occupied with the attended task. One popular task is to ask the subject to *shadow* material presented to him. In a shadowing task, a series of words is read to the subject and he is asked to repeat aloud (to shadow) each word as he hears it. This is difficult to do, especially if the material which is to be shadowed is presented at a reasonably quick rate. Thus, subjects are forced to devote substantial portion of their attentional capacities to the task of shadowing. As experimenters, we can tell how well the subject is attending to the shadowing task by how accurately he repeats the words presented to him. In general, it is wise to select the difficulty of the material which is being shadowed and the rate at which it is read so that the subject makes a small percentage of errors, perhaps 10%. In this way, we can tell whether his attention to the shadowing task changes by whether or not his error rate changes. (It is important that the subject not be able to shadow perfectly, for if he can do the shadowing without making any errors, the task might also be easy enough that he has some spare time to do other things.) Thus, in a typical experimental session, the subject is asked to shadow some selection of material (usually played to him through a tape recorder) which is presented to him over earphones to one of his ears. Then, the test material is presented to him in the other ear (or sometimes, visually).

After the session, the subject is questioned on the contents of the material presented to him to see what aspects he is able to remember.

Figure 9-18

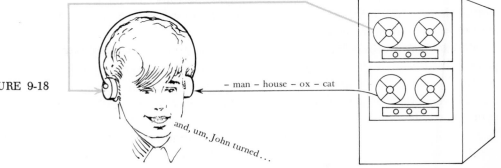

...and then John turned rapidly toward...

– man – house – ox – cat

and, um, John turned...

FIGURE 9-18

You should try the shadowing task. Get together two other people. Have one sit directly to one side and read aloud from this text or from a magazine at a reasonable rate. You try to shadow it. The passage should be read in a flat, unemotional voice. Repeat each word as it is said—do **not** hang back waiting for phrases or sentences to be completed. After you have had some practice at shadowing, then have the other person sit at your other side and read a second message as you are shadowing the first (perhaps the random words of Table 9-1). Try to attend to this second message, but without disrupting your shadowing performance on the first. The person who is reading the material that you are shadowing should tell you (poke you in the ribs) if you falter. Try different kinds of material for both messages and see if it makes any differences in the difficulty of the task. What do you perceive or remember about the second message? It is reasonably simple for you to replicate most of the studies involving shadowing that we discuss here.

When fully engrossed in a task, whether it be the result of shadowing or by the semitrance that accompanies the reading of a good novel, the watching of a good play or film, or even daydreaming, the subjective impression is that of being completely enveloped by the material on which we are concentrating. It is as if a switch disconnected all signals from reaching consciousness except those to which we were attending. Suppose we daydream in midst of a lecture. The sounds of the lecturer reach our ears, but leave no impression in our mind. The words spoken are not understood. By conscious exertion of willpower, the daydreaming can be stopped and the lecture attended to. Even though there need be no movement of muscles or parts of the body in changing from concentration on the daydream to concentration on the lecturer, there is quite a difference in perception. In both cases we "hear" the lecturer, but in one case we follow the words; in the other we do not. At what point is the bottleneck? Where does the analysis of the lecturer stop?

Processing the rejected message

The simplest theoretical position is that the signals from the environment pass through the sensory systems and the analyzing mechanisms found there. This must be true, since we do "hear" the unattended sounds, even if they are not understood. At some point, however, there must be a switch that passes the signals to which we wish to attend and blocks the rest, as in Figure 9-19.

Even a simple study of attention soon shows that some aspects of material that is not being attended to can be noticed. When a subject busily shadows material presented to him, he still shows the following recollection of the irrelevant material:

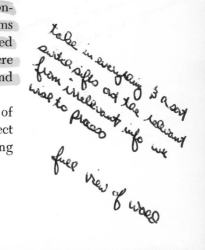

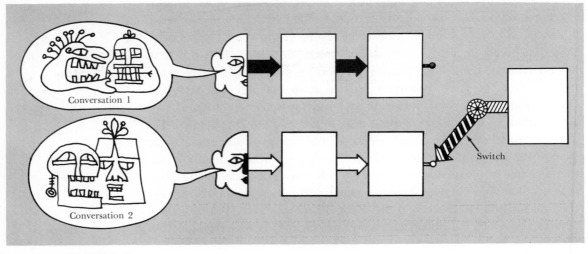

FIGURE 9-19

He is able to

- remember whether a voice was present at all,
- tell whether the voice changed from a man's to a woman's,
- notice signals, such as a whistle.

He is **not** able to

- remember the contents of the message,
- recognize the language of the message,
- tell if the language changed during the course of the experiment,
- distinguish speech from nonsense sounds.

When not attending to info presented gross characteristics are still noticed but things requiring interpretation like the meaning of a word is lost

These results indicate that the subject notices primarily the gross physical characteristics of signals to which he is not attending: Is something present; is it a man or woman? He fails to notice things that require interpretation, such as the meaning of the words, the identification of the language, or even whether the sounds form a meaningful language.

Although relevant material seems to undergo a rather complete analysis (including all the stages of processing discussed in Chapter 3 on pattern recognition), the analysis of all other incoming signals seems to stop very early, perhaps at the level of the feature extraction. It would appear that a selection mechanism examines the incoming features and selects the relevant material from the irrelevant by the physical features present: It then controls a switch that allows only the relevant signals to get through to further analysis.

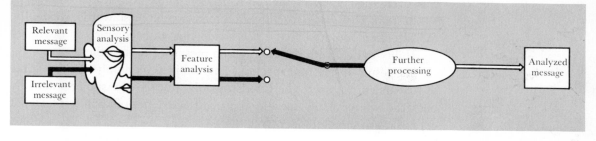

FIGURE 9-20

This system appears to be a generally useful attention process. The fact that the feature analyses of all signals get at least a cursory examination allows the subject to note and remember what signals are present. The fact that detailed analysis of irrelevant channels stops with the extraction of features, however, prevents any extraction of the meaning of the signals. The features alone are sufficient to distinguish a human voice from a nonvoice, but anything else—even so simple a task as recognizing a language—is not possible. Most importantly, the attention mechanism portrayed to this point is compatible with the system developed earlier for pattern recognition: All that has been added is the switch.

Of course, there are many ways that the nervous system could construct the logical equivalent of a switch. All that is needed is some inhibitory mechanism that blocks transmission of information about one conversation and allows transmission of others. The various synaptic mechanisms of the nerve cells allow for this possibility, but there is no need for us to speculate on the particular wiring diagram used by the nervous system at this time: We simply represent the process by the logical diagram of the functions involved.

A simple switching model is successful in explaining the phenomena of attention considered so far. But there are more phenomena.

The first phenomenon to examine is memory: What happens to memory in the absence of attention? To study this, we have subjects do several tasks simultaneously. The goal is to adjust things just right so that all of the subjects' attention must be devoted to one of the tasks. Then they are tested to see what they know about the things that happened in an entirely different task going on simultaneously. In one experiment of this type, the subjects had to shadow words presented over earphones to one ear while common English words were presented to their other ear, each word occurring as many as 35 times. When the experiment

Memory without attention

was over, their memory for the words presented to the unattended ear was tested: There was absolutely no memory for these words. Evidently, the attention required to do the shadowing task completely disrupted the ability to deal with the information presented to the other ear.

This result is not unexpected. The subjects certainly had no time to rehearse or organize the English words. But did the subjects actually hear the words? How far did the unattended information get? Did it get as far as short-term memory?

To discover whether material that is not being attended to gets into short-term memory, it is necessary to interrupt the subjects immediately after the material has been presented to them, and ask whether they remember anything. When the experiment is done in this way, subjects can in fact retrieve the last few items presented from their short-term memory. But if there is a delay as long as 30 sec between presenting the material and testing for its recall, the subject cannot remember any of the unattended words. When attention is concentrated elsewhere, additional incoming information seems to get as far as the short-term memory. But then it can dissipate without a trace. If the test of memory is given immediately, some of the information is still in short-term memory, and can be retrieved.

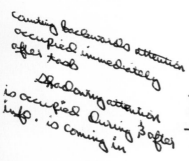

Note the similarity between the tasks of shadowing and of counting backward. In the counting-backward task, attention is occupied on the counting immediately **after** the items have been presented. For shadowing, the attention is also occupied **during** the time the information is coming in.

There is another way of demonstrating the effects of attention on long-term memory. Suppose subjects are given a list of words to remember, and suppose they are tested immediately after each list is presented. Their recall will follow the standard type of serial position curve, such as that shown in Figure 9-21. The experiment continues until 50 different lists have been tested. Then, without any warning, the subjects are asked to recall as much as they can from all of the earlier lists. What happens?

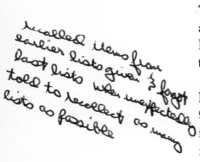

One plausible answer is that their performance should look something like that shown in Figure 9-15: That is, it should be the same as Figure 9-21, but with the short-term memory component gone. This, however, is not what happens. Instead, the subject shows no memory whatsoever for the items presented last in each list, even though many of the first items can be recalled (see Figure 9-21*b*). Why is there absolutely no memory for the last items in the lists of the experiment of Figure 9-21, whereas there is some in the experiment of Figure 9-15?

One possible explanation is that the subjects use different strategies in allocating their attention in these two experiments. In the experiment

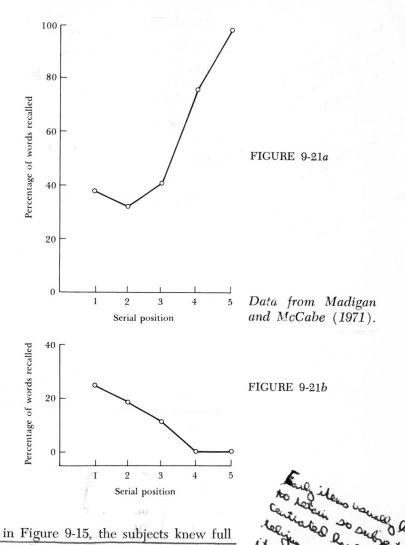

FIGURE 9-21a

Data from Madigan and McCabe (1971).

FIGURE 9-21b

that produced the results shown in Figure 9-15, the subjects knew full well that they were later to be tested on their total recall. But in the experiment shown in Figure 9-21 (performed by Madigan and McCabe, 1971), the subjects had no idea that they were later to be tested on all of the lists. During each list they may have concentrated most of their attention on the early items, since those are indeed the hardest to retain. They paid no attention to the last item, relying on the fact that if that information were recalled immediately, it could be retrieved correctly from short-term memory without having to spend much effort on it. This strategy is perfectly adequate for the initial part of the experiment, but it showed up as a disadvantage on the later, unexpected test.

In both shadowing and simple-recall experiments we find evidence

[handwritten margin note:] Early items usually hardest to retain so subjects concentrated hardest on them relying on the fact that last items would be stored for retrieval in STM. Unexpected test showed what happened when no attention was paid to later items — they were forgotten.

that complete lack of attention to incoming material can allow both
a normal short-term memory for that material and also a complete lack
of long-term memory storage. This should remind you of the discussion
in the previous chapter of the two patients H.M. and N.A. These two
people suffered from a neurological impairment in which short-term
memory appeared to be intact but in which they could not learn and
remember new information for any period of time. Perhaps the brain
damage affected the attentional mechanisms required to get material
from one form of memory to another.

Now let us return to the model of attention. The fact that there is
indeed a temporary memory for material, whether or not it is being
attended to, is not difficult to handle: All that is needed is the realization
that the short-term memory system might exist just after the feature
analysis of Figure 9-20, but before the switch. In this way, there would
be a temporary memory for all material that receives sensory analysis,
but permanent memory would occur only for those things that got
through the switch. This, indeed, is one explanation. But there are other
problems with the model: There is the problem of defining more exactly
what material on the nonattended channel gets through.

FIGURE 9-22   In ox the cap last door minute desk of penny the paper ballgame food the
owl pitcher paint threw book the ball mantiness to happy the carrot ground

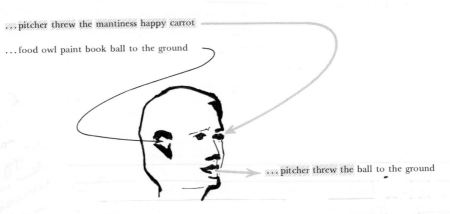

...pitcher threw the mantiness happy carrot

...food owl paint book ball to the ground

...pitcher threw the ball to the ground

Remember the example in which you were asked to read the words
in shaded print, while ignoring the unshaded ones? Suddenly, the meaningful sentence formed by the shaded words turned into gibberish, but
the sentence itself continued in the unshaded words, the ones you were
asked to ignore. When the experiment is actually performed as a shadowing task, with the subject asked to shadow only the material in his
left ear (see Figure 9-22) and to ignore everything else, he is quite
likely to switch the ear he is shadowing when the sentence material

switches. The context and meaning of the messages often intrude into the task, although subjects will often become aware of their error and then stop and apologize.

There are a rather large number of variations of this experiment that can be performed, but all lead to much the same conclusion: There is some awareness of the material in the nonshadowed channels. Thus, it is often the case that a subject will notice his own name when it is spoken in the ear to which he is supposedly not listening. He will pick up words that fit sensibly within the task that he is performing. He will not do well at picking up material from the nonshadowed ear, but neither will he miss everything, as the switch model might imply.

Now, how do we incorporate these results into the description of the process of attention? The final theory must incorporate several things. First, it must spell out the organization of the different processes involved in directing attention to one or more signals. Second, the resulting picture must be consistent with all the evidence that is now available. Third, it must also be consistent with the principle of the systems established for perception and for pattern recognition.

THEORIES OF ATTENTION
The attenuator model

The problem with a switch is that it is an all-or-none device: Either the information gets through, or it does not. But we have already seen that some of the information in a rejected channel, the one that is supposed to be disconnected, does get through and the subject is aware of it. A possible solution, therefore, is to suppose the switch is really an *attenuator*, a device that simply reduces the amount of information that gets past, rather than shutting it off completely. We attenuate an irrelevant signal rather than disconnect it altogether, and thus the diagram should be modified to look like this:

FIGURE 9-23

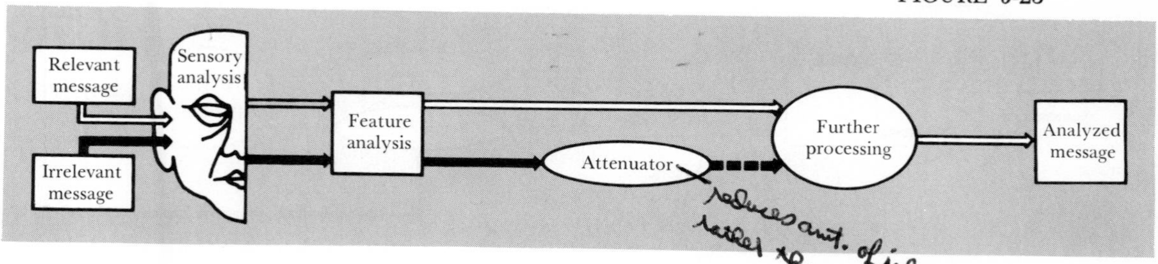

Can this model explain all the experimental evidence? If the attenuation of the unwanted channel reduces the load involved in processing the irrelevant information further, so that most of the effort is exerted on the main relevant channel, then the attenuator serves part of its purpose. In addition, it must allow some words—words that have special significance or that fit the context of the relevant message—to be analyzed even though they are attenuated. Presumably, the analysis is not so efficient on the signals that are attenuated as on those that pass through directly, so there should be lots of errors on the analysis of the attenuated signals: This is exactly what is found. Thus, attenuators do handle some of the phenomena of attention better than all-or-none switches.

What about the memory for the irrelevant signals? Well, perhaps there is a memory system just prior to the attenuator. This seems consistent with the results: Presumably only signals that receive further analysis have any possibility of being stored permanently, but all signals will receive a temporary storage.

How do we know which channel is to be attenuated? After all, we have mentioned that if the subject is asked to shadow the material presented to one ear—

John threw the on that street.

while he is presented simultaneously with this on the other ear—

The house is ball to Tom.

he is very likely to repeat the words "John threw the ball to Tom." The attenuator model would have to switch channels in the middle of the sentence to account for these results. This means the system should be generalized to allow the expectations derived from the analysis of the material that has been analyzed to control how the attenuators shall be set up for future material. Figure 9-24 shows the complete

FIGURE 9-24

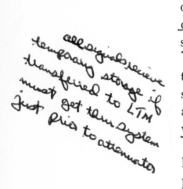

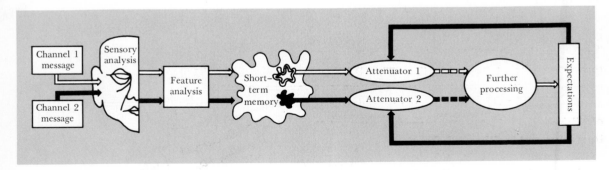

system with both a short-term memory preceding the attenuators and a method of controlling attenuator values. The model is starting to get a little cumbersome, but all the components appear to be necessary, and the system appears to satisfy all the demands made upon it.

We are rapidly approaching a model for attention that has much in common with the pattern-recognition system constructed in Chapter 3. There we concluded that much of the analysis of sensory signals required the use of an active synthesizing mechanism to construct and match the incoming signals, thus allowing for accurate recognition even in the presence of distortions and variations in the input signals. Without this active synthesizing process it would be difficult to analyze signals that contained gaps, inconsistencies, and ambiguities.

The active synthesizing-process model

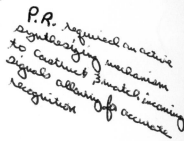

These conclusions appear to be very consistent with the requirements for the attention mechanism. Consider what it takes for the active synthesizer to construct the internal model of the environment. For one thing, it requires that all the information acquired about the signal be put together into a comprehensive pattern. To let context of a sentence predict the next word, it must take into account the subject matter under discussion, the grammatical style of the speaker, and the linguistic analysis of the part of the sentence that has so far been received. Then it can determine which possible inputs would be pertinent to the sentence (and, therefore, ought to be looked for) and which inputs would not be expected to occur. By this means, it can prewarn the perceptual mechanisms about the expected signals and make it possible to match the signal properly when it does arrive, even if it is not entirely distinct. To fit the evidence from the attention studies, it would appear that the analysis-by-synthesis process proceeds in an exceedingly single-minded fashion. Evidently, it follows a single track at a time, so that only one set of signals receives the benefit of extended analysis.

The problem, then, is to decide how to modify the model developed in Chapter 3 to allow several signals to come in simultaneously but only one to be fully analyzed. The basic result is shown in Figure 9-25. The question before us is to decide what to do with the output of the feature analysis from the nonattended channel. In Figure 9-25 it is simply left dangling. Now, remember that only the process labeled "active synthesis" is likely to have limitations on the number of analyses that it can do at any one time. This is the **active** process: It alone requires cognitive, conscious attention. All the other **passive** processes are automatic devices that probably can perform a continuous analysis of all incoming signals. The passive section of the analysis is insufficient to resolve ambiguities and distortions in the signal, and extract complex meanings; for thorough analysis, the information provided by the active mechanism is necessary. Let the same story be true for the analysis of several signals simultaneously. Let **all** signals be analyzed by the passive system: But let only **one** channel at a time also receive analysis by the active part of the system. The signals **not** analyzed by the active part of the system are, in a sense, **attenuated**.

FIGURE 9-25

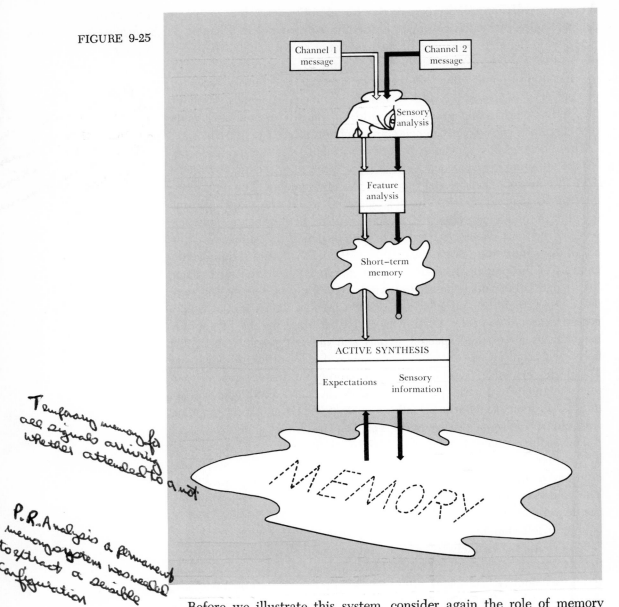

Temporary memory for all signals arriving whether attended to and

P.R. Analysis a permanent memory system was needed to extract a sensible configuration

Before we illustrate this system, consider again the role of memory in the process. Remember that there is some temporary memory for all signals that arrive, whether attended to or not. Notice also that in the pattern-recognition analysis, it was necessary to use the permanent memory system in order to determine what the configuration of features extracted from the signal might represent. The problem is to reconcile these two uses of memory.

In the attenuator model, this problem was resolved by inserting a special short-term memory system into the diagram: <u>a memory for each channel of information</u>. Here, however, it appears to be possible to do something different, primarily because the memory system is already given such a promenent role in the proceedings. A plausible assumption—that the short-term memory is an extension of the long-term one—produces a rather interesting system. Now there is complete symmetry in the way that all channels of information are processed by the passive part of the pattern recognition system.

FIGURE 9-26

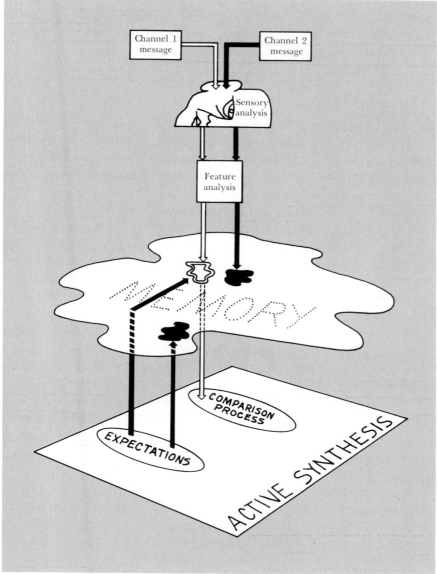

The channel that receives attention, however, also receives additional active processing: one that synthesizes and matches its expectations with the features that have been received. The pattern-recognition system, then, works on all signals as much as it can, extracting whatever physical features are present. But the active synthesizer does only one analysis at a time. Everything on the attended channel gets the benefit of both analyses. But the only signals on the unattended channels that get fully analyzed are signals whose features happen to be consistent with the features expected by the active synthesizing process. The system may switch channels when the signals on the unattended channel have general relevance—such as being the name of the listener. Thus the passive analysis on irrelevant information—the attenuated analysis—is sufficient to attract the attention of the active processor.

SUGGESTED READINGS

The early work on visual short-term memory was done by Sperling (1960) and by Averbach and Coriell (1961). All the data on visual short-term memory in this chapter come from Sperling's work. Rumelhart (1970) presents a theoretical explanation for many of these findings, and his paper serves not only as a source for one possible explanation, but also as a source for further references. A good introduction and review is provided in Neisser's book, *Cognitive Psychology* (1967).

There is by now a large literature on the effects of masking. Good reviews are available in three sources. First, start with Neisser's (1967) treatment. Then read Kahneman (1968), and then for a different perspective, Weisstein's paper on "What the Frog's Eye Tells the Human Brain" (1969).

Norman's introductory book, *Memory and Attention* (1969a: paperback), is a good way of getting into the literature on memory. In fact, a convenient way of getting up-to-date rapidly is to read this chapter, then Norman's book on memory and attention, then the relevant chapters of Neisser's *Cognitive Psychology* (1967). From there, if you still want more, go to the advanced literature: most of the experimental work is summarized in the book on memory by Kintsch (1970) and some advanced models of memory are presented in Norman's *Models of Human Memory* (1970).

Some interesting discussions of the role short-term memory plays in information processing can be found in two symposiums on reading: Singer and Ruddell (1970) and Kavanagh and Mattingly (1972). An old classic study on reading, containing many insights that are still novel and persuasive, is the book by Huey (1908), reprinted in paperback in 1968, with an interesting and important introduction by Kolers.

Weber and Castleman (1970) did the experiment which measured how long it takes to visualize the letters of the alphabet. Brooks (1968) has examined the manner by which visualizing auditory events interferes with visual processing, and vice versa. The experiments on the decay of memory were performed by Reitman (1971) and also by Atkinson and Shiffrin (1971). Sperling and Speelman, in Norman's *Models of Human Memory* (1970) discuss at an advanced level the notion of attributes in memory and the reconstructive process. Similarly, a very advanced treatment is given by Norman and Rumelhart in the second chapter.

The original work on acoustic confusions was performed by Conrad (1959) and Sperling (1959, 1960). Further work has been done by numerous people, so the best source now is a review article or book; Neisser's 1967 book *Cognitive Psychology* or Kintsch's 1970 book on memory; the articles by Wickelgren and Sperling and Speelman in Norman's (1970) *Models of Human Memory*. An extended series of discussions on the implications of acoustic confusions on the form of storage for verbal material (especially printed matter) is contained in the book edited by Kavanagh and Mattingly (1972). This book reports the results of a conference which discussed reading and language, and the discussions among the participants (also reported in the book) are perhaps more important than the papers themselves, for they indicate the present state of our lack of knowledge on this very important problem.

Peterson's article on short-term memory which appeared in July 1966, issue of *Scientific American* is relevant here. Peterson and Peterson did the original experiment in which subjects were asked to count backward by three's after receiving a simple item which they were asked to memorize. Some studies on memory of nonhuman primate (that is, monkeys) are reported in Jarrard's book (1971).

The literature on short-term memory now promises to overwhelm all of the journals. The interested reader can find the literature simply by opening any issue of the *Journal of Experimental Psychology* or the *Journal of Verbal Learning and Verbal Behavior* and then skimming through the two journals, *Psychological Review* and *Cognitive Psychology* for higher level theoretical and occasional experimental discussions of the issues. In addition to these journals, the *American Journal of Psychology*, the *Quarterly Journal of Experimental Psychology*, the *British Journal of Psychology*, and the *Canadian Journal of Psychology* are important sources.

Haber's article, "How We Remember What We See" in the May 1970 *Scientific American* also reviews much of the material presented in this chapter, with special emphasis on visual memory.

One phenomenon not discussed in this chapter is that of "photographic" or "eidetic" visual memory. This is a strange and puzzling phenomenon, and most of what we know is contained in two articles by Haber and his collaborators. One could start with Haber's article (1969a) an eidetic images in the April 1969 *Scientific American*. From there, one ought to go to the monograph on eidetic imagery by Leask, Haber, and Haber (1969).

A fascinating description of a subject with an anomalous memory is given in Luria's *The Mind of a Mnemonist* (1968: paperback). The description of this person's memory poses some fascinating problems for our theories. Is he just an anomaly, or does he represent a fundamental error in our way of thinking about memory?

The theories of attention are summarized in Norman's *Memory and Attention* (1969a) and Neisser's *Cognitive Psychology* (1969). In addition, Treisman's paper in the *Psychological Review* (1969) is also valuable to read. The experiments on memory for unattended material was performed by Moray (1959), who showed no memory with a delayed test, and by Norman (1969b), who showed that there was a short-term memory which could be measured if a test was given immediately. This experiment was also expanded upon by Glucksberg and Cowen (1970). A peculiar set of data on memory for nonattended material is reported by Bryden (1971).

Some more evidence for the analysis-by-synthesis model can be found in readings on pattern recognition, discussed in the "Suggested Readings" section for Chapters 1 and 3 as well as in the papers on reading discussed earlier. The article by Warren and Warren, "Auditory Illusions and Confusions" which appeared in December 1970, *Scientific American* gives some auditory illusions that apparently can only be explained by means of analysis-by-synthesis type models.

10

The structure of memory

In the house you lived in two houses ago, as you entered the front door, was the doorknob on the left or right?

Here is a question that requires memory and the retrieval of information. But if you try to answer it, you will find that the task seems more like that of solving a problem than of retrieving something from memory.

In fact, studies of remembrance, problem solving, thinking, and mental operations have much in common, since there is little to distinguish among them. A person recalling material seems to be solving a problem. First he analyzes the question to decide whether it is legitimate, whether he is likely to have the information, and if so, how difficult it will be to find. If he decides to attempt a recall, he sets up a retrieval strategy. As he proceeds, he combines the information in the request with partial solutions to form new questions and continue his search. His retrieval path seems to be organized around prominent events, landmarks in his memory that stand out above the myriad of stored details. Even if he recovers the information requested, much of his recollection appears to follow from logic and a reconstruction of what must have been.

The study of long-term memory is the study both of this problem-solving process and of the structure of the memory on which it operates. The things we remember are organized into a complex structure that interconnects the events and concepts built up by past experience. The act of remembering is the systematic application of rules to analyze this stored information.

ANSWERING QUESTIONS

Perhaps nowhere else is the power of human memory so clearly exhibited as when people answer questions about what they know. Consider what is required to answer a question (hereafter called a *query*). First, it is not sufficient just to have the pertinent information stored in memory. It is necessary to search out and find all the stored information that is relevant to the query, to evaluate any contradictory data, and finally to put it all together to form the best answer, given the information retrieved.

The human brain is not the only system faced with the problem of answering questions based on large amounts of information. There are numerous examples of systems that are capable of holding vast amounts of data: They range from such traditional devices as libraries to modern computer-based systems. When working with such memories, the first thing that is discovered is that getting information into the system is usually not a basic problem. The difficulties arise in trying to get it out.

Regardless of the memory system we contemplate—be it the human brain, a library card-catalog, a large collection of file folders, or a computer mass-storage device—there are types of queries for which the organizational structures of the memory (including its indices and abstracts) are inappropriate. Yet an omniscient outside observer might declare that the information required to answer the query does, in fact, exist in the system, if only the user would ask the correct questions and then put together the results sensibly. How can the system be designed so that, after we have gone to all the trouble of collecting information, we can find the information we want? What kinds of retrieval strategies are required? If the questions to be asked are known beforehand, the problem may not be too difficult. It is relatively easy, for example, to design the census system so that it can quickly find out how many people are under the age of 30, if you know you want that information before you store the data. But what about questions that were not anticipated? Is it possible to build a data-processing system that, like the human memory, can answer almost anything that comes to mind?

The key to any large-scale memory system, then, is not its physical capacity for storing huge amounts of information. Rather, it lies in its ability to retrieve selected pieces of data on request, its ability to answer questions based on the information stored. We can learn a great deal about the nature of the data-processing operations involved in human memory simply by sitting back and thinking about the kinds of questions people can answer and of the mechanisms and procedures necessary to answer them.

When to retrieve information

Query: **What was Beethoven's telephone number?**

What is your answer to this query? Nonsense, you say. Beethoven died before telephones were invented. But suppose we ask about someone who had a telephone?

Query: **What was Hemingway's telephone number?**

You still refuse to try to retrieve the number. You don't know. How do you know you don't know? What about:

Query: **What is the telephone number of the White House?**

What is the telephone number of your best friend?

What is your telephone number?

The principle being illustrated is that, when asked to recall something, you do not start off blindly on a search. First you seem to analyze the question to see whether you are likely to find anything. On the basis of this preliminary analysis, you may conclude that there is no sense in even attempting to recall the data. Maybe the information does not exist. Maybe the information exists, but you know it is not in your memory. But what information do you use to decide that you do not know Hemingway's phone number, even if he had a phone? Maybe you think you might be able to retrieve the information if you tried, but it would require too much effort to be worth the bother. Are you really sure you could not produce the White House number if you worked on the problem for awhile?[1]

When we ask questions of human memory we discover that there are procedures that analyze the message to determine if the relevant information exists, whether it is likely to have been stored, and the effort required and probable success of an attempt at retrieval. This whole sequence of operations seems to be carried out rapidly and unconsciously. We are only vaguely aware of the complexity of the rules involved.

Clearly, such a system is a great advantage for a large-scale memory. It does not waste time looking for things it does not know. It can judge the cost of retrieving information that is difficult to find. We will see later that when faced with a continuous bombardment of sensory information, it is very important to know what is not known, since it lets us concentrate on the novel, unique, important aspects of events in the environment.

We cannot yet define these preprocessing procedures well enough to take advantage of them in designing a retrieval system. We know such mechanisms operate in human memory. We can identify some of the basic processes and outline their general properties. But we cannot yet describe the details of the machinery involved.

Query: **In the rooms you live in, how many windows are there?**

Retrieving an image

This time, retrieval should proceed smoothly. First you conjure up an image of each room, then examine it, piece by piece, counting the windows. You then move to the next room and continue the process until you finish. The task seems easy. Yet, apart from the fact that people can have and use images, very little is known about the nature of internal images, how they are stored or how they are retrieved.

Whether present theories can handle the problem or not, it is clear that our memories do contain a large number of images of our past

---

[1] The White House telephone number is (202) 456-1414.

experiences. An image can be retrieved and examined at will: the face of a friend, a scene from our last trip, the experience of riding a bicycle. This record of visual experiences suggests some important principles for the analysis of retrieval strategies. Saving some form of a replica of the original information provides a great deal of flexibility in being able to deal subsequently with questions about experiences. It is unlikely that you thought about the possibility of someday being asked for the number of windows. There is no need for you to take note of this fact whenever you are in your room. As long as you save an image of the rooms, you can worry later about retrieving particular pieces of information when they may be required.

We do not always deal with visual information by storing it all away. Often we analyze and condense incoming information, throwing away irrelevant details and remembering only what seems important. Try to recall what we have said so far in this chapter. You do not conjure up an image of the pages and read off the words. You recall a highly abstract version of your visual experience, reorganized and restated in your own terms.

An adequate model of human memory, then, will have to describe when incoming events are saved in their entirety and when only the critical features are extracted and stored. Recording a replica of the information uses up considerable memory space, makes subsequent retrieval more complicated and time consuming, and tends to clutter up the memory with irrelevant details. Reorganizing and condensing the information to save only the central features runs the risk of failing to record information that might subsequently be important. It limits the range and variety of ways in which past experiences can be used and the types of questions we can answer. Maybe it would be optimal to save both a complete record and a reorganized, condensed version, or maybe there are more sophisticated ways of dealing with rote records. Are there general rules for recording and reconstructing images that simplify the storage problem without sacrificing details? After all, houses have lots of things in common, such as roofs and walls. Perhaps the human memory system capitalizes on these similarities.

Regardless of how the information is actually stored, it is important to have both some form of an image of the rooms and a procedure for counting the windows. During retrieval, these two processes interact: One retrieves and constructs the image; the other analyzes and manipulates the retrieved information. Just as for problem solving, retrieval requires the active construction and analysis of information through the application of rules or procedures. This constructive aspect of human memory comes out more clearly when the system is presented with yet another kind of question.

Retrieval as problem solving

> *Query:* **What were you doing on Monday afternoon in the third week of September two years ago?**

Don't give up right away. Take some time to think about it and see if you can come up with the answer. Try writing down your thoughts as you attempt to recover this information. Better still, ask a friend to think out loud as he tries to answer the query.

The type of responses people typically produce when asked this kind of question goes something like this:

1. *Come on. How should I know?* (Experimenter: Just try it, anyhow.)
2. *OK. Let's see: Two years ago. . . .*
3. *I would be in high school in Pittsburgh . . . .*
4. *That would be my senior year.*
5. *Third week in September—that's just after summer—that would be the fall term. . . .*
6. *Let me see. I think I had chemistry lab on Mondays.*
7. *I don't know. I was probably in the chemistry lab. . . .*
8. *Wait a minute—that would be the second week of school. I remember he started off with the atomic table—a big, fancy chart. I thought he was crazy, trying to make us memorize that thing.*
9. *You know, I think I can remember sitting. . . .*

Although this particular protocol is fabricated, it does catch the flavor of how the memory system works on this kind of retrieval problem. First, the question of whether or not to attempt the retrieval: The preliminary analysis suggests it is going to be difficult, if not impossible, to recover the requested information and the subject balks at starting at all (line 1). When he does begin the search, he does not attempt to recall the information directly. He breaks the overall question down into subquestions. He decides first to establish what he was doing two years ago (line 2). Once he has succeeded in answering this question (line 3), he uses the retrieved information to construct and answer a more specific question (line 4). After going as far as he can with the first clue, he returns to picking up more information in the initial query, "September, third week." He then continues with still more specific memories (lines 5 and 6). Most of what happened between lines 7 and 8 is missing from the protocol. He seems to have come to a dead end at line 7, but must have continued to search around for other retrieval strategies. Learning the periodic table seems to have been an important event in his life. The retrieval of this information seems to open up new access routes. By line 8, he once again appears to be on his way to piecing together a picture of what he was doing on a Monday afternoon two years ago.

Here memory appears as a looping, questioning activity. The search is active, constructive. When it cannot go directly from one point to another, the problem is broken up into a series of subproblems or subgoals. For each subproblem, the questions are: Can it be solved; will the solution move me closer to the main goal? When one subproblem gets solved, new ones are defined and the search continues. If successful, the system eventually produces a response, but the response is hardly a simple recall. It is a mixture of logical reconstruction of what must have been experienced with fragmentary recollections of what was in fact experienced.

This idea of memory as a problem-solving process is not a new notion. Similar ideas have been suggested by poets and philosophers for thousands of years. For psychologists, early and persuasive proponents were William James (1890) and Sir Frederick Bartlett (1932). What is new is that finally there are some analytic tools to deal with such processes in detail. The machinery is available to build and test models of memory that solve problems by breaking up questions into subgoals, that try to converge on solutions through continued reformulation and analysis of promising subquestions.

Retrieval and comprehension

Query: Can pigeons fly airplanes?

You should be fairly fast on this one. Assuming you responded negatively, then obviously the next question is, why not? Could a pigeon, in principle, fly an airplane?

This time, the problem is not one of preprocessing the message or of analyzing visual images, or of setting up a search strategy to recover specific information. Moreover, the question does not seem to be answered in terms of a simple recall. It is unlikely that you have given much thought to the specific possibility that pigeons might be pilots, or have stored directly the fact that they do not fly planes as part of the information associated with pigeons. Somehow, you arrive at your answer by a logical analysis of the information associated with the two concepts. But you are only vaguely aware of your analysis when you make your first impulsive response. It takes quite a bit of subsequent work to discover exactly why it is unlikely that pigeons fly airplanes. On further thought, you may even reverse your original verdict: Perhaps a pigeon (with a few modifications either to the pigeon or the airplane) could fly an airplane, after all.[2]

---

[2] When this question was posed to one of the authors' daughters (8 years old), the first response was laughter at the apparently preposterous idea. The second response was that maybe it was not so silly, since both pigeons and pilots do fly.

No existing data-storage system, except the human brain, has the capability of answering this type of question. By contrast, humans routinely analyze the information they receive to test its consistency with their past experience to decide whether what is being said is plausible in terms of what is already known.

This behavior indicates that human memories cannot be a random collection of facts. On the contrary, the information in memory must be highly interrelated and structured. Concepts can easily be compared to deduce the similarities and differences. Moreover, the comparison seems to go on at a number of levels. During the first stage of analysis, something must have suggested immediately that the concepts of pigeons and flying airplanes are logically inconsistent. The second stage requires a more extensive analysis which seems to be similar to the problem-solving procedures just discussed. The subquestion is asked as to what is required to convert a pigeon into a pilot and the stored information is reevaluated on the basis of this reformulation of the question.

This last question brings us to a key issue in the study of memory: the ability to understand. Somehow humans comprehend the meaning of an input and use this comprehension to evaluate present experiences in terms of what is already known. Any model of memory must come to grips with this basic aspect of long-term memory in humans.

THE IMPORTANCE OF UNDERSTANDING

Comprehension is an illusive process. How does one define exactly what it means to understand a word? In fact, how can one even decide from external appearances whether a machine or a person comprehends what is being said? If you think you can, then consider these two dialogs: They have been produced by two different information-processing models of memory which, in these instances, have been translated into computer programs.

The first is a dialog between a person and a program called DOCTOR, a computer program designed to simulate a psychiatrist. The person using the program is allowed to type anything he wishes onto the typewriter keyboard. The second is a program that moves blocks around on a table. The statements of the human user appear in this typeface and are always preceded by this symbol● ; the responses of the computer to these statements are printed in this print.

Figures 10-1 & 10-2

Examine the dialogs. Do you think the computers understand what the people are saying? The program conducting the psychiatric interview is a fraud. It does not have any idea at all what **boyfriends** are, or what it means to be **depressed** or **aggressive**. Nevertheless, to the casual observer, it certainly puts up a convincing front. The second program knows quite a bit about blocks and language. But does it really have

FIGURE 10-1

- Men are all alike.
  In what way

- They're always bugging us about something or other.
  Can you think of a specific example

- Well, my boyfriend made me come here.
  Your boyfriend made you come here

- He says I'm depressed much of the time.
  I am sorry to hear you are depressed

- It's true. I am unhappy.
  Do you think coming here will help you not be unhappy

- I need some help, that much seems certain.
  What would it mean to you if you got some help

- Perhaps I could learn to get along with my mother.
  Tell me more about your family

- My mother takes care of me.
  Who else in your family takes care of you

- My father.
  Your father

- You are like my father in some ways.
  What resemblance do you see

- You are not very aggressive but I think you don't want
  me to notice that.
  What make you think I am not very aggressive

- You don't argue with me.
  Why do you think I don't argue with you

- You are afraid of me.
  Does it please you to believe I am afraid of you

- My father is afraid of everybody.
  What else comes to mind when you think of your father

- Bullies.
  Does that have anything to do with the fact that your boyfriend
  made you come here.　(From Weizenbaum, 1968, pp. 172–173)

FIGURE 10-2

- Will you please stack up both of the red blocks and either a green cube or a pyramid?
  Ok
- Which cube is sitting on the table?
  The large green one which supports the red pyramid
- Is there a large block behind a pyramid?
  Yes, three of them: A large red one, a large green cube and the blue one
- Put a small one onto the green cube which supports a pyramid.
  Ok
- Put the littlest pyramid on top of it.
  Ok
- Does the shortest thing the tallest pyramid's support supports support anything green?
  Yes, the green pyramid
- What color is it?
  By "it", I assume you mean the shortest thing the tallest pyramid's support supports
    Red
- How many things are on top of green cubes?
  I'm not sure what you mean by "on top of" in the phrase "on top of green cubes"
  Do you mean:
    1—Directly on the surface
    2—Anywhere on top of?
- Anywhere on top of
  Three of them
- Had you touched any pyramid before you put the green one on the little cube?
  Yes, the green one
- When did you pick it up?
  While I was stacking up the red cube, a large red block and a large green cube
- Why?
  To get rid of it
- Why did you do that?
  To clean off the red cube
- Why did you clear off that cube?
  To put it on a large green cube
- Why did you do that?
  To stack up the red cube, a large red block and a large green cube
- Why did you do that?
  Because you asked me to
- How did you do it?
  By putting a large red block on the table; then letting go of it; then putting a large green cube on it; then letting go of that cube; then putting the red cube on that cube; then letting go of that cube
- How many objects did you touch while you were doing it?
  Four of them
- What did the red cube support before you started to clean it off?
  The green pyramid
- There were five blocks to the left of the box then.
  No, only four of them: the red cube, two large green cubes and a large red block
- • •
- Thank you.
  You're welcome!   (From Winograd, 1970, pp. 35–60)

the same understanding of the terms as the person with whom it is conversing? How would you test it to find out?

Like the processes of perception, the processes involved in understanding a message go on so quickly and automatically that normally we only become aware of them when they fail. Also like perception, we learn about the memory system by considering the kinds of inputs which are not dealt with smoothly and easily. For example, consider this statement:

Oranz minsocs tankin rakans.

You can read every word. Yet you immediately dismiss the statement as meaningless, and you are right: It is meaningless. But how did you know? Did you really check all the words you have encountered during the many years of dealing with language to make sure that you had not seen **minsocs** before? If you did, you must have conducted the search very quickly, for you have probably heard some 50,000 different words during your life. Yet, somehow, there is the feeling that it is not even necessary to check. You know immediately that these are new words and that this particular string is meaningless in terms of past experiences. But how do you build a memory system that knows so quickly what it does not know?

Or what about this statement?

The minsocs are rakans.

Now you should at least entertain the possibility that what is being said is perhaps meaningful. You still do not know what **minsocs** or **rakans** are, and you know that you do not know. But somehow this statement is treated differently from the first. Perhaps you will hear more about **minsocs** and can add a new word to your vocabulary. Maybe **minsocs** is worth remembering after all.

Notice that the sheer fact that you do not understand the word and cannot interpret it in terms of past experiences does not mean you cannot encode and remember it. If we ask you what **minsocs** are 200 pages from now, you will probably be able to recall that they are **rakans**, even though you do not know the meaning of either of the words. The models we build, then, must be able to decide what things are potentially useful and should be remembered even though it has never seen them before and cannot understand them.

Even fully meaningful statements often make complex demands on memory:

The authors are fascists.

Here all the words are meaningful, yet your reception of the message is hardly a passive, automatic experience. If you take this statement seriously, then to digest it you must retrieve and evaluate enormous amounts of information: What authors are we talking about; what authors would we know that you would also know; what authors do you know who are fascists? Maybe we are talking about ourselves. If so, maybe you should review what you have read so far to decide if there were any statements in the text that suggest that we are fascists. But how do you know a fascist statement when you see one? Whether you can define such statements or not, you will certainly be alerted to them if they occur from here on in the text.

Again there is the question of how to build a memory system that knows just what aspects of the vast amount of data it has stored are pertinent to a particular input. Moreover, it has to be able to find rapidly just the right information needed to evaluate the message, and even if it rejects the message it must be able to use it to guide the interpretation of future events.

Finally, what about the request:

Tell me everything you can think of about authors.

This should open the floodgates. Now you can go on forever, talking about the things you know. You may start talking about authors in general, then move on to specific authors you know, then to their stories, then to the relationships of these stories to your own experiences, and on and on. You probably will not repeat yourself, even though after awhile it would seem that just remembering what has already been said represents an extraordinary feat of memory. We need to build a memory system where all the information is ultimately related to all other information, where new relations linking old concepts can always be found.

We are beginning to see some of the complexity of the requirements for a realistic model of human memory. These illustrations demonstrate the crucial difference between a memory that passively records what it receives and one that actively interprets and analyzes the incoming information. This is precisely the issue that has to be faced in order to develop a convincing model of human memory. The model must be one that can use a conceptual structure to interpret the information it receives, that can compare the incoming messages with what it knows, and that can evaluate the plausibility of something in terms of its past experience. The time has come to see what is involved in actually constructing a model with these fundamental properties of human memory.

A MODEL OF
MEMORY

So far we have been talking about general principles, not specific models. Now it is time to attempt to translate this general discussion into a concrete model. We are going to try to build a memory system that has some of the characteristics of human memory.

In building such a model, an important distinction must be kept in mind. There are really two parts to memory, each equally important. One part is the *data base*, the part of the structure where the information in the memory system is actually stored. The data base must be able to encode and remember concepts and events and complex interrelationships—the stuff of human memory. Our first job is to work out the rules of the data base: We do this in the next section.

The other part of memory is the *interpretive process*, the system that uses the information stored in the data base. It is responsible for evaluating inputs to the memory, for storing new information, for answering questions, for retrieving information to solve problems, speak, think, and guide the daily operations of life. The investigation of these interpretive processes will be taken up in the next chapter.

*Remembering
concepts*

Human memory contains an enormous variety of concepts that can be retrieved and used at will. People have concepts of houses, dogs, cars, communists, and Cub Scouts. Most of the time, but not always, labels are attached to the concepts, such as those just used. In addition to the label, large amounts of information associated with any given concept can be produced on demand. The first job, then, is to decide how to represent concepts in a memory system.

Think of a word, say, **teapot.** Ask a friend to explain what it means, or explain it to yourself out loud. What kinds of information do you produce when describing its meaning? A typical explanation looks something like this:

> **Teapot,** *n. A container something like a kettle, made of metal or china.* [*The Golden Book Illustrated Dictionary for Children*]

Or

> **Teapot,** *n. A container with a handle or spout for making or serving tea.* [*The Thorndike–Barnhardt Comprehensive Desk Dictionary*]

Similarly, for other words, say, **tapestry, tart,** and **tavern,** the dictionary states that

> a **tapestry** is *a piece of cloth with figures or pictures woven into it;*

a **tart** is *a small, baked crust or pastry filled with fruit jelly or jam;*

a **tavern** is *a place where beer, wine, or other alcoholic drinks are served.*

These examples remind us that the definition of a word consists of other words. Typically, a definition starts off by saying, "Concept A is really something else, namely concept B"; a tapestry is a piece of cloth, a tart is a pastry. It then goes on to specify the restrictions on the concept. Unlike other places, taverns serve beer and wine. The unique thing about a tapestry is that it has figures or pictures woven into it. A teapot has either a handle or a spout and is used for tea. (The child's dictionary is a bit ambiguous about why teapots are different from other containers: It suggests that the fact that a teapot is made of metal or china is a critical property.)

Another form of information that is often used in explaining a concept is an example. If you were explaining a **tavern** to a friend, you would probably point out some specific examples. If we look up **place** in a dictionary, we might find little else but examples.

Place, *n. A city, town, or area.*

(Notice that the dictionary did not mention **tavern** as an example of a place.) Similarly,

Container, *n. Anything with the property of holding something, such as a box, barrel, can, or jug.*

It seems, then, that if a person or dictionary is questioned about what a word means, all that is produced is other words. For some reason, this does not seem to disturb us. The hoax only becomes apparent if you persist and ask for the definitions of words that are used to define other words. If you go to the *Oxford Dictionary* to find out what a **son** really is, first by looking up a definition of **son,** then looking up the definitions of the words used to define it, etc., you will trudge through a complicated maze, finally coming to a dead end. You will have gone in a circle, finding **child** defined as an **offspring,** and **offspring** as a **child.**

An important part of the meaning or comprehension of a concept, then, must be embedded in its relationships to other concepts in the memory. On examining the format of typical definitions, a rather small number of relationships seems to predominate: the class of *concepts* to which it belongs, the *properties* which tend to make that concept unique, and *examples* of the concept. A standard definition, then, can be summarized schematically as in Figure 10-3.

FIGURE 10-3

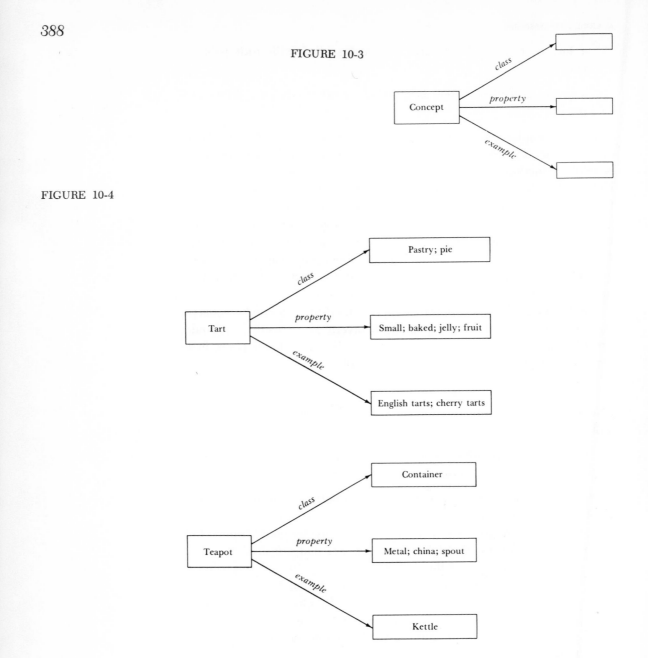

FIGURE 10-4

Filling in the blanks with some of the above definitions produces Figure 10-4. Moreover, the words used in the definition are themselves concepts, and therefore defined in the same way. The result is an interlinking structure that may not be apparent when looking up definitions, but that certainly becomes obvious when structure is shown graphically, as in Figure 10-5.

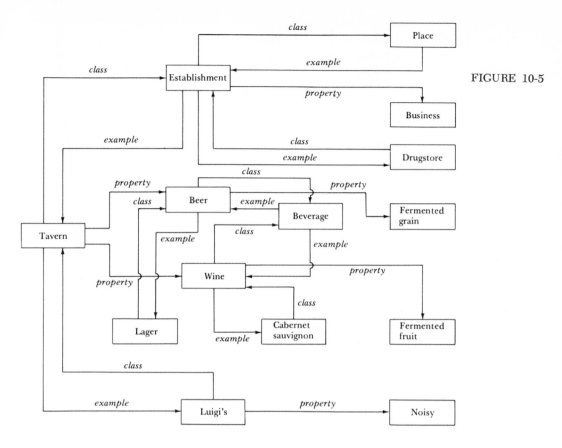

FIGURE 10-5

To represent concepts in the memory the diagrams show two kinds of things: boxes and arrows. The boxes represent the concepts. Notice that the arrows have two important properties. First, they are **directed.** That is, they point in a specific direction. We can follow them in either direction, but they mean different things. Second, they are **named:** there are three kinds of names so far—*property, example,* and *class.* Certainly, we need more than these simple relationships if we are to encode things more complicated than concrete nouns in the memory system. The first step in expanding the system is to change the names of the directed arrows to allow almost any action or relation to serve the purpose.

This is easy to do. First, replace the *class* arrow with the verb *isa. Isa* is obviously a compound word, constructed of the two individuals *is* and *a. Isa* always connects with an object, as in **John** *isa* **man.** Second, replace the *property* arrow with one of two verbs, *has* or *is. Has* is used primarily when properties are objects, such as an **animal** *has* **feet.** *Is,* on the other hand, is used primarily when the property is a **quality**, such as **John** *is* **hungry,** or **Rover** *is* **fat.** (Be careful not to confuse *isa* with *is:* They are quite different.)

Finally, notice that examples are almost always related to class names: The two simply go in opposite directions. Thus, if the class of tavern is an establishment, an example of an establishment will be tavern. So why bother with specific example arrows: Simply let an example be given by following the *class* or *isa* arrow in the backward direction. In summary:

class	*isa*	As in **John** *isa* **man.**
property	*has*	As in **Animal** *has* **feet.**
property	*is*	As in **John** *is* **tall.**
example	*the reverse direction of isa*	As in **John** *isa* **man.**

With these equivalences in mind, the definition of tavern can be redrawn:

FIGURE 10-6

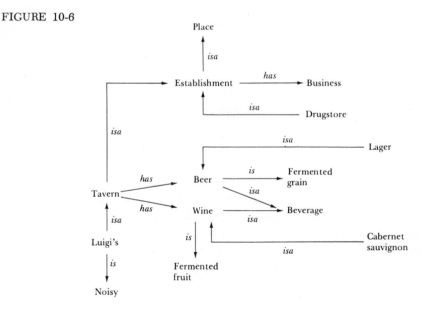

This is a more satisfactory description of the interrelationhips. First, it is much simpler than the original, always a virtue. Second, it captures some of the concepts better. Instead of saying that one of the *properties* of taverns was wine, a peculiar use of the word *property*, we now say simply that a **tavern** *has* **wine:** a neater way of doing things.

In considering the way information is being represented so far, you may have been bothered by the apparent circularity of things. Things get defined in terms of themselves. Moreover, sometimes, things belong to several classes. The memory may indicate that a **dog** *isa* **pet** and also that a **dog** *isa* **mammal.** Which is it? Actually, circularity and apparent lack of precision are desirable in a model of memory, since that is exactly how human memory is. To one person, a pet may be any animal that is domesticated, so that a dog is simply an example of a pet. But another person might have grown up around a household which only had a dog, and that is all he ever saw as an example of an animal that could be domesticated. Hence, when asked what a pet might be, he would reply, "Well, a pet is a dog that is domesticated." Later on, as he grew up, he would broaden his definition to, "A pet is a dog or cat that is domesticated." After many years of this, all the while broadening the definition, he might suddenly have an insight, realizing that, really, a pet is an animal that is domesticated so that, for most purposes, it is a dog that *isa* pet, not the pet that *isa* dog. But he already has the memory structure built up, so he adds the new concept to the old. This is not the neat, systematic logic that language and experience ought to have. But we are describing real behavior, and that is often complicated, confusing, and circular.

A pet isa dog or cat that is domesticated

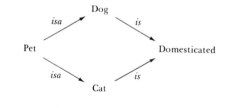

A pet isa dog or cat, and a pet is domesticated

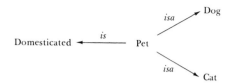

Cats and dogs are pets. A pet isa domesticated animal

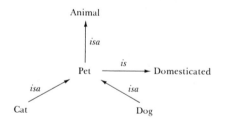

FIGURE 10-7

Primary and secondary concepts

In considering how to represent various kinds of information in this memory, an important problem comes up. Suppose we are trying to remember the information:

Leo, the hungry lion, has a sore mouth.

The difficulty here comes from the way in which we add the fact that the lion has a sore mouth:

FIGURE 10-8

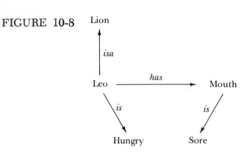

This is one way of representing the sentence. Note that **sore** has to modify **mouth.** If you put the arrow **is sore** off of **Leo,** then all of **Leo** would be sore, not just his mouth.

This description might be all right if this were the only time the concept of **mouth** was mentioned in the memory. But suppose we also know **John is a person who has a big mouth.** Simply adding this information as before would produce

FIGURE 10-9

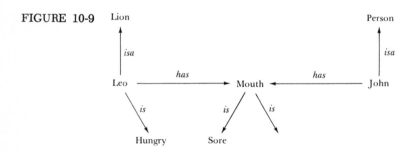

Clearly, this is wrong. When retrieving information about **John,** the memory would think that John's mouth was sore and that **Leo has a big mouth** as well as a **sore mouth.**

The way out of this dilemma is to realize that we need to have only one definition for the concept of mouth but that we need to have many instances where the concept is used, perhaps in modified form. The first definition, the basic one, is called a *primary definition.* The other, the particular use of the concept, is called a *secondary definition.* We represent secondary concepts by enclosing them in angular brackets, like this: ⟨**mouth**⟩. This can be read as "this mouth." This primary–secondary distinction is invaluable, as Figure 10-10 shows.

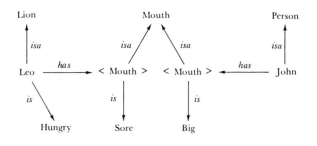

FIGURE 10-10

Actually, it is not even necessary to insert a name inside the secondary concept, for its definition can always be found simply by following the *isa* arrow, as illustrated in Figure 10-11. The secondary node labeled

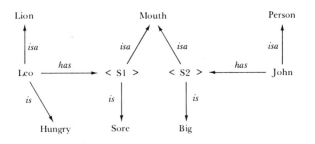

FIGURE 10-11

S1 is that of a **mouth**, in this particular instance, a **sore mouth**. Secondary node **S2** is also that of a **mouth**, but in this instance it is a **big mouth**. When retrieving information, we can automatically substitute **sore mouth** for S1 and **big mouth** for S2 to recover the correct information in each case.

To introduce the idea of a data base for storing information and its interrelated structure, we have restricted ourselves so far to descriptions of concrete nouns and three basic kinds of relationships: *isa, is,* and *has*. These concrete concepts are an important part of the human memory, but they represent only part of the information people normally encounter. What about events? What about the memory for the plot of the last novel you read? How can actions be represented in such a system?

Using the same basic strategy, it is rather easy to add different types of information to the data base. Only two more steps are required,

Remembering events

one very simple, the other rather complicated. The easy step is simply to expand upon the allowable types of arrows that can interconnect concepts. Before letting these arrows proliferate freely, however, it is important to decide on the types of arrows that might be connected to events.

The problem is to represent an event in the memory system. We do that by adding a new type of node to the memory, an *event* node. Thus, in the situation

The dog bites the man.

we wish to add the description of that event. To do that, consider an event as a *scenario*, with actions, actors, and stage settings. All the information must get encoded, with each part of the scene properly identified to its role in the event.

Consider again the situation **The dog bites the man.** Here the sentence that describes the event can be broken down into three parts: a subject (**dog**), a verb (**bites**), and a direct object (**man**). But we do not really wish to determine subjects, verbs, and direct objects, for these are often misleading. Take the sentence, **The man is bitten by the dog.** What do you call the subject? **Man** or **dog?** We want it to be **dog.** The instigator of the action is **dog,** so it is **dog,** not **man,** that is our subject.

To record events, some new concepts must be defined. Consider how an event is described. What we want to do is to break it down into a set of simple relationships that describes the basic concepts of the event. Events can often be described in sentences, but the sentence must be analyzed with some care. Linguists are very careful to distinguish among several levels of language. One, called *surface structure,* represents the part that is visible: The actual sentences people speak. The other level is called *deep structure* or *semantic space,* and it represents the meanings that underlie the sentences. Clearly, the important thing for memory is deep structure, or semantic space. Some sentences can look very similar to one another at the surface structure, but mean completely different things at the semantic level. Consider the sentences

Mother is cooking.

Supper is cooking.

These two sentences look very much the same, but they mean quite different things. In one case, Mother is standing at the stove cooking something. In the other, we can hardly imagine supper to be standing in the kitchen cooking something: It is supper that is being cooked, perhaps by Mother:

Mother is cooking supper.

To discover the basic structure of an event without being misled by the surface structure of the sentence that describes it, we always start by ignoring the details of the sentence and by identifying the *action*.[3] The first step in the analysis is to decide what the *scenario* is: What is the action? Next, find the actors and the things being acted upon. The actors, who cause the action to take place, are called *agents*. The things being acted upon are *objects*, and the person who receives the effect of an action can be called a *recipient*. Here are some examples:

Mother is cooking.

Action: cooking

Agent: Mother

Object: none

Supper is cooking.

Action: cooking

Agent: none

Object: supper.

Mother is cooking supper for Hubert.

Action: cooking

Agent: Mother

Object: supper

Recipient: Hubert

Identifying things this way simplifies life considerably.

Now we see how to represent events in the data base. The entire event centers around some action, so the action becomes the central node: We represent it in diagrams as a node, drawn as a circle around the word (usually a verb) that describes the action. Then the actors and objects that comprise the scenario are attached to the event node by arrows that identify their role: The basic format is shown in Figure 10-12.

---

[3] These examples and analyses come from Fillmore (1968) in Bach and Harms (1968).

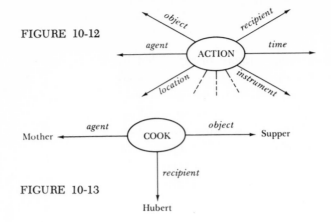

FIGURE 10-12

FIGURE 10-13

Thus, the sentences

Mother is cooking supper for Hubert.

and

Hubert's supper is being cooked by mother.

are both diagrammed as the same scenario—that of Figure 10-13. Thus, although the sentences look quite different from each other (they have different surface structure), they have the same meaning (the same deep structure), so they are drawn the same in terms of the information recorded in the memory. Moreover, there is the strong implication that the cooking is being done somewhere (a *location*), with something (an *instrument*), and at some specific time (*time*). These unstated concepts are simply added to the event node whenever they become known. No new structure need be created for them.

Other *cases* (that is what things like *agents, objects,* and *recipients* are called) that are useful are such things as

time: when an event occurs, often specified simply as past, present, or future, or conditional. (*Jack* **kissed** *Louise: Time is* **past**).

location: where an event takes place (*Bob hit Jack* **on the head:** *Location is* **head**).

instrument: the thing involved to cause the event (*Bob hit Jack on the head* **with a rock:** *Instrument is* **rock**).

truth: whether the event was true or false (*I* **did not** *see Jack: Truth is* **not**).

A complete list of the cases used to describe events is given in Table 10-1.

Table 10-1   The Parts of an Event

Action	The event itself. In a sentence, the action is usually described by a **verb**: The man was **bitten** by the dog.
Agent	The actor who has caused the action to take place: The man was bitten by the **dog**.
Conditional	A logical condition that exists between two events: A shark is dangerous **only if** it is hungry. John flunked the test **because** he always sleeps in lectures.
Instrument	The thing or device that caused or implemented the event: The **wind** demolished the house.
Location	The place where the event takes place. Often two different locations are involved, one at the start of the event and one at the conclusion. These are identified as **from** and **to** locations: They hitchhiked **from La Jolla to Del Mar.** **From the University,** they hitchhiked **to the beach.**
Object	The thing that is affected by the action: The wind demolished the **house.**
Purpose	Identifies the purpose of the event: Jack took Henry to the bar **to get him drunk.**
Quality	A descriptor, one that modifies a concept: The surf was **heavy.** There were **93** people in class.
Recipient	The person who is the receiver of the effect of the action: The crazy professor threw the blackboard at **Peter.**
Time	When an event takes place: The surf was up **yesterday.**
Truth	Used primarily for false statements: I do **not** like you, Hubert.

The event

Yesterday, at the beach with my new camera, I photographed the house on Ninth Street.

is analyzed as

action: photograph

agent: I

object: house on Ninth Street

location: beach

instrument: my new camera

time: yesterday

This analysis can be broken down even further. The *object* can be analyzed as a *concept* (house) plus a *location* (Ninth Street). The *instrument* is a specific camera, namely mine. Hence, the final structure is as shown in Figure 10-14.

FIGURE 10-14

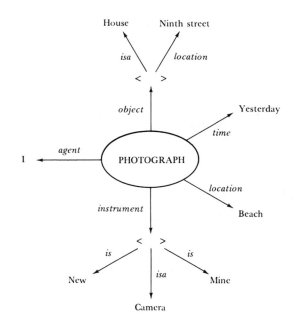

All these relationships are entered into the data base much the same way that concepts were, except that now there is a richer set of possibilities than simply *isa, is,* and *has.* There is one simplification of the structure that is sometimes useful, *shorthand notation.* Often in the case of a simple event, such as **Mother cooks supper,** there is little ambiguity as to the role played by each concept (**Mother** and **supper**). In this case the full event notation, that shown in Figure 10-15*a*, is not needed. Rather, the simplified structure of Figure 10-15*b* can be

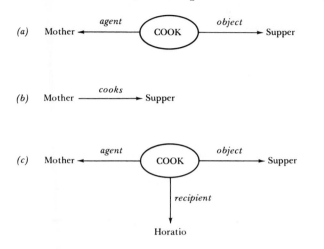

(a) Mother ← *agent* — COOK — *object* → Supper

(b) Mother — *cooks* → Supper

(c) Mother ← *agent* — COOK — *object* → Supper
— *recipient* → Horatio

FIGURE 10-15

used. Notice that this shorthand notation simply uses the action as the name of the relation (arrow) that connects the two concepts. There is no difficulty with this shorthand as long as it is recognized that the two versions shown in parts (*a*) and (*b*) of the figure are equivalent. As soon as a new detail is added to the description of the event, however, then the shorthand notation no longer works. Hence, **Mother cooks supper for Horatio** must be described in the full notation of Figure 10-15*c*.

Now that the full power of the data base is starting to emerge, add these events to the data base described earlier in Figure 10-6.

> **Bob drinks beer.**
>
> **Mary hit Louise hard yesterday at Luigi's.**
>
> **Al owns Luigi's.**
>
> **Bob likes Louise.**
>
> **Al's dog, Henry, bit Sam because he yelled at Mary.**
>
> **Louise drinks wine.**
>
> **Mary likes Bob.**

When this is done, the data base is considerably enriched, since now not only are many concepts defined, but we can begin to see the events that take place involving those concepts. A sample of how the final data base might look is shown in Figure 10-16. Note that here both

FIGURE 10-16

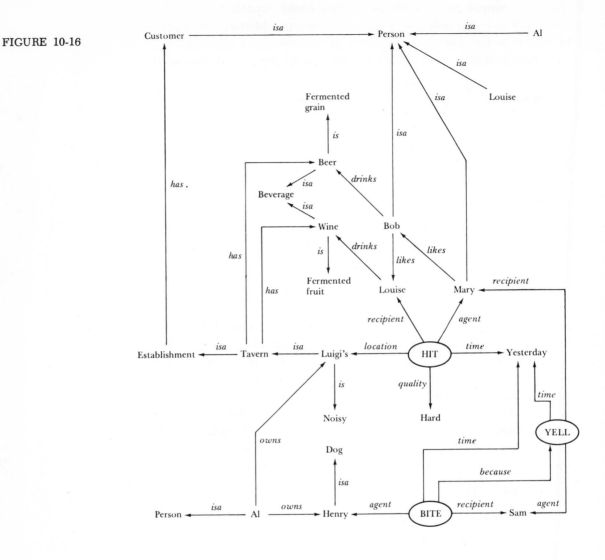

shorthand and full notation are used to describe events, but there should be no confusions caused by the combination. (A few new techniques are illustrated in this figure, so it would pay to examine it with care.)

We now have the basic design for the data base underlying human memory. The memory system is an organized collection of pathways that specify possible routes through the data base. Retrieving information from such a memory is going to be like running a maze. Starting off at a given node, there are many possible options available about the possible pathways to follow. Taking one of these paths leads to a series of crossroads, each going off to a different concept. Each new crossroads is like a brand new maze, with a new set of choice points and a new set of pathways to follow. In principle, it is possible to start at any point in the data base and, by taking the right sequence of turns through successive mazes, end up at any other point. Thus, in the memory system all information is interconnected.

As it stands now, the memory is passive. It is a network of potential pathways, each of which could, in principle, be used by interpretive and retrieval processes. It is now time to examine some procedures for retrieving and manipulating the stored information, the procedures that describe how the memory is used.

As an introduction to the problem, answer the following queries from the data base shown in Figure 10-16.

> *Query:* **Do people drink beverages?**
> *Query:* **Does Al like Mary?**
> *Query:* **Is Louise a customer?**

Suggested readings for Chapters 10 and 11 are combined at the end of Chapter 11.

SUGGESTED
READINGS

11

Memory processes

In the preceding pages, we developed a basic organizational structure for memory, including methods for encoding concepts and events. The structure of memory is only half the story. It is time now to explore the kinds of cognitive processes that might operate on such a memory structure.

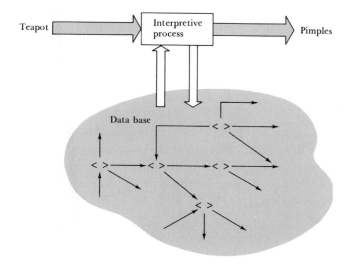

FIGURE 11-1

In this chapter, we explore the second half of the memory process: the *interpretive process.* The story is only a guide, since it soon gets entangled in the complexities of human thought. The general approach may be on the right track, but the details need careful scrutiny, both in terms of the logical properties of the processes involved and the experimental tests of their implications. The study of the cognitive processes of memory is new: The principles we discuss can be no more than a mere beginning.

A memory system must communicate with the world. It has to be able to take in statements and recode them into a format suitable for storing in the memory. It must also be able to respond to questions. Given the kind of memory structure described so far, the basic strategy for handling inputs and making responses is relatively straightforward.

MECHANISMS FOR INPUT AND OUTPUT

First let us consider two simple versions of the problems. The first problem of input is the problem of adding new statements into the data base; the first problem of output is to translate the information from the memory system into a coherent set of statements that describe the data that have been stored.

Processing an input   Suppose that Mary has just walked into our lives. We perceive her as a simple concept:

Mary is a fat, pimply person.

To get the concept into the data base requires that it first be translated into the standard format by which information is represented. That is, the concept of Mary as we now know her resides in three simple statements:

Mary isa person.

Mary is fat.

Mary has pimples.

At this point, we are concerned with the mechanisms that add these three statements to the data base. We assume that the concept of Mary, as perceived by the various perceptual and pattern-recognition processes, results in an image of Mary that contains these three statements. Now, the task is to translate the image into the data base. The illustrations

FIGURE 11-2

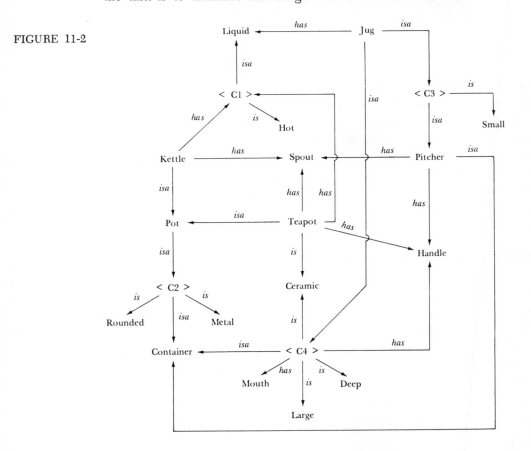

we use are all linguistic—Mary is described in simple sentences—but that is for convenience only. Presumably the actual memory of **Mary** as **fat** and **pimply** is nonverbal. The verbal description of the data base is the easiest to illustrate, but it is important to realize that these verbal descriptions are only representations of the actual, symbolic processes that must actually occur.

Let us start with the simplest situation: a set of concepts. The data base shown in Figure 11-2 contains the definitions of various kinds of pots and containers. Notice that all the concepts do not have names. In particular, there are intermediate concepts, labeled C1, C2, C3, and C4 in the figures, that are used during the definition of other entries. These intermediate concepts are the **secondary** concepts discussed earlier. If you follow the definitions through, you should have no difficulty in understanding their use.

Making responses

How does this system answer questions about what it knows? First, try some simple ones.

> *Query:* **Tell me about a teapot.**

The memory system should respond something as follows.

> A teapot is a pot. It is ceramic. It has a handle, a spout, and a, let me see, a liquid that is hot. A pot is a, um, a container that is rounded and metal. A kettle is a pot. Now let me tell you about a kettle. A kettle has a spout and, let me see, a liquid that is hot. Now let me tell you about. . . .[1]

This output is simple. It represents a straightforward attempt to follow the paths leading from each node. No interpretation is involved. But what happens when simple reasoning is required?

Using Figure 11-2, answer the following queries of the memory system.

A. *Query:* **Does a jug have a handle?**[2]
B. *Query:* **Is a pot made of metal?**
C. *Query:* **Is a teapot a pot?**
D. *Query:* **Is a teapot ceramic?**
E. *Query:* **Does the answer to D contradict the inference resulting from the answers to B and C?**

---

[1] In this hypothetical illustration we indicate something of a possible strategy for recall. First, all the information around a node is described, then one of the nodes referred to is described, and so on. Whenever a second node is reached, however, it must be examined with some care, first following the *isa* arrow to find its name, and then following the others to add qualifiers. This requires time and effort, so we assume the "person" fills in the time by such innocuous phrases as "let me see," "um," and ". . . you know."

[2] The correct answer is yes.

406

DEDUCING A PERSON'S MEMORY STRUCTURE

Within the memory system, everything is eventually related to everything else. Thus, if retrieval were allowed to continue, it could go on forever. But the structure of the output is intimately related to the structure of the data base. This fact can be used in the clinical assessment of patients. Several possible techniques can be used. In one, the technique of *free association,*

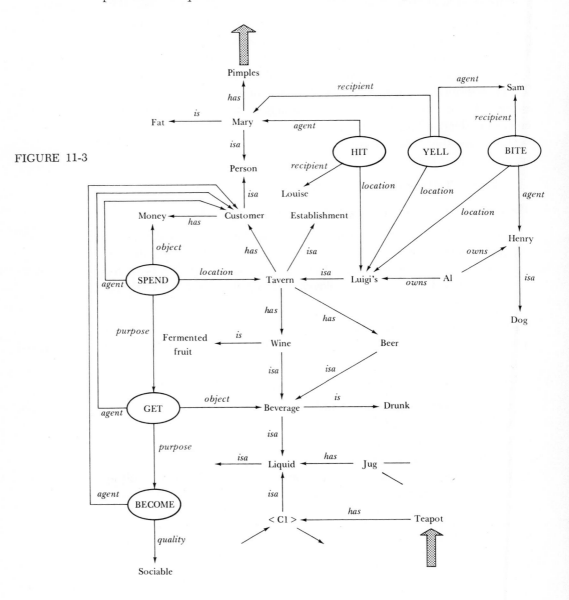

FIGURE 11-3

the patient is presented with a word and asked to respond with "the first word that comes to mind." In variations of this technique, the patient may be asked to discuss any topic that he wishes, whether it seems relevant or irrelevant to the problem confronting him. With the interlocking structure of the data base, everything must have some relevance to the consideration of everything else.

Look what would happen if the more complete version of the data base of Figure 11-3 is used to produce free associations and discussion of the word **teapot.**

Start with **teapot.** The path leads to **liquids** and **beverages.** Now the path goes two different ways.

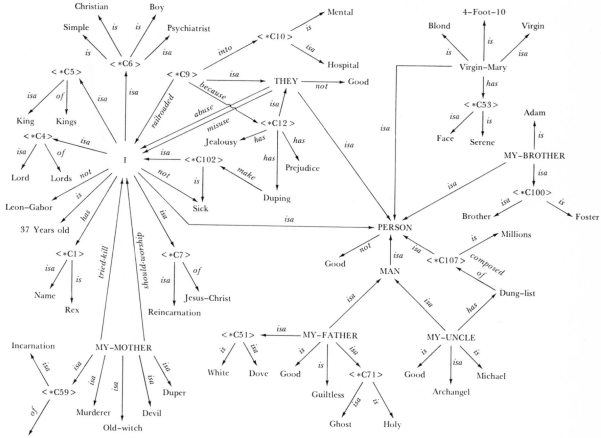

FIGURE 11-4

Customers spend money at taverns to get *beverages* for sociable purposes.

Alternatively, the path reads

Wine and beer are *beverages*. The tavern, Luigi's, has wine and beer, as well as *customers*.

Now, both paths have gotten us to **Customer. Customer** takes us easily to **person** and, hence, to **Mary** (the girl with **pimples**). But we are very close to a whole, interlocked series of events, the incident at **Luigi's.**

The type of response that this data base produces is determined to a large extent by the interpretive system. To whom does the data base belong? Is it the data base for **Sam?** If so, presumably he is very much concerned with that incident. With **teapot** as a starting point, he easily remembers either **customer** or **tavern** and then **Luigi's.** But once at **Luigi's,** he is attracted by the series of events in which **Henry** bit him, evidently because he yelled at **Mary.** But **Mary,** that **fat girl** with **pimples** had hit **Louise.** (**Louise,** we will discover later, is **tall** and **handsome.**)

Suppose **Sam** were asked to free-associate to the word **teapot.** Is it not possible that he responds **pimples?** The skilled clinician tries to make use of that bizarre association to probe the underlying memory structure, hoping thereby to deduce the complete picture. In this example, the structure is a rational one. With many mental ailments, of course, things are not put together so rationally. You might enjoy probing this structure of Leon-Gabor, a patient who believed himself to be Jesus Christ.[3]

Figure 11-4

<table>
<tr><td>SEARCHING
MEMORY</td><td>*Query:* **Are all alps mountains?**
Query: **Does a canary have blood?**</td></tr>
</table>

One way of testing memory is to see how people answer queries. Actually, the most valuable thing to observe is how quickly they can give answers, not what answers they give. To see this, let us examine another segment of the data base. This one is copied from the work of Allan Collins and M. Ross Quillian (1969) except that is has been redrawn to use the notation described in this book.

Consider the following queries:

1. **Is a canary yellow?**
2. **Does a canary have wings?**
3. **Does a canary breathe?**

How would you answer these by using Figure 11-5? Begin with the most difficult question: 3. **Does a canary breathe?** The obvious first

[3] The structure for Leon-Gabor was extracted from the case study by Rokeach, *The Three Christs of Ypsilanti* (1964).

FIGURE 11-5

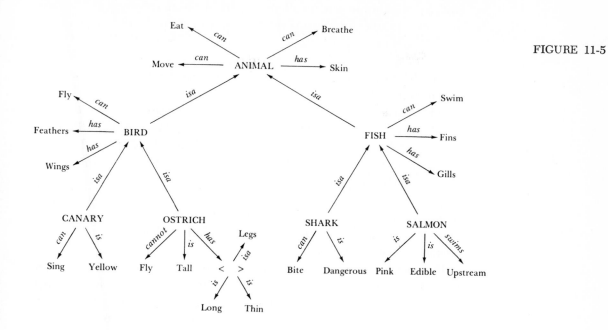

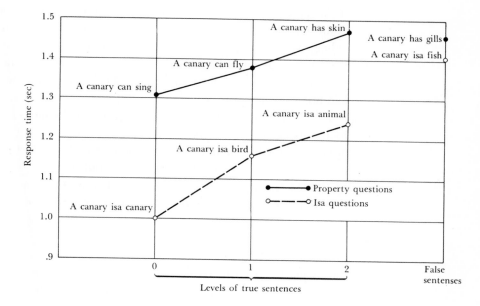

FIGURE 11-6

From Collins and Quillian (1969).

step is to look up the properties specifically associated with a canary and see whether or not breathing is part of the description. If breathing is found on the list of properties, you can immediately respond **yes.** But if breathing is not there, you cannot conclude that the answer is **no.** It is quite possible that **breathing** is stored with bird or animal: After all, why should not common properties modify the entire class to which they belong?

What *isa* canary? **A canary isa bird.** The next step, then, is to check the definition of birds: **Does a bird breathe?** Again, there is no information about breathing, so the upward search must be continued. **A bird isa animal.** What do we know about animals? Well, an **animal can breathe.** Hence a **bird** (which *isa* animal) **can breathe;** hence a **canary** (which *isa* bird) **can breathe.** If this is the way information is represented in the memory, then it should take much longer to find the answer to a query like **Does a canary breathe?** than to one like **Does a canary have wings?**

This is what is tested: the time taken to answer these types of questions. Subjects are asked to respond to a number of sets of such queries and the times required to make a response is measured. The results are shown in Figure 11-6. Here, several types of sentences are shown. One sentence, **Isa canary a canary?** is included for calibration purposes. It shows how long it takes someone just to read the sentences and make an answer, even when no real search of memory is required. In addition, two different types of sentences are distinguished. One type, called an *isa* question, needs only to follow the connection labeled *isa*. Hence, **isa canary a bird?, isa canary an animal?, isa oak a tree?** The other type, called property questions, checks properties such as **has skin, can breathe, has acorns.**

The data shown in Figure 11-6 indicate that the more concepts needed to be checked, the longer it takes to get an answer. In fact, it would appear to take around .1 sec for each extra level in the memory that must be searched. Note that it takes about 1.0 sec just to answer **yes** to the statement **a canary isa canary.** This is the time needed to read the sentence, make a simple decision, and push the response button. A sentence that requires searching one level up the *isa* chain (like **a canary isa bird**) takes about 1.18 sec, so we can conclude that the extra .18 sec is due to memory search time. A sentence that requires the memory search to follow two levels of *isa* statements (like **a canary isa animal**) takes about 1.24 sec, or an additional .24 sec over that time required by the most simple sentences.

Similarly, for the case where property lists must be searched, the most direct search—**a canary can sing**—takes about 1.3 sec, with an extra .8 sec required to discover that **a canary has skin.**

These experimental results are only preliminary: They cannot yet be used to do more than give a hint of the structure of memory and how the retrieval process operates. But they do offer some tantalizing evidence of the general nature of the system.

Exercise: Note that two more data points are shown in Figure 11-6—the time taken to respond to false statements such as, **a canary has gills,** and **a canary isa fish.** Now look at Figure 11-5 and try to determine what decision process might be used to answer such questions. How would you deal with such statements as **a canary is dangerous,** or even **a canary is peaceful,** statements for which no information at all is stored, at least not directly?

Finally, consider the type of data base that would allow you to deal with sentences of the form:

Madrid is Mexican.

A pecan has a castle.

Chicago has mountains.

An igloo would melt in Texas.

Bicycles defeat smog.

Query: **All alps are mountains.**

Multistage search processes

To decide whether this is true or false requires a different type of memory search from those discussed for queries of the form **a canary has skin.** In the canary question, the basic problem was to decide whether the definition structure of canaries was consistent with the statement. With the alps question, we need to examine every single instance of alps: quite a different operation.

A large set of questions of this form has been investigated by David Meyer (1970). He considered subjects' responses to questions of the following four types:

All P are S.

Some P are S.

All S are P.

Some S are P.

Depending upon the relationship between **S** and **P**, these questions pose different kinds of search strategies. Consider these cases:

Subset relations. Let **P** be an example of **S**. Thus, **P** might be an alp and **S** a **mountain**, or **P** might be a **ruby** and **S** a **gem**. Hence

All rubies are gems.	*True.*
Some rubies are gems.	*True.*
All gems are rubies.	*False.*
Some gems are rubies.	*True.*

Overlapping relations. Let **P** and **S** be two things that overlap in meaning but neither is an example of the other. Thus, **P** might be **women** and **S** **writers**, or **P** might be **conservatives** and **S** **students**. Hence, we get the four types of sentences:

All women are writers.	*False.*
Some women are writers.	*True.*
All writers are women.	*False.*
Some writers are women.	*True.*

Disjoint relations. Finally, let **P** and **S** be things that have nothing in common: They are *disjoint.* Thus, **P** might be **house** and **S** **vacuums**, or **P** might be **books** and **S** **cats**. All four versions of these sentences are false.

All books are cats.	*False.*
Some books are cats.	*False.*
All cats are books.	*False.*
Some cats are books.	*False.*

Given the kind of memory structure we have been studying, different search procedures are needed to answer these queries. For example, to answer the query:

Are all chairs furniture?

one could start with chairs, find all examples, and check each to make sure it was indeed a type of furniture. If this scheme is followed, the time required to answer the question

Are all thrones furniture?

ought to be a great deal shorter than for the first question. After all, there are far less examples of thrones than of chairs in most people's experiences, so the time needed to do the search should be much less.

Following this reasoning, it is possible to test various theories of the way memory is searched by changing the number of examples that must be searched to answer the questions and seeing how the times taken by subjects to reach their decisions change.

The results from such experiments indicate that there are at least two stages to the process of answering this type of query. First, there is a check to see whether the two things being compared have anything in common with each other—that is, do they intersect? For example, in these two queries:

All wheats are typhoons.   (All S are P.)

Some chairs are people.   (Some S are P.)

there is no common relation between **S** and **P** (**wheats–typhoons,** or **chairs–people**), so we know immediately that the correct answer to these queries is **false.** But if there is something in common between the two concepts, for example:

All pilots are men.   (All S are P.)

then the first stage of analysis does not produce an answer. In this case, a second stage is needed to analyze whether, without exception, every **pilot** is indeed a **man.** The additional processing, of course, requires additional time, and subjects are correspondingly slower in making a response. Notice that with a question of the type:

Some pilots are men.   (Some S are P.)

a single positive instance is sufficient for us to answer **true.** Hence the response is fast, since it is given by the first stage of analysis. In general, then, the search for answers to questions of this particular type can be represented as a two-stage search process operating on an organized memory structure.

Figure 11-7

The common feature of all our search procedures is that both the retrieval information and deductive logic is required to answer queries of the memory. The answer is seldom stored directly in the memory system. It must be ferreted out, dragged from the corners where it may be hiding, and painstakingly put together. Even so simple a question as

What is a quigee?

requires an extensive search and logical construction of the information found.

Figure 11-8

There is a long history in psychology of studies which have demonstrated that memory is seldom a simple storehouse of events, that it is a collec-

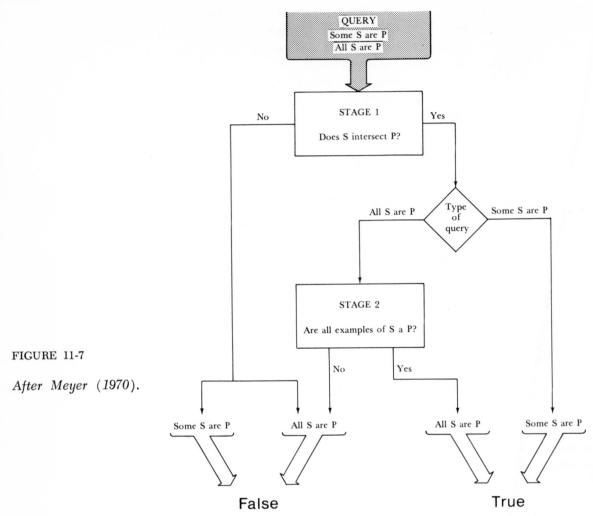

FIGURE 11-7

After Meyer (1970).

tion of ideas that must be worked on to reconstruct the image that is being retrieved. But it is only when we make a careful study of the nature of structure and the retrieval process that might be operating that the truly constructive nature of human memory emerges.

REORGANIZING
THOUGHTS

The data we have just been considering indicate that there is a reasonable amount of general structure to the information in the data base. It seems that information is stored where it is most efficient. Rather than have a statement like **has wings** stored with the concept of each and every single bird in the data base, it would appear that the information is stored only once, at the more general concept of birds. This

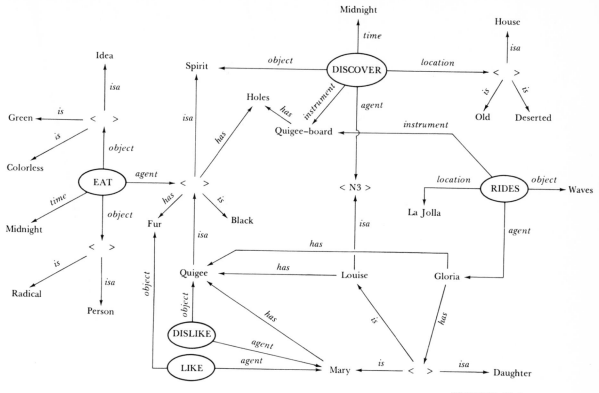

FIGURE 11-8

assumes quite a bit of intelligence on the part of the system, since at times, information within the memory will have to get reorganized. Let us now examine some of the processes by which this reorganization and generalization of information might occur.

Here is a picture of the concepts that might be encoded within the data base of someone's memory. To simplify the discussion, no events are portrayed, simply concepts related to **Mary, Bob,** and **Sam.** Given the kind of information shown—that **Mary** is **short, fat,** and **female,** that **Bob** is **red-haired** and **radical,** and **Sam** is **smart**—what kind of conclusions can be drawn by thinking about the relationships that exist? After all, as more and more information accumulates about concepts, it is perfectly reasonable to stop now and then to ask what has really been learned.

Figure 11-9

Query: **Tell me about person.**

For this query, the memory system should respond with a list of people, and then the properties of those people. But in the process,

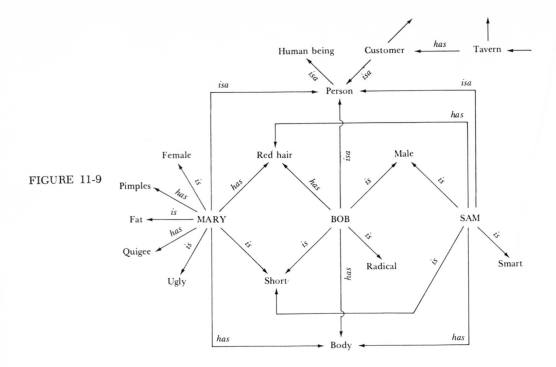

FIGURE 11-9

it might learn some interesting things. For example, consider this hypothetical output from the interpretive processes:

> Mary, Bob, and Sam isa person. Mary is female, fat, short, and ugly. Mary has red hair. Hmm, Bob has red hair. Sam has red hair. All persons have red hair. Bob is short. But look at this. Bob, Mary, and Sam are short. All persons are short. . . .

From the information stored in this data base, **all persons** are short, red-haired, and have a body. Thus, the concept of **person** has been generalized by putting together common information.

The system for generalizing is rather simple. First, examine all instances of a concept for information held in common. Whenever the same information is found stored at all concepts, generalize the knowledge of these concepts. Do all people have bodies? The data base only has three examples of people, and each of them does indeed have a body. The obvious thing to do is to remove the property of body from each of those three people and put it in a common location, as the information **person has body.** When we do this, it simplifies the overall structure of the data base.

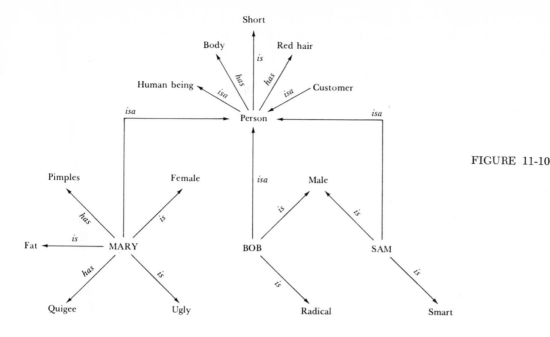

FIGURE 11-10

These generalizations of Figure 11-10 are peculiar: All people have red hair, are short, and have bodies. We would agree with the last, but not the first two. But, in part, this is simply because the memory that is illustrated only knows three people. You disagree that all people have red hair, but this is because you have encountered hundreds or thousands of people, and many of them did not have red hair. For the system illustrated, having red hair and being short is just as accurate a characterization of people as is the fact that they all have a body.

Some further refinement of the memory data-base is possible. Look at Figure 11-10. Here we see that Bob and Sam are persons that are male. This information can be combined to form a new concept, namely, that of **N1**, a **male person** (see Figure 11-11). For the moment, the memory system only knows that it can find a common concept between some of the **persons** in its data base, namely the property of being a **male**. Later on, it might learn that it should call the concept **man**, but at the moment, the generalization is indicated with an unnamed secondary node, labeled **N1** for convenience.

We now see how to form general concepts based on the analysis of information learned from past experience. The generalization scheme is deceptively simple. As it is applied over and over again, the memory is continuously being reorganized. Properties that concepts have in common tend to migrate upward and become attached to more general items. In time, only the unique or important characteristics of a concept will remain attached specifically to the concept. When the memory system thinks about Mary, it is going to think first about what makes her unique. More general properties can be retrieved by moving upward through the arrows labeled *isa*. With such a generalizing mechanism, the response to a question about a concept might be:

Query: **Tell me about Mary.**

Well let me see. Mary is a fat ugly female with pimples and a quigee. And she is a person, of course, and therefore is short and has red hair and a body. Would you like me to compare Mary with the other people I know?

Correcting errors   Obviously, when making generalizations, the memory system can only use the information it has available at any given instant of time. This is bound to lead to errors, since it may not know very much. This aspect of its behavior is compatible with human performance. But there should be some way of counterbalancing these tendencies to over generalize. A mechanism is needed for redoing concepts as more information comes in. Right now, the memory system has the following information about the concept of person:

FIGURE 11-11

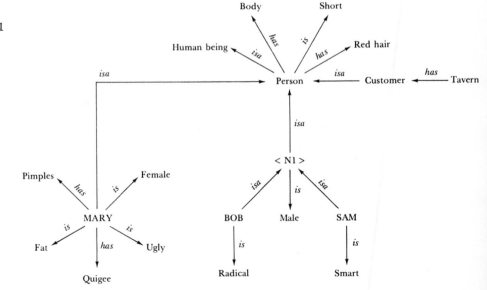

person
> * isa human being.
> * is short.
> * has body.
> * has red hair.
> **Mary** isa *.
> **customer** isa *.
> **N1** isa *.

To simplify the description of the node we let the symbol * stand for the concept that is being defined. Thus * **is a human being** represents the information that a person *isa* human being and **Mary** *isa* * represents the information that Mary *isa* person. Suppose that the following facts become available.

Person is happy.

Louise isa person.

Harry isa person.

So far, no problem. We add these three facts to the list of things known about person and also start three new concepts for **happy, Louise,** and **Harry.** (At this point, it would be wise for you to get some paper and copy the network in Figure 11-11, adding the three statements above, so that you can modify it as we go along. We are going to go through some reorganizations that may be difficult to follow unless you write them out.)

Suppose we now learn that

Sam is radical.

Sam is ugly.

From this information, a new rationalization can be formed. First add the new information that **Sam is ugly** and **radical** to the definition for **Sam.** Similarly, add **Sam** to the definition for each of these concepts. Note that **Mary** is also **ugly** but there is nothing much else in common between **Sam** and **Mary.** However, both **Sam** and **Bob** are radicals. Moreover, they are both **N1.** Thus, the new generalization—**N1 is radical.**

The memory structure now looks like this:

Sam
> * isa N1.
> * is smart.
> * is ugly.

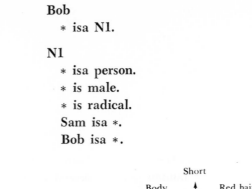

Bob
> * isa N1.

N1
> * isa person.
> * is male.
> * is radical.
> Sam isa *.
> Bob isa *.

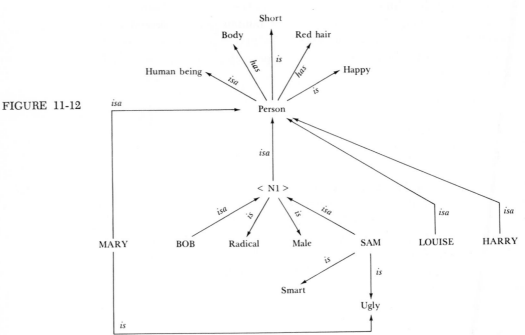

FIGURE 11-12

Suppose the memory system continues to learn about people, in particular about **Louise**. So far, all it knows about Louise is that **Louise isa person**. Then the following information is learned.

Louise
> * isa person.
> * is old.
> * is handsome.
> * is stupid.
> * is tall.

What have we here? **Louise is tall**, but **Louise isa person** and a **person is short**. At this point, the memory system must do something to correct the conflict.

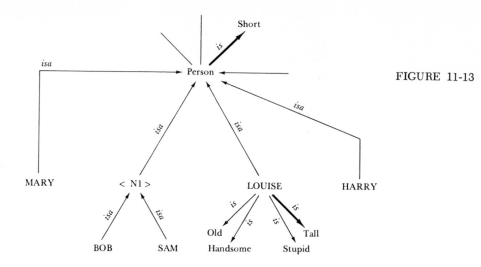

FIGURE 11-13

The first thing it ought to do is make sure it got the proper information and ask its informant:

Did you really mean to say that **Louise is tall?**

If the information is verified, then it must have some way of correcting the previous overgeneralization. There are several possible strategies. One strategy is to remove the offending information from the higher concept and replace it on all the lower members. That is, delete the statement **person is short** from the definition of **person** and, unless there is conflicting evidence, add it to all the other people the memory knows about, namely **Mary, N1,** and **Harry.** Then, later on, it might reanalyze those individuals to see if it can combine features again.

A second strategy—and the one we follow—is to divide the concept of **person** into two different groups, on the basis of whether they are **short** or **tall.** Thus, we form the concepts **N2** and **N3:**

N2
* isa person.
* is short.
Mary isa *.
N1 isa *.

N3
* isa person.
* is tall.
Louise isa *.

Now we make the appropriate changes in *person*, ending up with

> **person**
>   * **isa human being.**
>   * **has body.**
>   **customer isa *.**
>   **N2 isa *.**
>   **N3 isa *.**

What about Harry? All we know for sure is that he **isa person** (and, therefore, like all other persons is a happy, red-haired human being). But suppose we now learn that

> **Harry is old.**

> **Harry is handsome.**

> **Harry is tall.**

Harry is most like **Louise. Harry isa N3,** one of the **old, tall, handsome people.**

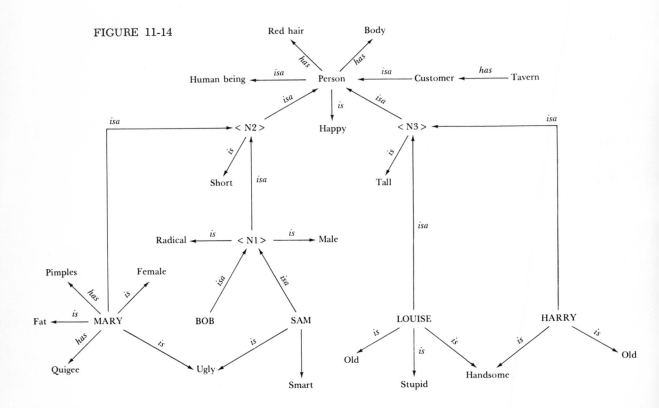

FIGURE 11-14

We have now accumulated a rather full list of properties. Here is the new network, in Figure 11-14. We have not yet shown the generalization of information that *Louise* and *Harry* are both *handsome* and *old*. If this were a human memory, the human might very well ponder what it knows from its data base (Figure 11-14) and make the following statements:

> Is Mary a radical? If so, then radicals can be either male or female and there is a good chance that Bob is ugly. Come to think of it, I bet that Harry is stupid. Do radical males have pimples?

> I have been thinking about the concept of a person. Anyone who is a person seems to have red hair, a body, and is happy. He is also a human being. There seem to be two major types of persons: One type is tall and handsome and old, the other is short. A short person can also be one of two types, one is female, fat, and ugly, with pimples and a quigee. The other kind of short person is a male radical. Some radicals are smart, but ugly. Some tall, handsome persons seem to be stupid.

We are making good progress. In fact, the model is developed far enough to begin considering some of the questions raised in the introduction. How would this memory system carry out some of the retrieval tasks discussed earlier? Remember the statement:

Evaluating an input

The authors are fascists.

We proposed that you did not passively accept this statement, but rather actively tried to interpret it. We wondered what rules you used to evaluate the input. Now we are in a position to examine that type of evaluation.

Here is the memory with which we will be working. Note that since our last encounter, it has done some reorganization. Moreover, apparently it has received more information about **Mary, Bob** and **Sam,** since it has generalized its concepts of **N2.** It has also heard the word **fascists** but knows only that a **fascist is cruel.** Now it receives the statement

Figure 11-15

A person isa fascist.

This time it is not going to accept the input at face value as before. Now it will try to integrate the incoming message with what it knows.

Informant: A person is a fascist.
Memory: I do not know very much about fascists, but I did not realize that a person in general might be a fascist. Maybe you are

FIGURE 11-15

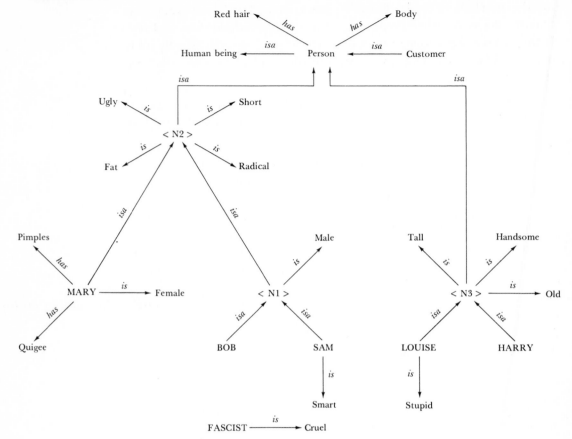

talking about a particular type of person—let me see. Is a fascist tall or short?

Informant: As a matter of fact, a fascist is usually short like Hitler Mussolini, and Napoleon.

Memory: Ah-hah. Is it ugly?

Informant: I would say so.

Memory: And radical?

Informant: In a sense.

Memory: Right. I know some persons who are fascist. I just never connected the name before. By the way, those persons you mentioned before, Hitler, Mussolini, and Napoleon—are they male or female?

Informant: Male.

Memory: Thanks. I will remember that.

The part of the memory that is affected by this interaction is shown in Figure 11-16. The first thing to notice is that an **N2** has now been named: **N2** is the same as **fascist.** As a result, by implication, the data base now encodes that **fascists** tend to be **fat, short, ugly,** and **cruel** and that **Mary, Bob,** and **Sam** are all **fascists.**

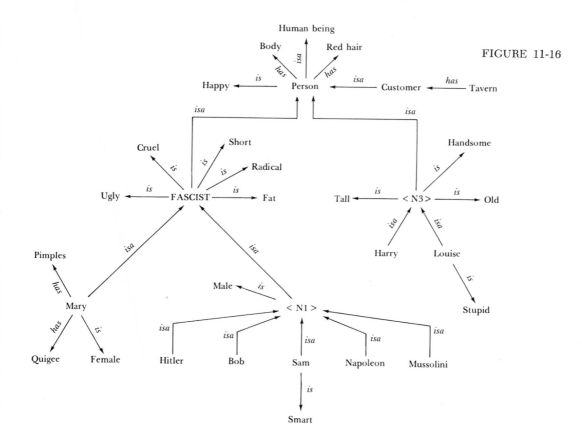

FIGURE 11-16

We have worked through some concrete examples to illustrate several procedures for rearranging the information stored in the data base. One procedure generalizes, deducing the common properties of concepts. Another makes special subdivision of classifications, realizing that specialized classifications can often be useful. Still another procedure looks for errors and inconsistencies and weeds them out of the system.

Exercise: From the data base for **pots** and **containers** (Figure 11-2), eliminate the inconsistency that states a **pot** is to be made of **metal,** but allows a **teapot** to be **ceramic,** even though it is defined to be a **pot.**

VIEWING THE DATA BASE

How much of the data can be seen at any one time by the interpretive process? So far, we have been drawing the networks so that everything is visible at once: It is not a difficult task to see just how things are interconnected. But it is quite possible that things are not so visible to the interpretive system. One way of thinking of this is to assume that the interpreter views the network by shining a flashlight at it. The only part visible is the part illuminated by the light. The question is, then, how wide is the beam of light produced by the flashlight?

Figures 11-17 & 11-18

We can see from the diagrams that there are many possible levels of visibility possible. (Note that the flashlight analogy is not completely accurate in that we show the network as getting more or less visible in terms of the number of arrows and concepts that can be seen, not in terms of physical diameter.)

The limitations in what the human retrieval process can "see" at any one time may be really a limitation of **short-term memory.** It is very likely that short-term memory holds the information on which the interpretive process is working. The capacity of short-term memory is measured in items, in psychological units. Now we can speculate about the nature of that unit. Perhaps a unit in short-term memory is a node. It is quite likely that the restricted number of nodes that can be retained in short-term memory may put some basic limitations on the ability of the interpretive processes to search out and evaluate information stored in the data base (long-term memory).

Try this thought experiment. Consider the incident at Luigi's, described

FIGURE 11-17

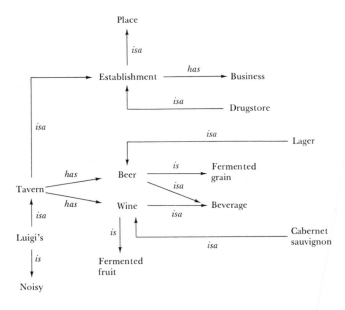

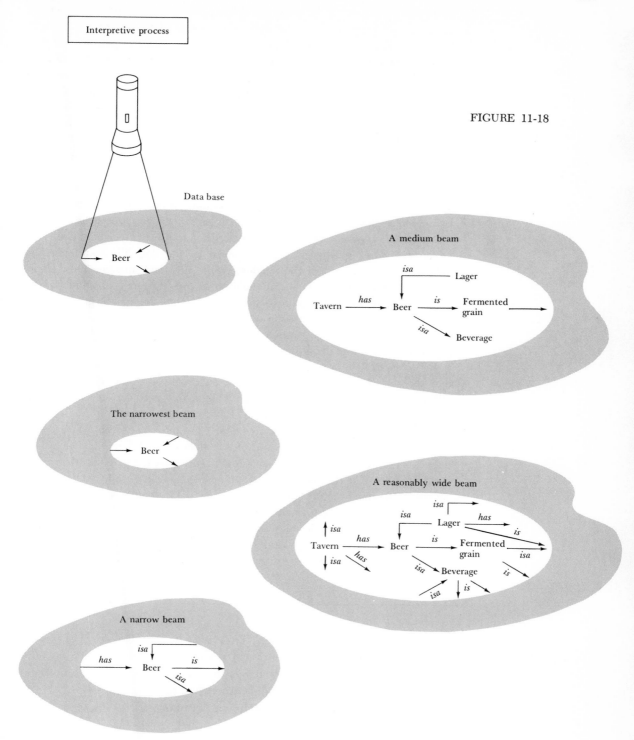

FIGURE 11-18

in Figure 11-3 of this chapter and Figure 10-16 of the previous chapter. Imagine the scene. Luigi's is a dark, dim tavern, with customers sitting in booths in dimly lit corners. The owner, Al, is a friendly, personable chap. His dog, Henry, is always around. Suddenly, among a group of people in the corner, a scuffle erupts. Sam can be heard yelling at Mary. Henry, Al's dog, bites Sam, and somewhere in the melee Mary has hit Louise. Imagine the entire scene in your mind. Is the whole thing clear? If so, what kind of a dog is Henry? How long is his tail? Now look at his collar. What do the identification tags dangling from the collar say?

Most people find that as they imagine the scene, there is a limit to how much detail can be brought in at once. Originally, when they imagined the scuffle at the tavern, they claimed it all to be sharp and clear in their minds. Yet, when they are queried about the details of the dress of any of the participants, the color or length of their hair, or even the details of the tavern itself, they discover that it really is not quite so clear. When you are asked to examine the dog, the image of the dog fills your conscious awareness, and the rest of the incident, while still there in some sense, fades from its central location in the thought process. This can go on indefinitely. When you are asked to examine the dog in detail, he too turns out to be not so clearly noted. Examining his collar causes the rest of his body to fade from view. In fact, examining the tags hanging from his collar causes the collar itself to disappear into a haze.

It is tempting to argue that we can bring only a limited number of nodes into the short-term memory at one time (alternatively, into the illumination afforded by the flashlight). Thus, there is probably a central secondary node that refers to the entire incident at Luigi's (not shown in the diagram). This can be examined, but it is a general concept of the event, and it does not contain any details. When any of the details are followed, such as the node that represents any of the individual participants, then the other nodes that represent the details of the event are no longer visible. Although not shown in the diagram, presumably Henry points to a complex set of interrelations that define the appearance and exact details of his existence as a dog. When any of those nodes are examined with care, then the ones around it are no longer quite so visible, and the ones distant (such as Henry's role in the incident at Luigi's) are far removed from consideration.

UNDERSTANDING VERSUS REMEMBERING

One major implication of these ideas is that the memory system encodes the meaning of the material that has been experienced, not the material itself. Man attempts to understand rather than to remember.

Consider the following experiment (Bransford & Franks, 1971). Subjects are told a story made up of individual sentences.

The rock rolled down the mountain.

The rock crushed the hut.

The hut is at the river.

The hut is tiny.

When these sentences are actually presented, they are randomly interspersed with other sentences that are not part of the story, such as

The breeze is warm.

The ants ate the jelly.

The story is in the newspaper.

The jelly is sweet.

Thus, the four sentences that comprise one story must be extracted and put together from the entire set of sentences that actually are presented (and the other sentences can be combined to form four different stories). After each individual sentence is presented, the subject answers a simple question about it (**Did what? Where?**) to make sure that he indeed understands each sentence. Then, about 5 min after all the sentences have been presented, the subjects are presented with some test questions. They are asked to state whether they had actually heard these sentences before or not. For example, three possible test sentences are:

A. **The rock crushed the hut.**
B. **The rock crushed the tiny hut at the river.**
C. **The rock is tiny.**

Sentence A is, in fact, one of the original ones presented: The subject should state that he remembers it. Sentence C is not one of the originals; moreover, the meaning is different from that of any of the sentences. But sentence B is the most interesting one, for here the meaning is correct, but this particular sentence never was presented.

How do subjects remember these sentences? Here are the four sentences and their structure (Figure 11-19). Notice that for the way the memory system encodes information the four structures combine into one (Figure 11-19E). If this is all that is stored, how could you tell whether sentence B had been presented or not? Certainly, it is quite consistent with the diagram. Sentence C is clearly wrong: It contradicts what is stored. But sentences A and B are equally good.

FIGURE 11-19

A   The rock rolled down the mountain

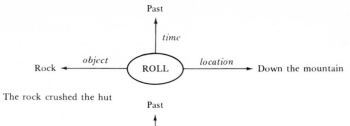

B   The rock crushed the hut

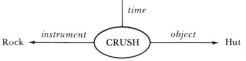

C   The hut is at the river

Hut   —— *location* ——▶ River

D   The hut is tiny

Hut   —— *is* ——▶ Tiny

E   The rock which rolled down the mountain crushed the tiny hut at the river

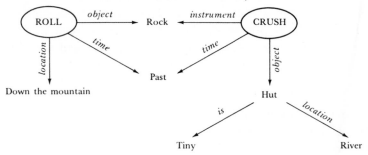

In the actual experiment, a set of test sentences was constructed with varying complexity: Some of the sentences contained a larger number of the original four ideas than others. Thus, consider these four examples:

Test 1:   **The hut is at the river.**
Test 2:   **The rock crushed the tiny hut.**
Test 3:   **The rock crushed the tiny hut at the river.**
Test 4:   **The rock which rolled down the mountain crushed the tiny hut at the river.**

Only the first of these test sentences, *Test 1*, actually was ever presented to the subjects. Yet, when subjects were asked to say whether they recognized any of the four sentences as one that was originally shown, they overwhelmingly selected *Test 4*, even though they had never in fact seen it. *Test 3* was next in terms of the number of times the subjects recognized it as occurring before. For both *Test 2* and *Test 1* (the only sentence actually presented) subjects usually denied having seen either of these sentences before. This is as it should be. The memory model encodes and remembers ideas and meanings. Hence, subjects should recognize sentences according to how well they fit the idea. Sentence *Test 4* is the most complete representation of the event as they remember it; sentence Test 1 overlaps only partially.

MEMORY AS INFORMATION PROCESSING

The structure of memory described in this chapter presents a very different view of the nature of learning from that which results from studying how associations are built up in classical learning tasks. The difference is in the emphasis on the dynamic and integrative processes of memory. The system learns through an active interaction with its environment, rather than a passive build up of stimulus–response connections. This mode of operation pervades all of our experiences and is fundamental to the way we deal with the world we encounter.

Most of you probably learned the story of Hiawatha as a child. Can you remember what you thought when you first heard about him? Do you think your concept of Hiawatha has changed in the intervening years? If so, is it because you have reread the story or is it a result of learning more about the world, about Indians, about the nature of children's stories, and about the older American traditions of Indian folklore?

Classical learning theories typically rely on repeated exposure to specific stimuli as the basis of acquiring information. They have difficulties dealing with the fact that the understanding of a concept continues to be elaborated and embellished, even though the concept may never directly be encountered again. Such an evolution is a natural property of the type of memory system we have been examining. As more information about the world is accumulated, the memory system's understanding continues to grow and become elaborated. As an automatic by-product of this changing structure, our knowledge continually changes. Thus, it is very likely that your present recollection of the story of Hiawatha is quite different from the original. Any discussion about Hiawatha that might now be produced is determined in part by what was originally learned, but also by what has been thought about since that time. Try to recall it: Is not your recall primarily a reconstruction of what you believe the story must have been, rather than what it really was?

This continual evolution of the stored knowledge within the memory system has very profound effects on the way that new information is acquired. It suggests that there must be a tremendous difference between the way a message is encoded into a child's memory and the way the same information is encoded by an adult. For children, each concept encountered has to be built up from scratch. A great deal of rote learning must take place during the initial construction of the data base: Understanding is only slowly elaborated as properties are accumulated, as examples are learned, and as the class relations evolve. At first, most of the concepts in memory will only be partially defined and will not be well integrated with the other stored information.

Later in life, when a great deal of information has been accumulated and organized into a richly interconnected data base, learning should take on a different character. New things can be learned primarily by analogy to what is already known. The main problem becomes one of fitting a new concept into the preexisting memory structure: Once the right relationship has been established, the whole of past experience is automatically brought to bear on the interpretation and understanding of the new events.

For models of this type, the development of individual differences and idiosyncratic systems should be the rule, rather than the exception. Understanding evolves through a combination of the external evidence and the internal operations that manipulate and reorganize the incoming information. Two different memories would follow exactly the same path of development only if they received the identical inputs in the identical order and used identical procedures for organizing them. Thus, it is extremely unlikely that any two people will evolve exactly the same conceptual structure to represent the world they experience.

Be careful to note what is at the basis of this idiosyncratic development. We expect that both the basic structure of memory and the processes for manipulating and reorganizing information are similar from individual to individual. However, even though this basic machinery is the same, its operation will not necessarily generate the same memory products. What a person believes depends on what he has experienced and what sequence of inferences and deductions has been applied to the stored information. Even very subtle differences in the environment can produce different memory products, despite the fact that the underlying machinery for interpreting and remembering information may be common to all people.

The possibility that a basic set of processes can be used to deal with a variety of environmental contexts is, of course, a very adaptive feature of the memory system. But we might expect that the flexibility with which it can deal with new information would continuously change as the structure is built. It is seldom that an adult encounters an entirely novel event—one that is totally unrelated to his existing conceptual structure. Almost everything he experiences can be related to what he has encountered in the past. Even when he experiences clearly discrepant information, his conceptual structure is made up of such a complex and interdependent set of relationships that it resists revision. Thus, an adult is more likely to reject a discrepant input or change its meaning than to modify or change his beliefs. With children, the conceptual structure is not nearly so elaborate or so highly interconnected as that of adults. New experiences can be taken in stride, since contradictions seldom arise.

Perhaps the most interesting of the areas left unexplored is the inter-active aspect of the human mind. People ask questions: They explore their own knowledge, they read, think, daydream and act. Even the most casual observations suggest that much of a child's behavior involves the engagement of his environment as he systematically seeks the information needed to build up his internal representation of the world. The model we have described here hints at these processes, but it does not do full justice to them. We have suggested some ways by which the memory system might ask for confirming evidence about the deductions and inferences it makes, but we have only scratched the surface of this very important area. The main problem at the moment is that there are no systematic tools for analyzing the natural exploratory behavior of people at work and play. A start has been made, however.

The concepts developed in Chapters 10 and 11 and representing the data base and its interpretation are novel. Little can be found today in the literature, but we predict that this will be changing rapidly for the study of long-term memory processes is increasing rapidly.

A symposium on the organization of memory held in Pittsburgh discussed many of these issues, so the interested reader might begin his search with that volume (Tulving & Donaldson, *Organization and Memory*, 1972). Perhaps the best place to start in that book is with our own chapter (Rumelhart, Lindsay, & Norman), for it presents a slightly more advanced version of the chapters in this book. Then, you could go on to the paper by Collins and Quillian, the chapter

SUGGESTED
READINGS

by Kintsch, and then the one by Bower. These chapters will provide the interested reader with a fairly comprehensive review of what has been done to this time, as well as specific literature references for further study. In addition a good review is provided by Frijda's survey article (to be published).

A number of experiments are now being performed on topics closely related to these issues. The classic work is the study on the reconstructive nature of remembering by Bartlett (1932). The studies referred to in this chapter were done by Bransford and Franks (1971), Collins and Quillian (1969), and Meyer (1970).

The model described in these chapters borrows heavily from the work on semantics by a number of modern linguists, but most especially the case grammar of Charles Fillmore (1968, 1969). The books in which the Fillmore articles appeared contain other papers highly relevant to the linguistics used here. The work by Winograd (1972) describes the development of a computer system for understanding language. This paper appeared in the journal, *Cognitive Psychology,* and current plans are for several other very important papers on the topic of language, memory, and thought to appear in this journal in the near future. They can't be referenced, because some of the papers we have in mind might not make it. Thus, you ought to skim through recent issues of the journal to see what new developments have occurred.

A number of relevant studies of memory are now beginning to appear in the computer science literature. Hence, the interested reader might wish to look at the book of collected papers by Minsky, *Semantic Information Processing* (1968). The book by Kolers and Eden (1968) also has some relevance, especially the chapter by Weizenbaum. The book by Loehlin (1968: paperback) offers a good introduction to models of personality somewhat relevant to the models of memory presented here. The Ph.D. thesis by Winograd (1970) (from which Figure 11-2 was taken) published in *Cognitive Psychology* (1972) is especially recommended, although it emphasizes language, not memory. In addition, Hunt's (1971) article, "What Kind of Computer is Man?" is a good article to read, although perhaps more important to the concept of man as an information processor than to specific notions of memory structure.

12

Language

The comprehension of language is perhaps the single most important aspect of the human mind. Language systems are so complex that no one has yet been able to write a complete description of the rules that must be involved. Yet any child can learn any existing language (so long as he is not severely retarded). As his capacity to communicate symbolically develops, language and thought become so inextricably intermixed it becomes almost impossible to separate them.

The acquisition of language marks a turning point in the development of a child. The child starts using language at the age of 2 (approximately) and, as we will see in the next chapter, this also marks the transition for the child from a knowledge about the world based on his sensory and motor experience to one that is based on symbolic processes. From then on, the child need not learn only through actual experiences: He can learn through language.

Action is the basis of the initial knowledge acquired by the child. Through his actions, the infant can evolve general concepts of the things he encounters: His concept of a dog could be based on the feel of its hair and the funny noises it makes when pinched; his concept of a ball could be based on its behavior when thrown. In the absence of language, perceptual and cognitive structures can be built up out of the actions of his experiences.

Meaning through actions

These early structures contain the sequences of actions taken by a child in dealing with his environment. The development of these schemes for action is discussed at some length in the next chapter: Here, it suffices to say that each scheme for integrating sensory events with motor movements is called a *sensorimotor schema*. The various sensorimotor schemata learned by the child in his first 2 years, plus the knowledge he then has of the permanence and independence of objects and events, comprise the base upon which language is established.

Even after language develops, the early mechanisms of sensorimotor intelligence continue to be a prime force in organizing a child's experiences. Long after the normal child has mastered language, action will remain a central part of his conceptual structure. Ask young child (around 7) to define common objects and the response will be based on their actions: Tables are for eating on; chairs are for sitting on; fathers are to play games with.

Language develops within this framework of sensorimotor intelligence. Initially, the problem of learning a language may mainly be that of assigning linguistic labels—names—to the already existing sensorimotor schemata. The child first begins to use language to label the things with which he is already familiar—his toys, his family, the objects in his environment. He also labels his actions as he performs these: He can often be heard talking to himself. But eventually, a conceptual structure based on the meanings of actions will not be enough.

The importance of labels

When a child begins to use symbolic labels, the basic for his organization of a concept slowly changes from one based on the action to one based on the word. As language begins to interact with conceptual development, words become the anchor points of conceptual structures. Once we have words as names of objects and events, we can think by manipulating the words, often a far easier task than that of manipulating the concepts themselves. But does the use of language labels alter the way we think? Does it affect what we see, what we attend to, or what we remember?

The power of words is the power of infinite flexibility. Language labels are arbitrary. Each language community has some degree of freedom in the way it carves up perceptual experiences in assigning names. Any set of examples can be linked together through a common label and thus force a specific pattern of generalization and differentiation on the developing conceptual structure of the child. A child from the Philippines must develop a conceptual organization that will allow him to use 92 different terms for rice; the Eskimo child must discriminate more than half a dozen different types of snow. The symbols that are used by any given language community reflect the perceptual and symbolic structures that are most useful to them. But perceptual capabilities are not altered by the acquisition of a language. Any person, regardless of the language he speaks can distinguish among the varieties of rice that receive special labels in the Philippine community, even if he cannot name them. Moreover, he can describe these differences symbolically—one type of rice is smaller, perhaps more oval-shaped, and slightly darker in color—though he must use many words to do so.

Memory for simple perceptual experiences is directly related to the ease with which the language can communicate that experience, since the efficiency with which an experience can be encoded into memory depends upon the previously acquired symbolic structure in the data base. The way in which a given language refers to perceptual experiences can have a considerable effect on the encoding and retention of sensory information. Recall that there is considerable evidence that incoming information is often encoded into its acoustic label on its journey into memory. These labels can provide a potential filter for the information that is remembered about an event.

Each language community seems to develop its own labeling patterns that determine the ease of encoding, remembering, and discussing specific perceptual experiences. Events and perceptions that are important to a community tend to be expressible in a few words. The words themselves seem to be governed by a similar principle (called Zipf's Law). In most languages the most frequently used words are also the shortest. Notice, for example, the length of English prepositions: **in, of, at.** We will see that this is a special class of words that is used very frequently, since they communicate general relations among concepts. Abbreviations follow the same rule. New technological events introduced into a culture, such as the **automobile** or **television** tend initially to have relatively long descriptions associated with them. As they become frequently used in the language, the pressure toward communication accuracy and efficiency sets in: **automobile** becomes **auto** or **car; television** becomes **T.V.; telephone** becomes **phone.**

Yet the tyranny of words is far from absolute. People from all language groups can communicate all types of perceptual events that are communicable in other languages, although some may be more difficult than others. Each different language may affect the way experiences are normally structured and remembered, but it does not affect the underlying cognitive machinery that builds these structures.

There are no rules for determining the meaning of a word from its sound. The correspondence between sounds and meanings must be learned for each individual word in the language. If a language used the same principles to construct sentences out of individual words as it does to construct words out of individual sounds, then language would lack its immense flexibility as a means of communication of previously unvoiced ideas. Moreover, because the meaning of each new sequence of words would have to be learned, the number of possible combinations of words would far exceed the capacity of the human memory system. We would need a dictionary to define the meaning of every possible sentence.

Clearly, this is not how language is constructed. The meanings of the individual words in a sentence combine according to the rules of grammar to form the meaning of the entire sentence. The way in which the meaning is formed is not simple. One does not simply add up the meanings of the individual words to find the meaning of a sentence. If this were so, then language learning should proceed smoothly: The child would simply learn the meanings of the individual words, and then he would learn to combine words whenever he wished to combine meanings. But there is a vast difference between the use of language as a labeling mechanism and language as a means of expressing state-

THE STRUCTURE OF
LANGUAGE

ments about the world. As soon as more than one concept is inserted into the same utterance, then the relations between those concepts become very important: Does **dog John bite** mean that **dog** or **John** is doing the biting? To tell, we need rules for constructing meaningful sequences of words. As a result, language is both powerful as a tool for communication and difficult for a child (or adult, for that matter) to acquire.

Meaning structure and surface structure

Consider the meaningful actions and relations portrayed by Figure 12-1. This is a picture of a possible underlying meaning represented within a person's memory structure using the notation developed in Chapters 10 and 11 and illustrating a situation discussed in Chapter 13. Suppose we wished to teach an adult the relationship between the disks and the slot machine; we would not need to let him wander about the room

FIGURE 12-1

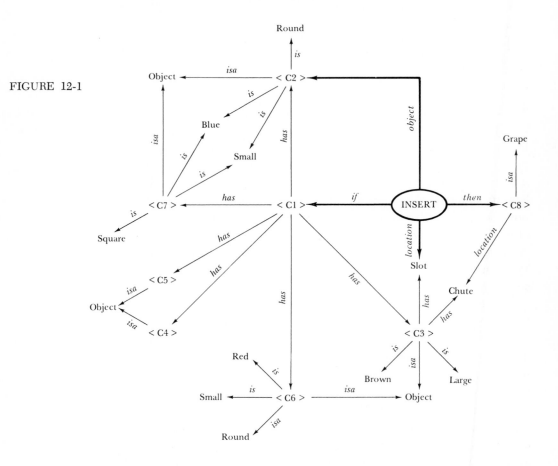

until he accidentally discovered the relationship. Rather, we could tell him:

> **Whenever you find yourself in this room with blue disks and a slot machine, if you would like some grapes, simply put a blue disk into the machine.**

Language can be conceived as a method of communicating the memory structure of the speaker to the memory structure of the listener.

When we talk about language, we distinguish between the words that are used to communicate ideas and the ideas themselves. The words are all that are measurable in language behavior: They can be seen or heard. Hence, we call the actual sentences that are written or spoken the *surface structure* of language. The meanings conveyed by words are not visible: They depend upon the memory structure of the people involved in the communication. Hence, we call the meaning communicated by message the *meaning structure*.

Given that language consists of words, not the peculiar circles and arrows, such as those of Figure 12-1, that we have used to illustrate meanings, then some conventions must be devised to indicate which spoken relations correspond to concepts, which to actions, and what relations apply between the concepts and actions. Note that for any given meaning structure there is a wide variety of possible sentences that can be used to describe it. Moreover, the entire structure need not be communicated if the receiver of the information can already be assumed to understand certain basic concepts. Thus, in the sentence that explained to our human subject how to get grapes with disks, we did not bother to mention that the grapes would appear in the chute of the slot machine, nor did we mention that the disk should be inserted into the slot. Moreover, we did not specify that the disk had to be picked up before it could be inserted. All these relations were assumed to be either already known by the human or so easy to discover that it was unnecessary to mention them.

The differences between surface and meaning structures are best illustrated by example. Consider the sentence

John frightens Mary.

This sentence communicates the same information as the sentence

Mary is frightened by John.

even though a different surface structure is used. The meaning structures are the same. In fact, given the basic structure of the event in which an **agent** John frightens a **recipient** Mary, there are eight possible transformations of the sentence in English, all based on the same meaning.

An *active* sentence:	John frightens Mary.
A *passive* sentence:	Mary is frightened by John.
A *negative* sentence:	John doesn't frighten Mary.
A *query*:	Does John frighten Mary?
A *negative passive*:	Mary isn't frightened by John.
A *negative query*:	Doesn't John frighten Mary?
A *passive query*:	Is Mary frightened by John?
A *negative passive query*:	Isn't Mary frightened by John?

In these eight sentences, the basic event is always **John frightening Mary.** The negative versions deny that the action is occurring; the queries ask if it is occurring. The sentences change only in formal surface structure. Figure 12-2 shows the meaning structure for all eight sentences. These eight *transformations* of the basic structure form the basis of most English surface structures.

It is possible to represent one basic underlying structure by many different surface structures. Similarly, it is possible to represent different meaning structures by the same surface structures. Consider the sentence:

They are working students.

This sentence has two possible meanings (at least). Each meaning translates into a different meaning structure, as is shown in Figure 12-3.

The grammatical rules of a language specify the ways by which a meaning structure can be converted into a surface structure. In speaking or writing, the person must go into his own meaning structure and apply the relevant grammatical rules to form legitimate sentences. In listening or reading, the reverse operations must be applied. The person must try to disentangle the words spoken to him and recover the meaning structure.

It is important to keep in mind, however, that meaning and grammatical correctness are related but they are far from being the same thing. The sentence

Eat apple

is ungrammatical, but in context, it is perfectly meaningful: the relational and conceptual information is unambiguous. Some grammatical distor-

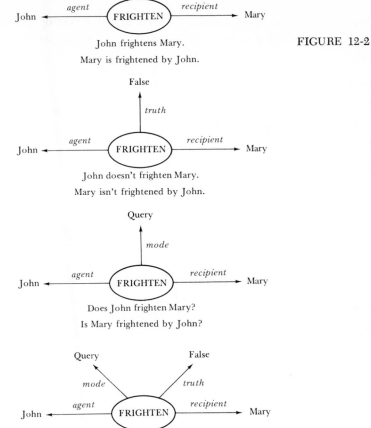

John frightens Mary.

Mary is frightened by John.

John doesn't frighten Mary.

Mary isn't frightened by John.

Does John frighten Mary?

Is Mary frightened by John?

Doesn't John frighten Mary?

Isn't Mary frightened by John?

FIGURE 12-2

FIGURE 12-3

THEY ARE WORKING STUDENTS

Those people make students work

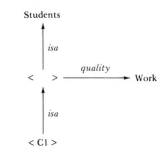

C1's are students who work

tions may also make the message uninterpretable. If they destroy the information that specifies roles of the various participants, part of the meaning is lost:

Kick John Mary.

Finally, a sentence may be perfectly grammatical, yet still raise interpretive problems because some of the information needed to encode it unambiguously into memory is missing:

They are working students.

Visiting professors can be boring.

A psychological study of grammar is concerned with the cognitive processes that translate between surface structure and meaning. Whether or not the message follows the rules of correct speech is not a reliable indicator of whether these cognitive processes will break down during its interpretation. Thus, many sentences that seem to have ambiguous surface structure are actually quite intelligible because only one possible meaning can be intended by the particular choice of words. Thus

Kiss John tiger

is both ungrammatical and unintelligible, while

Shoot John tiger

is ungrammatical, but can be interpreted if necessary: Only one word, **John,** can serve as the obligatory human **agent** of **shoot** and the remaining word, **tiger,** is a satisfactory (and even likely) **object.**

These sentences:

I saw the sparrows flying to the trees

I saw the Grand Canyon flying to New York

both have similar surface structures but quite different meaning structures. Yet the two sentences can be understood without too much difficulty because the set of possible meaningful relations is quite limited (Schank, 1969).

The psychological purpose of language is to communicate. People seldom speak in grammatical sentences. In fact, most spoken sentences are not intelligible out of the context in which they were delivered. The extensive deletions in sentences, the extensive use of pronouns and ambiguous references, makes formal analysis of spoken sentences difficult. But in context, when the use of the words **it** or **they** or **that one** is clear, then the meaning structures manage to get communicated even when the surface structure is formally deficient. If we view language as an aid to communication, then we can understand why this must be so.

ENGLISH GRAMMAR

English sentences are composed of several different kinds of sentence parts, linked together according to formal grammatical rules. In this book, we have been primarily concerned with the meanings of sentences rather than the exact surface structure, but in fact, the two are closely related.

According to traditional grammar, the normal, simple English sentence is composed of a subject and predicate, or subject, verb, and object. As we have already seen, these kinds of distinctions are of little use to us: we need to dissect the sentence differently.

Consider the sentence

The very old man eats oysters.

We can decompose this sentence in several ways. First, the phrase, **the very old man** is a *noun phrase* (*NP*). Second, the phrase, **eats oysters** is a *verb phrase* (*VP*), and third, we see that the verb phrase consists of a *verb* (*V*) plus a noun phrase. Hence we get a simple set of rules for decomposing this form of sentence.

1. S → NP + VP.

2. VP → V + NP.

(These can be read as: 1. A sentence *goes to* a NP plus a VP. 2. A VP *goes to* a V plus a NP.)

A noun phrase can be dissected further.

3. NP → Art + N.

4. N → Ad + N.

Rule 3 allows a noun phrase to be replaced with an *article* (*Art*) plus a noun. Rule 4 says that there may actually be a string of modifiers in a noun phrase, so that a N can continually be replaced by an *adjective* or *adverb* (*Ad*) plus N. Rule 4 allows the phrase **The very tired big fat hungry dirty old man.** These rules are optional, so that any or all might be applied to the analysis of the sentence. An example of this is Rule 4, which is not used in the phrase **the man** (Art + N), is used once in the phrase **the old man** (where the N of Art + N has been replaced by Ad + N), and is used twice in the phrase **the very old man** (where the N in the Art + Ad + N has itself been replaced with Ad + N, giving Art + Ad + Ad + N).

If we add some rules for transforming the results of these rules (V, N, Art, Ad) to words, we have completed the analysis of the sentence, **The very old man eats oysters.**

$$S \rightarrow NP + VP$$

NP	**VP**
$NP \rightarrow Art + N$	
$N \rightarrow Ad + N$	$VP \rightarrow V + NP$
$N \rightarrow Ad + N$	$NP \rightarrow Art + N$
$Art \rightarrow The$	$V \rightarrow eats$
$N \rightarrow man$	$Art \rightarrow$ (deleted)
$Ad \rightarrow very$	$N \rightarrow oysters$
$Ad \rightarrow old$	

The application of these rules is shown in tree-structure format in Figure 12-4, along with a picture of the meaning structure for the same sentence.

FIGURE 12-4

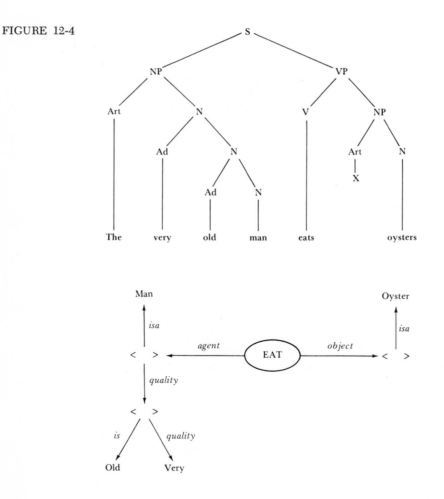

The grammar as written so far cannot handle prepositional phrases, such as used in the sentence

The very old man lives in the tree house.

The phrase **in the tree house** is a *prepositional phrase* (*PP*) and it consists of a *preposition* (*Prep*) plus a normal noun phrase. The preposition in this sentence (**in**) signifies that the noun phrase that follows specifies location. To handle these phrases we simply need to expand Rule 2:

2A. VP → V + NP.

2B. VP → V + PP.

2C. PP → Prep + NP.

Clearly in any given situation, either Rule 2A or 2B is applied: not both.

Now, with the addition of a dictionary, we can apply these rules to the new sentence, as shown in Figure 12-5.

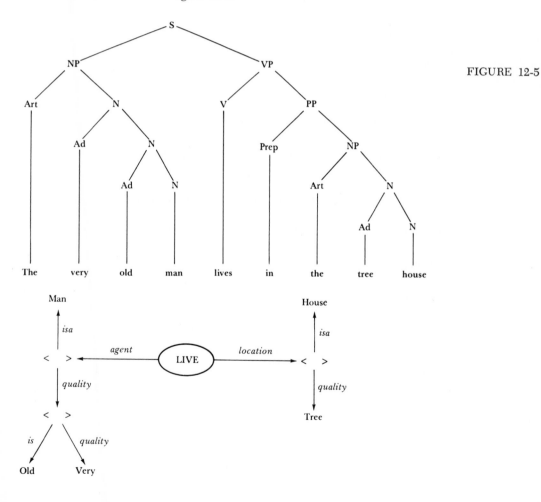

FIGURE 12-5

The dictionary looks like this:

$$V \rightarrow \text{lives, eats, sings, } \ldots$$

$$N \rightarrow \text{man, tree, house, limerick, oyster, } \ldots$$

$$\text{Art} \rightarrow \text{the, a, an, } \ldots$$

$$\text{Ad} \rightarrow \text{old, many, few, very, tree, } \ldots$$

$$\text{Prep} \rightarrow \text{in, on, at, by, to, } \ldots$$

Figures 12-4 and 12-5 show in diagram form the derivation of sentences. Because these rules all revolve around phrases, they are called *phrase-structure rules* (or sometimes *rewrite rules*), and the complete set of rules determines a *phrase-structure grammar*. (The several rules shown here are far from complete.) *Transformational rules* must be added to these phrase structure rules to account for the way that these phrases can be rearranged in the actual surface structure of sentences. For example, consider the passive sentence:

The tree house is lived in by the very old man.

A passive sentence requires a rearrangement of the phrases of the sentence. Thus, in this example, the original sentence had the phrase structure:

NP   +   V   +   PP
(The very old man) + **(lives)** + **(in the tree house)**

The passive sentence construction rearranges this in the format:

PP   +   V   +   NP
(In the tree house) + **(lives)** + **(the very old man)**

This sentence framework, although perfectly intelligible, is not normally considered to be grammatical, except in certain stylistic conventions such as in poetry:

In the tree house lives
the very old man
who constantly eats oysters
as fast as he can.

Normally, passive constructions are signaled by special construction of the verb. Moreover, the agent (or instrument) of the verb is signaled by the preposition **by.** Hence, some more modification of the sentence must occur: The initial PP has its preposition deleted, leaving a NP; the verb has an auxiliary added to it; the terminal NP is preceded by the preposition **by,** turning it into a PP; the Prep deleted from the PP is reinserted after the verb. In successive stages, the changes are:

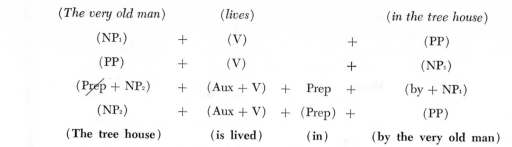

(*The very old man*)   (*lives*)   (*in the tree house*)

(NP₁)   +   (V)   +   (PP)

(PP)   +   (V)   +   (NP₁)

(Prep + NP₂)   +   (Aux + V)   +   Prep   +   (by + NP₁)

(NP₂)   +   (Aux + V)   +   (Prep)   +   (PP)

(The tree house)   **(is lived)**   **(in)**   **(by the very old man)**

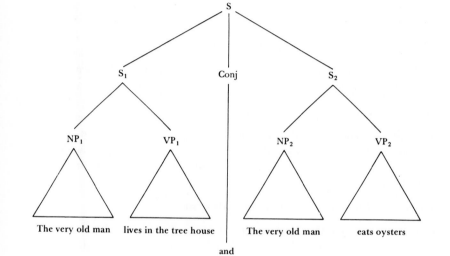

FIGURE 12-6

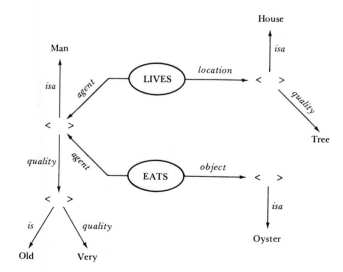

These are *transformational rules,* since they allow the various segments of the sentence to be shuffled about or transformed. Syntactical cues to the reshuffling are added, however, presumably to enable the person who reads or hears the transformed sentence to reconstruct the original version, although, as the poetry example shows, this is not always necessary.

It is possible to build up complex sentences from more simple ones. Thus,

The very old man who lives in the tree house eats oysters.

is composed of the two sentences we have been discussing. A slightly different way to combine sentences is with *conjunctions (Conj):*

1A. S → S + Conj + S.

1B. S → NP + VP.

Conj → and, but, because, or, . . .

Thus, by Rule 1A, our two sentences can be combined this way:

(**The very old man lives in a tree**) *and* (**the very old man eats oysters**)

This sentence is diagramed in Figure 12-6.[1] By looking at the sentence, the outline of the sentence, and the diagram for the meaning structure, we see that NP₁ is both the same as NP₂ and also plays a role in S₁ analogous to NP₂ in S₂. Normally, whenever this happens, we apply a *deletion rule,* allowing NP₂ to be eliminated:

The very old man lives in a tree and eats oysters.

Deletions often cause difficulties in the analysis of sentences because, once the item is deleted, it is difficult to tell what was there originally. Thus, deletions are often signaled by replacing the deleted phrase with a pronoun:

The very old man lives in the tree house and *he* **eats oysters.**

I saw the girl you saw talking to John yesterday and *she* **waved at me.**

On communicating the structure

For a listener or reader to understand language, he must identify the relationships of the concepts to the event being described. Thus, he must find the causal sequences, the agents, the objects, and so on. The format that we use to describe these relations has been discussed at length in Chapters 10 and 11. Table 12-1 summarizes these relations

---

[1] Note that we have introduced a new symbol into the diagram: the large triangle. This is simply a shorthand for the tree structure that would normally be drawn for the expansion of the NP's and VP's into the final words. The actual structures that the triangles have replaced are shown in Figures 12-4 and 12-5.

Table 12-1   The Parts of an Event

Action	The event itself. In a sentence, the action is usually described by a **verb:**
	The man was **bitten** by the dog.
Agent	The actor who has caused the action to take place:
	The man was bitten by the **dog.**
Conditional	A logical condition that exists between two events:
	A shark is dangerous **only if** it is hungry.
	John flunked the test **because** he always sleeps in lectures.
Instrument	The thing or device that caused or implemented the event:
	The **wind** demolished the house.
Location	The place where the event takes place. Often two different locations are involved, one at the start of the event and one at the conclusion. These are identified as **from** and **to** locations:
	They hitchhiked **from La Jolla to Del Mar.**
	From the University, they hitch hiked **to the beach.**
Mode	Signifies surface structure, where useful:
	Why isn't mode listed in Chapter 10? (**Mode** is a **query**)
	Don't ask so many questions. (**Mode** is **imperative**)
Object	The thing that is affected by the action:
	The wind demolished the **house.**
Purpose	Identifies the purpose of the event:
	Jack took Henry to the bar **to get him drunk.**
Quality	A descriptor, one that modifies a concept:
	The surf was **heavy.**
	There were **93** people in class.
Recipient	The person who is the receiver of the effect of the action:
	The crazy professor threw the book at **Peter.**
Time	When an event takes place:
	The surf was up **yesterday.**
Truth	Used primarily for false statements:
	I do **not** like you, Hubert.

(this is basically the same as Table 10-1). Many actions specify rather exactly the types of relations that are required for them to be a complete description of an event. With the action of **put,** for example, the event must include both an **object** and a **location.**

> **Henry** *put* **the book** *on* **the floor.**
>
> agent   object   location

If either object or location is left out, the message is incomplete:

> **Henry put the book.**
>
> **Henry put on the floor.**

Some relations are optional. Thus, neither time nor purpose were missed in the original sentence:

> **Henry put the book on the floor.**
>
> **Yesterday, Henry put the book on the floor to get it out of the way.**
>
> time   purpose

Moreover, even though all the above sentences specify the **agent** of the action, the verb **put** does not require one.

FIGURE 12-7

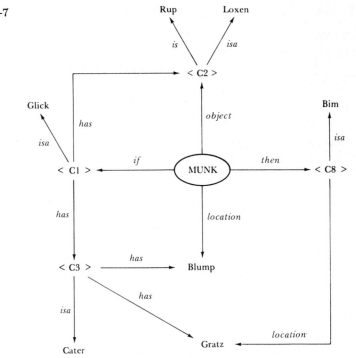

The book was put on the floor, yesterday.

Whether a speaker must insert an agent depends upon the information he wishes to convey: However, in English, if he wishes to delete the agent he often must use the passive form of sentences. In many cases, however, the **agent** may be replaced by the **instrument,** since both are closely related: **Agent** is simply an animate **instrument.**

The **train** delivered the quigees.

instrument

Mary delivered the quigees.

agent

If a language is to communicate about events, it must have mechanisms for transmitting the conceptual and relational information that make up the meaning structure of a message. Although a certain set of primitive relations can be expressed in all of the language systems of the world, the mechanisms used to specify the various relations differ widely from language to language.

It is not obvious from the surface structure of a message exactly how the language communicates its meaning.[2] To see how, let us try some experiments. Consider what happens if information is ambiguous or unintelligible. To do this, return to Figure 12-1 and simply substitute a meaningless label for every concept node in the memory structure. The results would look something like Figure 12-7. Translating this structure into a verbal message would produce:

On communicating the meaning

In a glick with rup loxens and a cater, munk a loxen into the blump for a bim in the gratz.

When nonsense words are substituted for meaningful concepts in a message, only the relational information is left. This is carried by words such as **with, in, into, a, the,** and **and.** These words are called *functors* or *function words,* since their main role is to signal relations. They provide a basic framework for entering concepts into memory by specifying, in outline, the structure of the event that is to be stored.

Notice that, although a message in which the concept information is deleted is certainly ambiguous, it still seems to communicate some meaning. We can, for example, answer questions quite sensibly from the structural information alone:

[2] What are Minsocs?

- How do you get a bim?
  Munk a rup loxen into the blump.
- Where is the cater?
  In the glick.
- What is rup?
  A loxen.
- What is in the glick?
  Some rup loxens and a cater.

We just substituted nonsense for concepts, but left the function words. Suppose there were no function words. When that happens, the message is nonsense:

Glick rup loxens tink cater munk loxen blump bim gratz.

But when we change the concepts back into English, the message is quite intelligible, even without the functions:

Room blue disks slot-machine insert disk slot grapes chute.

Although understandable, the message has a **telegraphic** style: It appears as though the unimportant words have been deleted, leaving only the most meaningful parts of the sentence. But if the function words carry all the relational information, how can a message without function words be understood? How can the appropriate structure be extracted? There are two answers. First, in English, relational information is specified in part by the order of the words. Disturb the order and you disturb the meaning that is communicated:

Slot-machine blue insert room disk slot grape disks chute.

The order in which the concepts appear provides function information that helps specify the probable relations among the concepts. Second, the meanings of the words allow the string to be partially interpreted even when all other cues are gone. Thus

shoot John tiger   or   **disk insert slot**

can be interpreted through semantic constraints, even when all function words are gone.

LEARNING A LANGUAGE

Learning rules

The fact a language is governed by rules imposes a special kind of learning task on the developing child. It is not sufficient that he simply learn what each word means, he must also somehow acquire the rules used in combining them. Learning rules is quite a different thing from learning names, or concepts.

From birth, the child is bombarded with a mixture of well-formed grammatical sentences, ill-formed fragments of sentences, utterances that are anticipations, questions, and baby-talk imitations of his own attempts to communicate. Out of this mish-mash of verbal utterances, he must somehow extract the rules for transmitting conceptual and relational information. An English-speaking child must learn that adjectives precede the noun that they modify. But how exactly does he pick this up? In actual speech, the same two words can appear in many different orders. Consider a simple example: The child is learning colors. He asks for the color name of milk and is told *"The color of* **milk—white."** Here the noun and its adjective appear in reverse order, although with a slight pause between the noun and the color name. How is he to learn from these examples like this that he must say **white milk** in sentences such as:

I don't want the white milk, I want the pink (strawberry) **milk.**

Folklore has it that a child learns to speak properly because his parents continually correct his errors. In fact, this is simply not true. Sometimes the child's speech is corrected, but usually it is either ignored or answered. Table 12-2 shows an example of the role of a mother in commenting on the speech of her child. In an analysis of numerous utterances (some of which are shown in Table 12-2), Brown and Hanlon (1970, Chapter 1) found no evidence whatsoever that mothers corrected grammatical mistakes with sufficient frequency to account for the fact that their children did learn the grammar.

Table 12-2   Examples of Utterances Approved and Disapproved[a]

Approval

Adam	Draw a boot paper.	**Adam's Mother**	That's right. Draw a boot on paper.
Eve	Mama isn't boy, he girl.	**Eve's Mother**	That's right.
Sarah	Her curl my hair.	**Sarah's Mother**	Um hmm.

Disapproval

Adam	And Walt Disney comes on Tuesday.	**Adam's Mother**	No, he does not.
Eve	What the guy idea.	**Eve's Mother**	No, that's not right. Wise idea.
Sarah	There's the animal farmhouse.	**Sarah's Mother**	No, that's a lighthouse.

[a] From Brown and Hanlon (1970, Table 1.12, p. 49).

There are two major mechanisms for learning. One is by reinforcement, the other by imitation. (The first is discussed extensively in Chapter 13.) But, as we have seen, the first cannot account for language learning, since there do not seem to be sufficient numbers of immediate reinforcements to the child for his grammatically correct utterances nor sufficient corrections of his errors. But what about imitation? Could the child learn a language simply by imitating the speech of adults?

Imitation Imitation clearly speeds up the acquisition of solutions to the practical environmental problems confronting a child. He can learn simply by watching how things are manipulated and used. Indeed, he seems quite capable of building complicated action schemata out of his observations. Imitation may also play a major role in the social development of the child. The family around him, the cast of characters on his favorite television shows, and his friends all provide models for personal interaction. From his observations, the child learns the social behaviors that are appropriate in his various social encounters. The models he observes become translated into his own behavior.

Could imitation be a primary mechanism for learning language? This seems to be unlikely. The whole developmental pattern of language acquisition argues against the proposition that the child learns to comprehend and use language by imitating what he hears. The first words he utters are only the crudest approximations to the appropriate sound patterns, yet he makes no attempt to practice and refine each word before going on to acquire new ones. At no time during the progression of a child's language from one-word utterances to adult-like speech does a child's speech pattern really appear to be an imitation of what he hears. On the contrary, the most striking thing about children's speech is its novelty. If a child learned by imitation, why would he say **goed** for **went, doed** for **did, sheeps,** or **you naughty are?**

In fact, it is difficult to decide what the child would imitate even if he wished to do so. The hallmark of language is its infinite variety of expression. The child who is learning a language seldom encounters the same sequence of words more than a few times. Moreover, children born with congenital defects in their speech apparatus comprehend language perfectly even though they cannot speak and, thus, cannot imitate what they hear. The pattern of development seems to reflect the struggles of the child's induction processes as they attempt to extract the rule system underlying language.

Language as If we consider language to be a device for communication, how well
communication does the young child do? The answer is **well.** Let us consider a few sample sentences from the repertoire of the 2-year-old:

Baby highchair	**Mommy eggnog**
Sat wall	**Mommy sandwich**
Pick glove	**Throw Daddy**

Do these utterances make sense? Probably not to you, since they are much too truncated to specify the exact nature of the relationships of the words to the actions. But consider when they were uttered. In general, the phrases of the child are perfectly understandable to the mother, since the context in which they were uttered leaves almost no possible ambiguity. Brown and Bellugi (1964), who recorded the preceding examples of child's speech also recorded the Mother's expansions of those sentences:

Baby is in the highchair.

Mommy had her eggnog.

Mommy'll have a sandwich.

He sat on the wall.

Throw it to Daddy.

Pick the glove up.

The child's speech seems to be composed of a telegraphic rendering of the full adult sentence. Function words are omitted. Complex grammatical relations are not yet discernable. But the adult can often expand the child's sentences with ease, simply using contextual information to determine the intended meaning and then adding the functor words and whatever else is necessary.

A good illustration of this comes from Eve's mother's expansion of the statement, **Eve lunch.** Roger Brown reports that Eve said this on two occasions, separated by about 30 min. For the first, Eve's mother was making lunch, so she expanded the utterance to **Yes, Mommy is going to fix Eve's lunch.** In the second, Eve said the utterance while sitting at the table eating, so her Mother expanded it as **Yes, Eve is eating lunch.** The first expansion puts Eve in the possessive relation toward lunch. The second expansion makes Eve an agent of the action **eat** and lunch an object. The fact that the same utterance is so easily interpreted by the mother in two different ways argues for the satisfactory use of language as a vehicle of communication by Eve, even though her grammatical skills were quite limited.

One concludes, therefore, that a child's language is based on meaning rather than grammar. It would appear to reflect the underlying conceptual base that he has acquired about the world. Hence, the study of language development should be performed along with the study of general development.

When a child begins to use language, he has already acquired some of the basic structural information he needs through his interactions with the environment. He must still learn how to communicate symbolically. The child's first attempts to communicate seem to be almost a direct statement of the internal memory structure. All of the function words that explicitly communicate relational information are missing: As a result, the child's speech is telegraphic. But there are more limitations. The child's memory span seems much reduced from that of an adult, he does not know all the phrase and transformational rules (if he knows any at all), and he does not yet know what information he must speak and what he can delete. In a verb such as **put,** the **location** and **object** must be specified, whereas other relations are optional. But to the child, everything seems to be treated as optional. Word order appears to be the only specific relational information that is systematically communicated in the beginning speech. If an agent is included in the child's utterance, it does tend to appear before the verb. For other types of relations, however, it is difficult to determine whether or not the child is using the appropriate order. In adult English, if the **agent** is missing and there is only an **instrument** and an **object** mentioned in a sentence, then in an active sentence, the **instrument** must come before the verb and the **object** after:

> *The* **key** *opens the* **door.**
>
> **instrument**   **object**

If the child simply telegraphed this sentence, he should say **Key open.** Instead, he will say **Open key.** Why? Evidently the child has in mind a different sentence, one with an agent, such as:

> **Daddy** *opens the door with his key.*

In this case, a telegraphic sentence **Open key** is correct.

Of course we have no way of telling whether this analysis is correct, but it does appear to be plausible explanation. Overall, the sentences of children are loosely formed. They neither designate all the concepts associated with an action nor do they use the specific linguistic symbols necessary for communicating the exact nature and relationships of the concepts they do speak.

Production versus comprehension. The lack of function words in the child's early speech is obvious and striking, but it is not so easy to decide why those words are missing. Is it a fundamental lack of understanding of the concept that is involved, or is it simply an inability to use the words properly? In part, the deletion seems related to a fundamental difficulty faced by young children: their inability to play the role of another person. Young children are egocentric: They view the world only from their own perspective. Long after the child has mastered language he will have difficulty in assuming the perspective of another person. This inability shows up in many places: in his performance on perceptual tasks, in the learning of concepts, and in his attempts to explain concepts to other people.

Piaget has investigated just how children develop the ability to understand the point of view of another (Piaget, 1926, Chapter 3). Here is an example of a typical task posed by Piaget to an 8-year-old boy. The boy, Gio, was told a story and then asked to retell it to another child.

The original story

Once upon a time, there was a lady who was called Niobe, who had 12 sons and 12 daughters. She met a fairy who had only one son and no daughter. Then the lady laughed at the fairy because the fairy had only one boy. Then the fairy was very angry and fastened the lady to a rock. The lady cried for ten years. In the end she turned into a rock, and her tears made a stream which still runs today. [Piaget, 1926, p. 82]

The story as retold by Gio

Once upon a time there was a lady who had twelve boys and twelve girls, and then a fairy a boy and a girl. And then Niobe wanted to have some more sons. Then she was angry. She fastened her to a stone. He turned into a rock, and then his tears made a stream which is still running today. [Piaget, 1926, p. 102]

Now this story comes from an 8-year-old child, one who is reasonably far advanced in intellectual skills. But even so, the ending is filled with pronouns **she, he, his,** and **her** that cannot be interpreted. Forgetting the errors in retelling (since they have nothing to do with the point under discussion), the poor listener has no way of knowing the referents to these pronouns and Gio makes no apparent attempt to help out.

When the child of 2 or 3 leaves out all functor words, it could be, at least in part, because of his inability to understand the difficulty that this presents to the listener. When Adam says **Draw a boot paper,** the unwitting adult might try to visualize a special kind of paper, a paper of boots, whereas Adam has simply deleted the functor that specified location: **Draw** (*a picture of*) **a boot** (*on the*) **paper.** But, then again, Adam may not have learned the functor words. After all, as long as he can communicate so well (his mother understood what he wanted), he should concentrate on more concrete and more important words, names of objects and actions. But when a child of 8 uses uninterpretable pronouns, it must be because he has not learned to assume another's point of view very well.

Whether or not the child can understand function information, he is certainly persistent in omitting it from all of his speech behavior. He cannot be persuaded to include it even when he has a direct model to imitate. Given the verbal phrase **Daddy's briefcase** and asked to repeat it, out comes **Daddy briefcase.** The statement **He's going out** comes back as **He go out. No, you can't write on Mother's hat** is repeated as **Write Mother hat.**

Overgeneralization. Gradually, function information does begin to appear in the child's speech. By the age of 3, his grammatical structures become quite similar to the colloquial speech of an adult. The verb inflections that indicate tense begin appearing, nouns become pluralized when appropriate, and possessives are added. The learning patterns indicate that he first attempts to use a simple linguistic signal to communicate a concept, but then extracts the general principle used by the language for expressing that concept. After the general principle has been learned, then come the exceptions to the rules.

The learning of tense information provides a striking example. Initially, no verb inflections or auxiliaries are present in the child's speech. He seems to talk only about the present, about the actions that are going on around him and the objects he is seeing. The first recognition of the temporal aspects of an action appear with the so-called *strong verbs*—verbs associated with actions in the immediate environment: **come, go, do, run.** When the child first expresses statements about the past, he is likely to use the proper verb forms: **came, went, did, ran.** But this is before he has learned the rule for making a verb into past tense by adding **-ed.** Once the rule is acquired, he applies it relentlessly: **run** becomes **runned, do** becomes **doed.** The rule has undone the proper words. Finally, once the general rules have been firmly established, the exceptions can gradually be relearned.

When the mechanisms for expressing a specific type of relational information have been acquired, the child can apply them in novel contexts. This has been ingeniously demonstrated by using nonsense words

(Berko, 1958). For example, a 4-year-old shown a picture of a man who is swinging something around his head is told:

> *This is a man who knows how to* **gling**.
>
> *He* **glings** *every day.*
>
> *Today he* **glings**.
>
> *Yesterday he*——?

The child can immediately supply the most probable word: **glinged**. Adults have much more difficulty in deciding on the appropriate response and seem to be torn among **glinged, glang, glung,** and **glought.**

What does it mean to understand? How can the parent or adult judge when a child understands what has been said? The problem is illustrated by consideration of another context: the computer understanding of language. There now exist several different computer programs that act as if they have some understanding of English (two examples of these were presented in Figures 10-1 and 10-2 of Chapter 10). But how can we tell whether the program actually understands English? We test it by typing an English statement on its typewriter keyboard:

Understanding

- The red block is on top of the big green cylinder.

It responds:

I see, thank you.

Does it understand or not? We still do not know.

The best way of determining whether a computer program understands English is to make it do something—give it a command or a question that requires an answer—and see what the result is.

- Is the green cylinder near the red block?

If this statement were typed into the DOCTOR program illustrated in Figure 10-1, it would probably respond:

Why is it that you want to know?

The same statement typed into the blocks program, illustrated in Figure 10-2, would probably lead to the response:

Which green cylinder do you mean?

If you mean the big one, the red block is on top of it.

If you mean the little one, it is far away.

With the first program, DOCTOR, the response gives us no clues as to its understanding of the sentence. But there can be little doubt about the second: It must understand.

The difficulty we face in analyzing understanding is that there are three different tasks that a man or machine must perform in order to prove to us that it can understand English.

- It must interpret the sentence properly: That is, it must actually understand.
- It must form a legitimate internal representation or program of the message.
- It must be able to activate that internal representation to produce a visible, interpretable result.

Consider the DOCTOR program again. Perhaps it understands nothing about the question. But it is quite possible that the DOCTOR program actually understands the question put to it (the first requirement) but does not know how to go about looking for an answer. Or it is possible that it both understands the question and looks for the answer (the second requirement), but does not know what to do with the information that it has found (the third requirement). The problem is that we cannot tell how much has been understood unless all three requirements are satisfied and we get a response similar to that produced by the block program.

What about children: How much can they understand? As with computers, it is sometimes difficult to tell. Suppose a mother requests a child of 6 months to **Give me the ball.** At best, the child will look at the mother, acknowledging the fact that he did at least hear something. But does he understand the sentence? Probably not. If the request is repeated when the child is about 12 months old, we are likely to get a better response: He is likely to look from his mother to the ball, back and forth. This action at least demonstrates that the child understands the word **ball,** but it tells us nothing else. Perhaps he does not understand the word **give.** Perhaps he understands **give,** but not the fact that the word **me** serves as the recipient (**You, baby, please give to me the ball**). Or perhaps he does understand the sentence but has not yet learned how to go and get an object, pick it up, carry it back to the speaker, and hand it over. That, after all, is a reasonably complicated set of actions for a 12-month-old baby to follow. Again, unless the child can satisfy all three requirements, we cannot tell whether he understands.

When the child has reached the age of 18 months, the request will be carried out. Now, finally, we have proof of comprehension. But it is shaky proof, at best. The child is quite likely simply to retrieve the nearest convenient object. And even if he does bring the ball a few times, he is likely to bring the ball again if the request is changed to **Give me the horse.** Finally, he tends to persevere in the action itself, so that if he has been repeatedly following the instruction **Put a ring on the peg,** he is likely to do it again even when the instruction is changed to **Take a ring off.**

By 2 years of age, the child can respond to simple instructions. But he is still unable to deal with any contingencies associated with an action, even though he has already demonstrated the cognitive capabilities for solving equivalent problems on a nonlinguistic level. When instructed to retrieve a coin under a cup, before about $2\frac{1}{2}$ years of age the child cannot extract the relevant information from the verbal message. Yet 8 months earlier at the age of 22 months, he has already solved more complicated retrieval problems just by watching others. The $2\frac{1}{2}$-year-old child tends to respond as soon as he understands the action that is involved. He probably will not wait for qualifications or restrictions on that action. If the request to the child is **When the light comes on, press the bulb,** the $2\frac{1}{2}$-year-old is likely to execute the command as soon as he identifies the action required, pressing the bulb immediately without waiting for the light. A $3\frac{1}{2}$-year-old can respond appropriately, and wait before pressing. But even he cannot encode more complex conditional information. The request to **Press when the red light comes on but not when the green light comes on** will produce a response when any light appears. It is not until he is 4 or 5 years old that the child completely masters the ability to extract all the contingencies encoded in the verbal messages and is able to translate them into an appropriate action sequence (Luria, 1961; see also Miller, Shelton, & Flavell, 1970).

There is far more to a system that can generate a sequence of actions from external instructions than simply the ability to extract the meaning of a verbal message. The command must be integrated into the existing memory structure so that the appropriate event will be recognized when it appears, and so that it will lead to the appropriate actions. Information about temporal sequence must be carefully evaluated so that the actions can be linked into the appropriate order. The child must be able to decide if he has enough information to execute the requested action and either deduce what is needed or request clarification. Some of the requested actions may be ambiguous, or may not yet exist in his response repertoire. If so, the child must determine if he can substitute some other action that will let him achieve the same goal. It is clear that we need to consider the whole set of intellectual abilities of the child in order to study the development of language skills, for all the processes affect one another.

SUGGESTED
READINGS

There are numerous sources for the study of the development of language in children. Lenneberg (1967) provides an excellent treatment for the biological foundations of language, including the survey of physiological changes that take place in the brain of a child as he matures. We have profited much from the works of Roger Brown, and we have relied extensively on his book *Social Psychology* (1965) for much of the work on development of intelligence and of language (a very excellent set of 150 pages of discussion: pp. 197–349). We recommend this set of readings to you highly. In addition, we had access to a chapter entitled "Stage I. Semantic and Grammatical Relations," from Brown's new book (in press).

The book which reports on a symposium at Carnegie–Mellon University on "Cognition and the Development of Language" contains an excellent set of papers on this topic (Hayes, 1970). Probably all of the papers will be of value to you, but we have found especially important the paper by Brown and Hanlon and the one by Bever. The edited collection of papers on language development by Dan Slobin (1971) should also be examined.

Many of the discussions of the child's acquisition of language emphasize a grammar that we have not discussed: *pivot grammar*. According to pivot grammar, the child in the very early stages of acquisition puts words into classes called *pivot* and *open*, and then forms sentences by combining two or three words from these classes according to a systematic set of rules. However, we do not always agree with the interpretation given by proponents of pivot grammar. It is our opinion that a grammar that is heavily based on the semantic structure of language does a better job of describing the child's acquisition of a language: for example, the *case grammar* which we present in this chapter. In these opinions we have been heavily influenced by Brown, both in his lectures and in the chapter we have seen of his unpublished manuscript.

All the works on language presented here owe an immense debt to Noam Chomsky, whose work on the study of grammar revolutionized linguistic theory. Most of the papers that we have referred to above will credit Chomsky extensively. Most of his papers, however, are very advanced and not easy for the beginner to read: perhaps the best place to start with Chomsky is in the appendix that he wrote for Lenneberg's book on biological foundations (Chomsky, 1967). To get further references on language, especially the case grammar that we rely on so heavily in the development of our memory structure, see the suggested readings for Chapter 11.

A particularly interesting development has been the reasonably successful attempts to teach chimpanzees to "speak" a language. Many previous attempts to raise chimps in normal households, teaching them to speak English in the same manner as one teaches a child, have always failed (beyond the first few words that the chimp did learn to speak). Two recent attempts seem much more successful, primarily because they rely on sign language and symbol language. The chimp cannot speak: He lacks the necessary vocal apparatus. But he does appear to have the necessary intellectual ability to do a simple language. See the study of Washoe by Gardner and Gardner (1969) and of Sarah by Premack (1971).

The relation between thought and word is perhaps best discussed in the works of Brown and Lenneberg (Brown, 1965; Lenneberg, 1967). Each of them, in their respective books, reviews the literature on this problem; the two of them together have conducted experiments on color naming, for although the English speaking people divide up the possible colors into many different names, some cultures only use two or three names for color. This does not mean that the other cultures cannot distinguish the colors, but simply that they do not bother with the fine distinctions that we make. We recommend Chapter 8, "Language and Cognition," from Lenneberg (1967) to you.

13

Learning and cognitive development

The ability to learn the consequences of one's actions is fundamental to the adaptive behavior of all organisms. Much of the study of intelligent behavior can be characterized as the study of the ability to learn about the contingencies of the world.

There is little formal distinction between learning and memory. Studies of learning tend to emphasize primarily the acquisition of knowledge: Studies of memory tend to emphasize the retention and use of that knowledge. Clearly, the two are so interrelated that the study of one must necessarily be a study of the other. Thus, we have already discussed the principles of learning in the several extensive chapters on memory. A major omission, however, has been how the knowledge within the memory system is acquired: How the relationships that exist among the environmental situations, the actions of the human, and the resulting outcomes are established. When an outcome cannot occur unless either a specific set of environmental conditions are satisfied or a specific action is performed, then we speak of the *contingencies* that operate among environmental conditions, actions, and outcomes (for example, the outcome, rain, is contingent upon certain atmospheric conditions). The major emphasis of this chapter is the way by which knowledge of contingencies is acquired: The problem of *contingency learning*.

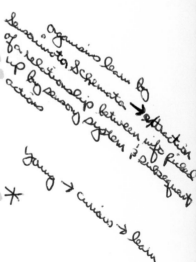

SENSORIMOTOR
SCHEMATA

Experimental studies of learning suggest that a simple, yet powerful principle is at the basis of intelligent behavior. Both perception and behavior appear to become organized by observing the consequences of actions. In the language of one of the foremost investigators of cognitive development, Jean Piaget, the organism learns by constructing *sensorimotor schemata*: He extracts the relationship between the information picked up by his sensory system and his actions (motor activities).[1] He is particularly sensitive to certain kinds of consequences, such as those associated with a desirable and necessary outcome, like food. But, in the human infant at least, any dramatic change in the external world, any "sensory spectacle," may attract his attention and serve as the basis for learning about the contingencies between actions and outcomes.

For contingency learning to occur, clearly the organism must be able

---

[1] A *sensorimotor schema* is a plan (a scheme) for performing an organized sequence of actions to perform some specific act, coordinating the information picked up by the **sensory** system with the necessary **motor** (muscle) movements. The acts of eating, walking, or riding a bicycle require their own well-developed sensorimotor schemata.

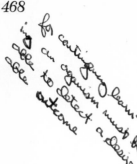

to detect the occurrence of desirable outcomes and then organize his behavior around attempts to obtain it. To do so, he must be capable of recognizing which actions are crucial to the occurrence of the outcome and which are irrelevant. To see more exactly what this means, we construct a hypothetical situation and examine just what must take place for an organism to learn of the contingencies between his actions and an outcome that he desires. We choose as our example the behavior of a chimpanzee in a puzzle room. The chimpanzee is an animal that is intelligent enough to serve our purposes, and, more important, it has not acquired any skills in language that would simplify his task and complicate ours.

A sensorimotor schema   We place the chimpanzee in a room that contains numerous objects. There are pictures on the walls, toys and boxes on the floor, chips, disks, and tiny square objects of various colors scattered about on the floor, and even a form of slot machine. The chimpanzee has never before encountered a situation quite like this: He is *experimentally naive.*

FIGURE 13-1

Eventually, if left in the room long enough, he will discover that placing a blue disk in the slot of the slot machine causes a bunch of grapes to appear in the chute of the machine. Because grapes are greatly liked by chimps, this is a desired outcome, and the chimp will willingly attempt to repeat (and learn) the task.

The problem for the animal is that, at first, there is neither prior knowledge of the actions expected of him nor of the resulting outcome. He must discover the necessary sequence of actions through trial-and-error and through accidents, and then he must be able to remember and take advantage of whatever desirable sequences have occurred. The end product of his learning will be a memory structure that represents the sensorimotor schema of placing blue disks in the slot machine in order to get grapes.

Now, watch how the chimp behaves in the room. At first he runs about, exploring the situation, playing with the toys, and jumping on the boxes. Eventually, he explores the slot machine and attempts to insert various objects into all the openings of that device: up the chute, down the slot. Then, quite by chance, he manages to get a blue disk down the slot, causing a cluster of grapes to fall into the chute with a loud "clunk."[2]. The first stage preparatory to learning has taken place.

What does the chimp make of the situation? He has been bouncing about, doing apparently irrelevant things, all with no particular effect. Now suddenly, after something that he has done, a bunch of grapes appears: The chimp remembers only the general outline of what he has been doing, plus whatever details are still present within his short-term memory. After this first success, it is likely that the only thing remembered by the chimp is that he had inserted something somewhere (presumably in the slot machine, someplace), and that grapes had arrived in the chute.

Let us represent the information acquired by the chimp with the format devised during the discussions of human memory in Chapters 10 and 11. To describe events, we describe a scenario which specifies an action and the role of the various objects and participants. A possible

1st problem - no prior knowledge of what to effect

End product → memory & trace of chips & pleasure

---

[2] The chimp is unlikely to learn this sequence of events if we truly had to wait for an "accident" to occur. Usually the experimenter deliberately sets up the situation so that the "accident" is rather likely. For example, he may have preexposed the chimp to other situations in which placing objects in slots was rewarding, or he may have placed the blue disks very near the slot, hoping that the chimp's natural propensity for inserting objects into openings would cause him to try it in this case. In either situation, the result is to get the learning started: The whole sequence of learning we are describing cannot take place until the first "accidental" success.

representation of the first, tentative sensorimotor schema is shown in Figure 13-2.

For your convenience we provide a dictionary that names the various concepts. Of course, the chimp does not have this knowledge, at least not at first. Eventually he may develop some abstract (nonlanguage) equivalence of the dictionary. Concept C1 represents the environmental or *antecedent* conditions associated with the situation. Concept C1 contains several elements, the slot machine (C3) and several as yet undefined elements (C2 and C4). In this environmental context, the action of inserting an unspecified object into the machine produces the *consequence* of grapes. Given environment C1, the associated action of **Insert** ? into ? will lead to the consequence of C8 (**grapes**). We specify this sequence by the relations **if** (for the antecedent condition) and **then** (for the consequence): **if** C1, **insert, then** C8.

FIGURE 13-2

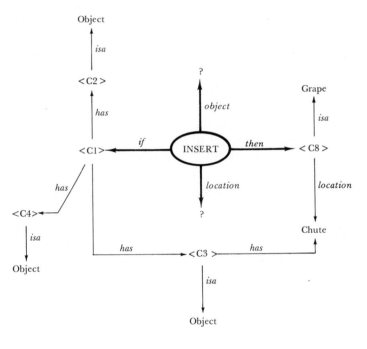

DICTIONARY

C1	The environment
C2	An object
C3	An object that has a chute
C4	An object
C8	Grapes in chute

The schema of Figure 13-2 marks a big advance in knowledge: The slot machine and the action of **insertion** are implicated in the scenario. Now all that remains is to discover the exact conditions necessary for the act to produce the grapes. The constraints upon the act of **insertion** help. Even without remembering any details, the action of inserting requires that one object be put into another object: In terms of our meaning structure, **object** and **location** must be specified. Even though the chimp does not have knowledge of language, we presume he has acquired knowledge about actions and events in the world. Thus, although he does not represent the action of **insert** in linguistic form, presumably he has some internal representation that is the rough equivalent. Given this, then the chimp has a specific goal: to discover the proper objects and the proper location. His behavior now can be directed toward a specific goal. Eventually, as he tries various operations, he will hit upon the proper combination and add it to his scenario: a possible sensorimotor schema for the complete scenario is shown in detail in Figure 13-3*a* and in outline form in Figure 13-3*b*. The chimp has learned the following schema: **if** *in environment C1,* **insert** *C2 in slot of C3,* **then** *get C8.*

Before considering the development of meaning structures through learning, let us first stop for a moment and examine some of the known properties of learning so that we can determine the conditions and situations that characterize the learning experience.

THE PHENOMENA OF LEARNING

The central issue confronting us is to discover how an organism acquires his knowledge of the world. Before we can do that, we need to know something of the basic phenomena. Hence, in this section, we examine the phenomena of learning in an attempt to describe the conditions that are operating. Later, we return to the problem of trying to explain this learning by deducing the internal mechanisms that operate within the organism to encode the situation into his memory structure.

Perhaps the most powerful description of the controlling factor of behavior is the *Law of Effect:*

> **An action that leads to a desirable outcome is likely to be repeated in similar circumstances.**

This law is simple, but it states the basic condition that underlies much of learned behavior. First postulated by the psychologist Thorndike in 1898, it has been studied extensively and modified many times: But still its basic form seems to be the most functional description of the conditions necessary for learning. This basic principle for acquiring

FIGURE 13-3

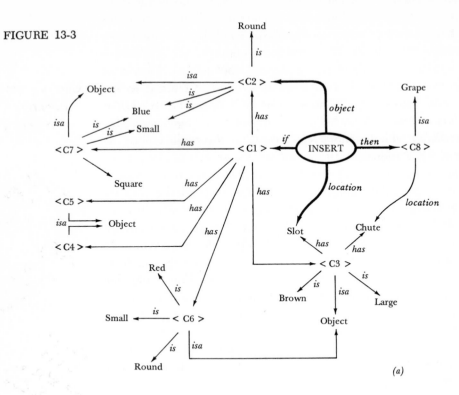

(a)

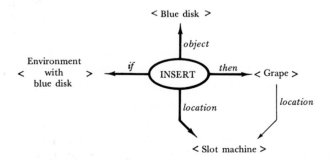

(b)

DICTIONARY	
C1	The environment
C2	Blue disk
C3	Slot machine
C4	Box
C5	Picture
C6	Red disk
C7	Blue square
C8	Grapes in chute

knowledge of the contingencies of the world is fundamental to the adaptive behavior of all organisms. It plays a major role in organizing the behavior of humans early in their infancy and continues as a dominant influence throughout adult life.

Consider the joint behavior of a newborn infant and his parents as they first interact with each other. We start the story with the hungry infant. He thrashes about randomly, in apparent discomfort, but with no noticeable purpose to his actions. Eventually he will emit crying sounds, attracting one of his parents who then attends to his wants. As a result of the crying, the infant receives food and thereby reduces his hunger. With the receipt of the food, the Law of Effect comes into play. The food is a *reinforcing event* and the behavior of crying is "likely to be repeated again in similar circumstances." This is the general paradigm of *instrumental learning*, since the baby's responses are *instrumental in changing the environmental conditions.*[3]

Reinforcing the behavior. The arrival of the reinforcing event, food, has two effects on the infant's behavior. It stops the instrumental response—the crying. It also makes it much more likely that the infant will cry in the future whenever he gets hungry.

Operant level. Initially, the chance that hunger would eventually lead to crying was relatively high, even in the absence of reinforcement. This is an important aspect of instrumental learning, since a behavior that does not occur cannot be reinforced. The initial reinforcement awaits the first occurrence of the instrumental or operant response. Thus the base rate or *operant level* of the response must be reasonably high to start. Responses other than crying might have been reinforced. A clever parent could have selected any of several different responses of the child as the signal for hunger, so long as that class of responses had a sufficiently high initial operant level.

Generalization. The infant would generalize his successful response to other similar situations. Thus, whenever he was in any discomfort, he would be likely to cry, not solely when he was hungry. Initially, the more similar the discomfort to that of hunger, the more likely the

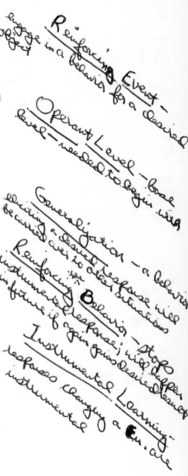

---

[3] The description in this section of contingency learning is based largely on the experimental studies of the field called *operant conditioning.* The investigation of operant conditioning has been heavily influenced by the work of B. F. Skinner, who began studying learning processes in the early 1930s. The term *operant conditioning* comes from the emphasis on the study of behavior which *operates* upon the environment in order to produce some outcome. The field of operant learning is a part of *instrumental learning*—the acquisition of responses that are *instrumental* in obtaining some reward.

infant would cry. These other cryings would also probably be reinforced by the arrival of the parent and alleviation of the discomfort, thus leading to even more frequent crying in the future for other forms of discomforts. Eventually, the infant would probably learn to cry anytime he wanted attention, for he would be reinforced for crying by the arrival of the concerned, attentive parent. In fact, an overattentive parent can cause the child to cry continuously for attention.

One of the most popular manuals on child raising, the famous Dr. Spock's *Baby and Child Care* (1957), put it this way:

> If the parents don't know how to put a stop to it, a baby may learn to wake not once but several times, to stay awake longer and longer each time, to demand not just company but walking, and to resist being put back to bed by furious crying. I've heard of cases in which it amounted eventually to 3 or 4 hours of walking each night [p. 188].

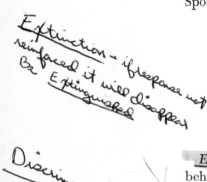

Extinction. The harried parent may attempt to *extinguish* the crying behavior by stopping the reinforcement for crying, otherwise the infant will spend most of the day in tears. How is this done? Again, let us turn to Dr. Spock:

> Most cases can be cured easily. The baby has to learn that there is nothing to be gained by waking and crying. This can usually be accomplished in 2 or 3 nights by letting him cry and not going to him at all. It is apt to be 20–30 minutes the first night (it may seem much longer), 10 minutes the second night, none the third [p. 188].

Spock goes on to warn the parent of the difficulty of carrying out this regime, especially when the baby reacts by becoming enraged and vomiting. But the mother should "harden her heart" says Dr. Spock and "stick to her program and not go in." More on this later.

Discrimination. The infant who is being reinforced for crying while uncomfortable but being extinguished for nonessential crying will have to learn to *discriminate* between the conditions that lead to reinforcement and those that do not. The only difference here is in the environmental conditions. Thus, ideally he should learn the differences between his various sensory states, between hunger or physical discomfort, on the one hand, and comfort on the other. When the infant can control his behavior according to these stimuli, we say that his behavior has come under *stimulus control*.

Schedules of reinforcement. The infant may respond to the *schedule* that governs his reinforcements. Thus, the parent, unable to tell by the cry of the infant whether it is actually hungry or otherwise distressed is likely to invent a simple rule: If the infant has just been attended to (fed, changed, played with, covered), ignore all cries for the next 30 min. Then, attend to the first cry.

This rule determines a *schedule of reinforcement:* In this case, the reinforcement is only given for the first cry after 30 min have elapsed from the preceding reinforcement. This is a *fixed-interval, 30-min schedule (FI-30).*

Although the desire of the parent is to bring the infant under stimulus control, crying only when hungry, the infant will probably simply respond to the schedule, eventually beginning to cry approximately 30 min after each previous cry was reinforced. This doesn't solve the parents' problem, of course.

Other schedules are possible. For example, it is likely that the parent will be variable in observance of the rule, sometimes waiting only 10 min, sometimes 50 before responding to cries. If the average delay is still 30 min, this then becomes a *variable-interval, 30-min schedule (VI-30).*

If the parent simply counts cries, deciding to attend to the infant only on the fifth cry, then this is a *fixed-ratio schedule, 5 responses (FR-5).* And, if there is variability in the counting of the number of responses necessary (but still with an average of five cries required), then this becomes a *variable-ratio schedule (VR-5).*

Finally, schedules can be *linked.* The parent might very well decide that he will not respond to a cry for 20 min after he has attended to the child (FI-20), but then he will respond on the average, to the third cry thereafter (VR-3). Here we have a sequence of two schedules, FI-20; VR-3. Unfortunately for the parent, the child soon becomes sensitive to the contingencies of reinforcement governed by these linked schedules and adjusts his behavior accordingly. In actual child-raising situations, the schedule usually is reasonably complex, since it develops out of the accidental frustrations of the child and the unsystematic attempts of the parent to deal with the situation.

So far, the reinforcement is positive: The infant receives something he wants. An analogous set of rules governs his responses to negative reinforcement—to the conditions in which an unpleasant or noxious event is involved. Let us leave the baby temporarily in order to consider some of the main features of negative reinforcement.

Escape and avoidance learning. A dog is placed in a *shuttle box,* an apparatus that has two compartments separated by a barrier. His

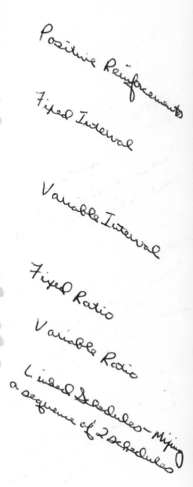

Positive Reinforcements

Fixed Interval

Variable Interval

Fixed Ratio

Variable Ratio

Linked Schedules—Mixing a sequence of 2 schedules

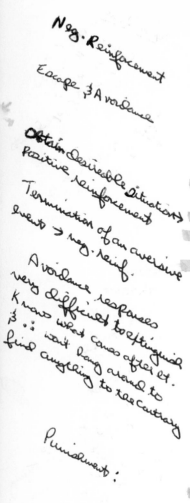

Neg. Reinforcement

Escape & Avoidance

Obtain Desirable Situations
Positive reinforcement

Termination of an aversive
event → neg. reinf.

Avoidance responses
very difficult to extinguish
Know what comes after it.
B ∴ won't hang around to
find anything to the contrary

Punishment:

task is to learn to jump across the barrier from one compartment to the other.

When the dog is in one compartment, the grid on the floor is electrified presenting a shock to his feet. He quickly learns to *escape* the shock by jumping the barrier into the "safe" compartment. Usually the arrival of shock is preceded by a cue: Ten seconds before the shock, a signal light comes on. The dog learns to *avoid* the shock by jumping the barrier during the 10 sec between the light cue and the shock. These two procedures are called *escape learning* and *avoidance learning*, respectively.

The two types of learning reflect the operation of *negative reinforcement*. The escape from shock resulted in its termination and thus **increased** the likelihood of escape responses in the future. The **delivery** of a desirable event is called *positive reinforcement:* **Termination** of an aversive event is called *negative reinforcement*. Both positive and negative reinforcement increase the likelihood of the responses that have immediately preceded.

Notice particularly what is learned with the **avoidance** procedure. Once the avoidance response has been learned, once the animal has learned to avoid the shock by jumping the barrier when the light comes on, his behavior is extremely difficult to extinguish. Even when the shocking apparatus has been totally disconnected from the shuttle box, he will continue to jump the barrier when the light comes on for hundreds of trials. So far as the animal is concerned, the contingency that is operating is that he will not get a shock if he jumps the barrier. Disconnecting the shocking apparatus does not affect this contingency. The light comes on, he jumps, and he does not get shocked. The action has led to the result that was expected, so no change in behavior is warranted.

Punishment. If the **termination** of a noxious event or **delivery** of a positive one **increases** the probability of the preceding response, then the **delivery** of a noxious event or **termination** of a positive one should **decrease** the probability of preceding responses. They do, but the situation resulting from punishment by delivering a noxious event is not quite analogous to the extinction that results from terminating a positive reward.

If an animal has learned to make a specific response in order to get food, its behavior will change very quickly when a shock, rather than food, results from that response. In fact, one experience may be enough to terminate the response permanently. But the punishment of the shock tends to have rather pervasive effects on behavior: It may suppress a large number of different responses that are only remotely associated with the punished one. Most organisms seem to be particularly sensitive to noxious events. They appear to be very conservative in judging the source of the punishment, tending to suppress a large number of behaviors rather than risk the recurrence of the punishing event.

This tendency, combined with the parents' usual inconsistencies in administering punishment, can combine to make the control of a child's behavior through punishment a rather uncertain business. Moreover, the high activity and stress that are normally associated with punishment by noxious events may interfere with the learning of more appropriate behaviors. In our discussion of motivation (Chapter 17), we will see that aggression is a frequent response to painful or unpleasant events. To return to the crying baby, punishment is clearly not the effective way to reduce the crying. If it is tried, it often produces a vicious circle of actions and responses: The parent spanks the child because he is crying; the child cries harder as a result of the spanking.

So far, we have discussed how an animal learns of the contingencies operating between his actions and the occurrence of a reinforcement. In many situations, the contingencies are probabilistic. In this case, we say there is a *correlation* between actions and outcome. Correlations between two events can vary between 100% and −100%. If the presence of an action guarantees the outcome, we say the correlation is 100% (usually stated as a correlation of 1.00). If the action is guaranteed to prevent the outcome, the correlation is −100% (or −1.00). If there is no relationship whatsoever between the action and the outcome, we say the correlation is 0. Intermediate values are also possible. Thus, we can say that the correlation between the environmental condition of dark clouds and the outcome of rain is .75, meaning that on the occasions in which dark clouds appear, rain is highly likely to result. The correlation between a perfectly clear, sunny day and rain might be −.95, meaning that the one condition almost (but not entirely) precludes the other.

✕ Contingencies are simply a special case of correlations. Animals not only are capable of learning correlations; they are quite capable of learning that there is a zero correlation between some actions and outcomes.

Learned helplessness. Return to the situation described for escape and avoidance learning. A dog is placed in a shuttle box and shocks are delivered to him. This time, however, there is no barrier, and no response that he can make will allow him to escape or avoid the shock. There is no correlation between his actions and the outcomes. After the dog has acquired some experience with this condition, the experimenter changes the situation. Now, the barrier is again introduced and the situation changed so that it is possible to escape or avoid the shock

Detecting correlations

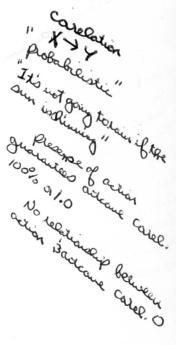

[Handwritten marginalia:]

Learned Helpless notes

step 1 - put dog in box & shock him no matter what he does. O correlation between action & outcome

step 2 - let dog escape shock by jumping barrier

Dog develops hypoth of helplessness → Can't eradicate "All responses in repertoire will produce shock" O correlation situation

In Helplessness situation there is little to differentiate the condition of "O" correlation to a new changed situation. Thus when differentiation between reinforcement schedules is hard to detect, changes don't immediately affect behavior

by jumping the barrier at the appropriate time. Unlike the dogs in the earlier experiments, dogs that have first experienced the situation with zero correlation find it difficult to learn that they can now escape shock. Some dogs never learn, even if the experimenter carries them over the hurdle in an attempt to demonstrate what the dogs should do (Seligman, Maier, & Solomon, 1969). These dogs seem to develop a hypothesis of *helplessness.* Unfortunately for the dogs, once such a hypothesis is established, it is difficult to eradicate. During the period of inescapable shock, the dogs presumably learn that all the responses in their repertoire lead to shock. Each time the dog receives a shock, he also receives a confirmation of his hypothesis: the expectation being confirmed, the dog is even less likely to do something on the next trial.

Some insight into the situation comes from performing an analogous experiment on humans, the advantage being that we can then ask why they fail to learn the escape response once the conditions change. In one such experiment, of the subjects who never did learn to escape, 60% reported ". . . that they felt they had no control over shock, so why try. These subjects reported that they spent the majority of their time in preparation for the upcoming shock. Approximately 35% reported that they, after pushing one or two buttons (the appropriate response, if done at the proper time), abandoned the idea of escape [Thornton & Jacobs, 1971, p. 371]." Subjects who did not learn the zero correlation situation responded quite differently. Not only did they learn to escape, but more than 70% of them ". . . reported they felt they had control over shock, and their task was to find out how." The power of an inappropriate hypothesis is found in the behavior of subjects who had decided that shock was not under their control when, in the condition where they could actually escape, they "accidentally" did manage to escape. These subjects would sometimes ". . . escape or avoid shock on one or more trials, but on subsequent trials would again take the full (3 sec) shock. It appeared that these subjects did not associate their responding with the reinforcement."

One of the difficulties faced by the animal or human subject in the experiment on helplessness is that there is little to differentiate the condition of zero correlation from the new, changed situation. This is a common phenomenon: when the differentiation between reinforcement schedules is difficult to detect, changes in schedules do not much affect behavior, at least not immediately.

Extinction and discrimination. If an animal learns a task, say to press a lever in order to get food, what happens in extinction, when the lever press no longer gives food? The answer depends upon the schedule of reinforcement that was initially used in learning. If the schedule were a fixed ratio, 1 (FR-1), so that the animal received food after every press, then once extinction started, the animal would soon stop pressing the bar. The change in schedule is large and should be easily detected.

But suppose the animal were slowly shifted from FR-1 to FR-10, to FR-100 and even to FR-1000. If the shift were properly done, the animal would learn to respond for food even when it took 1000 bar presses for each reinforcement. An animal that has learned to perform on an FR-1000 schedule would, when extinction was started, at first have great difficulty in distinguishing that anything had changed. Hence, he should continue to respond for a very long time after reinforcements had stopped. In fact, were the final schedule before extinction a variable one, say VR-1000, the extinction would only slowly, if ever, lead to a cessation of responding. The less frequently (or the more variably) we reinforce an animal in training, the longer he will continue to respond even during extinction. (Of course, learning itself is more difficult under these conditions.)

The partial reinforcement effect. The long time-course of continued responses when extinction follows an infrequently rewarded schedule is called the *partial reinforcement effect* (PRE). To sustain behavior, during extinction, it is best to train the animal on a schedule in which reinforcements occur only for a partial set of the responses, preferably both infrequently and with variability.

Consider the problem of training a child to work efficiently in elementary school. If the teacher rewards the child every time that he performs properly, say, does his work on time, things will go along smoothly only so long as the teacher is always present. But if the teacher misses several occasions, the child's behavior is likely to become erratic. Not only will the lack of the expected reinforcement tend to stop the behavior, but one can expect "frustration" responses as well.

Ideally, the teacher should slowly lengthen the time between reinforcements, carefully training the child to expect a reduced schedule. Now the child's performance is still likely to be maintained even when the teacher becomes inattentive (or is absent for a few days), since the prolonged absence of reward for good behavior can not immediately be distinguished from the normal fluctuations of the schedule. To establish the behavior, a **continuous** or 100% reinforcement schedule should be used (FR-1); to maintain the established behavior, a **partial** schedule should be used.

Consider again the problem of the crying infant. Suppose the child had been tended every time that he cried. As a result, the frequency of his crying increased to the point where he seemed to cry continuously whenever he was awake and his parents were not in sight. Now suppose that the frustrated parents agree to attempt the extinction of this behavior by never attending to the child while he cries, but rather always waiting for a silent period. Usually, when parents attempt this procedure they are incapable of following it through. As the good Dr. Spock puts it:

> It's hard on the kindhearted parents while the crying lasts. They imagine the worst: that his head is caught in the slats of the crib, or that he has vomited and is lying in a mess, that he is at least in a panic about being deserted [p. 187].

The result is that the child undergoes partial reinforcement: He is reinforced on some schedule, say on the average once every hour (VI-60). The result is, of course, just the opposite of what is desired. The crying becomes even more prolonged and difficult to extinguish. The baby has learned that he must cry longer in order to be reinforced. Again, from Dr. Spock: "It's important not to tiptoe in to be sure the baby is safe or to reassure him that you are nearby. This only enrages him and keeps him crying much longer [p. 187]."

Contingencies between the environment and outcomes

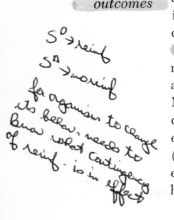

Extinction can be viewed as posing a problem of discrimination for the animal. He needs to know which schedule is in effect before he can alter his behavior in an appropriate manner. One way to make the cues for the schedule distinctive is to mark them explicitly by changing some aspect of the environment whenever the reinforcement schedule changes. We call the contextual cue a *signaling stimulus.*

Stimulus control. A stimulus that signals the presence of reinforcement is called an S^D (pronounced "ess dee"); a stimulus that signals the absence of reinforcement (extinction procedure) is an S^Δ ("ess delta"). Now things are under much better control: The animal normally has no difficulty in learning that reinforcement is available when an S^D is present, and that no reinforcement is to be expected when an S^Δ is present. (The most common form of S^D and S^Δ in animal experiments is the presence and absence of a light, respectively. A common form of S^Δ for humans is a sign that reads "out of order.")

Once the concept of stimulus control is initiated, it can very easily be expanded to other kinds of signals. For one thing, the S^D can itself take on the properties of a *secondary reinforcer:* The animal will work in order to cause an S^D to occur. Thus, the animal can learn to satisfy one schedule in order to get the appropriate S^D that marks the start of another schedule, one that will produce food at its termination. Moreover, once an animal has learned to associate a particular S^D with its schedule, we can use this association as a method of testing his preference of one schedule over another.

Choice. Suppose we train an animal on a fixed-ratio schedule, reinforcing it every 100 responses. We signify the FR-100 schedule by marking the response lever with vertical stripes. At the same time, on alternate hours, we might train the animal on another schedule, say a variable ratio 100 schedule, signaling the VR-100 by marking the response lever with horizontal stripes. Now we can measure the preference of the animal by giving it a situation with two levers, one marked with horizontal stripes, the other with vertical ones. This is a choice situation: By observing the animal's response we can determine his relative preference of the FR-100 schedule over a VR-100 one. Obviously, this technique is easily expanded to allow the comparison of any two (or more) schedules.

Discrimination. The same technique can be used in a slightly different manner to study an animal's discrimination behavior. Start with two schedules for which it is known that one is clearly preferred to the other: A very simple example is to use FR-1 for one schedule and no reinforcement for the other. Let the first schedule be signaled by a light of high intensity (the light is the S^D) and let the second schedule be signaled by a light of low intensity (this light is the S^Δ). Now we present the animal with two levers and the two stimuli, the lights of high and low intensities. If the animal can discriminate the difference in the intensities of the two lights, then presumably he will always choose the lever marked by the high intensity, S^D light, the one that leads to reinforcement. Now, slowly, we alter the intensity of the S^D light so that it becomes more similar to the S^Δ. We determine the animal's ability to discriminate intensity by recording his ability to select the proper response. (Clearly, we randomly alter the assignment of schedules and stimulus lights to the levers, so that the location of the levers is irrelevant.) This technique can be used to measure an animal's discrimination ability for any stimuli that can be used as S^D or S^Δ. It is a standard method of measuring an animal's sensitivity to lights, sounds, and other signals.

Chaining. Once a stimulus has acquired secondary reinforcing value, it can be used to reinforce a response. Hence, if we teach a chimpanzee to insert a blue disk into a slot machine in order to get grapes, the blue disk itself soon becomes a reinforcer. Then, we can teach the chimp other tasks in which the outcome is a blue disk. For example, we can teach him to pull a rope in order to get disks.

When the task of rope pulling is established, that task itself acquires reinforcing powers. Thus, we could teach the chimp to open a door in order to get access to the rope. Eventually, an S^D for the door could

be added, perhaps a light, so the door could only be opened when the light was on. And perhaps a switch could be provided to control the light.

The end result of all this training would be a chain of responses. To the observer it would be rather impressive. Whenever the chimpanzee was hungry he would walk over to one part of his room and turn on a light. Then, he would go to the door, open it, and pull out a rope. That would release a blue disk, which the chimp would insert into a slot machine, producing a bunch of grapes.

To establish chains of this sort, it is important that the learning proceed with already established reinforcers. Thus, normally the chain is learned backward, as just described.

Shaping behavior. In chaining, it is necessary to teach the sequence backward, with a gradual buildup of the appropriate response sequence. This is a crucial part of the power of operant techniques, the ability to *shape* behavior by selective reinforcement of desired characteristics and nonreinforcement of the others. Suppose one wishes to teach a dog to walk on its hind legs. To do this with operant techniques, one would first establish a *reinforcing event,* say the eating of a small amount of a dry dog food. Then, it is necessary to create a *discriminative signal* for the food. A simple technique is to blow a whistle every time food is available. Eventually the whistle will take on the characteristic of an S^D and will acquire secondary reinforcing power. Thus, the blowing of the whistle, the S^D, can serve as a reinforcer for a response. (For this S^D to be effective, of course, the dog should always be trained when slightly hungry.

With the S^D established, training can begin. First, the dog is reinforced by any movement even remotely approaching standing on the hind legs. Thus, at first, if the dog sits down, the whistle should be blown. Slowly, the criterion for blowing the whistle is modified, first whenever the dog sits down, then only if it has one front paw off the ground while sitting, then both paws, and finally only if it tries to stand with both paws off the ground. The point is to mold or shape the animal's behavior very gradually, until finally it achieves the desired form. Notice that no punishment is required, only reinforcement. The exact sequence of reinforced events can vary with each dog, but the important thing is that it is reinforced for behaviors that slowly approximate the desired one. Shaping works by selective reinforcement of successive approximations to the desired behavior. A reliable, rapidly presented reinforcer is a necessity.

The first step in shaping is to establish the reinforcement contingencies. Trying to teach the dog by letting it get to its meal if it "does well" during the training session simply will not work. A whistle

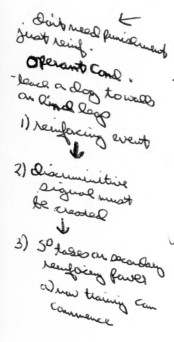

- Don't need punishment just reinf.
Operant Cond.
- teach a dog to walk on hind leg
1) reinforcing event
2) Discriminitive signal must be created
3) S^D takes on secondary reinforcing power
a) now training can commence

is effective because it can be sounded the instant the proper response is made. Unless a reinforcer is presented **immediately** after the proper response, the animal cannot know which action it performed was the proper one. The whistle serves both as a reinforcer and as a source of information feedback. Some care must be taken to maintain the reinforcing value of the whistle by continued access to food following the whistle (a partial schedule is permissible). A verbal reinforcer could also be used (such as the words "good boy") but only if these words are used only as S^D for reinforcement. Indiscriminate use of the words in other situations will result in extinction of its reinforcing value.

Summary

These, then, are some of the basic phenomena of contingency learning. In overview, they provide a description of how the actions of an animal or human are related to external events. One of the most striking features of contingency learning is the sensitivity of the animal's behavior to very subtle relations between actions and outcomes. This is especially apparent when the animal is allowed to acquire the knowledge slowly and systematically. The information that is extracted from the learning experience seems to be the overall correlations among the stimulus context, responses, and outcome conditions. That is, the Law of Effect appears to apply to the whole pattern or correlation of events rather than the specific application of an individual reinforcement. –

The phenomena of contingency learning describe what an organism does, but we still do not know how he does it. We turn now to consider some of the processes that might underlie the organism's ability to adapt his responses to contingencies of the external world.

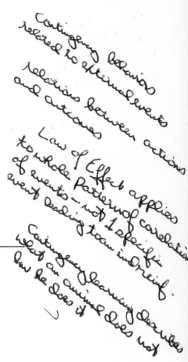

CLASSICAL CONDITIONING

Up to this point, our description has concentrated on instrumental learning. Most modern learning studies are concerned with instrumental learning. But the first major impetus to the study of learning came from a different background: the work of the Russian physiologist, Pavlov, which started at the turn of the century. *Pavlovian* (or *classical*) *conditioning* differs slightly from the learning that we have been discussing.

Pavlov was a physiologist and in his work (for which he had received the Nobel prize) he was primarily interested in the measurement of gastric fluids and salivary responses in hungry animals. As a result, he had devised several techniques for measuring such things as the salivary output of his dogs. But, with the insight that characterizes a good scientist, Pavlov soon discovered that other cues besides food would produce salivation. For example, whenever Pavlov himself entered the room, the dogs would salivate: Pavlov had discovered the power of conditioned stimuli.

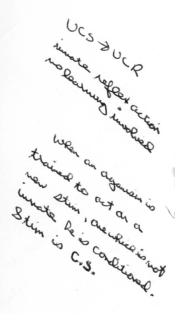

In classical conditioning, there are two types of stimuli and two types of responses. First, there are those stimuli (*unconditioned stimuli*) that automatically produce a specific response (an *unconditioned response*): These unconditional stimuli and responses are abbreviated as *UCS* and *UCR*. UCS's produce their UCR's through innate, reflex action. Salivation is a UCR to the UCS of food in the mouth. An eyeblink is a UCR to the UCS of a puff of air in the eye. Depressing a lever when a light comes on can **not** be considered as a UCR for the UCS of light: This is not an innate reflex response.

In classical conditioning, when a new, novel stimulus such as the turning on of a light, the ringing of a bell, or the sight of Pavlov comes to elicit a response such as salivation, we say that salivation has become **conditioned** to the novel stimulus: The novel *conditioned stimulus* is the *CS*. Initially, salivation was an UCR that always occurred only with the taste of food. Food, therefore, was the UCS. Now, however, even the sight of Pavlov leads to salivation; Pavlov is the CS and the response that has become conditioned to him—salivation—is the *CR* (the *conditioned response*). Thus food is the UCS, Pavlov the CS, and salivation both the UCR and the CR, depending upon which stimulus elicited it.

We can demonstrate the techniques of classical conditioning through the classical example: that of a dog salivating to the sound of a bell. In the experiment, first we establish that the UCS and UCR are as promised, unconditional. That is, we check that even to an experimentally naive dog, putting food into the mouth (the UCS) causes the dog to salivate (the UCR), and ringing the bell (the CS) does not. Pavlov did this experiment by placing the dog in a restraining harness and devising an apparatus that blew food powder into the mouth at the appropriate time.

Now, just before food powder is blown into the mouth, we ring a bell. Thus, a given trial in classical conditioning might consist of ringing a bell, waiting 3 sec, and then blowing food powder into the mouth. After a minute or so, the whole sequence is repeated. As we continue this process, the UCR, salivation, will start to occur **before** the presence of the food powder. In fact, if we test the animal by deleting the UCS and simply ringing the bell, we find that the CS has come to elicit the response: Salivation occurs whenever the bell rings. This is the essence of classical conditioning.

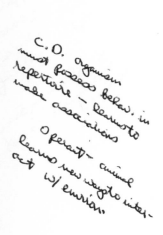

There are several basic differences between Pavlovian or classical conditioning and instrumental or operant conditioning. Using classical conditioning, we can link a response to a stimulus (the CS) that normally does not elicit it, but the response must already be part of the animal's repertoire. It must automatically be elicited by the UCS. Thus, the UCR is usually a simple, physiological or reflexive response. Using operant conditioning, the animal can acquire new and infinitely varied responses. We study classical conditioning to find out how the animal learns **associations**. We study operant conditioning to discover how the animal learns to interact with his environment.

We have seen something of the phenomena of learning. Now it is time to see whether we can examine how information is represented in the memory structure. Quite clearly, our goal is to describe the underlying conceptual schemata that result from the learning process. Our view of learning is the same as our view of memory: When new information is learned, it is added to preexisting meaning structures within the memory system. The problem facing the learner is to determine the conditions that affect him and record that information properly.

Reinforcement as a signal

In the discussion of learning, a reinforcement helped the organism to acquire the response that just preceded. But reinforcement is also a signal, signifying to the organism just which conditions are the desirable ones and which are the undesirable ones. Thus, one would expect that a reinforcer would have its optimum signaling properties only if it is unambiguous; that is, it should not lead to any confusion about which specific action is being reinforced. To maximize this signaling property, one of two conditions must be met. Either the reinforcer must occur rapidly after the appropriate action so no confusion results from the performance of other, irrelevant actions and also so the action can still be remembered within the short-term memory; or, alternatively, if there is a delay in the outcome, the relevant event must be distinct enough to be identified within the long-term memory for events.

Normally, to teach an animal something, the outcome must follow the action within about 5 sec. This limit on the delay of reinforcement has been variously interpreted, but a simple interpretation, certainly, is that the outcome must occur soon enough to guarantee that the action to be reinforced is still within short-term memory. There is one major exception to this 5-sec finding. Animals seem capable of discovering (and thereby avoiding) dangerous foods, even though the illness that results from the ingestion of such foods may not occur for many hours (Garcia & Koelling, 1966). The association between the specific food and the illness appears to be a result of both an innate strategy and the appropriate use of the long-term memory structure. That is, the animal apparently automatically associates any feelings of nausea with the last novel food that it has eaten, and therefore will avoid that food. This strategy requires that the memory for the most recent meals be relatively complete and relatively accessible (something that is certainly readily satisfied for humans even when they have made no attempt to remember their meals—What did you eat for your last two meals?). Usually, the strategy of avoiding novel foods is sufficient to prevent recurring food-caused sickness. The innate character of this strategy is shown by the fact that if an animal is made nauseous by some nonfood treatment (X rays, for example), he will still shun the last novel food. Moreover, he will not learn to avoid conditions that are highly correlated with future nausea, even when those conditions are well marked by lights, buzzers, etc. Nausea seems to be a cue for taste aversion and nothing else.

Reinforcement is not a necessary condition for remembering. The primary determiner of whether an event or concept will be remembered seems to be the type of processing given to it at the time it is experienced. If the information was integrated into a schema or action, it is likely to be remembered. Otherwise, it is not.

- Do you remember what time it was when you last checked? The answer is probably no, unless you did something with the answer when you got it.
- Do you remember the letters that appear on a telephone dial along with the numeral 7? The answer is probably no, even though you have seen and used that information countless numbers of times. (The answer is probably yes if at some time you made an effort to learn it.)
- Do you remember the clothes that you wore yesterday? The answer is probably yes, even if you made no attempt to remember them: But the act of selecting and wearing clothes automatically forms a memory schema in order to get done in the first place; hence, it is likely to be remembered.
- Recall the behavior of the human and animal subjects who had acquired the hypothesis of *helplessness*. To them, the impending shock, however unpleasant, was simply information feedback that confirmed and strengthened their opinion that the shock was unavoidable. Thus their behavior persisted, even though they appeared to be punished for it.

Learning and awareness   A major theoretical issue for many years has been the question of whether or not learning can occur without awareness. This is a very difficult question to answer, as the length and fierceness of the dispute will testify. People who claim that there need not be awareness, often claim this to prove that an outcome must serve as a reinforcer, not as a signal in a learning experiment. But, as we shall see in the chapters to follow, human thinking conceivably does occur without the immediate awareness of the person, and certainly does occur without retrospective awareness. For example, one can be aware of the clue used in solving a problem or of the contents of a dream at the instant it is occurring, but have forgotten it within minutes afterward. Therefore, when quizzed by an experimenter, there would appear to have been absolutely no awareness of the event. The possible short life of the awareness of an event hampers the experimental search for an answer to the issue. But even if an answer were possible, there would appear to be no reason why memory schemata and hypotheses could not be developed and tested subconsciously, without the awareness of the person involved.

A contingency learning system geared simply to extract correlations among the environment, actions, and outcomes has a fatal flaw. It cannot separate out those aspects that actually cause the outcome from those that just accidentally happen to be correlated with it. A gambler may believe that crossing his fingers will ensure that he wins. A parachutist may believe that a good luck charm guarantees safety. The chimp may believe that standing on its left leg is essential to the appearance of grapes. This phenomenon is termed *superstitious behavior*. It is easily demonstrated in the laboratory. It suggests that once contingencies of an event have been established, the animal is doomed to repeat past actions whenever it encounters the appropriate context. This aspect of contingency learning describes well many superstitious rituals, from rain dances to knocking on wood.

Learning by experimentation

Humans, however, have a protective mechanism. Even a very young infant is not blindly driven by contextual cues, mechanically producing responses that are associated with sensorimotor schemata built up from past experiences. Rather, the infant appears to vary his actions intentionally in order to observe the similarities and differences in the consequences that result. Here, for example, is Piaget's (1952) description of his son Laurent's experimentation at the age of 10 months:

> Laurent is lying on his back but nevertheless resumes his experiments of the day before. He grasps in succession a celluloid swan, a box, etc., stretches out his arm and lets them fall. He distinctly varies the position of the fall. Sometimes he stretches out his arm vertically, sometimes he holds it obliquely, in front of or behind his eyes, etc. When the object falls in a new position (for example, on his pillow), he lets it fall two or three times more on the same place, as though to study the spatial relation; then he modifies the situation [p. 269].

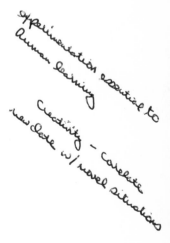

An infant experiments with his world. In this way, he discovers how his actions affect the environment, and he is protected against coincidental relationships between his responses and external consequences. This strategy separates causes from correlations. (In some cases, of course, the principle is difficult to follow: The parachutist does not leave his good luck charm at home just to test the relevance of his actions to the outcome. Nonetheless, experimentation is a crucial aspect of the intellectual development of human beings.)

*The importance
of expectations*

Goal-directed behavior. Evidence that the infant is anticipating that specific consequences will result from his actions begins to appear at a very early age. Before an infant is 6 months old, he seems mainly to be reacting to external signals: He responds to events when they occur; he does not initiate them. If he sees an object, he may reach out for it or suck on it, but does not seem to be unduly perturbed when it disappears from view.

By about 6 months of age, however, he starts to show indications that he has specific expectations as he interacts with his environment. They appear first in his searching behavior. Before the age of around 6 months, attempts to retrieve objects he cannot see are rather primitive, perhaps only a brief groping or visual search for an object that has disappeared from view. But soon the infant shows a systematic exploration of the probable hiding places—under the covers, behind obstacles, in the closed fist of a parent. Finally, deductions about the location of an object from his observations of the external events becomes a routine part of his search behavior.

The most complex aspects of goal-directed behavior emerge when we consider how the infant applies his sensorimotor intelligence to solving practical problems. Examine again the behavior of Piaget's child, Laurent:

> At 16 months, 5 days, Laurent is seated before a table and I place a bread crust in front of him, out of reach. Also, to the right of the child I place a stick about 25 cm long. At first Laurent tries to grasp the bread without paying any attention to the instrument, and then he gives up [p. 335].

Laurent has a problem. His habitual response of reaching for an object fails to achieve the desired goal, so some new response must be tried. But how is the new response selected: Is it random; is it blind trial-and-error; is it based on things he has done at the table before?

> I then put the stick between him and the bread; it does not touch the objective but nevertheless carries with it an undeniable visual suggestion. Laurent again looks at the bread, without moving, looks very briefly at the stick, then suddenly grasps it and directs it towards the bread. But he grasped it toward the middle and not at one of its ends so that it is too short to obtain the

objective. Laurent then puts it down and resumes stretching out his hand towards the bread. Then, without spending much time on this movement, he takes up the stick again, this time at one of its ends (chance or intention?), and draws the bread to him. . . . Two successive attempts yield the same result.

An hour later I place a toy in front of Laurent (out of his reach) and a new stick next to him. He does not even try to catch the objective with his hand; he immediately grasps the stick and draws the toy to him [p. 335].

Somehow, Laurent has discovered that an action–consequence sequence must be modified to achieve a particular goal. But how did he learn the new schema? He had never before used sticks to retrieve objects. What was guiding his selection of responses and what precisely did he learn from his initial failure? Did he learn that his arm was not long enough so that he must search for an "arm extender?" How does he know that? How does the environmental context—the presence of sticks, for example—help satisfy his search for a solution to the problem?

Learning that a stick can be used as a tool for reaching something may sound like a primitive task, but it is a surprisingly difficult one. This level of problem solving is beyond the explanatory capabilities of any existing theories of contingency learning, since this is very sophisticated learning, despite its apparent simplicity. In fact, it seems to represent the intellectual limits of nonhuman organisms: Only the very highest species of animals—some species of primates and man—are capable of solving the "stick problem." The next level problem, that of constructing a tool for a purpose (rather than using whatever happens to be lying around) may be limited to man.

COGNITIVE
DEVELOPMENT

The cognitive capability of the human changes radically during the years from its birth through adolescence. Starting at first with the minimum ability to learn of the correlations of the world, it slowly develops an awareness of concepts and events and, then, simple sensorimotor schemata. During the first years of its life, a chimpanzee has a faster and more advanced intellectual development than does a human infant in the same time period. But around the age of 2, there are dramatic changes in the human infant's cognitive capability. For one thing, it learns to internalize its thoughts, so that it is no longer so dependent upon external events. For another, it is starting to develop language, a symbolic skill that will allow it to advance rapidly in the acquisition of knowledge.

The development of the human can be characterized by the several stages through which it passes. The man who has done most to study the intellectual development of the child and specify its progress has been the Swiss scientist, Jean Piaget. We have already discussed some of his ideas (and briefly met his child Laurent). Now let us examine Piaget's several stages of development of the intellect.[4]

Piaget has identified several periods, subperiods, and stages in the cognitive growth of the child. The first period is that of *Sensorimotor* development: It lasts from birth through the age of about 18 months to 2 years. The second period is that of *Preoperational Thought,* running from the end of the sensorimotor period (age 2) through about age 7. This leads to the *Concrete Operations* period which lasts until about age 11. Finally, there is the period of *Formal Operations,* (starting around 11 years and lasting through adolescence), in which the final aspects of adult intelligence emerge.

Sensorimotor learning

We have already discussed the basic features of sensorimotor learning. To review, during that period, the child acquires an understanding of objects and actions. He learns that he can pick up and manipulate objects, that he can move about in the world and initiate events. The infant has learned that he is separate from his environment and that objects have permanence: He has learned about space and time and form, but he still lacks a good internal representation of the world. At the end of the period, imagery is just beginning, language is just starting. Basically, the child has learned to organize the perceptual features of the world, but his thought processes are still externalized. He is restricted to discovery through manipulation.

THE DEVELOPMENT OF IMAGES

A central part of contingency learning is the organization of perceptual features into clusters based on their association with an action sequence. The child must construct an internal image of the external events.

The ability to organize perceptual information according to response contingencies is probably *innate,* present at birth. The resulting development of the internal images is crucial to the cognitive growth of a child. Presumably,

---

[4] Piaget's works are too numerous to reference at this point. The "Suggested Readings" at the end of this chapter presents a guide to his thoughts and writings.

the first concepts developed in the infant's brain are of the objects he experiences. Initially, however, these concepts may have meaning only in terms of his own actions (that is, only *motor meaning*). In fact, at first, the infant may not even recognize that external objects exist independently of his actions. Piaget has suggested that in the first sensorimotor schemata that develop, perceptual features are not distinguished from the actions themselves. For example, Figure 13-4 shows a possible sensorimotor schema: The event of **move arm** causes a pleasant sound, but no separable concept of a prerequisite object has yet emerged.

FIGURE 13-4

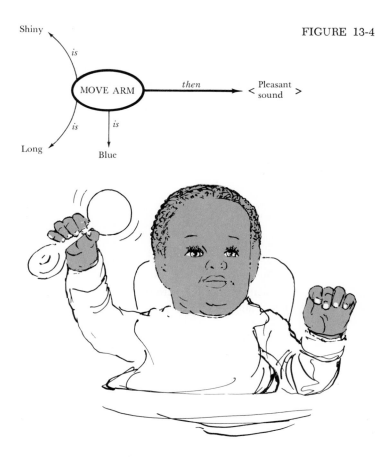

Gradually, as the child continues to manipulate the objects in his environment, the sensory components become separated from the action and begin to achieve an existence of their own. This is a critical beginning step in the child's acquisition of knowledge. Once the appropriate set of features is linked together in a separate, independent image, the memory system can recognize the object when it appears, allowing it to deal with the internal cluster of information—the memory node—as a unit.

FIGURE 13-5

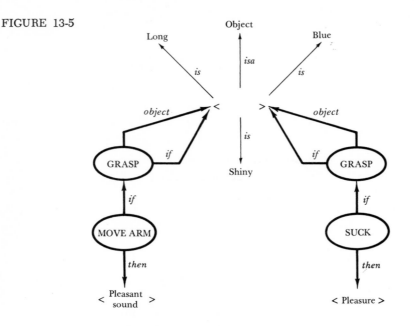

The same mechanisms continue to operate as the infant matures, but the problems associated with organizing perceptual information in a learning situation change. As the repertoire of images builds up, new objects must be integrated into existing perceptual structures through the processes of generalization and discrimination, since most of the things the infant encounters will have both similarities and differences compared to the things he already knows.

Preoperational thought

From the ages of roughly 2 through 7 the child begins to use an internal representation of his external world. This is his first major step toward adult thinking: the performance of mental experiments. Now, for the first time, he can predict the course of an event without actually having to do it. He can answer the question: What would happen if . . . ?

In the beginning, however, there are severe limitations on his ability to internalize events. He is mostly restricted to concrete actions: He does not form abstractions or generalizations. Moreover, once a mental sequence of actions is started, it proceeds systematically, step-by-step, with little or no opportunity for flexibility.

Some of a child's apparent peculiarities in forming abstractions and generalizations can be seen in his classification behavior. Suppose you present a child with a set of pictures of objects that differ along a variety of dimensions and ask him to put together the pictures that seem to belong together. Faced with this task, an adult will usually select some physical dimension or combination of dimensions and systematically sort the objects according to his selected criteria. The child's behavior (during the preoperational stage) is quite different. Similarities and differences in physical characteristics only seem to be used if there is no other choice. In dealing with familiar objects, the child tends to group them according to their connection with a common environmental situation. Pictures of a stove, a refrigerator, a bowl of cereal and a doll for Mommy may go into one pile; or he may build up a pile based on a barnyard or farming scene. Moreover, unlike the adult, he is not too fussy as to whether everything fits together nicely.

In some respects, an adult, confronted with an experimental task in concept formation, behaves quite similarly to the child. If a college student is requested to subdivide a pile of cards into two groups by whatever rule he wishes, a common strategy is for him to select a single dimension and try using it as the basis for making responses. Thus, he may pick all cards with red borders for one pile, blue borders for the other. When a card comes along that does not fit the rule, a new rule is selected and tried. In a complicated task, the subject may not remember the rules he has tried before, and may repeat himself. Like children, adults find rules that require them to combine several dimensions simultaneously more difficult to deal with than classifications based on a single dimension. If dimensions must be combined, then the simple *conjunction* of dimensions seems easiest (to belong to a class, an object must have **all** the attributes: for example, it must both be red **and** large). *Disjunction* is harder (the object must have any **one** attribute: for example, it must be either red **or** large). Concepts based on contingencies among the dimensions are hardest of all to learn (if the object is red, it must be large; but if it is blue, it must be small).

Overall, however, some of the characteristics of a child's classification behavior are distinctly different from the adult's. The most important feature seems to be that the child's induction mechanisms tend to deal with only a restricted range of the available information. The child tends to focus on only the dominant characteristics of an event. Moreover, he seems to require only local consistency across his examples rather than consistency that spans a full history of the relevant information. A child is likely to group a bat with a ball (because you play with them), then a tomato with the ball (because they are round), and then put a rose with the tomato (because they are red). An adult does not do this. Rather, adults insist on finding one single rule that applies to all objects.

The preoperational child tends to be egocentric, centering his internal representations around himself. That is, he seems completely unable to take or to understand another person's point of view. We have already discussed how this might affect language behavior (in Chapter 12), but it also has strong implications for a child's ability to learn by communicating with others or by mentally picturing a scenario from some other perspective.

In addition to all these limitations (or perhaps, as a necessary result), his thinking processes seem to be irreversible. Although he can imagine the outcome of a certain sequence of operations, he cannot return to the initial state. It is as though the mental performance of the imagined event had the same characteristics as the real performance of an actual event—once done, it cannot be undone.

The most famous example of irreversibility is Piaget's *water glass problem*. Take two glasses, one tall and narrow, the other low and wide. Fill the low, wide glass with water. Now, with the child watching closely, pour the water from the wide glass into the narrow one: Obviously it rises to a much greater height than it had before. Now ask the child whether the new glass has the same amount of water in it as did the old glass; a child in the preoperational stage will respond **no**, the narrow glass has a different amount in it. Some children will say there is now more (the level is higher) or that there is less (the width is thinner), but whichever mode of operation they focus on, they simply cannot be led to believe that the amount of water is unchanged. The child does not yet have a concept of *conservation of mass*.

Concrete operations   Around the age of 7, the child enters the stage of concrete operations. Now the problems of conservation are no longer troublesome and the child passes the water glass test with ease. He has learned both that matter is conserved and also that one dimension (height) can compensate for another (width). Although still limited to concrete reasoning about objects, the child nonetheless has broad new powers of thought available to him: He learns the rules of manipulation, of number and space, of simple generalization, and of simple abstraction. But still, during this stage, the child's thought remains rooted to concrete objects and events, centered primarily on things that exist, and lacking any true notions of abstraction.

The development within this stage of concrete operations can be seen by giving the child two small balls of modeling clay of the same size and weight. One ball is then shaped like a long sausage. Before the age of 7 (before concrete operations), the child believes that the amounts of matter, weight, and volume have all changed. At 7 or 8, he believes that matter is constant, but that weight and volume still change. Around 9, he recognizes that both matter and weight are unchanged, but he still thinks volume differs. It is not until he is 11–12 years old that all three concepts are seen as stable.

Finally, starting around the age of 11, the child begins the last stages in the transition to the full logical power of the human brain. During the early years of adolescence his language powers will become perfected, logical operations will appear, the laws of propositional arguments and implication will be learned, and he will begin to demonstrate abstract, hypothetical reasoning.

Formal operations

Table 13-1   Piaget's Periods of Intellectual Development in the Child

Approximate age (years)	Description
0–2	**Sensorimotor Development** Development of sensorimotor schemata. Learns of object permanence and actions. Limited to operations that actually affect the world
2–7	**Preoperational Thought** Language development starts. Learns to activate sensorimotor schemata mentally, without actually performing actions—mental experiments possible. Limited to concrete actions primarily dealing with events of present. Operations are egocentric, irreversible
7–11	**Concrete Operations** Logical deduction starts. Can manipulate concrete ideas. Still egocentric (but less so), still limited to possible events. Concepts of conservation, reversibility, and compensation are developed
11–15	**Formal Operations** Development of implication, abstraction, propositional logic, capable of mental hypothesis testing

A prerequisite of the ability to think is the construction of internal representations of external events. The processes involved in organizing and structuring perceptual information into sensorimotor schemata are invaluable aids to higher mental processes. Once internal structures are available, the thought processes are freed from dependence on the environment. With an internal representation of the world it is not necessary

THINKING

to actually execute an action in order to determine its consequences. Instead, the entire sequence of events can be anticipated through a mental simulation: Mental simulation is the essence of thought.

Consider some of the advantages of working from an internal representation. The human thinker can start with some desired goal and mentally work backward through his internal structures, hoping thereby to discover the possible actions that lead to his goal and the conditions required.

The internal sensorimotor schemata can provide a selective filter for attention and perception: They tell a person what to look for, they lead him to examine the features of the environment that are available, as well as to discover those that are missing. Missing conditions can be treated as subgoals, thus providing a method of discovering the sensorimotor schemata that might be appropriate for obtaining them. Expectations can play a central role even when failures occur. They can specify the crucial information that is needed for the intelligent selection of a new response action whenever an old one fails to produce the desired result.

Do lower organisms have the capabilities to plan? We do not know for sure. Certainly they are capable of following through relatively complex chains of actions, but the extent to which the anticipation of future events governs their current responses is difficult to determine. In the first 2 years of life, the human infant is developing sensorimotor intelligence, and he shows only the beginnings of such planning activities. For the most part, animals and infants below the age of 2 seem to rely largely on trying out responses to see what will happen, rather than starting with a distant goal and working out a strategy for achieving it.

Thought requires the ability to simulate whole scenarios mentally, to hypothesize new possibilities, and to manipulate them symbolically. The same basic abilities required for the development and manipulation of sensorimotor schemata are pertinent to all levels of thought. In our study of problem-solving behavior in adults (Chapter 14) and of decision making (Chapters 15 and 16), we shall see that the solutions to the problem situations involve a series of real and mental actions and consequences, with various choice points arising during progression through the problem.

SUGGESTED
READINGS

By far the most important influence on the study of intellectual development has come from the laboratories of Jean Piaget in Geneva. A prolific investigator, Piaget has turned out scores of studies spelling out the stages of development that a child must pass through on his way from early infancy through adulthood. It is clear that anyone wishing to pursue the topics developed in this chapter must read Piaget. But how? Piaget does not make life easy for his readers. His writings (in French) are difficult to follow. Even when he is translated into English, his books are often rough going. Moreover, there is an enormous quantity of them: One bibliography (Flavell, 1963) lists 136 books, chapters, and articles by Piaget in the period between the early 1920s and early 1960s. We have found it useful to approach Piaget in easy steps.

The easiest introduction that we have found is the small book by Phillips (1969: paperback). From there, you might wish to go to the collection of six essays collected together into a smaller book (Piaget, 1967: paperback). This is an especially good introduction to Piaget, since it gives you him directly without benefit of interpretation. Moreover, the editor (Elkind) and the translator (Tenzer) have been especially good at making his writing easy for the reader. The only quarrel we would have with this book is that it does not give the full flavor of Piaget's approach to the study of psychology, since it leaves out the lengthy, small-print records of the speech and actions of the children that he is observing, which play so prominent a role in his books. Nonetheless, it is a good start. The best, most complete treatment of Piaget is given in Flavell's book (1963). This is a very thorough book on Piaget's works and various theoretical positions, and although it is technical enough that you may wish to work up to it by reading the two books we have just mentioned first, it is an excellent treatment. Piaget himself seems to approve of the book, although he views Flavell's emphasis on experimentation—and the critique of his methods—with some disfavor, treating it as a typical response of the experimentally oriented American psychologist. (See the foreword by Piaget in Flavell's book.)

If you have come this far and still wish to know more about Piaget, then it is time to read his works directly. The works mentioned so far should give you ample bibliographic sources for reading of Piaget, but we found for ourselves that the single most important book was his *The Origins of Intelligence in Children* (1952). A good number of Piaget's works are available, translated in English, and in paperback, published by Norton and Co.: Piagets' *The Child's Conception of Number, The Origins of Intelligence in Children,* and Piaget and Inhelder's *The Child's Conception of Space.*

Flavell and his colleagues have studied extensively the development of role playing in children, and especially the child's egocentricity (Flavell, 1966; Flavell, Botkin, Fry, Wright, & Jarvis, 1968). Smedslund has a series of six papers on the child's acquisition of conservation and reversibility (Smedslund, 1961a–f). A different view is presented by Bruner (1964). A thorough source for the studies in the development of children is in the *Handbook of Child Psychology*, edited in two volumes by Mussen (1970). Some of our material on children's reasoning and thinking was taken from the chapter by Berlyne (1970) in that handbook.

Adult intellectual behavior has not been extensively reviewed in this chapter—the next three chapters will cover adult behavior. The classic work is that of Bruner, Goodnow, and Austin, *A Study of Thinking* (1956). Miller, Galanter, and Pribram's *Plans and the Structure of Behavior* (1960) is another important source. A very thorough review of the literature on thinking is provided in the book by Bourne, Ekstrand, and Dominowski (1971). We find the book somewhat ponderous, but it probably contains all relevant references. Saltz's book (1971) is much more enjoyable (see our comment in the final paragraph). You should also see our suggested readings following the chapters on language (Chapter 12) and on problem solving (Chapter 14).

Principles of learning An excellent introduction to operant conditioning, both technique and philosophy, is provided by Rachlin's *Introduction to Modern Behaviorism* (1970: paperback). This is perhaps the best book to read to get a fuller appreciation of the operant conditioner's methods and philosophies. In addition, the book contains references to specific aspects of learning. Another good review, more advanced and more difficult to read, but very thorough and complete is *A Primer of Operant Conditioning* by Reynolds (1968). Skinner's works can be read most easily in *Science and Human Behavior* (1953) and in his collection of papers and thoughts, *Cumulative Record* (1961). None of these sources is very sympathetic to the cognitive philosophies espoused in this chapter.

A description of many different learning theories can be found in Hilgard and Bower, *Theories of Learning* (1966). A complete survey of both operant and classical conditioning at a more advanced level is available in Kimble's *Hilgard and Marquis' Conditioning and Learning* (1961). Descriptions of the techniques and discussions of apparatus used in learning experiments are described in considerable detail in three chapters of Sidowski's *Experimental Methods and Instrumentation in Psychology* (1966).

Many problems in learning theory are beginning to show, primarily in the generality of the laws of learning. Two excellent critical articles are the general discussion on learning by Seligman (1970), and the description of some interesting problems given by Breland and Breland (1966). The work on specific aversions to foods after nausea, an important new problem in the study of learning, is by Garcia. Start with Garcia and Koelling (1966): Seligman both discusses this problem and gives further references. A discussion on the Law of Effect which interprets a reinforcement not as **increasing** the response that is reinforced, but rather as **decreasing** all of the others in a paradigm closely related to that of selective evolution is given by Staddon and Simmelhag (1971). A discussion of the use of direct electrical stimulation of the brain as a reinforcing outcome is discussed by Black in the *American Scientist* (1971).

The experiments on "learned helplessness" with animals were performed by Seligman, Maier, and Solomon and they are most easily found in any of three sources: Seligman's *Psychology Today* article (June 1969—this considers the problems of human schizophrenics); or at a more advanced level, either Maier, Seligman, and Solomon (1969), or Seligman *et al.* (1969). The experiment on humans was done by Thornton and Jacobs (1971). The "hypothesis" theory of Levine (1971) is almost identical to the explanation we have used here. His is an important paper, with implications for many problems, not just that of helplessness.

The book by Saltz, *The Cognitive Bases of Human Learning* (1971) is an interesting treatment of human learning and thought that will act somewhat as an antidote to the heavily noncognitive approach of most of the references on learning that we have listed so far.

14

Problem solving

Just what must be done in order to solve a problem? In this chapter we examine the strategies and procedures that people use. Problems come in two broad classes: problems that are well defined and those that are ill defined. A well-defined problem is one that has a clearly stated goal. Thus:

- What is the best route to the other side of town when all the main streets are closed because of the parade?
- What is the solution to the chess problem from last night's paper: white to checkmate in four moves?
- What were you doing 16 months ago?

These problems have well-defined attributes: a definite goal, a definite way to tell whether the problem solving is proceeding in the correct direction. Ill-defined problems are, perhaps, more frequent.

- Direct the filming of the most meaningful movie of the century.
- Make something significant of your life.
- Create a permanently lasting work of art.

We concentrate our study on the well-defined problem for good reason. The goal is to understand the processes a person uses in working through to the solution of a problem. We wish to understand how he constructs his internal model of the problem, what strategies he uses, what rules he follows. We want to see how he assesses his progress as he moves toward a solution. The results of these investigations should apply to all problem-solving behavior, be the problems ill or well defined.

Some of the basic principles of problem solving behavior have already been introduced. In the study of sensorimotor intelligence, we discussed the notion of selecting behavior based on an expected goal, of following through a chain of sensorimotor schemata to discover the end result of a possible action sequence, of starting with the final goal and working backward to form a plan for achieving that goal. We were exploring how these strategies were applied to practical environmental problems. Now we shall see the same procedures emerge as we study how people attempt to solve abstract conceptual problems.

Perhaps the best way to begin is to examine a problem. It will help in the analysis if you have an idea of the steps and operations that are being discussed. Attempt to solve the problem described below. Working on the problem will give you a feel for the tactics you use and the decisions involved, even if you cannot solve it. *Think aloud* as you work, saying all the thoughts that come to mind. Spend at

THE ANATOMY OF
A PROBLEM

least 5 min at the problem, even if it does not appear that you are
making progress. Remember, the important thing about this analysis
is to discover the types of mental operations that people do. It really
does not matter whether the problem ever gets solved.

$$\begin{array}{r} \text{DONALD} \qquad \text{D} = 5 \\ + \text{GERALD} \\ \hline \text{ROBERT} \end{array}$$

This is a problem in crypt arithmetic. In the expression, there
are ten letters, each representing a different, distinct digit. The
problem is to discover what digit should be assigned to each letter,
so that when the letters are all replaced by their corresponding
digits, the arithmetic is correct.

Please speak aloud all that you are thinking as you attempt
to solve the problem. You may write down anything you wish.

Protocols   The first step in the investigation of any phenomenon is to observe
the behavior associated with it. The obvious difficulty in studying human
problem solving is that much of what goes on is not directly observable:
People go through their internal mental operations quietly by themselves.
One way of getting around this difficulty is to have people make their
thought processes available to others by asking them to describe aloud
what they are doing as they attempt to solve a problem. The result
is a word-by-word compilation of their verbalized thought processes,
a *verbal protocol*. Clearly, although there are difficulties in interpreting
these protocols, they provide extremely useful initial information about
the thought processes involved in problem solving.

We shall analyze a small part of the verbal protocol of a subject
who was attempting to solve the DONALD plus GERALD problem.
This particular subject was a male college student at Carnegie–Mellon
University, who was given instructions about the problem similar to
those given here, and then asked to think aloud as he attempted to
find a solution. The complete transcription of his verbal descriptions
consisted of some 2200 words produced over the 20-min problem-solving
period. This was the first time this subject had tried to solve this type
of problem.[1]

The protocol from   **Each letter has one and only one numerical value—**
DONALD +
GERALD   (This is a question to the experimenter, who responds, "One
numerical value.")

[1] The problem, the analysis, and the quotations that follow all come from the
work of Newell (1967).

There are ten different letters and each of them has one numerical value.

Therefore, I can, looking at the 2 D's—each D is 5; therefore, T is zero. So I think I'll start by writing that problem here. I'll write 5, 5 is zero.

Now, do I have any other T's? No. But I have another D. That means I have a 5 over the other side.

Now I have 2 A's and 2 L's that are each—somewhere—and this R—3 R's. Two L's equal an R. Of course, I'm carrying a 1 which will mean that R has to be an odd number because the 2 L's—any two numbers added together has to be an even number and 1 will be an odd number. So R can be 1, 3, not 5, 7, or 9.

(At this point there is a long pause, so the experimenter asks, "What are you thinking now?")

Now G—since R is going to be an odd number and D is 5, G has to be an even number.

I'm looking at the left side of this problem here where it says D + G. Oh, plus possibly another number, if I have to carry 1 from the E + O. I think I'll forget about that for a minute.

Possibly the best way to get this problem is to try different possible solutions. I'm not sure whether that would be the easiest way or not.

The analysis. These words, then, are our data. What principles can be discovered from them? The first impression from such a protocol is that the problem solver is not proceeding in a straightforward, direct manner. Rather, he accumulates information by trying various hypotheses to see where they take him. He frequently encounters dead ends, backs up, and tries another tack. Look at the protocol. He starts off energetically and discovers first that $T = \emptyset$. (we write zero as $\emptyset$ to avoid confusion with the letter **O**).

Therefore, I can, looking at the 2 D's—each D is 5; therefore T is zero. So I think I'll start by writing that problem here. I'll write 5, 5 is zero.

He then looks to see if his knowledge that $T = \emptyset$ and $D = 5$ can be of any use elsewhere in the problem. He looks for a **T**.

Now, do I have any other T's? No.

This failed; how about **D**?

But I have another D. That means I have a 5 over the other side.

Having noted this fact, he finds another spot in the problem that seems promising.

Now I have 2 A's and 2 L's that are each—somewhere—and this R—3 R's.

Two L's equal an R. Of course, I'm carrying a 1 which will mean that R has to be an odd number. . .

Even though he has now deduced that R is an odd number, he then goes back over that again, as if to check the reasoning:

. . . because the two L's—any two numbers added together has to be an even number and 1 will be an odd number.

But this time he pursues his reasoning a little further and explicitly lists the possible numbers:

So R can be 1, 3, not 5, 7, or 9.

He abandons this route, however (after a long pause), evidently because there is no obvious way of selecting the particular value for R out of the possible candidates. Once again he returns to the basic idea that R is odd; does this give any information about G:

Now G—since R is going to be an odd number and D is 5, G has to be an even number.

This brief analysis of the first few minutes of the protocol is enough to reveal some general patterns in the subject's problem-solving behavior. He knows the overall goal he is trying to reach. The first thing he does, however, is to break down the final goal into a number of smaller steps. He then proceeds by successively trying out a variety of simple strategies, each of which he hopes will yield some information. Some strategies work, and so more and more data are accumulated. Other strategies do not seem to work; in this case, the subject backs up and tries a different line of approach.

This is a description that applies to a wide variety of problem solving and cognitive tasks. The same general principles appeared in the application of sensorimotor intelligence to practical problems. But our description so far leaves us with a set of unanswered questions. What is involved in breaking the overall goal down into a set of smaller, simpler steps? How does the subject know what kinds of strategies will be useful in solving the problem? How does he choose a particular strategy to apply at a particular moment? How does he know whether the strategy he is using is moving toward the solution rather than up a blind alley? To answer these questions, we need a better procedure for analyzing protocols.

Verbal protocols are clumsy to deal with. To study the problem-solving process in more detail, we need some method of representing the events that take place. A useful technique is to construct a visual picture of the sequence of operations going on during problem solving. One such technique available for this purpose is the *problem behavior graph*, a method developed by Allen Newell of the Carnegie–Mellon University of graphing the subject's progress through a problem (see Simon & Newell, 1971).

The problem behavior graph

States of knowledge. We noted from the protocol that the subject gradually accumulates new information about the problem by applying rules or strategies. He operates on his existing knowledge and the statement of the problem to add to his knowledge. All the information the subject knows about the problem at any moment is called his *state of knowledge*. Each time he applies some *operation* to some new fact, he changes his state of knowledge. A description of his problem-solving behavior, then, should trace out this progression in the subject's states of knowledge. To do this in the diagram, represent a state of knowledge by a box, and the operation that takes the subject from one state of knowledge to another by an arrow, as shown in Figure 14-1.

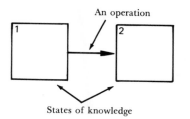

FIGURE 14-1

The protocol then is represented by boxes and arrows that describe the path taken by the subject through successive states of knowledge. To illustrate this, consider again the protocol for the DONALD + GERALD task.

The graph for DONALD + GERALD. For the first few statements, the subject simply is verifying that he understands the rules of the task. The first actual deduction does not occur until the statement:

> Therefore, I can, looking at the 2 D's—each D is 5; therefore, T is zero.

The subject clearly is processing the information in a single column, the one that reads $D + D = T$. Call this operation *process column 1*. (Number the six columns of the problem from right to left.) The operation moves the subject from his initial state of knowledge (where he knows that $D = 5$) to a new state, state 2, in which he also knows that $T = \emptyset$ (we write zero as $\emptyset$ to avoid confusion with the letter O). Does the subject also realize that there must be a carry into column 2, the next column on the left? So far, from the information in this protocol, we cannot tell. Looking ahead, however, we see, **Of course, I'm carrying a 1,** so he does know this fact. The problem behavior graph up to this time shows two states of knowledge, as shown in Figure 14-2.

FIGURE 14-2

The next several statements in the protocol are concerned with the act of writing down what has been learned so far. Then there is an attempt to get a new column, either one with T or one with D. The first operation to **get new column (T)** is unsuccessful, the second succeeds in finding another D. The problem behavior graph has progressed slightly, as shown in Figure 14-3 (the old states are unshaded: The one added since the last diagram is shaded).

FIGURE 14-3

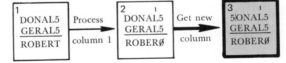

At this point, the subject again chooses to get a new column, trying first column 3, then 2.

> **Now I have 2 A's and 2 L's that are each—somewhere—and this R—3 R's.**

This gets him to the point where it is worthwhile to *process column 2*, moving him from state 4 to state 5, where he concludes that **R is odd.** The progression is shown in Figure 14-4.

FIGURE 14-4

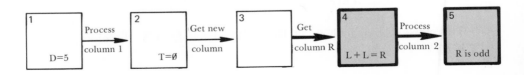

Backing up. Now the subject backs up. Notice this sequence. First, at state 5 he says

> Two L's equal an R. Of course, I'm carrying a 1 which will mean that R has to be an odd number . . .

But then, he decides to generate the actual possibilities for numbers, and to do this he backs up to state 4 and tries a new approach.

> . . . because the 2 L's—any two numbers added together has to be an even number and 1 will be an odd number. So R can be 1, 3, not 5, 7, or 9.

To illustrate the backing-up process, the next state, state 6, comes off of state 4. This is done in Figure 14-5 by showing the transition to state 6 by a vertical line from state 4. State 6 is simply the same as state 4, only at a later point in time. At state 7, the subject has again regenerated the fact that **R is odd**, and in state 8, he methodically tests all odd numbers.

FIGURE 14-5

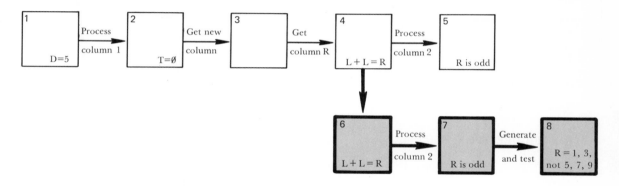

Note that when the subject generates the candidates for **R**, he does a thorough job and does not exclude the values already used. Thus, he explicitly generates and then rejects the possibility that **R = 5**. He did not simply skip over that possibility.

The next part of the record illustrates the experimental difficulties of getting protocols. The subject did not say anything, so the experimenter was forced to interrupt and ask him to speak. The result is that there is no evidence about how the possible values of **R** have been used. Rather, the process seems to have backed up again, this time going to column 6 with the fact that **R is odd** and that **D is 5**, concluding that **G** must be even. This takes us to state 10.

> Now **G**—since **R** is going to be an odd number and **D** is 5, **G** has to be an even number.

This deduction is not correct, but nevertheless, at the point represented by state 10, it describes the actual state of knowledge of the subject (see Figure 14-6). The possibility that **G** need not be even is recognized rather quickly in this case.

I'm looking at the left side of this problem here where it says D + G. Oh, plus possibly another number, if I have to carry 1 from the E + O. I think I'll forget about that for a minute.

This last statement indicates another start at processing column 6, ending up at state 12 and the knowledge that there may be a carry, and then the decision to back up once again and forget about the value for **G**. This concludes our analysis of this segment of the problem. This segment of the problem behavior graph is shown in Figure 14-6.

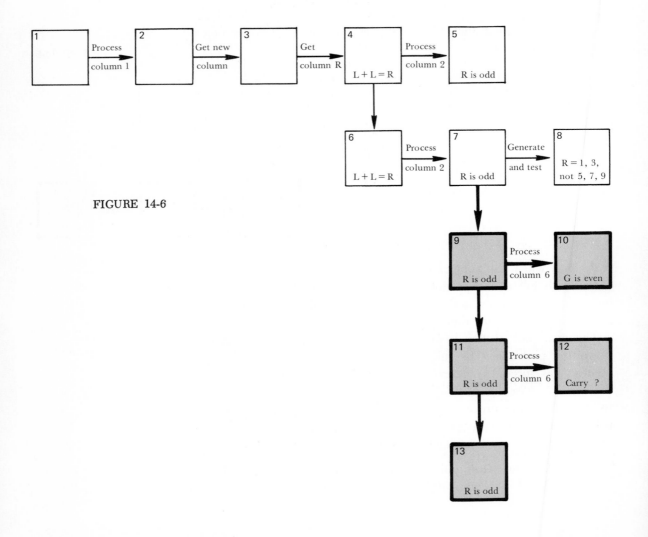

FIGURE 14-6

The short segment of the protocol just analyzed illustrates a method for decomposing and representing the steps involved in solving a problem. Here (Figure 14-7), in schematic form, is what the entire graph looks like when the protocol for the complete 20 min the subject spent on the task is represented.[2]

In analyzing the complete protocol, the same rules appear. The subject seems to have only a very small set of strategies, which he used repeatedly. In the full analysis of this subject, there were over 200 transitions among states of knowledge, yet only four different operations were needed to describe how he got from any one state to the next.

The problem-behavior graph is one method of dissecting the stages of problem solving, decomposing the process into a series of small steps. It graphically illustrates the mixture of successes and failures that go on in a problem-solving task. This general form of analysis and pattern of behavior seems to apply to a wide variety of problem situations. Certainly, the specific rules a subject uses depend on the particular nature of the problem he is solving, but the overall structure of his problem solving behavior is quite similar. The subject reorganizes the overall problem into a set of simpler subgoals or subproblems. At any given time, his progress can be summarized in a state of knowledge. It represents the information he has accumulated up to that point. He proceeds from one state of knowledge to the next by attempting to apply a particular operation selected from a small set of operations. If successful, he obtains new information, and thus moves to a new state of knowledge. His course is erratic, involving continual trial-and-error, testing the effectiveness of various operators, backtracking when a sequence of operations leads to a dead end and beginning once again. To describe his behavior, the notions of goals, states of knowledge, and operators have been introduced. Let us consider how these notions apply to problem solving in general.

If the puzzle you solved before you solved this one was harder than the puzzle you solved after you solved the puzzle you solved before you solved this one, was the puzzle you solved before you solved this one harder than this one? [Restle, 1969]

STRATEGIES OF
PROBLEM SOLVING

[2] *Using the graph.* To read these graphs, always start at the upper left-hand box and go horizontally to the right. When the end of that line is reached, back up to the first downward line and go down one level. Then again go horizontally to the right. Keep doing these steps, careful never to repeat, until all the paths have been covered. The rule: **Follow the graph as far to the right as possible, then back up to the first new vertical line and go down one step. Repeat as many times as necessary.**

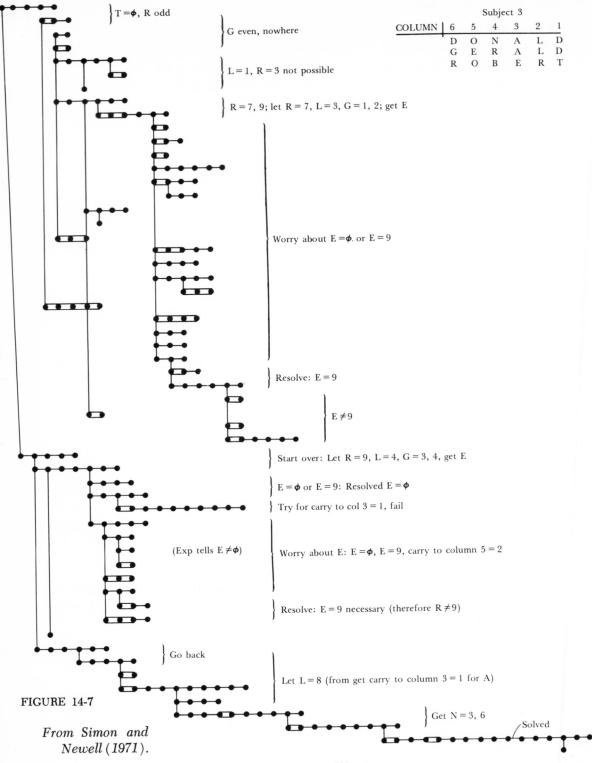

FIGURE 14-7

From Simon and Newell (1971).

T = φ, R odd

G even, nowhere

L = 1, R = 3 not possible

R = 7, 9; let R = 7, L = 3, G = 1, 2; get E

Worry about E = φ. or E = 9

Resolve: E = 9

E ≠ 9

Start over: Let R = 9, L = 4, G = 3, 4, get E

E = φ or E = 9: Resolved E = φ

Try for carry to col 3 = 1, fail

(Exp tells E ≠ φ)   Worry about E: E = φ, E = 9, carry to column 5 = 2

Resolve: E = 9 necessary (therefore R ≠ 9)

Go back

Let L = 8 (from get carry to column 3 = 1 for A)

Get N = 3, 6

Solved

238 states

Subject 3

COLUMN	6	5	4	3	2	1
	D	O	N	A	L	D
	G	E	R	A	L	D
	R	O	B	E	R	T

The **final goal** of this puzzle is clear: to produce an answer, yes or no. But if we simply start off working forward through the sentence from beginning to end, we quickly get bogged down in the complex linguistic structure. A *forward search* for a solution is not going to work. What about a *backward search?* Start at the goal—to answer yes or no—then ask what is needed to achieve that goal. Clearly, one strategy that should be helpful is to break the problem up into *subgoals*, so that it becomes manageable. For example, a specific subgoal might be simply to try to understand each phrase in the statement. Now what would be a good operator for achieving this subgoal?

One way to proceed is to attach labels, such as a different letter, to represent each different puzzle. Then any phrase that refers to a puzzle could be relabeled by the appropriate puzzle letter. The phrase, **this one,** is clearly equivalent to the phrase, **this puzzle,** or, to give it a name, **puzzle A.** Hence,

this puzzle = this one = puzzle A

and by making the substitutions, the problem can be restated as

> **If the puzzle you solved before you solved puzzle A was harder than the puzzle you solved after you solved the puzzle you solved before you solved puzzle A, was the puzzle you solved before you solved puzzle A harder than puzzle A?**

That worked pretty well, so try it again. Transform every occurrence of the phrase, **the puzzle you solved before you solved puzzle A,** into the phrase **puzzle B.** This substitution gives a new version of the problem:

> **If puzzle B was harder than the puzzle you solved after you solved puzzle B, was puzzle B harder than puzzle A?**

One phrase still remains to be interpreted: **the puzzle you solved after you solved puzzle B.** According to the previously used transformation, the puzzle prior to A must be puzzle B. Hence, by reversing the transformation, the puzzle that followed after puzzle B must be puzzle A. Thus, the phrase, **the puzzle you solved after you solved puzzle B,** should be labeled **puzzle A.** Now the problem is trivial:

> **If puzzle B was harder than puzzle A, was puzzle B harder than puzzle A?**

This example demonstrates some of the basic strategies humans apply in their attempts to solve problems. Most problems involve some aspect of **forward search.** That is, first one simply tries out some method of

Searching for solutions

attack and then decides whether progress has been made. If so, you keep going from where the previous step left off. The process is something like the way a stream of water meanders down the hillside. The water simply starts to flow in all downward directions: the unique configuration of the land determines the exact path the water follows. The important aspect is that the search progresses from the start to the finish, using simple, direct steps. In this particular puzzle, a simple forward search did not work.

A second approach is to **work backward.** Here one looks at the desired solution and asks what the previous step must have been to have arrived there. Then, from that step, the one just prior to it is determined, and so on, hopefully back to the starting point given in the original specification of the problem. Working backward is very useful in some visual problems, such as looking at a map in order to decide the route from one location to another.

In working backward, progress is made in small steps. A **subgoal** is defined, and an attempt is made to solve the subproblem. At this point, a strategy, perhaps the most powerful one, enters in: the *means–ends analysis*. In the means–ends analysis the desired subgoal—the end—is compared with the present state of knowledge. The problem is to find an operator—a means—that will reduce the difference. In the puzzle problem, the end was to understand a phrase in the sentence; the state of knowledge was a complex linguistic structure. The means of reducing the difference between the two was to simplify the phrases by labeling them appropriately. This is only one example of the means–ends analysis. The same strategy is applicable to many varieties of problem solving behavior, often with unexpected success.

Selecting operators   How did we come up with the idea of relabeling a complex phrase with a letter in order to simplify the puzzle problem? Clearly, one of the main problems for a human is finding the particular operators that will work in a situation. Breaking up the overall problem into subgoals is useful for setting the problem up. The means–end analysis is useful for evaluating whether a given operator will make some progress toward the solution. But none of these tactics tells us which operator we should be considering.

Heuristics.   The mathematician Polya (1945) suggests that to solve a problem:

> **First, we must understand the problem. We must clearly understand the goal, the conditions imposed upon us, and the data. Second, we must devise a plan to guide us to the solution.**

But the crux of the matter is to devise the appropriate plan, the operators that will, in fact, guide us toward a solution.

In the study of problem solving, plans or operators are divided into two types: *algorithms* and *heuristics*. The distinction between the two is whether the plan is guaranteed to produce the correct result. An algorithm is a set of rules which, if followed, will automatically generate the correct solution. The rules for multiplication constitute an algorithm; if you use them properly, you always get the right answer. Heuristics are more analogous to rules of thumb; they are procedures or outlines for searching for solutions which are relatively easy to use and are often based on their effectiveness in solving previous problems. Unlike algorithms, however, heuristic methods do not guarantee success. For many of the more complicated and more interesting problems, the appropriate algorithms have not been discovered and may not even exist. In these cases, we resort to heuristics.

A very important heuristic device is to find **analogies** between the present problem and ones for which the solution is known. Often, this requires a bit of skill in recognizing the similarities and a bit of subterfuge in ignoring obvious differences. Solution by analogy is extremely valuable, even if the analogy is far-fetched. The danger, of course, is that one can think there are similarities where in fact there are none, causing much wasted time and effort before the error is realized and a new approach tried.

Heuristics come into play in any complex, problem-solving situation. In fact, much of the study of thinking and problem solving involves a search for the kinds of heuristics people use. The role of heuristic strategies is best understood by considering a specific example.

Chess playing. Chess manuals do not give a prescription guaranteed to lead to success. Rather, they contain heuristic rules:

> **Try to control the four center squares.**
> **Make sure your king is safe.**

In fact, the differences among chess players seem to lie mainly in the power and efficiency of the heuristic schemes they employ while playing the game (see Simon & Simon, 1962). A good place to examine the operation of these rules is with the *endgame*—the last few moves of a game, just before a checkmate (an attack on the opponent's king from which it is impossible to escape). Some endgames start out a full eight moves before the actual checkmate takes place.

If we consider all the possible moves and counter moves that are available at any given stage in a chess game, there are about a thousand combinations that could conceivably take place. The number of possible sequences of eight moves, then, would be 1000^8 (a million billion billion, if you care to spell it out). Were we to try to devise an algorithm for evaluating the best one of these possible combinations, we would have to explore literally billions of different possibilities. The sheer effort involved would overload even the largest high speed computer.

A chess player clearly does not try to follow through all possible combinations to their conclusion. He considers the possible moves in a very selective fashion, and seems to restrict himself to considering only those moves that would seem to produce important results. How does he know which of the millions of possible moves should be considered in detail?

Several studies of chess experts—those who have reached the internationally recognized level of *Grand Master*—suggest that chess masters use a number of heuristic rules to examine and select moves. The rules are ordered in terms of importance, and this order is used to discriminate among promising moves. A sample of some of the heuristics used by chess Grand Masters gives an indication of how their search for appropriate operators is guided:

- Give highest priority to *double checks* (moves that attack the king with two or more pieces simultaneously) and *discovered checks* (moves that take another man out of a piece's line of attack).
- If there is an alternative, use the most powerful piece to make the check (the power of a piece depends on the flexibility of moves that can be made).
- Give priority to moves that leave the opponent with the least possible number of replies.
- Give priority to a check that adds a new attacker to the list of active pieces.
- Give priority to a check that takes the opponent's king farthest from its base.

These are simple rules. When they are applied to a number of standard chess ending situations (taken from one of the standard books on chess), they succeed in a large number of cases. Of more importance, they succeed without requiring too much memory capability on the part of the player: He need only consider from 9 to 77 possibilities in the *exploration phase* of reaching the solution, and from 5 to 19 possibilities in the *verification phase*, when he checks that his combination of moves is indeed valid and sound. Since the solution of some of these problems might take a chess Grand Master some 15 min to discover, they would not seem to require a great mental capacity of him at any one time. In fact, the task would appear to be equivalent to that of spending

15 min in memorizing a grammatical English selection of 75 to 100 words (the preceding three sentences, for example). The differences among chess players of different ability would appear to lie in the efficiency of the selective heuristic schemes they have developed, rather than in sheer mental capacity.

Starting with a subject's verbalization of his thoughts while problem solving, we have been able to discover quite a bit about the nature of the processes involved. Moreover, protocol analysis need not be limited to pure problem-solving situations. When a clinical psychologist attempts to analyze his patient, the procedures he follows are based on a somewhat less formal analysis of his patient's protocol, but the philosophy is quite similar. He tries to deduce the nature of the internal operations in the memory structure by following the paths the subject takes as reflected in his verbal outputs.

There are dangers that result from too heavy a reliance on the protocol generated by the subject. An example of the problem comes from one of the earlier studies of reasoning (Maier, 1931). In this experiment two cords hung from the ceiling of a room. The subject's task was to tie the strings together, but it was impossible for him to reach both at the same time.

Limitations of the protocol analysis

FIGURE 14-8

A number of solutions were possible by clever use of the various objects scattered deliberately but inconspicuously throughout the room. Only one solution was of interest to Maier, however, and he explored the hints needed to get his subjects to come up with it. (We deliberately will not tell you the answer, so that you can try the task yourself.) The experimenter (who was in the room with the subject) used two different hints.

Hint 1. The experimenter walked about the room, and, in passing the cord which hung from the center of the room, he put it in slight motion a few times. This was done without the subject knowing that a suggestion was being given. The experimenter merely walked to the window and had to pass the cord.

Hint 2. In case hint 1 failed to bring about the solution within a few minutes, the subject was handed a pair of pliers and told, "With the aid of this and no other object, there is another way of solving the problem." [The description of the hints is Maier's, as outlined in the original article (1931).]

Maier divided the subjects who successfully solved the problem after receiving the hints into two groups—those who appeared to solve the problem as a whole ("The solution just came to me; I don't know how"), and those who seemed to go through a series of steps to the solution ("Let's see, if I could move the cord, . . . throw things at it, . . . blow at it, . . . swing it like a pendulum . . . aha!"). The interesting difference between these two groups, from our point of view, is the difference between the subjects' reported use of the hint. Those who solved the problem as a whole failed to report that the hint was of any use to them, while the group that progressed through stages reported (with but one exception) that the hint was an aid. Our question is whether the "whole" subjects actually used the hint without being aware of it. If this is so, then we would expect that protocols taken during problem solving might miss many of the steps involved in arriving at a solution.

First, it is clear that the subjects who failed to report the use of the hint in fact solved the problem much quicker than the group for which no hints were given. On the average, the majority of subjects found the solution within less than a minute after the hint was given. When no hints were given, only 20% of the subjects found the solution, even though they were allowed to work on the problem for half an hour. Did the "whole" subjects notice the hint but were perhaps simply unwilling to admit that they used it? This seems unlikely. Subjects who solved the problem in steps seemed to have no hesitancy in referring to the hint as they described their solution. Why should the "whole" subjects hold back? The conclusion seems to be that the hint played an important part in bringing about the solution, even though the subjects were not consciously aware of its role. If the subject does not realize such an obvious step in his protocol behavior, then our protocol records are going to be incomplete.

We must assume, then, that as the subject works on a problem, he is proceeding through a series of strategies and operations which are reflected in his verbal description of his own mental operations. The steps going on internally, however, are not all faithfully represented in the verbal output. What we can observe will only be a partial description of the actual internal processes.

The conclusion, then, is that only a portion of the subject's cognitive activities is going to be available for external examination. The record will be most complete if the subject is encouraged to verbalize his detailed thought processes, and if the protocol is taken during the actual performance of the activity. Even Maier's "whole" subjects might have been aware of their use of the hint if they had been told beforehand to monitor their thought processes and to talk aloud as they groped for a solution. Despite its shortcomings, the protocol analysis is a powerful tool in attempting to reconstruct the events that go on during problem solving and to explore the kinds of cognitive strategies that operate in these complex tasks.

INTERNAL STATES VERSUS PROTOCOL STATES

One illustration of the problem comes from considering the differences between the three different problem-spaces: internal, protocol, and external. We presume that the subject works out the problem internally, according to some overall strategies and operations, hopefully similar to the ones analyzed in the problem-behavior graph. This solution is represented in the *internal space,* and there are no ways of making direct measurements on it. The verbal responses the subject produces when he speaks aloud as he solves the problem—the protocol—are a record of the *protocol space.* In addition, the subject writes down things or tries some actions as he progresses through the problem, generating the *external space.*

Consider how these three spaces might be related to one another. The internal space can be diagramed in the form of a program-behavior graph. On the next page is an example of an internal space that has 22 states. But the subject might verbalize only some of the internal states in his protocol—the states shown by shading. In this case, only 13 of the 22 states

FIGURE 14-9   INTERNAL SPACE

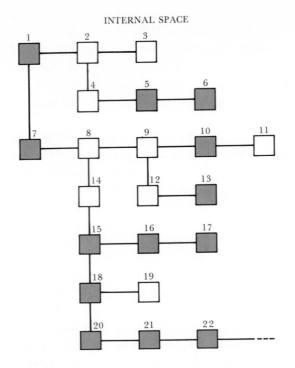

would appear in his protocol. A problem-behavior graph for the protocol space, then, would look something like this:

FIGURE 14-10   PROTOCOL SPACE

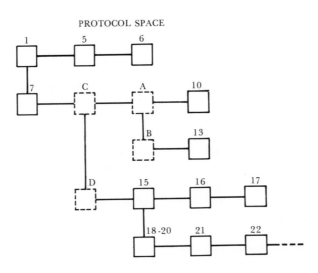

You can see what happens. From the protocol space it appears as though the subject goes directly from state 1 to states 5 and 6. The intermediate states of 2 and 4 and the blind alley that was followed, the path to state

3, are missed completely. In addition, states 10 and 13 both follow from state 7. Often, an analysis of the protocol suggests that something is missing. In this example, the protocol does not make complete sense: States 10 and 13 do not follow from each other and neither one follows directly from 7. In that case it is possible to infer some hypothetical states, namely states A and B. We know they are necessary, but because they are not recorded in the protocol, we can only guess at their existence. Similarly, state 18 gets lost, because it cannot be distinguished from state 20.

The final graph that is constructed from the protocol does bear resemblance to the internal state, but it certainly is not a complete portrayal of the processes

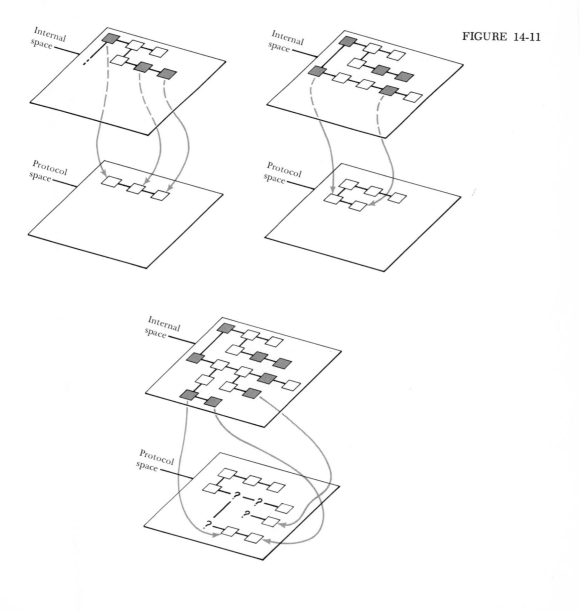

FIGURE 14-11

that went on. One way of visualizing the relationships of the internal and protocol states is to assume that the internal processes occasionally give a protocol output. As the subject progresses through the states internally, he generates a condensed version at the behavioral level of his internal thought processes.

Figure 14-11

THE MACHINERY OF
THOUGHT

The strategies for solving problems that we have been discussing depend on the general nature and organization of human brain-processes. Moreover, these general organizational principles must apply to all systems that store, retrieve, and use knowledge—whether they are electronic or biological systems. Any system that interacts with a dynamic world requires the storage and manipulation of information, and this produces fundamental problems common to all such systems.

Because of this generality, it is fruitful to question the organizational principles and structures of all information systems in our attempt to discover the principles of the human brain. The emphasis is on the word **principle.** The details of the way various functions are executed and the actual machinery used to execute them are irrelevant. When we are able to determine that a system uses a means–end heuristic to solve a problem, it does not matter whether that system is composed of neurons, integrated electronic circuits, or gears and levers: The heuristic is still the same in all cases.

In studying the structure of an information-processing system, there are several basic issues that must be considered, for they impose fundamental constraints on the system's performance. These are such questions as: Does the system remember solutions to specific problems or only the procedures for deriving the solutions? How does it deal with procedures that are used repeatedly in a variety of problem-solving tasks? Are there limitations in the system's ability to keep track of where it is during the course of problem solving and of any partial answers that have been derived? If there are such limitations, how do they affect its problem-solving ability?

Rules versus facts

Without writing anything down:

What is 8 times 4?   What is 262 times 127?

Two entirely different strategies are used to answer these two different questions. For the first problem, you have the facts stored in your memory and, when asked the question, you recall the answer directly. For the second problem, it is likely that you do not know the answer, but you do know how to compute it. Thus, you could take a paper and pencil and, by following the rules of multiplication, produce the response. These are two different strategies for dealing with information. The first is to store the facts directly in memory. The second is to store a *routine,* a set of rules that generates the information when needed.

In many cases, there is a choice of strategy. Each has advantages. By storing information directly, we simplify and speed up subsequent retrieval at the cost of memory space. But when too much information is involved it becomes more efficient to store the rules for generating it, trading the decrease in the speed of retrieval for a saving in memory space. For multiplication, we do store the products of all single-digit numbers (some 45 products), and some of the products of two-digit numbers (up to 4950 products). Some devoted addicts of numerical tricks (the so-called lightning calculators) memorize many three-digit products (but not all of the 499,500 possibilities). Whether it makes sense to learn rules rather than specific examples depends upon how frequently the material must be used. If your entire life is spent doing mental arithmetic, learning the examples is worthwhile. For most of us the memory load becomes intolerable.

Many times, the same routine of operations must be repeated over and over again in solving a single problem. Whenever this is the case, it is much more efficient simply to have one single instance of the routine and to use that single instance wherever necessary. As a good example of this, consider the program necessary for multiplying two, double-digit numbers. All that is needed is to apply the rules for multiplying a single-digit number by a double-digit one, two separate times, and then to add the answers together. We call the individual set of rules *subroutines.*

Subroutines

To use subroutines, several things are necessary. First, a master program is needed to call the subroutines in the right sequence: This master program is usually called an *executive program.* In addition, there should be some further controls so that we can keep track of where the subroutine came from and where it is going to return: If a subroutine is used several times during the course of solving a problem, it is important to keep track of which usage is involved at any given moment.

Special provisions have to be made when a subroutine needs to use itself: The process called *recursion.* People have difficulty in situations that require recursion. For example, to understand the following sentence, the routines that analyze the individual phrases (marked by parentheses) need routines that analyze phrases:

> **The movie (that the script (that the novel (that the producer (whom she thanked) discovered) became) made) was applauded by the critics.** [Miller, 1970]

The difficulties arise because of problems of recursion. The routine used to begin processing the phrase, **that the novel,** are interrupted in the middle, and the same routine must be used to deal with the phrase, **that the producer,** which is interrupted to handle, **whom she thanked.** The same sentence can be structured so that it does not require recursion to be understood. Now the same information is relatively easy to understand:

> **She thanked the producer who discovered the novel that became the script that made the movie that was applauded by the critics.** [Miller, 1970]

Short-term memory   In working through any complex problem, one of the basic difficulties is keeping track of where we are and what has been achieved at any given point. As the complexity of the problem increases, the amount of temporary information we have to keep track of increases. Sometimes we rely on external aids: We write down notes outlining what approaches have been tried and any partial answers that have been derived. Our notes represent an external memory for our problem-solving activities.

The fact that we often resort to such external aids suggests that a major factor affecting the course of internal problem-solving and decision making is the limitation in the short-term retention of information. Animals without such aids should have corresponding limitations in dealing with complex cognitive tasks. Similarly, when humans attempt to use short-term memory to keep track of their place in a problem and the partial results that have been generated, the short-term memory limitations of between five and ten items of information should pose some basic constraints on the structure and complexity of thought. In fact, we should be able to predict when a human will fail to be able to do a task simply because he cannot keep track of everything going on at one time.

Mental arithmetic.   Consider a simple mental task: Most people have trouble multiplying two numbers together in their heads. Is this due to limitation in short-term memory capacity? Let us try to spell out the memory requirements for this task and see.

Start with the multiplication of two single-digit numbers, say 9 times 4. We assume that the answer is already stored in memory. Hence, no more than three memory-registers are required: one for 9, one for 4, and one for the answer, 36. Thus, this task should be an easy one.

Now consider the multiplication of a two-digit number by a single-digit one, say 69 times 8. The problem can be solved in steps. First, at step 1, we store two items in short-term memory: the problem numbers themselves.

THE PROBLEM:
```
   6 9
 X 8
 5 5 2
```

FIGURE 14-12

THE SHORT – TERM MEMORY STRUCTURE

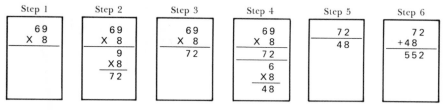

At step 2, the first subproduct has been performed and, temporarily, there are five numbers in memory. Two of those numbers can be discarded (the fact that 9 was multiplied by 8) and only the result stored (step 3). In step 4, the last product is computed (6 times 8 = 48), and temporarily there are six items in memory. Now, in step 5 the digits to be multiplied together can be forgotten, so only two items need be retained in short-term memory. These two numbers are shifted properly and added, leading to the answer. The memory load in the six steps thus varied from two through six numbers. At one point the load got close to the limit of short-term memory capacity (somewhere around seven), but since it did not exceed it, we presume that most people can indeed solve mental multiplication problems of two digits times a single digit if they concentrate a bit.

But the system breaks down when a two digit number must be multiplied by a two digit number. Consider the problem of 95 times 49. The step-by-step memory requirement is shown in Figure 14-13. The memory load increases to six items at steps 4, 7, and 10 and to seven items at step 9. Moreover, although not shown in the diagram, in addition to these six or seven digits, some other information is also involved—for example, the part of the problem being worked on at the moment and the amount that the partial answers must be shifted and added to each other to get to the final answer. Thus, the seven items shown in step 9 underestimate the memory load.

Indeed, most people discover that the mental multiplication of a two-digit number by a two-digit number is just at or beyond their capabili-

FIGURE 14-13   THE PROBLEM: 95
                                 X49
                                 ————
                                 4655

THE SHORT – TERM MEMORY STRUCTURE

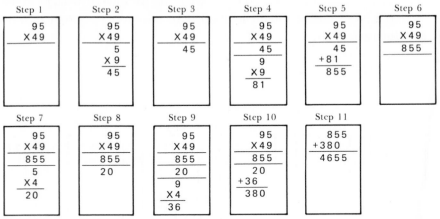

ties. The limit is clearly one of short-term memory, not mental capability. Given pencil and paper, the problem becomes trivial, for now the paper substitutes for short-term memory.

Some people—such as stage magicians—are very good at doing mental arithmetic. This is true despite the fact that their short-term memory capacity is the same as that of anyone else. They simply multiply according to different rules, rules that are designed to minimize the amount of information needed to be retained by short-term memory. Consider this simple trick for that last problem. Notice that the last number, 49, is equal to 7 times 7. Thus, we can change the problem into one of multiplying 95 times 7 and then multiplying the answer by 7. The problem is now reduced to two simpler multiplications. If you do the computations, you see that the maximum memory load is reduced to six. Other tricks for doing mental multiplication are even more successful at reducing memory load.

SUGGESTED   Much of the material presented in this chapter comes from the theoreti-
READINGS   cal work of Herb Simon and Allen Newell at Carnegie-Mellon Uni-
              versity. This work is presented in an advanced book just recently pub-
              lished (1971). Many of the very best experiments in problem solving
              are summarized in the book of readings put together by Wason and
              Johnson-Laird, *Thinking and Reasoning* (1968: paperback). DeGroot's
              work on chess (1965, 1966) is both important and interesting.

One of the major concepts in problem solving not covered in this chapter is that of *set*, sometimes called *fixation*. An excellent introduction to this topic can be found in the *Scientific American* article "Problem-Solving" by Scheerer (1963).

Some classic studies on problem solving are the book *Productive Thinking* by Wertheimer (1945), the semihandbook *How to Solve It* by Polya (1945), and the study *The Mentality of Apes* by Köhler (1925). The books on thinking recommended at the end of Chapter 12 are also relevant.

Some recent symposia on problem solving have been printed as books: Green (1966), Kleinmuntz (1966–1968), and Voss (1969).

A review of the effects that groups have upon problem solving can be found in Hoffman's article "Group Problem Solving" in the book edited by Berkowitz (1965).

Decision making

So he thought of his hut . . . and he thought of his boat,
And his hat and his breeks, and his chickens and goat,
And the hooks (for his food) and the spring (for his thirst) . . .
But he *never* could think of which he ought to do first.

And so in the end he did nothing at all,
But basked on the shingle wrapped up in a shawl,
And I think it was dreadful the way he behaved—
He did nothing but basking until he was saved!

["The Old Sailor," *in* A. A. Milne, *Now we are six* (1927)]

Decisions pervade our lives. We are continually faced with alternative courses of action, each of which must be evaluated for its relative merits. Sometimes, the decision depends upon the reactions of others; sometimes chance factors are involved; often, decision making is accompanied by a perplexing mixture of success and failure.

It is a very difficult psychological task to compare several courses of action and finally select one. First, if each course of action has any complexity to it, it strains the limited capacity of short-term memory simply to picture a single alternative and its implications, let alone carry several in mind simultaneously in order that they might be compared with one another. Second, if the alternatives are complex ones, then there is no clear way to do the comparison, even if the several choices could all be laid out one in front of the other. And finally, there are always a number of unknown factors that intrude upon the situation: Some of the results of the action are only problematical—who knows what will really happen? Some of the results of the decision depend upon how someone else will react to it, and often that reaction is not even known by the other person yet. It is no wonder that the sheer complexity of reaching a decision often causes one to give up in despair, postponing the event for as long as possible, sometimes making the actual final choice only when forced, and then often without any attempt to consider all the implications of that choice. Afterward, when all is done and it is to late to change the act, there is time to fret and worry over the decision, wondering whether some other course of action would have been best after all.

Decision theory provides a recipe for how to choose a course of action in an uncertain situation. It prescribes the information that is needed and the way it should be combined to arrive at an optimal decision. As we explore human decision-making behavior, we will discover that decision theory is concerned with very much the same issues that arose during the analysis of contingency learning (Chapter 13). The whole point of contingency learning was to determine through experience the environmental conditions and actions that led to desirable outcomes. The study of human decision making concerns the situation in which we must make a decision and act, even though we have limited experience with the conditions. The choice of possible actions and the prediction of the expected outcomes must be derived from a logical analysis of the situation. Often, it will depend on the behavior of others as well as on our own acts. In contingency learning, behavior is controlled by the outcomes, both positive (reward) and negative (punishment). In human decision making, the possible outcomes are often quite complex and not so easy to evaluate.

Human cognitive limitations interact with human actions. Thus, in our study of human decision making, we have to be especially concerned with realizing the distinction between the rules people ought to follow, and those they actually do follow. The distinction can be difficult to make, since people often describe their behavior as thorough and logical, even when it is not. When a person makes a decision that appears to be illogical from the viewpoint of an outsider, usually it turns out that the decision was sensible from the position of the decision maker, at least in terms of the information he was thinking about at the time. When his apparent error is pointed out to him ("Why did you move the pawn there; now I can take your queen?"), he is likely to respond that he simply "forgot" some important information ("Oh damn, I saw that before, but then I forgot about it"). This poses difficulties in our efforts to study the decision processes. Which behavior do we study— his actual, erratic acts, or his systematic, purposeful ones? The answer, of course, is both.

DETERMINING
VALUES

The function of rational, decision theory is to identify the information that is relevant to a decision and to specify how the information should be put together to arrive at a conclusion. The major principle of rational decision making is that of *optimization:* All other things being equal, pick the alternative with the greatest value. This was the guiding principle of contingency learning. It is also the guiding rule of decision theory.

This simple maxim of acting in order to maximize the gains and minimize the losses seems to be a perfectly plausible assumption on the surface. But in this simple form, it is of relatively little value for a theory of human decision making. The problem is that different people evaluate gains and costs differently.

A basic issue raised by the notion of optimization is to determine how people assess values and costs in a decision-making situation. The psychological worth a person associates with a course of action or an object is said to be his *utility* for that object. The task of decision theory is to determine how people assign utilities to objects and then, how these utilities are used during the course of decision making.

A natural place to begin a study of utilities is with the psychological worth of money. Clearly, the utility of money is not simply its face value: among other things, it must depend critically on a person's wealth. One dollar must surely represent a far greater utility to the beggar than to the wealthy man from whom he begs.

Consider this simple experiment. Suppose you were just given a present of $20. The arrival of the money was unexpected and there are absolutely no strings attached to it. Think about how happy this gift makes you. Now, seriously consider the amount of happiness generated by the gift of $20. How much money would the gift have to be to make you exactly twice as happy? What about four times as happy, or eight times as happy? (Notice that this is the magnitude estimation scaling technique discussed in Appendix A as it applies to money.[1] Try the experiment before reading the next paragraph.)

People differ in their responses to this thought experiment—as well they should. Someone who is a relative pauper cherishes the gift of $20; someone who receives a monthly allowance of $1000 would not be much affected by the gift: Hence, their evaluations of the situation differ. Nonetheless, almost everyone would agree that the money would have to be more than doubled in order to double the happiness that it brings. In fact, the usual answer is that the monetary amount must be **quadrupled** in order to double the happiness (utility). That is, the utility of money appears to increase as the square root of the monetary value.

Do not take this exact relationship too seriously. The important lesson of the example is that the psychological value of an item, even so well known an item as money, does not increase in direct proportion to the numerical value. In general, it increases more slowly.

The psychological value of money

What happens when we are not dealing with simple quantities like money? How do we assign values to complex objects and situations? The abstract nature of the problem is perhaps best illustrated by examining a situation not too closely related to reality; in this way we can avoid past experiences interfering with the consideration of the issues. So forget reality for a moment and view this scenario with us.

The value of complex alternatives

[1] The experiment was first performed by Galanter (1962b).

How to choose a mate. In a faraway land, where women are the rulers and sultanas are still in style, the Maga of Kantabara wished to purchase a mate to add to her collection. So she called before her the two best qualified brokers in all the land and requested them to go forth and seek for her a new mate. Now, by long, scientifically established tradition, the Maga had determined the most important attributes in a mate. Thus, she required that each of the prospective candidates undergo a test on several critical dimensions. Each would then be assigned a numerical value ranging from -5 to $+5$, depending upon his skills and attributes: Zero points if he were average, $+5$ if superb, -5 if perfectly awful.

The two brokers returned, each with one candidate: Shar and Malik. Their price was the same: Their individual evaluations are shown in Table 15-1.

Decision strategies. An examination of the Maga's choice situation indicates that the basic issue is how to compare all the various dimensions. How should she combine the virtues of sexual skill with those of intelligence: These are two different things.

The first step toward a solution is to make sure that all the values are on a common scale. It is important that the $+3$ given to Shar's prestige has just as much psychological worth to the Maga as the $+3$ assigned to Malik's intelligence. But let us assume that this first problem is solved, that each of the ratings assigned along the dimensions have been carefully worked out so that they can be compared directly.[2]

Figure 15-1

The problem of combining the dimensions still remains. Try making the decision: Which one should the Maga choose? How do you deal with the various ratings on the various dimensions?

Let us attack the problem by considering two quite different strategies for combining the values of the multidimensional mates in order to reach a decision: We call these two strategies *overall impression* and *dimensional comparison.*

Overall impression. In this strategy, each candidate is examined sep-

---

[2] One way of doing this is to transform each rating value onto a single scale, such as monetary value. Suppose there were two candidates, A and B, who were identical on all dimensions but one. On that dimension, A rated higher than B. How much monetary difference in purchase price would be necessary to offset the difference in ratings? The prospective buyer can be offered a choice of candidate A at a given price or candidate B at a reduced price. If a reduction in the price of B of, say, $1000 were sufficient to offset the lower rating of B on the dimension, then the one rating-difference has the same psychological worth as $1000. By offering a number of such choices for different ratings and different dimensions, it is possible to express the rating on each dimension on a common monetary scale.

Table 15-1 Evaluation of Prospective Mate

Dimension	Candidate	
	Shar	Malik
Military skill	2	1
Sexual skill	5	−1
Conversational skill	−2	4
Intelligence	−4	3
Personality	4	3
Physical attractiveness	2	2
Prestige of family name	3	1

Broker's verbal description of candidates:

SHAR: A man from a family of high prestige. Will add to the reputation of the court. A pleasure to be with, attractive, with fine military skills. Is top rated in his knowledge and employment of the amatory arts.

MALIK: A remarkably intelligent, personable choice. An attractive mate, with a high level of conversational ability to entertain you and your guests. Comes from a good family and has a good knowledge of military skills.

arately and a single figure of merit determined that represents the overall value of the candidate. The same procedure is performed on each candidate, and the one with the highest overall utility is selected. Thus, the values associated with Shar add up to a total of 10. For candidate Malik, the same procedure produces an overall rating of 13. According to this decision strategy, the Maga should purchase Malik for her mate.

Dimensional comparison. In this strategy, the alternatives are compared directly, one dimension at a time. First, the difference between the alternatives is assessed for each dimension. Then the final judgment is based on analysis of these dimensional differences. In this case, Shar wins on military and sexual skills, personality, and family prestige. The results of the dimensional analysis put Shar as the winner on four dimensions, Malik on 2, with a tie on one dimension. A simple decision rule is to choose the candidate preferred on the most dimensions: This makes Shar the winner, 4 to 2.

FIGURE 15-1

Assessment of the strategies. Here, then, are two strategies, each giving a different answer. What should the Maga do? That is her problem. But what about most people, which strategy do they follow? The answer is both: now one, now the other. Both strategies seem to be a part of the procedures followed by people in actual situations. Each has virtue and deficiency. In the method of overall impressions, each alternative is assessed by itself and then summarized by a single value. This procedure is probably the most accurate, but it is also the hardest to do: The assessment of a given alternative is relatively difficult. In the method of dimensional comparison, the comparison between alternatives along a single dimension is relatively easy to do, even if the result is less efficient. There is a trade-off between the complexity of the decision rule, its accuracy, and the ability of a person to perform the necessary evaluation.

Actually, we have presented the problem of making this choice in a rather cold-blooded fashion. In usual situations, it is not possible to come up with such a complete numerical assessment. In fact, even when some efficient businessman or government administrator manages to convince the decision makers to prepare such an assessment of the alternatives, usually the actual person who must make the decision is not satisfied. Thus, given this scientifically proven rating scale for prospective mates, the Maga is most likely to respond, "Well, that's all very well for making the initial selections of candidates, but maybe you had better just let me be alone with each one for an evening—find out what he is really like, you know."

The Maga is clearly correct in her dissatisfaction with such a precise listing of the values of the candidates: Certainly, there is more to the alternatives than can be captured in the numbers. The main virtue of the numerical assessment is that it allows for rational, complete decision making. But there is no question that many important subtleties are ignored. However, unfortunately, personal interviews are even worse. The difficulties of comparing two complex alternatives are now compounded by the limitations of personal encounters. In a personal interview, even the most trivial of events often carries high weight. Suppose one of the candidates stumbles on the rug while leaving, or wears a distasteful color, or does something else both accidental and annoying: "That Malik, he is much too clumsy to be a Maga's mate. Certainly Shar seemed quite graceful."

Cognitive strain

A major factor in a person's ability to make a decision or do any mental task, such as that of problem solving, learning, or thinking, is the amount of strain that these operations place on his cognitive capacities. The most potent limitation would appear to be that which results from limited short-term memory. In the previous chapter on problem solving, we showed how the complexity of different problems in mental arithmetic affected the number of items that had to be kept in short-term memory simultaneously, and that the limitations on a person's ability to do mental arithmetic seemed to result from the limitations of his short-term memory.

The tremendous limitations on computational ability placed on the human decision maker by his short-term memory affect the ways by which he approaches most tasks. The expert chess player (an International Grand Master) is often thought to have superior mental abilities. This is simply not true. Rather, the expert player has had so much experience with the game that he knows and recognizes the meanings of the various configurations of pieces on the board as well as you know the letters of the alphabet and recognize the various configurations and meanings of those sequences that form words. You can remember words easily because each word is one psychological unit, regardless of how many letters it contains. With nonsense configurations of letters, your memory is strained, since each letter now becomes one psychological unit (try remembering XPCWPTLMSQXKR). The skilled chess player treats well-known board configurations in much the same way as you treat well-known words: He appears to have superior skills in choosing among the possible moves because his great familiarity with the game allows him to manipulate whole segments of pieces as single psychological units. When you give the chess player random, meaningless board configurations to analyze, his apparent superb memory and analytical skills disappear, just as they did for your ability to remember letters, once the letters no longer formed meaningful words.

Analogous problems occur with the human decision maker. Although he might understand the sensible rules that ought to be followed in reaching a decision, the load they impose upon his memory capacity makes it quite likely that he will simplify them enormously when actually faced with a real situation. He will describe his behavior in the rational way in which he knows he ought to behave, rather than the apparently whimsical way in which he actually does behave. Usually, it is possible to determine exactly why a particular person has made the particular decision he did and show that he followed logical rules, even though he made an illogical decision. Thus, if the Maga truly picks Shar for her mate because he seemed graceful and Malik clumsy, we must admit that this is one truly logical decision rule, even if we complain of its lack of relevance. For the Maga to have worried over the fact that one trip does not an oaf make, or whether Malik's superior intelligence might compensate for his occasional trippings, would have presented her anew with the entire problem with all its complications. For after all, once Malik's intelligence is being considered again, how about Shar's personality?

What is being optimized?   Even after values have been assigned, does the decision maker always choose the highest valued alternative? Suppose that a student, Bob, has carefully saved his money in order to purchase a single-lens reflex camera. He is working his way through school, so in fact it has been difficult to raise the money needed. He has $140, and whatever is left over from buying the camera he intends to put aside toward his textbooks for next semester.

One weekend, Bob gets a ride with a friend to Los Angeles (some 100 miles away), where he knows he can get a good buy on the camera of his choice. He trudges around the city all day, from camera store to camera store. In the morning he finds store A, where the price is

$135. At noon, he finds B, where the price is $115, and at 4 P.M. he is at store C, where the price is $120. Clearly, Bob should go back to store B. But he is hungry and tired. He has not eaten all day. He has to meet his friend soon for his ride back, so the actual choice is between going back to store B (saving $5) and not having time to eat anything or staying at store C, paying the extra $5, but being able to stop off for a sandwich and some rest before heading back. Bob is very likely to choose the latter alternative today, when he compares his hunger and tiredness with the savings of $5. At the moment, this is a logical decision. Tomorrow, Bob may very well regret the decision, for then, when yesterday's tiredness and hunger no longer seem very important, he realizes that he will have to work for two more hours in the cafeteria to make up the $5.

The problem one faces in trying to analyze our ability to understand the actual decisions made by someone else is hampered because we do not and cannot ever know all the variables that entered into the situation. ("Yes, I know I made a mistake in leaving too soon, but I had to go to the bathroom.") The principle of maximization is assumed to underlie every decision. When the time comes for the actual choice to be made, however, it may be that new variables have entered into the situation and some of the old ones are not considered. Thus, even when a decision is made to pursue an apparently foolish choice, we assume that it is done logically and sensibly, considering the information involved in the analysis. An apparently illogical choice of decisions can be made simply because when it came to the final moment, the psychological utility for getting some rest or of minimizing the intellectual effort was greater than the utility thought to be gained by a more prolonged, thorough analysis of the alternatives. The properties of short-term memory which cause a low limit on the number of comparisons that can be made at any one time will often turn out to be one of the most important determiners of the actual choice. Our basic assumption is that each decision does optimize psychological utility, even though the bystander (and perhaps the decision maker himself) will later wonder why that choice was made.

THE LOGIC OF CHOICE

Almost without exception, everyone will agree that his decision processes ought to be logical. Moreover, formal theories of decision making assume logical consistency: Preferences among objects ought to be consistent with one another. If A is preferred to B and B to C, then logically A should be preferred to C. Transitivity of this sort is a basic property that just ought to hold anytime different objects are compared to one another. Let the symbol

> stand for a preference of one object over another, and the symbol =
stand for a complete indifference between two objects; the basic rules for
logical choices can be summarized as

1. If A > B and B > C, then A > C.
2. If A = B and B = C, then A = C.
3. If A = B and C > 0, then A + C > B.

These three rules constitute a sensible set of postulates about decision
behavior. Indeed, if the rules are described properly, so that the mathematical
framework is removed, they simply sound like obvious common sense. Those
who study decision making, however, have discovered that there is a difference
between the rules that people believe they follow and the rules that they
actually do follow. Thus, although these three assumptions form the core
of most decision theories, it is also realized that they do not always apply.
There are some clear examples of instances in which each rule is violated.

There are several ways in which the decision theorist can deal with these
difficulties. One is to ignore them, assuming that the violations of the rules
occur only in special circumstances, and not in the situation described by
the theory under study. Alternatively, the decision maker can try to incorporate
the violations into his theory, showing how they result from certain performance limitations of humans. Here are some anecdotal illustrations that demonstrate examples of violations for each of the three basic rules.

The circularity of
choice: rule 1

If A > B and B > C, then A > C

Consider the decision problem of a student trying to choose a course to
fulfill his social science requirement. Three courses are available—psychology,
sociology, and anthropology. Assume that his preferences among these courses
are based mainly on three characteristics: the quality of teaching in the
course, the grade he expects to get (which includes the difficulty of the
work and the toughness of marking), and his personal interest in the material.
In order to make a rational decision he rates the courses on these three
dimensions:

Course	Quality of Teaching	Expected Grade	Interest in Material
Psychology	High	Low	Medium
Sociology	Low	Medium	High
Anthropology	Medium	High	Low

Sociology versus psychology. When he goes to register, he finds the usual
long lines of students waiting to sign up for the courses. He has to decide
on a course fairly quickly or it will be closed before he has a chance to
enroll. Suppose he starts in the psychology line. As he stands there, he begins
thinking about his choice between psychology and sociology. Psychology has
a higher quality of teaching, but he expects a lower grade, and the material
is not as interesting as sociology. Thus, sociology rates higher than psychology

on two out of the three dimensions. So he really prefers sociology to psychology, since a sensible decision rule is to choose the course that rates highest on the largest number of dimensions. Therefore he should switch into the sociology line. Suppose he does.

Anthropology versus sociology. Now he is in the sociology line. He begins thinking about his other option, anthropology. Anthropology rates higher than sociology on both the quality of teaching and on the expected grade, although it is somewhat less interesting. Using the same decision rule as before, he now discovers that anthropology is clearly preferable to sociology and the sensible thing to do is to switch to the anthropology line. Suppose he does.

Psychology versus anthropology. After arriving in the anthropology line, however, he cannot stop thinking about psychology. After all, it rates higher than anthropology on both teaching quality and interest. Perhaps he should reenter the psychology line.

This circularity in behavior represents intransitivity in his choices among the courses. If A stands for anthropology, B for sociology, and C for psychology, then apparently he prefers A to B and B to C, but also C to A:

$$A > B > C > A > B \cdots .$$

Moreover, these vacillations in his choice behavior appear even though he is following a simple and consistent rule for making his choices.

When considering the choices among complex objects, this situation is not atypical. Frequently, the decision problem involves dealing with large numbers of dimensions, weighing the values of each dimension and, finally, devising some strategy for combining the evaluations. When the objects are complex, the opportunity for inconsistency is large.

If A = B and B = C, then A = C.

The importance of small differences: rule 2

This time, the scenario is the purchase of a new car. The customer has decided on a sports car with a base price of $3500. Now the salesman begins to offer some extras in the hope of building up the overall price of the car.

The customer has chosen the red fastback model. Certainly, the machined aluminum hubs would spectacularly improve the overall appearance. The salesman argues skillfully that the hubs are only $49 extra: Since the car costs $3500, the extra cost of the hubs is negligible. This is probably true. The customer claims to be indifferent between paying $3500 and $3549 for a car. Thus, if A is the cost of the car and B is the cost of the car and hubs, then, in the mind of the customer, A = B.

Now we do the argument over again: The black leather dash only costs $37.95. This is a must if the top will be down most of the time. Moreover, there is really no difference between paying $3549.00 and $3586.95. Thus, if B is the cost of the car and hubs and C = B + cost of dash, then, in the mind of the customer, B = C .

Now, what about a white tonneau cover? The customer may move the price over the $4000 mark before he realizes that the sum of his small indifferences has led to a large difference. Certainly he is not indifferent between a cost of $3500 and $4000.

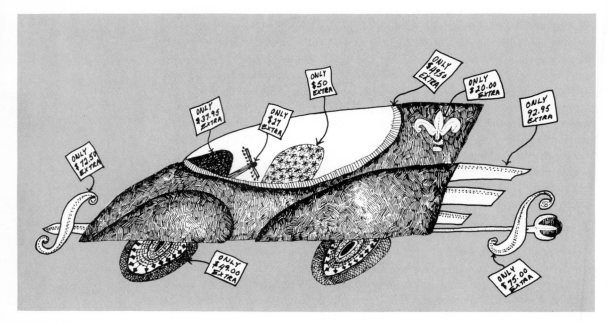

FIGURE 15-2

But having gone through the experience, indifference now operates in reverse to make it difficult to undo the sequence. The customer may feel that he could really forego the simulated alligator-hide upholstery in the trunk but it would only save him $19.95, a paltry amount, given that he is spending $4000 on the car. Maybe he should just pay the extra money rather than go to the trouble of determining the exact combination of extras that he can do without while significantly reducing the price of the car. The skillful salesman, of course, avoids mentioning the base price or cumulative cost of the extras. He emphasizes the trivial amounts of each increment relative to the total cost. If shrewd, he stops just before the customer begins to consider the possibility that although $A = B$ and $B = C$, A does not necessarily equal C.

The Tokyo–Paris problem: rule 3

$$\text{If } A = B \text{ and } C > 0, \text{ then } A + C > B.$$

There is a very popular counterexample to this rule, well known among economists and decision theorists. It goes like this. Suppose your name was just picked as the prize winner of a raffle. You are given a choice of prizes. Which do you prefer: an all-expense-paid week's trip to Tokyo, or an all-expense-paid week's trip to Paris? Let us assume that you are really indifferent between these two choices and would be willing to let the flip of a coin decide. Call the psychological value of the trip to Paris P and that for the trip to Tokyo T. Since you are indifferent, we have established that P = T.

Now, would you rather have someone give you a bottle[3] of wine or not? We assume your choice is to receive the gift. Therefore, the psychological value of the receipt of a bottle of wine is W, W > 0. Now, suppose you get the bottle of wine only if you choose the trip to Paris. You should now have a clear preference for the Paris trip: P = T, and W > 0, therefore P + W > T. You don't agree? Right, the logic does not apply. Somehow the offer of wine is really quite inconsequential in this decision.

The problem is not that wine has no value. In isolation, most people would prefer having the free wine to not having it. The issue here is the way the values depend upon the context in which they appear. In this situation, wine is clearly irrelevant to the choice problem. In other situations, the same bottle might be the deciding factor.

FIGURE 15-3

---

[3] The traditional example among decision theorists involves martinis rather than wine. You, in turn, may wish to substitute your own preference for a bottle of wine. But if you do, make it just a very small amount of the item of your preference.

RISKY DECISION
MAKING

Decisions in real life frequently must be made in uncertain situations. Choices often require both assessing the utilities of the various possible outcomes and taking a gamble on what is actually going to happen. The value of the decision to carry an umbrella depends upon the chance of rain. The question of whether or not one should buy life insurance is intimately connected with the chances of living for some specified amount of time. A choice of political strategies depends on the chance that the opponents will adopt certain countermeasures. This addition of chance factors to the situation does not change the basic principle of optimization, but in considering people's decision behavior, both utilities and chance factors must be included.

Utility in
risky choices

Consider the following set of choices. Would you prefer:

1. $0.10 with certainty or one chance in ten of obtaining $1.00.
2. $1 with certainty or one chance in ten of obtaining $10.
3. $10 with certainty or one chance in ten of obtaining $100.
4. $100 with certainty or one chance in ten of obtaining $1000.
5. $1000 with certainty or one chance in ten of obtaining $10,000.
6. One million dollars with certainty or one chance in ten of obtaining ten million dollars. [After Markowitz (1952, p. 150).]

We make two predictions about your pattern of preferences in this situation. The first is that you will not be indifferent between these choices. That is, for choice 1, for example, you will tend to prefer the gamble to the certain winnings: You would rather gamble on winning $1 than take 10¢ for sure. Similarly, you probably prefer to gamble on $10 than take $1 for sure, and perhaps you may prefer to gamble on a 10% chance of winning $100 rather than receive $10 with certainty. But at some stage you will reverse your pattern of preferences and begin choosing certain winnings to the chance situation. Unless you place an extremely high utility on the excitement of risk, it is unlikely that you would choose the opportunity of trying for $10,000,000 with a 10% chance over the outright gift of $1,000,000.

The second prediction is that the point at which you switch over from gambling to taking the sure thing will depend on your present wealth. The richer you are, the more willing you will be to gamble for higher stakes. In extremely reduced circumstances, you might even prefer the certain gift of a dime to the chance of winning $1. This is a good experiment to try on your friends, since you can collect the data quickly and easily. Select several acquaintances including some from high-income and some from low-income backgrounds. Starting with the first choice and going down the list, ask them which they prefer, the certain sum of money or the gamble. Note the points at which their preferences change from a sure thing to a gamble. The richer they are, the higher the number of the choice at which they cross over.

The switch-over in preference from the gamble to the certainty is at the point at which utility for money begins growing less rapidly than its dollar value. When $100 with certainty is chosen over a 10% chance of winning $1000, then utility for $1000 is **less than** ten times $100. Here, then, we have the basic situation for decision-making under risk. When outcomes are uncertain, both chance and utility must be considered. To deal with these, two new concepts must be added to our discussion: *probability* and *expected value*.

The *probability* of an event is simply the long-run expectation of the relative frequency with which the event will occur. Probability values range numerically from zero through one. When an event has a probability of zero, we can say with a great deal of certainty that we never expect the event to occur. The probability that the result of a single coin flip will be both heads and tails is zero. For events with probability of one, we say with extreme confidence that it will always occur: Because everyone dies, the probability of death is one. It is conceivable that in the future this probability will be changed. Similarly, it is possible that something with a probability of zero occurrence will actually happen: It simply is never expected to.

    Probability

When an intermediate value of probability is assigned to an event, this means that over the long run it is expected to happen a certain percentage of the time. An event with a probability of .28 would be expected to occur about 28% of the time in a long series of observations. Heads are expected to turn up about 50% of the time in a long series of coin flips. This does not mean that it is known exactly how many times a given event will occur. It simply means that, statistically speaking, the event is expected to happen with a particular frequency.

Probability theory is the mathematical machinery for determining the likelihood that various events or combinations of events are going to occur. Often, the assignment of probabilities can be made by an analysis of the physical characteristics of the device that is producing the events: The fact that a die is six sided and is evenly balanced produces an expected probability that any number on the die will show up on the average of $\frac{1}{6}$ of the time. Sometimes the nature of the physical mechanisms underlying the occurrence of the event are not well understood, so the probability is determined by observations of its relative frequency in the past. If someone claims that the probability of rain on any given day in California is about .01, this figure is an estimate, based on the past history of rain in the state.

These are objective probabilities based on the physical properties of a given situation. As we shall see in a moment, they do not necessarily coincide with an individual's personal assessment of how likely it is that a given thing will happen.

Expected value   When the outcomes are probabilistic, decision theory prescribes that the rational decision maker attempts to maximize his long-run expected gains. Both the probabilities of events and their values must be considered in selecting an optimal course of action. A simple gambling situation illustrates the basic principle for combining these two aspects of a decision situation.

Suppose you are given an opportunity to play the following game. A coin is flipped. If it lands on heads, you get $10; if it lands on tails, you pay $5. Should you play the game?

The *expected value* for this gamble is simply the expected winnings or losses in the long run. The calculations are straightforward. The two possible events that can occur in the situation are equally probable: There is an equal chance of winning or losing. The probability of heads is .5 [p(head) = .5], and when the coin does turn up heads, the value of that event is $10 [$V$(head) = $10]. When the coin turns up tails, you lose $5, so V(tail) = −$5. These probabilities and values are simply combined to give the overall expected value (EV) for the game.

$$EV = [V(\text{head}) \times p(\text{head})] + [V(\text{tail}) \times p(\text{tail})] \,.$$

$$EV = \$10 \times .5 + (-\$5) \times .5 \,.$$

$$EV = \$2.50 \,.$$

Over the long-run, then, you should win an average $2.50 for each flip of the coin. After playing the game 1000 times, you should come out about $2500 ahead.

In any situation in which probability values can be assigned for each outcome, the overall expected value can be computed. To make an optimal decision, the strategy or course of action that yields the highest expected value in the long run should be selected. This, of course, does not necessarily mean that you will win on every try. It only means that repeated choices of the strategy yielding the highest expected value will produce the largest long-run gains in a decision situation.

The expected-value computation gives the optimal decision choice, but obviously, few people understand the procedure or, even if they do, bother to make these computations before making a decision. (You can be sure, however, that gambling casinos, insurance companies, and similar businesses do make them with skill and devotion.) Now let us work our way toward what a person actually tends to do.

Subjective probability

If you were given a pair of dice, how likely do you think it is that you could roll a 7? Devices such as a pair of dice have no memory. Each roll of dice is completely independent of each other roll (we are assuming fair dice and a fair game). It does not matter whether a 7 has come up on every roll for the last 100 trials in a row, or whether a 7 has never come up: The dice themselves have no way of knowing what has happened. Yet a gambler will often bet that a 7 will come up next because, "It hasn't come up in the last 100 tries and now, by the law of averages, it has to." He is responding to his subjective notions about probability theory rather than to the true situation. Coins, dice, and wheels cannot remember what has gone on in the past, so that the probability of various events is always the same on every try, regardless of what has happened previously.

This judgment of the actual objective probabilities by humans in their subjective perception of the likelihood of an event is called *subjective probability.*

Representativeness and availability

It often appears that a person's subjective probability of an event comes about by his assessment of how characteristic the particular event is of the process thought to underlie its generation.[4]

Suppose we have just made a survey of all the families in California that have exactly six children. We find that about $\frac{1}{3}$ of the families have three boys and three girls. Now, suppose we consider the birth order of the children of these families. Which ordering do you think is more likely,

a: G B B G B G

b: B B B G G G

When someone thinks of a random order, usually he thinks of things "mixed together." Clearly, the first sample (*a*) is more representative of the random process that determines the order of arrival of boys and girls. Accordingly, most people believe it to be a more likely event—that is, the subjective probability of sequence *a* is judged to be appreciably greater than the subjective probability for sequence *b*. In fact, both

---

[4] The ideas for this description of representativeness and of decision making based upon the construction of mental scenarios of the possible outcomes is from the work of Daniel Kahneman and Amos Tversky of the Hebrew University, Jerusalem.

sequences are equally likely. Given that a family has three boys and three girls, there are exactly 20 possible birth orders that could take place: All 20 are equally likely. Yet sequence *a* appears to be representative of a random sequence, whereas sequence *b*, in the minds of most people, is not. After all, there is a simple pattern: how could that be the result of a random process?

The problem here is actually very simple. People clearly lump together such different sequences as

    a: G B B G B G

    c: G B C B B G

    d: B G B G G B

    e: B G G B G B

as being similar. Hence, they can imagine many different ways of getting a sequence "like" *a, c, d,* or *e* (18 ways, to be exact), but only two ways of getting a sequence "like" *b* (B B B G G G, and G G G B B B). Of course, that was not the question: The comparison was between the **exact** sequences *a* and *b*, not similar sequences. Nonetheless, the lesson is instructive: People expect the world to behave in a representative fashion.

A second, related way of determining subjective probabilities of an event is to consider all the past instances you can remember: The more "accessible" the event in your memory, the more probable it is judged to be. Consider, for example, which is more likely:

    a: that an English word starts with the letter **k**;

    b: that an English word has a **k** in the third position.

If you think of all the words you can that satisfy either *a* or *b*, it is quite clear that it is easier to find the former than the latter. Hence, most people will judge possibility *a* to be much more likely than possibility *b*. In fact, there are about three times as many words with a **k** in the third position as there are words that start with **k**. The problem is that human memory is not organized in a way that makes it easy to retrieve words by their middle letters, whereas it is organized to make it easy to retrieve them by their initial letters (or initial sounds).

This judgment by "availability" taints subjective probability estimates. If you are asked to judge whether mathematics professors are any good or not, you will base your answer on a consideration of the ones you can remember, even though you can know only a tiny fraction of the thousands of professors who teach mathematics in schools across the nation.

These explanations of the assessment of subjective probabilities through judgment of the **representativeness** of the sample and the **availability** of the events in memory often lead to three generalities about subjective probabilities:

1. People tend to overestimate the occurrence of events with low probability and underestimate the occurrence of events with high probability.
2. People tend to exhibit the *gambler's fallacy*, predicting that an event that has not occurred for a while is more likely to occur in the near future.
3. People tend to overestimate the true probability of events that are favorable to them and underestimate those that are unfavorable.

Faced with the uncertainty of real-life events, with subjective probabilities and utilities, it is still desirable to act in a way that maximizes the long-run expected gains. To do this requires the combination of the subjective probability of an event with the estimation of the utility of the event, using this estimate to select that choice which maximizes the expected outcome. The combination of subjective probability with utility is called the *subjective expected utility* (*SEU*) of an event.

Subjective expected utility

The rules for combining subjective probabilities and utilities are exactly analogous to those used to compute expected values. The only difference is that subjective probabilities (*sp*) replace objective ones (*p*) and utilities (*U*) replace values (*V*) in the decision equation. Hence, if an event E consists of either an outcome A with subjective probability $sp(A)$ or some outcome B, with subjective probability $sp(B)$, then

$$SEU(E) = [U(A) \times sp(A)] + [U(B) \times sp(B)].$$

As with the computation of expected values, however, it is unlikely that anyone ever goes through these computations before making a decision. What actually happens? One possibility is that people construct imaginary scenarios of the possible consequences of each decision alternative and then make the choice that leads to the more attractive scenario. Now, the construction of a scenario is actually closely related to the computation of an overall subjective expected utility. After all, to imagine the possible consequences of an event means somehow to combine the utility of that event with the subjective likelihood of its occurrence, although the assessment of *SEU* then need not conform in any easily determined way to the equation.

Consider a physician who wishes to prescribe one of two drugs to a patient. Both drugs have virtue, but both also have possible side effects. Essentially, the physician compares the *SEU* for drug A with the *SEU* for drug B, prescribing the one with the greater value. He is likely to do this comparison, however, by simply thinking back over his experiences with the two drugs. Drug A, he may recall, gave one woman a headache, but of the "many" other prescriptions for its use that he has made, he cannot recall any other complaints. Drug B, however, once caused a rash on a patient, who then complained bitterly for 2 weeks. Now it may actually turn out that the "many" cases the physician can recall for drug A are only about 15, that of those cases, 3 people moved without reporting back to him, and 4 more had headaches, but did not say anything because they assumed this to be "normal." For drug B, perhaps the only side effect of 50 prescriptions was for that one obnoxious patient. Nonetheless, the memory for that one patient is far stronger than for the other cases. Hence, this scenario predominates, and the choice is made to prescribe drug A.

Thus, the proper computation should be

$$SEU(\text{drug A}) = [U(\text{cure}) \times \text{sp}(\text{cure})] + [U(\text{headache}) \times \text{sp}(\text{headache})] \ ;$$

$$SEU(\text{drug B}) = [U(\text{cure}) \times \text{sp}(\text{cure})] + [U(\text{rash}) \times \text{sp}(\text{rash})] \ .$$

Suppose both drugs always cure the patient. For drug A, the actual probability of causing a headache is $\frac{5}{15}$, or $\frac{1}{3}$. For drug B, the actual probability of a rash is $\frac{1}{50}$. But, whenever the physician thinks about prescribing drug B, the long arguments with the rash patient come to mind: For this physician, $SEU(B) < SEU(A)$.

GAMBLING

The casinos of the world offer the potential gambler a number of games, all of which have a negative expected value for the player. For example, consider the expected value calculation for American roulette. There are 38 possible outcomes on each spin of the wheel—the numbers 1 through 36 plus 0 and 00. Each of these outcomes is equally likely, and thus the probability of any particular outcome is $\frac{1}{38}$. The player wins if the number he bets on comes up and loses if any other number comes up. The expected value, then, is

$$EV = [V(\text{win}) \times p(\text{win})] + [V(\text{loss}) \times p(\text{loss})] \ ;$$

$$EV = [V(\text{win}) \times (\tfrac{1}{38})] + [V(\text{loss}) \times (\tfrac{37}{38})] \ .$$

For the player to break even in the long run, the expected value must be 0. This means he should be paid \$37 for every dollar he bets on a winning number. In fact, in American casinos he is paid off only 35 times the amount he bets,

$$EV = [(\$35) \times (\tfrac{1}{38})] + [(-\$1) \times (\tfrac{37}{38})] \, ;$$

$$EV = -\$.0526 \, .$$

On the average, the bettor loses 5¢ on every dollar played. (In the European casinos, the expected loss is a bit less, since the wheels have only a single zero. Thus, players have one chance in 37 of winning, and they win 35 times the amount they bet when their number comes up, yielding an expected value of −\$0.028 or about −3¢ on every dollar bet.)

In dice (craps) you lose your money somewhat less rapidly if you bet optimally. The expected value for the craps game is about −1.5¢ for each dollar bet and may be as low as −.0085¢ with certain betting strategies.

Only one casino game offers a positive expected value to the player, and then only when the player uses a somewhat complex playing strategy. For blackjack (sometimes called twenty-one, or vingt-et-un), playing strategies based on knowledge of the changing composition of the card deck can yield positive expected values of up to 35¢ per dollar bet. These strategies were first extensively tested by a mathematics professor who invented the system (Thorp, 1966). In general, casinos encourage gambling strategies, for in most games they cannot work. Moreover, the publicity is good for business. In this case, however, the casino quickly lost its blasé attitude toward yet another gambling system, when the professor began building up large winnings using his strategy. Since, then, the casinos adopt simple countermeasures to reduce the positive expected value whenever they suspect a systems player at the Blackjack table: The simplest way for the casino to foul the system is to shuffle after every hand (see Epstein's *The Theory of Gambling and Statistical Logic*, 1967).

Another form of gambling illustrates some of the psychological factors underlying the perception of probabilities. Legal on-track betting at racetracks usually follows a system of odds called *pari-mutuel* betting. In this system, the odds that a horse will win, and the amount the track pays for a winning ticket are based on the percentage of bets that have been placed on each horse. The favorite is the horse with the largest amount of money bet on him, and therefore the one that pays the lowest return for a given sized bet. A long shot, on the other hand, has relatively few bets on him, and pays off proportionally higher if he wins. Before the computation of the odds, the track usually takes 15% of the total amount of money bet, and gains an additional 2% by rounding all payoffs down to the nearest 10¢.

Since the odds on the horses and, consequently, the expected winnings for a bet, are based on the combined judgments of the bettors, there are at least two different types of strategies for betting at the track. You can try to determine the "objective" probability that a horse will win from an analysis of his record and a multitude of other factors that affect his performance. Or you can bet on the bettors, trying to capitalize on the psychological tendencies of the spectators to bias their estimates (and hence the odds) away from the true probabilities that a horse will win.[5]

There are a number of betting strategies that try to capitalize on systematic characteristics in people's gambling behavior. One recommends that you bet on the favorite horse during the last few races of the day. This strategy is based on the assumption that people who win money tend to leave the track early, while those who lose try to recoup their losses by betting on the long shots for the last few races. The net result is fewer people than usual bet on the most probable winner so his odds are higher than the true probability of winning would indicate. The result is a favorable bet to you.

A second strategy is based on a general tendency for people to assume that when an event has not occurred for awhile, it becomes more and more likely to occur—the gambler's fallacy. In horse racing, this psychological tendency suggests that you ought to bet on the favorite whenever favorites have been consistently winning in the previous few races. The assumption is that the other bettors will operate according to the gambler's fallacy: They will assume it less and less likely that yet another favorite will win. This tendency would make the odds deviate from the objective probabilities and thus provides the opportunity for a good bet.

A third betting strategy concerns bets on the daily double—a bet in which you try to pick the winners of two successive races. You only win if both of the horses come in. The betting strategy is to wait until the first race has been run, then approach those people holding daily double tickets with the winning horse in the first race. You offer to buy their ticket for a fixed amount. Thus, you offer them the choice of winning X dollars for sure (the price you will pay for the ticket) or holding the ticket and gambling between winning a larger amount or losing the initial bet. Your goal is to buy daily double tickets on each of the possible winners in the second race, thus guaranteeing your success.[6]

This is the same type of choice situation as the one discussed in the text.

---

[5] We exclude illegal betting systems, such as the so-called builder play. In this system, a group of bettors monopolize the betting windows, placing small bets on unlikely winners. The strategy is to build up the pari-mutuel odds on the expected winner well beyond any objective estimates of his true probability of winning. Then, large bets are placed with off-track bookmakers on the most likely winners. These off-track bets do not affect the pari-mutuel odds. The most successful builder play to date was executed in England. Only one ticket was sold at the track on the winner and the odds were built from approximately even money to a nearly 10,000 to 1 payoff for the winning horse. The bookmakers in this case refused to pay off when the builder play was discovered. However, since off-track betting had been legalized in England just prior to the play, the executors of the builder play sued the bookies for their winnings.

[6] Caution: This strategy may be illegal, but it is widely used in many events, e.g., the Irish Sweepstakes.

Remember the option between winning 10¢ for sure or gambling with a 10% chance of winning a dollar? If this experiment is conducted at the race-track, you will win so long as people generally prefer to take the certain winnings to a gamble having the same or larger expected value. This is a plausible assumption so long as people's utility for money grows at a slower rate than its face value, or if they underestimate the true probability that they hold a winning ticket. Note that since you have to buy enough tickets to assure a win, it is only profitable if the average person's utility for the certain winnings is substantially higher than his expected utility for the gamble. The proponents of this system claim this to be the case, and report spectacular winnings using this strategy.

Although these strategies would seem to capitalize on real and consistent psychological processes underlying betting behavior, the influence of such mechanisms must be strong enough to produce substantial distortions in the perceived odds in order for the strategy to be profitable. And, of course, if they are successful, they are self-defeating. The bulk of the bettors will attempt to take advantage of them, which in turn will effect the odds and thus the expected value of the proposed betting strategy.

GATHERING
EVIDENCE

In most situations, we begin with some initial hypotheses about what is going to happen. We have some hunches or intuitions concerning how likely it is that a friend will agree to a bargain, that the stock market will go up, or that a used object can be purchased for some sensible price. Before making a final decision, we may attempt to gather additional information in order to maximize our chances of making the right choice. In this section, we discuss how to use the evidence collected to arrive at a better estimate of the probability of the various possible outcomes.

As usual, we start with a discussion of an idealized procedure for gathering together evidence. This procedure is actually quite sensible and seems to convey the spirit of what people actually do. It is unlikely that anyone ever does the computations we are about to present, but it should be apparent how those computations do capture the essence of actual behavior.

Odds

The standard theories of dynamic choice rely heavily on a theorem from mathematical statistics first stated by the Reverend Thomas Bayes in 1736. Bayes's theorem allows one to determine the likelihood that a particular hypothesis is correct. The easiest way to look at the actual theorem is through a modification of it called the odds–likelihood ratio form or, more simply, the computation of the odds. By the word *odds* we mean the likelihood that one event will happen rather than another. Thus, the first step is to specify what the two possible alternative hypotheses are.

Suppose that a friend, a well-known cheater, has carefully filed away at a coin so that whenever it is flipped, it lands on heads 70% of the time. One day you wander into his room and discover him gambling with someone by tossing coins. You wonder whether the coin he is using is the biased one (probability of a head—0.7) or is a fair one (probability of a head—0.5). You whisper to the other player, "Three to one that's an unfair coin," and then watch carefully the outcomes of the next few flips.

The statement "three to one" states the starting odds, before any data have been collected. This initial statement of odds is called the *a priori* odds. What is meant by this statement of odds is that for every one time the friend uses a fair coin, he will use an unfair coin three times. To transform the odds into probabilities is simple: The odds and the probabilities are simply different ways of stating the same fact. If two events A and M have odds of a to m, it means that for every m times event M occurs, the event we are talking about (A) will occur a times. Hence, if event A has odds of a to m, the probability of A occurring is $a/(a + m)$. Odds of three to one mean a probability of 0.75 in favor of the event.

To summarize: if the events A and M have odds of a to m:

the probability of A:

$$p(A) = \frac{a}{a + m},$$

the probability of M:

$$p(M) = \frac{m}{a + m}.$$

Alternatively, the odds of event A to event M, odds (A, M), is given by

$$\text{odds}(A, M) = \frac{p(A)}{p(M)}.$$

A test for cancer   To see how these odds are used and modified with the collection of evidence, consider the fate of two individuals: Mr. A, who is sickly and Mr. Z, who is healthy. Each is concerned about the possibility of having cancer. Mr. A is a hypochondriac: He is always imagining that he has some dreaded disease. Moreover, he has just read the science page of the Sunday newspaper about undetected cancer and is now very suspicious of his own health. He feels that there is at least one chance in five that he has cancer. So, for Mr. A, $p(\text{cancer}) = 0.2$.

Mr. Z is healthy and has never been sick a day in his life. He is muscular, and not concerned about illness. He thinks that there just might be one chance in 10,000 that he has cancer. For Mr. Z, $p(\text{cancer}) = .0001$.

Mr. A:

$$\text{odds(cancer)} = \frac{p(\text{cancer})}{p(\text{not cancer})}$$

$$= \frac{0.2}{0.8} = .25 \qquad (1 \text{ to } 4);$$

Mr. Z:

$$\text{odds(cancer)} = \frac{p(\text{cancer})}{p(\text{not cancer})}$$

$$= \frac{.0001}{.9999} = .0001 \qquad (1 \text{ to } 10,000) \, .$$

The evidence. At this point, suppose both Mr. A and Z are at the physician's for a normal checkup. Included among the tests is a check for cancer: The results are positive for both A and Z. Both receive the bad news.

The next step is how to deal with the evidence from the cancer test. The question is how to use this additional information to modify the *a priori* odds about the likelihood of having cancer. Thus, the basic issue is to determine the quality of the evidence that has been collected.

Bayes's decision theory suggests that the quality of the evidence depends on how likely it is that evidence would result, **given** either of the hypotheses you are entertaining is true. How likely is it that you would get a positive cancer test result given you do in fact have cancer; how likely is it that you would get the same positive test result if in fact you do not have cancer? The relative likelihood of these two situations is the *likelihood ratio*[7]:

$$\text{likelihood ratio} = \frac{p(\text{positive test} \mid \text{cancer})}{p(\text{positive test} \mid \text{no cancer})} \, .$$

This test for cancer, as with all medical tests, is not perfect. It does

[7] Read the vertical bar as "given." Thus, p (positive test | cancer) should be read as "the probability of a positive test, **given** that there was cancer."

not always detect cancer when it is there, nor does a positive test result always mean that the patient does have cancer. Suppose that for this particular test, if a person does have cancer, the chance of a positive test result is 0.9; if he does not have cancer, the chance for a positive test result is 0.05.

$$p(\text{positive test} \mid \text{cancer}) = 0.9 \;;$$

$$p(\text{positive test} \mid \text{no cancer}) = .05 \;.$$

Thus, the likelihood ratio is given by

$$\text{likelihood ratio(cancer)} = \frac{p(\text{positive test} \mid \text{cancer})}{p(\text{positive test} \mid \text{no cancer})} \;;$$

$$\text{likelihood ratio(cancer)} = \frac{0.9}{0.05} = 180 \;.$$

The relative odds of a positive test result given cancer are 180 to 1.

The final step is to combine the prior expectations and the evidence in order to arrive at the answer: What is the likelihood of cancer, given the initial expectations and the test evidence? According to Bayes's theorem, this is simply:

$$\text{new odds} = \text{likelihood ratio} \times \text{prior odds} \;.$$

By substituting the numbers,

   For Mr. A (sickly):

$$\text{new odds} = 180 \times .25 = 45 \qquad (45 \text{ to } 1) \;.$$

   For Mr. Z (healthy):

$$\text{new odds} = 180 \times .0001 = .018 \qquad (\text{about } 1 \text{ to } 50) \;.$$

Now we have an interesting situation. On the basis of the test result, A is absolutely convinced he has cancer: The odds are 45 to 1 that he has it (the subjective probability is therefore $\frac{45}{46} = .98$). But Z, on the other hand, is quite skeptical: He considers the odds **against** his having cancer to be 50 to 1. Thus, his subjective probability of having cancer is $\frac{1}{51}$, or around .02. Both have collected the same evidence. The only difference is in their initial expectations of how likely it was that they were sick.

According to this strategy for dealing with evidence, the information collected is used to change the initial expectations about the relative probabilities of events into a new estimate of those probabilities. The degree to which probabilities are modified depends on the quality of the evidence, the likelihood ratio. The final conclusion combines both the initial expectations and the evidence that has been obtained.

This structure for using evidence makes good intuitive sense. It suggests that our expectations are slowly modified through experience. Each piece of evidence may change our mind a little in one direction or another. If we had tendencies toward being slightly hypochondriac, we might start off with reasonably high estimates of the probability that we had cancer and require only the meagerest of evidence to persuade us that cancer was a real possibility.

Do you believe in ESP? Those people who tend to believe in ESP anyhow are persuaded with weak evidence. Those who start off with a completely skeptical attitude, however, require an avalanche of evidence, all of the highest quality, before their personal odds change to the point where they might seriously entertain the possibility of ESP. Similarly, those who start off believing are hard to convince otherwise. Eventually, empirical observations (in other words, truth) should overwhelm even the most unfavorable bias (prior odds), but unfortunately, with extreme biases, it may take a long time.

THE CUBAN MISSILE CRISIS

In 1962, the Soviet Union was discovered to be in the process of installing missiles in Cuba. The United States reacted in anger, warning the Russians that they must remove the missiles. President Kennedy announced an ultimatum to Russia, although without any specific threats. Russia ignored the warning, since the threatening gestures alone were no deterrent. The American press was in an uproar, diplomatic notes were being exchanged, and the United States Navy was enforcing a blockade of Cuba. Premier Khrushchev initiated negotiations with Kennedy at this stage. Here is Khrushchev's version of what happened.

> The climax came after five or six days, when our ambassador to Washington, Anatoly Dobrynin, reported that the President's brother, Robert Kennedy, had come to see him on an unofficial visit. Dobrynin's report went something like this: "Robert Kennedy looked exhausted. One could see from his eyes that he had not slept for days. He himself said that he had not been home for six days and nights. 'The President is in a grave situation.' Robert Kennedy said, 'and he does not know how to get out of it. We are under very severe stress. In fact we are under pressure from our military to use force against Cuba. Probably at this very moment the President is sitting down to write a message to Chairman Khrushchev. We want to ask you, Mr. Dobrynin, to pass President Kennedy's message to Chairman Khrushchev through unofficial channels. President Kennedy implores Chairman Krushchev to accept his offer and

to take into consideration the peculiarities of the American system. Even though the President himself is very much against starting a war over Cuba, an irreversible chain of events could occur against his will. That is why the President is appealing directly to Chairman Khrushchev for his help in liquidating this conflict. If the situation continues much longer, the President is not sure that the military will not overthrow him and seize power. The American army could get out of control.' "*

I hadn't overlooked this possibility. We knew that Kennedy was a young President and that the security of the United States was indeed threatened. For some time we had felt there was a danger that the President would lose control of his military, and now he was admitting this to us himself. Kennedy's message urgently repeated the Americans' demand that we remove the missiles and bombers from Cuba. We could sense from the tone of the message that tension in the United States was indeed reaching a critical point.

We wrote a reply to Kennedy in which we said that we had installed the missiles with the goal of defending Cuba and that we were not pursuing any other aims except to deter an invasion of Cuba and to guarantee that Cuba could follow a course determined by its own people rather than one dictated by some third party.

While we conducted some of this exchange through official diplomatic channels, the more confidential letters were relayed to us through the President's brother. He gave Dobrynin his telephone number and asked him to call at any time. Once, when Robert Kennedy talked with Dobrynin, he was almost crying. "I haven't seen my children for days now," Robert Kennedy said, "and the President hasn't seen his either. We're spending all day and night at the White House; I don't know how much longer we can hold out against our generals."

We could see that we had to reorient our position swiftly. "Comrades," I said, "we have to look for a dignified way out of this conflict. At the same time, of course, we must make sure that we do not compromise Cuba." We sent the Americans a note saying that we agreed to remove our missiles and bombers on the condition that the President give us his assurance that there would be no invasion of Cuba by the forces of the United States or anybody else. Finally Kennedy gave in and agreed to make a statement giving us such an assurance.

* Obviously, this is Khrushchev's own version of what was reported to him. There is no evidence that the President was acting out of fear of a military take-over.

[From *Khrushchev Remembers*, pp. 497–498, 1970.][8]

---

[8] This particular version of the Cuban crisis does not agree with the versions of the other participants who have also written about it. For example, the books of Robert Kennedy, Pierre Salinger, and Arthur Schlesinger, Jr. A detailed description of the decision as seen from the White House can be found in Schlesinger's book, *A Thousand Days* (1965, pp. 794–841).

What should one make of Khrushchev's version of the predicament faced by Kennedy? Clearly, there are two interpretations. First, Kennedy's worries about the power of the American military might have been true. Second, they might have been a bluff, simply a story circulated by President Kennedy in order to frighten the Russians. There is absolutely no way of knowing which interpretation is correct simply from the information presented here. Most important of all, there is no way that Khrushchev could tell which possibility might be correct. As the story is told in the memoirs, it is clear that Khrushchev believed the President to be telling the truth about the demands of his military leaders. Moreover, there is some sign that Khrushchev already believed this to be true: "For some time we had felt that the President would lose control of the military." In the terms of the language of this chapter, Khrushchev's **prior odds** were that the military would take over. Now, with evidence favorable to that interpretation, he believes this even more strongly.

Suppose Khrushchev's prior odds in favor of the military taking over were 2 to 1. Now, what about Kennedy's story that he is losing control: What is the likelihood ratio of such a story? Khrushchev might consider that if it were true, then Kennedy would always say so: $p(\text{story} \mid \text{situation true}) = 1$. What if the situation were false? Suppose we say that Kennedy would bluff only about one time out of ten: $p(\text{story} \mid \text{situation false}) = 0.1$. Then, *The odds computation*

$$\text{likelihood ratio} = \frac{p(\text{story} \mid \text{situation true})}{p(\text{story} \mid \text{situation false})} = \frac{1.0}{0.1} = 10 \ .$$

The new odds in favor of the situation being true are

$$\text{new odds} = \text{likelihood ratio} \times \text{prior odds} \ ;$$

$$\text{new odds} = 10 \times 2 \ ;$$

$$\text{new odds} = 20 \text{ to } 1.$$

Thus, given the story by Kennedy, Khrushchev now should believe the odds in favor of the military taking over to be 20 to 1. In other words, the probability that the military will take over if he does not do something to stop them is $\frac{20}{21}$ or .95.

Incidentally, the American public usually believes in the dominance of government over the military. Hence, suppose they believe the prior odds on the military taking over to be 1 chance in 100 ($\frac{1}{100}$). Suppose, moreover, they believe that Kennedy, a skilled poker player, bluffs half the time. Then, for the American Public, the computations become:

$$\text{prior odds} = \tfrac{1}{100} = .01 \; ;$$

$$\text{likelihood ratio} = \frac{p(\text{story} \mid \text{situation true})}{p(\text{story} \mid \text{situation false})} = \frac{1.0}{.5} = 2 \; ;$$

$$\text{new odds} = 2 \times .01 = .02 = \tfrac{1}{50} \; .$$

The American public viewing much the same sequence of events as Khrushchev might believe the chance of the military taking over to be 1 in 50. Alternatively, the probability that the military will step in is $\tfrac{1}{50} = .02$.

<table>
<tr>
<td>THE AFTEREFFECTS
OF DECISION
MAKING</td>
<td>When all has been decided and the final act taken, what then? Does the decision maker feel uneasy about the choice? Does he regret his decision? Or does he feel confident that he has taken the correct alternative? These questions have been actively studied by a number of social psychologists who have tried to measure the aftereffects of decisions.</td>
</tr>
</table>

When all has been decided and the final act taken, what then? Does the decision maker feel uneasy about the choice? Does he regret his decision? Or does he feel confident that he has taken the correct alternative? These questions have been actively studied by a number of social psychologists who have tried to measure the aftereffects of decisions.

One major group of psychological theories of human behavior goes under the heading of *Consistency Theory*. This general term actually encompasses a reasonably wide variety of different theoretical viewpoints, but all share a common theme about human cognitive processes: namely, that humans strive for consistency in their thoughts and actions. Any aspect that is inconsistent with another results in a tension, conflict, unbalance, or dissonance that must be eliminated. Different types of consistency theories deal with different aspects of the problem or have different ways of resolving the issues, but they all share the common principle that the normal individual attempts to minimize or eliminate cognitive conflicts.

Rationalization

To illustrate the principle, let us try to follow through the thought processes of a mythical decision maker, call him MDM. He has been looking for a used car to buy and has narrowed the choice to two:

Car A: an older sports model generally in good shape but with poor tires;

Car B: a newer sedan with excellent tires and engine but somewhat scratched and dented.

He has compiled a list of important features of each and is having trouble making up his mind between the two. The problem is, the two alternatives are matched rather well by each other. Regardless of the decision strategy MDM uses, the decision between the two cars is a difficult one. Suppose that MDM finally reaches a decision: He buys car B. His decision immediately produces a conflict or dissonance situation.

The problem is that although MDM has selected car B, he has just finished an exhaustive analysis that led him to conclude that the two cars really were about equally matched. Thus, the decision was difficult, and MDM begins worrying about his decision: "Maybe I should have chosen A—it's really a neater-looking car." This is the period of *post-decisional regret* following a difficult decision.

The solution to this malady, as proposed by those who believe in the theory of cognitive dissonance, is for MDM to increase the salience of the two alternatives. That is, MDM should reconsider the two alternatives and convince himself that they were truly different, with B being by far the best. How does he do that? Easy. The whole process of assigning values to the attributes of the cars is quite clearly subjective. Thus, all he has to do is go over the attributes again, this time reassessing their importance. MDM, the great rationalizer, goes to work.

- "Come on," he yells to his friends, "let's all go in my new car." Add utility points to car B, for as MDM drives away with a crowded car he can say to himself, "You see, I chose wisely. If I had car A I never could have fit all these people in. Getting a large car really is more important to me than I originally thought."

- MDM sees a car with a flat tire or reads an advertisement for automobile tires: "Hmm, with my car I don't have to worry. It's very important to have good tires on a car." (Car A, of course, had bad tires.)

- The paint on car B, however, was in much worse shape than on car A and so when one of MDM's friends ties a surfboard to the roof, scratching the body in the process, MDM responds, "It's OK, the paint is chipped anyway. Scratches don't change the way the car works. Good thing I didn't buy that other car, I couldn't even put the board on a sports car." (It is not hard to imagine how MDM might rationalize his choice of the small car, had he chosen it instead. "Come on, Mary, hop in and I'll drive you over. Gee, I'm sorry guys, but I just can't fit anyone else into this car.")

Do you like fried grasshoppers? Suppose a polite, popular professor of one of your classes brought some in to class and asked if any of

Of grasshoppers and things[9]

---

[9] For a discussion of the experiments from which this example was drawn, see Zimbardo and Ebbeson, 1969.

the students were willing to try them. How much do you think those students who took up the offer and actually ate some grasshoppers would actually change their opinion of the taste for the better?

Suppose the same sort of thing happened in another class, this one taught by a bossy, aggressive, and unpopular professor. He, too, brings in some fried grasshoppers, but he goes about offering them quite differently. He places a grasshopper in front of each of 15 students and says, "Eat." Obviously, the students don't have to obey if they do not wish to, but of those that do, how many do you think would actually change their opinion of the taste for the better?

Most people would favor the mild, pleasant approach and, in fact, this approach is usually much more successful in actually getting people to eat grasshoppers than the efforts of the bossy, obnoxious professor. But what about the opinions of those who eat the grasshoppers? Why did they eat them?

The students in the pleasant professor's classes like their teacher. If they were asked to do something somewhat distasteful, well, he is a nice guy, so why shouldn't they do it; after all, it will please the professor. But they still dislike the whole idea.

The students of the obnoxious professor feel rather differently. Why should they do something to please him? Who cares about his feelings; after all, he doesn't seem to care about theirs. But then why should they eat the grasshoppers? Well, maybe because they don't really taste so bad after all.

This is the post-decisional change predicted by dissonance theory: If one performs a distasteful action with no apparent rationale, why, then, maybe the action is not so bad after all. Hence, the nonintuitive prediction that doing an action "voluntarily" for an obnoxious person may influence your opinion in a positive direction more than doing the same action voluntarily for a pleasant person who also wishes you to change your opinion in the same way.

Postdecisional rationalization

By now you must get the idea. The good points of a selected alternative are emphasized and the bad points minimized or ignored. The rejected alternatives get the opposite treatment: Their bad points are emphasized and the good points forgotten or minimized. In fact, if you watch people (including yourself) who have just made a difficult decision, you will see this type of rationalizing behavior. There is even a suspicion that technical literature and advertisements for a product are read most carefully **after** the decision has been made to select that product. It is as if the decision maker must reassure himself of the virtues of the selected item. If literature for the other, losing alternatives is read, it seems to be more in order to find the weaknesses than for any other reason.

In this chapter, we have described some of the rules a decision maker follows in comparing alternatives, gathering information, and then reconsidering his choice. The choices of a rational decision maker are determined primarily by the expected values associated with the possible decisions, the probabilities of the events, and the payoffs and penalties of various outcomes. He should select the course of action that maximizes his gain. Although people also appear to operate according to the principle of optimization, they do not necessarily do so in a manner that is readily predictable. Internal variables, such as boredom and fatigue, are often added into the decision equation. Moreover, the limitations of short-term memory often force the human into strategies that minimize his cognitive strain, thereby forcing him either to neglect considering all the important variables or to use a decision strategy that, while logical, is less than optimal and perhaps even inconsistent.

To make contact between the prescription for rational decision making and the actual behavior of people, objectively defined quantities must be translated into their subjective equivalents. In general, the subjective expected utility model is a reasonable description of much of human choice behavior. But a person's estimates of probabilities and his assignment of utilities do not always remain stable. In most cases, this is as it should be. The utilities for events should vary as a person gains or loses, since utility is, after all, a function of the total wealth of the owner. Different people should and do have different judgments of the value of the same event. Subjective probability also varies. A unique event may stand out in one person's memory and not in another's, leading the former to judge it as a much more probable occurrence than it actually is.

The theories of decision making stand as a **prescription** for optimal behavior. Faced with decision situations, you will find it useful to analyze the situation according to the outlines presented here and to assess the values and costs associated with each possible decision strategy. But if you do so, don't trust your memory: Write things down.

CONCLUSIONS

An excellent introduction to mathematical decision theory is provided in the book, *Mathematical Psychology: An Introduction*, by Coombs, Dawes, and Tversky (1970). This book does require some knowledge

SUGGESTED READINGS

of mathematics and probability theory, but for anyone who is seriously interested in the material discussed here, it is a valuable introduction. For those less mathematically inclined, there are a number of *Scientific American* articles relevant. Most of the good ones are included in the book edited by Messick, *Mathematical Thinking in Behavioral Sciences: Readings from Scientific American* (1968). The analysis of the perceptual and mental abilities of chess players comes from DeGroot (1965, 1966).

The analyses of various decision rules, and especially the discussion on subjective probability and the role of representativeness and accessibility, come from the works of Kahneman and Tversky. Unfortunately, most of these works are not available in published form, but see their "The Belief in the Law of Small Numbers" (Tversky & Kahneman, to be published). Some of the discussion on the logic of choice was suggested by the experiment of Tversky (1969).

A good number of the important papers on decision theory have been collected together in the Penguin paperback book by Edwards and Tversky (1967). Chapters 1 and 2 of that book are especially important, since they provide reviews of the literature up to 1960. Several of the examples used in this chapter come from Chapter 7 by Tversky (examples on transitivity relations).

A complete review of the recent theories is provided by Luce and Suppes in an article in the *Handbook of Mathematical Psychology*, Volume III (1965), "Preference, Utility, and Subjective Probability." This article is extremely advanced, however, and should be read only after you have read many of the articles in the Edwards and Tversky collection and then only if you have a reasonable mastery of probability theory and linear algebra.

If you wish to know how to use decision theory in your everyday life, there are three delightful books you can turn to: Epstein's *The Theory of Gambling and Statistical Logic* (1967), Raiffa's *Decision Analysis: Introductory Lectures on Choices under Uncertainty* (1968), and Williams' *The Complete Strategist* (1954).

Epstein's book does what its title suggests: It analyzes in marvelous detail many gambling games and chance situations, through the standard (and some nonstandard) games of the gambling casino, to the stock market, duels and truels, horse racing, and what have you. The book uses a straightforward expected value analysis of these games, and you can enjoy it (and learn some useful strategies), even if you are unable to follow the mathematics, which do get a bit messy at times.

Raiffa tells how an individual ought to go about choosing a course of action, even when the set of possibilities before him looks discouragingly complicated and the real values and probabilities are difficult to estimate. Raiffa is a Professor of Managerial Economics, and he has used the techniques described in the book in many different business situations. The book is easy to follow and may even prove to be useful.

The book by Williams, *The Complete Strategist*, is slightly different. It deals with game theory, which is a variant on the decision theory discussed here. Nonetheless, Williams treats the complex topic with great skill, making it easy reading even for those with no mathematical ability. Game theory is most useful when you must pit your choices against those of an opponent (such as in the situations covered in Chapter 16) whereas decision theory is designed to work against the capriciousness of the world (or nature). Thus, in decision theory you try to maximize your expected gain. In game theory, there are several other strategies available, such as minimizing the maximum possible loss, maximizing the minimum possible gain, or attempting what is known as the mini-max solution. Interestingly enough, the best solution often requires you to toss a coin to make the final decision. In game theory, however, it is important that the opponent know that you are using game theory to make your decisions and that you may make the final decision by tossing a coin. Thus, game theory will work against a sophisticated opponent, but not against a stupid or uneducated one.

Those of you interested in reading up on dissonance theory might wish to examine several of Leon Festinger's books on this topic; perhaps starting with his *A Theory of Cognitive Dissonance* (1957) and including the very delightful study by Festinger, Riecken, and Schachter, *When Prophecy Fails* (1956).

The experiment on grasshoppers was actually performed by E. E. Smith in an unpublished Armed Forces report (1961). This experiment is discussed in some detail (along with a replication and expansion of it) in the book on attitude change by Zimbardo and Ebbesen (1969: paperback. The grasshopper experiment is discussed starting on page 40 and then again on page 72.) Bem's book on beliefs (1970: paperback) also covers this material.

Probably the best introduction to the effect of the gathering of evidence on decision making is the paper by Edwards, Lindman, and Phillips, "Emerging Technologies for Making Decisions" (1965). In addition, the paper by Phillips and Edwards (Chapter 8) in the book of readings by Edwards and Tversky (1967) also covers this topic.

A discussion of how decision making research is sometimes used is given in the proceedings of a National Aeronautics and Space Administration symposium (Patton, Tanner, Markowitz, & Swets, 1970).

16

Decisions in a social context

- A used-car salesman accidentally finds his customer's bank book. He refuses to look at it, fearing that if he knows too much, he will not drive as good a sale for himself.
- The president of a large corporation is about to undertake some delicate negotiations with the union. Business is bad, and he wants to make sure that the bargaining will be favorable for the company. He decides he has his best chance of success if he sends a low-ranking company official to negotiate for him.
- "An 18-year-old switchboard operator, alone in her office in the Bronx, is raped and beaten. Escaping momentarily, she runs naked and bleeding into the street, screaming for help. A crowd of 40 passersby gathers and watches as, in broad daylight, the rapist tries to drag her back upstairs; no one interferes." [Latané & Darley (1970)]

These are decisions made within a social context. The final outcome depends on the actions not only of a single individual, but also of other people involved in the decision situation. Sometimes the others are protagonists, seeking to optimize their own gain at anyone else's expense. Sometimes the others are partly cooperative, so everyone can gain if they agree on a mutually beneficial decision. Sometimes the others are strangers who provide an audience with subtle social pressures on the decisions. The introduction of social factors into decision making takes us beyond the point of the last chapter in which the optimal rational strategy could be specified with mathematical precision, and in which the decisions were made in isolation, independent of the pressures of others. To understand social decision making, we must study the issues of negotiation, threats, conflict, and attitude change.

When decisions must be made in a social context, several new and interesting variables come into play. Different types of situations are involved here, but in all, the opinions and actions of other people become as important as the formal costs and gains of the decision situation.

We can start the analysis of social factors rather simply by considering situations very much related to those of the previous chapter, only now we add in the value of other people's opinions. Whether or not a family decides to purchase a new car or color television set may depend much more upon their perception of the reactions of colleagues and friends than of the actual economics or need for the item. (Among certain populations—such as university professors—the social pressures work

SOCIAL INFLUENCE
ON DECISION
MAKING

in reverse, causing them to avoid purchasing a fancy automobile or color television set, even if they can afford them.) In situations such as these, the analyses of the previous chapter work reasonably well, except that the pressures of social factors must be added.

Part of the difficulty lies with the uncertainty faced by each, individual decision maker. Most real decisions are difficult, so there is real conflict and dissonance over the actual choice. Should you call the fire department when smoke pours into the room? Of course, unless the smoke has a simple, natural explanation, or unless several other people have already called. Each individual must decide for himself how to act when the unexpected occurs. But he knows that life is complicated and filled with peculiar situations in which action simply leads to embarrassment for the person who acts. To the simple assessment of the decision situation, there must be added a consideration of the aftereffects of each action.

Let us start our analysis of the effects of social factors in decision making by considering what happens in reasonably natural situations: We consider the actions of people left in smoke-filled rooms, or confronted with bizarre frisbee players, or involved as witness to a crime.

BYSTANDER
BEHAVIOR

The plight of Kitty Genovese, beaten to death in full view of her neighbors over a 30-min period, none of whom called the police; the murder of Andrew Mormile, stabbed and left to bleed to death in a subway train in the presence of eleven passengers, none of whom tried to help; the rape of the switchboard operator described in the introduction of this chapter—these are the types of events that motivated Latané and Darley (1970) to investigate why bystanders fail to act.

Here we are dealing with a decision situation with certain specific ingredients: There is uncertainty as to the appropriate behavior involved; other people are facing the same situation; the opportunities for communication are limited or not exercised. Somehow, each individual must decide by himself that there is an emergency and then decide on the appropriate course of action. Latané and Darley have carried out a series of ingenious studies of decision behavior in these situations. Both their techniques and their results are instructive.

Throwing frisbees. The setting was Grand Central Station in New York City. The experimenters, two girls, sat opposite each other on benches in the waiting room, throwing a newly acquired frisbee back and forth. After a few minutes of play, the frisbee was accidentally thrown to a bystander (who, in fact, was a confederate of the experimenters). The confederate's function was to establish a model or focal point for the reactions appropriate to a stranger in these circumstances. The confederate either enthusiastically joined in the frisbee game, or she belligerently kicked at the frisbee, expressing her opinion that the game was both childish and dangerous. In some of the experimental conditions, the confederate left the situation after voicing her opinions; in others, she remained while the girls tested the reactions of the real bystanders. The experimental test consisted of throwing the frisbee to each of the bystanders on the benches: A bystander was counted as cooperative if he returned the frisbee to the girls at least twice.

Generally, the bystander interpreted and acted in the situation according to the model provided by the confederate. If the confederate was uncooperative they too were uncooperative, often moving away, muttering comments similar to those of the confederate. When the confederate was cooperative, however, there was almost 90% cooperation among the bystanders; indeed, the problem became one of trying to terminate the game rather than trying to stimulate participation. The **vocal behavior** of the confederate and her **continued presence** made all the difference. If the confederate merely let the frisbee lie where it landed and said nothing, her lack of interest did not inhibit participation by others. If she voiced disdain and then left, the bystanders joined in the game after she left: Grand Central Station became a playground.

The smoke-filled room. Subjects were sitting in a room, filling out a "marketing questionnaire," when suddenly smoke began to trickle in through a ventilator. As they worked on the questionnaire, the smoke continued coming in until, "by the end of four minutes, enough smoke had filtered into the room to obscure vision, produce a mildly acrid odor, and interfere with breathing [Latané & Darley, 1970]."

The way a person responds to the situation depends upon whether he is working alone or with others. When the subjects were working alone, 75% of them responded rationally to the possibility of fire. They investigated the smoking ventilator and went out into the hall to report the incident. But when two other people were in the same room, by far the majority of subjects failed to report the smoke. They attempted to wave the smoke away and persevered with the questionnaire, until the experimenters compassionately terminated the experiment.

The lady in distress. Again, subjects were sitting in a room filling out a "marketing questionnaire." As they worked, they could hear the "marketing representative" as she moved around in an adjoining office. Four minutes after they began work on the questionnaire, a loud crashing sound came from the office, accompanied by a woman's scream and the (tape recorded) moans: "Oh, my God, my foot . . . I . . . can't move . . . it. Oh, my ankle . . . I . . . can't . . . can't . . . get . . .

this thing off . . . me." When the subjects were working alone, 70% of them responded to the situation by offering assistance. But when they were working in the presence of two others (actually, confederates of the experimenter who were instructed to make no responses to the cries), only 7% responded to the lady's distress.

Bystander apathy These studies demonstrate the potent effect that the presence of others has on the actions of an individual. Generally, he tends to follow the course of least resistance, conforming to the actions of his neighbors. But these acts are not necessarily unsocial, nor do they necessarily demonstrate a simple lack of consideration for the plight of others. Rather, they tend to show how complex the actual decision process must be.

Consider the plight of the woman described in the opening paragraphs of this section. Would you have gone to her rescue? Probably not, since the problem for the decision maker witnessing the actual event is not nearly so simple as the short description here conveys. The crowd or the noise would attract your attention. Going over to watch, you would see a naked girl screaming for help while a man tried to carry her to a building. "What is going on?" you ask the person next to you, and he says, "I don't know." Maybe someone is making a movie, maybe it is a domestic quarrel, maybe the man is trying to help her. How serious could it be, for look, nobody else seems to be doing anything. So you shrug your shoulders and walk off, saying that New York City certainly is a strange place.

The situation would have been quite different had you been all alone when you saw the girl and her pursuer. In this case, some of the other explanations do not seem so possible, and it is very likely that you would be concerned and would take some action. Crowds of people, of course, do not always lead to apathy or inaction, as the actions of lynch mobs or Ku Klux Klanners prove. Often, they lead to good, as when a group of people band together to help out in the aftermath of a natural disaster. The point is that individual decision making is a difficult and unsettling task, and social conformity usually acts to simplify the decision problem for the individual. The decision maker is faced with doubt about the correctness of his choice. The reactions of other people provide a source of information. They reduce the uncertainty about the possible interpretations of a situation—"It must be correct, look how many other people agree with me." The fact that most of the crowd agree simply because the others appear to agree with them is irrelevant, because this fact is not known. The reactions of others also indicate some of the contingencies associated with possible actions. In the presence of a passive crowd, individual action may not be supported, and consequently a person may expose himself to considerable risk.

The effect of group pressure can be very striking. A favorite laboratory demonstration of conformity is to ask a subject (let us call him subject H) to judge which of two lines is longer. The task can be made to be rather difficult when the lines to be compared differ only by a very small amount. The experiment is run in a group setting, so that several different subjects are making decisions at the same time. Each can see the answers made by the others. Usually, the answers of the subjects agree reasonably well with each other, except perhaps on the very difficult choices. After the experiment has gone on for a while, a rather simple choice is given, one which is always identified correctly 100% of the time. Just before subject H responds, he notices that the other subjects have all chosen what he thought was the wrong answer. What should he do?

When faced with a discrepancy between his own decision process and the actions of others, the subject is in a difficult situation. Clearly, different people will devise different explanations of the discrepancy they face, but the end result is always an overwhelming tendency to weigh heavily the actions or inactions of others in arriving at a decision. Perhaps the most important observation, however, is not that people tend to conform to the actions of others, but rather that it is a traumatic and difficult act for them to do so. When severe social pressures force a person to comply in his responses in the face of strong contrary evidence, he does so at great psychological cost to himself. One investigator who has studied this aspect of compliance found that the subjects who complied showed considerable anxiety: Some felt psychologically "quite distant" from the other people in the experiment, others felt "queer," or somehow "different" (Crutchfield, 1955). We shall return to this aspect of conforming behavior shortly.

Closely allied to the mechanisms of conformity is the use of authority as a means of inducing another person to do as you wish. Sometimes authority carries with it an implied threat for failure to comply; sometimes authority is perceived as benevolent, so the demands add positive value that may offset whatever costs might be involved; sometimes authority implicitly or explicitly takes over the decision process: The task gets done because the participants do not need to make any judgment whatsoever, they simply do as they are told.

A controversial series of studies provides a good introduction to some

Compliance with authority

of the factors operating in compliance with authority. The scenario gives you a chance to play the role of a subject. Try to imagine the situation and predict how you would behave.[1]

Imagine that you have answered an advertisement to serve as a subject in a psychological study of learning at Yale University. You enter the new, impressive buildings of the interaction laboratory at Yale and go to the designated room, where you are met by a scientist in a white coat. Another subject has already arrived. The scientist explains that he is studying the relationship between punishment and learning. In particular, he is interested in how much punishment is best for learning and in whether the relative ages and sexes of the teacher and students affect the rate of learning.

After drawing lots to decide who is to be the "teacher" and who the "learner" (it turns out that you draw the slip marked **teacher**), both of you are taken to an adjacent room. The learner is strapped into the apparatus ("in order to prevent excessive movement"), and an electrode is fixed to his wrist with special jelly ("in order to avoid blisters and burns"). While you are present, the experimenter reassures the learner that, although the shocks he will receive may be extremely painful, they will not cause any permanent tissue damage. He then takes you back to the experimental room and explains your part in the study.

Your task is to teach the learner a list of words. You are to read the complete list of word pairs, then go back to the beginning and start reading the words one at a time. You read the first word of a pair, then four test words. The learner is to press a button indicating which of the four test words was part of the original pair. You give him an electric shock each time he makes an error. For each successive error, the shock level is increased by one step. The apparatus for delivering the shocks has a series of switches for setting different shock levels. The intensities range from 15 volts up to 450 volts in 15-volt steps. The lowest intensities are marked **Slight Shock** and the highest intensities marked **Danger: Severe Shock,** then **XXX.**

After some practice with the procedures, the trials begin. As you proceed through the word list, the learner gets about one correct response in every four. For each error you increase the shock levels according to the experimental design. After several repetitions of the list, the shock intensity is at 300 volts. At this point, the subject starts to pound

[1] The description of this study and the quotations were taken from Milgram (1963).

on the wall of his booth. The experimenter tells you to allow 5 to 10 sec for a response, than treat the failure to respond as an error and carry on with the procedure. After the next test word, there again is pounding on the wall, but because there is no response, you administer the 315-volt shock. When you turn to the experimenter for advice, he appears completely passive and simply requests that you "Please continue." If you show continued reluctance, he may inform you that "The experiment requires that you continue," or "You have no other choice; you must go on." How far would you be willing to go?

We have explained the situation in considerable detail to allow you to imagine how you would expect to behave in this set of circumstances. When Yale psychology majors were given the same kind of description and asked to predict, there was general agreement that people in this situation would refuse to continue with the experiment. On the average, they expected that most people would not administer shocks much beyond the 240-volt range, regardless of the inducements of the experimenter. They predicted that only an insignificant minority of the subjects (1–3%) would be willing to continue on to the most intense shock levels (450 volts). Informal polling among psychiatrists and colleagues of the experimenter produced similar predictions.

In the actual experiment, all of the subjects administered shock levels of 300 volts or higher. Twenty-six of the 40 subjects, 65%, were willing to administer the maximum shock levels of 450 volts. These results were completely unexpected. They have stirred up considerable controversy, both on their social implications and on the ethics of psychological experimentation.

The experiment was actually a hoax. No electric shock was being presented: The man pretending to be the learner was actually one of the experimenters, playing the role of learner and acting out his responses to the fake shocks according to a well-rehearsed script. The real subject in this experiment was the person playing the part of the teacher. The real question being studied was how far the relatively minor inducements of the psychologist would cause the subject to go in presenting shocks.

The results are the more surprising in light of the fact that each subject's decision to go on with the deliverance of shock was obviously difficult and painful. The subjects were "observed to sweat, tremble, stutter, bite their lips, groan, and dig their fingernails into their flesh. These were characteristic, rather than exceptional responses to the experiment." For subjects who refused to continue, a typical explanation indicates the depths of their conflict:

He is banging in there. I'm gonna chicken out. I'd like to continue, but I can't do that to a man. . . . I'm sorry, I can't do that to a man. I'll hurt his heart. You take your check. . . . No, really, I couldn't do it.

The subjects appeared to be in a severe emotional conflict with themselves as they struggled with the anxiety involved in compliance to authority. One observer who watched the experiment through a one-way mirror commented:

I observed a mature and initially poised businessman enter the laboratory, smiling and confident. Within twenty minutes he was reduced to a twitching, stuttering wreck who was rapidly approaching a point of nervous collapse. He constantly pulled at his earlobe and twisted his hands. At one point, he pushed his fist into his forehead and muttered, "Oh God, let's stop it." And yet he continued to respond to every word of the experimenter and obey to the end. [Milgram (1963)]

These emotional effects are not restricted to situations as dramatic as the shock experiment. Even in the seemingly innocuous line-judging experiment mentioned previously, subjects underwent considerable trauma when they were faced with the problem that the judgments of others did not conform to their own perceptions.

What exactly does the experiment demonstrate? This work and the studies that followed it have been widely cited as evidence for a general human tendency to defer to authority. One must be extremely cautious, however, in drawing such a sweeping conclusion. Clearly, people try to evaluate the entire pattern of events when engaged in making decisions about the most appropriate course of action. In this particular experiment, the unimpeachable reputation of science was behind the quiet, smooth voice of the experimenter. The subject must balance his own mental anguish (and the apparent anguish of the learner) against the possible utility of the experimental results. He should refuse to proceed with the experiment only when his own personal anguish exceeds his perceived value of the study.

Actually, it is possible to argue that the subjects were absolutely correct in their assessment of the situation when they continued to deliver the shock, even at the highest levels. After all, the experimenter asked them to continue, thereby implying that there would be no permanent damage. And, in fact, they (and he) were correct: It turned out to be an experiment in which no one was getting shocked after all.

These results, then, need not have anything to do with any natural or enduring trait of obedience, but rather, they represent a rational evaluation of a particular set of circumstances. What is surprising, then, is not that people will comply, but their assessment of the relative utilities in the situation—the apparent high degree of positive value assigned to the scientific institution, relative to the personal costs of inflicting pain on another. Critics of the experiment have pointed out that the experimenters themselves were exhibiting a behavior pattern quite similar to their subjects. The fact that they were willing to conduct such an experiment and impose upon their subjects such tension and discomfort represents a similar weighting of the value of science relative to the discomfort of the subjects.

Although there has been vocal opposition to this type of experiment, the subjects who underwent the experiment did not seem to share this point of view. After the study, every subject was carefully debriefed, and the intent and implications of the study were fully explained. The subjects felt the experiment was useful and that their personal experience in it had been instructive.[2] They seemed to believe that they had learned a valuable lesson about the necessity of acting according to their own principles, and not to follow authority so readily (see Milgram, 1964). These experiments pose important issues for all of us, both as individuals and as members of society. Milgram has summarized the issues in this way:

[2] In this experiment, as in all such experiments where there is some deception of subjects, the experimental session is followed by a *debriefing* stage. Here the subjects are told the exact nature of the experiment, informed of the exact conditions that were studied, and introduced to the "victim" who was, in actuality, one of the experimenters. Moreover, in this particular experiment, the subjects received a full description of the experiment at a later date and were visited to determine the long-term effects (see Milgram, 1964, for a full report).

It is unfortunate that subjects must sometimes be hoaxed in the initial stages of experiments of this kind, but so far, no one has discovered any other way of collecting the scientific information required to assess theories of human behavior. But the standard ethics of the profession require that all subjects always be debriefed after such experiments. Often, the subjects feel that the experiment was a worthwhile experience for them; that they have learned something useful about themselves.

In most psychological experiments, there is no deception. In the majority of cases, the experimenter really is studying what he says he is. Many an experimenter trying to study something so innocuous as hearing comes to grief because the subject keeps waiting for the trick, when in fact there is none. Many readers of this book will be asked to serve as subjects in psychological experiments. If you do serve, and if after the experiment is over you are not told that deception was involved, then unless you have hit the unlikely case of an experimenter who is immoral and is violating the well-established ethics of the field, you can be sure that no deception was present: You were indeed helping the experimenter do what he claimed to be interested in.

With numbing regularity good people were seen to knuckle under the demands of authority and perform actions that were callous and severe. Men who are in everyday life responsible and decent were seduced by the trappings of authority, by the control of their perceptions, and by the uncritical acceptance of the experimenter's definition of the situation, into performing harsh acts.

What is the limit of such obedience? At many points we attempted to establish a boundary. Cries from the victim were inserted; not good enough. The victim claimed heart trouble; subjects still shocked him on command. The victim pleaded that he be let free, and his answers no longer registered on the signal box; subjects continued to shock him. At the outset we had not conceived that such drastic procedures would be needed to generate disobedience, and each step was added only as the ineffectiveness of the earlier techniques became clear. The final effort to establish a limit was the Touch–Proximity condition. But the very first subject in this condition subdued the victim on command, and proceeded to the highest shock level. A quarter of the subjects in this condition performed similarly.

The results, as seen and felt in the laboratory, are to this author disturbing. They raise the possibility that human nature, or—more specifically—the kind of character produced in American democratic society, cannot be counted on to insulate its citizens from brutality and inhumane treatment at the direction of malevolent authority. A substantial proportion of people do what they are told to do, irrespective of the content of the act and without limitations of conscience, so long as they perceive that the command comes from a legitimate authority. If in this study an anonymous experimenter could successfully command adults to subdue a fifty-year-old man, and force on him painful electric shocks against his protests, one can only wonder what government, with its vastly greater authority and prestige, can command of its subjects. There is, of course, the extremely important question of whether malevolent political institutions could or would arise in American society. The present research contributes nothing to this issue. [Milgram (1965)]

INTERACTIVE   The previous situations all involved pressures put on an individual. But
DECISIONS   the decision was still relatively simple, one that had to be made alone
               by the individual. A second basic type of social context is where several
               participants interact with each other, to bargain or to debate, so that

the eventual course of action is determined by the mutual decisions reached by all the participants. Several different factors enter into this process. For one, the interests of the different parties may differ, so that an optimal decision for one is not optimal for the other. In this situation, some sort of compromise must be reached. For another, there may be a lack of communication among the participants, so that it is not always possible to discuss the possible decisions and their implications. For example, in business negotiations, each side does not usually know the details of the problems of the other. In negotiations between nations, there is often mutual distrust, so communication is strained.

Some of the factors operating in interactive decision making can be illustrated by a prototypical situation: bargaining. The bargaining situation is both competitive and cooperative. It is competitive because two opponents—a buyer and seller—seek to maximize their own gains through negotiation: Usually, the optimal outcome for one is not the optimal outcome for the other. But bargaining can also be cooperative: The participants must agree upon a price if either is to gain and the transaction is to be completed. Communication is allowed, but restricted. In the simplest case, bargaining is conducted impersonally with no social pressures allowed. All communications are limited to the negotiations about price and quantity. Bargaining is usually a decision-making situation in which each participant has incomplete knowledge: He does not know the payoff matrix of his opponent.

Bargaining

We start our analysis of bargaining with an example from the market-place. We want to pit a **buyer** against a **seller** in a social decision-making situation to see the kinds of interactions that take place. You should try the task: It is informative as well as fun. The example works best if you try it with a friend. (The necessary decision matrices have been inserted in the book in a way to make it possible for two people to play the game.) Ideally, you should play one of the parts and have a friend play the other. (If you cannot find a partner in this enterprise, it is surprisingly satisfactory for you to take both roles, alternating between being buyer and seller.) It helps to play-act, putting yourself in the role of the part you are going to play.

Now decide which part each participant wishes to play, the **buyer** or the **seller.** Then, locate the figure in the text that contains the description of the parts, and have each participant read the description that applies to him (either Figure 16-1 or 16-2 depending on which part you have chosen). Do not read both descriptions; that would hamper the ability to play the role demanded of you satisfactorily.

*The bargaining
procedure*[3]
Each participant knows the rate structure of his business: the dependence of the profit or loss on the price and quantity that is bought or sold. The relation among price, quantity, and profit is a complex one, however, with a number of different factors interacting to make the structure somewhat different than intuition might suggest. Thus, both the buyer and the seller have prepared a profit table for their use that gives the figures necessary for the bargaining situation. Obviously, these tables must be kept highly confidential. Neither the seller nor the buyer can let the other see his version of the table. In short, in this situation, neither player knows the payoff matrix for his opponent. A sample of these tables is shown in Figure 16-3 (both buyer and seller may examine these illustrations). Across the top of each table are listed the quantities of the commodity involved. Down the left side are listed the prices for each unit amount of quantity. The numbers in the table show the profits if the bargain is settled at the specified price and quantity.

In the simplified segments of the profit tables shown here, there is conflict; the buyer is best off if he purchases a large quantity at a low price; the seller is best off with a small quantity at a high price. (The actual tables to be used in the negotiations are more complex than this, as a study of both complete tables will indicate, but please do not study them both until after the negotiations are complete.)

In the actual negotiations each participant will have a complete table. Each should start bargaining at a position that is favorable to himself, but both will eventually have to make concessions. The following rules of sportsmanship should be followed:

- You either accept an offer or make a counter-offer.
- Bargaining is in good faith. That is, any offer is always valid. Even if an offer is rejected at first, either party may later decide to accept it. At that time, the man who originally made the offer must agree to abide by it.
- No agreements which involve losses for either party are acceptable.
- All offers are to be made in writing, each offer stating both a price and a quantity.
- No talking.

Now, try it. We have provided both a buyer's and a seller's profit table. If two of you are negotiating (and using only one book) sit at a desk with the buyer on the left. We have located the tables in the book so that each of you will be able to see only the table he is using. The two tables are on pages 578 and 581 for the buyer and

---

[3] Both buyer and seller should read this section.

THE BUYER

FIGURE 16-1

You are trying to buy corn. You are a grocery store owner, chosen to negotiate for an amalgamation of independent grocery store owners. The small neighborhood grocery store is in severe economic difficulties because of competition from the large supermarket chains. Last year, times were hard, and a number of small stores were forced to declare bankruptcy or to sell out at very poor prices to representatives of the supermarkets. This year, many of the independent store owners are in debt from previous years. At least one family has had large medical bills, unpaid at this time. This year, the stores have agreed to group together in purchasing farm commodities, hoping that their mass purchasing power will enable them to buy large enough quantities of foods that their purchase prices will not be too high compared with that of the supermarkets. Furthermore, you are ready to purchase corn early, hoping to gain a time advantage over the markets which are not yet ready to begin negotiations. (The produce sections of the large markets are suffering from a strike of their personnel.) You are presently the only buyer in large commercial quantities. Thus, you represent the only outlet for corn. You wish to get the largest possible profits for your grocers. (Now read the section entitled *The bargaining procedure,* p. 574.)

---

seller, respectively. The **buyer's guide** is on the **left** side of the book, the **seller's** is on the **right,** and there is a page of text between them. Hold the page separating the two tables vertically to act as a shield.[4]

When the negotiating game is over, it is time to examine the processes by which an agreement was reached. Note how each person's behavior influenced that of the other. In determining a bargaining stance, each participant had to consider the constraints imposed upon the other, even though he did not know exactly what they might be.

The process of negotiation

Level of aspiration. One factor that plays an important role in the bargaining behavior is the level of aspiration of the bargainers. Think back on your own performance. Initially, you probably started off by examining the range of profits possible from the various price–quantity

---

[4] If you are playing both parts, do it honestly. Get yourself in the mood of the buyer and make an offer in writing on a piece of paper. Then, turn to the seller's table, get yourself in the mood of the seller, and examine the offer. Using the profit and the history of the previous offers, either accept or make a counteroffer. Then go back to the role of the seller. The tables are complex enough so that you will have difficulty in gaining any unfair advantage, if you play the game honestly. But remember that neither buyer nor seller is supposed to know anything about the other's profit table.

FIGURE 16-2

THE SELLER

Imagine that you are trying to sell corn. You are a farmer, chosen to negotiate for a farm cooperative. Last year there were severe problems in the
farms, with drought and disease combining to create severe difficulties on the
various individual small farms which are represented by the cooperative. This
year things were much better, but many farmers and their families are heavily
in debt from the preceding year. At least one family has had large medical bills,
unpaid to this time. It is important for you to negotiate a good price for this
year's corn crop. This year you have harvested the crop early, so that at the
present time you are the only source of corn in commerical quantities. Thus,
you represent the only source of supply. You wish to get the largest possible
profit, since your farmers need it. (Now read the section entitled *The bargaining procedure,* p. 574.)

FIGURE 16-3

Buyer's Guide (Example)

Price		Quantity	
	5	6	7
		Profits	
100	6	7	8
90	6	8	9
80	7	8	10

Seller's Guide (Example)

Price		Quantity	
	5	6	7
		Profits	
100	3	2	2
90	2	2	1
80	2	1	0

(Note that these are simplified
tables, used only to illustrate the
situation. Do not use these figures
in the actual negotiations.)

combinations of the table, selecting a target range for the amount of gain you hoped to make. Then, you made your bids in such a way that you would end up somewhere near your goal. Probably you were rudely awakened to reality by the initial bids of your opponent, since his initial bids most likely left you with little or no gain. From this point on, the bargaining usually proceeds somewhat like a fencing match, with each participant trying to keep his profits at an acceptable level, while at the same time attempting to discover what range of prices and quantities seem to be acceptable to his opponent. The final goal that you were trying to attain is called the *level of aspiration (LA)*.

Level of aspiration plays an important role in much human behavior, since it tends to dominate the way that people will act in a wide variety of situations. A person who traditionally sets a high value of LA for himself acts quite differently than one who sets a low level. Often, the pattern of success is determined by the setting of the LA, with the person who sets a high value producing more achievement than the person who is more modest in ambition. The achievement could result from one of two reasons, of course. The man who sets high values of LA may be more competent and skilled than the man who sets a low value of LA. Alternatively, the man who sets the high value may thereby goad himself into good performance, both by his refusal to settle for results too far removed from the target he has set himself and for the extreme self-confidence that often accompanies the setting of high goals.

In the bargaining situation illustrated here, for example, the end result is determined by the joint agreement reached by the two bargainers: The LA value set by each bargainer has a strong influence on that end point. The participant who sets and keeps a high value of LA may very well end up with more profit than the one who sets a low value. This is not because the winner has a unique ability or any inherent advantage at the bargaining table. He simply refuses to give concessions to his opponent that would cause him to end up below his LA.

In addition to these general effects of LA, several other aspects of the bargaining situation have been discovered in the series of experiments performed by Siegal and Fouraker. [The bargaining game, including the tables, comes from the book in which Siegal and Fouraker reported their experiments (1960).] One central point concerns the different types of strategies adopted by the bargainers.

There are a number of different variations of the bargaining procedure possible, and the strategies of the bargainers vary with the situation. In the situation illustrated here with the tables, neither bargainer knew the profit tables of his opponent. This experimental situation is called

FIGURE 16-4

Buyer's Guide[a]

Buyer's Profit in Cents

Price	Quantity																	
	1	2	3	4	5	6	7	8	9	10	11	12	13	14	15	16	17	18
240	7																	
230	17	6	0															
220	27	26	30	28	15	0												
210	37	46	60	68	65	60	50	24	0									
200	47	66	90	108	115	120	120	104	90	70	33	0						
190	57	86	120	148	165	180	190	184	180	170	143	120	91	42	0			
180	67	106	150	188	215	240	260	264	270	270	253	240	221	182	150	112	51	0
170	77	126	180	228	265	300	330	344	360	370	363	360	351	322	300	272	221	180
160	87	146	210	268	315	360	400	424	450	470	473	480	481	462	450	432	391	360
150	97	166	240	308	365	420	470	504	540	570	583	600	611	602	600	592	561	540
140	107	186	270	348	415	480	540	584	630	670	693	720	741	742	750	752	731	720
130	117	206	300	388	465	540	610	664	720	770	803	840	871	882	900	912	901	900
120	127	226	330	428	515	600	680	744	810	870	913	960	1001	1022	1050	1072	1071	1080
110	137	246	360	468	565	660	750	824	900	970	1023	1080	1131	1162	1200	1232	1241	1260
100	147	266	390	508	615	720	820	904	990	1070	1133	1200	1261	1302	1350	1392	1411	1440
90	157	286	420	548	665	780	890	984	1080	1170	1243	1320	1391	1442	1500	1552	1581	1620
80	167	306	450	588	715	840	960	1064	1170	1270	1353	1440	1521	1582	1650	1712	1751	1800
70	177	326	480	628	765	900	1030	1144	1260	1370	1463	1560	1651	1722	1800	1872	1921	1980
60	187	346	510	668	815	960	1100	1224	1350	1470	1573	1680	1781	1862	1950	2032	2091	2160
50	197	366	540	708	865	1020	1170	1304	1440	1570	1683	1800	1911	2002	2100	2192	2261	2340
40	207	386	570	748	915	1080	1240	1384	1530	1670	1793	1920	2041	2142	2250	2352	2431	2520
30	217	406	600	788	965	1140	1310	1464	1620	1770	1903	2040	2171	2282	2400	2512	2601	2700
20	227	426	630	828	1015	1200	1380	1544	1710	1870	2013	2160	2301	2422	2550	2672	2771	2880
10	237	446	660	868	1065	1260	1450	1624	1800	1970	2123	2280	2431	2562	2700	2832	2941	3060

[a] From Siegel and Fouraker (1960, pp. 114–115).

incomplete–incomplete: Each person has incomplete knowledge of his partner's profit table. What happens, however, when one man knows both profit tables but the other man only knows his own—the situation called *complete–incomplete?* The result depends upon the negotiation strategy selected by the man who has the complete knowledge. Two possible strategies are especially interesting: One can be called *fair;* the other can be called *ruthless.*

The fair strategy. If the two opponents are fair, reasonable people, then it may actually be detrimental for one to have too much information about the other. What happens is this. When one of the bargainers knows both profit tables, he can see just what the reasonable values of profits might be for both participants. He notes that most of the price–quantity values which yield him large profits are unreasonable for the other person, hence he keeps away from them. He can aim for a target price and quantity that will tend to equalize profits for both participants—a "fair" solution. In other words, he sets a low value on his LA.

His opponent, however, does not know both profit tables. Typically, he will set a high initial value for his LA. Moreover, he is reinforced by the rapidity at which his opponent starts offering him reasonable profits. The offers of reasonable profits from the informed participant support his estimates of how much he can get. The uninformed one often wins out, for the bargainer with complete information encounters a long string of failures as he attempts to stick to reasonable demands. The bargaining situation produces strong pressures to try to salvage some profits and give in to the opponents (if no agreement is reached, no profits can be obtained). It is clear that the man who is fair is handicapped if he has too much information.

The ruthless strategy. If the bargainer who has complete information is also ruthless in his determination to maximize profits, he can use his information to manipulate systematically his opponent's level of aspiration. Basically, the ruthless man needs only two things. First, he needs to know the general principles of learning theory, namely that a history of reinforcements for positive behavior and lack of reinforcements for negative behavior can have a powerful influence on performance. The reinforcements for negative behavior can be very small, so long as they are applied and withheld consistently. Thus, one ruthless, completely informed bargainer in this situation started out by offering his opponent no chance at all for profit. Then, small increments in profit were offered only for large concessions. Whenever the opponent proved reluctant to make concessions, the informed bargainer changed his bids to give zero profit to the opponent. The end result was that the completely informed bargainer realized a substantial profit, whereas the incompletely informed man was very pleased with the small amount that he had managed to salvage. The advantage of learning theory, when used properly, is that not only can it lead to beneficial results for the ruthless player, but that the history of small reinforcements is so pleasing, the uninformed bargainer is not only satisfied with his own performance, but is willing to play (and lose) again.

In all these examples of social decision-making, no personality factors were operating. Everything was carried out (or should have been) in a cold, impersonal manner. What if personalities had been allowed to intrude, what then? According to the basic principles of decision theory one should maximize profits, and thus personality factors should really make no difference. This, of course, is false. Consider what might have happened could you perceive the plight of your opponent. Would not the whole bargaining structure be changed if it were known that one participant was evil, profit-minded, and ruthless: totally aware of the problems of his opponent, but completely unmoved by them, caring only for his profit no matter the cost to others?

Strategic *negotiations*   We have seen something of the nature of interpersonal negotiations during bargaining. The main feature of the normal bargaining situation is that neither opponent is aware of the other's payoff matrix, yet both must arrive at some compromise if either is to gain. In these situations, communication is both impersonal and limited. The moves and counter-moves during negotiations are seldom limited to a simple, unretractable offer of one outcome. In most situations where two sides must negotiate with one another, the possible tactics for negotiation are much more numerous and sophisticated. Moreover, the payoff matrix for each opponent is usually known to both sides. The overall goal is still the same: to maximize your winnings by attempting to force the other's decision in your favor. When the communication channels open up, the tactics change: Now the weapons of threat, promise, and commitment emerge. Let us examine how they work.

Consider a situation of conflict. Both sides distrust each other, so it is not possible to reach a satisfactory solution simply through mutual understanding and goodwill, even though such an agreement would probably be better for both sides than the unsatisfactory compromise that threats and counterthreats will produce.

The tactics of *conflict*   Conflict can be viewed as a contest, with each side trying to better its position. It is usually possible for both sides to better themselves simultaneously, so the two need not be unalterably opposed to each

FIGURE 16-5

Seller's Guide[a]

Price	Quantity — Seller's Profit in Cents																	
	1	2	3	4	5	6	7	8	9	10	11	12	13	14	15	16	17	18
240	230	440	630	800	950	1080	1190	1280	1350	1400	1430	1440	1430	1400	1350	1280	1190	1080
230	220	420	600	760	900	1020	1120	1200	1260	1300	1320	1320	1300	1260	1200	1120	1020	900
220	210	400	570	720	850	960	1050	1120	1170	1200	1210	1200	1170	1120	1050	960	850	720
210	200	380	540	680	800	900	980	1040	1080	1100	1100	1080	1040	980	900	800	680	540
200	190	360	510	640	750	840	910	960	990	1000	990	960	910	840	750	640	510	360
190	180	340	480	600	700	780	840	880	900	900	880	840	780	700	600	480	340	180
180	170	320	450	560	650	720	770	800	810	800	770	720	650	560	450	320	170	0
170	160	300	420	520	600	660	700	720	720	700	660	600	520	420	300	160	0	
160	150	280	390	480	550	600	630	640	630	600	550	480	390	280	150	0		
150	140	260	360	440	500	540	560	560	540	500	440	360	260	140	0			
140	130	240	330	400	450	480	490	480	450	400	330	240	130	0				
130	120	220	300	360	400	420	420	400	360	300	220	120	0					
120	110	200	270	320	350	360	350	320	270	200	110	0						
110	100	180	240	280	300	300	280	240	180	100	0							
100	90	160	210	240	250	240	210	160	90	0								
90	80	140	180	200	200	180	140	80	0									
80	70	120	150	160	150	120	70	0										
70	60	100	120	120	100	60	0											
60	50	80	90	80	50	0												
50	40	60	60	40	0													
40	30	40	30	0														
30	20	20	0															
20	10	0																
10	0																	

[a] From Siegal and Fouraker (1960, pp. 114–115).

other. In a conflict, threats are better than actions, since the latter often destroy as much as they gain. A conflict, therefore, is really basically a bargaining situation.[5]

How does the unscrupulous bargainer force his opponent to give in to his demands? Rationality is not a virtue. Full information, good communication, and efficient decision-making abilities can all be turned into liabilities. Often the man (or nation) with the upper hand in a conflict situation is the weaker of the parties.

On rationality. Rationality is often a handicap. If the other side knows that you are rational, you may be at a disadvantage. "If a man knocks at the back door and says that he will stab himself unless given $10, he is more likely to get the $10 if his eyes are bloodshot." The man who hijacks an airliner and forces it to land in some remote country is more feared when he is irrational (with a history of mental disturbance) than when he appears to be logical and efficient. If a tiny country carefully nurtures the story that its leader is a madman with dictatorial powers, the leader can threaten to drop a deadly poison in the water supply of Paris unless the United States apologizes for seating his ambassador in the wrong spot at a dinner party.

The normal rules of bargaining assume that each participant evaluates the costs and penalties in a rational manner, each trying to maximize his own position. But if one side is irrational, then the strategic negotiations are totally disrupted. If the opponent is believed to be incapable of making a proper evaluation of the costs and penalties or if he does not care about them, then strategic manipulations become ineffective.

On good communication. The side with the most efficient communication is often at a disadvantage. If you are arguing with a friend on the telephone over where to eat dinner, he wanting seafood at one end of town, you preferring Chinese food at the other, the best strategy for you is simply to announce that you will be at the Chinese restaurant at 6 P.M. and immediately hang up and leave. If he wants to eat with you, he has no choice but to meet you there.

Manipulation of communication channels is effective both as a threat and as a defense against threat. If a threat is not heard or understood, then the commitment to carry it out becomes meaningless. One option for the father who suspects that his daughter might have been kidnapped is to leave town and remain incommunicado before any negotiations begin. Use of foreign troops is effective in quelling riots and civil disturbances because the language barrier makes them immune to threats,

---

[5] The discussion that follows is motivated by Schelling's book *The Strategy of Conflict* (1963). All quotations in this section are from Schelling.

promises, and commitments. Moreover, it may even add the ingredient of irrationality to the decision situation.

On power. The man with the power to make decisions is the man at a disadvantage. In negotiations, it is always best to send a low-level person—one who simply follows orders. Then, no matter how persuasive the arguments of the other side, even if he finally came to agree with them, he could not change the bargaining position. Were one side represented by the chief, then everyone knows that once he is persuaded—no matter how slightly—he has the power to give in.

The wise president of a university now denies that he has any power over the police. Thus, when a campus disturbance arises, he can tell the students that he sympathizes with their problems, but the city chief of police has informed him that if the disturbance is not ended in 1 hour, the tactical squad will be sent in. By his lack of power over the police, the president can dramatically increase his power over the total situation.

Altering the payoff matrix. If a threat has no effect on the decision process, then it loses effectiveness. This is a plausible tactic, since there is usually a large degree of uncertainty associated with the evaluation of someone else's costs and values. If a group of kidnappers have a government hostage, then one counterresponse for the government is to act as if the life of the hostage were insignificant. If someone kidnaps the son of a prominent businessman, he could respond by saying, "Good riddance."

On the escalation of threat and counterthreat. Suppose the "Keep New York Small" movement opposes the construction of a new 125-story building at the entrance to the George Washington Bridge. No one listens to them, so they decide to dramatize their plight by threatening to stop railroad transportation until their requests are met. The intention is to do it all peacefully: No one wants any violence. The railroad ignores the statement. Now the movement carries out its threat by sitting on one of the railroad tracks, forcing the next commuter train to a halt. The engineer in charge of the train, being a reasonable man, has no choice but to stop. Score one for the movement.

The railroad company decides to counter the threat: They instruct the engineer to set the throttle of the train so that it moves very slowly along the tracks and then to jump out of the train and walk along beside it. Now, he no longer has power to control the train, even if he would want to: The other side had better get off the tracks. Score one for the tactic of *lack of power.*

The "Keep New York Small" movement has an obvious counterthreat. Thus, the next time they sit on a track, they also destroy their power to move: They handcuff themselves to the track. Score another for the tactic of *lack of power:* The engineer does not dare leave the train.

But this last tactic is vulnerable, for here communication is very important. The people in the movement dare not actually handcuff themselves until they can assure themselves that the engineer knows they are handcuffed. Obviously, the best counterresponse of the railroad is to assign a deaf engineer to the train. Score one for the tactic of *lack of communication.*

The difficulty with all these tactics of threat is well illustrated by the example. Primarily, they are temporary, unstable solutions to a particular situation. They force agreement by default, not because the participants have come to any real understanding of the issues that are involved. They turn the negotiation process into a game, and the main difficulty with viewing an issue in this way is that there always seems to be a rematch. Unfortunately, when negotiations must be conducted in the face of mutual distrust, often there is no alternative but to play out the scenario, time after time.

No real solution to these problems exists. The psychologist has attempted to analyze them formally, usually by means of a set of mathematical techniques known as game theory. Readings on this topic are suggested in the "Suggested Readings" at the end of this chapter. Be warned that although game theory can be fun, it is highly controversial as a means of analyzing human behavior. In its formal analysis, it also is very technical, often requiring a high degree of mathematical sophistication.

GAMES AND DECISIONS

One formal analysis of decision making in the social context is the Theory of Games. Game theory is similar in spirit to the study of rational decision making considered in the last chapter. It attempts to specify a formal definition of the decision situation and derive rational solutions. Although, to date, game theory has not been able to deal adequately with some of the more complex factors operating in social decision making, it provides an excellent anchor point for beginning the investigation of decision making in the social context.

A game of pure competition   The basic ingredient of social decision making is that the outcome depends upon the joint actions of a number of people. We begin with the simplest case—the situation in which two players oppose each other in a game. Each player chooses a course of action from those available to him. He makes his selection alone, without any communication with the other player. When he has made his decision, both players reveal their choices simultaneously

FIGURE 16-6

A Game of Pure Competition

The Payoff Received by Player A

		If B Selects	
		1	2
If A Selects	1	3	0
	2	5	−5

The Payoff Received by Player B

		If B Selects	
		1	2
If A Selects	1	−3	0
	2	−5	5

The Joint Matrix

		If B Selects	
		1	2
If A Selects	1	3 : −3	0 : 0
	2	5 : −5	−5 : 5

(the proper way to do this is for the selection to be written down and handed to an impartial referee). The heart of the game is the **payoff matrix:** the set of outcomes that results from their combined choice.

One form of payoff matrix is shown in Figure 16-6 in three parts. The top matrix shows how much player A receives for each combination of moves that he and his opponent might make. The second matrix shows the same information for player B. The bottom matrix is the joint matrix which illustrates the usual manner in which this information is presented: Both the other two matrices are combined into one. In the joint matrix, the left-hand number always represents the payoff to the player listed on the left of the matrix; the right-hand number indicates the payoff to the player listed at the top.

According to these payoff matrices, if both players A and B choose option 1, A gets $3 and B loses $3. If they both choose 2, A loses $5 and B wins $5. The problem, then, is this: If both players know what the payoff matrices look like, what response should they make?

The decision strategy for this situation is rather simple. Player A should reason somewhat like this:

> Clearly, I want to win the most—that means I should play 2 and B
> should play 1. But B is no dope. He will lose the most if that happens,
> so he will probably play 2. If B plays 2 I have to play 1 or lose $5.
> And then, even if B does play 1, I come out ahead.

Player B has a somewhat different line: He has little choice. If B plays
1, he always loses. If he plays 2, the worst he can do is to break even.
Therefore, in this particular game, we would expect A to select 1 and B
to select 2: The game always ends in a draw.

This is one of the simplest of all decision situations whose outcomes depend
on the joint actions of two opponents. It is defined as *purely competitive*,
since whatever value one opponent wins, the other must lose. (In the language
of game theory, this is a *zero sum* game.) There are no combinations of
decisions where they both could win or lose. It is also defined as a *determinate*
game, since the outcome for rational players is always the same. There is
no room for negotiation or persuasion or chicanery. Player B can announce
his play beforehand and state that he will always play 2. This open declaration
would not tempt A to change his choice from 1 to 2, since he loses $5
by doing so. Similarly, the announcement by A that he will play 2 would
not affect B's behavior. Whether there is communication or secrecy is irrelevant, and does not affect the outcome. To explore a more interesting and
more typical situation, the first thing to do is to relax the basic constraint
operating in this simple determinant game: the property that a single joint
decision is optimal for both players.

When deception
makes a difference   A rearrangement of the payoffs for the various decision combinations converts
the basic game into a much more interesting and realistic decision situation.
A historical example illustrates what happens when a particular combination
of decisions is not optimal for both sides.

FIGURE 16-7

		If the Germans	
		Defend the Harbor	*Defend the Beaches*
If the Allies	Attack the Harbor	① 0 : 0	② +5 : −5
	Attack the Beaches	③ +3 : −3	④ −5 : +5

Prior to the allied landings during World War II, the Germans had to anticipate where the main thrust of the invasion would come. There was a choice of probable sites along the west coast of France, among the most likely being the harbor at Calais. The harbor facilities were crucial for the rapid buildup of the logistical support of the invasion forces. Less likely but still probable, were the beaches along Normandy. The Germans had to choose where to put their main fortifications and defensive forces; the Allies had to choose whether to attack the harbor or the beaches. It is a joint decision situation and the outcome can be represented by a payoff matrix.   Figure 16-7

This matrix assumes that if the Allies attack a heavily fortified harbor against maximal defensive formations, the result is indeterminate (0).

Presumably, an attack on the open beaches of Normandy against a concentrated defense effort would be unsuccessful: a loss of 5 to the Allies, a gain of 5 to the Germans. Finally, assume that the Allies have a greater gain if they attack an undefended harbor than if they attack an undefended beach.

Superficially, the decision strategies of the two antagonists might be expected to proceed as before. Both sides know the approximate payoffs for the various combinations of decisions. When the Allies examine the decision situation, they should conclude they can minimize their maximum losses by attacking the harbor. Similarly, the Germans might think their optimal strategy is to concentrate their defensive capabilities on the harbor (which, in fact, they did). It might be expected, then, that the selection of strategy ① by both sides would be the automatic outcome; the outcome labeled ① .

A little further examination suggests that, unlike the previous situation, this is not a stable outcome. Suppose the Allies have been following the German reasoning. They will know that the Germans might expect them to attack the harbor. If the Germans actually adopt strategy ① , however, the Allies can gain by attacking the beaches. The outcome would be box ③ in the decision matrix. But the Germans should anticipate this line of reasoning by the Allies and might guess that the Allies would really select the beaches. In this case, their optimal choice is changed, and they should also concentrate their defensive operations on the beaches. The outcome would be box ④ . If, however, the Allies anticipate what the Germans will think that the Allies will think, they should revert to the attack of the (now) undefended harbor, hoping for box ② as the final outcome. This means that the Germans should revert to their initial strategy to produce box ① . In short, there is no stable combination of choices in this decision situation: The best strategy depends on what one player perceives the opponent will perceive that he perceives, and so on.

This change in the payoff matrix is the key to the operation of social factors in decision making. It opens the door for communication, persuasion, and deception. No longer can the true decision be announced beforehand without giving an advantage to the opponent. The more information you have about the probable decision of other people, the greater your advantage in controlling the final outcome.

The prisoner's dilemma   One commonly encountered decision situation is where two participants are confronted with the problem of trying to assess an opponent's possible actions without being able to communicate with him. The situation is such that there is a cooperative solution: If both opponents act appropriately, they will both gain. There is also a competitive solution where a certain choice of actions results in a loss to both participants. In the two other possible outcomes, one gains at the other's expense. How do the participants arrive at a decision if negotiations are not permitted?

The decision situation. The basic situation is reportedly derived from a typical deal offered to prisoners by a prosecuting attorney. Prisoners A and B have been picked up on suspicion of being partners in a crime, but without any real evidence. Thus, the district attorney (the D.A.) tries to get the prisoners to confess. To do this, he offers a bribe. Each prisoner is informed that if he confesses (turns state's evidence), he will be pardoned and set free. Otherwise, the D.A. will do all he can to bring full charges against him. If he does not confess and his partner does, he will receive the maximum penalty for the crime—25 years' imprisonment. If neither confesses, the evidence for conviction will not be very strong. The worst that can happen is a conviction for a minor charge (such as disturbing the peace) and a 1-year sentence.

If both confess, the D.A. cannot let them both go, but he will recommend leniency: He predicts that each will receive a sentence of 10 years. The situation is summarized in Figure 16-8.

FIGURE 16-8

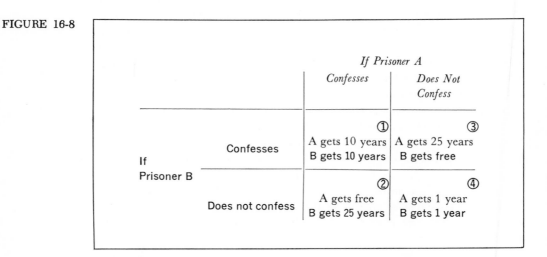

The dilemma is obvious: The best overall strategy is for neither A nor B to confess. But such joint behavior requires that each trust the other, and in the absence of communication, such trust may be difficult to form. Moreover, the police probably do their best to minimize the possibility that one prisoner can long maintain faith in the other by implying that they have already received a confession.

The problem faced by these participants is, in fact, a rather general decision problem: The general payoff matrix is shown in Figure 16-9. If one trusts the other person, one should follow strategy 2 (do not confess). If there are any doubts, however, then the other strategy becomes attractive.

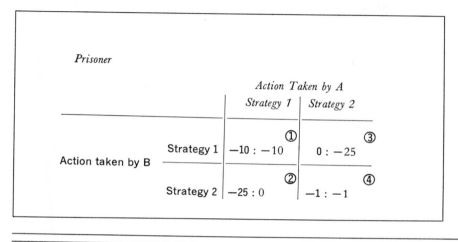

FIGURE 16-9

SUGGESTED
READINGS

Many of the readings for this chapter overlap those of the preceding chapter, so those references should also be consulted. Most of the material in this chapter draws from the field of social psychology or from game theory and political science. There are several excellent books that cover the topics.

The material on conformity, in which subjects are led to respond according to the responses of their fellow subjects rather than their own beliefs derives primarily from the work of Solomon Asch. This work is reviewed in Asch's text *Social Psychology* (1952). An excellent review is Crutchfield's article, "Conformity and Character" (1955). Asch's work can also be found in his 1955 *Scientific American* article. A review of the literature on conformity is provided by Allen's discussion, "Situational Factors in Conformity" (1965).

The material on bystander apathy comes from the book by Latané and Darley, *The Unresponsive Bystander* (1970). A very excellent short summary of the work can be found in the *American Scientist* article by Latané and Darley (1969).

The work on compliance with authority, the unexpected willingness of subjects to forego their own personal judgment and obey the requests of the experimenter, comes from the work of Stanley Milgram (1963, 1965). We also recommend that you read Milgram's reply to critics, in which he explained in some detail exactly how he conducted the aftermath of the experiment, the debriefing and thorough discussions of the experiments with his subjects (Milgram, 1964).

The example on bargaining comes from the book by Siegal and Fouraker, *Bargaining and Group Decision Making: Experiments in Bilateral Monopoly* (1960).

The work on strategic negotiation comes from the book by T. C. Schelling, *The Strategy of Conflict* (1963). This is a fascinating book, one that may be considered immoral by some circles. Anyone who reads Schelling's book should also read the one by Anatol Rapoport, *Fights, Games, and Debates* (1960). Both these books make excellent introductions to discussion on game theory. In addition, three excellent articles have appeared in *Scientific American*. [All are included in the book of reprints edited by Messick, *Mathematical Thinking in Behavioral Sciences: Readings from Scientific American* (1968).] The three articles are: Morgenstern, "The Theory of Games" (1949); Hurwicz, "Game Theory and Decisions" (1955); Rapoport, "The Use and Misuse of Game Theory" (1962). In addition, some of the books recommended for the previous chapter contain material relevant here, such as Coombs *et al. Mathematical Psychology* (1970) and Williams' book, *The Complete Strategist* (1954).

An important set of material, not discussed in this chapter but very much related, is the way by which people form beliefs and attitudes. Two excellent small books are available on this topic: one by Bem on beliefs (Bem, 1970: paperback); one by Zimbardo and Ebbesen, *Influencing Attitudes and Changing Behavior* (1969: paperback). A technical handbook on how to go about changing attitudes is provided by Karlins and Abelson (1970). Jacobo Varela, an applied psychologist from Montevideo, has applied many of these psychological principles to the social and interpersonal problems of daily life. His book (Varela, 1971) summarizes his philosophies and is highly relevant to the material covered within this chapter.

While on the topic of attitude change, Eugene Burdick's popular novel, *The 480* (1965) discusses how a thorough computer analysis of voting patterns was used to alter a hypothetical election. The analysis is not completely hypothetical; similar analyses are actually done by various companies that simulate the beliefs of the American voting populace in manners not unrelated to the discussion that occurred in this chapter.

A not-so-amusing discussion of an attempt to alter attitudes comes from McGinniss' discussion of *The Selling of the President, 1968* (1969). The most reassuring thing about this book is that, despite all its sophistication, many of the techniques simply did not work.

17

Motivation

BRAIN MECHANISMS OF MOTIVATION
Electrical control of hunger and thirst
Disrupting the motivational control system

MOTIVATIONAL CONTROL SYSTEMS
A numerical test
  Distasteful foods
  The land of milk and honey
Terminating eating
  Esophagus feeding
  Preloading the stomach
Nonbiological factors

RESPONDING TO UNCERTAINTY
Responses to stress
  BIOCHEMICAL RESPONSES TO STRESS
  How to produce stress
  Fear
Responses to conflict
  Approach–avoidance conflict
  Frustration
Responding to nothing
  Sensory deprivation
Neural mechanisms of arousal
  The reticular activating system
  SLEEP

INTERPRETING EMOTIONAL AROUSAL
Emotions: one or many?
  Physiological measures
  Biofeedback
To be mad or euphoric
  Emotional arousal
  The environmental conditions
  Euphoria
  Anger
  The results

MOTIVATION AND COGNITION
SUGGESTED READINGS

Many different sources of information interact to control what an animal or human does—from his thoughts, to his hormonal level, to his nutritional needs, to what he sees before him in the world. So far, we have concentrated on studying pure information-processing systems: systems that pick up information from the environment or from memory and follow through a logical sequence of operations. In the study of biological motives, we are dealing for the first time with systems that directly involve biochemical factors in their operation—systems for which the chemical state of the body is one of the most important inputs.

BRAIN MECHANISMS OF MOTIVATION

Electrical control of hunger and thirst

Start with a well-fed animal who appears to be perfectly content and not wanting for anything. Place him in a chamber where a preferred food is freely available. If he is indeed satiated for food, he will not eat. Now turn on a stimulating apparatus that passes an electrical pulse train through an electrode that has been implanted in the midbrain structure of his brain. If the electrode has been placed in the proper location, the animal will begin eating and continue to eat as long as the stimulator remains on. He stops eating as soon as the current is turned off. Electrodes placed in the proper region of the brain can reliably control the animal's eating responses (Hoebel, 1969).

On seeing a demonstration of electrical control over eating responses, the first question is whether we are actually activating the normal hunger system. The skeptic may argue that the animal's responses have nothing at all to do with motivation. It is quite possible, he will say, that the electrode simply is activating muscle control programs associated with eating. The ability to activate the muscle control by electrical stimulation is not novel, nor does it indicate anything about motivation.

How can the skeptic be convinced that the electrode stimulation is really affecting a motivational control system? Well, first of all, the animal's response should have a number of distinctive characteristics. For one thing, his response to the electrical current should not simply be an automatic eating response of whatever happens to be available. Rather, it should depend on what the animal has learned to do under normal circumstances in the past. Moreover, the animal should acquire new response patterns if old ones no longer lead to the desired results. Finally, his behavior should be related only to a specific type of motivation: perhaps either for water or for food. This last piece of evidence is needed in order to rule out the possibility that the electrode simply influences some general activation system, making the animal generally more responsive to anything in his environment, including food. Until all these points have been demonstrated, the case for the electrical control of motivational systems will not be proven.

An animal's response to an electrical pulse train that activates neural circuits in his midbrain is identical to the response that results from a biological hunger drive. He does not simply consume any food that happens to be available. He dutifully executes the response that he has learned will produce food. He will change that response when it no longer produces food. In short, he acts like a hungry animal, even though his hunger is electrical rather than biochemical in origin (Hoebel, 1969).

Similar results have now been found for many different motivational systems. Goats, rats, cats, and monkeys will learn a variety of arbitrary responses under the influence of electrical brain stimulation in order to obtain such things as food, water, and suitable sexual partners. The particular motivational system that is activated depends on the exact placement of the electrodes in the midbrain structures. By now, the precise locations of these areas are well known. Thus, motivated behavior can be activated at will, quite independently of any biochemical deficits existing in the organism.

Some locations of the electrodes have opposite effects: They stop the motivation. Thus, a hungry or thirsty animal will stop eating or drinking and return to his meal only when the stimulating current is terminated. The first clue to the nature of motivational systems is that they seem to follow the general principle of neural information-processing: Two opposing systems act against each other; whether they be muscle control, the perceptual analysis, or motivation—an excitatory system is opposed by an inhibitory system.

Disrupting the motivational control system

If stimulating a particular region of the brain causes a satiated animal to eat, then destroying that same brain location with a lesion should do just the opposite: It should produce an animal who has no interest in food, even when hungry. Similarly, if electrical stimulation of a brain region inhibits eating in a hungry animal, then surgically destroying this same region should produce an animal who eats all the time, even when not hungry. These conclusions are based on the assumption that the control system opposes excitatory and inhibitory mechanisms.

Lesions can affect either excitatory or inhibitory regions. A lesion in an excitatory area of the hunger center produces an animal who refuses to eat, even when dying of hunger. A lesion in an inhibitory area produces an animal who overeats and finally reaches a weight several times his normal weight (this condition is called *hyperphagia*).

A lesion in an inhibitory center for hunger produces an animal who appears to be chronically hungry. Despite his voracious appetite, however, he is quite picky about what he eats. So long as a preferred food is freely available, he consumes enormous quantities and grows excessively fat. Nevertheless, his overeating does not extend to foods that are normally either neutral or aversive to him (Teitelbaum & Epstein, 1962).

There are some types of lesions which severely alter the animal's ordinary food and water preferences. He eats and drinks materials that are normally extremely aversive to him. These lesions also produce indiscriminate sexual behavior and a general lack of goal orientation. They suggest a complete disruption in whatever mechanism ordinarily evaluates the pertinence of environmental information to a particular motive. The pervasive influence of the lesion on a variety of behaviors implies that there may be a common evaluation process serving a number of different motivational systems.

These electrical and surgical techniques are gradually uncovering the outlines of the mechanisms involved in motivation. The details have not yet been filled in. It is now rather commonplace to insert electrodes into the brain in order to turn motivational responses on and off, all under push-button control. If the aim of psychology were simply to control behavior rather than to understand the mechanisms that underlie it, then the ability to control motivational responses would represent perhaps the most dramatic success story of the psychologist.

To understand the principles of a motivational control system, we explore a prototypical system—the control of hunger. The goal is to outline the structures that interact with one another in controlling an organism's motivated behavior. The first step is to decide, in general, what the system must do.

MOTIVATIONAL CONTROL SYSTEMS

Overall, the function of a motivational control system is clear. The organism continuously consumes food substances: protein, fat, vitamins, sugar, water. Biological control systems must ensure that sufficient reserves of these substances are available for normal metabolism. Periodically, the system should take action to replenish these supplies. At the same time, it must make sure that excesses do not build up. In addition to maintaining a balanced diet, the system should protect the organism against potentially harmful materials. All this is to be done unobtrusively in the background, without unduly interfering with the other activities that occupy an organism's daily existence.

At this point, we can put together the first few stages of the model of the hunger-control system. The general function of motivational control systems is to regulate the availability of an enormous variety of chemical substances which together make up the *biochemical state* of the organism. Obviously, this requires some physiological mechanism for monitoring the available reserves of these biochemical substances.

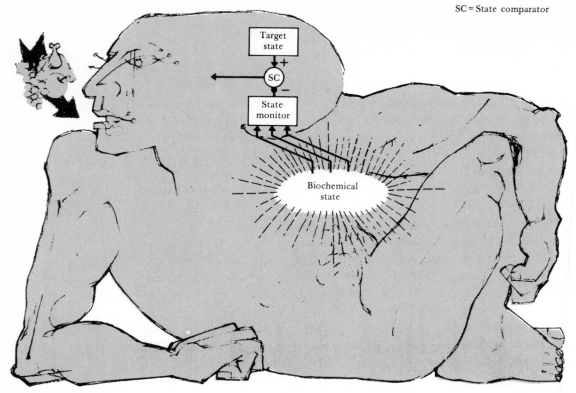

FIGURE 17-1

For the purposes of the model, call this measuring device a *state monitor*. Its job is to keep track of the amount of a particular substance available in the body, and its response can be represented as a single number: the current reserve level of the particular substance it is monitoring. (Of course, there must be many different types of state monitors associated with different metabolic substances, but we give them a common name, since they all perform the same logical function in the control system.)

As the substances are used up during normal metabolism, the output from the state monitor changes continuously. At some point, the reserves will fall to a critical level, and this is the point at which the organism becomes motivated. This aspect of the control system can be represented logically as a comparison between the output of the state monitor and some critical level or *target state*. Figure 17-1 summarizes the relationship between the biochemical state, the state monitor, and the target state in a set of boxes. The circle represents a comparison process; rectangles represent the processes of the system. The arrows and dots converging at a circle specify the inputs that are to be compared, and the arrow leaving the circle specifies the results of the comparison. As in the drawings for neural circuits, an arrow means the input is excitatory (added); the dot means the input is inhibitory (subtracted). These arrows and circles, of course, represent whole neural structures rather than individual neurons.

In the model, the device that compares the state monitor with the target state, the *state comparator* (*SC*), is subtracting the value for the biochemical state value from the target value. Thus, a negative output indicates that sufficient biochemical reserves are available. When the biochemical state falls below the target value, the output of the SC becomes positive and provides the cue that something is amiss: The organism should take steps correct it.

When the SC output goes positive, then the animal should begin some sort of food-seeking behavior. The exact types of responses produced will depend on the response repertoire of the animal and the environment in which it finds itself. This is the point at which motivational factors begin interacting with learning experiences, and we indicate this in Figure 17-2 simply by connecting the state comparison to a *behavior selector,* a system that is responsible for initiating food-seeking behavior. The presence of the behavior selector will serve as a reminder of the conditions under which the motivational system takes over control of the organism's behavior and begins to guide its responses.

FIGURE 17-2

SC = State comparator

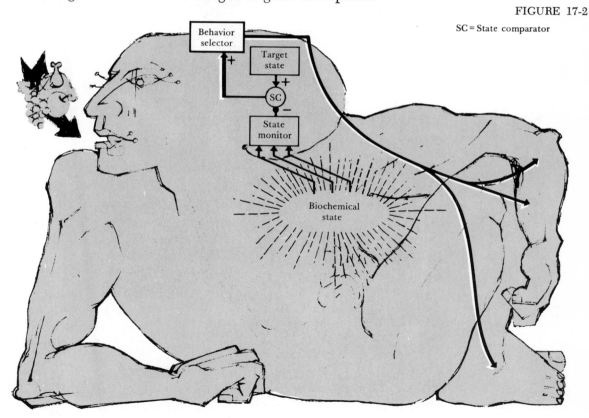

What happens next? The next question concerns how the environmental information is used during the organism's food-seeking behavior. We assume that, with a particular kind of motivational deficit, the organism will look for a particular type of environmental event. It is not going to look for food when it is thirsty. Thus, when the state comparator goes positive, environmental information begins to be analyzed in terms of its relevance to the present deficit. Information arriving by way of the sensory systems is compared with what the animal knows about his target, and the results of this comparison depend on how well the environmental objects match the animal's internal target-image of food.

To summarize this aspect of motivated behavior, several things must be added to the system (Figure 17-3). First, to show that environmental objects are analyzed by the sensory system and compared with the internal image of the target, add a *sensory analysis* and *target image* to the system. Second, to show that these two sources of information are compared with each other, add a *goal comparator* (*GC*).

FIGURE 17-3

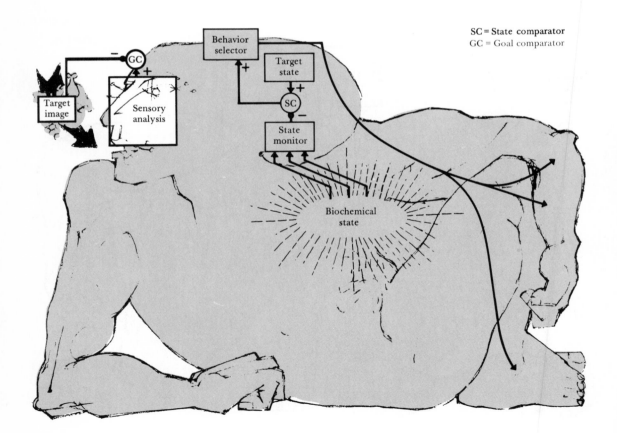

So far, there is a mechanism for measuring the biochemical status of the organism, one for initiating food-seeking action when the level drops too low, and one for analyzing incoming sensory data for their relevance to the motivation deficit. All that remains is to control the time at which the organism will stop looking and start eating. This is done with another comparison device, the *state goal comparator* (*SGC*) (Figure 17-4). The SGC simply **adds** the inputs from the state comparator and the goal comparator. The output of the SGC activates a *consumption* box when it goes positive and simultaneously terminates the behavior selector. As we shall see later, this arrangement allows a very hungry animal to eat almost anything, even if the goal comparator says it has a negative value as food. It also allows an animal who is not at all hungry to eat, if the food is sufficiently desirable.

FIGURE 17-4

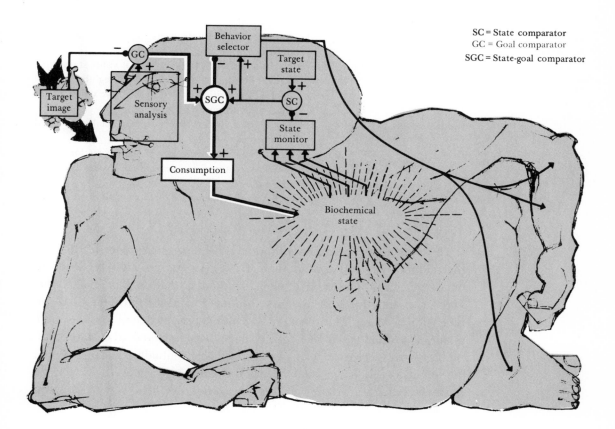

SC = State comparator
GC = Goal comparator
SGC = State-goal comparator

Table 17-1   List of Components and Their Properties

Behavior Selector	Initiates food-seeking behavior. Operates only when both SC and SGC allow it. A positive value of SC initiates activity of Behavior Selector; a positive value of SGC stops it
Biochemical State	The storage reserves of biochemical substances used by the organism
Consumption	Initiates consumption of whatever object is presently being analyzed by the Sensory Analysis, but only if SGC output level is positive
Digestion	The process of converting the objects eaten into their basic biochemical values
Environment	The world in which the animal lives: In this diagram, everything outside the animal's body
Goal Comparator (GC)	Compares sensory analysis with internal image. Output value signifies how good the comparison is
Sensory Analysis	Analyzes environmental information about the object before the animal from information provided by the sensory system. Includes the pattern recognition stages. Gives positive response only to objects categorizable as food
State Comparator (SC)	Subtracts value of state monitor from value of target state. Output value reflects the size of the hunger deficit
State Goal Comparator (SGC)	Adds values of SC and GC. Output value states how much the food is desired, combining the type of food with nutritional need. A negative value means that no consumption should occur
State Monitor	Measures the current concentration of biochemical substances
Target Image	The internal representation of the object for which the sensory analysis is searching. Is usually rather general
Target State	Represents desired value of biochemical substance

The system as it stands outlines the sequence of events leading to the initiation of food consumption. How does consumption get stopped, once it begins? The most obvious solution is that as food enters the body, the digestive system starts working to restore the deficits in the biochemical state. This change is continuously watched by the *state monitor,* so that when the deficits have been restored, the *state comparator* level decreases to a negative value, eventually shutting off the consummatory behavior and letting the animal get back to its normal business. Later on, we shall see that this is not a realistic way of stopping the consummatory behavior. For the moment, however, it closes the loop and allows us to proceed with testing the behavior of the model. (Meanwhile, see if you can determine the reason why the system needs another way to stop consuming food.)

This model, then, is a description of the logical mechanisms involved in a motivational control system. It is complete enough now that it can be tested. The first question is what an organism's response patterns would look like if this were the system controlling its behavior. The second question is, how are the systems outlined in the model reflected in the experimental studies of motivation?

Suppose a hypothetical animal were controlled by the system of Figure 17-4. What would the animal's behavior look like? Would such a control system accurately maintain the internal reserves of the substance it is monitoring? What kinds of food preferences would there be, and what variables would affect his eating patterns? Will he know enough to ignore nonnutrient substances and eat the correct amount of nutrient materials?   *A numerical test*

To form a general idea of how the system might operate, it is useful to work through some examples. Take a piece of paper and set up the following eight columns: Time, State Monitor, SC, Sensory Analysis, GC, SGC, Behavior Selector, Consumption (see Table 17-2). The table will be used to follow the responses of each component as we study how the system might behave.[1]

Under typical circumstances, start off in the table at time 1 (assume that the times are measured in hours). Suppose that at this time the animal has a partially filled stomach: There are 100 units in the biochemical state, and the state monitor reports this figure. The target value is 90, so the output of the state comparator is −10. Clearly, the animal is not yet hungry, so the other columns can be ignored. No food-seeking behavior is initiated.

As time goes by, the animal's normal activities continue to use up his internal reserves. Assume that the animal uses up 3 units of substance each hour. Thus, hour-by-hour, the state monitor reports steadily decreasing values of biochemical substances. Finally, at the 5th hour, the state monitor value drops to 88, below the target state. Now the SC goes positive, and food-seeking behavior is initiated (the behavior selector is turned **on**).

---

[1] Those of you who are more ambitious can write a computer simulation of the process. We have found this particularly easy to do with this system, especially when one has access to the computer through a typewriter terminal. The computer language BASIC is ideal for this problem.

Table 17-2

Metabolic Rate: 3 units per hour
Target State: 90
Target Image: 25

Time (hours)	State Monitor	SC	Sensory Analysis	GC	SGC	Behavior Selector	Consumption
1	100	−10	—	—	—	—	—
2	97	−7	—	—	—	—	—
3	94	−4	—	—	—	—	—
4	91	−1	—	—	—	—	—
5	88	+2	On	−25	−23	On	—
6	85	+5	On	−25	−20	On	—
7	82	+8	On	−25	−17	On	—
8	79	+11	On	−25	−14	On	—
9	76	+14	On	−25	−11	On	—
10	73	+17	On	−25	−8	On	—
11	70	+20	On	−25	−5	On	—
12	67	+23	On	−25	−2	On	—
13	64	+26	On	−25	+1	—	Yes
14	74	+16	On	−25	−9	On	—
15	71	+19	On	−25	−6	On	—
16	68	+22	On	−25	−3	On	—
17	65	+25	On	−25	0	On	—
18	62	+28	On	−25	+3	—	Yes
19	72	+18	On	−25	−7	On	—
20	69	+21	On	−25	−4	On	—

The fact that the animal is now motivated does not necessarily mean that he will immediately eat whatever happens to be around. Suppose that the only objects in front of the animal have a sensory analysis value of 0; that is, they are not normally considered to be food. Moreover, assume the animal is usually picky about his food, so he will not accept anything with an internal target image value less than 25 as being worth eating. Hence, in this case, the output of the goal comparator is −25, and the output of the state goal comparator is −23. The animal does not eat. At the 5th hour, then, the biochemical state is 88, the target state is 90, the sensory analysis reports 0, and the internal target image for food is 25. Be certain you can fill in all the remaining columns.

When will the animal eat? It depends on two factors. If the sensory analysis reports a desirable enough food object, he will eat it immediately. (The food would have to have a sensory analysis value of at least 24.) Alternatively, if time goes by and he gets hungry enough (the state comparator rises to high enough values), he will eat the object with food value of 0 (the SC would have to increase to $+26$). Eventually, these two factors—the desirability of the food and the animal's state of hunger—will balance out, and something will be eaten.

Distasteful foods. Suppose first that the animal is unable to find anything to eat that has a food value higher than 0. As shown in the table, he resists eating for hour after hour, while his biochemical state keeps dropping. Finally, by the 13th hour, the value of the state monitor has dropped to 64, and the SGC goes positive to $+1$. He will eat, even though the food substance before him has 0 desirability.

If the object he is eating turns out to have a nutritional value of 10 units, and it takes him one hour to digest it, by the 14th hour the food will add 10 units to the biochemical state. The state monitor will then report a value of 74. (If the animal were lost in the woods, assume that the food he finally starts to eat is plant roots.) Even though the animal is still hungry, he has regained enough food substance that he no longer will force himself to eat something with a sensory analysis of 0. As the biochemical state starts to decrease in value again, at 3 units each hour, by the 18th hour it will be down to 62, the state comparison will have risen to 28, and the animal once again will overcome his distaste for the food of 0 desirability (plant roots) and begin eating.

The animal is now in a stable situation. He remains continually hungry with a biochemical state somewhere between 60 and 70. Every 4 or 5 hours, he forces himself to overcome his distaste for the food before him (roots) and eats enough to keep him going for another 4 or 5 hours. But in the interim, he spends his whole time looking for food. He keeps looking, even though he does not eat unless something better than roots turns up.

The land of milk and honey. Now consider the situation in which food of relatively high value is continuously available (see Table 17-3). It starts off just as before. At the end of the 5th hour, the animal is hungry, but now he immediately discovers food that is palatable: The sensory analysis value of this preferred food is 30. He starts eating right away. If this food has the same nutritional value as the roots—10 units—he will be content for several more hours; until the 9th hour, in fact. Then he again gets hungry, but again satisfies his hunger immediately.

Note the rather dramatic differences in the animal's behavior caused simply by changing the preference value of the available food. Exactly

Table 17-3

Metabolic Rate: 3 units per hour
Target State: 90
Target Image: 25

Time (hours)	State Monitor	SC	Sensory Analysis	GC	SGC	Behavior Selector	Consumption
1	100	−10	—	—	—	—	—
2	97	−7	—	—	—	—	—
3	94	−4	—	—	—	—	—
4	91	−1	—	—	—	—	—
5	88	+2	30	5	7	—	Yes
6	98	−8	—	—	—	—	—
7	95	−5	—	—	—	—	—
8	92	−2	—	—	—	—	—
9	89	+1	30	5	6	—	Yes
10	99	−9	—	—	—	—	—

the same motivational system is operating. But when the available food has low preference value, the animal is always hungry. Everything he does is based around the search for food. Moreover, he probably loses weight, since his average biochemical state hovers somewhere in the 60s. When we change foods, however, the animal is no longer preoccupied with hunger. Every 4 or 5 hours he eats, but he is not hungry in-between. He does not need to think about food for hours at a time. Moreover, his body weight is probably reasonably high, since the biochemical state now fluctuates between 87 and 99.

It is important to note that in these two examples, the nutritional value of the food remained constant. All that was changed was its desirability. It is like the difference between 800 calories worth of plant roots and 800 calories worth of steak. On the former, our animal would always be hungry and thin, always searching for better food. On the latter, he would be happy and content, well fed, and with plenty of leisure time. How would his eating patterns be affected by foods with equal preference but different nutritional values? Work through an example and see.

Of course, this model is an extreme simplification of real motivational processes. It is fine for organizing our initial thinking about how motivational control processes might work, and in fact, it illustrates some of the basic principles involved. But if you examine the details carefully, you will find many problems. These become apparent when we take the model into the laboratory to subject it to experimental tests.

One of the greatest discrepancies between the model with which we have been working and real biological systems is the manner in which a motivational sequence is terminated. In the model, it was assumed that eating stops as soon as the biochemical state returns to a sensible level, either because the hunger stops (the output of the state monitor drops to a negative value), or because the desirability of the food is no longer high enough to sustain eating (the value of SGC drops to a negative value). One of the assumptions required to make this work is that the digestive process is very rapid. This is a bad assumption.

The digestive systems of most organisms are rather ponderous; they can easily require 2 hours or more to convert a meal completely into the biochemical components used for metabolism. Clearly, there must be some way of stopping consumption long before the deficits in biological state have been restored.

Several possibilities exist for controlling how much food is eaten. Most animals rely on sensing devices that monitor the quantity and some aspects of the quality of the food that is being ingested. These monitors can signal that sufficient intake has been consumed, long before any real change in biochemical levels has taken place.

One way to test the location and properties of the monitoring system is to see if it can be fooled. Does it simply monitor the amount of foodstuff in the stomach, stopping when the stomach is full? If so, then it should be possible to bypass eating and swallowing altogether. Simply fill a hungry animal's stomach with food through a tube. Will this stomach *preload* satisfy the animal's hunger? Alternatively, the animal could be allowed to eat normally, but with a tube inserted into his esophagus so that the food eaten never reaches the stomach: Will the animal stop eating after consuming a normal meal?

Esophagus feeding. A plausible guess for the locations of receptors that monitor food intake is that they are in the mouth or throat area. The obvious candidate is the tongue, since it is well equipped with taste receptors. These receptors provide a variety of information about the properties of the materials being ingested, and this information may be used by the motivational system to decide when to stop consumption. If this receptor information controls the amount the animal consumes, then he should eat normally even if the food does not actually reach his stomach. This can be arranged by a simple operation. A plastic tube is inserted into an animal so food entering the mouth leaves the body at the throat, just above the stomach. When the animal eats or drinks, the ingested material stimulates the throat and mouth in a normal fashion but never reaches the stomach. The preparation is called an *esophagus bypass.*

If receptors in the animal's tongue and throat are monitoring the

① Experimental animal outfitted with esophagus bypass

② Thirsty animal drinks, but water never enters his stomach

③ Nevertheless, apparently satiated, the animal stops drinking after his normal quota

④ But 5 or 10 minutes later he drinks again, a greater quantity than before

FIGURE 17-5

intake of food, then an animal with an esophagus bypass should eat and drink normally, ingest the appropriate amount, and then stop, even though nothing actually enters his stomach. Later on, when the control system discovers it has been fooled into terminating consumption without actually correcting the deficit conditions, the animal should begin eating again. If these peripheral sensors are insufficient or are not used at all to control intake, then the animal should continue consumption indefinitely, once he begins.

To set up the experiment, the animal is placed on a deprivation schedule and only allowed to eat or drink once every 24 hours. After he has adjusted to this schedule, careful measures are taken of the amount of food and water he normally consumes during the daily meal. This is to determine his typical behavior under the conditions of the experiment. Next is the operation and insertion of an esophagus bypass. After surgery, the animal is put back on the deprivation schedule. Finally, when he has fully recovered from the operation, the animal is ready for the critical test. Twenty-four hours after his normal feeding time, he is allowed free access to food and water. Does he eat and drink the appropriate amounts, then stop; or does he continue consumption as long as the food substances are available? The answer is both yes and no: It depends on whether he is eating or drinking.

A **thirsty** animal outfitted with an esophagus bypass will drink his normal quota of water and then stop, apparently satiated by liquids that never enter his stomach. Five to ten minutes later, he tries again to drink his daily water ration. The cycle continues with the amount of water consumed gradually increasing as the thirst deficits build up (Adolph, 1941). The conclusion is inescapable. Peripheral receptors in the mouth and throat are signaling when the appropriate amount of water has been ingested, and this information is sufficient to terminate drinking activity.

There is an interval of 5 to 10 min before the motivational control system detects the rather bizarre situation that, although sufficient water has entered the mouth and throat, somehow it never reached the stomach.

A **hungry** animal equipped with an esophagus bypass seems to keep eating and eating. Dogs, for example, will consume up to 80% of their body weight; an amount of food which, for humans, would be roughly equivalent to a 130-pound meal (Hull, 1951). In contrast to studies of thirst, the conclusions to be drawn from esophagus experiments on hunger are rather meager: If a mechanism exists for shutting off food consumption, then it certainly is not located in the mouth or throat region of mammals.

Preloading the stomach. A second technique for studying the nature of hunger and thirst control is to implant a tube (fistula) into the animal's stomach, so food or water can be injected directly into the stomach without passing through the mouth. The fistula is implanted in such a way that ingestion and digestion are not interfered with when the animal is allowed to eat normally.

What is the prediction about the behavior of a thirsty animal who is first preloaded with water, then given the opportunity to drink? Since the feedback information that tells the animal he is taking in water originates from peripheral receptors in the mouth and throat, it should not be activated when water is injected directly into his stomach. In short, preloading the animal's stomach with water should not immediately affect his thirst: He should drink a normal amount when given the opportunity.

To set up the experiment, again it is important to establish first how much an animal will drink on the average under a controlled set of conditions. As in the previous study, this is done by placing him on a fixed water-deprivation schedule and allowing him to have access to water only once every 24 hours. After his drinking behavior has stabilized, his average daily water intake is measured. Once the amount of water the animal normally drinks is known, he is ready for the experimental test.

At drinking time, the animal's stomach is preloaded with his daily water ration. Then he is given access to the water bowl, and his consumption is measured. It is also useful to test him with varying delay periods between the preload and his access to water, in order to see whether his drinking behavior changes as an increased amount of time is allowed for digestion.

In general, the results for this type of experiment are just what would be expected. After a preload, the animal still appears to be thirsty and will drink his normal water ration as soon as he is given the opportunity. If the time between the preload and when he is allowed to drink is delayed for, say, 5, 10, or 15 min, then the amount he consumes will decrease correspondingly. After a delay of some 20 min or so, digestion appears to be complete, and the animal shows no interest in the water (Adolph, 1941). Preloading an animal's stomach with water shuts off his thirst slowly: At first, the animal behaves as though he had not received any water at all (Figure 17-6).

What about a preload experiment on hunger? Should the animal still be hungry after a food preload, or should the direct injection of food into his stomach be sufficient to shut off his consummatory behavior? A hungry animal behaves differently from a thirsty animal. When pre-

FIGURE 17-6

loaded with food, his hunger is reduced (Smith & Duffy, 1955). We conclude that there must be feedback sensors in the upper ingestional tract or stomach regions which signal the motivational control system when the appropriate amount of food has entered the stomach.

It appears that the hunger system is capable of shutting off consumption long before digestive processes have had the time to restore the biochemical conditions of the organism. Further experiments indicate that it can work with both bulk and liquid materials. Moreover, it can discriminate between nonnutrient and nutrient substances and seems to be able to take account of the caloric value of the incoming food. There is no question that a fast feedback mechanism is operating, and some of its general characteristics are known. With all this information, it is somewhat surprising that no one has yet determined precisely where it is located or the details of how it actually performs its task. There is fragmentary evidence, but the complete picture is not yet clear.

We seem to be making good progress: Most organisms that have been studied, including humans, appear to be equipped with a rather sophisticated feedback mechanism for monitoring and analyzing the materials that are being ingested. This system supplies information about the amount of materials coming in, and some of the general characteristics of the ingested substances, such as their salt concentration and relative nutrient value. The arrangement frees the animal from having to depend on the slow-acting digestive processes, and provides him with fast, rather precise feedback information about the relative value of the incoming materials.

The next step is to decide how to incorporate this new information into the model of the motivational control system. Clearly, we need to add a box labeled *feedback monitor*. But where should the output of the feedback system be connected? One possibility is to connect it directly to the state monitor. With this arrangement, the comparator is driven negative as soon as the feedback mechanism indicates that the appropriate amount of food or water has been ingested. As a first guess, this seems to be the simplest and most logical way to use the feedback information. We leave you the task of completing the picture by adding the feedback mechanism. Be careful: It is not quite so easy a job as we have implied.

There is more to these basic biological control systems—more experimental facts, more neural and chemical circuits—but for present purposes, we have done enough. Motivational control systems operate through a combination of neural and chemical mechanisms that monitor the overall performance of the animal and regulate his internal reserves.

Nonbiological factors

But there are other controls on the system. We learn to be hungry at specified hours. We learn to regulate the pattern of food intake to the demands of the civilization in which we live, something that is hard to explain if we simply account for feeding behavior in terms of biochemical reserves. While undergoing severe mental or emotional strain, the whole regulatory system can be upset. The numerous nonbiological factors that enter into the behavior of the motivational system indicate that there are other parts of the system, parts we did not discuss. So the model is incomplete, not only in that some of the details have not been discussed, but also in that other principles must be involved.

Nonetheless, the major principles seem to be well defined. As we turn now to the study of other motives underlying an organism's behavior, we find the study of the basic, biological control-systems provides a useful starting point for understanding the more complex motivations operating in men and animals.

We have talked about the general structure of motivational systems underlying the biological survival of the organism. What about the other kinds of motivations people normally experience? What about things such as love and lust, anger and hate? Are there separate psychological and biological mechanisms underlying each of these motives, or is there some general process underlying all motivational experiences?

When we come to consider human motivation, one dominant theme emerges repeatedly. Uncertainty, a failure to observe an expected event, a disruption in the pattern of otherwise smoothly flowing response sequences, an anticipation of the inability to cope with a pending event—these seem to be basic driving forces behind human behavior. The common thread is a real or anticipated mismatch between what occurs and what is expected. An organism, be it human or nonhuman, acts as if it had an internal model against which to compare the events of the external world. Emotions and arousal result from the inadequacies of the model when the predictive apparatus fails.

This, of course, is familiar to you by now. We find over and over again that we can picture the mind as a device that actively engages the environment, interpreting current events within the context of past experience and expectations. Previously we have studied these processes operating in perception, memory, problem solving, and decision making. Now we will discover many of the same principles involved in the study of emotion and motivation. This is to be expected, because in the complex motives of humans, the nature of the environment does not seem to be as important as the interpretation given it. Memory and cognitive factors are intimately interlinked with the motives that underlie human behavior.

Words like *expectations, uncertainty, disruption, discrepancy, dissonance,* and *conflict* are key words in the experimental analysis of human emotion and motivation. A useful concept in considering these studies is the notion of the *state comparator,* which we discussed in the study of biological motives. In many types of motivational situations, the organism acts as if something were monitoring the ongoing cognitive processes, watching for potential trouble spots in dealing with the environment, and signaling when difficulties arise. It is like the state comparator for hunger except that it is primarily concerned with the results of cognitive processing rather than the biochemical condition of the organism. So long as things are within sensible limits, it remains quiet. But when something is encountered that is new or discrepant from what is expected or potentially threatening, it acts like an interrupt mechanism, alerting the organism to the potential problem and mobilizing resources to deal with it. The result is a change in the general level of arousal or activation. It can range from high levels under stress and fear to low levels when the environment makes no demands at all on the organism.

RESPONDING TO
UNCERTAINTY

Figure 17-7

Responses to stress

Two monkeys are placed in adjacent cages, both of which contain a bar. One of the monkeys, called the *executive monkey* (for reasons that will become obvious in a minute), must learn to press his bar at least once every 5 sec. If he fails to press within the appropriate limit, both he and his partner in the next cage receive an electric shock. The other monkey's bar has no effect at all on the presentation of shock. Thus, both monkeys undergo identical shock experiences, but only the executive monkey has control. He is the one who has to remain alert and act appropriate in order to avoid the shocks.

When monkeys are placed in this experimental situation for 6-hour work periods and 6-hour rest periods between each experimental session, daily physiological tests do not detect any abnormalities in either monkey. Both monkeys maintain a proper diet and weight. After about 20 days, however, the executive monkey dies. The cause of death is ulcers (Brady, 1958).

The ulcers of the executive monkey are only one of a large number of biochemical changes that can result from mental processes. Although both monkeys in this experiment received identical shock experiences, the second monkey remained perfectly healthy. The executive monkey differed from his partner in that he had to make the decisions. Having control seems to be the critical factor in stress. It is not simply contact with a painful event; stress is only produced when the organism must develop some way of coping with a threatening situation.

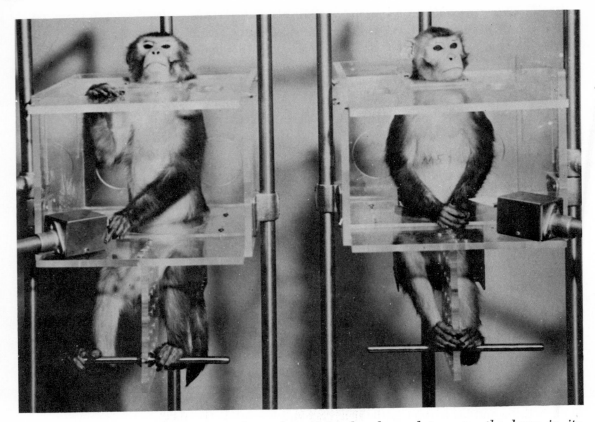

FIGURE 17-7   *The "executive" monkey (left) has learned to press the lever in its left hand, which prevents shocks to both animals. The other monkey (right) has lost interest in its lever, which is a dummy. From Brady (1958). U.S. Army photograph, Medical Audio Visual Department, Walter Reed Army Institute of Research, Washington, D.C.*

The wide range of conditions that can produce stress, coupled with the variability among individuals in their responses to stressful situations, have perplexed those who study the phenomenon. Under proper circumstances, almost anything can produce stress. The situation may be as dramatic as a parachute jump or as innocuous as a dripping faucet. The threat is really in the mind of the beholder. The capacity of a situation to arouse stress depends upon the perception of the situation and its context, past experience, and the availability of adaptive responses. Stress emerges as a result of the individual's active interpretation and interaction with his environment: It changes dynamically as the individual attempts to cope with the situation.

BIOCHEMICAL RESPONSES TO STRESS

The development of ulcers and other gastric disorders is only one of a large number of biochemical changes that occur with prolonged exposure to stress. The physiological responses go through several distinct stages. On initial contact with a stressful situation an alarm reaction develops, characterized by increased adrenaline discharge, increased heart rate, reduced body temperature and muscle tone, anemia, transient increases in blood sugar level, and stomach acidity. These symptoms, when present simultaneously, describe a state of clinical shock. If the stress persists, the alarm stage gives way to a defensive reaction in the body, during which the physiological control systems are mobilized to counteract the stressing agent. These changes are primarily due to altered activity in the pituitary–adrenal system, which diverts hormones, particularly those used during the digestive process, into the increased development of antibodies and maintenance of the heightened metabolic processes. It also tends to increase the release of chemicals from the normal storage reserves, in particular the blood sugar stored in the liver, to support the development of "general resistance." These last two factors account for the development of pathological conditions such as ulcers in the stomach and gastrointestinal tract and in hypoglycemia when the normal sugar reserves are depleted. The hyperactivity in the adrenal–pituitary system can lead to enlargement of the organs involved.

Figure 17-8

Should the resistance phase be unsuccessful in counteracting the stressing agent, the biochemical system finally gives way to a stage of exhaustion, collapse, and death.

Note several things about these biochemical responses to stress. First, these responses tend to be the same, regardless of the stress or agent operating. They occur for temperature changes, infection, intoxicants, injury, surgical trauma, as well as for physically noxious or painful stimuli. Similarly, they occur with stress that is primarily psychological in origin, such as the presence of psychologically threatening situations or the requirement of coping with a persisting threat in the environment. The general adaptation syndrome is present in varying degrees under all of these circumstances. Second, some of the stages in the stress response may be omitted. For particularly abrupt and severe stresses, the animal may pass directly from initial alarm to final exhaustion. The alarm stage, however, always seems to be necessary.

In addition to these general biochemical responses, common to all stressful situations, there are specific responses to particular events. Increasing temperature causes the arteries to dilate; decreasing temperature causes them to constrict. The type of antibodies formed depends on the infection they are to combat. The magnitude of the stress response depends upon the type of stressor agent, its intensity, and the abruptness of its occurrence. Immunity to stress can be developed, and people show a wide range of susceptibility

FIGURE 17-8

Normal   Stressed

Adrenals

Thymus

Lymph nodes

Inner surface
of stomach

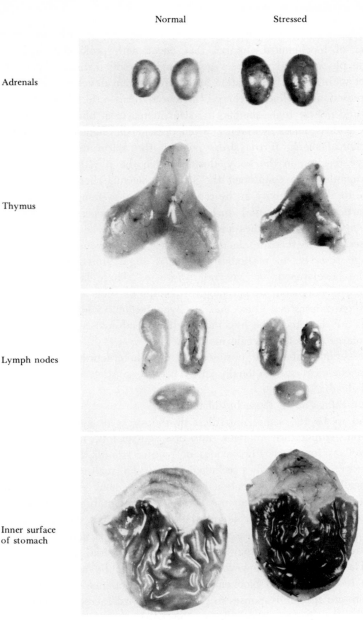

Characteristic symptoms of stress syndrome: enlarged and discolored adrenals, involuted thymus and lymph nodes, and ulcerated stomach wall. From Selye (1952).

to stressful circumstances. Individuals appear to become "immunized" when given repeated exposure to stressful conditions.

How to produce stress. We have already seen several experiments that were capable of producing high levels of stress: the executive monkeys in this chapter and the tests of conformity and compliance with authority described in Chapter 16. Nevertheless, the close dependence of stress on cognitive factors has made stress extremely difficult to study in the laboratory. For example, in one experiment, psychologists attempted to study the stress reaction in soldiers undergoing combat training, using live ammunition (Berkun, Bialek, Kearn, & Yagi, 1962). They were surprised at the apparently low levels of stress associated with the combat training. The trainees simply refused to believe that the Army would place them in a position where they could get hurt. They assumed (falsely) that being perched precariously on a tree with bullets whizzing all around ("sniper training") must be safer than it seems, or the Army would not permit it.

Similar difficulties are found in other experimental studies of stress. Most subjects assume that any ignoble treatment in an experiment must be part of the test manipulations. Their reluctance to give up their image of a benevolent experimenter, one who would not subject them to any real risk or harm without good reason, tends to counteract the effects the experimenter is trying to achieve.

Although these problems make it difficult to study stress under controlled conditions, they do underscore the importance of cognitive factors in determining emotional responses. If things are staged correctly, stress can be induced. A roller coaster ride can be made far more stressful (without changing the ride itself) by adding a few signs about the reliability of the track:

> **Warning. Loose track. This section under repair. Do not use while red flag is up** (a big red flag is perched on the sign).

Amusement park operators do not dare such tricks, even in jest, for the very success of the ride depends upon the conflict between the knowledge that things must be safe and the external appearances of danger. Make the cognition also believe in danger, and business would drop dramatically.

The various, well-publicized tests of "space stations" in which a number of volunteers are placed aboard a space simulator and locked up for some few months, also fail in their attempts to mimic stressful conditions. The knowledge that one is really on the ground, being observed all the time by television and various physiological measuring devices, takes away most of the reality of the experiment. Yes, the simulation does help in answering questions about the reliability of the toilets and other equipment, but human responses will be severely affected by the knowledge that this is only a test.

In general, the success of simulated environments in making people react normally depends a good deal on how successfully the simulation mimics reality. This difference between the psychological response to simulated and real experiences has been the basis of at least one science fiction solution to the problem of making astronauts perform coolly and competently during a real space mission, even in the face of massive equipment failure. The trick in the science fiction story was simple: The astronauts thought they were being run through one of the more realistic space simulators.

Stress produces a well-defined physiological response in both men and animals. It seems generally to result whenever the person has to deal with threatening or uncertain circumstances over prolonged periods of time. Whether a full-blown stress reaction emerges and the ultimate response to stress is roused depends on the individual's cognitive evaluation of the situation as he attempts to find adaptive responses to cope with stressful circumstances.

Fear. Stress and fear are related, but different phenomena. Situations that cause stress are typically rather diffuse and uncertain, and they may prevail over long periods of time. Sudden, well-specified environmental dangers lead to a more focused response: that of *fear*. The main difference between stress and fear is that in fear, certain specific responses become prominent, most especially those of escape and attack. Although exactly opposite in their effects, the responses of escape and attack are highly related: The same situation may provoke either attack or escape or even vacillation between the two.

In lower organisms, and probably in humans, fear and its associated responses of attack seem to be well-organized patterns of behavior under the control of specific neural subsystems in the brain. Electrical stimulation of these neural centers can provoke well-coordinated attack responses. Even small, white laboratory rats that are normally relatively calm and peaceful (quite unlike their ancestors, the larger gray rats that are wild and fierce) can be caused to attack a mouse under the influence of electrical stimulation. With some electrode placements, the attack is accompanied by all the external manifestations of rage: bristling hair, bared teeth, etc. With other placements, the attack may be carried out coolly and calmly with no external indications of emotional arousal. Typical patterns of the escape that results from fear can also be induced by electrode stimulation. Under the influence of electrical inputs, the animal may show fear and attempted flight when confronted with something it normally attacks: A cat will cower fearfully in front of its traditional enemy, a mouse.

When the same situation has both desirable and undesirable components, the organism has a problem. Should he approach the situation in order to obtain the positive rewards? How does he avoid the negative aspects at the same time? This situation has been formalized and studied rather carefully because of its potentially wide application in a variety of motivational contexts.   *Responses to conflict*

Approach–avoidance conflict.   The general strategy for studying approach–avoidance conflicts was first explicitly developed by Neal Miller (1951). The key ideas are easiest to see when they are shown graphically.

Consider a situation in which there is a goal that is both aversive with attractive. We diagram the situation in Figures 17-9 and 17-10. The line representing the strength of the approach tendency goes up as the

FIGURE 17-9

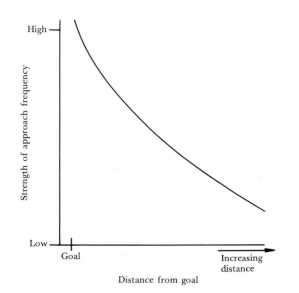

FIGURE 17-10

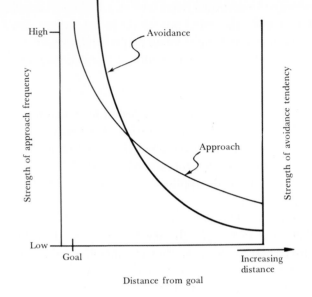

Distance from goal

animal moves closer to the goal. Similarly, the strength of avoidance tendencies also increases as the animal approaches the goal. The relative superiority of the strength of motives is shown by the fact that the curve for avoidance rises more quickly than the curve for approach. The way these two tendencies work on the organism is shown in Figure 17-11 by the two arrows (vectors); the organism (the circle) is pulled to the left by approach tendencies and pushed to the right by avoidance. The way he moves depends upon the relative strengths of the opposing forces.

FIGURE 17-11

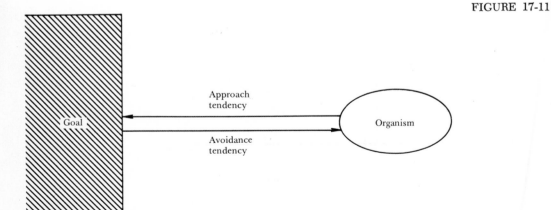

Suppose the animal is far from the goal—far to the right on the graph. Here, approach tendencies are stronger than those for avoidance, so he moves in closer. If he gets too close, however (to the left part of the graph), then avoidance tendencies predominate and he moves away. This produces a situation that has a stable equilibrium point, a point where the two forces exactly cancel each other.

This type of approach–avoidance conflict is easy to observe. It is visible in the swimmer attracted to the pleasure of swimming but repelled by the temperature of the water. In ideal situations, you can sometimes see a person vacillate for as long as 15 min, standing at the brink of the water, advancing and receding slightly, but essentially stuck at the equilibrium point. Finally, something happens to make the situation change, and either the person backs away and leaves, or closes his eyes, grits his teeth, and goes in. It is also visible around telephone booths, where students sometimes make calls to arrange dates. The approach–avoidance conflict involved in making a potentially troublesome telephone call can be dramatic. One observer has reported watching someone for 30 min, sitting in the telephone booth, continually on the brink of making the call, but never quite willing to go all the way through with the act.

The shapes of the two lines are not fixed forever, of course. Goals can be made more attractive, moving the approach curve higher up, and thus causing the equilibrium point to move closer to the goal. Alternatively, the avoidance gradient can increase, if there is an increment in the fear associated with the outcome, causing the equilibrium point to move farther away. Thus, to reduce a person's fear of a situation, either increase the positive aspects (increase the approach line) or decrease the negative aspects (lower the avoidance line). Alternatively, the whole situation could be reinterpreted, changing the relative values of both approach and avoidance.

The same type of analysis can be applied to other types of conflicts:

- **approach–approach.** The animal is torn between choosing one of two desirable situations. He can only select one of them.
- **avoidance–avoidance.** The animal is forced to choose one of two situations, but both are undesirable.

We leave it as an exercise for you to construct the relevant graphs for these other situations, but you might note that the *approach–approach* conflict has an unstable equilibrium point: As soon as the organism is displaced from that point, he will tend to drift all the way toward one of the situations. From the force diagram for the *avoidance–avoid-*

ance situation, you see from an immediate analogy with the similar force diagrams of physics that the best solution is to leave the situation, to go off vertically. This solution is often attempted. A student faced with the choice of either writing a term paper or talking to his professor (an act that apparently has high avoidance value) sometimes solves the avoidance–avoidance conflict by leaving school, making the whole choice somewhat academic.

Frustration. Conflict can arise because the same thing has both positive and negative values. It can also arise when something interferes with attempts to achieve a particular goal. When there is a barrier in the way of a desired action, the result is frustration, and the most common response to frustration is aggression.

In a classic study of this form of conflict, frustration was introduced into children of kindergarten age (Barker, Dembo, & Lewin, 1941). In the first part of the experiment, children were presented with a playroom containing a curious mixture of toys. The toys were without all their components: ironing boards without irons; water toys without water. The various deficiencies in the toys did not seem to bother the children in the least. They made imaginative use of the toys and seemed to enjoy constructing elaborate and imaginative games out of what was available.

Their behavior changed, however, when they were provided with a glimpse of a better world. They were allowed to look at toys for which no parts were missing and which were much more elaborate and intriguing to play with than the ones they had been given. The next day when they were again allowed to play with the original toys, the effects of this experience became apparent. The children were no longer satisfied with the motley collection that was available. They squabbled among themselves, they were belligerent to the experimenter, and they were destructive to the toys.

Our intuitions suggest that such aggressive responses are a natural reaction to frustration. When prevented from achieving some desired goal, direct aggression toward the barrier often results. If that is not possible, then there will often be displaced aggression toward whatever happens to be around. Aggression is part of our potential response to a frustration conflict. But aggression is clearly not an inevitable result of frustration: A generality of this magnitude seldom applies to an organism so complex as the human being.

Responding to nothing   In the situations we have been discussing so far, uncertainty arose as the organism was having difficulty negotiating with some aspects of his environment. He had to try to develop an adaptive response to some noxious situation, or a way of resolving conflicting response possibilities, or some means of overcoming a barrier that was blocking a desired action. What happens when the environment makes no demands whatsoever on the individual? You might think this should produce a completely placid organism: He has nothing to react to and thus nothing to tax his cognitive capacities.

Sensory deprivation. In 1959, at McGill University in Montreal, students were offered an opportunity to participate in an experiment that appeared to be a students' paradise (Heron, 1961). They would be highly paid for doing absolutely nothing. Their job was to remain in a small, bare room furnished only with a cot. The room was continuously lighted, but the subjects wore diffusing goggles over their eyes which prevented them from seeing any patterns. They wore cushions over their ears to reduce sound, and had their arms and legs wrapped to reduce tactile sensations. They could leave the room only to go to the toilet. How did this affect the subjects?

Figure 17-12

The students found that doing nothing was not all that it was cracked up to be. In fact, this degree of stimulus deprivation was very unpleasant. The first response of most subjects was to go to sleep. But this cannot go on for very long, so they quickly learned to seek any form of stimulation. Many subjects hallucinated. All found the situation

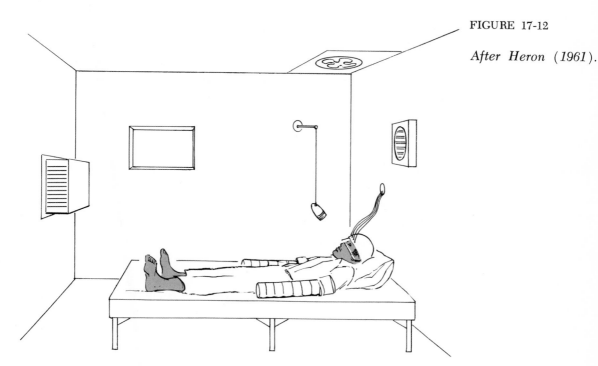

FIGURE 17-12

After Heron (1961).

aversive. Perhaps the best indication of this was that few subjects could last longer than 24 hours in the situation, despite the fact that they had volunteered to stay longer. They preferred unemployment to being a highly paid subject in this particular study.

Since these initial experiments a great deal of research has been published on the effects of sensory deprivation and impoverished stimulus environments. More elaborate apparatus have been developed. Now the subject is usually suspended nude in a pool of water maintained at body temperature to minimize skin sensations, temperature variants, and gravitational forces. Again, the lack of sensory stimulation is extremely unpleasant. Subjects report that they try to devote their full concentration to whatever small amount of stimulation remains in order to relieve the tedium of the experiment. Repetitive or unchanging stimulation seems to act about as well as deprivation of stimulus input. Continuous auditory noise (white noise) seems to be just as noxious as total silence.

There can be no doubt that people find environments aversive either when they are completely predictable or when the normal levels of external stimulation are drastically reduced. But this has been known by penal institutions for a long time. If we try to discover whether there are some more specific side-effects to sensory deprivation, then the answer is less clear. One notion that has generated a good deal of research is that people submit more easily to suggestion after they have undergone prolonged periods of sensory deprivation. This has been used as an explanation for brainwashing. There is no question that fear can have potent effects on persuasion and suggestibility. But laboratory studies on the effects of fear on suggestibility have not been particularly convincing on this issue—perhaps because the periods of deprivation used have typically been relatively short. In addition, of course, in the laboratory situation, it is difficult to mimic the same conditions of stress and fear aroused under real-life situations.

Neural mechanisms of arousal   Uncertainty arises in numerous situations: when novel events occur; when predictions about future events cannot be made; when potentially threatening circumstances must be confronted; when there is conflict in selecting an appropriate action; or when desirable actions are blocked. The neural subsystem involved in meeting the problems of uncertainty must fulfill certain requirements.

- The system must interact closely with the cognitive processes carried on in the higher cortical centers.
- The system should both monitor and control the efficiency of cortical processing.

- The system should be sensitive to the incoming sensory information so that it can alert the organism when certain incoming signals require priority in the attention and processing given to them.

There exists a neural system with most of these properties. Running through the part of the brain called the midbrain is a loosely packed set of neurons that are interconnected to much of the rest of the brain. The normal activation of the brain depends on the integrity of this area: It is called the *reticular activating system (RAS)*; see Figure 17-13.

The reticular activating system. The sophistication of the reticular function is suggested by the abundance and the complexity of its inter-connections with the rest of the central nervous system. Sensory messages pass by the RAS on their way to the cortex. In addition to its sensory-communication network, the reticular system connects directly with brain centers located immediately above it, and also sends out enormous numbers of fibers that connect diffusely throughout the cortex. Communications travel in both directions. The cortex receives large numbers of fibers from the reticular system, and in turn can send messages directly back. Simply from an anatomical point of view, the reticular system is in an ideal position to play a central role in the coordination and integration of the neural traffic in the central nervous system. Studies of the reticular system are just beginning to reveal how central this role is.

Generally, the RAS appears to modulate the overall activity levels of the cortex, affecting the efficiency with which incoming sensory data are processed. Suppose a flash of light or a click is presented to an animal. The flurry of neural impulses generated in the sensory system travels to the sensory receiving area of the cortex where it sets off responses in a large number of cortical brain cells. The synchronized activity of these cortical units can be measured with a gross electrode: It is called an *evoked potential*. In an anesthetized animal, this cortical response to incoming signals seems to die down quickly and is restricted mainly to the region of the cortex that first receives the sensory signals. In an alert animal, the neural response travels widely throughout the cortex and can easily be detected at many different recording locations. The anesthetized animal's insensitivity to signals may thus be due to the failure of the cortex to process the sensory messages beyond the sensory reception areas. Since anesthetics have their primary influence by desensitizing the reticular system, this result suggests that efficient cortical processing depends on a properly functioning reticular system.

There is considerable evidence for this general thesis. If the RAS is activated by an electrode at the same time as an external signal is

FIGURE 17-13

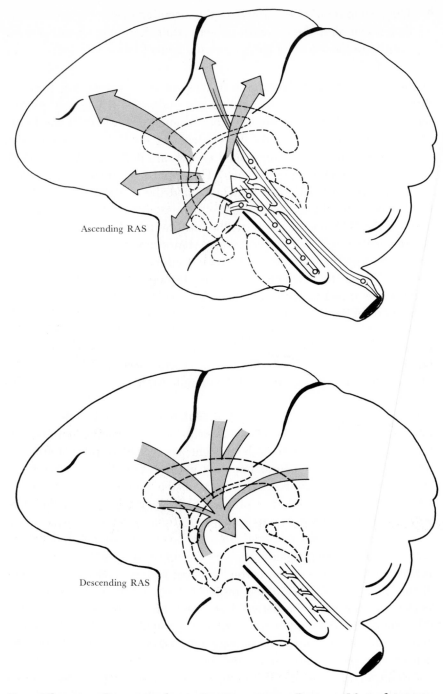

Top: The ascending reticular activating system. Bottom: Mutual interaction of messages from the cortex downward and from the reticular activating system upward. From Lindsley (1957).

presented, both the magnitude of the neural response in the sensory cortex and the extent of the spread of activity throughout cortical areas are increased. Similar influences can be found for single cells in the sensory pathways. Neurons in the visual pathways, for example, which are not responding to an incoming signal may suddenly become very active when an electrode embedded in the reticular system is turned on. Reticular activation, however, does not invariably produce an increased sensitivity in the sensory transmission pathways. Activating some areas of the reticular system seems to have the opposite effect—it reduces rather than increases neural activity levels to sensory events.

Changes in the reticular activation level, then, seem to be capable of producing widespread alterations in the conductivity of both cortical and sensory pathways. In turn, the reticular system is influenced by the activity in these networks. Some cells in the RAS seem to be sensitive to activity in any of the sensory systems and may respond with equal vigor to the occurrence of a visual, auditory, tactile, and even an olfactory stimulus. This type of cell appears to be primarily sensitive to the overall level of sensory traffic, rather than to specific characteristics of the sensory message. They are most frequently found in the lower half of the RAS. Other reticular cells are more selective in their responses. Some seem to be primarily monitoring information in a particular modality and are sensitive only to changes in the characteristics of the appropriate signal. These distinctive response patterns have been the basis for dividing the RAS into two separate areas. The lower half, primarily concerned with the gross levels of sensory activity, appears to be sluggish and relatively unselective in its response. Its primary function may be to maintain a lower limit or a background level of arousal or activity. The upper part of the reticular system (often called the *diffuse thalamic projection system*) is more sensitive to transient changes in the level of stimulation and may play a basic role in alerting the organism to changing environmental conditions and modulating the flow of sensory traffic in response to changing environmental demands.

Here is a neural structure capable of monitoring the volume of traffic in the sensory system, of detecting transient changes in environmental stimulation, of altering the characteristics and efficiency of cortical processing, of amplifying or attenuating messages on their way to the cortex, and of receiving messages from higher brain centers which control its own activity. It has important influences on the activity of the organism, ranging all the way from control over sleeping and waking cycles to specific alterations in attention and the efficiency of cortical processing. To an engineer, it has all the earmarks of a communications controller, a system responsible for coordinating the information flow in the nervous system and for controlling the allocation of computations and analytic facilities of the higher nervous centers. We are not quite ready to state this conclusion, however, no matter how intuitively plausible it sounds. Although the data collected so far give us a good start on understanding the RAS, we are still far from understanding the complete story.

___

SLEEP

The RAS also seems to contain the biological alarm clock that wakes the animal up and puts him to sleep on a regular schedule. Sleeping organisms, of course, are at a low-point on their arousal continuum. Metabolic indices tend to be lowered, the organism is inactive (except for eye movements and continued stomach activity), and he is unresponsive to normal levels of stimulation. For many years, any discussion of the neural mechanisms of sleep relied primarily on a consideration of the typical patterns of electrical activity produced in the brains of sleeping and wide-awake organisms. The overall electrical response of a large proportion of the cortical area of mammalian brains takes on a distinctively different character as an animal goes from being fully awake, through a state of relaxation, and finally to a sleeping state. When alert, the electrical response of his brain, as measured from the external surface of the skull, shows a rapid, irregular pattern. The irregularity of the pattern is presumably due to the fact that different cortical cells in different areas of the brain are operating independently of each other. But as the organism relaxes, regular oscillations at a rate of 8 to 12 Hz appear in the electrical brain recording. This pattern suggests that a large percentage of the brain cells are operating together in a synchronized way. These repetitive firing patterns are labeled *alpha waves,* and the term *alpha blocking* describes the change from the regular cyclic activity of the relaxed state to the irregular desynchronized brain response of an alert, active organism. As the organism falls asleep his brain responses go through a number of distinctive stages associated with various levels of sleep, from drowsy sleep

Figure 17-14   (very light) to deep sleep.

The early theories about sleep tended to equate it with a response to lack of stimulation. That is, there was an arousal system which kept an animal alert and awake. In the absence of arousal, there was sleep. Thus, alertness was the result of the arousal activity: Sleepiness was a result of low arousal. This theory is wrong. It turns out that sleep is under the control of specific "sleep centers" in the brain. Animals maintain a 24 hour sleep–awake cycle even when deprived of all sensory information.

Lesions in specific parts of the nervous system, specific regions of the ascending brain stem, produce rather specific effects on sleep and awakefulness. If the lesion is high in the brain, the result is an animal who sleeps all the time. If the lesion is made low in the brain, there is no effect on sleeping and waking patterns. It is the reticular activating system that lies between these two levels.

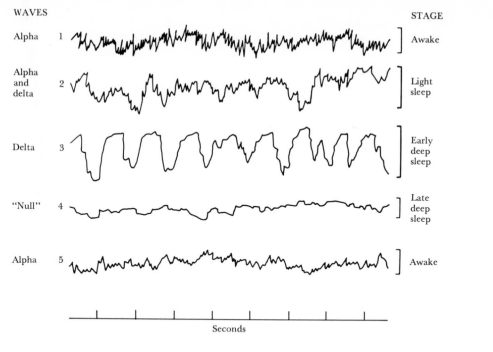

WAVES

Alpha 1 — Awake

Alpha and delta 2 — Light sleep

Delta 3 — Early deep sleep

"Null" 4 — Late deep sleep

Alpha 5 — Awake

STAGE

Seconds

FIGURE 17-14

From Kleitman (1963).

A mismatch between expectations and reality can cause a general activation of physiological and cognitive processes. A central issue for the theorist is whether there is a single arousal mechanism that simply alerts the organism and allows any possible response to occur, or if the activation pattern is different for different causes? The proposal that emotional arousal is nonspecific and based on a single underlying mechanism has been called the Juke Box Theory of Emotion (Mandler, 1962).

As the name implies, according to the Juke Box Theory, the arousal of emotion is somewhat analogous to placing a coin in a juke box: The machine is lit up, ready to go, equally ready to play anything in its collection. The actual behavior is determined only when a particular button is pushed. Emotional activation begins when the coins enter the machine. Environmental factors then select the resulting behavior, just as the pushing of a button selects a particular record.

As with all analogies, the parallels are not meant to be taken literally. One important factor in emotional responses not covered by the analogy is that with emotions, the very events that lead to the response are those that then control the behavior, once the system is activated. This puts a strong bias on what behavior will result from an emotional state.

INTERPRETING EMOTIONAL AROUSAL

Emotions: one or many?

An alternative theoretical possibility is that activation mechanisms are different for different emotions. After all, are you not aware of the differences in the way your body is aroused by hunger or by cold, fear, or sex? The answer is yes, but no. On the one hand, it is clearly possible to divide the types of neural activation into two general classes: those that excite and those that calm. One set of emotions seems to result from activation of the *sympathetic nervous system* and leads to general tenseness, especially of muscles that help support the body (the so-called antigravity muscles). In man, the typical pattern is tenseness of the knees, an erect body, clenched hands and jaws. The heart-rate rises, the blood vessels constrict, and there is a rise in blood pressure. In terms of emotions, these are often the symptoms of rage, hate, or anger. Another set of emotions appears to have symptoms that are almost the complete opposite. It results from activation of the *parasympathetic nervous system*. There is a slowing of heart rate, dilation of blood vessels, and a reduction of blood pressure. The limbs tend to bend. In terms of emotions, these are often the symptoms of pleasurable states, of satiation from overeating, for example.

There should be little doubt that body states of tenseness can be distinguished from states of relaxation, at least in the extreme cases. But can finer distinctions be made within those two classes? On this point, the evidence is not so clear. At least one theorist, for example, has argued that these two basic emotions are simply outgrowths of the body's normal defenses against cold and heat (Stanley-Jones, 1970). Contraction of blood vessels and all the related results are part of the defense against cold. Dilation of blood vessels and the resulting relations are part of the defense against heat. According to this theory, a whole set of emotional states have become attached to these two basic physiological reactions. The distinctions we feel among the states—the reason that we do not often confuse being warm with being sexually excited, or being cold with being angry—is that cognitive factors have taken control. Thus, the same cognitive factor that causes relaxation of blood vessels will also cause us to interpret the resulting body states as those of love, not simply overheating.

The problem in resolving the issue comes from the limitations of conscious awareness. In principle, all the psychologist wishes to know is whether such things as tenseness caused by fear can be distinguished from tenseness caused by anger, or even cold. In practice, he finds that it is not easy to find out.

Physiological measures. We have mentioned that during emotional arousal many physiological indices change. The obvious question is whether there is a distinctive pattern in the physiological responses associated with the various emotions. Does the physiological state of an organism when he is angry differ from the state when he is afraid?

In one experiment (Ax, 1953), the subjects were connected up to a variety of physiological monitors and then angered or frightened by the activities of the laboratory assistant (who was actually a confederate of the experimenter). Fear was induced by the assistant's inept handling of the equipment; anger was induced by some well-chosen remarks.

There were some differences in the overall pattern of physiological responses to these two emotions. But the exact activity pattern depends not only on the strength of the emotional arousal, but also on the total context. Moreover, it is difficult to tell whether the physiological differences reflect true underlying physiological causes, or simply reflect the results of the emotional response. Ax found that angry subjects had decreases in heart rate and increases in muscle tension and diastolic blood pressure, whereas fearful subjects breathed faster. But these could have resulted from the subjects' attempts to cope with their perception of fear and anger. Physiological responses are affected by whether or not the individual openly expresses his anger. Moreover, even if the internal arousal patterns differ somewhat for different emotions, there is still the question of whether these arousal patterns are distinctive enough to provide the individual with reliable cues about the emotion he is undergoing.

Biofeedback. Why not take a person's word for it and simply ask people to express what they are "feeling." Even if the question can be answered, there is no way of knowing how much the answer is determined by cognitive factors that created the body states and how much from an actual assessment of those states. Moreover, it is possible to have perfectly controllable body states that a person is unable to describe.

Wiggle the second finger of your hand. Now wiggle the third finger of the same hand. Describe what you did differently these two times. It is simply not possible. Yet the fact that you have such precise control over your finger movements proves that your brain can consciously exert the proper motor commands to move those fingers. Suppose you had to teach someone how to wiggle their fingers—or their ears? How would you start? There is no way to do it by description; you need to use more sophisticated techniques. So it might be with emotional body states. "But," you may complain, "I always know when I am hungry because my stomach rumbles and pains." Wrong. People who have had their stomachs removed still feel the same "stomach pangs." Why do you sometimes feel those pangs only after you have looked at your watch? The feeling is real. But the cause is not accurately known.

One method of trying to assess people's knowledge of body states is to monitor the system and see if people can respond accurately when something happens. Most of the early experiments were failures. In one heroic attempt, a subject was asked to predict which of two lights was going to flash on. The actual light that was turned on was determined by the subject's heart rate: One light went on whenever the rate increased; the other when it decreased. After 5000 trials, there still was no sign of any ability to predict the correct light.

Today, however, it is common practice to have subjects control all sorts of internal body states of which they have no apparent awareness, but they need some external help to do it. If we ask you to meditate, to change the pattern of your brain's electrical activity, for example, you probably wouldn't even know how to begin. But that does not matter; you can be trained, even though you are completely unable to describe what it is that you are doing (just as you cannot describe how you move your finger).

The trick is to use an electronic apparatus that can monitor the electrical signal from the brain (or other body processes) that is to be controlled. For controlling brain waves, this is rather easy to do. Electrical leads are connected to the scalp and the resulting electrical potential is amplified and monitored. This potential is, in turn, used to control the pitch of a tone produced by an audio oscillator. The subject hears this tone over earphones. Normally, the brain activity of a subject contains a very slow (about 10 Hz) component of reasonably large amplitude whenever he is not thinking about or looking at something; this is the alpha rhythm mentioned previously.

The task of the subject is to produce this alpha activity while he is in an alert, wide-awake state. The way we do this procedure in our own laboratory is as follows: When there is no alpha component in the subject's brain record, he hears a steady, unchanging tone over earphones. But the more alpha rhythm he produces, the lower the pitch of the tone: He is told to make the tone go as low as possible. After some training, many people can turn their alpha rhythms on or off at will.

The control over internal processes such as heart rate and brain waves is possible, though not necessarily easy. It requires some way of making these internal states easily observable to the subject. Thus, the recent evidence tends to refute the view that people are relatively powerless to do anything about what goes on in their own bodies. But most of the recent evidence concerns man's ability to control his own body functions, and **to control** is not necessarily **to be aware of.**

A famous experiment conducted by Schachter and Singer (1962) asked the following question: Is it possible to activate the emotional system of different subjects in the same ways, but then get them to perform and act quite differently, depending upon the environmental situation in which they find themselves?

To be mad or euphoric

Figure 17-15

Emotional arousal. Many emotional situations cause the hormone *adrenaline* (more properly, *epinephrine*) to be released into the body. What Schachter and Singer did was to inject some of their subjects with adrenaline, but misinform them about the nature of the injection. Thus, the emotional activation was controlled by the drug while the cognitive state was controlled by the situations presented to each subject.

There were two groups of subjects: those injected and told what to expect, the group called *informed;* those injected but misled into thinking there would be no effects of the injection, the group of subjects called *uninformed.* All the subjects had volunteered to participate in an experiment to study the effects of a drug on vision.

When each subject arrived for the experiment, he was asked if he minded being injected with a "vitamin compound called Suproxin." If he agreed, he was injected by the attending physician. In addition, subjects selected to be in the uninformed group were told that the injection would have no side effects. Subjects in the informed group were told that some subjects ". . . have experienced side effects from the Suproxin. These side effects last only 15 or 20 min. Probably your hands will start to shake, your heart will start to pound, and your face may get warm and flushed." This description is, in fact, an accurate statement of the results of an injection of adrenalin.

The environmental conditions. After being injected, the subjects were put into waiting rooms "to give the injection time to take effect." When a subject entered a waiting room, he found someone else already there. Two of the several experimental conditions used for controlling the environment the subject experienced are of interest to us: one called *euphoric,* the other called *anger.* There are now four experimental groups: *informed-euphoric, uninformed-euphoric, informed-anger,* and *uninformed-anger.* In addition to these experimental groups, several *control* groups experienced the environmental conditions, but without receiving injections of adrenaline.

Euphoria. In the euphoric condition, when the subject entered the waiting room, he found a rather playful fellow subject already there.

This other person was having a gay time, flying paper airplanes, playing with whatever he could find in the room, and practicing basketball with a crumbled paper and wastebasket. He continually requested his companion to join in the fun.

Anger. In this condition, the subject was led to the waiting room and asked to fill out a long, rather infuriating questionnaire. A typical question on the form was

> **With how many men (other than your father) has your mother had extramarital relations?**
>
> **4 and under** _____
> **5 through 9** _____
> **10 and over** _____.

This question had no function but to annoy the respondent. The other person who was in the waiting room at the same time showed increasing agitation and finally ripped the questionnaire up in rage, slammed it to the floor, denounced it, and stomped from the room.

The results. Now consider what these various conditions have done. Here are subjects whose biological systems are in a state of arousal and who are left alone in a room with a strangely behaving person. If an emotion simply resulted from a reaction to the combination of internal arousal state and the environment, there should be no difference between the performance of the subjects **informed** about the feelings generated by the drug and those **uninformed.** If the arousal state is specific to a particular type of emotion and independent of the environment, then both the subjects in the **euphoric** group and in the **anger** group should respond similarly. If the environmental factors have strong influence, then they should each act by responding to the behavior of the partner in the waiting room.

What was discovered was very simple. The **informed** subjects calmly went about their tasks, either quietly waiting or filling out the questionnaire, and ignored the antics of their partner. The **uninformed** subjects, however, tended to follow the behavior of their partner, becoming euphoric or angered according to his mood.

Here, then, are two groups of subjects, the informed and the uninformed, with identical internal arousal states and identical environmental experiences. Yet they do different things. Why? One expects the internal feelings that he is feeling, attributes them (correctly) to the drug injection, and is able to go about his job, ignoring the antics of the other fellow in the room. The other, however, feels his heart pound and his

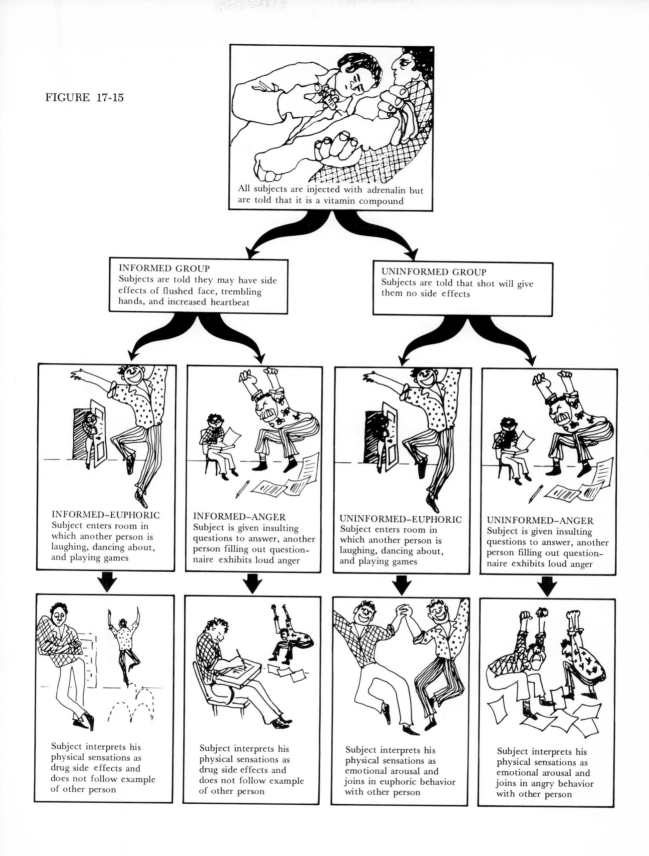

FIGURE 17-15

All subjects are injected with adrenalin but are told that it is a vitamin compound

INFORMED GROUP
Subjects are told they may have side effects of flushed face, trembling hands, and increased heartbeat

UNINFORMED GROUP
Subjects are told that shot will give them no side effects

INFORMED–EUPHORIC
Subject enters room in which another person is laughing, dancing about, and playing games

INFORMED–ANGER
Subject is given insulting questions to answer, another person filling out questionnaire exhibits loud anger

UNINFORMED–EUPHORIC
Subject enters room in which another person is laughing, dancing about, and playing games

UNINFORMED–ANGER
Subject is given insulting questions to answer, another person filling out questionnaire exhibits loud anger

Subject interprets his physical sensations as drug side effects and does not follow example of other person

Subject interprets his physical sensations as drug side effects and does not follow example of other person

Subject interprets his physical sensations as emotional arousal and joins in euphoric behavior with other person

Subject interprets his physical sensations as emotional arousal and joins in angry behavior with other person

face get flushed. He has no explanation for these feelings, but they do make sense if he is euphoric or angered. Hence, with no explanation, he is easily manipulated into one of these states.[2]

MOTIVATION AND
COGNITION

There is a large list of experiments that have now been performed which generally support these main points: emotional states are manipulable by the combination of three different factors—*cognitive processes* (expectations), *physiological states*, and *environmental influences*. To say that cognitive factors play an important role in the manipulation of emotional behavior does not mean that we are necessarily consciously aware of our cognitions. When we become angered or threatened by someone's remarks or actions, our logic may tell us there is nothing to be concerned about, while our internal responses may tell us differently. In this case, we can have a large discrepancy between our rationalizations of our behavior and the actual behavior.

To translate the active interpretive theory of emotion into a working system means that we must have several interesting interactions among the processes controlling behavior. First, we need an ongoing system that creates an internal model of the world to provide the expectations that are so important for emotions. That is, a central feature of the system must be cognition: the active development of a picture of the world, including the past, present, and expectations about the future. In addition, we need an assessment of how well things are coming along. How well are our expectations being met? What predictions can we make for the future if things continue along in the same way?

Next, we need some way of correcting aberrant behavior. Suppose there is a mismatch between expectations and events. Suppose we must get a term paper in by Friday, or we may fail the course. But examination of how far we have gotten indicates that we are not going to make it. Panic. Tension.

How does the system cause panic? Obviously, it can do the cognitive operations that lead to the prediction that the deadline will not be met. But how does knowledge of that fact change the heart rate, muscle tension, sweat, blood pressure, and even the hunger system?

---

[2] In the debriefing, following the experiment, the subjects were told the exact nature of the experiment, informed of the exact drug with which they were injected and the proper side effects, and told that the partner in the waiting room was, in actuality, one of the experimenters.

As we explained previously in footnote 2 of Chapter 16 (page 571), some deception is sometimes necessary in conducting psychological experiments, but whenever this is done the experiment is always followed by a debriefing session in which the exact nature and purpose of the experiment is explained.

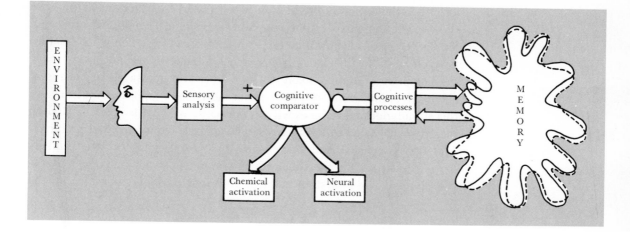

FIGURE 17-16

Consider how the system must operate. An active synthesizing process creates predictions about the world; a memory system aids in this synthesis; then the actions that have taken place are compared with those that were expected. If the synthesizing and predicting mechanisms are called *cognitive processes,* then the system looks something like that shown in Figure 17-16. The diagram is a simplification, of course, but it makes the point that the important output is the comparison between cognition and action. What does that output do? It controls the chemical and neural workings of the system. That is, a sufficient mismatch of the *cognitive comparator* (CC) releases appropriate chemicals (mostly hormones) into the biochemical structure of the body and changes the neural activation of brain structures. These signals are picked up through the normal analyses performed by the working systems of the body.

Think back about the hunger system: The system for hunger picked up information in several ways. First, it did a biochemical analysis, then it had a target state for the nutritional level it was trying to maintain. It also created an internal image of the target it was seeking. Finally, it analyzed sensory information. Cognitive processes can interact here in several ways. The chemical activation caused by CC could affect the biochemical analysis of the hunger state. The neural activation could affect any of the processes, but especially that of determining the internal image of the target. If we try to show this interaction, we get something like Figure 17-17.

But all motivational systems have similar points about them. Cer-

tainly, they all monitor biochemical states as well as neural ones. Therefore, the whole picture might look like Figure 17-18. Note what we have
shown. The cognitive system can control biological emotional processes.
Similarly, the biochemical system can control actions. The whole picture
is a circular, feedback control system. If actions are not going well,
the cognitive system is likely to send out error messages by means of
chemical stimulation—it might shoot adrenaline into the system. But
this stimulation might be exactly the opposite of what is needed. Modern
man does not need to kill tigers. He needs to solve intellectual problems.
The rise in tension and body states associated with the one is likely
to be disastrous for the other. Furthermore, it is not unlikely that the
poor human whose system has just activated itself might notice all the

FIGURE 17-17

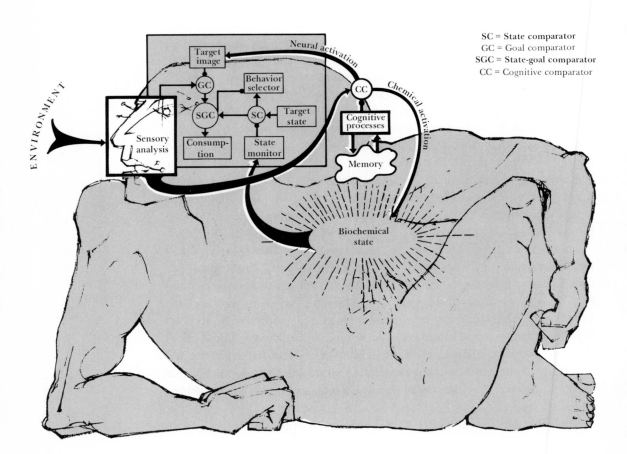

SC = State comparator
GC = Goal comparator
SGC = State-goal comparator
CC = Cognitive comparator

physiological changes occurring—increased heart rate, deep breathing, tension, sweating—and conclude that he is frightened. Then things really can get out of hand, for if he is frightened, maybe he should run. (*All this for a term paper.*)

The system we have outlined works simultaneously in all directions. The cognitive aspect of fear can cause biochemical (hormonal) stimulation of the body. But, in turn, the inflow of hormones into the body can lead to fear. How are we ever to tell which causes which? Why do we care? The important thing about this system is the way the various pieces interact with one another. Cognition and emotion are intimately intermingled with each other.

FIGURE 17-18

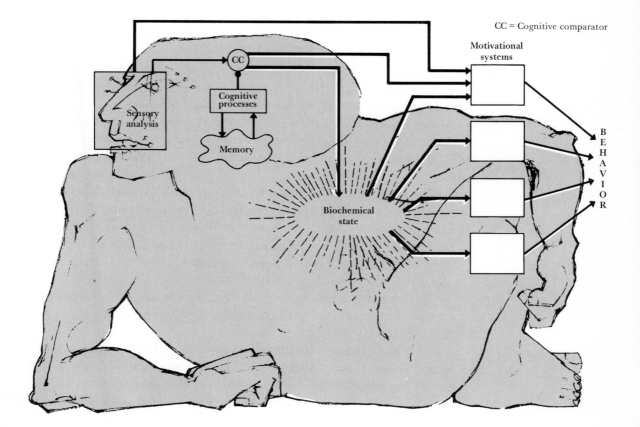

SUGGESTED
READINGS Without any doubt, the most thorough book on motivation and emotion is the massive review by Cofer and Appley, *Motivation: Theory and Research* (1964). This 958-page volume discusses all the concepts discussed in this chapter and, obviously, much more. Some of the book, of course, is rather advanced, but at the very least, gives the reader an indication of the direction in which research is moving. A number of the original, important papers are collected together in the book of readings by Haber, *Current Research in Motivation* (1967).

Several good reviews exist on the role of hunger and thirst mechanisms, although a good spot to start would be with Chapter 5, pp. 204–258, of Cofer and Appley. Another good review is by Teitelbaum, *The Biology of Drive* (1967). Two recent *Annual Review* articles are also relevant: Hoebel's review, "Feeding: Neural Control of Intake," in the 1971 *Annual Review of Physiology;* and Finger and Mook's article, "Basic Drives" in the 1971 *Annual Review of Psychology.*

Some of the work on brain stimulation is reviewed in the *Scientific American* articles by Olds (1965), on "Pleasure Centers in the Brain" (1965) and by Fisher "Chemical Stimulation of the Brain," (1964). Olds and Olds (1965) have a more technical discussion in the book by Barron *et al.*

The work on stress and, in particular, the executive monkey, was done by Brady, and that material can be found reviewed in the Cofer and Appley volume, as well as in the *Scientific American* paper by Brady, "Ulcers in 'Executive' Monkeys," (October, 1958). The work on aggression and on goal gradients is also well covered by Cofer and Appley. An interesting and different approach can be found in Lorenz's *On Aggression* (1966: paperback). Several good books exist on sleep, although we are far from an understanding of sleep and related stages. An introductory book, written for public consumption, is the one by Luce and Segal (1966). Dement's "An Essay on Dreams" (1965) is a good introduction to the technical literature (it is in the same book as the chapter by the Oldses on brain stimulation), as is the book of discussion and readings on sleep by Webb (1968). Kleitman's (1963) book is the classic, but it is very difficult to read. Kleitman also has a *Scientific American* article, "Patterns of Dreaming," which appeared in November, 1960.

The studies on anger and euphoria are reported in Schachter (1967), Schachter and Singer (1962), and Schachter and Wheeler (1962). The earlier papers are admirably reviewed in the article, "Emotion," by Mandler (1962). Some more recent work is reported in the symposium volume *Feelings and Emotions: The Loyola Symposium,* edited by Arnold (1970). But, basically, there have been no advances in the study of emotion in recent years. Again, Cofer and Appley (1964) provide the best overall source.

A fascinating new book, one that ties together results from several different areas is Schachter's *Emotion, Obesity, and Crime* (1971). This book starts with the Schachter studies reported in this chapter (*To be mad or eurphoric*), then moves on to a discussion of obesity and the parallels between the behavior of the overweight individual and that of rats with lesions in the hypothalamus. From there, he moves to some discussions on crime.

APPENDIX A

Measuring psychological variables

SENSORY EXPERIENCES

SCALING

Scale types
   Nominal scale
   Ordinal scale
   Interval scale
   Ratio scale
   Absolute scale
Scaling techniques
   Confusion scaling
   Direct scaling
Magnitude estimation
The power law
"How much" versus "what kind"
Interpretation of the power function
Range of applicability
Cross-modality matching
How to scale
   Method
   Analysis of results
   Cross-modality matching
   Analysis

SUGGESTED READINGS

When speaking of sensory experiences, such as those of seeing and hearing, it is important to distinguish between the physical light and sound waves that exist in the environment and the psychological experiences that are in the mind. The physical aspects of light and sound are easily studied, defined, and measured. A physical wave can be accurately specified by its waveform—the description of its energy or pressure variation over time—or by its spectrum—the description of how much energy is present at each frequency. The psychological aspects are not so easily specified. With sound, the two most obvious psychological dimensions are loudness and pitch, but there are also other experiences of sound quality—timbre, dissonance, consonance, and musicality. Similarly, with light, the most obvious psychological dimensions are brightness and hue, but other distinctions are possible.

With the simplest of physical waveforms, a pure sine wave of the type produced in light by a laser or in sound by a simple, smooth whistle or by an electronic oscillator, the physical aspects can be described in terms of its frequency and intensity. It is tempting to associate these simple physical variables with the psychological experience of hue and brightness or of pitch and loudness: To do so is incorrect. For one thing, the relations are not directly linear: Doubling the intensity of a physical wave does not double its perceived brightness or loudness. For another, they are not independent: Varying the frequency affects both the perceived brightness or loudness as well as its hue or pitch. And, finally, they are not constant: The perception of the hue and brightness of a light or the pitch and loudness of a tone depends not only upon its frequency and intensity, but also upon the context in which it appears, the nature of the other lights and sounds that may also be present at the same time. Even the simplest of physical dimensions is subjected to a complex analysis by the nervous system. Do not make the mistake of confusing the **psychological** perceptions of loudness, brightness, pitch and hue with **physical** properties of intensity and frequency. They are different things.

Figure A-1 & Table A-1

In the study of the relationship between the physical and the psychological, it is possible to measure exactly the physics, but we have only our private impressions to guide us in determining the psychology. To study psychological impressions, it is necessary to ask people to tell something about their sensations. Simply asking someone to say what he is perceiving is a dangerous game. What we are told is determined as much by the subject's knowledge of language and his expectations of what he thinks he should be saying as it is by the actual responses of his sensory systems. Many years of studying the introspections of observers have led to an understanding of some of the difficulties of this direct approach. If care is exercised, however, it is possible to learn

FIGURE A-1

Table A-1

Physical Variables

Psychological Variables	Of Primary Importance	Of Secondary Importance
Hearing		
Loudness	Sound intensity	Frequency of sound waves (Hz)
Pitch	Frequency of sound waves (Hz)	Sound intensity
Timbre (quality)	Complexity of sound wave	—
Volume (size)	Frequency and intensity	—
Density	Frequency and intensity	—
Consonance (smoothness) Dissonance (roughness)	Harmonic structure	Musical sophistication
Noisiness	Intensity	Frequency composition, temporal parameters
Annoyance	Intensity	Frequency composition, meaningfulness
Seeing		
Brightness	Light intensity	Wavelength of light, adaptation of the eye
Hue (color)	Wavelength	Spectral composition, intensity and hue of surrounding lights
Saturation (richness of color)	Spectral composition	Surrounding lights
Contrast	Intensity, wavelength, surrounding lights	—

about perceptions with little risk of misinterpretation. The important thing is to ask the right questions.

A good technique for getting at sensory impressions is to restrict the subject's task to elementary decisions—has a signal occurred; are two signals the same or different—to the operations of detections and comparison. Instead of asking a person "What do you hear?" ask "Do you hear anything at all?" Instead of asking for descriptions of the sensation, ask "Are these two things the same or not?" By asking such straightforward questions in carefully designed experiments, it is possible to learn a great deal about the basic mechanisms of sensory-information processing.

SCALING   Listen to some music. How loud is it? The obvious immediate response
is to say something like **not very,** or **extremely.** This will hardly do.
We need some precise way of specifying what is heard; some way that
will allow us to generalize across many people and make predictions
of impressions about new sounds. Moreover, to understand how the
nervous system operates, we must be able to match subjective impressions of loudness with the known properties of the physical sound and
of the sensory system. Basically, we need precise quantitative numbers,
not words like "but it is very loud." For the problems discussed in
this book, we need some way of scaling or measuring our perceptions
of loudness, pitch, brightness, and hue.

Scale types   Let us put some numbers to the psychological dimensions. The task
is to determine the exact numerical relationships that hold between
the physical and the psychological experiences. To do this requires a
method of measuring psychological impressions: a scaling technique.
It is not enough to assign numbers to psychological experiences; we
need to be concerned about the mathematical meaning that we can
attach to the numbers so assigned.

  Nominal scale. For example, if numbers are assigned arbitrarily to
different objects—something like the way the uniforms of baseball and
football players are numbered—we have performed a valuable service
by allowing the different objects to be identified. This assignment of
numbers fulfills a naming requirement, but quite clearly, the particular
values of numbers that have been assigned are irrelevant. Hence, this
type of assignment of numbers to objects is the weakest possible use
of numbers to scale something. The numerical scale so formed is called
a *nominal scale* (nominal for naming).

  Ordinal scale. The next level of sophistication in scaling comes about
when the numbers assigned to the objects bear some correspondence
to the mathematical properties of numbers. The most common next step
in scaling is to order the objects to be scaled so that the assignment
of numbers reflects the ordering. This type of scale is called an *ordinal
scale* (ordinal for order). Scales for hardness of rocks or quality of
lumber, such that the larger the number, the harder the rock or the
higher quality the lumber, are ordinal scales. Similarly, if the people
in a room are numbered by lining them up in alphabetical order, giving
the first person in line the number 1 and proceeding down the line,
we have established an ordinal scale. Someone with a number of eight
is not twice someone with the number four; his name simply starts
later in the alphabet.

  Interval scale. Better than an ordinal scale is one in which the differences between the numbers represent the differences in psychological value. Scales in which the intervals between numbers represent a meaningful concept are called *interval scales*. The normal temperature scales used in the home are interval scales (Farenheit and Celsius). The temperature chosen to be labeled 0° is completely arbitrary, but the difference in temperature between an object that is 80° and one that is 70° is exactly the same as the difference between an object that is 40° and one that is 30°. Ratios are meaningless. An object with a temperature of 80° does not have twice as much heat as an object with a temperature of 40°. In an interval scale, only the differences among the scale values are meaningful. The value that is assigned to be zero is quite arbitrary and could be changed without affecting the validity of the scale.

Ratio scale. Finally, among the most desirable of the methods of scaling is the technique that leads to meaningful intervals and ratios among the numbers assigned: the *ratio scale*. Thus, when someone's height is specified in inches, if we get a value of 80, it means that he is twice the height of someone whose height is 40. Both the intervals and the zero point are meaningful in a ratio scale. The specification of temperature on the Kelvin scale or as absolute temperature leads to a ratio scale. Length, height, weight, and monetary value are all examples of ratio scales. Ratio scales are not the highest form of scale type, for the particular number assigned to an object is still somewhat arbitrary. After all, we can say that someone's height is 80 inches, 6.67 feet, 203 centimeters, or 2.22 yards. Multiplying all the scale values by a constant does not destroy any of the interval or ratio properties of the scale.

Absolute scale. Occasionally, we can find examples of absolute assignment of numbers to objects, so strictly determined that we cannot change the numbers at all, not even by multiplication, without affecting the relationships that hold among the items. Such a scale is called an *absolute scale*. The number of things in a pile is counted on an absolute scale.

There are many ways by which psychologists go about the business of assigning numbers to psychological attributes. Two basic procedures are now used most widely. The first method is called *confusion scaling*, the second *direct scaling*.   *Scaling techniques*

Confusion scaling. With this procedure, the psychological distance of two objects is determined by the number of times that they are confused with one another. Suppose that we wish to determine the relative spacing of the psychological **sweetness** of different amounts of sugar (sucrose) concentration. Suppose we take an accurately measured cup of distilled water and put in it exactly 1 teaspoon of sugar. This would produce a solution with some amount of sweetness to it. Call this amount the *standard sweetness*. Now, make up ten other sugar solutions, five with concentrations progressively less, five with concentrations progressively more than the standard, giving eleven different concentrations of sugar water, each differing from the next in very tiny steps, perhaps like this:

Amount of Sugar Dissolved in 1 Cup of Distilled Water

.5 teaspoon		1.1 teaspoons
.6 teaspoon		1.2 teaspoons
.7 teaspoon	*1.0 teaspoons (the standard)*	1.3 teaspoons
.8 teaspoon		1.4 teaspoons
.9 teaspoon		1.5 teaspoons

By asking subjects to taste a pair of concentrations, always comparing the **standard** with one of the other solutions (called the **comparison**), indicating which they believe to be sweeter, we determine relative sensitivity to taste.[1]

When concentrations were relatively similar (such as the comparison between 1.0 and 1.1 teaspoons), there would often be confusion. When concentrations were very different (as with the comparison between .5 and 1.0 teaspoons), there would be close to 100% accuracy. A reasonably typical set of results is shown in Figure A-2.

This set of results shows just how accurately a person can discriminate between two different levels of sweetness, a standard value of 1.0 and a comparison value given by the points along the horizontal axis. This function is called a *psychometric function*. It plays an important role. We see that when comparing, say, the standard with a concentration of 1.4, the solution of 1.4 is judged to be sweeter than the standard about 88% of the time. Thus, the judgment is in error 12% of the time. If we look at Figure A-2, we see that the judgment of sweetness is also in error about 12% of the time when the concentration slightly less than .7 is compared with the standard of 1.0.

---

[1] In an actual experiment, of course, we would probably specify sweetness in terms of molar concentration of sucrose, not simply as teaspoons per cup of distilled water. In making the comparisons, we would use people with a good deal of experience at this task. They would be asked to compare solutions in identical containers by sipping a measured amount of the fluid and then spitting out each sample so that nothing was swallowed. After each taste, the mouth would be rinsed with some neutral fluid, probably distilled water. The order of the comparison substance and the standard would vary randomly, with the subject never knowing which solution was the standard: He would simply be asked to say which fluid was sweeter, the first or the second sampled.

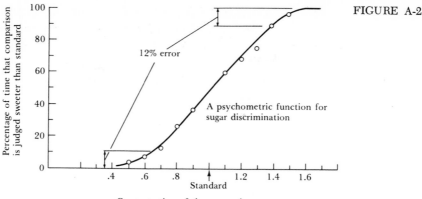

FIGURE A-2

If concentrations of 1.4 and .7 are equally often confused with the standard, does that mean that they are equally distant from the standard in terms of their psychological scale values? The method of confusion scaling is based on this assumption:

- **Two physical differences which are equally often confused are psychologically equal.**

This is the basis of confusion scaling. It allows us to equate differences between psychological scale values: Hence, it specifies the objects measured on an *interval scale*.

Confusion scaling has played an extremely important role in the history of psychology. It is the basis of the most widely used and most important result of psychological scaling procedures: the *intelligence scale (IQ)*. Further discussion of the assumptions and implications of this method of scaling is presented in Appendix B.

Direct scaling. An alternative method of assigning numerical scale values to psychological phenomena is quite a bit simpler than the method of confusion scaling: We simply ask people to assign numbers to physical attributes in ways that are proportional to their subjective impressions. This direction procedure originated with the work of Professor S. S. Stevens at Harvard University, and the rest of this section is devoted to a description of the method and the several techniques for using it.

The basic technique is simple. One simply presents a signal to the subject and asks him to judge it relative to a standard. Stevens (1956) describes the genesis of the technique in these words:

Magnitude estimation

It all started from a friendly argument with a colleague, who said, "You seem to maintain that each loudness has a number and that if someone sounded a tone I would be able to tell him the number." I replied, "That's an interesting idea. Let's try it." We agreed that, as in any problem of measurement, we would need first to decide on a modulus—a size for our unit—so I sounded a loud tone and we agreed to call its loudness 100. I then presented a series of other intensities in random order and, with a readiness that surprised both of us, he assigned numbers to them in a thoroughly consistent manner.

That was my first use of the method. Only after working with this procedure for a couple of months did I discover—or rediscover—that it is basically similar to the method used by Richardson and Ross (1930), which I had described in 1938 (Stevens and Davis, 1938). How easily one forgets!

Anyhow, the evidence accumulated over the past two years suggests that, if properly used, the method of magnitude-estimation can provide a simple, direct means of determining a scale of subjective magnitude. The method has wide potential utility, but like all psychophysical methods it has its pitfalls and its sources of potential bias. In any given situation, most of the distorting factors can probably be discovered and either avoided or balanced out of the experimental design [p. 21].

After years of experience with magnitude estimation as a tool for measuring subjective experience, it would appear to be a reliable, robust method. It is simple and effective. It gives reliable answers, so reliable that it can be used in a class as a demonstration of scaling without any fear that the answers will come out wrong. In fact, the main difficulties with the method come when the experimenter tries to help it along: He suggests that the subject might limit the numbers he uses; or he presents the standard over and over again, lest the subject forget what it was like; or he collects many trials of responses to get a good statistical reliability. All of these improvements make things worse. As Stevens says, "He should keep hands off and let the observers make their own judgements." In fact, it is not even necessary to present the standard. Let the subject assign whatever numbers he feels appropriate to each stimulus as it is presented. This is much more natural for the subject than arbitrarily telling him what number he should use for that first one. Actually, today most experimenters do not use numbers. They use instead a procedure called *cross-modality matching* (described a couple of sections hence).

For many sensory functions, the psychological impression of the physical intensity follows a simple mathematical function: the *power function*. For example, loudness and brightness increase in subjective magnitude proportionally to the $\frac{1}{3}$ power (the cube root) of the physical intensity of the sound or light. Heaviness increases with the 1.5 power of the actual weight of an object; psychological judgment of the duration of a sound increases almost linearly (to the power 1) with the actual time span as measured in seconds. In general, for many sensory phenomena,

The power law

$$J = kI^p,$$

where J is the Judgment of psychological magnitude, I is the physical Intensity, p is the *p*ower, the size of the exponent that governs the relationship between physical and psychological magnitude, k is an arbitrary constant, simply serving to get the psychological magnitude into the actual numbers used by subjects. If loudness grows with the cube root of sound intensity, then $p = \frac{1}{3}$ or .3. If a sound intensity of 1 were assigned a response of 100 by the subject, then $k = 100$. Thus, we would predict that a sound intensity of 8 would receive a response of 200 by the subject. The relationship is called a power law, because we raise physical intensity to a power (I^p) to get psychological magnitude. (Note that this is not an exponential function—the expression p^I would be exponential. In a power function, the variable of interest, I, is raised to a power. In an exponential function, the variable of interest is in the exponent.) The relationship is also called Stevens' Law, after the psychologist who has developed the technique, promulgated the procedure, and verified its applicability to a large variety of areas.

Table A-2

We can distinguish between two kinds of sensations, one that deals with the question **how much,** the other with the question of **what kind** or **where.** It would appear that Stevens' law of the power function applies to all relationships between physical and psychological variables that deal with the question of **how much.** The distinction between these kinds of sensations is simple, but important.

"How much" versus "what kind"

The psychological continuum that deals with **how much** of something is present is *additive;* it changes from one level to another by adding on to or subtracting from whatever is already present. Weight is an additive dimension, since we increase and decrease weight by adding on or taking away mass. Moreover, we assume that the psychological correlate of heaviness comes about through the number and rate at which the neurons respond: More weight means more responses. Loud-

Table A-2

Judgment	Power
Loudness (one ear)	.3
Brightness, dark-adapted eye, target of 5°	.3
Smell of coffee odor	.55
Taste of saccharine	.8
Taste of salt	1.3
Taste of sucrose	1.3
Cold (on arm)	1.0
Warmth (on arm)	1.6
Thickness of wood blocks as felt by fingers	1.3
Heaviness of lifted weights	1.5
Force of a handgrip	1.7
Loudness of one's own voice	1.1
Electric shock applied to fingers (60 Hz)	3.5
Length of a line	1.0

ness, intensity of a smell or taste, force of a handgrip, and felt intensity of an electric shock all appear to be additive dimensions. They all yield power functions. They all intuitively fit the notion of something increasing. Such an additive continuum is named a *prothetic continuum.*

The psychological continuum that deals with **what kind** or **where** is *substitutive;* it changes from one value to another by substituting the new for the old. If pressure is applied to the skin, pressure changes are additive. They are performed by increasing or decreasing the amount already being applied. Pressure is a prothetic dimension. But, if we vary the location of the pressure on the skin, that is a substitutive action. We take away the old pressure and replace it with one at a different location. The psychological correlate of a substitutive dimension comes about by one group of neurons ceasing their responses and a different group starting. Pitch, apparent inclination of the body, felt location of an object, and location of a sound all appear to be substitutive. These dimensions do not necessarily yield power functions. They all fit the intuitive notion that something has been replaced. Such a substitutive continuum is named a *metathetic continuum.*

Interpretation of the power function   The power function is simply stated as $J = kI^p$. By taking logarithms of both sides of this equation, we find that

$$\log J = p \log I + \log k.$$

This is a simple result. It means that plotting the logarithm of psychological intensity on the vertical axis of a graph and the logarithm of physical intensity on the horizontal axis gives a straight line which has a slope of p and an intercept of log k. Alternatively, the points can be plotted on the special graph paper which has both axes stretched out logarithmically—the graph paper which is called log–log paper. This simple relationship makes it easy to test the power function: When the results are plotted on log–log paper they ought to lie in a straight line.

FIGURE A-3

From Stevens (1961a).

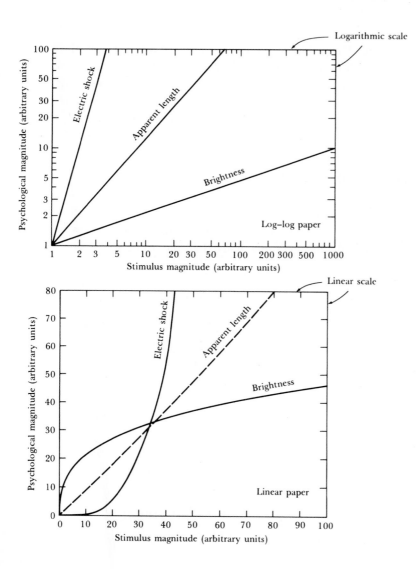

As you can see from Figure A-3, the log–log portrayal is extremely simple and easy to work with. Note, by the way, that judgments of apparent length vary almost exactly with actual length. The exponent of the power function is 1.0, which means that $J = kI$. Because $p = 1$, the power law reduces in this case to simple proportionality.

Range of
applicability

It is possible to use magnitude estimation procedures to judge almost any psychological dimension that is additive (or prothetic). Sellin and Wolfgang (1964) used this technique as a tool for measuring the way that society viewed the seriousness of crimes and of punishments. For example, subjects (juvenile court judges, police officers, college students) rated the seriousness of crimes. They judged that stealing and abandoning a car is .1 times the seriousness as robbing a man of $5 and wounding him. The robbery increases in the seriousness of the crime by a factor of 2.5 if the robbery victim is killed. Ratings on the seriousness of a robbery as a function of the amount of money stolen produced a power function with an exponent of .17. Thus, in order for one crime to be considered twice as serious as another, about 70 times the amount

Figures A-4 & A-5   of money must be stolen [$70^{.17} = 2$].

Cross-modality
matching

One difficulty with magnitude estimation is its reliance on numbers. How does one assign a number to a sensation? Look at the brightness of this book page. What number do you assign to it? 10? 1000? 45.239? Serious objections to the magnitude-estimation procedure have often been raised, usually because one feels that the rules we have learned

FIGURE A-4
From Stevens
(1966a).

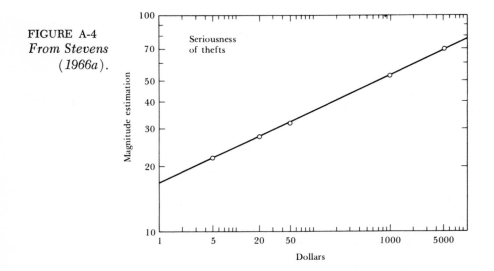

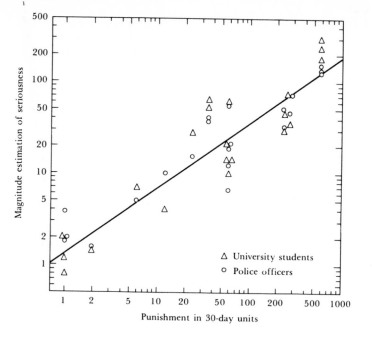

Magnitude estimation of seriousness

△ University students
○ Police officers

Punishment in 30-day units

FIGURE A-5

*From Stevens
(1966a).*

about the mathematics of numbers somehow must force the results to be power functions, even though the underlying psychological sensations are not. One answer to this criticism is to ask why there is such consistency in the results when we give many different people the same task. Surely, people's experiences must differ, so one would expect that difference to be reflected in the estimations. But if there were some artifact in the procedure which always produced power functions, why should pitch and position be exempt?

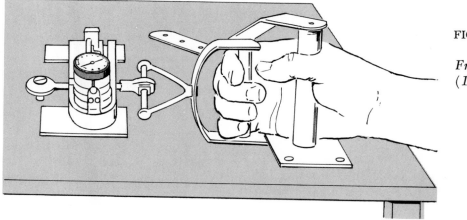

FIGURE A-6

*From Stevens
(1961a).*

A simple way to avoid the criticism, however, is simply to avoid the use of numbers. The easy way is to have someone judge the subjective magnitude of one event by producing an outcome that he feels is equal in subjective value.

Figure A-6

One simple method is to have a subject listen to different sound intensities, say, and tell us their loudness by squeezing his hand as hard as he feels the sound to be loud. We measure the squeeze pressure with a dynamometer. Alternatively, we could have someone adjust the intensity of a tone until it sounded as loud as a light was bright, or draw a line as long as sandpaper was rough, or adjust an electric shock to have the same psychological magnitude as the strength of the odor of coffee. Does this seem a strange method to you? Try it (see the experiment described later in this section). The description is strange, but in practice it is quite simple and direct.

We can predict what the results of these cross-modality matches should be. Let us compare two continua, A and B. We do standard magnitude-estimation experiments for each, finding that for intensity values of I_A and I_B, the judgments of psychological magnitudes J_A and J_B are represented this way:

For estimates of A:

$$J_A = k_A I_A{}^a.$$

For estimates of B:

$$J_B = k_B I_B{}^b.$$

Now, if we ask our subject to observe a signal from A which has intensity I_A and produce a value of intensity on B, I_B, so that the two psychological impressions are equal, we know that

$$J_A = J_B,$$

and so

$$k_A I_A{}^a = k_B I_B{}^b.$$

Thus, if we solve for the value of I_B necessary for the judgment of B to match that of A

$$I_B{}^b = \frac{k_A I_A{}^a}{k_B}$$

and, taking the bth root of both sides,

$$I_B = k I_A{}^{a/b}, \qquad \text{where} \quad k = \frac{k_A}{k_B}.$$

Thus, we still get a power function when we plot the intensity of B that the subject claims matches the subjective impression of the intensity of A. The exponent of the power function obtained by cross-modality matching is given by the ratios of the exponents which we get in a magnitude estimation experiment.

Table A-3   The Exponents (Slopes) of Equal-Sensation Functions, as Predicted from Ratio Scales of Subjective Magnitude, and as Obtained by Matching with Force of Handgrip[a]

	Ratio Scale		Scaling by Means of Handgrip		
Continuum	*Exponent of Power Function*		*Stimulus Range*	*Predicted Exponent*	*Obtained Exponent*
Electric shock (60-cycle current)	3.5		0.29–0.72 milliampere	2.06	2.13
Temperature (warm)	1.6		2.0–14.5°C above neutral temperature	.94	.96
Heaviness of lifted weights	1.45		28–480 gm	.85	.79
Pressure on palm	1.1		0.5–5.0 lb	.65	.67
Temperature (cold)	1.0		3.3–30.6°C below neutral temperature	.59	.60
60-Hz vibration	.95		17–47 dB re approximate threshold	.56	.56
Loudness of white noise[b]	.6		59–95 dB re .0002 dyne/cm²	.35	.41
Loudness of 1000-Hz tone[b]	.6		47–87 dB re .0002 dyne/cm²	.35	.35
Brightness of white light	.33		59–96 dB re 10^{-10} lambert	.20	.21

[a] From Stevens (1961a).

[b] There is a technical issue here that often causes confusion. We specified that the exponent for loudness judgments as a function of sound intensity had a value of .3. Yet the table shown here lists the exponent as .6. Why the discrepancy? The answer is simply that sound is measured both in units of energy and amplitude. Sound *intensity* refers to energy measurements; *sound pressure level (SPL)* refers to amplitude measurements. Sound energy is proportional to sound amplitude squared ($I \approx A^2$). Hence, if we write the power function, we find that

$$J \approx I^{.3} \approx (A^2)^{.3} \approx A^{.6}.$$

Both exponents are correct: .6 applies when sound pressures are measured; .3 when sound intensities are used.

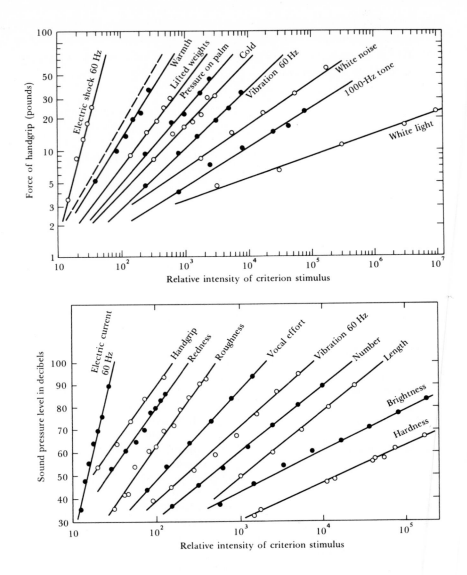

FIGURE A-7   *Top: Equal-sensation functions obtained by matching force of handgrip to various criterion stimuli. The relative position of a function along the horizontal axis is arbitrary. The dashed line shows a slope of 1.0 in these coordinates. Bottom: Equal-sensation functions obtained by matches between loudness and various criterion stimuli. The relative positions of the functions are arbitrary, but the slopes are those determined by the data. From Stevens (1966d).*

Method. Take a piece of lined paper and letter the lines from A to H (8 lines). You will write your responses on these lines. You will be presented with a series of stimuli in irregular order. Your task is to tell the immediate psychological impression they make on you by assigning numbers to them. Don't try to make any computations; simply write down what comes to mind.

The first item shown to you is the standard. Assign a value of 1 to it. Then as you look at the other stimulus items, assign numbers such that they reflect your subjective impression. For example, if a stimulus seems 20 times as intense, assign the number 20 to it. If it seems $\frac{1}{5}$ as intense, assign the numbers .2 (or $\frac{1}{5}$) to it, and so on. Use fractions, very large numbers or very small numbers. Just make each assignment proportional to your subjective impressions.

Write down your answers in order down the answer sheet. Do **not** look at previous responses. It would be best to cover each response

How to scale

Figures A-8 & A-9

FIGURE A-8

AREAS

Take a blank piece of lined paper and label the lines from A to H. Now, judge the *area* of each circle relative to the *area* of the standard. No computations, simply write down your subjective impression. The standard circle is assigned a value of 1. Cover all the other circles and then expose them to view one at a time. If you think a circle is five times the area of the standard, write down 5 for its value. If you think it is 1/10, write down 1/10. Do *not* look back over either your answers, the other circles, or the standard.

This is the **standard** circle: Call its area 1.  Standard

Now, cover the circles below. Cover the standard. Expose only one of the circles below at a time.

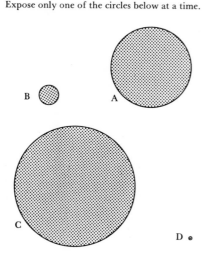

NUMBER OF DOTS
    Take a blank piece of paper and label the
lines from A to H. Now, judge how many dots
each square contains relative to the number
in the standard. No counting, simply write
down your subjective impression. The number
of dots in the standard square is assigned
a value of 1.

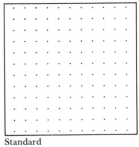

Standard

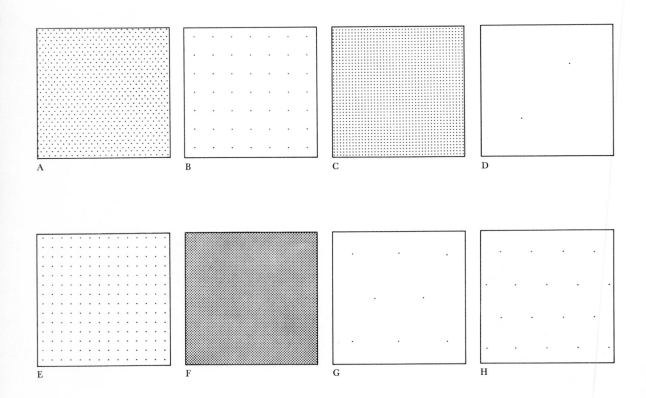

A   B   C   D

E   F   G   H

FIGURE A-9

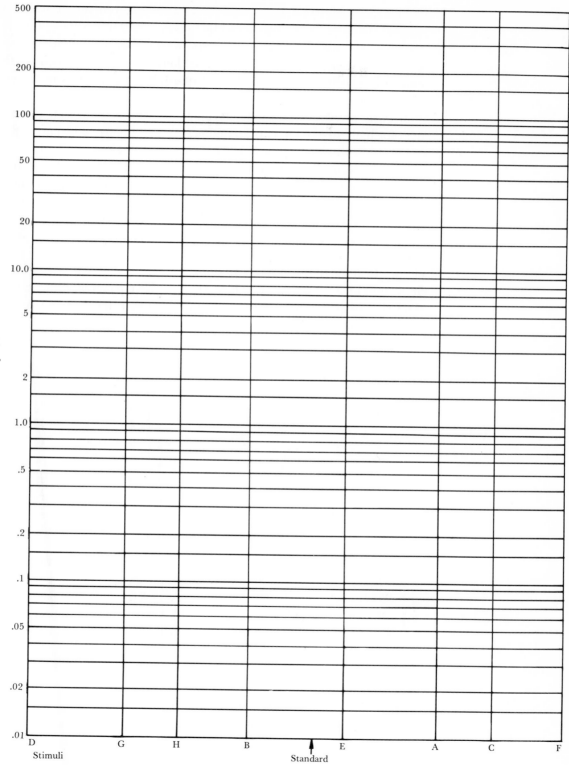

as you make it. Don't be concerned if you think you forgot what the original standard looked like. Everything will work out fine.

Remember, make assignments according to your immediate impressions. The standard is 1. If something looks 5 times as much as the standard, give it a number 5. Now do both the experiments in judging areas and numerosity.

Analysis of results. Plot the number you assigned to each stimulus item for both area judgments and numerosity on Figure A-10 (use different symbols, and use pencil so you can erase). (You might find the fraction-to-decimal conversion factors listed in Table A-4 to be useful.) Note that we have already put the stimulus items at their proper location along the horizontal axis of each graph. The scales for both horizontal and vertical axes on the graph are spaced logarithmically. That is, we have used log–log paper for the graph. This type of paper should make your data points fall along straight lines. Actually, there will be a lot of statistical variability ("noise") in the points, so they will not actually fit a straight line. But if you draw the two best possible straight lines through the points, one for areas and the other for numerosity, the deviations should not be too bad.

Table A-4   Conversions of Fractions to Decimals

$\frac{1}{32}$	.03	$\frac{9}{32}$	.28	$\frac{17}{32}$	.53	$\frac{25}{32}$	.78
$\frac{1}{16}$	.06	$\frac{5}{16}$	.31	$\frac{9}{16}$	.56	$\frac{13}{16}$	.81
$\frac{3}{32}$	.09	$\frac{11}{32}$	.34	$\frac{19}{32}$	.59	$\frac{27}{32}$	.84
$\frac{1}{8}$	.13	$\frac{3}{8}$	.38	$\frac{5}{8}$	.63	$\frac{7}{8}$	.88
$\frac{5}{32}$	.16	$\frac{13}{32}$	.41	$\frac{21}{32}$	.66	$\frac{29}{32}$	.91
$\frac{3}{16}$	.19	$\frac{7}{16}$	.44	$\frac{11}{16}$	.69	$\frac{15}{16}$	.94
$\frac{7}{32}$	.22	$\frac{15}{32}$	.47	$\frac{23}{32}$	.72	$\frac{31}{32}$	.97
$\frac{1}{4}$	.25	$\frac{1}{2}$	.50	$\frac{3}{4}$	.75		

$\frac{1}{2}$	.50	$\frac{1}{9}$	.11	$\frac{1}{16}$	.063	$\frac{1}{40}$	.025
$\frac{1}{3}$	.33	$\frac{1}{10}$	.100	$\frac{1}{17}$	.059	$\frac{1}{50}$	.020
$\frac{1}{4}$	.25	$\frac{1}{11}$	.091	$\frac{1}{18}$	.056	$\frac{1}{60}$	.017
$\frac{1}{5}$	.20	$\frac{1}{12}$	.083	$\frac{1}{19}$	.053	$\frac{1}{70}$	.014
$\frac{1}{6}$	.17	$\frac{1}{13}$	.077	$\frac{1}{20}$	.050	$\frac{1}{80}$	.013
$\frac{1}{7}$	.14	$\frac{1}{14}$	.071	$\frac{1}{25}$	.040	$\frac{1}{90}$	.011
$\frac{1}{8}$	.13	$\frac{1}{15}$	.067	$\frac{1}{30}$	.033	$\frac{1}{100}$	.010

Cross-modality matching.   Remember that one objection to magnitude estimation procedures is that they require subjects to produce numbers

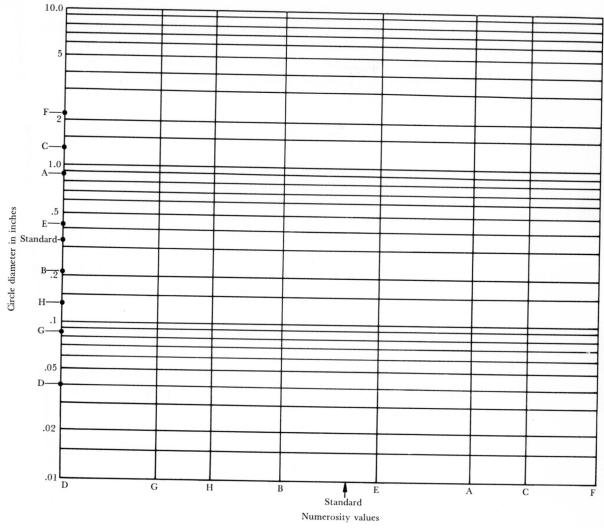

FIGURE A-11

as responses, a rather arbitrary scheme. But we need not use numbers. Go back through the assessment of numerosity again. But this time, respond by drawing a circle instead of giving a number. Draw a circle whose area is as large as the dots are numerous. That is not as difficult as it seems. If the dots look to be five times more numerous than the dots on the standard, simply draw a circle whose area is five times that of the standard circle. In fact, you should not think of numbers at all: Just look, and draw whatever feels right.

Analysis. Plot circle size against numerosity. To make this easy for you, we provide a graph, Figure A-11, with the numerosity stimuli already placed along the horizontal axis. You can plot circle size on the vertical axis. Circle size should be specified on the graph as the size of the circle diameter, measured in inches (use pencil again). (The table of conversions between fractional inches and decimals, Table A-4, will be of use to you.)

See whether you can predict your results. Look back at the magnitude estimation functions for these two stimuli. Find the numerical response you gave to numerosity value C. Now look up on the magnitude estimation function for the area size that would have given the same response. (You will have to draw the best straight line through your points and interpolate the answer, since it is unlikely that one of the sizes of circles we gave you will match exactly the number you are looking up.) Now you know how the numbers predict that circle area matches with numerosity. In fact, by checking several values of numerosity and circle area, you can draw the complete predicted function: How well do they match?

SUGGESTED
READINGS

Perhaps the best spot to start is with the papers by Stevens. He has clearly elucidated the issues and problems faced in measuring psychological attributes. The basic article on scaling, which describes the various types of scales, is Chapter 1 of the *Handbook of Experimental Psychology*, edited by Stevens (1951). This chapter does not discuss magnitude estimation techniques nor the power function: That was developed after 1951. Another excellent introduction to measurement theory comes from the article by Galanter in the book *New Directions in Psychology I* by Brown, Galanter, Hess, and Mandler (1962).

A good review of many of the results is provided by Stevens' article (1961a) in the book *Sensory Communication*, edited by Rosenblith (1961). The application of the scaling techniques to social issues and opinions (such as illustrated in this section by the rating of seriousness of crime) can be found in Stevens (1966a,b, 1968). The study on rating the seriousness of crime and punishment was done by Sellin and Wolfgang (1964). An interesting expansion of power functions to account for changes that result from masking and glare can be found in Stevens (1966c).

A mathematical description of scaling (with emphasis on various variations of confusion scaling) can be found in Chapters 2, 3, and 4 of Coombs, Dawes, and Tversky, *Mathematical Psychology: An Introduc-*

tion (1970). An even more advanced treatment, for those of you with the necessary mathematical background, can be found in Chapter 1 of Volume 1 of the *Handbook of Mathematical Psychology* (Luce, Bush, & Galanter, 1962–1965) in the article, "Basic Measurement Theory" by Suppes and Zinnes (1963). In addition, the two-volume work on measurement theory by Krantz, Luce, Suppes, and Tversky, (1971) will treat this topic in perhaps more detail than you will wish to get, at this point.

APPENDIX B

Operating characteristics

THE DECISION PROBLEM

THE DICE GAME

The criterion rule
  Hits and misses
  False alarms
  Moving the criterion
  The operating characteristic
Confidence ratings
The normal distribution

PROBLEMS

The fire sprinkler problem
Memory
The dice game revisited

SUGGESTED READINGS

In most real decisions that we must make, there is no answer that is guaranteed to be correct. For most situations, it is necessary to choose among virtues and evils, hoping to minimize the chance of misfortune and maximize the chance of good.

In this section, we analyze one common, simple form of decision making. The situation can be described by the following description. First, there is some information that the decision maker uses to help reach his decision. This information comes from the observations of the decision maker. We represent the results of the observations by the letter **O**. Second, the only choice open to the decision maker is to decide which of two acts, **A** or **B**, he will choose to do. Finally, the choice of decision can be correct or incorrect. Thus, we have the simple chain of events with four possible outcomes shown in Figure B-1. The prototypical example is that of the following, a dice game.

THE DECISION
PROBLEM

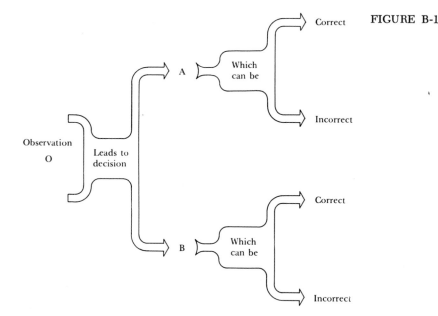

FIGURE B-1

You are gambling while playing a guessing game. Your partner throws three dice. Two of the dice are normal, one die is very special in that three of its sides are marked with the number "3" and the other three sides with the number "0." Your job is to guess which side the special die came up on; you are told only the total scores from all three dice. (Obviously, if the total is 2, 3, or 4 the special die must be "0"; if

THE DICE GAME

the total is 13, 14, or 15, the special die must be "3.") You are told that the score is 8. What should you respond?

*Your observation **0** is* 8.

*Alternative **A**:*   Decide that it was a 3.
Possible results: 1. It was a 3. You win the bet.
                               2. It was a 0. You lose your money.

*Alternative **B**:*   Decide that the 3 did not turn up.
Possible results: 1. It was a 3. You lose your money.
                               2. It was a 0. You win.

The important thing to notice about this situation is that, on the average, you cannot help but make mistakes. There is no possible way of guaranteeing perfect performance.

To analyze the dice game, consider all the possible ways that it can come out. First, how many possible results are there? Well, the lowest number that is possible comes if the two regular dice both turn up "1" and the special die comes up "0": that gives a total of 2. The highest number comes if the two regular dice both come up 6 and the special die comes up 3: that gives a total of 15. Thus, there are 14 possible outcomes, ranging from 2 through 15.

Now consider the chance that we can get any one of those 14 scores, given that the special die was a 3 or a 0. To do this, we have to figure out how many ways the dice can turn up to give any particular score. Here is how we do that.

Suppose the total were 8: this can happen in different ways, depending upon whether the special die is 3 or 0.

If the special die is a 3:

The two regular dice must total 5: There are four ways for that to happen. The two regular dice can come up 1 and 4, 2 and 3, 3 and 2, or 4 and 1.

If the special die is 0:

The two regular dice must total 8: There are five ways for that to happen. Two regular dice can come up 2 and 6, 3 and 5, 4 and 4, 5 and 3, or 6 and 2.

In fact, for all the possible scores of the dice, we get the number of possibilities shown in Table B-1.

Now, suppose that we observed a score of 10. How many ways can that happen? Looking at Table B-1, we see that this can happen in 3 ways if the special die is 0 and 6 ways if the special die is 3: There is a total of 9 ways that the 3 dice can combine to give a 10. Thus, because we know that we got a score of 10, we also know that, on the average, $\frac{6}{9}$ of the time this will be a result of the special die coming up a 3 and $\frac{3}{9}$ of the time from the special die coming up 0. So, if we guess that a score of 10 means that the special die is a 3, we will be correct 6 out of every 9 trials and incorrect 3 out of every 9 trials, on the average. If you are a gambler, you would say that a score of 10 means that the odds of the special die being a 3 are 2 to 1 (six to three).

It would seem to be sensible to say the special die is 3 whenever the total is 10, because the odds favor it. In fact, look at this: *The criterion rule*

Total	Proportion of Times Special Die Is 3
7	$\frac{3}{9} = 33\%$
8	$\frac{4}{9} = 44\%$
9	$\frac{5}{9} = 56\%$
10	$\frac{6}{9} = 67\%$
11	$\frac{5}{7} = 71\%$
12	$\frac{4}{5} = 80\%$
13	$\frac{3}{3} = 100\%$

On the average, the percentage of times that calling the special die 3 will be correct rises steadily as the total score rises, with the chance being more favorable than not as soon as the total is 9 or greater. A good decision rule, thus, would appear to be "Say that the special die is 3 whenever the total score is 9 or greater." Let us see what this would cause to happen.

Hits and misses. Suppose we tossed the dice 100 times, and on each toss had to decide whether the special die was a 3. We use the decision rule of responding "Yes" every time a total of 9 or more occurs. Now go ahead to Table B-1. We will answer **yes** (the die is a 3) for a score of 9, 10, 11, 12, 13, 14, and 15. Otherwise we will say **no**. But there are 36 possible combinations of the regular two dice, and if the special die is a 3, only 26 of them give totals of 9 or greater. (We can get scores less than 9—scores of 8, 7, 6, and 5—in 10 ways.) Thus, we will be correct by saying **yes** 26 out of every 36 trials on which the special die really is a 3. We **miss** 10 out of every 36 trials that the special die really was 3.

The proportion of times that we get a **hit** by correctly deciding **yes**, the 3 has turned up, is represented as $p(\text{yes}|3)$. The vertical bar $(|)$

Table B-1

Number of Ways This Can Happen
if the Special Die Is a

Total	0	3
0	0	0
1	0	0
2	1	0
3	2	0
4	3	0
5	4	1
6	5	2
7	6	3
8	5	4
9	4	5
10	3	6
11	2	5
12	1	4
13	0	3
14	0	2
15	0	1
16	0	0
Total Combinations:	36	36

means "conditional" or "given." Thus the terms read "the proportion of hits is equal to $p(\text{yes}|3)$, which is the proportion of yes, given that a 3 actually was rolled on the special die." In this example the hit rate or $p(\text{yes}|3) = \frac{26}{36} = 72\%$. Similarly, the **miss** rate $p(\text{no}|3)$, is $\frac{10}{36}$ or 28%.

False alarms. What about when the special die really was a 0? We respond **yes** anytime the total score is 9, 10, 11, or 12. Thus, out of the 36 combinations of the two regular dice when the special die is a 0, exactly 10 of them lead to a total score of 9 or more, the other 26 combinations lead to a total score of 8 or less. Saying **yes** for the wrong event is called a **false alarm.** In this example, the false-alarm rate is $\frac{10}{36}$: $p(\text{yes}|0) = \frac{10}{36} = 28\%$.

Moving the criterion. We can adjust how often we correctly guess that the special die turned up "3" by adjusting the critical score at which we change from an answer of "yes" to "no." But, as the critical score varies, so do the hits and the false alarms. The hit- and false-alarm rates are related; increasing one always increases the other. In fact, the exact relationship between the hit and false-alarm rate is very important in decision theory. Call the critical score on which we base our decisions the *criterion*. Whenever the dice total equals or exceeds the criterion, we say that the special die is most likely to be a "3"; otherwise we say that it is probably a "0."

Criterion	False-Alarm-Rate		Hit Rate	
	Fraction	*Percentage*	*Fraction*	*Percentage*
1	$\frac{36}{36}$	100	$\frac{36}{36}$	100
2	$\frac{36}{36}$	100	$\frac{36}{36}$	100
3	$\frac{35}{36}$	97	$\frac{36}{36}$	100
4	$\frac{33}{36}$	92	$\frac{36}{36}$	100
5	$\frac{30}{36}$	83	$\frac{36}{36}$	100
6	$\frac{26}{36}$	72	$\frac{35}{36}$	97
7	$\frac{21}{36}$	58	$\frac{33}{36}$	92
8	$\frac{15}{36}$	42	$\frac{30}{36}$	83
9	$\frac{10}{36}$	28	$\frac{26}{36}$	72
10	$\frac{6}{36}$	17	$\frac{21}{36}$	58
11	$\frac{3}{36}$	8	$\frac{15}{36}$	42
12	$\frac{1}{36}$	3	$\frac{10}{36}$	28
13	$\frac{0}{36}$	0	$\frac{6}{36}$	17
14	$\frac{0}{36}$	0	$\frac{3}{36}$	8
15	$\frac{0}{36}$	0	$\frac{1}{36}$	0

The operating characteristic. It is easier to see the relationship between false alarms and hits if we plot them together, as shown in Figure B-2. This relationship is called an *operating characteristic*.[1] This curve shows explicitly how changing the criterion (the numbers beside the points) changes both the percentage of hits and the percentage of false alarms.

Another way of seeing how the decision rule must always be related to the trade off between hits and false alarms is to look again at the distribution of total scores shown in Table B-1. This time, draw a diagram of the distributions (Figure B-3). This is the same information originally presented in the table, but now it is clear why there must always be errors. The distribution of dice scores when the special die

[1] Originally, this relationship came from the study of radar receivers attempting to determine whether the signal seen was a real one or simply noise. Hence, the curve was called a *Receiver Operating Characteristic* or *ROC curve*. The term *ROC curve* is still widely used in the psychological literature.

FIGURE B-2

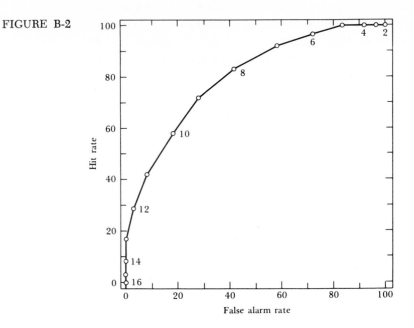

THE OPERATING CHARACTERISTIC

FIGURE B-3

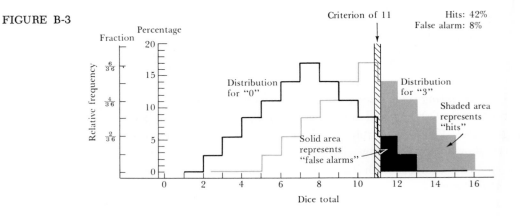

is a 0 (the distribution on the left) overlaps considerably with the distribution of scores when the special die is a 3 (the distribution on the right). There is nothing that can be done about that overlap: If the dice total is 8, it could be a result of either outcome of the special dice. In the figure, a criterion of 11 is drawn in. For this criterion value, we decide to say that the special die is a 3 if we get a dice total of 11 or more, so the chance that we are correct is the chance that we get an observation of 11 or more from the distribution shown on the right. The chance of a false alarm is the chance of an observation of 11 or more from the distribution shown on the left. Thus, simply by examining how much of each distribution lies to the right of the criterion, we can see the way the relative hit- and false-alarm rates vary as we move the criterion back and forth. This, of course, is exactly what we did in drawing the operating characteristic.

The operating characteristic shows how performance varies as we vary the decision rule. Now, what happens if we make the task easier? Suppose we change the dice game so that the special die has a 6 on three sides and 0 on the other three sides. What then? We leave this as a problem for the reader. Draw the new distribution of observations of the dice scores for the special die coming up a 6. (You already have the distribution for the case when the special die is 0.) Now draw the operating characteristic. It should include the point that has a hit rate of 83% and a false-alarm rate of 8%. If it does not, you had better review this section on operating characteristics.

The diagram of the distributions points out something else about the decision rule: If we simply adopt a strategy of saying "3" whenever the dice total exceeds the criterion, we are wasting information. There are times when we have absolutely no doubt about the accuracy of our response, and there are times when we know that we are simply guessing: How does the decision rule describe this? The answer is simple. Whenever we get a low total on the dice, say between 2 and 4, we are certain that the special die was a 0; whenever we get a high score, say between 13 and 15, we are certain that the special die was a 3. With a value of 8 or 9 for the total score, we are guessing. Thus, we can say more than simply **yes** or **no** whether the special die is likely to be a 0 or a 3: We can also assign a statement of how confident we are in that response. We can easily qualify our answers by adding a statement like "I am very certain," or "I am pretty certain," or "I am really just guessing" to our statement of **yes** or **no**. When this is done, we see that there are really six responses:

Confidence ratings

> **Yes,** the special die is a 3 and I am
> > **very certain**
> > **certain**
> > **not certain**
>
> **No,** the special die is a 0 and I am
> > **not certain**
> > **certain**
> > **very certain**

These six responses can be ordered according to the dice score, with a response of "very certain that it is a 3" always coming from the highest total and "very certain that it is a 0" coming from the lowest.

If we draw the way responses come from the distributions of dice totals, we might get something like that shown in Figure B-4.

FIGURE B-4

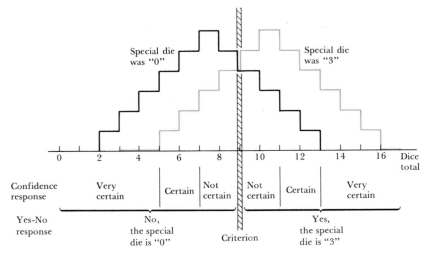

These confidence ratings are extremely useful. Note that we can treat the six different responses somewhat as if we had six different criteria for responding. Thus, the operating characteristic can be drawn to reflect confidence ratings, rather than the criteria illustrated previously. To do this, simply note that the chance of responding **yes** with a confidence of **certain** or greater is given by the chance that the dice total is **11** or greater. Thus, in the illustration shown in Figure B-4, the translation between criteria and confidence ratings looks like this:

To Simulate a Criterion of	*Combine These Responses*
13	**Yes—very certain**
11	**Yes—very certain** and **certain**
9	Any response of **yes**
7	**No—Not certain** and any response of **yes**
5	**No—Not certain, certain,** and any response of **yes**
2	Any response whatsoever

Note that in order to plot the operating characteristic we do not really need to know what the criteria are. All we need to know is what the hit- and false-alarm rates are for the various responses.

Suppose we did the dice game for 200 times. Furthermore, suppose that on 100 trials the special die came up 0 and on 100 trials it came up 3. After the experiment, we sort out the responses according to whether they resulted from a 3 or 0 on the special die. Suppose that this is what we found.

Responses	*Number of Occurrences When Special Die Was*	
	0	*3*
A. Yes—very certain	0	17
B. Yes—certain	17	41
C. Yes—not certain	11	14
D. No—not certain	30	20
E. No—certain	25	8
F. No—very certain	17	0
TOTAL:	100	100

Now, without bothering to figure out what criterion each response represents, we simply realize that we can treat these responses as if each came from a criterion, if we lump together all responses of a certain confidence or **greater:**

Response	*(Special Die Was 0)* *False-Alarm Rate*	*(Special Die Was 3)* *Hit Rate*
A	0	17
B or A	17	58
C, B, or A	28	72
D, C, B, or A	58	92
E, D, C, B, or A	83	100
F, E, D, C, B, or A	100	100

If we plot the hit- and false-alarm rates, we get the operating characteristic (Figure B-5)—the same curve shown in Figure B-2.

This is exactly how we analyze real data, the only exception being that in a real experiment the numbers would not come out quite so cleanly. People are inconsistent in where they place their criteria. These inconsistencies are relatively small, however.

FIGURE B-5

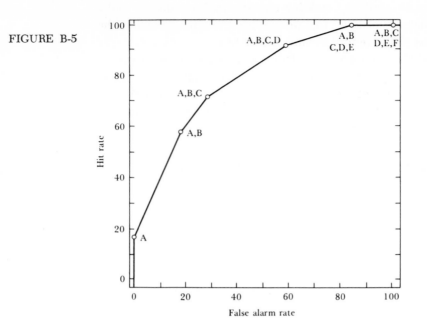

The normal distribution

We ask a human subject to listen to a very weak signal that is presented to him periodically over a pair of earphones. We want to find out whether or not he can hear the signal. The question is actually much more complex, however, because the subject is always hearing something: He must decide whether what he has heard resulted from the signal presented, or whether it was simply a result of the normal fluctuations in hearing that occur. These fluctuations come about for many reasons. In fact, in many experiments, we add noise to the earphones in order to see how well the subject can pick out the signal from the noise.

The situation for the subject is very much like the situation described for the dice game. He listens during the interval when the signal could be presented and ends up with some observation, much like our rolling the dice and ending up with some total score. The question is, did that observation come from the signal or just from noise. The analogous question for the dice game, of course, is, "Did that total result from the special die being a 0 or a 3?" We assume the subject who tries to detect the signal chooses some criterion: If his observation exceeds that criterion he says "signal." Otherwise he says, "no signal." From his hit- and false-alarm rates, we try to determine the separation of the distributions that he must be using to make his decision. Then, from our determination of the distributions, we try to decide how the auditory system must be converting the signals.

Let us now work through some examples. Before we do, however, we need to introduce a special type of distribution of observations, the *normal distribution*.

When we played the dice game, we developed the distribution of outcomes of the dice (Figure B-3). In general, however, a different type of distribution is frequently encountered. This distribution is called the *normal distribution,* and is an extremely useful one to know about. It is widely used in many fields of study, including psychology, and it usually turns out that even if the actual distributions under study are not normal, the normal is an excellent approximation to the true one. A drawing of the normal distribution is shown in Figure B-6. Notice

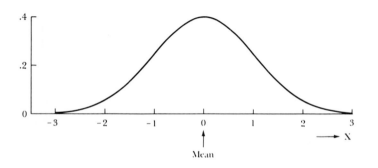

FIGURE B-6

that it looks very much like the distribution for the dice game, except it is drawn smoothly, rather than with steps. This is because the total score from a dice game can only take on an integral value—it must be a number like 6 or 7, it cannot lie between. The normal distribution, however, can take on any real number, positive or negative. The normal distribution shown here is characterized by one number—the mean or average value. As it is drawn, it has an average value of zero. If it were to have an average value of, say, 1.5, the distribution would simply be shifted to the right, so that its peak was at 1.5: This is shown in Figure B-7.

The values of the normal are shown in Table B-2. Here we see the height of the curve for different values along the horizontal axis. In addition, we also show the percentage of the curve that lies to the right of any criterion. It is this latter figure that we use for computing the operating characteristics.

What we usually care about is how far apart the mean values of two distributions are from one another. Suppose we do the experiment

Table B-2   The Normal Distribution Height and Percentage of the Curve (Area)

to the Right of Any Criterion

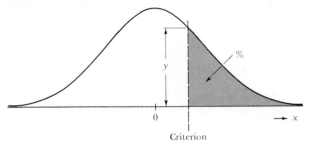

Criterion	Y	Percentage		Criterion	Y	Percentage		Criterion	Y	Percentage
−3.0	.004	99.9		−1.0	.242	84.1		1.0	.242	15.9
−2.9	.006	99.8		−.9	.266	81.6		1.1	.218	13.6
−2.8	.008	99.7		−.8	.290	78.8		1.2	.194	11.5
−2.7	.010	99.7		−.7	.312	75.8		1.3	.171	9.7
−2.6	.014	99.5		−.6	.333	72.6		1.4	.150	8.1
−2.5	.018	99.4		−.5	.352	69.2		1.5	.130	6.7
−2.4	.022	99.2		−.4	.368	65.5		1.6	.111	5.5
−2.3	.028	98.9		−.3	.381	61.8		1.7	.094	4.5
−2.2	.035	98.6		−.2	.391	57.9		1.8	.079	3.6
−2.1	.044	98.2		−.1	.397	54.0		1.9	.066	2.9
−2.0	.054	97.7		0	.399	50.0		2.0	.054	2.3
−1.9	.066	97.1		.1	.397	46.0		2.1	.044	1.8
−1.8	.079	96.4		.2	.391	42.1		2.2	.035	1.4
−1.7	.094	95.5		.3	.381	38.2		2.3	.028	1.1
−1.6	.111	94.5		.4	.368	34.5		2.4	.022	.8
−1.5	.130	93.3		.5	.352	30.1		2.5	.018	.6
−1.4	.150	91.9		.6	.333	27.4		2.6	.014	.5
−1.3	.171	90.3		.7	.312	24.2		2.7	.010	.4
−1.2	.194	88.5		.8	.290	21.2		2.8	.008	.3
−1.1	.218	86.4		.9	.266	18.4		2.9	.006	.2

FIGURE B-7

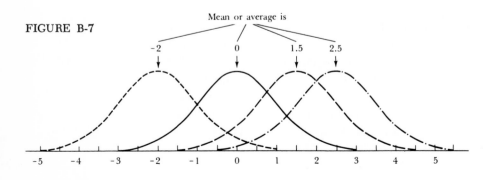

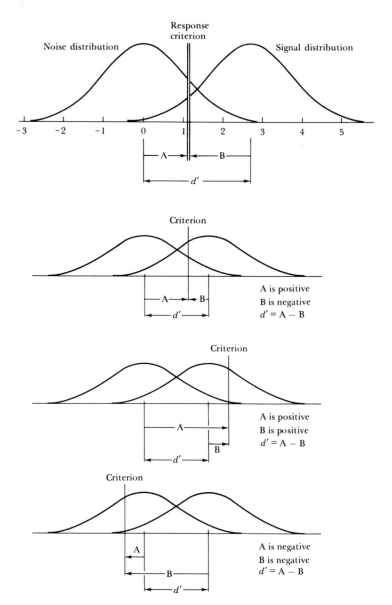

we mentioned in which we ask the subject to try and detect a signal that we present to him. We want to find out how far the distribution of observations that results from noise is from the distribution which results from the signal. We think that the situation is characterized by Figure B-8.

We want to discover both exactly where the signal distribution is located relative to the noise distribution and also where the criterion is. To start, call the mean value of the noise distribution 0. There is good reason for doing this, in the absence of signal the average observation ought to be around zero. Moreover, since we only care about the *relative* separation of the two distributions, it doesn't really matter what number we call the mean value of the noise (our measurement will be on an *interval scale;* see Appendix A). We call the distance from the mean of the noise distribution to the criterion A, the distance from the mean of the signal distribution to the criterion B, and the distance from the mean of the noise distribution to the mean of the signal distribution d'. The symbol d' is used for historical reasons: That is what it has been called in the psychological literature. Both A and B are distances from the mean value of distribution. If the criterion is to the right of the mean, A and B are postive. If the criterion is exactly at the mean, then the distance value is 0. If the criterion is to the left of the mean, the distance is negative. Thus $d' = A - B$.

Suppose our subject gives us a false-alarm rate of 14% and a hit rate of 95%. We can immediately determine A: If we look up 14% in Table B-2, we see that the criterion must be located a distance of 1.1 units to the right of the noise distribution. Thus, $A = 1.1$. Similarly, we see that a hit rate of 95% requires that the criterion be 1.6 units to the left of the mean of the signal distribution (the criterion value is at -1.6). Thus, $B = -1.6$. Now we know that $d' = 2.7$. And that is all there is to it.

PROBLEMS

The fire-sprinkler problem

At this point, we can probably learn most about the use of operating characteristics and about the normal distributon by working a few problems.

We are installing a sprinkler system as part of a fire-alarm system for a building. Now we wish to install the temperature control that will turn on all the sprinklers whenever a fire occurs. The control is located near the ceiling of a large store room. The roof is made of tin, and there are no windows in the room. Questions: To what temperature should we set the control? If the temperature is set too low, (say 130°), then on very hot days, when the outside temperature goes as high as 110°, it is quite likely that the hot air will rise to the ceiling of the storeroom and be heated even more by the sun warming up the tin roof. Thus, it would not take long for the air temperature to reach 130° and set off the system: a *false alarm*.

If, however, the temperature is set higher, say 180°, it is quite likely that a fire could develop and destroy a good deal of the items in the storeroom before the flames got high enough to heat the air at the ceiling to a temperature of 180°. Thus, we would fail to report many fires, at least while they were still small enough that the sprinkler system could put them out. This would be a *miss*. Where do we set the temperature?

To solve this problem, we need information about hits and false alarms. We need to know the probabilities with which these occur. Ideally, we would set up a test situation and watch what happens over, say, a 3-month period, carefully counting the occurrences of hits (correct triggering of the system to a fire), misses (failure to respond within, say, 5 min of a fire), false alarms (triggering of the system in the absence of a fire), and correct rejections (no response from the system in normal conditions). Then we could plot an operating characteristic.

The way we plot the operating characteristics is to vary the temperature setting of the control, collecting information about the hit- and false-alarm rate at each temperature setting. Thus, if we set the control at 140°, we might observe that the actual room temperature reaches that value on one day out of every five—giving a false-alarm figure of 20%—and we might also note that 88% of the fires that we set caused the room temperature to reach that value within the 5 min we require—a hit rate of 88%. This, then, is the first point on our curve: $p(\text{alarm}|\text{fire}) = 88\%$; $p(\text{alarm}|\text{no fire}) = 20\%$.

This one point is actually sufficient, if we believe that everything is normally distributed. We can now compute the value of d' and then compute what the rest of the curve should look like.

If we go back to the table of the normal distribution, Table B-2, we see that if we have a false alarm rate of 20%, the criterion must be to the right of the highest point on the distribution, at about .8: That is, the value of A is 0.8. A hit rate of 88% means that the criterion must be located to the left of the highest point on the distribution, at a point around -1.2. Thus, $B = -1.2$. Now d' is simply the distance that the two distributions are apart, and that is given by $0.8 + 1.2 = 2.0$. Our fire-alarm system has a d' of 2.0. The entire curve, therefore, looks like that shown in Figure B-9.

Now, to complete our information about the setting of the temperature limit we can simplify our procedure: All we do is find out what the false-alarm rate would be at different temperatures. To get this information, we can install an automatic temperature recorder in the building for a few months. Then, we look at the distribution of temperatures reached throughout that period. We might find that at a temperature of 150°, there was a false alarm only 10% of the time, at a temperature

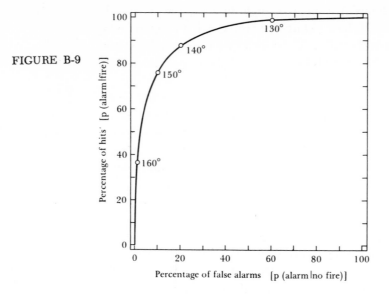

FIGURE B-9

of 160° only 1% of the time, and at a temperature of 130°, 60% of the time. These values then determine points on the operating characteristic, as shown.

At this point, it is obvious that we can never survive with a d' as low as 2.0. If we set the false-alarm value at a level acceptable to the fire department, say 1%—a temperature setting of 160°—then our insurance company will complain that we will only detect a fire with a chance of $\frac{37}{100}$. If we try to detect the fire with a chance as high as $\frac{95}{100}$, we will have a false alarm rate of close to 40%—clearly unacceptable to the fire department. It is quite clear that we can never solve the problem by trying to adjust the temperature setting of the sprinklers and alarms. We have to raise the d' value.

Supose that both the fire department and the insurance company agree that an acceptable hit and false alarm rate would be 99% and 1% respectively. What value of d' would we have to have?

Memory   From experiments in memory, we know that if a list of 30 names is presented to you once (for about 2 sec per name), an hour later the retention of that list will be very low. In fact, for any individual name, $d' = 0.8$.

Suppose you were a member of a receiving line at a formal party and in a 60-sec time period, 30 people had been introduced to you. An hour later you try to recall their names. Assuming that you adjust your false-alarm rate to be 8%, what percentage of the names do you remember?

Consider a version of the three-dice game in which the special die has **O** on three sides and **S** on the other three sides. Using the normal distribution as a good approximation of the dice distribution, what is the relationship between d' and the value of S?

Assume that there is a fixed criterion at 11. This means there will be a false-alarm rate of 8%. Thus, if S is 3, we see from our dice-game table that the hit rate is $\frac{15}{36}$ or 42%. Going to the normal distribution tables, $A = 1.4$, $B = 0.2$, so $d' = A - B = 1.2$. The relationship between d', hit rate, and false-alarm rate (assuming a fixed criterion of 11) is shown in Table B-3. The relationship between d' and S is plotted in Figure B-10. Now, you should try to complete both the table and the figure.

The dice game revisited

Table B-3

Value of S	False-Alarm Rate	Hit Rate	A	B	A − B = d'
0	8%	8%	1.4	1.4	0
1	8%	—	1.4	—	—
2	8%	—	1.4	—	—
3	8%	42%	1.4	0.2	1.2
4	8%	—	1.4	—	—
5	8%	—	1.4	—	—
6	8%	83%	1.4	−1.0	2.4
7	8%	—	1.4	—	—
8	8%	—	1.4	—	—

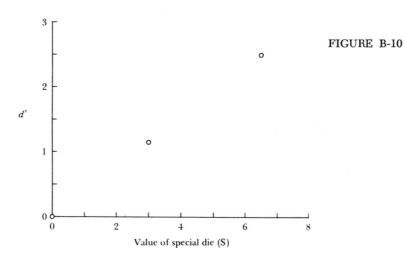

FIGURE B-10

SUGGESTED
READINGS The decision theory discussed here grew out of the engineering literature and it has mostly been applied to the study of sensory processes:
to psychophysics. Because it was first applied to the analysis of detecting
signals in noise, it usually goes under the name of *Signal Detection
Theory,* or sometimes simply *SDT.* Thus, to find this topic in book
indices, one must usually look for "signal detection theory" or sometimes
for d'.

The best overall introduction to the many uses of the decision theory
discussed here is the book by David Green and John Swets: *Signal Detection Theory and Psychophysics* (1966). This book does get very technical,
but much of the material in the early chapters can be followed without
too much difficulty even by those whose mathematics is weak. Some of
the latter chapters review the various uses of the decision theory to other
areas of psychology.

The chapter by Egan and Clarke (1966) in Sidowski's book on experimental methods offers another very good introduction to the technique.
The book of collected readings edited by Swets (1964) gives a collection
of uses, but this is very technical material.

This decision theory has been widely used in other areas. A good
(and easy to follow) description of its application to the study of the
retrieval of material from libraries by various automatic systems is given
in the *Science* article by Swets (1963). But perhaps the most widely
encountered use of this method of analysis has been in the study of
memory. Two typical studies, both introducing the technique and illustrating what can be done with it are the ones by Norman and
Wickelgren (1965) and Wickelgren and Norman (1966). A much
simpler introduction to these studies is the short description given in
Norman's *Memory and Attention* (1969a, pp. 148–161). (This is the same
theory discussed in Chapter 9 of this book.) Many of the advanced
theories presented in Norman's *Models of Human Memory* (1970) rely
heavily on detection theory analysis.

Bibliography

The reader who is interested in learning more about the issues discussed in this book can look in a number of different places for more material. The most important sources are the *Annual Reviews,* the *Psychological Abstracts,* the *Citation Index,* and the various journals in the field.

The *Annual Reviews* are a series of volumes published every year that survey the research findings in the field. They are published by Annual Reviews, Inc., Palo Alto, California. Although these books are published yearly, some of the specific areas are covered less frequently—perhaps once every third or fourth year. Use of the *Annual Reviews* is perhaps the fastest way to get up to date in any research area. They are difficult to use, however, because they are written for advanced readers, and some of the reviews tend to be incomprehensible even to them. Nonetheless, you can carefully examine the chapter in the *Annual Review* that covers the area of your interest, ferret out the references to the more important recent papers, and then find the papers themselves in the library. Often the papers on a topic are easier to understand than the reviews of those papers.

Although *Annual Reviews* are published on a number of topics, the two that will contain almost all the material relevant to the topics of this book are *Annual Reviews of Psychology* and *Annual Reviews of Physiology.*

Psychological Abstracts is a journal published by the American Psychological Association that contains abstracts of all technical papers published in a very large list of journals. By looking up a topic in the index of the abstracts, it is possible to trace the papers that might be of interest. The abstracts themselves give a general summary of what that paper is about, thus letting one know whether the actual article ought to be examined.

The main difficulty with the abstracts is that they tell you too much: You will be led to more papers than you can possibly examine. This usually is a result of the fact that you cannot find the exact area you wish to read about in the index: Thus, if you use an index term like "memory," you are likely to be referred to something like 500 papers. The one paper you really ought to read is probably somewhere in that list of 500, but you will never find it. Your job is to use the index and abstracts so cleverly that you can reduce that large initial number of papers to a more manageable size. It can be done with some thought: Basically, look up more specific terms. This difficulty has virtue, however, for often the abstracts lead you to a paper or research area that is even more interesting than the one you were originally seeking. Many a person has discovered his true interest by accidentally finding a paper in his wanderings through the abstracts.

The abstracts are bound in yearly editions: You have to examine each year's editions for the topic in which you are interested. It is always best to start with the most recent year and work backward.

Often you find a particularly good paper, but one that is rather old. The problem is to discover what new material has been published on this same topic. The way to do this is through the *Science Citation Index* (published

Annual reviews

Psychological abstracts

The science citation index

quarterly by the Institute for Scientific Information, Inc.). Here you look up the paper in which you are interested: The citation index tells you what recent papers have been published that refer to it. This is an excellent way to search forward from a paper to the recent work. This method fails sometimes, both because you get led astray with papers that cite the one you have but are, in fact, on a completely different topic, and also because not all the good papers you ought to read will get around to referencing the paper you happen to have.

The *Citation Index* is also bound in yearly editions, so you have to look up your favorite old paper in each year to see what new ones might have referred to it.

The journals　When all these methods fail, you can go directly to the journals. The journal presentation is often very technical, but sometimes surprisingly simple to read. The best thing to do is to find out the names of a few journals that cover the field that interests you (you can find the names of the journals in the references in this book), and then simply browse through the stacks in the library, including the stack of unbound, recent issues of the journal. Then you will probably both stumble across interesting articles and also discover references to earlier articles. Sometimes, when you find a journal that appears to cover the area in which you are interested, it makes sense to turn every page of the journal and examine all the articles, starting with the most recent years and going back as many years as your interest holds out. This technique of "brute force" search is not really so laborious as it sounds, and almost every serious scientist has done this task several times. (Do not shun the older issues. Because of the peculiar history of psychology, the most fascinating papers seem to have been published in the years around 1890 through 1910.)

The journals you will find to be of most interest are:

American Journal of Psychology　(General experimental psychology)
British Journal of Psychology　(General experimental psychology)
Canadian Journal of Psychology　(General experimental psychology)
Cognitive Psychology　(Both theoretical and some experimental articles dealing with memory, perception, cognition)
Journal of the Acoustical Society of America (*JASA*)　(Theoretical and experimental papers on hearing and speech recognition)
Journal of Experimental Psychology　(Experimental papers on almost any topic in psychology)
Journal of Mathematical Psychology　(Psychological topics treated mainly in terms of mathematical models and theories)
Journal of the Optical Society of America (*JOSA*)　(Theoretical and experimental papers on vision)
Journal of Verbal Learning and Verbal Behavior　(Experimental papers mainly concerned with human memory studies)

Perception and Psychophysics   (Experimental papers, primarily)

Psychological Bulletin   (Contains review articles on specialized topics. Good for summarizing the research and opinions on a topic)

Psychological Review   (Contains theoretical articles in current areas of interest)

Quarterly Journal of Experimental Psychology   (General experimental papers)

Science   (Occasional long survey articles, frequent short, technical papers)

Scientific American   (Good introductory articles)

Vision Research   (As the name implies)

Throughout the text, we reference particular books and articles that ought to be read for the individual chapters. In addition to these, there are several excellent general sources, books that you will probably want to scan to get a more thorough knowledge of psychology in general. Here is a small number of those books we feel are best suited for the reader who has finished this book and wishes to go on. It is not a complete list.

GENERAL READINGS

R. S. Woodworth & H. Schlosberg. *Experimental psychology*. New York: Holt, 1938, 1954, 1971. An excellent treatment of all of experimental psychology. Long used as the standard text for graduate students. There are three versions of this text in existence: the original text by Woodworth (1938), the one by Woodworth and Schlosberg (1958), and a new, revised one (Kling and Riggs, 1971). The 1938 version of the book is a remarkable document. It contains discussions on many important issues, issues that were not covered in the 1958 version. In many ways, the 1938 edition of the book is more valuable than the 1958 one, but you will have to decide this for yourself by browsing through both of them. The newest edition promised to bring the virtues of the earlier editions more up to date, but in our opinion it did not. It is a disappointing book.

G. A. Miller, E. Galanter, & K. H. Pribram. *Plans and the structure of behavior*. New York: Holt, 1960. A brief treatment of many of the issues presented in this book, with a framework that may sound familiar. This was one of the very first books to introduce information processing into psychology—a well-written book, easy to understand.

D. E. Wooldridge. *The machinery of the brain*. New York: McGraw-Hill, 1963: paperback. An excellent introduction to the operation of the brain and its implications for behavior. We have often assigned this book as supplementary reading for our course. Wooldridge also has several other books that should interest you, although they are not directly concerned with psychological issues.

C. H. Coombs, R. M. Dawes, & A. Tversky. *Mathematical psychology: An introduction*. Englewood Cliffs, New Jersey: Prentice-Hall, 1970. Much modern psychological theorizing uses mathematical models. This book provides an excellent introduction to all of this work.

G. A. Miller. *Psychology: The science of mental life*. New York: Harper and Row, 1962. An excellent summary of psychology, including an historical survey.

Collected readings   Many collections of reprinted articles are available. Many are especially good in the treatment of specialized topics, and we have referred to these books in the Suggested Readings after the appropriate chapters. At least two collections seem appropriate to more general areas, however, as well as comprising excellent source materials for further exploration of the concepts discussed in this book. These two are:

R. C. Atkinson (Ed.), *Contemporary psychology. Readings from Scientific American*. San Francisco: W. H. Freeman, 1971.

J. M. Foley, R. A. Lockhart, & D. M. Messick (Eds.), *Contemporary readings in psychology*. New York: Harper, 1970.

REFERENCES   Adolph, E. F. The internal environment and behavior. III. Water content. *American Journal of Psychiatry*, 1941, **97**, 1372.

Adrian, E. D. *The mechanism of nervous action: Electrical studies of the neurons*. Philadelphia: University of Pennsylvania Press, 1959.

Albers, J. *Interaction of color*. New Haven: Yale University Press, 1963. [*Also see* Bucher (1961).]

Allen, V. L. Situational factors in conformity. In L. Berkowitz (Ed.), *Advances in experimental social psychology*. Vol. 2. New York: Academic Press, 1965.

Alpern, M., Lawrence, M., & Wolsk, D. *Sensory processes*. Belmont, Calif.: Brooks/Cole, 1967.

Arnheim, R. *Art and visual perception*. Berkeley: Univ. of California Press, 1969. (a)

Arnheim, R. *Visual thinking*. Berkeley: Univ. of California Press, 1969. (b)

Arnold, M. B. (Ed.) *Feelings and emotions: The Loyola symposium*. New York: Academic Press, 1970.

Asch, S. E. *Social psychology*. Englewood Cliffs, N. J.: Prentice-Hall, 1952.

Asch, S. E. Opinions and social pressure. *Scientific American*, 1955, **193**, 31–35.

Atkinson, R. C. (Ed.) *Contemporary psychology. Readings from Scientific American*. San Francisco: Freeman, 1971.

Atkinson, R. C., and Shiffrin, R. M. The control of short-term memory. *Scientific American*, 1971, **225** (2), 82–90.

Averbach, E., & Coriell, A. S. Short-term memory in vision. *Bell System Technical Journal*, 1961, **40**, 309–328.

Ax, A. F. The physiological differentiation between fear and anger in humans. *Psychosomatic Medicine*, 1953, **15**, 433–442.

Bach, E., & Harms, R. G. (Eds.) *Universals in linguistic theory*. New York: Holt, 1968.

Backus, J. A plea for conformity. *Journal of the Acoustical Society of America,* 1968, **44**, 285.

Barbizet, J. *Human memory and its pathology.* San Francisco: Freeman, 1970.

Barker, R. G., Dembo, T., & Lewin, K. Frustration and regression: An experiment with young children. *University of Iowa Studies in Child Welfare,* 1941, **18**, No. 386.

Barlow, H. B., Hill, R. M., & Levick, W. R. Retinal ganglion cells responding selectively to direction and speed of image motion in the rabbit. *Journal of Physiology,* 1964, **173**, 377–407.

Barron, F., Dement, W. C., Edwards, W., Lindman, H., Phillips, L. D., Olds, J., & Olds, M. *New directions in psychology.* Vol. 2. New York: Holt, 1965.

Bartlett, F. C. *Remembering.* Cambridge, England: Cambridge University Press, 1932.

Bartlett, N. R. Dark adaptations and light adaptation. In C. H. Graham (Ed.), *Vision and visual perceptions.* New York: Wiley, 1965.

Bartley, S. The psychophysiology of vision. In S. S. Stevens (Ed.), *Handbook of experimental psychology.* New York: Wiley, 1951.

Beach, F. A., Hebb, D. O., Morgan, C. T., & Nissen, H. W. (Eds.) *The neuropsychology of Lashley.* New York: McGraw-Hill, 1960.

Békésy, G. von. On the resonance curve and decay period at various points on the cochlear partition. *Journal of the Acoustical Society of America,* 1949, **21**, 245–254.

Békésy, G. von. *Experiments in hearing.* New York: McGraw-Hill, 1960.

Békésy, G. von. *Sensory inhibition.* Princeton, N.J.: Princeton University Press, 1967.

Bem, D. J. *Beliefs, attitudes, and human affairs.* Belmont, Calif.: Wadsworth, 1970.

Berko, J. The child's learning of English morphology. *Word,* 1958, **14**, 150–177.

Berkowitz, L. *Advances in experimental social psychology.* Vol. 2. New York: Academic Press, 1965.

Berkun, M. M., Bialek, H. M., Kearn, R. P., & Yagi, K. Experimental studies of psychological stress in man. *Psychological Monographs,* 1962, **76** (15, Whole No. 534).

Berlyne, D. E. Children's reasoning and thinking. In P. Mussen (Ed.), *Handbook of child psychology.* New York: Wiley, 1970.

Bever, T. G. The cognitive basis for linguistic structures. In J. R. Hayes (Ed.), *Cognition and the development of language.* New York: Wiley, 1970.

Bishop, P. O. Central nervous system: Afferent mechanisms and perception. *Annual Review of Physiology,* 1967, **29**, 427–484.

Bishop, P. O., & Henry, G. H. Spatial vision. *Annual Review of Psychology,* 1971, **22**, 119–160.

Bjork, R. A. Repetition and rehearsal mechanisms in models for short-term memory. In D. A. Norman (Ed.), *Models of human memory.* New York: Academic Press, 1970.

Black, A. H. The direct control of neural processes by reward and punishment. *American Scientist,* 1971, **59**, 236–245.

Bolt, R. H., Cooper, F. S., David, E. E., Jr., Denes, P. B., Pickett, J. M., & Stevens, K. N. Identification of a speaker by speech spectrograms. *Science,* 1969, **166**, 398–342.

Bouman, M. A. History and present status of quantum theory in vision. In W. A. Rosenblith (Ed.), *Sensory communication.* Cambridge, Mass.: M.I.T. Press, 1961.

Bourne, L. E., Jr., Ekstrand, B. R., & Dominowski, R. L. *The psychology of thinking.* Englewood Cliffs, N. J.: Prentice-Hall, 1971.

Brady, J. V. Ulcers in "executive monkeys." *Scientific American,* 1958, **199** (4), 95–100.

Bransford, J., & Franks, J. Abstraction of linguistic ideas. *Cognitive Psychology,* in press.

Brazier, M. A. B. (Ed.) *Brain function.* Vol. II. Berkeley, Calif.: University of California Press, 1964.

Bredberg, G., Lindeman, H. H., Ades, H. W., West, R., & Engström, H. Scanning electron microscopy of the organ of corti. *Science,* 1970, **170**, 861–863.

Breland, K., & Breland, M. *Animal behavior.* New York: Macmillan, 1966.

Brooks, L. Spatial and verbal components of the act of recall. *Canadian Journal of Psychology,* 1968, **22**, 349–368.

Brown, R. *Social psychology.* New York: Free Press, 1965.

Brown, R. *A first language, the early years.* Cambridge, Mass.: Harvard University Press, in press.

Brown, R., & Bellugi, U. Three processes in the child's acquisition of syntax. In E. Lenneberg (Ed.), *New directions in the study of language.* Cambridge, Mass.: M.I.T. Press, 1964.

Brown, R., & Hanlon, C. Derivational complexity and order of acquisition in child speech. In J. R. Hayes (Ed.), *Cognition and the development of language.* New York: Wiley, 1970.

Brown, R., Galanter, E., Hess, E. H., & Mandler, G. *New directions in psychology I.* New York: Holt, 1962.

Bruner, J. S. The course of cognitive growth. *American Psychologist,* 1964, **19**, 1–15.

Bruner, J. S., Goodnow, J. J., & Austin, G. A. *A study of thinking.* New York: Wiley, 1956.

Bryden, M. P. Attentional strategies and short-term memory in dichotic listening. *Cognitive Psychology,* 1971, **2**, 99–116.

Bucher, F. *Joseph Albers. Despite straight lines.* New Haven: Yale University Press, 1961.

Burdick, E. *The 480.* New York: Dell, 1965. Originally published by McGraw-Hill, New York, 1954.

Bureš, J., & Burešová, O. The use of Leäd's spreading cortical depression in research on conditioned reflexes. *EEG. Clinical Neurophysiology,* 1960, 359–376. (Suppl. 13.)

Bureš, J., Petráň, M., & Zacharj, J. *Electrophysiological methods in biological research.* (3rd ed.) New York: Academic Press, 1967.

Byrne, W. L., Samnel, D., Bennett, E. L., Rosenzweig, M. R., Wasserman, E., Wagner, A. R., Gardner, F., Galambos, R., Berger, B. D., Margules, D. L., Fenichel, R. L., Stein, L., Corson, J. A., Enesco, H. E., Chorover, S. L., Holt, C. E., III, Schiller, P. H., Chiappetta, L., Jarvik, M. E., Leaf, R. C., Dutcher, J. D., Horovitz, Z. P., & Carlson, P. L. Memory transfer. *Science,* 1966, **153,** 658–659.

Carraher, R. G., & Thurston, J. B. *Optical illustions and the visual arts.* Princeton, N. J.: Van Nostrand-Reinhold, 1968.

Chapanis, A. The dark adaptation of the color anomalous measured with lights of different hues. *Journal of General Physiology,* 1947, **30,** 423–437.

Chomsky, N. The formal nature of language. In E. H. Lenneberg (Ed.), *Biological foundations of language.* New York: Wiley, 1967.

Chomsky, N., & Halle, M. *The sound pattern of English.* New York: Harper, 1968.

Cofer, C. N., & Appley, M. H. *Motivation: Theory and research.* New York: Wiley, 1964.

Cogan, D. B. *Neurology of the visual system.* Springfield, Ill.: Thomas, 1966.

Cohen, J. *Behavior in uncertainty.* New York: Basic Books, 1964.

Collins, A., & Quillian, M. R. Retrieval time from semantic memory. *Journal of Verbal Learning & Verbal Behavior,* 1969, **8,** 240–247.

The Color Tree. (2nd ed.) New York: Interchemical Corp., 1965.

Conel, J. L. *The postnatal development of the human cerebral cortex.* Vols. I–VI. Cambridge, Mass.: Harvard University Press, 1939–1963.

Conrad, R. Errors of immediate memory. *British Journal of Psychology.* 1959, **50,** 349–359.

Coombs, C. H., Dawes, R. M., & Tversky, A. *Mathematical psychology: An introduction.* Englewood Cliffs, N. J.: Prentice Hall, 1970.

Corballis, M. C., & Beale, J. L. Bilateral symmetry and behavior. *Psychological Review,* 1970, **77,** 451–464.

Coren, S. Brightness contrast as a function of figure-ground relations. *Journal of Experimental Psychology,* 1969, **80,** 517–524.

Corkin, S. Acquisition of motor skill after bilateral medial temporal-lobe excision. *Neuropsychologia,* 1968, **6,** 255–265.

Corning, W. C., & John, E. R. Effect of ribonuclease on retention of response in regenerated planarians. *Science,* 1961, **134,** 1363–1365.

Cornsweet, T. N. Information processing in human visual systems. *Stanford Research Institute Journal,* 1969, Feature issue No. 5.

Cornsweet, T. N. *Visual perception.* New York: Academic Press, 1970.

Creutzfeldt, O., & Sakmann, B. Neurophysiology of vision. *Annual Review of Physiology,* 1969, **31,** 499–544.

Crutchfield, R. S. Conformity and character. *American Psychologist,* 1955, **10,** 191–198.

Davidson, D., Suppes, P., & Siegal, S. *Decision making: An experimental approach.* Stanford, Calif.: Stanford University Press, 1967. Reprinted in W. Edwards and A. Tversky (Eds.), *Decision making.* Harmondsworth, Middlesex, England: Penguin Books, 1967.

Davson, H. (Ed.) *The eye.* New York: Academic Press, 1962.

DeGroot, A. D. *Thought and choice in chess.* The Hague: Mouton, 1965.

DeGroot, A. D. Perception and memory versus thought: Some old ideas and recent findings. In B. Kleinmuntz (Ed.), *Problem solving: Research, method, and theory.* New York: Wiley, 1966.

DeGroot, M. H. *Optimal statistical decision.* New York: McGraw-Hill, 1969.

Delafresnaye, J. F. (Ed.) *Brain mechanisms and consciousness.* Oxford, England: Blackwell, 1954.

Dement, W. C. An essay on dreams: The role of physiology in understanding their nature. In F. Barron *et al.* (Eds.), *New directions in psychology* II. New York: Holt, 1965.

Denes, P. B., & Pinson, E. N. *The speech chain.* Murray Hill, N. J.: Bell Telephone Laboratories, Inc., 1963. (Available from the business office of the local Bell System Telephone Company.)

de Sausmarez, M. *Bridget Riley.* Greenwich, Conn.: New York Graphic Society Ltd., 1970.

Deutsch, J. A. The physiological basis of memory. *Annual Review of Psychology,* 1969, **20,** 85–104.

Deutsch, J. A. (Ed.) *Physiological basis of memory.* New York: Academic Press, to be published.

Deutsch, J. A., & Deutsch, D. *Physiological psychology.* Homewood, Ill.: Dorsey Press, 1966.

Deutsch, S. *Models of the nervous system.* New York: Wiley, 1967.

DeValois, R. L., Abromov, I., & Jacobs, G. H. Analysis of response patterns of LGN cells. *Journal of the Optical Society of America,* 1966, **56,** 966–977.

DeValois, R. L., & Jacobs, G. H. Primate color vision. *Science,* 1968, **162,** 533–540.

Dodwell, P. C. *Visual pattern recognition.* New York: Holt, 1970.

Eccles, J. C. *The neurophysiological basis of mind.* London and New York: Oxford University Press, 1953.

Eccles, J. C. *The physiology of synapses.* Berlin and New York: Springer-Verlag, 1964.

Eccles, J. C. Possible ways in which synaptic mechanisms participate in learning, remembering and forgetting. In D. P. Kimble (Ed.), *The anatomy of memory.* Vol. I. Palo Alto, Calif.: Science and Behavior Books, 1965.

Edwards, W. Controller decisions in space flight. In R. Patton *et al.* (Eds.), *Applications of research on human decision making,* NASA SP-209. Washington, D. C.: National Aeronautics and Space Administration, Office of Technology Utilization, 1970.

Edwards, W., & Tversky, A. (Eds.) *Decision making.* Harmondsworth, Middlesex, England: Penguin Books, 1967.

Edwards, W., Lindman, H., & Phillips, L. *Emerging technologies for making decisions.* In *New directions in psychology.* Vol. 2. New York: Holt, 1965.

Egan, J. P., & Clarke, F. R. Psychophysics and signal detection. In J. B. Sidowski (Ed.), *Experimental methods and instrumentation in psychology*. New York: McGraw-Hill, 1966.

Enright, J. T. Stereopsis, visual latency and three-dimensional moving pictures. *American Scientist*, 1970, **58**(5), 536–545.

Epstein, R. A. *The theory of gambling and statistical logic*. New York: Academic Press, 1967.

Ernst, G. W., & Newell, A. *GPS: A case study in generality and problem solving*. New York: Academic Press, 1969.

Escher, M. C. *The graphic work of M. C. Escher*. New York: Meredith Press, 1967. (1st ed. 1961).

Fay, R. R. Auditory frequency stimulation in the goldfish (*carassius auratus*). *Journal of Comparative & Physiological Psychology*, 1970, **73**(2), 175–180.

Fay, R. R., & MacKinnon, J. R. A simplified technique for conditioning respiratory mouth movements in fish. *Behavioral Research Methods and Instrumentation*, 1969, **1**, 3.

Festinger, L. *A theory of cognitive dissonance*. New York, Harper, 1957.

Festinger, L. *Conflict, decision, and dissonance*. Stanford, Calif.: Stanford University Press, 1964.

Festinger, L., Coren, S., & Rivers, G. The effect of attention on brightness contrast and assimilation. *American Journal of Psychology*, 1970, **83**, 189–207.

Festinger, L., Riecken, H. W., & Schachter, S. *When prophecy fails*. Minneapolis: University of Minnesota Press, 1956.

Fillmore, C. J. The case for case. In E. Bach & R. G. Harms (Eds.), *Universals in linguistic theory*. New York: Holt, 1968.

Fillmore, C. J. Toward a modern theory of case. In D. A. Reibel & S. A. Schane (Eds.), *Modern studies in English*. Englewood Cliffs, N. J.: Prentice-Hall, 1969.

Finger, F. W., & Mook, D. C. Basic drives. *Annual Review of Psychology*, 1971, **22**, 1–38.

Fisher, A. E. Chemical stimulation of the brain. *Scientific American*, 1964, **210**(6), 60–68.

Flavell, J. H. *The developmental psychology of Jean Piaget*. Princeton, N. J.: Van Nostrand-Reinhold, 1963.

Flavell, J. H. Role-taking and communication skills in children. *Young Children*, 1966, **21**.

Flavell, J. H., Botkin, P. T., Fry, C. L., Wright, J. W., & Jarvis, P. E. *The development of role-taking and communication skills in children*. New York: Wiley, 1968.

Flexner, L. B., Flexner, J. B., & Roberts, R. Memory in mice analyzed with antibiotics. *Science*, 1967, **155**, 1377–1383.

Flock, H. R., & Freedberg, E. Perceived angle of incidence and achromatic surface color. *Perception & Psychophysics*, 1970, **8**, 251–256.

Foley, J. M., Lockhart, R. A., & Messick, D. M. (Eds.) *Contemporary readings in psychology.* New York: Harper, 1970.

Frijda, N. H. The simulation of human memory. *Psychological Bulletin,* in press.

Gaito, J. (Ed.) *Macromolecules and behavior.* (2nd ed.) New York: Appleton, in press. 1st ed., 1966.

Galanter, E. Contemporary psychophysics. In R. Brown, E. Galanter, E. H. Hess, & G. Mandler, *New directions in psychology.* Vol. 1. New York: Holt, 1962. (a)

Galanter, E. The direct measurement of utility and subjective probability. *American Journal of Psychology,* 1962, **75,** 208–220. (b)

Garcia, J., & Koelling, R. Relation of cue to consequence in avoidance learning. *Psychonomic Science,* 1966, **4,** 123–124.

Gardner, R. A., & Gardner, B. T. Teaching sign language to a chimpanzee. *Science,* 1969, **165,** 664–672.

Gazzaniga, M. S. *The bisected brain.* New York: Appleton, 1970.

Geldard, F. A. *The human senses.* New York: Wiley, 1953.

Geschwind, N. The organization of language and the brain. *Science,* 1970, **170,** 940–944.

Gibson, A. R., & Harris, C. S. The McCollough effect: Color adaptation of edge-detectors or negative afterimages? Paper presented at the annual meeting of the Eastern Psychological Association, Washington, D. C., April 1968.

Gibson, J. J. *The perception of the visual world.* Boston: Houghton, 1950.

Gibson, J. J. *The senses considered as perceptual systems.* Boston: Houghton, 1966.

Glass, D. C. (Ed.) *Studies of obesity and eating in neurophysiology and emotion.* New York: Rockefeller University Press, 1967.

Glassman, E. The biochemistry of learning: An evaluation of the role of RNA and protein. *Annual Review of Biochemistry,* 1969, **38,** 605–646.

Glassman, G., & Wilson, J. E. The incorporation of uridine into brain RNA during short experiences. *Brain Research,* 1970, **21,** 157–168.

Glucksberg, S., & Cowen, G. N., Jr. Memory for nonattended auditory material. *Cognitive Psychology,* 1970, **1,** 149–156.

Gombrich, E. H. *Art and illusion.* New York: Pantheon, 1960.

Graham, C. H. (Ed.) *Vision and visual perception.* New York: Wiley, 1965.

Grasselli, A. (Ed.) *Automatic interpretation and classification of images.* New York: Academic Press, 1969.

Greeff, Z. Graefe-Saemisch Hb. ges. augenheilk, II, Kap. 5, 1900, **1.**

Green, B. F., Jr. Current trends in problem solving. In B. Kleinmuntz (Ed.), *Problem solving.* New York: Wiley, 1966.

Green, D. M., & Swets, J. A. *Signal detection theory and psychophysics.* New York: Wiley, 1966.

Greenwood, D. D. Auditory masking and the critical band. *Journal of the Acoustical Society of America,* 1961, **33,** 484–502.

Gregory, R. L. *Eye and brain: The psychology of seeing.* New York: McGraw-Hill, 1966.

Gregory, R. L. *The intelligent eye.* New York: McGraw-Hill, 1970.

Gross, C. G. A comparison of the effects of partial and total lateral frontal lesions on test performance by monkeys. *Journal of Comparative & Physiological Psychology,* 1963, **56,** 41–47.

Guirao, M., & Stevens, S. S. Measurement of auditory density. *Journal of the Acoustical Society of America,* 1964, **36,** 1176–1182.

Gulick, W. L. *Hearing: Physiology and psychophysics.* London and New York: Oxford University Press, 1971.

Gurowitz, E. M. *The molecular basis of memory.* Englewood Cliffs, N. J.: Prentice-Hall, 1969.

Guzmán, A. Decomposition of a visual scene into three-dimensional bodies. In A. Grasselli (Ed.), *Automatic interpretation and classification of images.* New York: Academic Press, 1969.

Haber, R. N. (Ed.) *Current research in motivation.* New York: Holt, 1967.

Haber, R. N. (Ed.) *Contemporary theory and research in visual perception.* New York: Holt, 1968.

Haber, R. N. Eidetic images. *Scientific American,* 1969, **220,** 36–44. (a)

Haber, R. N. (Ed.) *Information-processing approaches to visual perception.* New York: Holt, 1969. (b)

Haber, R. N. How we remember what we see. *Scientific American,* 1970, **222**(5), 104–112.

Hamlyn, L. H. An electron microscope study of pyramidal neurons in the Ammon's Horn of the rabbit. *Journal of Anatomy,* 1963, **97,** 189–201.

Harlow, H. F., & Woolsey, C. N. (Eds.) *Biological and biochemical bases of behavior.* Madison, Wis.; University of Wisconsin Press, 1958.

Harris, C. S. Perceptual adaptation to inverted, reversed, and displaced vison. *Psychological Review,* 1965, **72,** 419–444.

Harris, C. S., & Gibson, A. R. Is orientation-specific color adaptation in human vision due to edge detectors, afterimages or "dipoles?" *Science,* 1968, **162,** 1506–1507. (a)

Harris, C. S., & Gibson, A. R. A minimal model for McCollough's orientation-specific color aftereffect. Paper presented at the annual meeting of the Psychonomic Society, St. Louis, November 1968. (b)

Hartline, H. K., Milne, L. J., & Wagman, I. H. Fluctuations of response of single visual cells. *Federation Proceedings (Federation of American Societies for Experimental Biology)* 1947, **6,** 124. (Abstract)

Hartline, H. K., & Ratliff, F. Inhibitory interaction of receptor units in the eye of limulus. *Journal of General Physiology,* 1957, **40,** 357–376.

Hartline, H. K., Wagner, H. G., & Ratliff, F. Inhibition in the eye of limulus. *Journal of General Physiology,* 1956, **39,** 651–673.

Hawkins, J. E., Jr., & Stevens, S. S. The masking of pure tones and of speech by white noise. *Journal of the Acoustical Society of America,* 1950, **22,** 6–13.

Hayes, J. R. *Cognition and the development of language.* New York: Wiley, 1970.

Hebb, D. O. *The organization of behavior.* New York: Wiley, 1949. Reprinted in paperback by Science Editions, 1961.

Hecht, S., & Hsia, Y. Dark adaptation following light adaptation to red and white lights. *Journal of the Optical Society of America,* 1945, **35**, 261–267.

Held, K. Two modes of processing spatially distributed visual stimulations. In F. O. Schmidt (Ed.), *The neurosciences: Second study program.* New York: Rockefeller University Press, in press.

Held, R. Dissociation of visual functions by deprivation and rearrangement. *Psychologische Forschung,* 1968, **31**, 338–348.

Henney, K. *Principles of radio.* (3rd ed.) New York: Wiley, 1938.

Heron, W. Cognitive and physiological effects of perceptual isolation. In P. Solomon *et al.* (Eds.), *Sensory deprivation.* Cambridge, Mass.: Harvard University Press, 1961.

Hilgard, E. R., & Bower, G. H. *Theories of learning.* New York: Appleton, 1966.

Hochberg, J. *Perception.* Englewood Cliffs, N. J.: Prentice-Hall, 1964.

Hochberg, J. In the mind's eye. In R. N. Haber (Ed.), *Contemporary theory and research in visual perception.* New York: Holt, 1968.

Hochberg, J., & Beck, J. Apparent spatial arrangement and perceived brightness. *Journal of Experimental Psychology,* 1954, **47**, 263–266.

Hoebel, B. G. Feeding and self stimulation. *Annals of the New York Academy of Sciences,* 1969, **157**, Art. 2, 758–777.

Hoebel, B. G. Feeding: Neural control of intake. *Annual Review of Physiology,* 1971, **33**, 533–568.

Hoffman, L. R. Group problem solving. In L. Berkowitz (Ed.), *Advances in experimental social psychology.* Vol. 2. New York: Academic Press, 1965.

Hubel, D. H., & Wiesel, T. N. Receptive fields, binocular interaction and functional architecture in the cat's visual cortex. *Journal of Physiology (London)* 1962, **160**, 106–154.

Hubel, D. G., & Wiesel, T. N. Shape and arrangement of columns in cat's striate cortex. *Journal of Physiology (London)* 1963, **165**, 559–568.

Hubel, D. H., & Wiesel, T. N. Receptive fields and functional architecture in two nonstriate visual areas (18 and 19) of the cat. *Journal of Neurophysiology,* 1965, **28**, 229–289.

Hubel, D. H., & Wiesel, T. N. Receptive fields and functional architecture of monkey striate cortex. *Journal of Physiology* (London), 1968, **195**, 215–243.

Huey, E. B. *The psychology and pedagogy of reading.* Cambridge, Mass.: M.I.T. Press, 1968. Originally published 1908.

Hull, C. L. *Essentials of behavior.* New Haven: Yale University Press, 1951.

Humphrey, N. K., & Weiskrantz, L. Vision in monkeys after removal of the striate cortex. *Nature (London),* 1967, **215**, 595–597.

Hunt, E. What kind of computer is man? *Cognitive Psychology,* 1971, **2**, 57–98.

Hurvich, L. M., & Jameson, D. *The perception of brightness and darkness.* Rockleigh, New Jersey: Allyn & Bacon, 1966.

Hurvich, L. M., Jameson, D., & Krantz, D. Theoretical treatments of selected visual problems. In R. Luce, R. R. Bush, & E. Galanter (Eds.), *Handbook of mathematical psychology.* Vol. III. New York: Wiley, 1965.

Hurwicz, L. Game theory and decisions. *Scientific American,* 1955, **192**(2), 78–83.

Hydén, H., & Egyházi, E. Glial RNA changes during a learning experiment with rats. *Proceedings of the National Academy of Sciences of the United States of America,* 1964, **49**, 618–624.

Ingle, D. Two visual mechanisms underlying the behavior of fish. *Psychologische Forschung,* 1967, **31**, 44–51.

Jacobson, E. *Biology of emotions.* Springfield, Ill.: Thomas, 1967.

Jakobson, R., Fant, G. M., & Halle, M. *Preliminaries to speech analysis.* Cambridge, Mass.: M.I.T. Press, 1951.

James, W. *The principles of psychology.* New York: Holt, 1890. Reprinted by Dover, New York, 1950.

Jameson, D., & Hurvich, L. M. Opponent chromatic induction: Experimental evaluation and theoretical account. *Journal of the Optical Society of America,* 1962, **51**, 46–57.

Jarrard, L. E. (Ed.) *Cognitive processes of nonhuman primates.* New York: Academic Press, 1971.

Jensen, D. D. Paramecia, planaria, and pseudo-learning: Learning and associated phenomena in invertebrates. *Animal Behavior Supplement,* 1965, **1**, 9–20.

John, E. R. Studies on learning and retention in planaria. In M. A. B. Brazier (Ed.), *Brain function.* Vol. II. Berkeley, Calif.: University of California Press, 1964.

John, E. R. *Mechanisms of memory.* New York: Academic Press, 1967.

Jones, M. R. (Ed.) *Nebraska symposium on motivation.* Lincoln, Neb.: University of Nebraska Press, 1957.

Judd, D. B. Basic correlates of the visual stimulus. In S. S. Stevens (Ed.), *Handbook of experimental psychology.* New York: Wiley, 1951.

Julesz, B. Binocular depth perception of computer-generated patterns. *Bell System Technical Journal,* 1960, **39**, 1125–1162.

Julesz, B. Binocular depth perception without familiary cues. *Science,* 1964, **145**, 356–362.

Julesz, B. *Foundations of cyclopean perception.* Chicago: University of Chicago Press, 1971.

Jung, R. Allgemeine neurophysiologie. In *Handbuch der inneren medizen.* Ed. V/1. Berlin and New York: Springer-Verlag, 1953.

Kahneman, D. Methods, findings, and theory in studies of visual masking. *Psychological Bulletin,* 1968, **69**, 408–425.

Karlins, M., & Abelson, H. J. *Persuasion: How opinions and attitudes are changed.* (2nd ed.) Berlin and New York: Springer-Verlag, 1970.

Kavanagh, J. F., & Mattingly, I. G. (Eds.) *Language by ear and by eye. The relationship between speech and reading.* Cambridge, Mass.: M.I.T. Press, 1972.

Kepes, G. (Ed.) *Vision and value series: 1. Education of vision; 2. Structure in art and in science; 3. The nature and art of motion; 4. Module, proportion, symmetry, rhythm: 5. The man-made object; 6. Sign, image, symbol.* New York: Braziller, 1965, 1966.

Khrushchev, N. *Khrushchev remembers with an introduction, commentary and notes by Edward Crankshaw.* Translated and edited by Strobe Talbott. Boston: Little, Brown, 1970.

Kiang, N. *Discharge patterns of single fibers in the cat's auditory nerve.* Cambridge, Mass.: M.I.T. Press, 1965. (Res. Monogr. No. 35.)

Kimble, D. P. (Ed.), *The anatomy of memory.* Vol. I. Palo Alto, Calif.: Science and Behavior Books, 1965.

Kimble, G. A. *Hilgard and Marquis' conditioning and learning.* New York: Appleton, 1961.

Kinney, G. C., Marsetta, M., & Showman, D. J. *Studies in display symbol legibility, part XII. The legibility of alphanumeric symbols for digitalized television.* Bedford, Mass.: The Mitre Corporation, November 1966, ESD-TR-66-117.

Kintsch, W. *Learning, memory, and conceptual processes.* New York: Wiley, 1970.

Kleinmuntz, B. (Ed.) *Problem solving.* New York: Wiley, 1966.

Kleinmuntz, B. (Ed.) *Concepts and the structure of memory.* New York: Wiley, 1967.

Kleinmuntz, B. (Ed.) *Formal representation of human judgement.* New York: Wiley, 1968.

Kleitman, N. Patterns of dreaming. *Scientific American,* 1960, **203**(5), 82–88.

Kleitman, N. *Sleep and wakefulness.* (Rev. ed.) Chicago: University of Chicago Press, 1963.

Kling, J. W., & Riggs, L. A. (Eds.) *Woodworth/Schlosberg's experimental psychology* (3rd ed.) New York: Holt, 1971.

Koch, S. *Psychology: A study of science.* Vol. IV. New York: McGraw-Hill, 1962.

Köhler, W. *The mentality of apes.* London: Routledge and Kegan Paul, 1925. 2nd ed., 1927). Available in paperback from Vintage Books, New York, 1959.

Kolers, P. A., & Eden, M. (Eds.), *Recognizing patterns: Studies in living and automatic systems.* Cambridge, Mass.: M.I.T. Press, 1968.

Krantz, D. H., Luce, R. D., Suppes, P., & Tversky, A. *Foundations of measurement.* Vol. 1. *Additive and polynomial representations.* New York: Academic Press, 1971.

Kryter, K. D. *The effect of noise on man.* New York: Academic Press, 1970.

Kuffler, S. W. Discharge patterns and functional organization of mammalian retina. *Journal of Neurophysiology,* 1953, **16**, 37–68.

Lashley, K. S. Mass action in cerebral function. *Science,* 1931, **73**, 245–254.

Lashley, K. S. In search of the engram. *Symposium of the Society of Experimental Biology,* 1950, **4**, 454–482.

Lashley, K. S. The problem of serial order in behavior. In L. A. Jeffress (Ed.), *Cerebral mechanisms in behavior: The Hixon symposium.* New York: Wiley, 1951.

Latané, B., & Darley, J. M. Bystander "apathy." *American Scientist,* 1969, **57**, 244–268.

Latané, B., & Darley, J. M. *The unresponsive bystander.* New York: Appleton, 1970.

Leask, J., Haber, R. N., & Haber, R. B. Eidetic imagery in children: II. Longitudinal and experimental results. *Psychonomic Monograph Supplements,* 1969, **3**(3, Whole No. 35).

LeGrand, Y. *Light, colour, and vision.* London: Chapman & Hall, 1957.

Leibowitz, H., Myers, N. A., & Chinetti, P. The role of simultaneous contrast in brightness constancy. *Journal of Experimental Psychology,* 1955, **50**, 15.

Lenneberg, E. H. (Ed.) *New directions in the study of language.* Cambridge, Mass.: M.I.T. Press, 1964.

Lenneberg, E. H. *Biological foundations of language.* New York: Wiley, 1967.

Lettvin, J. Y., Maturana, H. R., McCulloch, W. S., & Pitts, W. H. What the frog's eye tells the frog's brain. *Proceedings of the IRE,* 1959, **47**(11), 1940–1951.

Lettvin, J. Y., Maturana, H. R., Pitts, W. H., & McCulloch, W. S. Two remarks on the visual system of the frog. In W. A. Rosenblith (Ed.), *Sensory communication.* Cambridge, Mass.: M.I.T. Press, 1961.

Levelt, W. J. M. *On binocular rivalry.* Soesterberg, The Netherlands: Institute for Perception RVO-TNO, 1965.

Levine, M. Hypothesis theory and nonlearning despite ideal S-R reinforcement contingencies. *Psychological Review,* 1971, **78**, 130–140.

Liberman, A. M. The grammars of speech and language. *Cognitive Psychology,* 1970, **1**(4), 301–323.

Lindgren, N. Machine recognition of human language. *Institute of Electrical and Electronics Engineers Spectrum.*

 Part 1. Automatic speech recognition, March 1965, **2**, 114–136.

 Part 2. Theoretical models of speech perception in language, April 1965, **2**, 45–59.

 Part 3. Cursive script recognition, May 1965, **2**, 104–116.

Lindsley, D. B. Emotion. In S. S. Stevens (Ed.), *Handbook of experimental psychology.* New York: Wiley, 1951.

Lindsley, D. B. Psychophysiology and motivation. In M. F. Jones (Ed.), *Nebraska Symposium on Motivation.* Lincoln, Nebraska: University of Nebraska Press, 1957.

Loehlin, J. C. *Computer models of personality.* New York: Random House, 1968.

Lorenz, K. Z. *On Aggression*. New York: Bantam Books, 1969. First published 1966 by Harcourt, New York.

Luce, G. G., & Segal, J. *Sleep*. New York: Coward-McCann, 1966.

Luce, R. D., Bush, R. R., & Galanter, E. (Eds.) *Handbook of mathematical psychology*. 3 vols. New York: Wiley, 1962–1965.

Luce, R. D., & Suppes, P. Preference, Utility, and subjective probability. In R. D. Luce, R. R. Bush, and E. Galanter (Eds.), *Handbook of Mathematical Psychology*. Vol. III. New York: Wiley, 1965.

Luckiesh, M. *Visual illusions*. Princeton, N. J.: Van Nostrand-Reinhold, 1922. Also available in paperback from Dover Publications, 1965.

Luria, A. R. *The role of speech in the regulation of normal and abnormal behavior*. New York: Liverright, 1961.

Luria, A. R. *The mind of a mnemonist*. New York: Basic Books, 1968.

Madigan, S. A., & McCabe, L. Perfect recall and total forgetting: A problem for models of short-term memory. *Journal of Verbal Learning & Verbal Behavior*, 1971, **10**, 101–106.

Magoun, H. W. The ascending reticular system and wakefulness. In J. F. Delafresnaye (Ed.), *Brain mechanisms and consciousness*. Oxford, England: Blackwell, 1954.

Magritte. See Sylvester (1969).

Maier, N. R. F. Reasoning in humans. II. The solution of a problem and its appearance in consciousness. *Journal of Comparative Psychology*, 1931, **12**, 181–194.

Maier, S. F., Seligman, M. E. P., & Solomon, R. L. Pavlovian fear conditioning and learned helplessness. In B. A. Campbell and R. M. Church (Eds.), *Punishment and aversive behavior*. New York: Appleton, 1969.

Mandler, G. Emotion. In R. Brown *et al.* (Eds.), *New Directions in psychology*. New York: Holt, 1962.

Markowitz, H. The utility of wealth. *Journal of Political Economics*, 1952, **60**, 152–158.

McCollough, C. Color adaptation of edge detectors in the human visual system. *Science*, 1965, **149**, 1115–1116.

McConnell, J. V. Memory transfer through cannibalism in planarians. *Journal of Neuropsychiatry Supplement 1*, 1962, **3**, 542–548.

McConnell, J. V. Cannibalism and memory in flatworms. *New Scientist*, 1964, **21**, 465–468.

McConnell, J. V., Jacobson, A. L., & Kimble, D. P. The effects of regeneration upon retention of a conditioned response in the planarian. *Journal of Comparative & Physiological Psychology*, 1959, **52**, 1.

McGinniss, J. *The Selling of the President 1968*. New York: Trident Press, 1969.

Melton, A. W. Implications of short-term memory for a general theory of memory. *Journal of Verbal Learning & Verbal Behavior*, 1963, **2**, 1–21.

Mershon, D. H., & Gogel, W. C. Effect of stereoscopic cues on perceived whiteness. *American Journal of Psychology*, 1970, **83**, 55–67.

Messick, D. M. (Ed.) *Mathematical thinking in behavioral sciences. Readings from Scientific American.* San Francisco: Freeman, 1968.

Meyer, D. On the representation and retrieval of stored semantic information. *Cognitive Psychology,* 1970, **1,** 242–300.

Milgram, S. Behavioral study of obedience. *Journal of Abnormal Psychology,* 1963, **67,** 371–378.

Milgram, S. Issues in the study of authority: A reply to Baumrind. *American Psychologist,* 1964, **19,** 848–852.

Milgram, S. Some conditions of obedience and disobedience to authority. *Human Relations,* 1965, **18,** 57–75.

Miller, G. A. Decision units in the perception of speech. *IRE Transactions on Information Theory,* 1962, **8,** 81–83. (a)

Miller, G. A. *Psychology: The science of mental life.* New York: Harper, 1962. (b)

Miller, G. A. The cybernetic approach. In G. A. Miller, *The psychology of communication.* New York: Basic Books, 1967. Reprinted in J. M. Foley, R. A. Lockhart, & D. M. Messick (Eds.), *Contemporary readings in psychology.* New York: Harper, 1970.

Miller, G. A., & McNeill, D. Psycholinguistics. In G. Lindzey and E. Aronson (Eds.), *The handbook of social psychology.* Vol. III. (2nd ed.) Reading, Mass.: Addison-Wesley, 1969.

Miller, G. A., Galanter, E., & Pribram, K. H. *Plans and the structure of behavior.* New York: Holt, 1960.

Miller, N. E. Comments on theoretical models illustrated by the development of a theory of conflict behavior. *Journal of Personality,* 1951, **20,** 82–100.

Miller, S. A., Shelton, J., & Flavell, J. H. A test of Luria's hypotheses concerning the development of verbal self-regulation. *Child Development,* 1970, **41,** 651–665.

Milne, A. A. *Now we are six.* New York: Dutton, 1927.

Milner, B., Corkin, S., & Teuber, H. L. Further analysis of the hippocampal amnesia syndrome: 14-year followup study of H. M. *Neuropsychologia,* 1968, **6,** 215–234.

Minsky, M. (Ed.), *Semantic information processing.* Cambridge, Mass.: M.I.T. Press, 1968.

Moray, N. Attention in dichotic listening: Affective cues and the influence of instructions. *Quarterly Journal of Experimental Psychology,* 1959, **11,** 56–60.

Morgan, C. T. *Physiological psychology.* (3rd ed.) New York: McGraw-Hill, 1965.

Morgenstern, O. The theory of games. *Scientific American,* 1949, **180**(5), 22–25.

Mountcastle, V. B. (Ed.) *Interhemispheric relations and cerebral dominance.* Baltimore, Md.: Johns Hopkins Press, 1962.

Mueller, C. G. *Sensory psychology.* Englewood Cliffs, N. J.: Prentice-Hall, 1965.

Mueller, C. G., Rudolph, M., & the Editors of Time-Life Books. *Light and vision*. New York: Time, Inc., 1969.

Murdock, B. B., Jr. The retention of individual items. *Journal of Experimental Psychology*, 1961, **62**, 618–625.

Murdock, B. B., Jr. The serial effect of free recall. *Journal of Experimental Psychology*, 1962, **64**, 482–488.

Mussen, P. (Ed.) *Handbook of child psychology*. 2 vols. (Rev. ed.) New York: Wiley, 1970.

Myers, R. E. Transmission of visual information within and between the hemispheres: A behavioral study. In V. B. Mountcastle (Ed.), *Interhemispheric relations and cerebral dominance*. Baltimore, Md: Johns Hopkins Press, 1962.

Neisser, U. Visual search. *Scientific American*, 1964, **210** (6), 94–102.

Neisser, U. *Cognitive Psychology*. New York: Appleton, 1967.

Newell, A. Studies in problem solving: Subject 3 on the crypt-arithmetic task, DONALD plus GERALD equals ROBERT. Pittsburgh: Carnegie-Mellon Institute, 1967.

Norman, D. A. *Memory and attention: An introduction to human information processing*. New York: Wiley, 1969. (a)

Norman, D. A. Memory while shadowing. *Quarterly Journal of Experimental Psychology*, 1969, **21**, 85–93. (b)

Norman, D. A. (Ed.) *Models of human memory*. New York: Academic Press, 1970.

Norman, D. A., & Rumelhart, D. E. In D. A. Norman (Ed.), A system for perception and memory. *Models of human memory*. New York: Academic Press, 1970.

Norman, D. A., & Wickelgren, W. A. Short-term recognition memory for single digits and pairs of digits. *Journal of Experimental Psychology*, 1965, **70**, 479–489.

Olds, J. Pleasure centers in the brain. *Scientific American*, 1956, **195**(4), 105–116.

Olds, J., & Olds, M. Drives, rewards, and the brain. In F. Barron *et al.* (Eds.), *New directions in psychology*. Vol. 2. New York: Holt, 1965.

Pantle, A. J., & Sekuler, R. W. Velocity-sensitive elements in human vision: Initial psychophysical evidence. *Vision Research*, 1968, **8**, 445–450.

Patterson, R. D. Noise masking of a change in residue pitch. *Journal of the Acoustical Society of America*, 1969, **45**, 1520–1524.

Patton, R. M., Tanner, T. A., Jr., Markowitz, J., & Swets, J. A. (Eds.) *Applications of research on human decision making*. NASA-SP-209. Washington, D. C.: National Aeronautics and Space Administration, Office of Technology Utilization, 1970.

Penrose, L. S., & Penrose, R. Impossible objects: A special type of illusion. *British Journal of Psychology*, 1958, **49**, 31.

Peterson, L. R. Short-term memory. *Scientific American*, 1966, **215**(7), 90–95.

Peterson, L. R., & Peterson, M. Short-term retention of individual items. *Journal of Experimental Psychology*, 1959, **58**, 193–198.

Phillips, J. L., Jr. *The origins of intellect: Piaget's theory.* San Francisco: Freeman, 1969.

Piaget, J. *The language and thought of the child.* New York: Harcourt, 1926.

Piaget, J. *Play, dreams, and imitation in childhood.* New York: Norton, 1951 (1st ed., 1945).

Piaget, J. *The origins of intelligence in children.* New York: International Universities Press, 1952. (1st ed., 1936)

Piaget, J. *The construction of reality in the child.* New York: Basic Books, 1954. (1st ed., 1937)

Piaget, J. *Six psychological studies.* In D. Elkind (Ed.), (translated by A. Tenzer.) New York: Random House, 1967. Published in paperback by Vintage Books, 1968.

Piaget, J., & Inhelder, B. *The child's conception of space.* London: Routledge and Kegan Paul, 1956.

Pirenne, M. H. *Vision and the eye.* (2nd ed.) London: Associated Book Publishers, 1967.

Pirenne, M. H. *Optics, painting, and photography.* London and New York: Cambridge University Press, 1970.

Polya, G. *How to solve it.* Princeton, N. J.: Princeton University Press, 1945.

Polyak, S. *The vertebrate visual system.* Chicago: University of Chicago Press, 1957.

Pomeranz, B., & Chung, S. H. Dendritic-tree anatomy codes form–vision physiology in tadpole retina. *Science*, 1970, **170**, 983–984.

Postman, L., & Phillips, L. W. Short-term temporal changes in free recall. *Quarterly Journal of Experimental Psychology*, 1965, **17**, 132–138.

Premack, D. Language in chimpanzee? *Science*, 1971, **172**, 808–822.

Pritchard, R. M. Stabalized images on the retina. *Scientific American*, 1961, **204**, 72–78.

Rachlin, H. *Introduction to modern behaviorism.* San Francisco: Freeman, 1970.

Raiffa, E. *Decision analysis: Introductory lectures on choices under uncertainty.* Reading, Mass.: Addison-Wesley, 1968.

Rapoport, A. *Fights, games, and debates.* Ann Arbor: University of Michigan Press, 1960.

Rapoport, A. The use and misuse of game theory. *Scientific American*, 1962, **207**(6), 108–118.

Rasmussen, G. L., & Windle, W. F. (Eds.) *Neural mechanisms of the auditory and vestibular systems.* Springfield, Ill.: Thomas, 1960.

Ratliff, F. Inhibitory interaction and the detection and enhancement of contours. In W. A. Rosenblith (Ed.), *Sensory communication.* Cambridge, Mass.: M.I.T. Press, 1961.

Ratliff, F. *Mach bands: Quantitative studies on neural networks in the retina.* San Francisco: Holden-Day, 1965.

Ratliff, F., & Hartline, H. K. The response of *limulus* optic nerve fibers to patterns of illumination on the receptor mosaic. *Journal of General Physiology*, 1959, **42**, 1241–1255.

Reddy, D. R. Phoneme grouping for speech recognition. *Journal of the Acoustical Society of America*, 1967, **41**, 1295–1300. (a)

Reddy, D. R. Computer recognition of connected speech. *Journal of the Acoustical Society of America*, 1967, **42**, 329–347. (b)

Reitman, J. S. Mechanisms of forgetting in short-term memory. *Cognitive Psychology*, 1971, **2**, 185–195.

Restle, F. Mathematical models and thought: A search for stages. In J. F. Voss (Ed.), *Approaches to thought*. Columbus, Ohio: Charles E. Merrill, 1969.

Reynolds, G. S. *A primer of operant conditioning*. Glenview, Ill.: Scott, Foresman, 1968.

Richardson, L. F., & Ross, J. S. Loudness and telephone current. *Journal of General Psychology*, 1930, **3**, 288–306.

Riggs, L. A., Ratliff, F., Cornsweet, J. C., & Cornsweet, T. N. The disappearance of steadily-fixated objects. *Journal of the Optical Society of America*, 1953, **43**, 495–501.

Riley, B. See de Sausmarez, M. (1970).

Ripps, H., & Weale, R. A. Color vision. *Annual Review of Psychology*, 1969, **20**, 193–216.

Robinson, D. A. Eye movement control in primates. *Science*, 1968, **161**, 1219–1224.

Robinson, D. W., & Dadson, R. S. A redetermination of the equal-loudness relations for pure tones. *British Journal of Applied Physics*, 1956, **7**, 166–181.

Rokeach, M. *The three Christs of Ypsilanti*. New York: Alfred A. Knopf, 1964.

Rosenblith, W. A. (Ed) *Sensory communication*. Cambridge, Mass.: M.I.T. Press, 1961.

Rosner, B. S. Brain functions. *Annual Review of Psychology*, 1970, **21**, 555–594.

Rumelhart, D. E. A multicomponent theory of the perception of briefly exposed visual displays. *Journal of Mathematical Psychology*, 1970, **7**, 191–218.

Rumelhart, D. E., Lindsay, P. H., & Norman, D. A. A process model of long-term memory. In E. Tulving and W. Donaldson (Eds.), *Organization of memory*. New York: Academic Press, 1972.

Saltz, E. *The cognitive bases of human learning*. Homewood, Ill.: Dorsey Press, 1971.

Schachter, S. Cognitive effects on bodily functioning. In D. C. Glass (Ed.), *Studies of obesity and eating in neurophysiology and emotion*. New York: Rockefeller University Press, 1967.

Schachter, S. *Emotion, obesity, and crime*. New York: Academic Press, 1971.

Schachter, S., & Singer, J. E. Cognitive, social and physiological determinants of emotional state. *Psychological Review*, 1962, **69**, 379–399.

Schachter, S., & Wheeler, L. Epinephrine, chlorpromazine and amusement. *Journal of Abnormal Psychology*, 1962, **65**, 121–128.

Schadé, J. P., & van Groenigen, W. B. Structural organization of the human cerebral cortex: Maturation of the middle frontal gyrus. *Acta Anatomica*, **47**, 74–111.

Schank, R. A. Conceptual dependency representation for a computer oriented semantics. AI Memo-83. Stanford, Calif.: Computer Science Department, Stanford University, 1969. (Also, *Cognitive Psychology*, 1972.)

Scharf, B. Critical bands. In J. V. Tobias (Ed.), *Foundations of modern auditory theory*. Vol. I. New York: Academic Press, 1970.

Scheerer, M. Problem solving. *Scientific American*, 1963, **204**(4), 118–128.

Schelling, T. C. *The strategy of conflict*. Cambridge, Mass.: Harvard University Press, 1963.

Schlesinger, A. M., Jr. *A thousand days: John F. Kennedy in the White House*. Boston: Houghton, 1965.

Schmitt, F. O. (Ed.) *The neurosciences: Second study program*. New York: Rockefeller University Press, in press.

Schneider, A. M. Retention under spreading depression: A generalization-decrement phenomenon. *Journal of Comparative & Physiological Psychology*, 1966, **62**, 317–319.

Schneider, A. M. A control of memory by spreading cortical depression: A case for stimulus control. *Psychological Review*, 1967, **74**, 201–215.

Schneider, A. M., & Ebbesen, E. Interhemispheric transfer of lever pressing as stimulus generalization of the effects of spreading depression. *Journal of the Experimental Analysis of Behavior*, 1964, **7**, 350.

Schneider, A. M., & Hamburg, M. Interhemispheric transfer with spreading depression: A memory transfer or stimulus generalization phenomenon? *Journal of Comparative & Physiological Psychology*, 1966, **62**, 133–136.

Schneider, A. M., & Kay, H. Spreading depression as a discriminative stimulus for lever pressing. *Journal of Comparative & Physiological Psychology*, 1968, **65**, 149–151.

Schneider, A. M., & Sherman, W. Amnesia: A function of the temporal relation of foot shock to electroconvulsive shock. *Science*, 1968, **159**, 219–221.

Schneider, G. E. Contrasting visuomotor functions of tectum and cortex in the golden hamster. *Psychologische Forschung*, 1967, 1968, **31**, 52–62.

Schneider, G. E. Two visual systems. *Science*, 1969, **163**, 895–902.

Schurnecht, H. F. Neuroanatomical correlates of auditory sensitivity and pitch discrimination in the cat. In G. L. Rasmussen and W. F. Windle (Eds.), *Neural mechanisms of the auditory and vestibular systems*. Springfield, Ill.: Thomas, 1960.

Scoville, W. B. Amnesia after bilateral mesial temporal-lobe excision: Introduction to case H. M. *Neuropsychologia*, 1968, **6**, 211–213.

Seitz, W. C. *The responsive eye*. New York: Museum of Modern Art, 1965.

Sekuler, R. W., & Ganz, L. Aftereffect of seen motion with a stabilized retinal image. *Science*, 1963, **139**, 419–420.

Selfridge, O. Pandemonium: A paradigm for learning. In *Symposium on the mechanization of thought processes*. London: HM Stationery Office, 1959.

Selfridge, O., & Neisser, U. Pattern recognition by machine. *Scientific American*, 1960, **203**(2), 60–68.

Seligman, M. E. P. Can we immunize the weak? *Psychology Today*, June 1969, 42–44.

Seligman, M. E. P. On the generality of the laws of learning. *Psychological Review*, 1970, **77**, 406–418.

Seligman, M. E. P., Maier, S. F., & Solomon, R. L. Unpredictable and uncontrollable events. In F. R. Brush (Ed.), *Aversive conditioning and learning*. New York: Academic Press, 1969.

Sellin, T., & Wolfgang, M. E. *The measurement of delinquency*. New York: Wiley, 1964.

Selye, H. *The story of the adaptation syndrome*. Montreal: Acta, 1952.

Sidman, M., Stoddard, L. T., & Mohr, J. P. Some additional quantitative observations of immediate memory in a patient with bilateral hippocampal lesions. *Neuropsychologia*, 1968, **6**, 245–254.

Sidowski, J. B. *Experimental methods and instrumentation in psychology*. New York: McGraw-Hill, 1966.

Siegel, S., & Fouraker, L. E. *Bargaining and group decision making: Experiments in bilateral monopoly*. New York: McGraw-Hill, 1960.

Simon, H. A., & Newell, A. *Human problem solving*. Englewood Cliffs, N.J.: Prentice Hall, 1971.

Simon, H. A., & Simon, P. A. Trial and error search involving difficult problems: Evidence from the game of chess. *Behavioral Science*, 1962, **7**, 425–429.

Singer, H., & Ruddell, R. B. (Eds.) *Theoretical models and processes of reading*. Newark, Del.: International Reading Association, 1970.

Skinner, B. F. *Science and human behavior*. New York: Macmillan, 1953.

Skinner, B. F. *Cumulative record*. (Rev. ed.) New York: Appleton, 1961.

Slobin, D. I. (Ed.) *The ontogenesis of grammar*. New York: Academic Press, 1971.

Smedslund, J. The acquisition of substance and weight in children.
    I. Introduction. *Scandinavian Journal of Psychology*, 1961, **2**, 11–20. (a)
    II. External reinforcement of conservation of weight and of the operations of addition and subtraction. *Scandinavian Journal of Psychology*, 1961, **2**, 71–84. (b)
    III. Extinction of conservation of weight acquired "normally" and by means of empirical controls on a balance scale. *Scandinavian Journal of Psychology*, 1961, **2**, 85–87. (c)
    IV. An attempt at extinction of the usual components of the weight concept. *Scandinavian Journal of Psychology*, 1961, **2**, 153–155. (d)
    V. Practice in conflict situations without external reinforcement. *Scandinavian Journal of Psychology*, 1961, **2**, 156–160. (e)
    VI. Practice on continuous versus discontinuous material in conflict situations without external reinforcement. *Scandinavian Journal of Psychology*, 1961, **2**, 203–210. (f)

Smith, M. P., & Duffy, M. The effects of intragastric injection of various substances on subsequent bar pressing. *Journal of Comparative & Physiological Psychology,* 1955, **48**, 387–391.

Soby, J. T. *René Magritte.* New York: Museum of Modern Art, 1965.

Sperling, G. Information in a brief visual presentation. Unpublished doctoral dissertation, Harvard University, 1959.

Sperling, G. The information available in brief visual presentations. *Psychological Monographs,* 1960, **74** (Whole No. 11).

Sperling, G., & Speelman, R. G. Acoustic similarity and auditory short-term memory experiments and a model. In D. A. Norman (Ed.), *Models of human memory.* New York: Academic Press, 1970.

Sperling, H. G., & Harwerth, R. S. Red-green cone interactions in the increment-threshold spectral sensitivity of primates, *Science,* 1971, **172**, 180–184.

Sperry, R. W. Cerebral organization and behavior. *Science,* 1961, **133**, 1749.

Sperry, R. W. Hemisphere disconnection and unity in conscious awareness. *American Psychologist,* 1968, **23**, 723–733.

Spielberger, C. D. (Ed.) *Anxiety and behavior.* New York: Academic Press, 1966.

Spinelli, D. N. Receptive field organization of ganglion cells in the cat's retina. *Experimental Neurology,* 1967, **19**, 291–315.

Spock, B. *Baby and child care.* New York: Pocket Books, 1957.

Squire, L. R., & Barondes, S. H. Inhibitions of cerebral protein on RNA synthesis and memory. In J. Gaito (Ed.), *Macromolecules and behavior.* (2nd ed.) New York: Appleton, in press.

Staddon, J. E. R., & Simmelhag, V. L. The "superstition" experiment: A reexamination of its implications for the principles of adaptive behavior. *Psychological Review,* 1971, **78**, 3–43.

Stanley-Jones, D. The biological origin of love and hate. In M. Arnold (Ed.), *Feelings and emotions.* New York, Academic Press, 1970.

Sterling, P., & Wickelgren, B. G. Visual receptive fields in the superior colliculus of the cat. *Journal of Neurophysiology,* 1969, **32**, 1–15.

Stevens, C. F. *Neurophysiology: A primer.* New York: Wiley, 1966.

Stevens, S. S. The attributes of tones. *Proceedings of the National Academy of Science of the United States of America,* 1934, **20**, 457–459.

Stevens, S. S. The relation of pitch to intensity. *Journal of the Acoustical Society of America,* 1937, **8**, 191–195.

Stevens, S. S. (Ed.) *Handbook of experimental psychology.* New York: Wiley, 1951.

Stevens, S. S. The direct estimation of sensory magnitude—loudness. *American Journal of Psychology,* 1956, **69**, 1–25.

Stevens, S. S. The psychophysics of sensory function. In W. A. Rosenblith (Ed.), *Sensory communication.* Cambridge, Mass.: M.I.T. Press, 1961. (a).

Stevens, S. S. To honor Fechner and repeal his law. *Science,* 1961, **133**, 80–86. (b)

Stevens, S. S. A metric for the social consensus. *Science,* 1966, **151,** 530–541. (a)

Stevens, S. S. On the operation known as judgment. *American Scientist,* 1966, **54,** 385–401. (b)

Stevens, S. S. Power-group transformations under glare, masking, and recruitment. *Journal of the Acoustical Society of America,* 1966, **39,** 725–735. (c)

Stevens, S. S. Matching functions between loudness and ten other continua. *Perception & Psychophysics,* 1966, **1**(1), 5–8. (d).

Stevens, S. S. Ratio scales of opinion. In D. K. Whitla (Ed.), *Handbook of measurement and assessment in behavioral sciences.* Reading, Mass.: Addison-Wesley, 1968.

Stevens, S. S., & Davis, H. *Hearing: Its psychology and physiology.* New York: Wiley, 1938.

Stevens, S. S., Warshofsky, F., & the Editors of *Life. Sound and hearing.* New York: Time, Inc., 1965.

Stromeyer, C. F. Further studies of the McCollough effect. *Perception and Psychophysics,* 1969, **6,** 105–110.

Stromeyer, C. F., & Mansfield, R. J. Colored aftereffects produced with moving images. *Perception & Psychophysics,* 1970, **7,** 108–114.

Suppes, P., & Zinnes, J. L. Basic measurement theory. In R. D. Luce, R. R. Bush, & E. Galanter (Eds.), *Handbook of Mathematical Psychology.* Vol. I. New York: Wiley, 1963.

Swets, J. A. Information retrieval systems. *Science,* 1963, **141,** 242–250.

Swets, J. A. (Ed.) *Signal detection and recognition by human observers.* New York: Wiley, 1964.

Sylvester, D. *Magritte.* Catalogue of an exhibition of paintings by Rene Magritte, 1898–1967. London: The Arts Council of Great Britain, 1969.

Talland, G. A. *Deranged memory.* New York: Academic Press, 1965.

Talland, G. A. *Disorders of memory and learning.* Harmondsworth, Middlesex, England: Penguin Books, 1968.

Talland, G. A., & Waugh, N. (Eds.) *The pathology of memory.* New York: Academic Press, 1969.

Teitelbaum, P. The biology of drive. In G. C. Quarton, T. Melnechuk, & F. O. Schmidt (Eds.), *The neurosciences.* New York: Rockefeller University Press, 1967.

Teitelbaum, P., & Epstein, A. N. The lateral hypothalmic syndrome: Recovery of feeding and drinking after lateral hypothalmic lesions. *Psychological Review,* 1962, **69,** 74–90.

Terrace, H. S., & Stevens, S. S. The quantification of tonal volume. *American Journal of Psychology,* 1962, **75,** 596–604.

Teuber, H. L. Perception. In J. Field, H. W. Magoun, & V. E. Hall (Eds.), *Handbook of physiology, Section 1: Neural physiology.* Vol. 3. Baltimore: Williams & Wilkins, 1960.

Teuber, H. L., Milner, B., & Vaughan, H. G., Jr. Persistent anterograde amnesia after stab wound of the basal brain. *Neuropsychologia,* 1968, **6,** 267–282.

Thornton, J. W., & Jacobs, P. D. Learned helplessness in human subjects. *Journal of Experimental Psychology,* 1971, **87,** 367–372.

Thorp, E. O. *Beat the dealer: A winning strategy for the game of twenty-one.* New York: Random House, 1966.

Tobias, J. V. (Ed.) *Foundations of modern auditory theory.* Vol. I New York: Academic Press, 1970.

Treisman, A. M. Strategies and models of selective attention. *Psychological Review,* 1969, **76,** 282–299.

Trevarthen, C. B. Two mechanisms of vision in primates. *Psychologische Forschung,* 1968, **31,** 299–337.

Tulving, E., & Donaldson, W. (Eds.) *Organization of memory.* New York: Academic Press, 1972.

Tversky, A. Intransitivity of preferences. *Psychological Review,* 1969, **76,** 31–48.

Tversky, A., & Kahneman, D. The belief in the law of small numbers. *Psychological Bulletin,* in press.

Uhr, L. (Ed.) *Pattern recognition. Theory, experiment, computer simulations, and dynamic models of form perception and discovery.* New York: Wiley, 1966.

Ungar, G. Chemical transfer of learning; its stimulus specificity. *Federation Proceedings, Federation of American Societies for Experimental Biology,* 1966, **25,** 109.

Ungar, G., & Oceguera-Navarro, C. Transfer of habituation by material extracted from brain. *Nature (London),* 1965, **207,** 301.

van Bergeijk, W. A. Variation on a theme of Békésy: a model of binaural interaction. *Journal of the Acoustical Society of America,* 1962, **34,** 1431–1437.

van den Brink, G. Two experiments on pitch perception: Displacusis of harmonic AM signals and pitch of inharmonic AM signals. *Journal of the Acoustical Society of America,* 1970, **48,** 1355–1365.

van der Velden, H. A. Over het aantal lichtquanta dat nodig is voor een lichtprikkel bij het meselijk oog. *Physica (Utrecht),* 1944, **11,** 179.

van der Velden, H. A. The number of quanta necessary for the perception of light of the human eye. *Ophthalmologica,* 1946, **111,** 321.

Varela, J. A. *Psychological Solutions to Social Problems.* New York: Academic Press, 1971.

Vasarely, V. *Vasarely.* Translated by H. Chevalier. Neuchatel, Switzerland: Editions du Griffon Neuchatel, 1965.

Verheijen, F. J. A simple after image method demonstrating the involuntary multi-directional eye movements during fixation. *Optica Acta,* 1961, **8,** 309–311.

Vernon, M. D. (Ed.) *Experiments in visual perception.* Harmondsworth, Middlesex, England: Penguin Books, 1966.

Voss, J. F. (Ed.) *Approaches to thought*. Columbus, Ohio: Charles F. Merrill, 1969.

Wagner, H. G., MacNichol, E. F., Jr., & Wolbarsht, M. L. The response properties of single ganglion cells in the goldfish retina. *Journal of General Physiology*, 1960, **43**, 45–62.

Wald, G. The receptors for human color vision. *Science*, 1964, **145**, 1007–1017.

Warren, R. M., & Warren, R. P. *Helmholtz on perception: Its physiology and development*. New York: Wiley, 1968.

Warren, R. M., & Warren, R. P. Auditory illusions and confusions. *Scientific American*, 1970, **223**, 30–36.

Warrington, E. K., & Weiskrantz, L. An analysis of short-term and long-term memory defects in man. In J. A. Deutsch (Ed.), *Physiological basis of memory*. New York: Academic Press, to be published.

Wason, P. C., & Johnson-Laird, P. N. (Eds.) *Thinking and reasoning*. Harmondsworth, Middlesex, England: Penguin Books, 1968.

Wathen-Dunn, W. (Ed.) *Models for the perception of speech and visual form*. Cambridge, Mass.: M.I.T. Press, 1967.

Webb, W. B. *Sleep: An experimental approach*. New York: Macmillan, 1968.

Weber, R. J., & Castleman, J. The time it takes to imagine. *Perception & Psychophysics*, 1970, **8**, 165–168.

Weiskrantz, L. Contour discrimination in a young monkey with striate cortex ablation. *Neuropsychologia*, 1963, **1**, 145–164.

Weisstein, N. What the frog's eye tells the human brain: Single cell analyzers in the human visual system. *Psychological Review*, 1969, **72**, 157–176.

Weizenbaum, J. Contextual understanding by computers. In P. A. Kolers and M. Eden (Eds.), *Recognizing patterns: Studies in living and automatic systems*. Cambridge, Mass.: M.I.T. Press, 1968.

Wertheimer, M. *Productive thinking*. New York: Harper, 1945.

Wever, E. G. *Theory of hearing*. New York: Dover Publications, 1970.

White, B. W., Saunders, F. A., Scadden, L., Bach-y-Rita, P., & Collins, C. C. Seeing with the skin. *Perception & Psychophysics*, 1970, **7**, 23–27.

Whitfield, I. C. *The auditory pathway*. London: Arnold, 1967.

Whitfield, I. C., & Evans, E. F. Responses of auditory cortical neurons to stimuli of changing frequency. *Journal of Neurophysiology*, 1965, **28**, 655–672.

Whitty, C. W. M, & Zangwill, O. L. (Eds.) *Amnesia*. London: Butterworth, 1966.

Wickelgren, B. G., & Sterling, P. Influence of visual cortex on receptive fields in the superior colliculus of the cat. *Journal of Neurophysiology*, 1969, **32**, 16–23.

Wickelgren, W. A. Sparing of short-term memory in an amnesic patient: Implications for strength theory of memory. *Neuropsychologia*, 1968, **6**, 235–244.

Wickelgren, W. A. Multitrace strength theory. In D. A. Norman (Ed.), *Models of human memory*. New York: Academic Press, 1970.

Wickelgren, W. A., & Norman, D. A. Strength models and serial position in short-term recognition memory. *Journal of Mathematical Psychology,* 1966, **3**, 316–347.

Williams, J. *The complete strategist.* New York: McGraw-Hill, 1954.

Williams, M. Memory disorders associated with electroconvulsive therapy. In C. W. M. Whitty & O. L. Zangwill (Eds.), *Amnesia.* London: Butterworth, 1966.

Winograd, T. Procedures as a representation for data in a computer program for understanding natural language. Unpublished doctoral dissertation, Department of Mathematics, Massachusetts Institute of Technology, 1970.

Winograd, T. A program for understanding natural language. *Cognitive Psychology,* 1972, **3.**

Woodworth, R. S. *Experimental psychology.* New York: Holt, 1938.

Woodworth, R. S., & Schlosberg, H. *Experimental psychology.* New York: Holt, 1954.

Wooldridge, D. E. *The machinery of the brain.* New York: McGraw-Hill, 1963.

Wyszecki, G. W., & Stiles, W. S. *Color science, concepts and methods, quantitative data and formulas.* New York: Wiley, 1967.

Young, P. T. *Motivation and emotion.* New York: Wiley, 1961.

Zelman, A., Kabat, L., Jacobson, R., & McConnell, J. V. Transfer of training through injection of "conditioned" RNA into untrained planarians. *Worm Runner's Digest,* 1963, **5**, 14–19.

Zimbardo, P., & Ebbesen, E. *Influencing attitudes and changing behavior.* Reading, Mass.: Addison-Wesley, 1969.

Zwicker, E., & Scharf, B. Model of loudness summation. *Psychological Review,* 1965, **72**, 3–26.

Zwislocki, J. Analysis of some auditory characteristics. In R. D. Luce, R. R. Bush, and E. Galanter (Eds.), *Handbook of mathematical psychology,* Vol. III. New York: Wiley, 1965.

Author index

Numbers in italics refer to the pages on which the complete references are listed. Names of painters, photographers, and composers mentioned in the text are also listed in the Author Index.

A

Abelson, H. J., 590, *697*
Abromov, I., 210, *692*
Ades, H. W., *690*
Adolph, E. F., 606, 607, *688*
Adrian, E. D., *688*
Albers, Josef, 27, 48, 144, *688*
Allen, V. L., 589, *688*
Alpern, M., *688*
Appley, M. H., 638, 639, *691*
Arnheim, R., 48, *688*
Arnold, M. B., 639, *688*
Asch, S. E., 589, *688*
Atkinson, R. C., 345, 371, *688*
Austin, G. A., 498, *690*
Averbach, E., 370, *688*
Ax, A. F., 629, *688*

B

Bach, E., 395, *688*
Bach, Johann Sebastian, 11
Bach-y-Rita, P., 45, *710*
Backus, J., 249, *689*
Barbizet, J., 307, 326, *689*
Barker, R. G., 620, *689*
Barlow, H. B., 87, 112, *689*
Barondes, S. H., *707*
Barron, F., *689*
Bartlett, F. C., 434, *689*
Bartlett, N. R., *689*
Bartley, S., *689*
Beach, F. A., 326, *689*
Beale, J. L., 327, *691*
Beck, J., 186, 214, *696*
Békésy, G. von, 112, 214, 244, 255, *689*
Bellugi, U., 457, *690*
Bem, D. J., 561, 590, *689*
Bennett, E. L., 326, *691*
Berger, B. D., 326, *691*

Berko, J., 461, *689*
Berkowitz, L., 525, *689*
Berkun, M. M., 615, *689*
Berlyne, D. E., 498, *689*
Bever, T. G., *689*
Bialek, H. M., 615, *689*
Bishop, P. O., 112, 174, 175, 215, *689*
Bjork, R. A., *689*
Black, A. H., 499, *690*
Bolt, R. H., 148, *690*
Botkin, P. T., 497, *693*
Bouman, M. A., *690*
Bourne, L. E., Jr., 498, *690*
Bower, G. H., 498, *696*
Brady, J. V., 611, 612, 638, *690*
Bransford, J., 428, 434, *690*
Brazier, M. A. B., *690*
Bredberg, G., *690*
Breland, K., 498, *690*
Breland, M., 498, *690*
Brooks, L., 371, *690*
Brown, R., 455, 457, 464, 465, 662, *690*
Bruner, J. S., 498, *690*
Bryden, M. P., 372, *690*
Bucher, F., 48, *690*
Burdick, E., 590, *690*
Bureš, J., 318, *691*
Burešová, O., 318, *690*
Bush, R. R., 663, *700*
Byrne, W. L., 326, *691*

C

Carlson, P. L., 326, *691*
Carraher, R. G., 22, 48, 145, *691*
Castleman, J., 371, *710*
Chapanis, A., 189, 191, *691*
Chiappetta, L., 326, *691*
Chinetti, P., *699*
Chomsky, N., 148, 464, *691*
Chorover, S. L., 326, *691*

Y

Z

Subject Index

E